MICHELIN
CHARMING PLACES TO STAY

1 000 Charming Hotels and Guesthouses in France

SUMMARY

ALSACE — 9
67 Bas-Rhin – 68 Haut-Rhin

AQUITAINE — 37
24 Dordogne – 33 Gironde – 40 Landes
47 Lot-et-Garonne – 64 Pyrénées-Atlantiques

AUVERGNE — 91
03 Allier – 15 Cantal – 43 Haute-Loire – 63 Puy-de-Dôme

BURGUNDY — 123
21 Côte-d'Or – 58 Nièvre – 71 Saône-et-Loire – 89 Yonne

BRITTANY — 157
22 Côte-d'Armor – 29 Finistère – 35 Ille-et-Vilaine
56 Morbihan

CENTRE AND UPPER LOIRE VALLEY — 187
18 Cher – 28 Eure-et-Loir – 36 Indre – 37 Indre-et-Loire
41 Loir-et-Cher – 45 Loiret

CHAMPAGNE-ARDENNE — 215
08 Ardennes – 10 Aube – 51 Marne – 52 Haute-Marne

CORSICA — 227
2A Corse-du-Sud – 2B Haute-Corse

FRANCHE-COMTÉ — 237
25 Doubs – 39 Jura – 70 Haute-Saône – 90 Ter.-de-Belfort

ÎLE-DE-FRANCE AND PARIS — 253
75 Seine (Paris) – 77 Seine-et-Marne – 78 Yvelines – 91 Essonne
92 Hauts-de-Seine – 93 Seine-Saint-Denis
94 Val-de-Marne – 95 Val-d'Oise

LANGUEDOC-ROUSSILLON — 271
11 Aude – 30 Gard – 34 Hérault – 48 Lozère
66 Pyrénées-Orientales

LIMOUSIN — 295
19 Corrèze – 23 Creuse – 87 Haute-Vienne

LORRAINE — 305
54 **Meurthe-et-Moselle** – 55 **Meuse** – 57 **Moselle** – 88 **Vosges**

MIDI-PYRÉNÉES — 315
09 **Ariège** – 12 **Aveyron** – 31 **Haute-Garonne** – 32 **Gers**
46 **Lot** – 65 **Hautes-Pyrénées** – 81 **Tarn** – 82 **Tarn-et-Garonne**

NORD-PAS-DE-CALAIS — 361
59 **Nord** – 62 **Pas-de-Calais**

NORMANDY — 377
14 **Calvados** – 27 **Eure** – 50 **Manche** – 61 **Orne** – 76 **Seine-Maritime**

PAYS-DE-LA-LOIRE — 417
44 **Loire-Atlantique** – 49 **Maine-et-Loire** – 53 **Mayenne**
72 **Sarthe** – 85 **Vendée**

PICARDY — 437
02 **Aisne** – 60 **Oise** – 80 **Somme**

POITOU-CHARENTES — 451
16 **Charente** – 17 **Charente-Maritime** – 79 **Deux-Sèvres**
86 **Vienne**

PROVENCE-ALPS - FRENCH RIVIERA — 467
04 **Alpes-de-Haute-Provence** – 05 **Hautes-Alpes**
06 **Alpes-Maritimes** – 13 **Bouches-du-Rhône** – 83 **Var** – 84 **Vaucluse**

RHÔNE-ALPS — 523
01 **Ain** – 07 **Ardèche** – 26 **Drôme** – 38 **Isère** – 42 **Loire**
69 **Rhône** – 73 **Savoie** – 74 **Haute-Savoie**

LOW PRICE HOTELS AND MAISONS D'HÔTE — 575
WINING & DINING BREAKS — 580
ACTIVITY BREAKS — 582
ALPHABETICAL LIST OF HOTELS AND MAISONS D'HÔTE — 584

REGIONAL MAPS

- ALSACE
- AQUITAINE
- AUVERGNE
- BURGUNDY
- BRITTANY
- CENTRE AND UPPER LOIRE VALLEY
- CHAMPAGNE-ARDENNE
- CORSICA
- FRANCHE-COMTÉ
- ÎLE-DE-FRANCE AND PARIS
- LANGUEDOC-ROUSSILLON
- LIMOUSIN
- LORRAINE
- MIDI-PYRÉNÉES
- NORD-PAS-DE-CALAIS
- NORMANDY
- PAYS-DE-LA-LOIRE
- PICARDY
- POITOU-CHARENTES
- PROVENCE-ALPS - FRENCH RIVIERA
- RHÔNE-ALPES

Symbols used in the guide

Number of the establishment
in the guide and on the regional map:
blue for hotels
red for maisons d'hôte

Hotel

Maison d'hôte

Hotel or maison d'hôte offering rooms
for under €50 per night
for a double room

The little extra that makes the hotel
or maison d'hôte different

INTRODUCTION

The guide

Michelin's 1000 Charming Hotels and Guesthouses features a selection of establishments at reasonable prices throughout France, chosen by our inspectors for their authenticity, character, warmth and setting. The most expensive rooms cost no more than €110, most of the prices are below €80 and a quarter of the establishments offer rooms for less than €50.
A few words, indicated by our ⌂ symbol, highlight the little extra that we particularly liked: "Exploring the underwater depths of Scandola nature reserve", for example.

How the Guide works

The guide is divided into 19 French regions. Within these regions, the establishments are listed in ascending order of the number of the *département:* Aquitaine, for example, is split into the *départements* of Dordogne 24), Gironde (33), Landes (40), Lot-et-Garonne (47) and Pyrénées-Altantiques (64). Within the *département,* towns or villages where we list an establishment are given in alphabetical order and the establishments are numbered in this order. Hotels are marked in blue ⌂ and maisons d'hôte in red ⌂.

Maps

The maps of France at the beginning of the guide shows the 19 regions and their *départements.*
At the beginning of each chapter is a regional map with the hotels marked as blue dots and the maisons d'hôte as red dots; each dot has a number which corresponds to the number at the top of the establishment's description. The maps and directions in this guide use the metric system for reasons of practicality; as a reminder 1km = c0.6miles.

Maisons d'hôte

Maisons and chambres d'hôte are, loosely speaking, bed & breakfast establishments with between three and six rooms. Often converted mills, country houses, farmsteads or hunting lodges, and typically in quiet countryside or the residential area of a town, they are also the private homes of the people who will welcome you and endeavour to make your stay as pleasant as possible. We definitely recommend booking ahead, particularly during the summer or the long spring weekends. You should also call if you think you may arrive late in the evening.

Hotels

Many of our hotels are in converted castles, mansions, convents, abbeys and the like. As with the chambres d'hôte, all have been selected for their character, tranquillity and hospitality. There is no point, however, in attempting to compare a simple seaside holiday home with rooms at under €40 with accommodation in a luxurious medieval château: each has its own distinctive charm. Most hotels have a restaurant and offer half-board rates (i.e. for dinner and accommodation). If they do, we point this out: the establishment will confirm the details. Remember to confirm your reservation if you're running late – guests are usually expected to arrive by 6pm.

The information provided by the maisons d'hôte and hotels and reproduced in good faith should be considered as an indication only. Despite our best efforts, it is always possible that some of the information is not complete or accurate. Michelin Travel Publications cannot be held responsible for such changes.

Tables d'hôte

If a hotel or restaurant has dining facilities, we say so. Some maisons d'hôte offer a "table d'hôte". This home-cooked set menu at a fixed price may be served to you at your own table, or you may join the rest of the guests at a communal table.

Prices

All prices are inclusive of tax and service, the prices indicated in this guide were supplied to us by the proprietors of the hotels in 2005 for the year 2006 and may thus be liable to change during the year. Prices refer to the high season. Such prices are not contractual and Michelin Travel Publications may under no circumstances be held responsible for any possible changes.

Rooms: The prices given are the highest and lowest rates for a double room in high season. Always confirm the price when booking. Out of season, many establishments offer special deals; again, its best to ask when making the reservation.

Breakfast: Breakfast is sometimes included in the price of the room. Whenever this is not the case, we have indicated the price of breakfast per person.

Deposit and Instalments

Visitors should be aware of the conventional difference between a deposit ('arrhes' in French) and an instalment ('acompte'). In the first case, the customer may cancel his booking and so forfeit his deposit; if the hotelier is unable to provide his guest with the room, he repays double the amount his customer paid. An instalment, on the other hand, is considered a binding commitment to pay the whole tariff.

Credit Cards

If an establishment does not accept credit cards, we indicate this in its entry. Note that in giving your credit card number to secure your reservation, you are entitling the hotelier or owner of the maison d'hôte either to charge an instalment equal to the minimum tariff for your stay, to be reckoned against your final bill, or to take payment for what you have ordered and reserved, in such cases where the reservation is not cancelled within the time determined by the hotelier or the owner of the maison d'hôte.

Access and Facilities

For each establishment we give details of
• how to get there from the nearest town.

• facilities including television, swimming-pool, tennis court, sauna, children's games and an indication of whether dogs are allowed.
• handicapped access where special adaptations or arrangements have been made.

Places with that little bit extra

Three themed indexes can be found at the back of the book:

Low price: this index lists all the establishments which offer double rooms at under €50 a night.

Wining and dining breaks: all the gastronomic establishments whose cooking we found particularly good.

Activity breaks: this includes all the establishments which have a swimming pool and also offer at least one other sport (hiking, riding, tennis, golf, canoeing etc.).

Index

In addition to the themed indexes, all of the establishments are listed in alphabetical order.

Exploring France?

Don't forget to stock up with the latest Michelin REGIONAL and LOCAL maps and titles from The Green Guide Collection. Michelin also offers an online route-planning service at www.ViaMichelin.com.

Your viewpoint

We have aimed to make this guide practical and readable and trust that it will accompany you on family outings and romantic weekends: it's written for you and you can help to make the next edition even better. Please point out any errors and ommissions you spot and fill in the questionnaire at the back of the guide: all your comments and suggestions for new addresses are very welcome.

ALSACE

Alsace is perhaps the most romantic of France's regions, a place of fairy-tale castles guarding the foothills of the mountains, gentle vine-clad slopes and picturesque dolls' house villages perched on rocky outcrops or nestling in lush green valleys. From Colmar's Little Venice with its flower-decked balconies and famous storks to Strasbourg's Christmas market whose multicoloured lights illuminate the magnificent cathedral or the half-timbered houses of Little France reflected in the meanders of the River Ill, an inner warmth radiates from Alsace that even the cold winter winds cannot chill. So make a beeline for the boisterous atmosphere of a brasserie and sample a real Alsace beer or head for a picturesque *winstub* – wine bar – and tuck into a steaming dish of choucroute – sauerkraut with smoked pork – and a huge slice of *kugelhof* cake, all washed down with a glass of fruity Sylvaner or Riesling wine.

- Bas-Rhin (67)
- Haut-Rhin (68)

ALSACE

ANDLAU - 67140

1 ZINCKHOTEL
M. Zinck

13 rue de la Marne
67140 Andlau
Tel. 03 88 08 27 30
Fax 03 88 08 42 50
zinck.hotel@wanadoo.fr
www.zinckhotel.com

Open all year • 18 rooms with bath/WC or shower/WC and television • €55 to €95; breakfast €8 • No restaurant • Terrace, park, private car park. No dogs admitted

 Relaxing in the flower-decked garden and fruit orchards on a summer's day.

A building in the tanners' quarter in the 16C, a mill until 1830, a hosier's shop and now a hotel complete with a contemporary wing - if the walls of the Zinckhotel could speak, what tales they would tell! The old millwheel still takes pride of place in the breakfast room, reminding visitors of the building's past. However guests are often even more surprised by the unusual decorative themes of the rooms ranging from "English" to "Zen" and "The Arabian Nights".

Access : By the D 500, exit 13 Mittelbergheim

BALDENHEIM - 67600

2 LES PRÉS D'ONDINE
M. Dalibert

5 route de Baldenheim - Rathsamhausen-le-Haut – 67600 Baldenheim
Tel. 03 88 58 04 60
Fax 03 88 58 04 61
message@presdondine.com
www.presdondine.com

Open all year • 12 rooms, on 2 levels, with bath/WC and television, 1 with disabled access • €70 to €90; breakfast €10; half-board available • Table d'hôte evenings only (closed Sun and Wed); menus €22 to €32 • Garden, private car park. No dogs admitted in restaurant • Fitness room, library

 The pastoral charm of this riverside setting on the banks of the Ill.

This former forest house built in the early 20C near the river has been treated to a recent makeover. Its bright colourful façade invites visitors to venture through the garden gate. Inside, you will be delighted first by the sitting room-library and then by the trim restaurant with its attractive woodwork and tasty table d'hôte. Carefully-chosen furniture, warm colours, matching fabrics and knick-knacks give the rooms an elegant flavour.

Access : 5km eastbound of Sélestat on the D 21

ALSACE

BETSCHDORF - 67660

3 KRUMEICH
M. Krumeich

23 rue des Potiers
67660 Betschdorf
Tel. 03 88 54 40 56
Fax 03 88 54 40 56

Open all year • 3 rooms • €48 to €53, breakfast included • No table d'hôte • Garden, car park. Credit cards not accepted. Dogs not admitted • Pottery courses

The warm welcome from the owner, who is also a potter.

Situated in the heart of a village renowned for its stoneware pottery, this large property provides clean, quiet rooms decorated with elegant period furniture – including beautiful wardrobes – and a lovely shaded flower garden. The owner, the proud descendant of a long line of potters, organises introductory pottery courses all year long.

Access : 15km north-east of Haguenau, towards Wissembourg on the D 263 then the D 243

BIRKENWALD - 67440

4 AU CHASSEUR
M. Gass

7 rue de l'Eglise
67440 Birkenwald
Tel. 03 88 70 61 32
Fax 03 88 70 66 02
hotel.au-chasseur@wanadoo.fr
chasseurbirkenwald.com

Closed in Jan • 24 rooms with bath/WC or shower/WC and television • €60 to €79; breakfast €12; half-board available • Non-smoking restaurant closed Mon and Tue lunchtimes and Thu lunchtimes; menus €15 (weekday lunchtimes) to €65 • Terrace, garden, car park. No dogs admitted in rooms • Heated indoor swimming pool, sauna, jacuzzi

Taking the time to enjoy the covered heated swimming pool, sauna, Jacuzzi and solarium.

This family-run hostelry, hidden behind an inviting flower-decked façade, dominates the village of Birkenwald, guaranteeing nights of peaceful slumber to even the lightest sleepers. The rooms are comfortable, pleasant and extremely well kept; a few command a view over the Vosges mountains. The owner takes pleasure in concocting tasty dishes which are a happy blend of classical and regional cooking, served in a dining room whose multicoloured wainscoting is the work of a local artist.

Access : In the centre of the village between Saverne and Mosheim

ALSACE

BLIENSCHWILLER - 67650

5 **WINZENBERG**
Mme Dresch-Horning

58 route des vins
67650 Blienschwiller
Tel. 03 88 92 62 77
Fax 03 88 92 45 22
winzenberg@visit-alsace.com
www.winzenberg.com

Closed 3 Jan to 18 Feb • 13 rooms all with bath/WC or shower/WC and television • €41 to €50; breakfast €6 • No restaurant • Private car park. Dogs not admitted

 Ideally located in a village along the Wine Route.

A little village surrounded by vineyards provides the backdrop to this former wine-grower's house, now restored and transformed into a hotel. Although not exactly enormous, the rooms are pleasantly appointed with colourfully painted furniture and some have sloping ceilings while others boast balconies. The current owners, also wine-growers, enjoy taking guests on a guided tour of the cellar, finishing up with a tasting session.

Access : In the main street of the village

CLEEBOURG - 67160

6 **KLEIN**
Mme Klein

59 rue Principale
67160 Cleebourg
Tel. 03 88 94 50 95
Fax 03 88 94 50 95
annejp.klein@laposte.net
www.chez.com/cleebourg

Open all year • 4 rooms • €40, breakfast included; half-board available • Table d'hôte €12 (evening only) • Garden, car park. Credit cards not accepted. Dogs not admitted

 The lovingly preserved, authentic Alsatian décor.

This 18C-19C Alsatian house in the heart of an acclaimed wine-growing village could well prove irresistible: there's no mistaking the true Alsatian style. The peaceful rooms, all on the ground floor, are decorated with pristine antique furniture; wood is the predominant feature of the dining room which serves typical regional cuisine. Guests can relax in the pretty garden to the rear.

Access : 7km south-west of Wissembourg on the D 7, in the centre of the village

ALSACE

DAMBACH-LA-VILLE - 67650

7 LE VIGNOBLE
M. Boulanger

1 rue de l'Église
67650 Dambach-la-Ville
Tel. 03 88 92 43 75
 Fax 03 88 92 62 21

Closed from 24 Jun to 8 Jul and 24 Dec to 23 Mar • 7 rooms, one of which has disabled access, most have bath/WC, all have television • €48 to €55; breakfast €7 • No restaurant • Private car park. Dogs not admitted

 Walking along the Dambach wine path.

This hotel's architecture is characteristic of the modest wine-growers houses dotted along the Wine Route. A narrow façade facing onto the street, only the upper residential storey of which has the traditional half-timbering, and a ground floor devoted to grape pressing equipment and the cellar. The peaceful rooms have retained their oak beams and the bells of the neighbouring church remain considerately silent during the night. Family breakfast room.

Access : In the centre of the village

DIEFFENBACH-AU-VAL - 67220

8 LA ROMANCE
M. Geiger

17 route de Neuve-Église
67220 Dieffenbach-au-Val
Tel. 03 88 85 67 09
Fax 03 88 57 61 58
corinne@la-romance.net
www.la-romance.net

Open all year • 6 rooms, one of which is split-level, two have sitting rooms • €75 to €85, breakfast included • No table d'hôte • Garden, car park. Credit cards not accepted, dogs not admitted • Sauna and spa

 The modern comfort of this pretty regional residence.

Although rather difficult to find, this snug house is so comfortable that, once over the threshold, you may not want to leave! Warm welcome and spotless interior. The well-appointed, tastefully decorated rooms are named after flowers and trees and two of them overlook the valley. Add to this a warm welcome, spotless housekeeping and a garden on the edge of the forest which is the perfect spot for breakfasts in the summertime.

Access : 12km north-west of Sélestat on the N 59 and the D 424, towards Villé

ALSACE

ENTZHEIM - 67960

9 PÈRE BENOIT
M. Massé

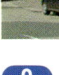

34 route de Strasbourg
67960 Entzheim
Tel. 03 88 68 98 00
Fax 03 88 68 64 56
hotel.perebenoit@wanadoo.fr
www.hotelperebenoit.com

Closed from 30 Jul to 21 Aug and from 24 Dec to 2 Jan • 60 rooms on 2 floors, 4 of which have disabled access, all have bath/WC and television • €60; breakfast €8 • Air-conditioned restaurant; menu €19 to €24 • Terrace, garden, private car park. No dogs admitted in restaurant • Fitness room, sun deck

 A farmhouse full of character near Strasbourg airport.

Behind the half-timbered, red façade of this genuine 18C Alsatian farmhouse, a range of dining choices reveals a real love of good food. Take your pick from a family dining room, the adorable balcony-cum-terrace installed under a wooden gallery, a snug "winstub" – literally a "wine room", with paintings, wood panelling and earthenware stove – or a vaulted cellar serving local tartes flambées. Snug rooms, most overlooking a peaceful flowered courtyard.

Access : 12 km from Strasbourg on the A 35 (exit no 8), then take the D 400 and D 392

FOUDAY - 67130

10 JULIEN
M. Goetz

12 route Nationale
67130 Fouday
Tel. 03 88 97 30 09
Fax 03 88 97 36 73
hoteljulien@wanadoo.fr
www.hoteljulien.com

Closed 8 to 24 Jan and Mon • 46 rooms, 8 of which are split-level, all have bath/WC or shower/WC and television • €72 to €117; breakfast €11; half-board available • Menus €18 (weekdays) to €36 • Terrace, garden, indoor swimming pool, car park. No dogs admitted in restaurant • Aquatic leisure centre. Organised tours of Alsace

 The scenic valley view with the hotel's footbridge in the foreground.

Even though the street façade with its copper-roofed overhang may strike visitors as unusual, it is nothing in comparison to the breathtaking sight of the garden side simply overflowing with flowers. In just a few years this family-run establishment has evolved immensely and the rooms reflect this renovation, ranging from comfortable to luxurious. Another of the establishment's appeals is its delicious regional cuisine.

Access : On leaving the village drive towards Schirmeck

ALSACE

GIMBELHOF - 67510

11 GIMBELHOF
M. Gunder

67510 Gimbelhof
Tel. 03 88 94 43 58
Fax 03 88 94 23 30
info@gimbelhof.com

www.gimbelhof.com

Closed 15 Nov to 26 Dec and during the February holidays • 9 rooms, most of which have shower/WC • €40 to €55; breakfast €6; half-board available • Restaurant closed Mon and Tue; menus €11 (weekdays) to €28 • Car park

 The ruins and caves of Fleckenstein Castle.

A narrow forest road leads to this unassuming family inn hidden away in the dense woodland of Northern Vosges. The countrified rooms and dining room are simply furnished but there is no better starting point for nature lovers, walkers and history enthusiasts to explore the surrounding countryside. A footpath lined with fir trees winds its way past four ancient fortresses, along the Franco-German border affording superb views over the Palatinate countryside.

Access : Leave Lembach on the D 3, after 3.5km take a right onto the D 925, then the forest road on the right

INNENHEIM - 67880

12 AU CEP DE VIGNE
M. Schaal

5 route de Barr
67880 Innenheim
Tel. 03 88 95 75 45
Fax 03 88 95 79 73

www.aucepdevigne.com

Closed from 15 to 28 Feb, 1 to 15 July, Sun evening (except the hotel) and Mon • 37 rooms, one of which has disabled access, all have bath/WC or shower/WC and television • €57 to €66; breakfast €8; half-board available • Menus €15 to €41 • Garden, car park

 Hospitality in the old French tradition.

The steep eaves, impressive half-timbered façades and wooden balconies are in keeping with the consistently high hotel standards and attention to detail shown by the Schall family, owners of this traditional establishment since 1902. The rooms vary from functional and light to rustic and a little dark; ask for one of the quieter ones overlooking the garden. Cosy dining room with dark wood panelling and carved ceiling.

Access : Between Strasbourg and Obernai, in the village

ALSACE

ITTERSWILLER - 67140

13 **ARNOLD**
M. Arnold

98 route des vins
67140 Itterswiller
Tel. 03 88 85 50 58
Fax 03 88 85 55 54
arnold-hotel@wanadoo.fr
www.hotel-arnold.com

Closed 25 and 26 Dec • 29 rooms, 10 of which are in a separate wing, 1 with disabled access; all have bath/WC or shower/WC and television • €90 to €111 (€77 to €99 low season); breakfast €12; half-board available • Menus from €23 (weekdays) to €46 • Terrace, garden, car park

 Filling up our shopping basket from the regional produce boutique.

The Arnold Hotel epitomises Alsace from its vineyard landscape to its spruce half-timbered façades and smart, immaculately cared-for interior. Recent renovations have added to guests' comfort and well-being without detracting from the regional character of its three buildings. The comfortable welcoming rooms overlook either the picturesque village or the vineyards. As for the winstub, its typical local décor and regional cuisine are an invitation to sample its excellent fare.

Access : In the heart of the village, south of Obernai

LA WANTZENAU - 67610

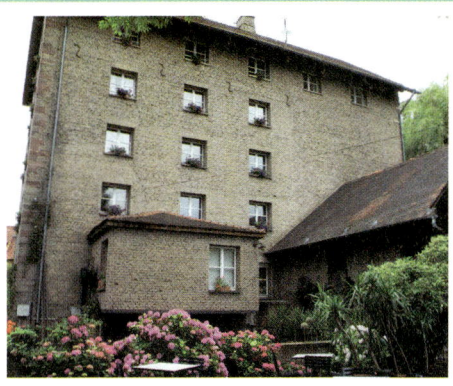

14 **LE MOULIN DE LA WANTZENAU**
Mme Wolff B. et Mme Dametti A.

3 impasse du Moulin
67610 La Wantzenau
Tel. 03 88 59 22 22
Fax 03 88 59 22 00
moulin-wantzenau@wanadoo.fr
www.moulin-wantzenau.com

Closed from 24 Dec to 2 Jan • 20 rooms and 1 split-level apartment on four levels with lift, with bath/WC or shower/WC and television • €70 to €98; breakfast €11; half-board available • Air-conditioned restaurant, closed 7 to 28 Jul, 27 Dec to 8 Jan, Sun and public holidays; menus €26 to €32 • Terrace, garden, private car park • Nearby: golf, tennis, horse riding, fitness

 Charm and tranquillity just a few minutes from Strasbourg.

This former mill on the banks of a branch of the Ill enjoys a superbly quiet countryside setting. Pastel-coloured striped wallpaper, matching hangings, exposed beams and light-coloured wooden furniture give the welcoming rooms an incredibly cosy feel. The sitting room with its fireplace is equally inviting and is the setting for delicious breakfasts of carefully selected country fare. The restaurant opposite the Moulin is run by the same family.

Access : 12km north-east of Strasbourg on the D 468

ALSACE

LE HOHWALD - 67140

NATZWILLER - 67130

15 LA PETITE AUBERGE
M. Hubrecht

6 rue Principale
67140 Le Hohwald
Tel. 03 88 08 33 05
Fax 03 88 08 34 62
hrpetiteauberge@aol.com
www.lapetiteauberge-hohwald.com

Closed 2 Jan to 6 Feb, Tue lunchtime and Wed • 7 rooms with bath/WC and television • €60; breakfast €8; half-board available • Non-smoking restaurant; menus €15 to €27 • Terrace, car park

16 AUBERGE METZGER
M. Metzger

55 rue Principale
67130 Natzwiller
Tel. 03 88 97 02 42
Fax 03 88 97 93 59
auberge.metzger@wanadoo.fr
www.hotel-aubergemetzger.com

Closed from 3 to 24 Jan, 21 June to 4 July, Sun evening and Mon. • 16 rooms all with bath/WC or shower/WC and television • €59 to €73; breakfast €9; half-board available • Menus €13 (weekdays) to €53 • Garden

 The split-level rooms are wonderfully spacious.

 The lush green garden filled with flowers.

The accommodation wing of La Petite Auberge is located behind a long brand-new wooden façade. The rooms are most pleasant: 36m^2 in size, a private terrace, tastefully decorated with light wooden furniture, functional bathrooms and a sleeping area upstairs under the timber-framed roof. Meals are served in a more traditionally-inspired house with a choice of classical cuisine in the restaurant or regional dishes in the Caveau le Relais.

Set in the heart of a peaceful village in the midst of Alsace's green countryside, everything about this appealing country inn conjures up an image of peace and quiet. The rooms are tastefully and individually decorated in a modern decorative style which provides the backdrop to period and contemporary furniture. Appetising, liberally-served regional cuisine is served in a welcoming dining room or in the shade of a pleasant terrace.

Access : In the heart of the village

Access : In the upper reaches of the village

ALSACE

NIEDERSTEINBACH - 67510

17 **AU CHEVAL BLANC**
M. Zinck

11 rue Principale
67510 Niedersteinbach
Tel. 03 88 09 55 31
Fax 03 88 09 50 24
contact@hotel-cheval-blanc.fr
www.hotel-cheval-blanc.fr

Closed 30 Jan to 9 Mar, fortnight in late Jun and a fortnight early Dec • 26 rooms, 3 of which are apartments, with bath/WC or shower/WC and television • €49 to €69; breakfast €8; half-board available • Menus €18 (weekdays) to €53 • Terrace, garden. No dogs admitted in restaurant • Outdoor swimming pool, tennis, children's play area

The owners' gracious welcome.

An impressive traditional country inn set in the midst of a land of medieval fortresses dating from the Holy Roman Empire. Most of the slightly old-fashioned, but comfortable and well-kept rooms overlook wooded vales; ask for one which doesn't face the street. Tuck into generously served regional dishes served in cosy, regional dining rooms, modelled after the "winstub" wine-bar. Half-timbered reading room. Former German leader and keen gastronome, Helmut Kohl, is said to be a regular!

Access : 8 km north-west of Lembach on the D 3, towards Bitche

OBERNAI - 67210

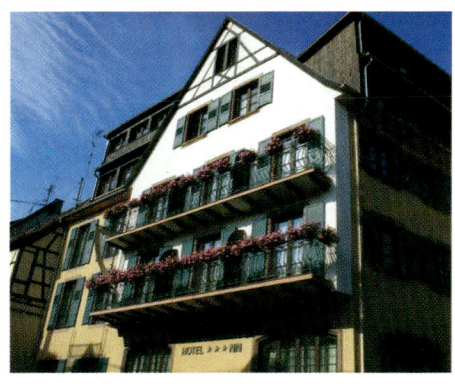

18 **COLOMBIER**
M. Baly

6/8 rue Dietrich
67210 Obernai
Tel. 03 88 47 63 33
Fax 03 88 47 63 39
info@hotel.colombier.com
www.hotel.colombier.com

Open all year • 44 air-conditioned rooms with bathrooms and television; 2 have disabled access • €81 to €110; breakfast €10 • No restaurant • Garage

Leave your car in the hotel garage and discover the charm of Obernai on foot.

The Colombier is proof that regional architecture and contemporary interior design can coexist happily. The flower-decked façade, which fits so perfectly into the lovely Alsace city, hides a surprising interior which is a mixture of designer furniture, modern light fittings, metal structures, half-timbered walls and bare beams. Most of the rooms are spacious and a few boast a balcony overlooking the street.

Access : In the heart of the village

ALSACE
OTTROTT-LE-HAUT - 67530   PFETTISHEIM - 67370

19 À L'AMI FRITZ
M. Fritz

8 rue des Châteaux
67530 Ottrott-le-Haut
Tel. 03 88 95 80 81
Fax 03 88 95 84 75
ami-fritz@wanadoo.fr
www.amifritz.com

Closed from 18 Jan to 4 Feb and one week in Feb • 22 rooms, 11 are air-conditioned, with bath/WC or shower/WC and television, half are air-conditioned and 1 has disabled access • €69 to €99; breakfast €11; half-board available • Restaurant closed Wed; menus €22 to €59 • Terrace, park, private car park, garage

 Sipping the red wine of Ottrot while digging into one of the chef's tasty dishes.

The hotel's name, taken from a novel by Erckmann-Chatrian, also refers to the owner of this trim Alsace house located on the heights of the village. Personalised, cosily comfortable, impeccably-kept and stunningly quiet bedrooms set the scene of the establishment. The chef's tasty regional fare is served in a pleasant dining room or in a picturesque winstub. The annex (Le Chant des Oiseaux), located 500m away in the heart of the countryside, is home to simply furnished small rooms.

Access : 4km to the west of Obernai on D 426

20 LA MAISON DU CHARRON
Mme Gass

15 rue Principale
67370 Pfettisheim
Tel. 03 88 69 60 35
Fax 03 88 69 85 45
mdc67@free.fr

 www.maisonducharron.com

Open all year • 5 rooms, 2 are split-level and 2 are gîtes • €44 to €53, breakfast included • No table d'hôte • Garden. Credit cards not accepted, dogs not admitted

 The personalised decoration of each room.

The owners of these two 1858 houses enthusiastically took a hand in their renovation. The master-carpenter husband undertook the individual decoration of the rooms, each of which takes its inspiration from a different type of tree - birch, maple, larch, among others - while his wife, a gifted seamstress, decorated the house with her patchworks. The small garden is very pleasant in the summer and the horses are always popular with children.

Access : 13km north-west of Strasbourg on the D 31

ALSACE

REICHSTETT - 67116

21 AIGLE D'OR
Mme Jung

5 rue de la Wantzenau
67116 Reichstett
Tel. 03 88 20 07 87
Fax 03 88 81 83 75
info@aigledor.com
www.aigledor.com

Closed from 24 Dec to 1 Jan and 4 to 20 Aug • 17 rooms with bath/WC or shower/WC and television • €64 to €99 (€59 to €97 low season); breakfast €10 • No restaurant • Car park • Nearby: walks along the banks of the canal from the Marne to the Rhine

 A deliciously sophisticated small family establishment.

The attractive white, half-timbered façade of the Aigle d'Or Hotel stands near the church of this picturesque market town near Strasbourg. Original stained-glass windows flood the hall with light and the breakfast room, in the basement, is most appealing. Upstairs, wrought-iron or Louis XVI-style furniture, wainscoting and warm fabrics more than make up for the small size of the bedrooms.

Access : 7km northbound of Strasbourg on the D 468 and D 37, or via the A 4 and the D 63

SAULXURES - 67420

22 LA BELLE VUE
Mme Boulanger

36 rue Principale
67420 Saulxures
Tel. 03 88 97 60 23
Fax 03 88 47 23 71
labellevue@wanadoo.fr
www.la-belle-vue.com

Closed from 21 to 30 Mar, 27 Jun to 6 Jul, 14 to 30 Nov and 24 to 26 Dec • 11 rooms, 7 split-level, with shower/WC and television • €82 to €119; breakfast €10; half-board available • Restaurant closed Tue and Wed, non-smoking room; menus €19 to €50 • Terrace, car park • Tennis

 The delightful interior decoration, an intelligent mix of old and new.

This village inn founded in the 19C and run by the same family for five generations has evolved admirably over the decades. The present-day accommodation features modern, spacious fittings and personalised decoration with bright woodwork, original paintings and brightly-coloured curtains; the split-level rooms have a pleasant sitting room. The inventive cuisine is served in a non-smoking restaurant which sports exposed timber-work and contemporary frescoes.

Access : In the village between Saales and St-Blaise-la-Roche

ALSACE

SAVERNE - 67700

23 LE CLOS DE LA GARENNE
Mme Schmitt

88 route du Haut-Barr
67700 Saverne
Tel. 03 88 71 20 41
Fax 03 88 02 08 86
clos.garenne@wanadoo.fr
www.closdelagarenne.fr.st

Open all year • 15 rooms with bath/WC or shower/WC and television • €46 to €86; breakfast €8; half-board available • Menus €15 to €65 • Car park, park

The landscaped gardens.

This early 20C family residence is peacefully located on the edge of a forest of fir trees. It is impossible to resist the temptation to snuggle up in the individually decorated rooms furnished in a tasteful period or country style. The all-wood, snug dining room is reminiscent of an old mountain inn. The terrace overlooks a landscaped park on a hillside.

Access : From place des Dragons take the road to Haut Barr Castle

SAVERNE - 67700

24 L'HÔTEL EUROPE
M. Kuhry

7 rue de la Gare
67700 Saverne
Tel. 03 88 71 12 07
Fax 03 88 71 11 43
info@hotel-europe-fr.com
www.hotel-europe-fr.com

Closed 17 to 31 Dec • 28 rooms, 20 of which have shower/WC, 8 have bath/WC, all have television • €63 to €87; breakfast €9 • No restaurant • Garage, public car park nearby • Visits to the nearby Château des Rohan

The individual decoration of each room.

Within easy reach of the station and the castle on the banks of the canal which links the Marne to the Rhine, this family-owned business has recently been partly refurbished. In keeping with the hotel's namesake, each spacious room features a different European style: the choice includes "Scandinavian", "French", "English" and "contemporary". A delightful sitting room decorated with frescoes and an Art Nouveau-style breakfast room. Private garage and car-park opposite.

Access : Near the railway station

ALSACE

VILLÉ - 67220

25 LA BONNE FRANQUETTE
M. Schreiber

6 place du Marché
67220 Villé
Tel. 03 88 57 14 25
Fax 03 88 57 08 15
bonne-franquette@wanadoo.fr

Closed from 13 to 27 Feb, 26 June to 3 July and 23 Oct to 6 Nov • 10 rooms, 2 non-smoking, all with bath/WC or shower/WC and television • €39 to €53; breakfast €7; half-board available • Menus €20 to €40

 Being so close to the Regional Park of the Ballons des Vosges.

The white façade, hidden by flowers during the summer, invites you to venture inside this aptly named country inn, which roughly translates as "A good, simple meal". The owner's kindness and friendly welcome immediately make it clear that he has his guests' welfare at heart. Unpretentious, practical and spotlessly clean rooms. The restaurant - a favourite with the locals, which is always a good sign - has a basement and an upper room, both serving traditional fare.

Access : In the town centre

WISSEMBOURG - 67160

26 HOSTELLERIE DU CYGNE
M. et Mme Kientz

3 rue du Sel
67160 Wissembourg
Tel. 03 88 94 00 16
Fax 03 88 54 38 28
hostellerie-cygne@wanadoo.fr

Closed from 15 Feb to 3 Mar, 3 to 16 Jul and 8 to 23 Nov and Wed • 16 rooms in two adjacent houses, with bath/WC or shower/WC, all have television • €50 to €65; breakfast €8; half-board available • Restaurant closed Thu lunchtime and Sun evening; menus €25 (weekdays) to €58 • Terrace. Dogs not admitted in rooms

 The Salt House (1448) and its amazing roof.

This inn's two buildings, one of which was built in the late 14C and the other in 1535, typify the style of this well-preserved small town, where over 70 of the houses date from before 1700. The bedrooms, somewhat old-fashioned but still comfortable, are ideal for an overnight halt. The restaurant's two dining rooms are lit by stained-glass windows; the cosiest has recently been embellished with a lovely marquetry ceiling. A terrace in the courtyard overlooks a handsome half-timbered façade.

Access : In the town centre, next to the town hall

ALSACE
WISSEMBOURG - 67160   AMMERSCHWIHR - 68770

27 AU MOULIN DE LA WALK
M. Schmidt

2 rue de la Walk
67160 Wissembourg
Tel. 03 88 94 06 44
Fax 03 88 54 38 03
info@moulin-walk.com
www.moulin-walk.com

Closed from 2 to 25 Jan and from 19 Jun to 4 Jul • 25 rooms, one of which has disabled access, with bath/WC or shower/WC and television • €58 to €65; breakfast €8; half-board available • Menus €30 to €45 • Terrace, garden, car park. Dogs not admitted in rooms

 A slice or two of raisin cake - the famous "kugelhof" - at breakfast time.

This cluster of buildings built on the foundations of an old mill, whose well-preserved wheel is still in working order, stands on the banks of the Lauter on the outskirts of the town. Most of the rooms have been refurbished with modern fittings and brand new bathrooms. Tasty, traditional fare is served in a cosy, wainscoted dining room and a pretty flower-decked terrace.

Access : Out of the town centre, on the banks of the Lauter

28 AUX ARMES DE FRANCE
M. Gaertner

1 Grand' Rue
68770 Ammerschwihr
Tel. 03 89 47 10 12
Fax 03 89 47 38 12
aux.armes.de.france@wanadoo.fr
www.aux-armes-de-france.com

Closed Wed and Thu • 10 rooms with bath/WC and television • €67 to €82; breakfast €12 • Menus €25 to €42 • Garden, private car park • Located in the heart of the Alsace vineyards. Golf 1km away

 Good taste abounds in this warm Alsatian inn.

Numerous famous chefs have learnt their craft in this handsome house rebuilt after the air raids of the Second World War. Its long culinary tradition dates back to the Thirties, when the grandmother of the present chef ruled the kitchen. Spacious rooms and a bourgeois-style dining room where mouth-watering dishes are served under the watchful eye of ancestors' portraits. Definitely worth tasting!

Access : At the entrance to the town centre

ALSACE

AMMERSCHWIHR - 68770

 MAISON THOMAS
Famille Thomas

 41 Grand'Rue
68770 Ammerschwihr
Tel. 03 89 78 23 90
Fax 03 89 47 18 90
thomas.guy@free.fr
 www.maisonthomas.com

Open all year • 4 rooms with a kitchenette • €43 to €46, breakfast included • No table d'hôte • Garden, car park. Credit cards not accepted • Sauna

 Extremely well-appointed rooms.

This former wine-grower's house – painted an unmissable turquoise – stands in the most picturesque part of the village. Each of the spacious, well-equipped rooms carries a name and all have kitchenettes. The well thought-out garden has something for everyone: a shaded corner for afternoon naps, bower, barbecue, swings, table-tennis and boules, not forgetting the view over the vineyards. The house also boasts a sauna and keep-fit equipment.

Access : In the village

BERGHEIM - 68750

 CHEZ NORBERT
M. Moeller

 9 Grand'Rue
68750 Bergheim
Tel. 03 89 73 31 15
Fax 03 89 73 60 65
labacchante@wanadoo.fr

Closed from 12 to 18 Jan, 5 to 31 Mar and 6 to 13 Jul • 12 rooms and 1 apartment, some split-level, most have bath/WC, all have television • €69 to €110; breakfast €12; half-board available • Air-conditioned restaurant, closed Wed lunchtime, Fri lunchtime and Thu; menus €22 (weekdays) to €48 • Terrace, courtyard, private car park

 Home-made cakes and jams for breakfast.

The cachet of this group of wine-growers' farms is undeniable. The colourful, half-timbered façades (14C) vie for pride of place with the other picturesque houses of this town on the Alsace Wine Route. Some of the contemporary, practical rooms are located under the eaves; avoid those overlooking the road, which are noisier. Good country fare served in a typically Alsatian restaurant or on a pleasant terrace, bedecked with geraniums in the summer.

Access : On the main street in the centre of the village

ALSACE

COLMAR - 68000

31 TURENNE
Mme Helminger

10 route de Bâle
68000 Colmar
Tel. 03 89 21 58 58
Fax 03 89 41 27 64
helmlinger@turenne.com
www.turenne.com

Open all year • 85 rooms, 42 of which are non-smoking, all have bath/WC or shower/WC, air-conditioning and television • €60 to €68; breakfast €8 • No restaurant • Garage

 A convenient distance from the old town.

Conveniently located two minutes away from the picturesque Little Venice district, you can't miss the distinctive pink and yellow façade of this large house. Spacious, refurbished double rooms some of which have traditional regional furniture. Smaller, single rooms, equally well-kept and soundproofed, are also available. Breakfasts are served in a typically Alsatian dining room. Wainscoted sitting room and bar, heaven-sent private garage and friendly family welcome.

Access : Coming from the railway station, head for the A 35 motorway and turn left at the Elf petrol station

ILLHAEUSERN - 68970

32 LES HIRONDELLES
M. et Mme Muller

33 rue du 25-Janvier
68970 Illhaeusern
Tel. 03 89 71 83 76
Fax 03 89 71 86 40
hotelleshirondelles@wanadoo.fr
www.hotelleshirondelles.com

Closed 29 Jan to 10 Mar and 19 to 27 Dec • 19 rooms, most have shower/WC, all have television • €70 to €74, breakfast included • No restaurant • Garden, private car park • Outdoor swimming pool

 The swallows, which really do make the summer.

Rustic painted furniture and oak beams set the tone of the relatively soberly-decorated rooms which overlook a flowered inner courtyard or a picture-book landscape of kitchen gardens. The recent swimming pool, complete with teak sun-deck and air-conditioning in the adjacent accommodation building makes the hotel very pleasant during the hot summer months.

Access : In the centre of the village

ALSACE

KAYSERSBERG - 68240

33 **L'ARBRE VERT**
Famille Kieny-Wittner

 1 rue Haute du Rempart
68240 Kaysersberg
Tel. 03 89 47 11 51
Fax 03 89 78 13 40
arbrevertbellepromenade@wanadoo.fr
http://perso.wanadoo.fr/arbrevertbelle
promenade

Closed from 6 Jan to 12 Feb • 20 rooms with bath/WC or shower/WC and television, 14 in a separate wing • €62 to €71 (€59 to €70 low season); breakfast €8; half-board available • Non-smoking restaurant; menus €23 to €38 • Dogs not admitted in restaurant

 A walk round this tiny Alsatian town rich in points of interest.

The birthplace of the humanitarian Dr Schweitzer, the most famous inhabitant of Kayserberg, stands side by side this hostelry comprised of two Alsace houses located on either side of a square of greenery. The low-key countrified rooms and the restaurant, renowned for its regional-inspired classical cuisine, are located in the main house. The other, called the Belle Promenade, offers more spacious, pleasant accommodation, furnished in particular with pieces painted by the lady of the house.

Access : 6km westbound of Colmar in the centre of the village

KIENTZHEIM - 68240

34 **HOSTELLERIE SCHWENDI**
M. et Mme Schillé

 2 place Schwendi
68240 Kientzheim
Tel. 03 89 47 30 50
Fax 03 89 49 04 49
hotel-schwendi@wanadoo.fr
www.hotel-schwendi.com

Open all year (by reservation from 24 Dec to 15 Mar) • 25 rooms all with bath/WC and television, 9 with air-conditioning • €78 to €95; breakfast €9; half-board available • Restaurant closed Thu lunchtime and Wed and from 24 Dec to 15 Mar; menus €23 to €59 • Terrace, private car park

 The delightful welcome of the hotel owners-cum-winegrowers.

An old well, around which the terrace is laid in the summer, stands in the paved courtyard of this 17C inn with its elegant, pale yellow facade. Guests are accommodated in renovated rooms with original timber ceilings. A likeable blend of classical Louis XIII chairs and bare stone walls adds a cosy combination of rustic and bourgeois to the dining room, where wholesome country cooking is served with delightful home-made wines.

Access : 3km to the east of Kaysersberg on the D 28

ALSACE
LAPOUTROIE - 68650   LAPOUTROIE - 68650

 35 LES ALISIERS
M. et Mme Degouy

 36 DU FAUDÉ
M. et Mme Baldinger

 Lieu-dit Faudé
68650 Lapoutroie
Tel. 03 89 47 52 82
Fax 03 89 47 22 38
jacques.degouy@wanadoo.fr
www.alisiers.com

 28 rue du Général-Dufieux
68650 Lapoutroie
Tel. 03 89 47 50 35
Fax 03 89 47 24 82
info@faude.com
www.faude.com

Closed 6 Jan to 5 Feb, 25 Jun to 1 Jul (except hotel), 21 to 25 Dec, Mon, Tue (except evenings in season) and Wed lunchtime • 18 rooms, one of which has disabled access and 5 are non-smoking. Rooms have bath/WC or shower/WC • €50 to €122; breakfast €9; half-board available • Menus €15 to €44 • Terrace, garden, car park

Closed from 12 to 31 Mar and from 6 to 24 Nov • 31 rooms, 2 of which are apartments, with bath/WC or shower/WC, all have television • €74 to €95; breakfast €13; half-board available • Restaurant closed Tue and Wed; menus €20 to €75, children's menu €10 • Garden, terrace, private car park • Indoor swimming pool, fitness room, hammam, jacuzzi, skiing

 The kindness of the staff and the owners.

 A riverside country garden.

All the windows of this extended farmhouse built in 1819 overlook the pleasant, rolling countryside of the Béhine Valley, whether it be from the snug and countrified or more contemporary rooms; you can choose your favourite on the hotel's website. The veranda restaurant shares the same great view; generous helpings of regional cooking, with an accent on local produce, are served in the non-smoking dining room. Pleasant garden overlooking the village of Lapoutroie.

The Baldinger family has run this traditional country inn for over 40 years and have certainly learnt a thing or two about making their guests feel at home. Well-soundproofed bedrooms are spacious and comfortable. The restaurant staff, dressed in traditional Alsatian costume, serves tasty, locally sourced food whose continued popularity is due to the chef's ability to move with the times, introducing lighter dishes and vegetarian meals. Attractive indoor swimming pool and a fitness room.

Access: In the upper reaches of the village, 3km to the south-west on a minor road

Access: In the centre of the village

ALSACE

LOGELHEIM - 68280

37 À LA VIGNE
M. Bauer

5 Grande-Rue
68280 Logelheim
Tel. 03 89 20 99 60
Fax 03 89 20 99 69
restaurant.alavigne@calixo.net
www.reperes.com/la-vigne

Closed from 22 Jun to 9 Jul and from 23 Dec to 7 Jan • 9 rooms with bath/WC or shower/WC and television • €52 to €70; breakfast €6; half-board available • Restaurant closed Sat lunchtime Mon evening and Sun; menus €21 (weekdays) to €27 • A few parking spaces. No dogs admitted in rooms

The simple, friendly atmosphere.

An attractive village house with a redbrick façade and a totally renovated interior. Only 10min from Colmar, this tranquil hotel is an excellent choice for an overnight stop. The tastefully decorated rooms are pleasant and spotless. Wood is the predominant feature of the family dining room which offers a menu of French classics, while the bar serves the region's famous tartes flambées – light pizzas on an extra-thin crust – by the warmth of an earthenware stove.

Access : To the south-east of Colmar, on the D 13 then the D 45

LUTTER - 68480

38 AUBERGE ET HOSTELLERIE PAYSANNE
Mme Guérinol

1 rue de Wolschwiller
68480 Lutter
Tel. 03 89 40 71 67
Fax 03 89 07 33 38
aubergepaysanne2@wanadoo.fr
www.auberge-hostellerie-paysanne.com

Closed for 2 weeks late Jan-early Feb, 2 weeks early Jul • 16 rooms at the Auberge and 9 in the separate wing (L'Hostellerie) 200m away. Rooms have bath/WC or shower/WC, all have television • €48 to €68; breakfast €7; half-board available • Restaurant closed Tue lunchtime out of season and Mon; menus from €9 (weekdays) to €38 • Terrace, garden, car park

The picturesque, unspoilt landscapes of the Sundgau.

This establishment does offer its own modern accommodation, but most people prefer the annexe, 200m away: a 1618 farmhouse typical of the Sundgau region, which was actually taken apart brick by brick and rebuilt here, a short distance from the Swiss border. Some of the rooms, of varying quality it must be said, have oak beamed ceilings, and a pretty flowered garden leads out towards the fields. Check-in at the main inn and sample the regional specialities and seasonal game in its dining room.

Access : Leave Ferrette south-east bound on the D 23, at Sondersdorf take the D 21B, then at Raedersdorf go back onto the D 23

ALSACE

MITTELWIHR - 68630

39 DOMAINE DU BOUXHOF
M. et Mme Edel

Rue du Bouxhof
68630 Mittelwihr
Tel. 03 89 47 93 67
Fax 03 89 47 84 82

Closed Jan • 3 rooms with television and fridge • €50, breakfast included • No table d'hôte • Garden, car park. Credit cards not accepted, dogs not admitted

Staying in a wine-growing property and trying a glass — it would be impolite to refuse!

This 17C castle flanked with square towers seems to rise out of a sea of vines. Guests can choose between two types of accommodation: modern, spotless rooms or very well-equipped cottages; those with a balcony overlooking the vineyards are the most attractive. The superb breakfast room is housed in a 15C chapel. Don't pass up a chance to visit the cellar and its oak vats where the estate's wine is made, finishing with a wine-tasting session.

Access : In the upper part of the village, on the wine-growing estate

MOERNACH - 68480

40 AUX DEUX CLEFS
Mme Enderlin

218 rue Hennin Blenner
68480 Moernach
Tel. 03 89 40 80 56
Fax 03 89 08 10 47

 auxdeuxclefs@wanadoo.fr

Closed for two weeks in February, one week early Nov and from late Jul to early Aug • 7 rooms with shower/WC and television • €42 to €47; breakfast €6; half-board available • Restaurant closed Wed evening and Thu; menus €21 (weekdays) to €44. Daily set menu €9.50 • Garden, car park, garage

An afternoon nap in the pretty tree-lined garden.

A handsome half-timbered and gabled country house, characteristic of the Sundgau; look for its attractive wrought-iron sign of two crossed keys. Taste the local delicacy, fried carp, in the welcoming wood-panelled dining room, tastefully decorated with paintings. Comfortable, inviting rooms, which are being progressively renovated, occupy a wing which dates from the Sixties.

Access : At Vieux-Ferrette leave the D 432 for the D 473 which goes through Koestlach and Moernach

ALSACE

OLTINGUE - 68480

41 **MOULIN DE HUTTINGUE**
M. Thomas Antoine

68480 Oltingue
Tel. 03 89 40 72 91
Fax 03 89 07 31 01

Closed in Jan and Feb • 4 rooms • €55 to €65, breakfast included • Car park, garden, terrace. Credit cards not accepted. Dogs not admitted

 The decorative features which bear witness to the mill's long history.

The Franco-Swiss border is only a short distance from this 17C wheat mill on the banks of the Ill, which is little more than a stream here. The rooms, all upstairs, are quite simply appointed on the whole. The superb loft under the eaves has been fitted with a useful kitchenette. Breakfast is served in a dining room complete with magnificent wooden pillars or on the terrace when the weather permits.

Access : 1.5km south of Oltingue on the D 21e

ORBEY - 68370

42 **FERME DU BUSSET**
Mme Batôt

33 lieu-dit Busset
68370 Orbey
Tel. 03 89 71 22 17
Fax 03 89 71 22 17
fabienne.batot@wanadoo.fr
 www.fermedubusset.com

Closed 23 to 26 and 29 to 31 Dec • 6 rooms • €48, breakfast included • No table d'hôte • Garden, car park. Credit cards not accepted. Dogs not admitted

 The panoramic view over the Orbey Valley.

A steep road winds its way up to this farmhouse, which still breeds its own poultry and sheep, high on a lush green plateau at an altitude of 600m. Choose from self-catering cottages or bed and breakfast rooms: the latter are lined in wood and while not enormous are very well-kept and quiet. Before leaving, make sure you stock up on cheese, cooked meats and home-made jams.

Access : 1km to the east of Orbey on a minor road

ALSACE
RIQUEWIHR - 68340   RIQUEWIHR - 68340

43 L'ORIEL
Mme Wendel

3 rue des Écuries-Seigneuriales
68340 Riquewihr
Tel. 03 89 49 03 13
Fax 03 89 47 92 87
info@hotel-oriel.com
www.hotel-oriel.com

Open all year • 22 rooms, 3 of which are split-level, with shower/WC or bath/WC, all have television • €67 to €97; breakfast €10 • No restaurant • Terrace

44 LE SARMENT D'OR
M. et Mme Merckling

4 rue du Cerf
68340 Riquewihr
Tel. 03 89 86 02 86
Fax 03 89 47 99 23
info@riquewihr-sarment-dor.com
www.riquewihr-sarment-dor.com

Closed from 9 Jan to 12 Feb, from 3 to 10 Jul • 9 rooms, 2 of which are split-level, most have bath/WC, all have television • €60 to €80; breakfast €8 • Restaurant closed Sun evening, Tue lunchtime and Mon; menus €20 to €52 • No dogs admitted in rooms

 Breakfast served in the inner courtyard in summertime.

 The owners' attentive welcome.

The frontage of this 16C country home is adorned with a handsome two-storey oriel window and an amusing wrought-iron sign; the delightful maze of corridors and staircases bear witness to the house's old age. The rooms, in the progress of being renovated, are decorated in a variety of styles, ranging from rustic to more modern – families generally prefer one of the split-level rooms.

The Sarment d'Or – or golden vine – has put down its roots in a quiet street lined with handsome 16C houses. A spiral staircase leads up to the cosy, modern bedrooms. The snug, warm dining rooms are characteristic of Alsatian interior decoration with pine panelling and dark beams lit up by the crackling flames of a welcoming log fire.

Access : From the town hall take Rue du Général de Gaulle then the first street on the right

Access : From the town hall square, drive to the end of Rue du Général de Gaulle and turn left (pedestrian street)

ALSACE

RIXHEIM - 68170 **SAINT-AMARIN - 68550**

  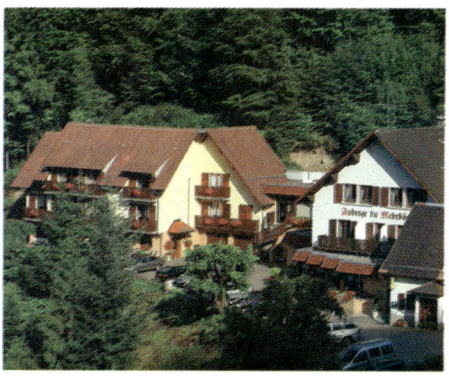

45 LE CLOS DU MÛRIER
Mme Volpatti

42 Grande-Rue
68170 Rixheim
Tel. 03 89 54 14 81
Fax 03 89 64 47 08

Open all year • 5 rooms with kitchenettes, bathrooms with separate WC • €62; breakfast €8 • No table d'hôte • Garden, car park. Dogs not admitted

46 AUBERGE DU MEHRBÄCHEL
M. et Mme Kornacker

Route de Geishouse
68550 Saint-Amarin
Tel. 03 89 82 60 68
Fax 03 89 82 66 05
kornacker @ cegetel.net

Closed for one week early Nov, Mon evening, Thu evening and Fri • 23 rooms located in 2 buildings, with bath/WC or shower/WC • €54 to €58; breakfast €9; half-board available • Air-conditioned restaurant; menus €16 (weekdays) to €45 • Car park. Dogs not admitted • Ideal for rests and walking

The spacious, comfortable rooms.

Toasting your toes by the warm stove after a hard day's trekking.

This venerable 16C Alsatian house has been tastefully renovated. Old beams blend well with a modern décor and each bedroom has its own kitchenette. On the leisure side, the house has a pleasant walled courtyard and the owners are happy to lend bicycles to guests.

This old farmhouse built on the edge of a forest of fir trees, so characteristic of the Vosges scenery, has been in the family since 1886. Half the simple but spacious and well-kept rooms have balconies and most of them overlook the wonderful Rossberg mountain range. Game and regional dishes are served in the air-conditioned dining room, its walls are adorned with hunting trophies. A hiking trail runs past the inn, ideal for walkers!

Access : 6km eastbound from Mulhouse, drive towards Basle, in the centre of Rixheim

Access : Between Thann and Bussang, drive for 4km on the Mehrbächel road

ALSACE
SAINTE-CROIX-EN-PLAINE - 68127　　　SAINTE-MARIE-AUX-MINES - 68160

47　AU MOULIN
M. et Mme Woeffle

Route d'Herrlisheim
68127 Sainte-Croix-en-Plaine
Tel. 03 89 49 31 20
Fax 03 89 49 23 11

Open from 1 Apr to 3 Nov • 17 rooms with bath/WC, almost all have television • €56 to €68; breakfast €8 • Menus from €12 to €25 • Garden, car park • Small museum about Alsace in the inner courtyard

Lingering over breakfast in the enchanting flowered courtyard.

With its flowered courtyard and half-timbered buildings, this former flour-mill, built in 1880, represents a haven of peace and quiet, just a short distance from an interchange on the A 35! The sizeable rooms are practical and tastefully decorated with cane furniture. Some overlook the peaks of the Vosges, while others look down on the plain; all are wonderfully quiet. Interesting mini-museum on the Alsace of yesteryear.

Access : 10km southbound from Colmar on the D 201, then at Sainte-Croix-en-Plaine take the D 1

48　AUX MINES D'ARGENT
Mme Willmann

8 rue du Docteur-Weisgerber
68160 Sainte-Marie-aux-Mines
Tel. 03 89 58 55 75
Fax 03 89 58 65 49

Open all year • 9 rooms with shower/WC and television • €45 to €55; breakfast €6; half-board available • Menus €10 to €32 • Terrace

The busy atmosphere surrounding the famous Mineral, Gem And Fossil Show (June).

The mullioned windows of the façade testify to the old age of this house, said to have been built in 1596 by a miner who would appear to have struck it rich! The original spiral staircase leads up to the rooms, graced with large windows and furniture dating from 1900 or thereabouts. The family dining room, in the "winstub" style, is embellished with wood carvings which depict the miners' lives: the seam at Ste Marie was mined from the 9C to the 18C.

Access : In the centre, in the street parallel to the main road (where the town hall is)

ALSACE

SEWEN - 68290

49 **LA VILLA DU LAC**
Mme Rioual

2 route du Ballon
68290 Sewen
Tel. 03 89 82 98 38
Fax 03 89 82 98 38
villadulac.sewen@tv-com.net

Closed Jan • 6 non-smoking rooms, all with bath/WC or shower/WC • €50 to €55, breakfast included • Table d'hôte €20, drinks included • Garden, library, television room, car park. Credit cards not accepted, dogs not admitted

 The pleasant peaceful environment of the house.

This 1930's style villa, at the foot of the Ballon d'Alsace and opposite Lake Sewen, makes a perfect departure point for walking trips. On your return, dig into the tasty Alsatian dishes prepared by the mistress of the house with local farm produce. Then, after a good night's sleep in one of the rooms overlooking the lake or the forest, devour a generous breakfast, composed of, depending on the season, strudel, Christmas cake or fruit pie.

Access : 400m outside the village, towards Ballon d'Alsace on the D 466 opposite Lake Sewen

SIERENTZ - 68510

50 **AUBERGE ST-LAURENT**
M. et Mme Arbeit

1 rue Fontaine
68510 Sierentz
Tel. 03 89 81 52 81
Fax 03 89 81 67 08
info@auberge-saintlaurent.fr
www.auberge-saintlaurent.fr

Closed Mon and Tue and fortnight in Mar and fortnight in Aug • 10 rooms upstairs, all are air-conditioned with bathrooms and television • €100 to €130; breakfast €13; half-board available • Menus €39 to €70 • Terrace, car park

 Deliciously classical home cooking spiced up with a touch of modernity.

A stopover in this former staging inn is a treat for the eyes, soul and palate! It is impossible not to give in to the infectious good humour of the owners' charming welcome. The decoration of the spruce bedrooms evokes the ancestors of the Arbeit family: Sophie the baker, Marie the grandmother, Gustave the labourer and others, and is full of charming details. The restaurant, furnished in soft colours, has a collection of cockerels, knick-knacks and paintings, and a lovely terrace.

Access : On the way through the village

ALSACE

THANNENKIRCH - 68590   WINKEL - 68480

51 AUBERGE LA MEUNIÈRE
M. et Mme Dumoulin

30 rue Sainte-Anne
68590 Thannenkirch
Tel. 03 89 73 10 47
Fax 03 89 73 12 31
info@aubergelameuniere.com
www.aubergelameuniere.com

52 AU CERF
M. Koller

76 rue Principale
68480 Winkel
Tel. 03 89 40 85 05
Fax 03 89 08 11 10
g.koller@tiscali.fr

Open from 21 Mar to 19 Dec • 25 rooms at the rear of the building. Rooms have bath/WC or shower/WC, all have television • €50 to €80; breakfast €7; half-board available • Restaurant closed Mon-Wed lunchtimes; menus €17 (weekdays) to €36 • Terrace, car park, garage • Sauna, fitness room, table-tennis, billiards

Closed Feb • 6 rooms upstairs with bath/WC, some have television • €47 to €50 (€42 to €47 low season); breakfast €7; half-board available • Menus €10 to €25 • Dogs not admitted • Hiking

 The restful view of the forest, from some of the bathrooms!

 The family atmosphere behind these red walls.

The imposing flowered façade of this inn conceals a host of attractions. Almost all the rooms are rear-facing – avoid those overlooking the street – with a view of the Bergenbach Valley and the towers of Haut-Koenigsbourg Castle, which film buffs may recognise as the location of Jean Renoir's anti-war masterpiece "La Grande Illusion". The restaurant is decorated in a delightful rustic style and the terrace opens out onto the splendid Vosges scenery.

The smart red frontage of this inn near the Swiss border cannot be missed. The rather bare rooms are tiled and furnished practically; nearly all have been recently renovated and the proverbial Swiss obsession with cleanliness has clearly made it over the border here. Family dining rooms in an up-to-date "winstub" style. Bring a rucksack and walking stick and explore the beautiful Sundgau region and the source of the Ill along countless footpaths.

Access : Between Ribeauvillé and Sélestat, in a village very near Haut-Koenisbourg

Access : In the centre of the village

AQUITAINE

Friendly Aquitaine has welcomed mankind since prehistoric times. Its varied mosaic of landscapes is as distinctive as its inhabitants' dedication to hospitality, invariably spiced with a generous sprinkling of forthright rural humour. No stay in Aquitaine would be complete without visiting at least one of Bordeaux' justly famous châteaux and vineyards. Afterwards head for the "Silver Coast", prized by surfers and rugby fans alike, and sample delicious Basque gâteau, have a drink in a tapas bar or even take ringside seats for a bullfight! This rugged yet sunny land between the Pyrenees and the Atlantic has always been fiercely proud of its identity and the inhabitants of the Basque country still celebrate their time-honoured traditions in truly vigorous style. If you spend a little time in one these sleepy Basque villages, all of which sport the region's colours, red and green, you will be astounded by the ease with which they suddenly burst into spirited song and games.

- Dordogne (24)
- Gironde (33)
- Landes (40)
- Lot et Garonne (47)
- Pyrénées Atlantiques (64)

AQUITAINE

BADEFOLS-SUR-DORDOGNE - 24150

1 CÔTÉ RIVAGE
Mme De Roton-Couderc

Au bourg
24150 Badefols-sur-Dordogne
Tel. 05 53 23 65 00
Fax 05 53 22 56 01
coterivage@online.fr
www.cote-dordogne.com

Open 30 Apr to mid-Oct, closed Sun • 7 air-conditioned rooms • €55 to €90; breakfast €9; half-board available • Menu €25 to €32 including beverages • Terrace, garden

We most liked Cutting through the garden to walk along the banks of the Dordogne.

This welcoming, restored house is located between the presbytery and a fishermen's house, a few steps from the Dordogne River. Spotless walls, colourful curtains, antique furniture and air-conditioning make the rooms very pleasant. The bar and sitting room are decorated with old advertising gadgets, while beams, bare stone walls and wrought iron furniture set the contemporary tone of the dining room which leads into a pleasant terrace. Fresh, local produce and a fine wine menu of local vintages.

Access : On the banks of the Dordogne

BAYAC - 24150

2 LE RELAIS DE LAVERGNE
Mme Pillebout

« La Vergne »
24150 Bayac
Tel. 05 53 57 83 16
Fax 05 53 57 83 16
relaisdelavergne@wanadoo.fr

Open all year • 4 rooms upstairs, one apartment with disabled access, all have bathrooms • €60 to €65, breakfast included • Table d'hôte €23 (evening only) • Park, terrace, car park. Credit cards not accepted, no dogs admitted in restaurant • Outdoor swimming pool

We most liked The tranquillity of this handsome 17C manor house.

The peaceful appeal of this house is such that guests often wish they had planned to stay longer. The attentive welcome of the two hostesses, the tranquil atmosphere and mouth-watering smells wafting from the kitchen never fail to enchant. Light, airy bedrooms combine the charm of yesteryear with modern-day comforts. The spacious restaurant and inner courtyard provide a perfect setting for elegant dining.

Access : 10km to the south-east of Lanquais, on the Beaumont road

AQUITAINE

BERGERAC - 24100

3 LA FLAMBÉE
M. Delage

153 avenue Pasteur
24100 Bergerac
Tel. 05 53 57 52 33
Fax 05 53 61 07 57
laflambée@hotmail.fr
www.laflambee.com

Open all year • 21 rooms, 7 of which are in a separate wing. Rooms have bath/WC, some have shower/WC, all have television • €74 to €82 (€65 to €76 low season); breakfast €8; half-board available • Menus €18 to €37 • Terrace, park, car park • Swimming pool, tennis

A tennis match and swim in the pool, or a quiet glass of Bergerac for the less energetic!

This pleasant old country home on the doorsteps of the tobacco capital of France has been recently renovated. The rooms, practical and spacious with a personal touch, are named after one of the surrounding vineyards; those in the annexe are more simply decorated but have private terraces overlooking the flowered grounds. The stylish dining rooms feature cosy armchairs, wrought-iron furniture, oak beams, log fires and a veranda.

Access: Leave Bergerac on the N 21 towards Périgueux

BOURDEILLES - 24130

4 HOSTELLERIE LES GRIFFONS
M. et Mme Lebrun

Le bourg
24310 Bourdeilles
Tel. 05 53 45 45 35
Fax 05 53 45 45 20
griffons@griffons.fr
www.griffons.fr

Open from 14 Apr to 14 Oct, closed Mon and Fri lunchtimes in Jul-Aug, lunchtimes except weekends and national holidays from Sep to Jun • 10 rooms with bath/WC or shower/WC and television • €86 to €96 (€75 to €94 low season); breakfast €10; half-board available • Non-smoking restaurant; menus €24 to €39 • Terrace, car park

A visit to the two castles of Bourdeilles.

This 16C mansion, at the foot of a medieval and a Renaissance castle, stands on the banks of the River Dronne close to its picturesque old bridge. Exposed stonework and beams, antiques and curios help to give the rooms a rustic feel; those on the first floor boast decorative fireplaces, while the rafters upstairs under the eaves add a distinctly romantic flavour. The stylish dining room opens out onto a pleasant terrace overlooking the river.

Access: In the centre of the village between the château and the river

AQUITAINE
BOURDEILLES - 24310   BOURG-DES-MAISONS - 24320

5 CHAMBRE D'HÔTE L'AMBROISIE
M. Joch

Grand'Rue
24310 Bourdeilles
Tel. 05 53 04 24 51
Fax 05 53 04 67 45
jc.joch@wanadoo.fr

Closed 1 week in Feb and during Nov school holidays • 4 rooms, all have bath/WC or shower/WC • €51 to €65, breakfast included • Table d'hôte €23, drinks included • Terrace, garden, television room. Credit cards not accepted, no dogs admitted

We most liked The availability and kindness of the owners.

The spirit and charm of Périgord reign throughout this handsome 18C property located in the town centre just a few steps from the castle. The rooms, furnished with antiques, sport the fresh tangy colours of the spices after which they are named (Curry, Paprika, Anis, etc.); some have retained the original bare walls and beams. The tasty dishes concocted by the lady of the house are served in the garden under the shade of olive trees in fine weather.

Access : In the town centre

6 DOMAINE DE TEINTEILLAC
M. Pin

Route de Chapdeuil
24320 Bourg-des-Maisons
Tel. 05 53 91 51 03
Fax 05 53 91 51 03
www.teinteillac.com

Open all year • 4 non-smoking rooms, all have bathrooms • €60, breakfast included • Table d'hôte €18 to €28 • Terrace, park, private car park. Credit cards not accepted, no dogs admitted

We most liked The authentic beauty of the château, parkland and surrounding countryside.

This immense estate tucked away in the countryside and removed from the bustle of urban life, is home to a remarkable 15C château, currently undergoing renovation. The elegantly furnished bedrooms further enhance the appeal of the location. The farm-inn serves excellent regional dishes made from locally grown organic produce. The untamed parkland is perfect for long country walks.

Access : 2km northbound on the D 99 and D 106, Chapdeuil road

AQUITAINE

BRANTÔME - 24310

BRANTÔME - 24310

7 LES HABRANS
M. Falcoz

Les Habrans
24310 Brantôme
Tel. 05 53 05 58 84
Fax 05 53 05 58 84

Closed from 30 Oct to 1 May • 5 rooms, 4 of which are on the first floor • €60 to €70, breakfast included • No table d'hôte • Terrace, garden. Credit cards not accepted

8 LA MAISON FLEURIE
M. et Mme Robinson

54 rue Gambetta
24310 Brantôme
Tel. 05 53 35 17 04
Fax 05 53 05 16 58
info@maisonfleurie.net
www.maisonfleurie.net

Closed 14 Feb to 1 Mar • 5 non-smoking rooms • €60 to €85, breakfast included • No table d'hôte • Credit cards not accepted, no dogs admitted • Outdoor swimming pool

Boating down the Dronne.

The riverside setting of this unpretentious little house is without question its main asset. The simple rooms are tastefully decorated; those on the first floor under the eaves have sloped ceilings and windows overlooking the river. When the weather is fine, guests can tuck into breakfast on the delightful terrace.

Staying in the heart of the hometown of the 16C court chronicler Brantôme.

This 19C property, in the shadow of the elegant Romanesque belfry of the abbey, boasts a number of attractions: a convenient town centre location, exemplary welcome, excellent value for money and above all, its charming, comfortable rooms. Whenever the weather permits, generous breakfasts are served in the flowered courtyard and the small swimming pool is always appreciated during the hot weather.

Access : In the lane opposite the gendarmerie (police station)

Access : In the town centre

AQUITAINE

CAMPAGNE - 24260

9 HÔTEL DU CHÂTEAU
Mme Petit

Le Bourg
24260 Campagne
Tel. 05 53 07 23 50
Fax 05 53 03 93 69
hotduchateau@aol.com

Open from Apr to 15 Oct • 16 rooms with bath/WC or shower/WC, all with television • €46 to €50; breakfast €7; half-board available • Menus €18 to €50 • Terrace, car park. No dogs admitted in rooms

We most liked The simple authenticity of this family home.

A handsome country house in the midst of an enchanting Périgordian hamlet. The charming, old-fashioned rooms are spacious, comfortable and well kept, and stay cool even in the height of summer thanks to their thick stone walls. From the windows of the dining room, diners can see Campagne Castle while they sample the chef's carefully prepared regional cooking. Pleasant, shaded terrace, decked in flowers in the summer.

Access : Leave Le Bugue south-east bound on the D 703 and drive for 4km

CÉNAC-ET-SAINT-JULIEN - 24250

10 LA GUÉRINIÈRE
M. et Mme Demassougne

« Baccas »
24250 Cénac-et-Saint-Julien
Tel. 05 53 29 91 97
Fax 05 53 30 23 89
contact@la-gueriniere-dordogne.com
www.la-gueriniere-dordogne.com

Closed from 2 Nov to 1 Apr • 5 rooms upstairs and 2 gîtes • €75 to €90, breakfast included • Table d'hôte €22 (except Sun) • Terrace, park, car park. Credit cards not accepted, no dogs admitted • Outdoor swimming pool, tennis, bicycles, golf

We most liked Sampling the tasty meals made with fresh farm produce.

This 18C manor farm, extensively remodelled over the centuries, is reminiscent of a charterhouse. Each of the extremely spacious rooms - with bare stone walls, period furniture and tasteful fabrics - is named after a flower. Cats, dogs and farmyard animals enjoy the run of the extensive grounds, to the invariable delight of children.

Access : On the D 46 road to Gourdon

AQUITAINE

CÉNAC-ET-SAINT-JULIEN - 24250

11 LA TOUILLE
M. et Mme Barry

Route de l'Église
24250 Cénac-et-Saint-Julien
Tel. 05 53 28 35 25
Fax 05 53 28 35 25
sbarry.latouille@wanadoo.fr
www.sarlat-en-perigord.com/latouille

Open all year • 4 non-smoking rooms, all with bathrooms • €31 to €36; breakfast €5 • No table d'hôte • Garden, car park

We most liked: The immaculately cared for rooms.

The rooms of this villa tucked away in one of the village's peaceful streets, have all been renovated: those on the ground-floor feature the simple charm of iron bedsteads and pretty fabrics, while the one upstairs is slightly cosier with wooden country-style furniture. Depending on the season, breakfast is served in the veranda or under the pergola. Children's play area in the garden. Friendly welcome.

Access : 5km southeast of La Roque-Gageac on the D 703 and D 46, towards Gourdon then the D 50 towards Saint-Cybranet, at Cénac

JOURNIAC - 24260

12 LES LANDETTES
M. Stocklouser

24260 Journiac
Tel. 05 53 54 35 19
Fax 05 53 54 35 19

Open all year • 2 rooms on garden level, with bathrooms • €50, breakfast included • No table d'hôte • Credit cards not accepted, no dogs admitted • Outdoor swimming pool

We most liked: The scenery of the Vézère Valley.

The setting of this wonderfully renovated 1850 Périgordian farmhouse couldn't be more rural. The bedrooms, fitted-out in the outhouses, make up in charm what they lack in dimensions, with pastel shades, white tiled floors, colourful fabrics and old furniture; all overlook the swimming pool. The shade of a giant lime-tree makes the inner courtyard very pleasant in the summer.

Access : 13km westbound from La Madeleine

AQUITAINE

LA ROQUE-GAGEAC - 24250

13 AUBERGE LA PLUME D'OIE
M. et Mme Walker

Le Bourg
24250 La Roque-Gageac
Tel. 05 53 29 57 05
Fax 05 53 31 04 81
laplumedoie@wanadoo.fr
www.hotels-restau-dordogne.org

Closed from 20 Nov to 20 Dec, mid-Jan to 14 Feb, Sun evening, Mon and Tue lunchtimes • 4 non-smoking rooms upstairs, reserved mainly for the restaurant clients, with bath/WC and television • €70 to €80; breakfast €12 • Menus €45 to €58

We most liked: The picturesque site of La Roque-Gageac.

This old residence, built on the flanks of the cliff, stands in the heart of the idyllic medieval town. A spiral staircase leads up to a few refreshingly cool bedrooms decorated with pastel fabrics. The pretty dining room features light wooden beams, painted straw-bottomed chairs and bare stone walls. Diners can enjoy a view of the picturesque "gabarres" and canoes floating down the Dordogne. Imaginative menu.

Access: In the village, on the banks of the Dordogne

LA ROQUE-GAGEAC - 24250

14 LA BELLE ÉTOILE
M. Ongaro

Le bourg
24250 La Roque-Gageac
Tel. 05 53 29 51 44
Fax 05 53 29 45 63
hotel.belle-etoile@wanadoo.fr

Open from late Mar to early Nov • 15 rooms with bath/WC and television • €50 to €75; breakfast €8; half-board available • Menus €23 to €38 • Terrace, garage • Canoeing, swimming, fishing

We most liked: Floating down the Dordogne in a "gabarre".

This fine old creamy-coloured stone house perched on the cliff commands a wonderful view over the peaceful meanders of the Dordogne. The bedrooms have been painted white and most are furnished in a period style. The typical Périgordian repertoire, served in two pleasant dining rooms, or in the summer, under a trellis, will tempt even the most refined of palates. Numerous nearby leisure activities, including canoeing, swimming and fishing.

Access: On the D 703, between the cliff and the river

AQUITAINE

LANQUAIS - 24150

15 DOMAINE DE LA MARMETTE
Mme Rose

« La Crabe »
24150 Lanquais
Tel. 05 53 24 99 13
lamarmette@aol.com
http://www.bergerac-tourisme.com/annonces/chbmarmette.asp

Closed 1 Jan to 1 Apr • 5 rooms on garden level • €59 to €69, breakfast included; half-board available • Table d'hôte €18 to €23 (evenings only) • Garden, terrace, car park. Credit cards not accepted, no dogs admitted • Outdoor swimming pool

Back to basics in a land of open fields.

This 16C farm and outbuildings dotted with lawns and countless clumps of flowers is almost a little hamlet in itself. The former loose-boxes have been turned into bedrooms on the ground floor and each one is decorated with a personalised fabric, chest of drawers and a wrought-iron bed. A sitting room, library and dining room-conservatory are located in the main house. A kitchen is also available for use by guests.

Access : Take the Faux road then turn left towards Bournaz after leaving town and continue for 200m

LAVEYSSIÈRE - 24130

16 MAISON DE LA FORÊT
M. Swainson

Pas de l'Eyraud
24130 Laveyssière
Tel. 05 53 82 84 50
Fax 05 53 82 84 51
info@aubergerac.com
www.aubergerac.com

Closed 24 to 26 Dec • 5 rooms with bathrooms • €65 (€49 to €59 low season), breakfast €5 • No table d'hôte • Park, garden, car park. Credit cards not accepted, no dogs admitted • Outdoor swimming pool

Staying just 10min away from Bergerac without suffering the hordes of tourists.

This welcoming white house stands in its own extensive grounds, surrounded by forest. Run by a delightful English couple, the establishment offers colourful rooms under the eaves, on the small side but all with views of the countryside. The prettiest rooms are to the rear of the house. Breakfast is served on the terrace in fine weather.

Access : 14km northbound from Bergerac on the D 709, then take a minor road

AQUITAINE

LE BUGUE - 24260

17 MAISON OLÉA
Mme Nardou

La Combe-de-Leygue
24260 Le Bugue
Tel. 05 53 08 48 93
Fax 05 53 08 48 93
info@olea-dordogne.com
www.olea-dordogne.com

Open all year • 5 rooms, all with bath/WC or shower/WC • €65 to €75 (€55 to €65 low season); breakfast €5 • No table d'hôte • Garden, car park. Credit cards not accepted • Heated outdoor swimming pool

We most liked **Lazing about on terraces of the rooms, overlooking the swimming pool and valley.**

Though recently built, this house has faithfully upheld the style and tradition of local architecture. South-facing, it overlooks a superb overflow saltwater swimming pool with the Vézère Valley in the distance. On the ground floor you will be met with Moorish touches, murals, red-brick floor tiles and a stunning veranda-cum-winter garden. The immense (air-conditioned) rooms upstairs feature immaculate walls, pedestal tables draped in lace, antique furniture and exquisite bedding. Blissfully calm!

Access : 5km to the east of Le Bugue on the D 703, towards Sarlat-la-Canéda and then a minor road on the left

LES EYZIES-DE-TAYAC - 24620

18 HOSTELLERIE DU PASSEUR
M. Brun

Place de la Mairie
24620 Les Eyzies-de-Tayac
Tel. 05 53 06 97 13
Fax 05 53 06 91 63
hostellerie-du-passeur@perigord.com
www.hostellerie-du-passeur.com

Open early Mar to early Nov • 19 rooms on 3 floors, most have shower/WC, some have bath/WC, all have television • €65 to €100; breakfast €8; half-board available • Restaurant closed Mon and Tue lunchtimes (low season); menus €19 to €50 • Terrace, car park

We most liked **The home-made foie gras which can be bought in the hotel or from its website.**

This handsome stone house covered in Virginia creeper stands in the heart of the Périgord capital, known for its prehistoric heritage. The stylish, cheerful rooms all sport bright colours; some overlook the cliffs dotted with oak trees. Diners can choose from a traditional dining room complete with an attractive stone fireplace, a bright conservatory or a country terrace under lime-trees facing the Vézère, in all of which guests can relax and savour the hotel's renowned regional dishes.

Access : In the town centre, not far from the Vézère

AQUITAINE

LES EYZIES-DE-TAYAC - 24620

19 LE MOULIN DE LA BEUNE
M. Soulié

2 rue du Moulin-Bas
24620 Les Eyzies-de-Tayac
Tel. 05 53 06 94 33
Fax 05 53 06 98 06
contact@moulindelabeune.com
moulindelabeune.com

Open from Apr to Oct • 20 rooms with bath/WC or shower/WC, all have television • €59 to €69; breakfast €7; half-board available • Restaurant closed on Tue, Wed and Sat lunchtimes; menus €29 to €50 • Terrace, garden, car park. No dogs admitted in restaurant

Talking into the early hours of the morning on the riverside terrace.

The attractive stone walls of this former seed and sawmill now house a charming hotel-restaurant. All the pleasant, tastefully decorated rooms enjoy peace and quiet and the stylish wood-panelled dining room commands views of the wonderfully preserved paddle wheel and the garden and river. The setting, on the banks of the Beune, is quite idyllic in fine weather.

Access: In the town centre, off the road on the banks of the Beune

LES EYZIES-DE-TAYAC - 24620

20 LE PANORAMIQUE
M. et Mme Spadi

Beune
24620 Les Eyzies-de-Tayac
Tel. 05 53 06 98 82
Fax 05 53 05 24 04

Open all year • 4 rooms • €28 to €37; breakfast €5 • No table d'hôte • Park, car park. Credit cards not accepted, dogs not admitted • Swimming pool

An unmatchable view of the village and site of Eyzies-de-Tayac.

One hectare of parkland protects these three regional-style houses, which dominate the "prehistoric capital", from the outside world. The rooms are deliberately understated in spirit but most pleasing, and two boast wonderful panoramic terraces. On your way to the breakfast room under the veranda, look out for the collection of coffee and pepper mills picked up by the delightful owners over the years. Two gîtes are also available.

Access: 4km south-east of Eyzies-de-Tayac on the D 47, towards Sarlat, then take the Saint-Cyprien road

AQUITAINE

LISLE - 24350

21 LE PIGEONNIER DE PICANDINE
M. et Mme Lacourt

La Picandine
24350 Lisle
Tel. 05 53 03 41 93
Fax 05 53 03 28 43
picandine@aol.com
www.picandine.com

Closed 15 Nov to 1 Mar • 5 rooms with shower/WC or bath/WC • €50, breakfast included; half-board available • Table d'hôte €19 • Terrace, car park. Credit cards not accepted, no dogs admitted • Outdoor swimming pool

We most liked The sweeping view over the Périgord countryside.

This lovely 17C farmhouse is graced with two-hundred-year-old chestnut trees in the inner courtyard. Stone walls and wood beams set the tone for the bedrooms in the main wing, while two suites in the renovated barn are well suited to families. It's an ideal place to unwind: snuggle up with a good book in the cosy sitting room-library or treat yourself to a game of billiards.

Access: From Lisle, take D 1 towards Périgueux, then take the third turning on the right

MARNAC - 24440

22 LA GRANDE MARQUE
Mme Cockcroft

24440 Marnac
Tel. 05 53 31 61 63
grande.marque@perigord.com
www.lgmfrance.com

Open all year • 5 rooms with bathrooms • €65 to €75; breakfast €7 • Table d'hôte €22 • Terrace, park, car park. Credit cards not accepted • Outdoor swimming pool

We most liked Strolling round the magnificent ten-acre parkland.

This wonderful 17C Périgord estate commands a sumptuous view of the Dordogne Valley and the quaint, riverside village of Siorac-en-Périgord. The rooms under the eaves have recently been treated to a simple, tasteful facelift. The estate boasts a wide range of leisure activities including a fitness room, sauna and tennis court.

Access: 9km to the north-east on the D 703, take the road to Sarlat and then turn right

AQUITAINE

MARQUAY - 24620

23 HÔTEL DES BORIES
M. et Mme Dalbavie

Le bourg
24620 Marquay
Tel. 05 53 29 67 02
Fax 05 53 29 64 15
hotel.des.bories@wanadoo.fr
www.membres.lycos.fr/hoteldesbories/

Open from 1 Apr to 2 Nov • 30 rooms, 20 of which are in a separate wing, 5 have private terraces, all have bath/WC or shower/WC and television • €33 to €61 (€31 to €57 low season); breakfast €8; half-board available • Menus €15 to €38 • Terrace, garden, car park • 2 outdoor swimming pools

Peace and quiet guaranteed.

Despite the name, you won't have to sleep in a "borie", one of the somewhat Spartan dry-stone huts that abound in the region. The accommodation in this family home may not be luxurious, but it is well equipped with modern comforts. Some rooms also have a terrace where you can take breakfast, and the most stylish of all has a superb stone fireplace and wooden beams. Relax in the swimming pool overlooking the countryside.

Access : On leaving Sarlat-la-Canéda, drive towards Les Eyzies-de-Tayac and follow the D 6 on the right

MEYRALS - 24220

24 LA BÉLIE
Mme Baltzer

L'Abeille
24220 Meyrals
Tel. 05 53 59 55 82
Fax 05 53 59 56 04
contact@perigord-labelie.com
www.perigord-labelie.com

Closed 15 Feb to 15 Mar • 3 non-smoking rooms, 1 in a separate wing, all have shower/WC • €70 to €100, breakfast included • Table d'hôte €18 to €23 (evenings only) • Terrace, garden, car park. Credit cards not accepted, dogs not admitted

The owners' affable hospitality.

This traditional Perigord house has been beautifully renovated by a young architect, who endeavoured to retain the site's original appeal whilst adding contemporary touches: the bathrooms combine modern wash basins with old beams and the bedrooms sport a tasteful mixture of unusual objects and furniture and extremely tasteful fabrics. The table d'hôte is essentially regional in inspiration, but the owner also adores preparing dishes gleaned from her well-travelled past.

Access : 8km along the Sarlat road, towards Meyrals and a place known as l'Abeille

AQUITAINE

NONTRON - 24300

25 CHRISTINE ET MAURICE BIRON
M. et Mme Biron

Le Domaine du Petit-Houx "Brégou"
24300 Nontron
Tel. 05 53 60 78 82
Fax 05 53 60 78 81
layourte@wanadoo.fr
www.perigord.com/lepetithoux

Open all year • 3 rooms upstairs, all with bath/WC • €57, breakfast included; half-board available • Table d'hôte €18 (evening only) • Park, car park. Credit cards not accepted, no dogs admitted • Hiking, horse riding, mountain biking

We most liked **Strolling through the grounds overlooking Périgord's rambling landscape.**

Nearly 10 acres of open fields planted with magnificent mature oaks surround this former smallholding. The barn, sheepfold and main building have been treated to a painstaking makeover, with priority given to retaining regional features. The main wing houses a pleasant sitting room-library heated in the winter by an open fire and attractive, brightly coloured, comfortable rooms with new bedding, rush matting on the floors and full bathrooms. The establishment also offers stabling for horses.

Access : 6km to the east of Nontron on the D 707, towards Thiviers and then left onto the D 85 towards Châlus

SAGELAT - 24170

26 LE BRANCHAT
M. et Mme Ginioux

Lieu-dit de Branchat
24170 Sagelat
Tel. 05 53 28 98 80
Fax 05 53 28 98 80
info@lebranchat.com
www.lebranchat.com

Open Apr to Oct • 6 rooms, all with bath/WC or shower/WC • €63 to €69 (€53 to €63 low season); breakfast included • Table d'hôte €20 to €25 • Children's play area, park, car park. Dogs not admitted • Outdoor swimming pool, ponies

We most liked **The two rooms with a private terrace and a view of the lofty village of Belvès.**

The quality of the restoration lavished on the sheepfold, cowshed, barn and farmhouse, now turned into chambres d'hôte, is quite outstanding. White walls and parquet flooring and wooden furniture set the tone. Surrounded by some 12 acres of valleys, woods and hazel trees, you won't have time to count the sheep at night! On the leisure side: swimming pool, walks in the park or pony riding.

Access : 3km south of Belvès on the D 710, towards Fumel and then a minor road on the left

AQUITAINE

SAINT-AUBIN-DE-LANQUAIS - 24560

27 L'AGRYBELLA
Mme Raby

Place de l'Église
24560 Saint-Aubin-de-Lanquais
Tel. 05 53 58 10 76
legall.ma@wanadoo.fr
www.agrybella.fr.st

Closed Jan and Feb • 4 non-smoking rooms, 1 with disabled access, all have bath/WC • €75, breakfast included • No table d'hôte • Terrace, garden, private car park. Credit cards not accepted, dogs not admitted • Outdoor swimming pool, sitting room-library and board games

We most liked: The amazing decoration of the "Surprise" apartment.

The handsome 18C property and its outhouses stand in the heart of attractive grounds complete with swimming pool. Each room is individually and very tastefully decorated: the "Colonial" boasts a mosquito net and soft lights, the "Retro" has turn-of-the-century furniture and objects picked up in antique stores, the "Perigourdine" is full of sweet country air while the Surprise apartment sports a... theme we'll leave you to discover for yourself! Delightful welcome.

Access: In the town centre

SAINT-CRÉPIN-ET-CARLUCET - 24590

28 LES CHARMES DE CARLUCET
M. et Mme Edgar

Carlucet
24590 Saint-Crépin-et-Carlucet
Tel. 05 53 31 22 60
lescharmes@carlucet.com
www.carlucet.com

Closed from 1 Dec to 1 Feb • 5 non-smoking rooms on two floors, one with disabled access, and 1 gîte, all have bath/WC or shower/WC and television • €75 to €99 (€65 to €89 low season), breakfast included • Table d'hôte €23 (evenings only by reservation) • Terrace, park, car park. Dogs not admitted • Outdoor swimming pool, sauna

We most liked: The peace and quiet which reigns in this superb Périgord property.

A delicious address in the heart of the Périgord noir region. This handsome property set in 2 hectares of grounds is home to spacious bedrooms, two of which are under the eaves. The rooms are decorated simply, but warmly and carefully with rustic or modern furniture, pastel colours, wooden floors and paintings. An extremely comfortable gîte for up to 8 people, complete with private terrace and swimming-pool, has been created in the pigeon-house. Faultless hospitality extended by the English-born owners.

Access: 13km northbound of Sarlat-la-Canéda, on the D 704 Montignac road and right onto the D 60

AQUITAINE

SAINT-CRÉPIN-ET-CARLUCET - 24590

29 LES GRANGES HAUTES
M. Fauste

Le Poujol
24590 Saint-Crépin-et-Carlucet
Tel. 05 53 29 35 60
Fax 05 53 28 81 17
fauste@netcourrier.com
www.les-granges-hautes.fr

Closed 15 Dec to 28 Feb • 6 non-smoking rooms, all have baths or showers • €64 to €102 (€57 to €96 low season); breakfast €7 • No table d'hôte • Garden, car park. No dogs admitted

We most liked **The sophisticated charm of a French country house.**

It is hard to resist the charm of this 18C-19C Périgord country house, surrounded by superb gardens and a salt-water swimming pool. The stylish rooms feature oak beams, warm, sunny colours and immaculate bathrooms. The sitting room, whose central feature is a large fireplace, is the perfect place to relax and read. The charming owners are delighted to recommend interesting places to visit in the region.

Access: 12km to the north-east of Sarlat towards Brive then Salignac

SAINTE-ALVÈRE - 24510

30 LE MOULIN NEUF
MM. Chappell et Shippey

Paunat
24510 Sainte-Alvère
Tel. 05 53 63 30 18
Fax 05 53 63 30 55
moulin-neuf@usa.net
www.the-moulin-neuf.com

Closed from 15 to 31 Oct, 25 Dec • 6 rooms with bathrooms • €60 to €65; breakfast €10 • No table d'hôte • Terrace, garden. Credit cards not accepted, no dogs admitted

We most liked **The laughter of children playing in the estate's pond.**

This attractive old mill house is hidden in the heart of a country estate complete with pond. The cosy interior features light colours, roomy sofas and floral print fabrics. The modest-sized rooms are tastefully decorated and located in a beautifully restored old barn. In the summer months, breakfast is served under an arbour and by the fireside in the sitting room in the winter.

Access: Take the D 2 southbound

AQUITAINE

SAINT-JULIEN-DE-CREMPSE - 24140

31 LE MANOIR DU GRAND VIGNOBLE
M. Scotti

Le grand vignoble
24140 Saint-Julien-de-Crempse
Tel. 05 53 24 23 18
Fax 05 53 24 20 89
grand.vignoble@wanadoo.fr
www.manoirdugrandvignoble.com

Open from late Mar to mid-Nov • 44 rooms with bath/WC and television • €82 to €109 (€58 to €79 low season); breakfast €9; half-board available • Menus €23 to €45 • Park, car park • Swimming pool, tennis, golf practice, sauna, Jacuzzi, fitness, riding centre, wine tasting lessons

We most liked **A canter around the estate thanks to the riding school on site.**

This 17C manor house enjoys a wonderfully tranquil setting in the midst of over 100 acres of parkland. In the main wing are the reception, sitting room and pleasantly unassuming dining room, where guests are invited to sample regional fare and wines (Bergerac, Pécharmant). A dozen or so rooms, some with four-poster beds, can also be found in this wing. The other wing of the hotel is located in the outbuildings where the extra space has given rise to a more contemporary feel.

Access : 16km northbound from Bergerac on the N 21 as far as Campsegret, then left on a minor road towards Saint-Julien-de-Crempset, before Saint-Julien

SAINT-MARTIAL-VIVEYROLS - 24320

32 HOSTELLERIE LES AIGUILLONS
M. Beeuwsaert

Le Beuil
24320 Saint-Martial-Viveyrols
Tel. 05 53 91 07 55
Fax 05 53 91 00 43
lesaiguillons@aol.com
www.hostellerielesaiguillons.com

Open 1 May to 1 Oct • 8 rooms, one of which has disabled access, all have bath/WC and television • €50 to €91; breakfast €8; half-board available • Menus €25 to €42 • Terrace, park, car park • Outdoor swimming pool

We most liked **Woods, hills and open fields for as far as the eye can see.**

Here you will find total peace and quiet and a place in the sun, disturbed only by the twittering of birds and the occasional distant murmur of country life. Built on the ruins of an old farmhouse, this hotel offers fresh, spacious rooms, a restaurant in hacienda style and a terrace overlooking the grounds, surrounded by countryside. If you find yourself suffering withdrawal symptoms, the traffic jams, pollution and stress of Paris are a mere 500km stone's throw away!

Access : 5km to the north-west of Verteillac on the D 1, then right on the D 101, the C 201 and finally a minor road

AQUITAINE

SAINT-PIERRE-DE-CÔLE - 24800

33 DOUMARIAS
M. et Mme Fargeot

24800 Saint-Pierre-de-Côle
Tel. 05 53 62 34 37
Fax 05 53 62 34 37
doumarias@aol.com

Closed from 30 Sep to 31 Mar • 6 rooms • €58, breakfast included • Table d'hôte €16 • Garden, car park. No dogs admitted • Outdoor swimming pool

Hooking a fish in the River Côle just a step away.

The leaves and branches of a great lime-tree throw a welcome shadow over the courtyard of this pleasant country property curtained in Virginia creeper, at the foot of the crumbling towers of Bruzac Castle; the charm of the Périgord at its best. The stylish, peaceful rooms are lavishly adorned with period furniture, ornaments and paintings. The swimming pool and garden are most appreciated, as is the staff's friendly welcome.

Access: 12km eastbound from Brantôme on the D 78

SAINT-RABIER - 24210

34 VILLA DES COURTISSOUS
M. et Mme Dalibard

24210 Saint-Rabier
Tel. 05 53 51 02 26
Fax 05 53 50 73 55
villa.courtissous@libertysurf.fr
www.bienvenue-montignac.com

Closed from Nov to Mar; by reservation in season • 4 rooms with bathrooms • €74, breakfast included • No table d'hôte • Terrace, garden, car park. Credit cards not accepted, no dogs admitted • Outdoor swimming pool

Visiting the nearby Hautefort Castle.

This dignified villa was built in 1800 in the middle of a landscaped garden. The recently renovated, well-proportioned rooms are painted white, adorned with the occasional photo, carefully chosen fabrics and lovingly restored old furniture. The bathrooms are faultless, with all mod-cons to hand. Depending on the season, breakfast is served at the large kitchen table in front of the open fire or on the terrace next to the swimming pool.

Access: 12km southbound from Hautefort on the D 704

AQUITAINE

SAINT-VINCENT-SUR-L'ISLE - 24420

35 CHAMBRE D'HÔTE LA CALMADE
M. Margo Collin

Le Bourg
24420 Saint-Vincent-sur-l'Isle
Tel. 05 53 07 87 83
margo@lacalmade.com
www.lacalmade.com

Open all year • 5 rooms one of which has disabled access, all have bathrooms • €60; breakfast included • No table d'hôte • Garden, car park. Credit cards not accepted • Outdoor swimming pool

We most liked
The warm, simple family welcome.

Thhis farm located on the town's doorstep is said to date back to 1750. The tastefully decorated rooms, located in the main wing and in a restored barn, are furnished with a combination of family heirlooms, antiques and modern pieces. Pastimes include a library complete with piano and board games and swings for the children in the garden under the shade of a superb chestnut tree.

Access : 15km north-east on the N 21 towards Limoges and then right on the D 705

SARLAT-LA-CANÉDA - 24200

36 CHAMBRE D'HÔTE LE CLOS-VALLIS
M. Bosio

Le Clos Vallis
24200 Sarlat-la-Canéda
Tel. 05 53 28 95 64
Fax 05 53 28 95 21
br.b@wanadoo.fr
www.leclosvallis.com

Open all year • 4 non-smoking rooms, 2 of which are upstairs, all have bathrooms • €60; breakfast included • No table d'hôte • Garden, car park. Credit cards not accepted, no dogs admitted • Outdoor swimming pool

We most liked
The calm of the countryside just a few kilometres outside Sarlat.

The buildings and outhouses of this carefully restored farmhouse are laid out around a pleasant Périgord-style courtyard. An old barn is now home to light, airy rooms, decorated in a refreshingly simple style with bare stone or white-washed walls, tiles or coconut matting and pine furniture. The sitting room, complete with fireplace, displays the same welcoming simplicity as does the teak-furnished breakfast room. Discreetly cordial welcome.

Access : 3km north-east of Sarlat-la-Canéda on the D 47 Sainte-Nathaléne road and then a lane to the left

AQUITAINE

SARLAT-LA-CANÉDA - 24200

37 HÔTEL DE LA MADELEINE
M. Mélot

1 place de la Petite-Rigaudie
24200 Sarlat-la-Canéda
Tel. 05 53 59 10 41
Fax 05 53 31 03 62
hotel.madeleine @ wanadoo.fr
www.hoteldelamadeleine-sarlat.com

Closed 1 Jan to 12 Feb • 39 rooms, 2 of which have disabled access, with bath/WC or shower/WC, all have air-conditioning and television • €76 to €98 (€64 to €77 low season); breakfast €9; half-board available • Menus from €27 to €46 • Terrace

Ideally located a step from the centre of historic Sarlat.

Freshly painted sky-blue shutters, restored frontage, stylishly renovated rooms with modern amenities, a brand-new dining room in shades of red and orange and a spacious sitting room decorated with prints and green plants. This fine hotel, said to be the oldest in town, dating from 1840, has just been renovated from top to bottom. Extremely practical garage (at an extra cost).

Access : On a main square at the entrance to the medieval town

SARLAT-LA-CANÉDA - 24200

38 HÔTEL DES RÉCOLLETS
M. Larequie

4 rue Jean-Jacques-Rousseau
24200 Sarlat-la-Canéda
Tel. 05 53 31 36 00
Fax 05 53 30 32 62
contact @ hotel-recollets-sarlat.com
www.hotel-recollets-sarlat.com

Open all year • 18 rooms with bathroom and television • €43 to €63; breakfast €7 • No restaurant • Car park

The tranquillity of this hotel in the heart of the medieval city.

The cloisters of the Récollets convent, which dates back to the 17C, is now home to a characterful hotel, whose attractive stone walls are covered in wisteria and climbing roses. A narrow staircase leads up to small, well-restored rooms. Each one is different, but all feature the same happy blend of contemporary furniture and original beams and walls. Breakfast is served in a handsome room, where stone prevails, or on a delightful patio. Baggage service available from the public car park.

Access : In the old town

AQUITAINE

SARLAT-LA-CANÉDA - 24200

39 LE MAS DE CASTEL
Mme Charpenet-Castalian

Sudalissant
24200 Sarlat-la-Caneda
Tel. 05 53 59 02 59
Fax 05 53 28 25 62
castalian@wanadoo.fr

Open from Easter to 11 Nov • 13 rooms, half of which are on garden level, with bath/WC or shower/WC and television • €56 to €68 (€50 to €58 low season); breakfast €7 • No restaurant • Garden, car park. Dogs not admitted • Outdoor swimming pool

We most liked The enchanting countryside feel of this authentic farmhouse.

Located in the heart of an unspoilt countryside, this farmhouse has been turned into a welcoming hostelry with rustic rooms upstairs or level with the garden (our favourites). A cockerel, the last remaining survivor of the hen house, joyfully serenades guests with a not-too-early morning call. Enjoy the relaxed pace of a traditional Périgord home and take a dip in the swimming pool before breakfast. The nights are so peaceful that you'll even be philosophical about the rooster's morning chorus.

Access: 3km from Sarlat-la-Canéda on the D 704 towards Gourdon, right onto the Canéda road, then take a minor road

SORGES - 24420

40 CHAMBRE D'HÔTE AU VILLAGE
M. Valentini

Le Bourg
24420 Sorges
Tel. 05 53 05 05 08
Fax 05 53 05 05 08

Closed in Oct • 3 rooms with shower/WC and television • €34; breakfast €5 • No table d'hôte • Terrace, garden. Credit cards not accepted

We most liked Sampling the "black diamond" that has made Sorges famous.

This tiny village house, probably built in the 15C, is just next door to the Tourist Office and the Truffle Museum, devoted to the local "black diamonds". Bedrooms in a charming rural style feature wooden floorboards, stone walls, wooden ceilings and antique furniture. In the summer, breakfast is served in the lovely inner courtyard under the welcome shade of an enormous lime-tree.

Access: In the village

AQUITAINE

TOURTOIRAC - 24390

41 L'ENCLOS
M. et Mme Ornsteen

Pragelier
24390 Tourtoirac
Tel. 05 53 51 11 40
Fax 05 53 50 37 21
rornsteen@yahoo.com
www.hotellenclos.com

Closed from Oct to Apr • 5 rooms • €70 to €100; breakfast €9 • Table d'hôte €20 to €30 • Park, car park. Credit cards not accepted • Outdoor swimming pool

The unusual complex of seven independent cottages.

You too will fall under the charm of this unusual hamlet of cottages, also a favourite with a number of American film stars! The luxuriously decorated, personalised rooms are dotted around the garden in various outhouses, such as the former chapel, bakery and estate manager's house. Definitively rustic in character, all feature beautiful provençal fabrics. Walnut and fruit trees abound in the beautiful parkland which is well worth a ramble.

Access: 5km westbound from Hautefort on the D 62, then the D 67

VAUNAC - 24800

42 FERME DES GUEZOUX
M. Fouquet

Les Guezoux
24800 Vaunac
Tel. 05 53 62 06 39
Fax 05 53 62 88 74
escargot.perigord@wanadoo.fr
www.escargotduperigord.com

Open all year • 3 rooms • €43 (€39 low season); breakfast €4 • No table d'hôte • Garden, car park • Outdoor swimming pool

Delicious home-made walnut cake served at breakfast time.

Hidden by dense woodland, this stone farmhouse was restored in 1990 and makes a wonderfully peaceful retreat for anyone hoping to get away from it all. Whitewashed walls, tiled floors and pine furniture paint the picture of the simple, but impeccably kept bedrooms. The genial proprietor loves showing his guests his very own snail farm.

Access: 9km northbound on the RN 21, then take the lane on the right

AQUITAINE

ANDERNOS-LES-BAINS - 33510

43 LES ALBATROS
M. et Mme Malfère

10 bd de Verdun
33510 Andernos-les-Bains
Tel. 05 56 82 04 46
jmalfere@club-internet.fr
www.lesalbatros.com

Closed Nov to Jan • 3 non-smoking rooms • €60 to €68; breakfast included • No table d'hôte • Garden. Credit cards not accepted, dogs not admitted

We most liked **The owners who bend over backwards for their guests.**

This attractive white house surrounded by a beautifully cared-for garden full of flowers is ideally located just 100m from the beach and town. Each of three personalised rooms bears an evocative name, "Romantic", "Sea" and "Safari"; the latter is the most spacious and perfect for longer stays. Generous breakfasts, complete with home-made jams, are served on a covered terrace or in the dining room which boasts a crystal chandelier and cosy furniture.

Access : 100m from the beach, near the town

ARÈS - 33740

44 LE GRAIN DE SABLE
Mme Bécaud

37 avenue de la Libération
33740 Arès
Tel. 05 56 60 04 50
Fax 05 57 17 14 98
hotel.legraindesable@wanadoo.fr
www.hotelgraindesable.com

Open all year • 14 rooms, all have bath/WC or shower/WC, television and telephone • €52 to €66; breakfast €7 • No restaurant • Garden, car park, meeting room

We most liked **A matchless location between the Atlantic and the Regional Nature Park of the Landes de Gascogne.**

This enchanting recently restored house has retained the stylish regional character in its interior decoration where the theme of evasion takes pride of place. The spacious rooms are personalised on a variety of themes ranging from "Ouarzate" and "Bali" to "Cottage". The breakfast room and sitting room, inspired by the Arcachon basin, are a happy marriage of sandy colours and cane furniture.

Access : On the church square in the town centre, head towards Arcachon/Andernos, the hotel is 400m further on to the left

AQUITAINE

BERNOS-BEAULAC - 33430

45 DOUSUD
M. et Mme Chapdelaine

33430 Bernos-Beaulac
Tel. 05 56 25 43 23
Fax 05 56 25 42 75
info@dousud.fr
www.dousud.fr

Open all year • 5 non-smoking rooms, all with bath/WC or shower/WC and television • €76 (€61 low season), breakfast included • Table d'hôte (evenings only) €16 • Terrace, park, kitchenette, car park • Outdoor swimming pool, riding, walking, canoeing, kayaks, bicycles

We most liked: The peace and quiet surrounding this lovely Landes farmhouse.

Nature is the centre of attraction of this farmhouse set in the heart of immense grounds and the perfect departure point for walking, cycling and even riding excursions. The attractive rooms, each with its own individual outdoor access, are located in the renovated riding stables. A small kitchen and barbecue are available to guests, unless you wouldn't rather prefer putting your feet under the table and tucking into the dishes concocted by the owner, who trained as a chef.

Access: In the town

BOMMES-SAUTERNES - 33210

46 PEYRAGUEY MAISON ROUGE
M. et Mme Belanger

33210 Bommes-Sauternes
Tel. 05 57 31 07 55
Fax 05 57 31 03 95
belanger@club-internet.fr
www.peyraguey-sauternes.com

Open all year • 3 non-smoking rooms, 2 of which are on the ground floor with private entrance and 1 upstairs • €68 to €79, breakfast included • No table d'hôte • Garden, car park. Credit cards not accepted, dogs not admitted • Outdoor swimming pool

We most liked: Each room has its own independent entrance.

The mouth-watering names, "Sauternes", "St-Émilion" and "Médoc", of these enchanting spacious guestrooms located in the heart of the Sauternes vineyards set the stage for your stay. A bottle of Bordeaux is offered to each guest on arrival and tasting sessions are organised in the evenings, all of which is guaranteed to make you feel at home. What's more the house itself is full of character with its regional stone façade, red tile floors and antique furniture.

Access: Sauternes road

AQUITAINE

BORDEAUX - 33000

47 UNE CHAMBRE EN VILLE
M. Labory

35 rue Bouffard
33000 Bordeaux
Tel. 05 56 81 34 53
Fax 05 56 81 34 54
ucev@bandb-bx.com
www.bandb-bx.com

Open all year • 5 non-smoking rooms, all with bath/WC or shower/WC and television • €75 to €85; breakfast €7 • No table d'hôte

We most liked: The tasteful, understated contemporary decoration.

This building in the heart of the historic district of Bordeaux has been fully restored and the old stone walls and staircase now make a handsome setting for modern furniture and fittings. The rooms are personalised and immaculately cared for: the "Bordelaise" apartment features warm colours and period furniture, the "Nautique" is decorated on a maritime theme while the "Orientale" sports the bright colours and furniture of North Africa...

Access: In the town centre

BORDEAUX - 33000

48 LA TOUR INTENDANCE
M. Brandt

16 rue de la Vieille-Tour
33000 Bordeaux
Tel. 05 56 44 56 56
Fax 05 56 44 54 54
contact@hotel-tour-intendance.com
www.hotel-tour-intendance.com

Open all year • 22 non-smoking rooms, all with bath/WC or shower/WC and television • €78 to €100 (€68 to €94 low season); breakfast €8 • No restaurant • Car park

We most liked: The exemplary restoration of this hotel in the town centre.

The recent renovation of this hotel in the heart of the town centre is above reproach: a handsome façade, typical of Bordeaux with bare stone walls and red tile floors inside. The comfortable, modern and personalised rooms (matching fabrics and fittings, pebble-stone bathroom floors, etc), add to the property's charm. Delightful smiling welcome.

Access: In the town centre

AQUITAINE

CAPIAN - 33550

49 CHÂTEAU DE GRAND BRANET
Mme Mainvielle

859 Branet-Sud
33550 Capian
Tel. 05 56 72 17 30
Fax 05 56 72 36 59
chateaugrandbranet@entredeux
mers.com
www.entredeuxmers.com/chateau
grandbranet

Closed in Jan • 5 non-smoking rooms upstairs, all have bathrooms • €60, breakfast included • No table d'hôte • Park, car park. Credit cards not accepted

A tour of the restored spirit store houses.

This handsome 17C castle, renovated in the 19C, stands in the heart of grounds planted with trees, some of which are several hundred years old. The ground-floor dining room commands a fine view of the surrounding vineyards. Upstairs, five rooms – bare stone walls and antique furniture – can accommodate 3 or 4 people each. The charming owner can generally be depended on to take guests on a guided tour and explanation of his estate and store houses, followed by a tasting session of course!

Access : 9km south of Créon towards Cadillac

CASTELNAU-DE-MÉDOC - 33480

50 DOMAINE DE CARRAT
Mme Péry

Route de Sainte-Hélène
33480 Castelnau-de-Médoc
Tel. 05 56 58 24 80
Fax 05 56 58 24 80

Closed Dec 25 • 5 rooms • €54 to €60, breakfast included • No table d'hôte • Park, car park. Credit cards not accepted

Romance pervades this country estate.

This red-shuttered country seat, built in 1885, nestles in its own grounds, surrounded by 50 acres of woodland. Formerly the stables of the neighbouring castle, it now houses comfortable, quiet bedrooms, graced with family heirlooms. The most pleasant, on the ground floor, open directly onto the lawn. A roaring open fire welcomes guests in the winter, while the summer months ring to the voices of children swimming in the Jalette. Extremely attentive staff.

Access : 1km to the south-west of Castelnau-de-Médoc

AQUITAINE

COUTRAS - 33230

51 HENRI IV
Mme Dri-Stragier

Place du 8-Mai-1945
33230 Coutras
Tel. 05 57 49 34 34
Fax 05 57 49 20 72
hotel-henriIV.gironde@wanadoo.fr
www.hotelcoutras.com

Open all year • 15 rooms on 2 floors with bath/WC or shower/WC and television • €45 to €65; breakfast €8 • No restaurant • Garden, car park

We most liked **The hotel's polished service.**

Coutras rose to fame following a battle fought here in 1587 by Henry of Navarre, the future Henry IV. The 19C mansion with a graceful courtyard-garden to the front now houses a well-kept hotel with pine furnished rooms. Double-glazing efficiently blocks out the rumble of the nearby railway and the attic rooms on the top floor are air-conditioned.

Access : In the town centre, opposite the railway station

GENSAC - 33890

52 LES REMPARTS
M. Parker

16 rue du Château
33890 Gensac
Tel. 05 57 47 43 46
Fax 05 57 47 46 76
info@lesremparts.net
www.lesremparts.net

Closed from 17 to 31 Dec • 7 rooms, one of which has disabled access; all have bath/WC or shower/WC and television • €60 (€55 low season); breakfast €8; half-board available • Menus €18 to €29 • Car park, garden

We most liked **The warm, friendly welcome from the whole family.**

Exceptionally well-located, this house stands on the site of the former ramparts, dominating the old village and the surrounding countryside. The 11C presbytery now houses simple, but appealing rooms furnished in a rustic style and hung with bright, colourful fabrics. The dining room, which affords a splendid panoramic view of the Durèze Valley, lies on the other side of a delightful little garden.

Access : Very close to the church

AQUITAINE

LATRESNE - 33360

LESTIAC-SUR-GARONNE - 33550

53 CHÂTEAU COULON LAURENSAC
M. Ronald Rens

1 chemin de Meydieu
33360 Latresne
Tel. 05 56 20 64 12
Fax 05 56 21 79 44
coulonlaurensac@wanadoo.fr
www.clbx.com

Open all year • 1 non-smoking room and 2 apartments, all with bathrooms, independent access and private terrace • €95 to €110, breakfast included • Table d'hôte €58, including drink • Terrace, park, car park. Credit cards not accepted, dogs not admitted • Outdoor swimming pool

We most liked: A peaceful haven of greenery just 5min from Bordeaux.

The delightful young owners, of Dutch origin, have created three lavish guestrooms in the wine store-house of their castle. The rooms are particularly exquisitely finished, sporting bare stone and timber beams, contemporary furnishings and all the modern comforts. All have a private terrace. Breakfasts are served in the summer room of the main wing of the house or outdoors in fine weather.

Access: 5km southeast from Bordeaux, in the ZI de Latresnes, on the banks of the Garonne

54 LES LOGIS DE LESTIAC
M. Dejean

71 route de Bordeaux
33550 Lestiac-sur-Garonne
Tel. 05 56 72 17 90
philippe@logisdelestiac.com
www.logisdelestiac.com

Open all year • 5 non-smoking rooms on two levels, all have bath/WC or shower/WC (1 has a power shower) television and internet access • €80 to €95, breakfast included; half-board available • Table d'hôte €25 (evenings only) • Terrace, garden, car park. Credit cards not accepted, dogs not admitted • Outdoor swimming pool

We most liked: The interior decoration, both understated and elegant, of this mansion.

The young owner of this magnificent 18C manor house clearly indulged himself when he began restoring his home. A keen antiques collector and interior decorator, he has already restored four rooms on the theme of the seasons: "Autumn Loft" for example is an exquisite combination of burgundy-red fabrics and unusual objects (sewing machine, old suitcases); the equally unusual "Chambre de Philippe" will soon be finished. An immense garden and heated salt-water swimming pool complete the picture.

Access: In the town centre

AQUITAINE

LIBOURNE - 33500

55 LA TOUR DU VIEUX PORT
M. Segonzac

23 quai Souchet
33500 Libourne
Tel. 05 57 25 75 56
Fax 05 57 25 01 45
latourduvieuxport@free.fr
http://atourduvieuxport.com

Open all year • 14 non-smoking rooms, all with bath/WC, telephone and television • €48 to €68; breakfast €6; half-board available • Menus €15 to €29 • Terrace

We most liked
The personalised decoration of each room.

This hotel-restaurant next to the Tour du Port and opposite the Dordogne welcomes guests into a pleasant tastefully restored setting, full of imagination and comfort. The decoration of the spacious, personalised rooms is the work of the owner who has adorned each bed-head with a fresco which matches the room's fabrics. A traditional menu made from fresh market produce is served in one of three dining rooms.

Access : In the town centre

MARGAUX - 33460

56 LE PAVILLON DE MARGAUX
Mme Laurent

3 rue Georges-Mandel
33460 Margaux
Tel. 05 57 88 77 54
Fax 05 57 88 77 73
le-pavillon-de-margaux@wanadoo.fr
www.pavillondemargaux.com

Open all year • 14 rooms with bath/WC and television, 5 in a separate wing, 10 are air-conditioned • €81 to €110 (€60 to €90 low season); breakfast €12; half-board available • Restaurant closed Wed from 16 Nov to 31 Mar and Tue; menus €12 (weekday lunchtimes) to €51 • Private car park • Surrounded by vineyards

We most liked
The hotel's remarkable wine cellar.

As you contemplate this entrancing 19C abode on the edge of the vineyards, it is difficult to imagine that it was formerly home to the village school. The shouts and laughter of the playground have given way to sophisticated decoration and a much calmer atmosphere. Each room is named after and decorated in the spirit of a Médoc château; those in the new wing are smaller but just as comfortable as the others. Elegant dining room and veranda overlooking the vineyards.

Access : On the way into the village of Margaux

AQUITAINE

MARTILLAC - 33650

57 CHÂTEAU LANTIC
Mme Ginèbre

10 route de Lartigue
33650 Martillac
Tel. 05 56 72 58 68
Fax 05 56 72 58 67
mginebre@wanadoo.fr
www.chateau-de-lantic.com

Open all year • 6 non-smoking rooms, all have bath/WC or shower/WC, small kitchen, some have a television • €70 to €135, breakfast included • No table d'hôte • Terrace, garden, car park • Outdoor swimming pool

We most liked **The charm of this small restored castle.**

Murielle Ginèbre, owner of the premises since 2003, has restored her 18C property with faultless taste. The splendid rooms, some of which with a kitchenette, all boast antique furniture and matching fabrics. The immense "Romeo and Juliet" suite with its sumptuous four-poster bed is the height of romanticism. Whatever your purpose, business trip or honeymoon night, you are sure to full in love with this delightful château.

Access : Turn left before the church, the castle is on the left beyond the vineyards

MAUBUISSON - 33121

58 VILLA ASHRAM
Mme François

18 rue des Genêts-d'Or
33121 Maubuisson
Tel. 05 56 03 49 19

Open all year • 3 rooms, all have shower/WC • €50 to €70; breakfast €6 • No table d'hôte • Terrace, garden. Credit cards not accepted, no dogs admitted

We most liked **The proximity of the forest and the ocean.**

If you are in search of a quiet relaxing stay, Madame François has just what you need: a haven of peace and quiet in a residential neighbourhood just 500m from Lake Hourtin-Carcans. The three guest-rooms and self-contained gîte have been masterfully decorated by the lady of the house who has added here own artistic works here and there. Breakfasts can be taken either in the villa or on one of the countless café terraces which line the neighbouring beach.

Access : 500m from the lakeside and the town centre

AQUITAINE

PAREMPUYRE - 33290

59 DOMAINE DU MASCARET
M. Marin

44 avenue de Labarde
33290 Parempuyre
Tel. 05 56 95 21 47
Fax 05 56 35 22 56
info@domainedumascaret.com
www.domainedumascaret.com

Open all year • 6 rooms with private access, all have bath/WC and television • €80 to €100, breakfast included • No table d'hôte • Terrace, park, car park

We most liked: Each room offers a glimpse of distant lands.

When he took over this 18C building located on the banks of the Garonne, Jean-Bernard Marin deployed his talents to turning each of the 6 bedrooms into a bona fide invitation to voyage: red walls, coconut matting and round bathtub for the "Asian", warm African fabrics and pearls for the "Moroccan", etc. Whatever your "destination", you will be invited to breakfast in the country-style dining room or charming terrace.

Access: 8km north of Bordeaux on the D 210 then right on a minor road

PUJOLS - 33350

60 LES GUÉS RIVIÈRES
M. et Mme Bernard

5 place du Général-de-Gaulle
33350 Pujols
Tel. 05 57 40 74 73
Fax 05 57 40 73 26
margotte-sarl@wanadoo.fr
http://perso.wanadoo.fr/margotte.olivier

Open all year • 3 non-smoking rooms upstairs, all have private bathrooms • €52 to €60, breakfast included • Table d'hôte €23 (by reservation) • Terrace, garden. Credit cards not accepted, dogs not admitted • Nearby: tennis, golf, swimming pool, mountain bikes, cycling paths, rowing, canoeing

We most liked: Relaxing on the panoramic terrace.

This handsome property full of character stands on the main village square, commanding a splendid view of the vineyards of the Entre-Deux-Mers from its terrace. Take the time to savour the view on a deckchair or seated in front of a generous breakfast table laden down with cakes and home-made jams. Upstairs the three simply but tastefully decorated rooms all sport a romantic air. Regional produce takes pride of place on the table d'hôte, booking essential.

Access: 6km southbound of Castillon-la-Bataille on the D 17

AQUITAINE

RIMONS - 33580

61 LE GRAND BOUCAUD
M. Levy

4 l'Aubrade
33580 Rimons
Tel. 05 56 71 88 57
Fax 05 56 61 43 77
grandboucaud @ free.fr
http://grandboucaud.free.fr

Open from Feb to late Sep • 3 non-smoking rooms upstairs, two with bath/WC and 1 with shower/WC • €65, breakfast included • Table d'hôte (evenings only) €23 to €35 • Terrace, garden, car park. Credit cards not accepted, dogs not admitted • Outdoor swimming pool

Strolling around this haven of greenery.

Swimming pool, shaded garden, cosy rooms with bare stone walls... This handsome 18C property extends an invitation to relax in a pleasant landscape of wooded hills and vineyards. The gourmet couple of owners pay equal attention to the quality of the meals. While Monsieur waxes lyrical on the marriage between local produce and wine, offering to accompany guests to local wine-growers should they so fancy, Madame invites guests to try their hand at local recipes in her kitchen.

Access: 3km west of Rimons on the D 230, Monségur road and a left turning

SAINT-ÉMILION - 33330

62 CHÂTEAU MEYLET
Mme Favard

La Gomerie
33330 Saint-Émilion
Tel. 05 57 24 68 85
Fax 05 57 24 77 35
chateau.meylet @ free.fr
www.chateau.meylet.free.fr

Open all year • 4 rooms with bathrooms • €52 to €58, breakfast included • No table d'hôte • Garden, car park. Credit cards not accepted

The rustic charm of the rooms.

A five-acre vineyard surrounds this elegant 1789 property. The rooms boast polished parquet floors and lovely 18C furniture inherited by the family or unearthed in the local flea markets. Some bedrooms enjoy a view of the vineyard, while others overlook the garden's magnificent Indian bean tree. Breakfast is served in the conservatory in the winter and under the arbour in the summer.

Access: 1.5km westbound from Saint-Émilion on the Libourne road (D 243)

AQUITAINE

SAINT-HIPPOLYTE - 33330

SAINT-MACAIRE - 33490

63 CHÂTEAU MONLOT
M. et Mme Rivals

33330 Saint-Hippolyte
Tel. 05 57 74 49 47
Fax 05 57 24 62 33
mussetrivals@belair-monlot.com
www.belair-monlot.com

Open all year • 6 rooms with bath/WC • €70 to €98, breakfast included • No table d'hôte • Garden, car park

64 LES FEUILLES D'ACANTHE
Mme Bielsa

5 rue de l'Église
33490 Saint-Macaire
Tel. 05 56 62 33 75
Fax 05 56 62 33 75
info@feuilles-dacanthe.fr
www.feuilles-dacanthe.fr

Closed from 19 Dec to 20 Jan • 10 rooms and 1 apartment, all with disabled access, and bathrooms • €60 to €80; breakfast €8 • Menus €18 to €29 • Car park • Jacuzzi

The personalised decoration of the rooms.

This château, with its chalk façade and lovely tiled roof is typical of the many stately homes of the region. Each room, stylishly furnished with antiques, paintings and old photos, is named after a variety of grape: Merlot, Cabernet, Sauvignon and so on. The vine theme is also prominent in the pleasant breakfast room. The lovely shaded garden is at its most idyllic in summer.

The charm of this old merchant's house.

This handsome 14C and 17C house, located in the heart of the medieval district of Saint-Macaire, has been faultlessly restored, both inside and out. The rooms and the apartment are enchanting: Gironde tile floors, oak furniture, bare stone or orange roughcast walls. On the leisure side, a counter-current swimming pool and Jacuzzi surrounded by loungers await guests in the inner courtyard.

Access : 3km eastbound from St-Émilion, towards Castillon on the D 245

Access : In the historic town

AQUITAINE

SAINT-MARTIN-DE-LERM - 33540

65 LA LÉZARDIÈRE
M. et Mme Mattei

Boimier-Gabouriaud
33540 Saint-Martin-de-Lerm
Tel. 05 56 71 30 12
Fax 05 56 71 30 12
lalezardiere@free.fr
www.lalezardiere.free.fr

Open 1 Mar to 31 Dec • 4 rooms and one gîte with shower/WC or bath/WC • €60, breakfast included; half-board available • Table d'hôte €20 • Garden, car park. Credit cards not accepted • Outdoor swimming pool, bicycles, children's games, petanque, table tennis

We most liked
Lazing by the swimming pool in the immense garden.

A beautifully restored 17C farmhouse enjoying a stunning view over the Dropt Valley. Stone and wood add warmth to the welcoming rooms in the renovated cowsheds. The exposed beams, terracotta tiled floor, huge table and fireplace and original mangers lend the breakfast room a real country character. Ask to see the owner's fine collection of works on the local wines and produce.

Access: 8km to the south-east of Sauveterre-de-Guyenne on the D 670, the D 230 and then the D 129

SAINT-PALAIS - 33820

66 LA SAUVAGEONNE
M. Bienfail

2 les Mauvillains
33820 Saint-Palais
Tel. 05 57 32 92 15
marc@relax-in-gironde.com
www.relax-in-gironde.com

Open all year • 3 non-smoking rooms all have bath/WC or shower/WC and television; 2 gîtes • €80 (€65 low season), breakfast included • Table d'hôte €26, drinks included (evenings only) • Terrace, park, car park. Credit cards not accepted, dogs not admitted • Outdoor swimming pool

We most liked
The elegance of this 18C property tucked away in the heart of the countryside.

This establishment's name, which roughly translates as wilderness, used to suit the property very well with its former abandoned garden... However things have changed with the arrival of the new owners and the surrounding woodland and vineyards now add to the charm of this well-tended property. The elegant bedrooms are gracefully proportioned and in the kitchen, garden produce takes pride of place in the dishes rustled up by one of the partners, a former pastry chef.

Access: 200m from the town

AQUITAINE

VILLENAVE-DE-RIONS - 33550

ANGRESSE - 40150

67 LES BATARELLES
M. Tandonnet

103 Deyma
33550 Villenave-de-Rions
Tel. 05 56 72 16 08
Fax 05 56 72 33 30
tandonnet.danielle@wanadoo.fr
http://lesbatarelles.free.fr

Open all year • 4 rooms, 2 of which are upstairs, all have bathrooms • €50 to €60, breakfast included • Table d'hôte €20 to €25 • Terrace, garden, car park. Credit cards not accepted, dogs not admitted

The warmth of this house is most contagious.

Fancy a cosy jaunt into the heart of Bordeaux's vineyards? Les Batarelles is the place for you! The attractive comfortable rooms have been tastefully fitted out by the owner who bends over backwards to make sure her guests' stay is as pleasant and relaxing as possible. On the breakfast table you will be treated to homemade jams and honey, served by the fireside in winter or on a terrace lined in vines in summer.

Access : 1.5km westbound on the D 237

68 TY-BONI
M. et Mme Boniface

1831 route de Capbreton
40150 Angresse
Tel. 05 58 43 98 75
Fax 05 58 43 98 75
info@ty-boni.com
www.ty-boni.com

Open all year • 5 rooms • €75 (€55 low season), breakfast included • No table d'hôte • Park, car park. Credit cards not accepted, no dogs admitted • Outdoor swimming pool

The owners' warm, generous welcome.

Only the chirping of birds and gentle breezes rustling through the pine trees interrupt the peace and quiet of this contemporary house in regional style. The soberly decorated rooms are very pleasant. Guests can cook their own meals in a guest kitchen. The park and swimming pool next to the pond are particularly pleasant during the summer months. An ideal situation within easy reach of the beach and the lively seaside village of Hossegor.

Access : 3km eastbound from Hossegor on the D 133

AQUITAINE

BETBEZER-D'ARMAGNAC - 40240

69 LE DOMAINE DE PAGUY
M. et Mme Darzacq

Domaine de Paguy
40240 Betbezer-d'Armagnac
Tel. 05 58 44 81 57
Fax 05 58 44 68 09
albert.darzacq@wanadoo.fr

Closed Wed from 1 July to 15 Sep • 6 rooms • €40 to €66, breakfast included • Table d'hôte from €16 (weekdays) to €31 • Park, terrace, car park. Credit cards not accepted, dogs not allowed in rooms • Outdoor swimming pool. Guided tours of the Armagnac cellars

We most liked: The tour and commentary of the Armagnac cellars.

This 16C manor house stands in the centre of a vast wine-growing estate overlooking the Douze Valley. Spacious, attractive rooms, partly renovated, open onto the landscaped park and the vineyards, where hens and ducks roam free. Fine local Landes cuisine takes pride of place in the kitchen of this handsome property.

Access : 5km to the north-east of Labastide-d'Armagnac on the D 11 then the D 35

CRÉON-D'ARMAGNAC - 40240

70 LE POUTIC
M. Subra

Route de Cazaubon
40240 Créon-d'Armagnac
Tel. 05 58 44 66 97
lepoutic@wanadoo.fr
www.lepoutic.com

Open all year • 3 non-smoking rooms, all with shower/WC • €45 to €55, breakfast included • Table d'hôte €18, including drinks • Terrace, park, car park. Credit cards not accepted, dogs not admitted • Library-sitting room, jacuzzi. Theme weekends

We most liked: The theme weekends.

The restoration of this old regional farmhouse has enhanced the appeal of its old stone walls, beams and timber frame. The same attention to detail has been lavished on the tastefully decorated and well-tended rooms. A spa and a 100m^2 summer room, located in converted outhouses, further encourages guests to relax. The owners also organise theme weekends: horse-riding, golf, woodpigeon shooting...

Access : On the way out of Créon-d'Armagnac, on the D 51 Cazaubon road

AQUITAINE

HAGETMAU - 40700

71 LES LACS D'HALCO
M. et Mme Demen

Route de Cazalis
40700 Hagetmau
Tel. 05 58 79 30 79
Fax 05 58 79 36 15
contact@hotel-des-lacs-dhalco.fr
www.hotel-des-lacs-dhalco.com

Open all year • 24 rooms with bath/WC and television, 2 have disabled access • €68 to €98 (€64 to €85 low season); breakfast €10; half-board available • Air-conditioned restaurant; menus €27 to €50 • Car park. No dogs admitted in restaurant • Indoor swimming pool, tennis, bicycle rentals

The resolutely futuristic architecture blends in perfectly with the Landes countryside.

Steel, glass, wood and stone comprise the surprising modern architecture overlooking the lakes and forest. The countless bay windows of this semi-circular construction invite guests to gaze out on the countryside. A spacious hall, contemporary bar and unusual dining room, built on a rotunda which seems to float on the water, are located on the ground-floor. Upstairs, the ample, modern bedrooms are decorated in a pleasantly unfussy style. Covered swimming pool, rowing boats and crazy golf.

Access: 3km south-west of Hagetmau on the Cazalis road

HOSSEGOR - 40150

72 BARBARY-LANE
M. Duclau

156 avenue de la Côte-d'Argent
40150 Hossegor
Tel. 05 58 43 46 00
Fax 05 58 43 95 19
barbary-lane@wanadoo.fr
www.barbary-lane.com

Closed Jan and Feb • 18 rooms, including 2 apartments, all with bathroom and television • €100 (€45 low season); breakfast €7; half-board available from 15 Jun to 15 Sep • Half board available from 15 June to 15 Sep • Terrace, equipped meeting room • Outdoor swimming pool

Lounging around the swimming pool.

This regional-style house, in a quiet tree-lined residential neighbourhood, has been renovated from top to bottom. The personalised, prettily-decorated rooms sport colourful fabrics, antique furniture, old box beds fixed to the wall and painted chinaware. In summer, the establishment offers a half-board formula and breakfast – served until midday – becomes brunch.

Access: In the town

AQUITAINE

MIMBASTE - 40350

73 CAPCAZAL DE PACHIOU
Mme Dufourcet

606 route de Pachiou
40350 Mimbaste
Tel. 05 58 55 30 54
Fax 05 58 55 30 54

Open all year • 4 rooms • €47 to €65, breakfast included • Table d'hôte €20 (closed Sun) • Car park. Credit cards not accepted

We most liked **The authenticity of the house and the welcome.**

This wonderful old house has been in the same family since it was built in the 17C. Its loving restoration has preserved countless traces of its illustrious past, such as a dovecote, bird cage, original panelling and parquet floors. The house exudes history, as the canopied beds, carved fireplaces and old prints illustrate, and this same proud commitment to tradition is in evidence in the kitchen, where duck and goose feature prominently in mouth-watering local dishes.

Access : 11km on the N 947 towards Dax-Orthez

SABRES - 40630

74 LES ARBOUSIERS
Mme Labri

Le Gaille
40630 Sabres
Tel. 05 58 07 52 52
Fax 05 58 07 52 52
lesarbousiers@aol.com
www.chambres-landes.com

Open all year • 6 rooms • €49 (€45 low season), breakfast included; half-board available • Table d'hôte €18 (evenings only) • Park, car park. Credit cards not accepted, dogs not admitted

We most liked **The enchanting picture of this half-timbered house.**

Set in a clearing in a pine forest, this half-timbered home, typical of the region, never fails to attract admiring glances. The comfortable new rooms are bright and airy. The large bay windows of the restaurant also flood the dining room with light, while diners can enjoy the view of a park which makes no secret of the owner's passion for wildlife and ornithology. What's more, the owner's simple, unaffected welcome is quite irresistible.

Access : 7.5km westbound from Sabres on the D 44

AQUITAINE

SOUSTONS - 40140

ST-MICHEL-D'ESCALUS - 40550

75 DOMAINE DE BELLEGARDE
M. Bouvy

23 avenue Charles-de-Gaulle
40140 Soustons
Tel. 05 58 41 24 06
Fax 05 58 41 33 60
domainedebellegarde@wanadoo.fr
www.domainebellegarde.com

Open all year • 4 non-smoking rooms, all with shower/WC and television, 2 have a private sauna • €90 to €175 (€60 to €150 low season); breakfast €10 • No table d'hôte • Terrace, garden, car park. Credit cards not accepted, dogs not admitted • Outdoor swimming pool, billiards, tennis

76 LA BERGERIE ST-MICHEL
M. Verdoux-Loustau

40550 St-Michel-d'Escalus
Tel. 05 58 48 74 04

Closed Oct 6 to Apr 30 • 5 rooms, all with bath/WC, television, direct access to rooms • €90 (€80 low season), breakfast included • No table d'hôte • Garden, car park. Credit cards not accepted, no dogs admitted

Every nook and cranny of this establishment oozes with charm.

The sophisticated contemporary bedrooms of this handsome country house built in the early 20C combine a pleasing mixture of styles and materials (coconut matting, wrought iron beds, etc); one has its own private sauna while another one opens onto a private terrace. The inviting sitting rooms, billiards room, tennis court, swimming pool and extensive wooded grounds further enhance the property's appeal.

Waking up to the smiling the owner and his sumptuous breakfasts!

This magnificently restored former sheepfold is tucked away deep in the Landes forest not far from the 12C church of St Michael. The rooms, situated in the outhouses, boast lovely antiques, splendid hi-tech bathrooms and a private terrace. The largest, fully independent, was for a time the studio of an American artist. Breakfasts are served in the main house, behind the lovely half-timbered façade, or in the garden.

Access : On the way out of the town, on the Saint-Geours-de-Maremne road

Access : 5km eastbound from St Michel d'Escalus on the D142, opposite the church

AQUITAINE

TARNOS - 40220

77 CHAMBRE D'HÔTE M. LADEUIX
M. et Mme Ladeuix

26 avenue Salvador-Allende
40220 Tarnos
Tel. 05 59 64 13 95
Fax 05 59 64 13 95
heleneladeuix@hotmail.com
www.enaquitaine.com

Open all year • 5 rooms and one gîte • €65 (€53 to €55 low season), breakfast included • No table d'hôte • Park, car park. Credit cards not accepted • Outdoor swimming pool

The pleasant surprise of the woodland to the rear of the house.

From the road, it is impossible to imagine that this house covered in wisteria opens onto such a sumptuous park of oak, chestnut, maple, mimosa, banana and pear trees. Most of the rooms are relatively simply decorated, except one which has a distinctly Basque accent. Guests have the use of a laundry room and a kitchen. Children will love the sheep pen, as well as the nearby rabbit and poultry cages.

Access: 5km northbound from Bayonne on the N 10

AGEN - 47000

78 CHÂTEAU DES JACOBINS
M. et Mme de Capmarty-Bujan

1 ter place des Jacobins
47000 Agen
Tel. 05 53 47 03 31
Fax 05 53 47 02 80
hotel@chateau-des-jacobins.com
www.chateau-des-jacobins.com

Open all year • 15 rooms with bath/WC or shower/WC and television, 13 are air-conditioned • €98 to €107; breakfast €12 • No restaurant • Park, private car park

The pleasantly old-fashioned atmosphere which reigns throughout this characterful abode.

The central location combined with tranquillity is greatly appreciated by the patrons of this private mansion built in 1832. A shady courtyard leads visitors into the establishment. On the ground-floor are two prettily decorated sitting rooms and a handsome staircase which leads up to the bedrooms. Of varying sizes, all are comfortably appointed and decorated individually in a deliciously outmoded style. A perfect antidote to those who abhor hotel chains!

Access: In the town centre near the Jacobins Church

AQUITAINE

BARBASTE - 47230

MONCLAR-D'AGENAIS - 47380

79 LA CASCADE AUX FÉES
Mme Mazurier

La Riberotte - Chemin du Moulin des Tours
47230 Barbaste
Tel. 05 53 97 05 96
Fax 05 53 97 05 96
gmazurier@aol.com
www.cascade-aux-fees.com

Closed Jan and Feb • 4 non-smoking rooms, all have bath/WC or shower/WC • €80 to €95 (€64 to €76 low season); breakfast €7; half-board available • Table d'hôte €15 to €25 • Sittong room, garden, terrace, car park. Credit cards not accepted • Swimming pool, petanque, angling and mountain bikes

80 CHÂTEAU DE LA SEIGLAL
M. et Mme Decourty

47380 Monclar-d'Agenais
Tel. 05 53 41 81 30
decourty-chambres-hotes@worldonline.fr

Open all year (by reservation) • 5 rooms • €53, breakfast €5; half-board available • Table d'hôte €20 including beverages (evening only) • Park, car park. Credit cards not accepted, dogs not admitted • Outdoor swimming pool, table-tennis, table football, football pitch, fishing, cycling

We most liked: The view of the restored Moulin des Tours.

This 18C property, partly built into the rock, commands a view of magnificent flowered grounds and the shady banks of the Gélise. The wide range of facilities include a swimming pool, hammock, riverside summer dining room and bar. Indoors, the bedrooms and sitting rooms, furnished with period pieces, are all refreshingly simple and understated in style. The overall impression of charm is further enhanced by the delightful welcome extended by the mistress of the house.

We most liked: The friendly atmosphere of this 19C castle.

Hidden by a park planted with ancient trees, this small château built in 1820 is a haven of peace and quiet. The renovated, well-proportioned, comfortable rooms, named after the owner's five sisters, overlook the park and the surrounding meadows. The dining room is a treasure trove of period furniture, carved hunting scenes and a superb fireplace. Not to be outdone, the menu boasts garden- and farm-produce as well as delicious home-made pastries.

Access: 6km northeast of Nérac on the D 930 and D 655 Casteljaloux road

Access: 6km northbound from Fongrave on the D 238 then left onto the D 66 Miramont-de-Guyenne road

AQUITAINE

NÉRAC - 47600

81 LE DOMAINE DU CAUZE
SCI du Cause- Mlle Pope Isabelle

47600 Nérac
Tel. 05 53 65 54 44
Fax 05 53 65 54 44
cauze.pope@wanadoo.fr
www.domaineducauze.com

Closed from 23 Dec to 2 Jan • 4 rooms • €53, breakfast included; half-board available • Table d'hôte €18 (€24 in evening) • Car park. Dogs not admitted • Outdoor swimming pool

We most liked: The tranquillity of this hundred-year-old establishment.

This superbly restored old farmhouse has it all. First and foremost, an idyllic situation on a hillside with sweeping views of the dense forests of the Landes and the Gers on fine days. Add to this the tranquillity of the tastefully decorated rooms and last, but not least, the meals, served under the arbour in the summer and whipped up with rare enthusiasm by the imaginative owner-chef. Friendly, hospitable hosts.

Access: 2.5km eastbound from Nérac towards Agen (D 656)

SAINT-EUTROPE-DE-BORN - 47290

82 MOULIN DE LABIQUE
Mme Boulet

47290 Saint-Eutrope-de-Born
Tel. 05 53 01 63 90
Fax 05 53 01 73 17
moulin-de-labique@wanadoo.fr
www.moulin-de-labique.fr

Open all year (by reservation) • 6 non-smoking rooms on 2 floors, all have bath/WC or shower/WC • €90; breakfast €8; half-board available • Table d'hôte €30 • Garden, car park • Sitting room-library, tennis, outdoor swimming pool, ponies

We most liked: The immaculate interior decoration.

The delicious inner courtyard planted with high plane trees is at the heart of this estate. The bedrooms, created in former barns and stables and the main house, which sports a Colonial-style façade, are all located off the courtyard. The personalised bedrooms feature a tasteful blend of furniture, objects and paintings. After a bout of angling, a dip in the pool or a read in the sitting room, you will be ready to do justice to the tasty dishes rustled up by the talented lady of the house...

Access: 4km southeast of Saint-Eutrope-de-Born on the D 153

AQUITAINE

SAMAZAN - 47250

83 CHÂTEAU CANTET
M. et Mme Raitrie

47250 Samazan
Tel. 05 53 20 60 60
Fax 05 53 89 63 53
jbdelaraitrie@wanadoo.fr

Closed 15 Dec to 15 Jan • 3 rooms and 1 apartment with bath or shower and separate WC • €57 to €70, breakfast included • Table d'hôte €25, including beverages (by reservation) • Park, car park. Credit cards not accepted, dogs not admitted • Outdoor swimming pool. Children's games room

We most liked **The wide range of leisure activities.**

An elegant 16C manor house set in well-tended grounds in the heart of the countryside. The bright colour scheme of the rooms sets off a smart but homely interior, with a hint of rustic style. Meals are served in the Louis XIII-style dining room or under the arbour around the pool. The choice of leisure activities is vast: play room, bicycles, lawn croquet, billiards, table-tennis, basketball, pétanque and only 10km away, a golf course and tennis courts.

Access: 10km southbound from Marmande towards Casteljaloux

ASCAIN - 64310

84 CHAMBRE D'HÔTE ARRAYOA
M. Ibarburu

Ferme "Arrayoa"
64310 Ascain
Tel. 05 59 54 06 18

Open all year • 4 rooms with bathrooms • €52, breakfast included • No table d'hôte • Living room with a kitchen and library. Credit cards not accepted

We most liked **Getting away from it all without entirely forgoing the social whirl of the Basque coast.**

This lovely house seems to have been designed with the good life in mind, from the charming countrified rooms to the tempting home-made foie gras and other delicacies served in the former cowshed. If your waistband feels a little tight, you can try your hand on the establishment's private pelota court or don your walking boots and hike up the Rhune. The superb view is more than worth the effort, but those with fewer calories to burn may prefer to catch the little train from the Col de St Ignace.

Access: 800m from the pelota court

AQUITAINE

BUZY - 64260

85 MAÏNADE
Mme Augareils

6 place Cazenave
64260 Buzy
Tel. 05 59 21 01 01
Fax 05 59 21 01 01
rolande.augareils@free.fr

Closed in Jan • 6 rooms • €52 to €54, (€20 to €51 low season), breakfast included; half-board available • Table d'hôte €18 to €22 • Car park. Credit cards not accepted, dogs not admitted

We most liked
The warm welcome extended by the lady of the house, Rolande, and her staff.

This attractive Béarn farmhouse with its wrought-iron gate, flowered window boxes and courtyard, lies in the heart of the village. Don't stand on ceremony, just sit down with the other guests and Rolande's family at the huge open-air table, which can seat up to 25, and enjoy a wonderful meal, invariably accompanied by a song or two. The rooms are lovingly decorated with old lace and family heirlooms, but, beware, none are heated. 100 % authentic Béarn cooking.

Access : 4km northbound from Arudy on the D 920

CASTAGNÈDE - 64270

86 LA BELLE AUBERGE
M. et Mme Vicassiau

64270 Castagnède
Tel. 05 59 38 15 28
Fax 05 59 65 03 57

Closed from 1 to 15 Jun, 20 Dec to 31 Jan, Sun and Mon evenings • 14 rooms with bath/WC or shower/WC, all have television • €39 to €43; breakfast 6; half-board available • Menus €12 to €22 • Terrace, garden, car park • Outdoor swimming pool

We most liked
Killing time around the swimming pool.

Nothing could be more welcoming than this family-run establishment nestling in a picturesque hamlet on the fast-flowing Gave d'Oloron river. The bar and two country-style dining rooms, serving generous helpings of hearty, local dishes, are located in the main wing of the old house. The bedrooms, in a later wing, are not luxurious but they are well looked-after and all overlook the spacious garden and unusually-shaped swimming pool.

Access : Leave Salies-de-Béarn on the D 17 (towards Peyrehorade), then left onto the D 27 and right onto the D 384

AQUITAINE

FÉAS - 64570

87 LE CHÂTEAU DE BOUES
Mme Dornon

64570 Féas
Tel. 05 59 39 95 49
Fax 05 59 39 95 49

Closed from late Sep to Apr • 4 rooms • €60, breakfast included • No table d'hôte • Garden, car park. Credit cards not accepted, dogs not admitted • Outdoor swimming pool

The kindness of the hospitable owners.

On the doorstep of Baretous Valley, the pristine walls of this lofty 18C castle dominate the surrounding Béarn countryside. The bedrooms, located in the central wing – the owners occupy the towers – enjoy views of the garden, swimming pool and superb kitchen garden. Breakfast is a lively, friendly affair and guests are made to feel like friends of the family.

Access : 8km to the south-west of Oloron-Ste-Marie on the D 919

GUÉTHARY - 64210

88 BRIKÉTÉNIA
M. et Mme Ibarboure

142 rue de l'Église
64210 Guéthary
Tel. 05 59 26 51 34
Fax 05 59 54 71 55

Open from 15 Mar to 15 Nov • 16 rooms, 12 of which have balconies, 1 has disabled access, all have bath/WC and television • €65 to €68 (€60 to €65 low season); breakfast €8 • No restaurant • Car park

Grab a "makhila" – a traditional Basque walking stick – and explore this seaside resort.

The coaching inn, built in 1680 on the heights of Guéthary, is a fine example of traditional Basque architecture: steep tiled roof, balcony, whitewashed walls, timber frames and red shutters. Perhaps it was the ocean view from some of the rooms that appealed to one Napoleon Bonaparte, an illustrious former guest? Be that as it may, the energetic proprietors are not the sort to rest on their laurels and the inn has recently been renovated from top to toe.

Access : Near the church

AQUITAINE

ISPOURE - 64220

89 FERME ETXEBERRIA
M. Mourguy

64220 Ispoure
Tel. 05 59 37 06 23
Fax 05 59 37 06 23
domainemourguy@hotmail.com
www.domainemourguy.com

Open all year • 4 rooms • €44, breakfast included • No table d'hôte • Car park. Credit cards not accepted, no dogs admitted • Tour of the cellars and wine-tasting

Donkey rides through Irouleguy's vineyards.

What better way to really get to know the Basque country than by staying in this attractive farmhouse surrounded by vineyards. The converted barn houses modern, soberly decorated and very pleasant rooms. Guests have the use of a kitchenette, an attractive breakfast room and a conservatory which overlooks the vines. The owners, who also produce wine and raise donkeys, are happy to help guests organise hikes throughout the region.

Access: 0.8km to the north-east of Saint-Jean-Pied-de-Port on the D 933

ISSOR - 64570

90 LA FERME AUX SANGLIERS
M. Delhay-Cazaurang

Micalet
64570 Issor
Tel. 05 59 34 43 96
Fax 05 59 34 43 96

Open all year • 5 rooms with bathrooms • €43 to €55, breakfast included • Table d'hôte €15 to €22 (evenings only) • Car park. Credit cards not accepted, dogs not admitted • Tasting and sale of homemade "charcuterie"

The stunning view from all the bedrooms.

A narrow road winds its way up to this lovingly restored Béarn farmhouse. You can be sure of a warm, generous welcome, together with comfortable rooms, all of which command sweeping views of the valley and the Pyrenean peaks. The focus is on healthy, local produce and the owner, who breeds animals, adores taking visitors round his boar parks, to the delight of children.

Access: 10km westbound from St-Christau on the D 918 as far as Asasp, then the N 134 and the D 918 towards Arette

AQUITAINE

ITXASSOU - 64250

91 HÔTEL DU CHÊNE
Mme Salaberry

64250 Itxassou
Tel. 05 59 29 75 01
Fax 05 59 29 27 39

Closed in Jan and Feb, Tue from Oct to Jun, and Mon • 16 rooms with bath/WC, some have television • €45 (€43 low season); breakfast €7; half-board available • Menus €15 to €38 • Terrace, garden, car park. Dogs not admitted in restaurant

The superb Villa Arnaga, nearby, one-time home to Edmond Rostand, creator of Cyrano de Bergerac.

The doors of this hospitable country inn have been open since 1696. The bedrooms, some of which are graced with marble fireplaces and old Basque furniture, overlook the cherry trees of Itxassou – a sight to behold in the spring! Make sure you sample the famous blackcherry jam under the colourful blue beams of the dining room or in the shade of the sweet-scented wisteria.

Access : Near the church

ITXASSOU - 64250

92 SOUBELETA
Mme Régérat

64250 Itxassou
Tel. 05 59 29 78 64

Open all year • 5 rooms • €49 to €55, (€48 to €52 low season), breakfast included • No table d'hôte • Garden, car park. Credit cards not accepted, dogs not admitted

The tranquil mood of this peaceful 17C mansion.

This imposing mansion, built in 1675, certainly makes the most of a lovely spot in the upper part of the village. The generously proportioned rooms, graced with gleaming family antiques, look over meadows and the orchard; two have marble fireplaces. The light, airy sitting room is very pleasant and children will love visiting the cows in the neighbouring dairy farm.

Access : In the village, stay on the D 918 until the Nive bridge, then turn right

AQUITAINE

IZESTE - 64260

93 CHAMBRE D'HÔTE M. ET MME ASNAR
M. Asnar

4 avenue Georges-Messier
64260 Izeste
Tel. 05 59 05 71 51
Fax 05 59 05 71 51
jean-lili.asnar@tele2.fr
www.vallee-ossau.com/hebergement/asnar

Closed 2 weeks in Oct • 3 rooms, all with shower/WC and television • €43, breakfast included • No table d'hôte • Terrace, garden, car park. Credit cards not accepted

A simple smiling welcome.

A beautifully tended garden planted with flowers and plane, linden, palm and fruit trees, surrounds this handsome stone house facing the mountain. The owner offers a gîte and three rooms, all on the ground-floor, with an independent entrance; each room is different and all are furnished simply but with no lack of modern comforts.

Access : In the town

LANNE EN BARÉTOUS - 64570

94 MAISON RACHOU
M. Masero

64570 Lanne-en-Barétous
Tel. 05 59 34 10 30
Fax 05 59 34 10 30
www.gites64.com/maison-rachou

Open all year • 5 rooms, 1 with disabled access, all with shower/WC • €46, breakfast included • Table d'hôte €17, drinks included • Terrace, garden, car park. Credit cards not accepted • Outdoor swimming pool

The view of the village and the Pyrenees.

The owners of this old farmhouse located on the heights of the town have taken great care to ensure that you will be welcomed in an immaculately maintained establishment: renovated façade, vast dining room with fireplace and timber beams... The rooms are all more or less identical with wooden ceilings and floors, white walls and functional bathrooms. The master of the house, formerly a chef, prepares dinner himself.

Access : In the village, opposite the baker's, follow the signposts

AQUITAINE

LESCAR - 64230

95 LA GRANGE DU MOULIN
Mme Dubosc

Moulin du Batan
64230 Lescar
Tel. 06 88 25 39 20
Fax 05 59 81 29 01
lagrangedumoulin@club-internet.fr
www.lagrangedumoulin.com

Open all year • 4 non-smoking rooms upstairs, all with shower/WC and modem access • €90 (€68 low season), breakfast included • No table d'hôte • Terrace, park, library, private car park. Credit cards not accepted, dogs not admitted

Relaxing in the heavenly garden by the water's edge.

The owners welcome their guests in their exquisitely restored former water mill. The personalised and tastefully decorated rooms are full of charm, as is the breakfast room with its bare stone walls, large fireplace and inviting table. If you then add the owners' warm welcome, you will have all the ingredients for a memorable stay in the Béarn region.

Access : At Lescar, go towards Bayonne on the N 117 and a minor road to the left

PAGOLLE - 64120

96 MAISON ELIXONDOA
M. et Mme Walther

64120 Pagolle
Tel. 05 59 65 65 34
Fax 05 59 65 72 15
jean.walther@wanadoo.fr
www.elixondoa.com

Open all year • 4 rooms • €48, breakfast included • Table d'hôte €20 (evening only) • Garden, car park. Credit cards not accepted

The pastoral charm of this remote spot.

Those in need of a serious break should head for this 17C farm, set among open fields, on one of the old pilgrim roads to Santiago de Compostela. The bedrooms, recently fitted-out with all the modern comforts, overlook the surrounding hillsides. Meals are taken in the vast dining room where the exposed stone work and timbers cannot fail to catch the eye. Friendly service.

Access : 13km westbound from Mauléon-Licharre on the D 918 then the D 302

AQUITAINE

SAINT-JEAN-DE-LUZ - 64500

97 VILLA ARGI-EDER
M. Basset

Avenue Napoléon III
64500 Saint-Jean-de-Luz
Tel. 05 59 54 81 65
Fax 05 59 54 81 65
villa-argi-eder @ wanadoo.fr

Open all year • 4 rooms • €50; breakfast €5 • No table d'hôte • Terrace, garden, car park. Credit cards not accepted

Admire the reckless surfers braving the giant waves.

This handsome Basque villa, recently spruced up with a new coat of paint, has something for everyone: tranquillity, a well-tended lawn lined in flowers and a superb location just 100m from the surfing beach. The brand-new spacious bedrooms are an invitation to meditation and those overlooking the garden have private terraces. The bathrooms are neat and well appointed. One of the resort's most pleasant hotels.

Access: 5km to the north-east of Saint-Jean-de-Luz on the N 10 towards Biarritz, then take a minor road

SALIES-DE-BÉARN - 64270

98 LA CLOSERIE DU GUILHAT
Mme Potiron

Le Guilhat
64270 Salies-de-Béarn
Tel. 05 59 38 08 80
Fax 05 59 38 31 90
guilhat @ club-internet.fr
www.holidayshomes.com/guilhat

Open all year • 4 rooms and one gîte • €49 to €55, breakfast included; half-board available • Table d'hôte €20 (evenings only except Thu) • Park, car park. Credit cards not accepted, dogs not admitted

Whiling away the evenings on the terrace facing the Pyrenees.

It is difficult to find a fault with such a lovely old country house, especially one with a sumptuous landscaped park and an exquisite terrace overlooking the valley, set against a backdrop of Pyrenean peaks. A bold colour scheme distinguishes the quiet, well-dimensioned rooms, each of which is named after a flower. The mistress of the house makes guests feel truly welcome and dining on the winter veranda or summer terrace is an unforgettable experience.

Access: 4km northbound from Salies towards Puyoo, in the upper reaches of Salies

AQUITAINE

SALIES-DE-BÉARN - 64270

99 LA DEMEURE DE LA PRESQU'ÎLE
M. Sclafer

22 avenue des Docteurs-Foix
64270 Salies-de-Béarn
Tel. 05 59 38 06 22
Fax 05 59 38 06 22
www.demeurepresquile.com

Open all year • 3 rooms upstairs, all with bath/WC or shower/WC, 2 have a television • €61 (€54 low season), breakfast included • Table d'hôte €23 • Terrace, park, library, garage. Credit cards not accepted

We most liked: The mouth-watering home-made pastries.

This 18C abode, a short walk from the town centre, is home to an authentic interior full of character: lovely tiles in the entrance hall, a period dining room lined in mirrors in which the pretty wooden fireplace is reflected and a delightful sitting room-library. A handsome staircase leads up to the spacious elegant rooms furnished with period pieces. Regional influences feature prominently in the kitchen. Splendid magnolia in the immense grounds.

Access: In the town

SALIES-DE-BÉARN - 64270

100 MAISON LÉCHÉMIA
Mme Camougrand

Quartier du Bois
64270 Salies-de-Béarn
Tel. 05 59 38 08 55
Fax 05 59 38 08 55

Open all year • 3 non-smoking rooms, 2 in a separate wing, all with bath/WC or shower/WC • €52 (€48 low season), breakfast included • Table d'hôte €23, including drinks • Terrace, garden, private car park. Credit cards not accepted

We most liked: The owner's unaffected friendly welcome.

This old farm hidden in the country has been faultlessly restored. We recommend booking one of the two attractive rooms in the converted stables. At mealtimes, after choosing between the winter dining room, complete with fireplace, or the covered terrace in summer, you will be served delicious country fare made with home-made and home-grown produce: garden vegetables, home-made jams with fruit from the orchard, etc.

Access: In the town, take the Carresse road by the D 17 and turn right onto a minor road at the Quartier du Bois

AQUITAINE
SARE - 64310

101 ARRAYA
M. Fagoaga

64310 Sare
Tel. 05 59 54 20 46
Fax 05 59 54 27 04
hotel@arraya.com
www.arraya.com

Closed 2 Nov to 30 Mar • 23 rooms, most have bath/WC, some have shower/WC, all have television • €69 to €110; breakfast €9; half-board available • Restaurant closed Sun evening and Mon lunchtime (except 3 Jul to 12 Sep); menus €21 to €31 • Terrace, garden. No dogs admitted in rooms • Shop with Basque linen and local produce

Chugging up the Rhune in an old train (1924).

This village, nestling at the foot of the Rhune, is a treasure chest of Basque heritage. In keeping with its historic past, the 17C coaching inn, which formerly welcomed pilgrims of St James, is a fine example of regional interior design with dark timbers, old furniture and colourful fabrics. The surrounding countryside, a former "smugglers' paradise" is now heaven on earth: footpaths criss-cross the region, winding through meadows where the local ponies and sheep graze peacefully.

Access : In the heart of the village, near the main square, next to the pelota court

AUVERGNE

Shh! Auvergne's volcanoes are dormant and have been for many millennia, forming a natural rampart against the inroads of man and ensuring that this beautiful wilderness will never be entirely tamed. If you listen very carefully, you may just make out a distant rumble from Vulcania, where spectacular theme park attractions celebrate the sleeping giants. The region's windswept domes and peaks, sculpted by long-extinguished fires, are now the source of countless mountain springs that cascade down the steep slopes into brooks, rivers and crystal-clear lakes. Renowned for the therapeutic virtues of its waters, the region has long played host to countless well-heeled *curistes*, come to take the waters in its elegant spa resorts. It has to be said that many find it impossible to follow doctor's orders when faced with the enticing aroma of a country stew or a full-bodied Cantal cheese.

- Allier (03)
- Cantal (15)
- Haute-Loire (43)
- Puy-de-Dôme (63)

AUVERGNE

BOURBON-L'ARCHAMBAULT - 03160

1 G. H. MONTESPAN-TALLEYRAND
M. Livertout

Place des Thermes
03160 Bourbon-L'Archambault
Tel. 04 70 67 00 24
Fax 04 70 67 12 00
hotelmontespan@wanadoo.fr
www.hotel-montespan.com

Open from 1 Apr to 20 Oct • 44 rooms, 4 of which have kitchenettes, all have bath/WC or shower/WC and television • €58 to €103; breakfast €10; half-board available • Menus €22 (weekdays) to €45 • Garage. No dogs admitted in restaurant • Outdoor swimming pool, fitness room

We most liked: The attractive flowered garden at the foot of a medieval tower.

These historic houses stand next door to the spa centre with the Castle of the Dukes of Bourbon in the background. Practically all the ceilings feature traditional dark-timbered beams, while simple white-stone walls, adorned with elegant fireplaces, light up the cosy, personalised rooms. Talleyrand, and a number of noble ladies, including Mme de Montespan and Mme de Sévigné resided here while taking the waters. A grand old establishment which is definitely a cut above your average spa hotel.

Access: In the centre of the resort, next to the spa

CHARROUX - 03140

2 LA MAISON DU PRINCE DE CONDÉ
M. Speer

Place d'Armes
03140 Charroux
Tel. 04 70 56 81 36
Fax 04 70 56 81 36
jspeer@club-internet.fr
www.maison-conde.com

Open all year • 6 non-smoking rooms, including 1 apartment in tower, all have bath or shower and WC and television • €56, breakfast included • No table d'hôte • Garden. Credit cards not accepted, dogs not admitted

We most liked: Chatting with the owner, ever available for guests.

The tiny medieval city of Charroux is home to this delightful guesthouse run by a couple of retired Canadians. Five of the six rooms are situated in the main building, but the "Porte d'Orient", a split-level apartment with balneo bathtub and four-poster bed is tucked away in a tower up a narrow irregular staircase. Meals are served in an unusual and attractive 13C vaulted dining room.

Access: In the centre of the village

AUVERGNE

COULANDON - 03000

3 LE CHALET ET MONTÉGUT
M. Navarro

28 route du Chalet
03000 Coulandon
Tel. 04 70 46 00 66
Fax 04 70 44 07 09
hotel-chalet @ cs3i.fr
www.hotel.lechalet.com

Closed from 18 Dec to 10 Jan • 28 rooms, 19 of which are in a separate wing, one has disabled access. Rooms have bath/WC or shower/WC and television • €66 to €81; breakfast €9; half-board available • Menus €18 (weekdays) to €39 • Terrace, park, car park • Outdoor swimming pool

We most liked
Generous breakfasts with a distinctly Alpine flavour; the landlord is Swiss.

A cluster of three buildings make up this 10-acre country estate, complete with a large pond for fishing, hundred-year-old parkland and a swimming pool. The rooms are situated in the "chalet", which also houses the reception and in the former stables, while the restaurant is in a more recent building. Savour the pleasure of waking up in the heart of the peaceful Bourbon countryside.

Access : 7km to the south-west of Moulins on the D 945 (towards Souvigny), then right on a minor road

COULANDON - 03000

4 LA GRANDE POTERIE
M. Pompon

9 rue de la Grande-Poterie
03000 Coulandon
Tel. 04 70 44 30 39
Fax 04 70 44 30 39
jcpompon @ lagrandepoterie.com
www.lagrandepoterie.com

Closed in Jan • 4 rooms, 1 on ground floor, all have bathrooms • €58 to €64, breakfast included • Menu €20 • Terrace, garden, car park, small kitchen. Credit cards not accepted • Outdoor swimming pool, bicycles on request

We most liked
The kindness and availability of the owner.

Extremely well-kept tree-lined and flower-decked grounds surround this restored farmhouse, perfect for a peaceful halt. The refreshingly simply decorated yet sophisticated rooms are particularly pleasant and attractive. Local Auvergne produce takes pride of place on the table d'hôte in the form of mouth-watering specialities: pâté bourbonnais, pompe aux pommes, brioche aux grattons... Don't worry though – you can burn off those excess calories in the heated swimming pool!

Access : From Coulandon, take the Savigny road, after the level crossing, continue for 600m then take the first left and follow the signs

AUVERGNE

LA FERTÉ-HAUTERIVE - 03340

5 DEMEURE D'HAUTERIVE
M. Lefebvre

03340 La Ferté-Hauterive
Tel. 04 70 43 04 85
Fax 04 70 43 00 62
j.lefebvre@demeure-hauterive.com
www.demeure-hauterive.com

Open all year • 5 rooms, one of which is on the ground floor • €75 to €83 (€70 to €78 low season), breakfast included • Table d'hôte €20 to €25 • Park, car park • Swimming pool, horse-drawn carriage outings possible

Strolling through the park bedecked in autumn colours.

It would be difficult to find a more gracious establishment than this opulent mansion, built in 1850 in the heart of an 8-acre park. The exquisitely decorated rooms, particularly those on the ground floor, are spacious. The house also provides its guests with a wide range of leisure activities, including billiards, badminton and table tennis, but the most pleasant of all is a stroll through parkland dotted with ornamental pools and follies. Highly friendly atmosphere.

Access: 12km northbound from St-Pourçain-sur-Sioule on the N 9 then the D 32

LE THEIL - 03240

6 CHÂTEAU DU MAX
M. Mazet-Pesar

03240 Le Theil
Tel. 04 70 42 35 23
Fax 04 70 42 34 90
chateaudumax@club-internet.fr
www.chateaudumax.com

Open all year • 4 rooms with private bathrooms and television • €70, breakfast included • Table d'hôte €22 to €25, drinks included • Garden, car park. Credit cards not accepted

This magnificent castle still boasts its original moat.

The entrance to this 13C and 15C castle is through a porch, which used to be a drawbridge in former times. A spiral staircase in the paved courtyard leads up to the medieval style dining room and rooms. Each of the different coloured rooms has been tastefully decorated by the owner, a former Parisian theatre set designer. Her ebullient personality and excessive kindness make it a pleasure to join her at dinner time and taste the local produce.

Access: West of Theil, 2.5km on the D 235

AUVERGNE

POUZY-MÉSANGY - 03320

7 MANOIR LE PLAIX
Mme Raucaz

03320 Pouzy-Mésangy
Tel. 04 70 66 24 06
Fax 04 70 66 25 82
leplaix@yahoo.fr

Closed 15 Dec to 15 Mar • 4 non-smoking rooms, all have bathrooms • €44, breakfast included; half-board available • Table d'hôte €16 (evenings only, by reservation) • Sitting room, car park. Credit cards not accepted • Nearby: tennis, mini golf

We most liked Walking along the banks of the Bieudre, which meanders its way through the immense property.

This welcoming 16C stronghold stands in the heart of a working farm. One of the chambres d'hôte is reached by a handsome spiral staircase. Red-brick floor tiles, wooden beams, old furniture and stone fireplaces set the scene for a pleasantly, relaxed stay. In the evenings, don't miss the chance to sample the delicious local produce, including the tender Charolais beef raised on the estate. Depending on the season, you can go walking, fishing or mushroom picking.

Access : Drive for 1.5km to the north-west on a minor road

THENEUILLE - 03350

8 L'OMBRE DE GOZINIÈRE
Mme Pamela Line

03350 Theneuille
Tel. 04 70 67 59 17
Fax 04 70 67 59 17
pamelaline@wanadoo.fr

Open May to Sep • 3 rooms • €50, breakfast included • Table d'hôte €18 (by reservation only) • Sitting room, garden, car park. Credit cards not accepted • Outdoor swimming pool

We most liked Taking a dip in the circular swimming pool set in a garden opening onto the countryside.

The owners of this attractive 17C building, a former outhouse of the neighbouring manor, have every right to be proud of its renovation. It now boasts fetching rooms with sloping ceilings where gingham fabrics, massive beams and rustic-style furniture create a pleasing, countrified atmosphere. Breakfasts and dinners are served in a cosy dining room which leads into a sitting room.

Access : On the way out of the village on the D 953

AUVERGNE

VALIGNAT - 03330

9 CHÂTEAU DE L'ORMET
M. et Mme Laederich

Lieu-dit l'Ormet
03330 Valignat
Tel. 04 70 58 57 23
Fax 04 70 58 54 36
lormet@wanadoo.fr
http://membres.lycos.fr/ormet

Closed 17 Dec to 2 Mar • 4 non-smoking rooms on two floors, all with bathrooms • €63 to €79, breakfast included • Table d'hôte €25, Fri and Sat by reservation • Garden, park, car park. Credit cards not accepted, dogs not admitted • Outdoor swimming pool

We most liked The toing-and-froing of the small trains that run through the garden in the evenings.

At an altitude of 465m on a plateau dominating the Limagne plain, this 18C manor house, altered countless times over the years, has lost none of its original class. The tastefully decorated personalised rooms overlook the park, the saltwater swimming pool and the amusing "garden trains" built by the railway enthusiast owner. Meals begin with a glass of Birlou (local aperitif made from white wine and sweet chestnut liqueur), followed by a main course, Auvergne cheeses and home-made desserts.

Access : 8km eastbound of Charroux on the D 183, at Valignat, L'Ormet

YGRANDE - 03160

10 LE CHALET DE LA NEVERDIÈRE
M. et Mme Vrel

Les Ferrons
03160 Ygrande
Tel. 04 70 66 31 67
Fax 04 70 66 32 64

Open all year • 4 rooms located in a small house 100m from the farm • €45, breakfast included • No table d'hôte • Garden, car park. Credit cards not accepted, dogs not admitted

We most liked The gargantuan breakfasts.

This early 20C house with its ochre edged façade and steep roof nestling in the heart of the Bourbon countryside, looks nothing like the chalets the region abounds in, but who cares? Its well-proportioned and well thought-out rooms overlook lush, green countryside. Tronçais Forest, 12km away, is perfect to walk off the extremely generous breakfasts. Very friendly staff.

Access : 10km to the south-west of Bourbon-l'Archambault on the D 953, then a minor road

AUVERGNE

CALVINET - 15340

11 · BEAUSÉJOUR
M. Puech

15340 Calvinet
Tel. 04 71 49 91 68
Fax 04 71 49 98 63
beauséjour.puech@wanadoo.fr
www.cantal-restaurant-puech.com

Closed from 9 Jan to 12 Feb • 10 rooms with bath/WC or shower/WC, all have television • €58 to €100; breakfast €10; half-board available • Menus €20 (weekdays) to €60 (booking recommended) • Private car park

We most liked
An unforgettable dining experience.

A larger than life genius reigns over the kitchens of this traditional Auvergne house in the middle of nowhere. The master chef whips up imaginative recipes based on wholesome local produce in which mushrooms, chestnuts and pork figure prominently. Guests feast on his inspired creations in an elegant brick-coloured dining room-veranda. The rooms, practical rather than charming, are amply compensated for by the quality of the cooking.

Access : On the Figeac road to Aurillac, leave the N 122 at Maurs for the D 19. In the centre of the village

CHAMPS-SUR-TARENTAINE - 15270

12 · AUBERGE DU VIEUX CHÊNE
Mme Moins

34 route des Lacs
15270 Champs-sur-Tarentaine
Tel. 04 71 78 71 64
Fax 04 71 78 70 88
danielle.moins@wanadoo.fr

Closed 1 Nov to 1 Apr, Sun and Mon out of season • 15 rooms on 2 floors with bathrooms, some have television • €57 to €80 (€52 to €71 low season); breakfast €9 • No restaurant • Terrace, garden, car park

We most liked
The picturesque Artense region, somewhat reminiscent of Scandinavia.

The frontage of this historic 19C farmhouse is almost hidden by Virginia creeper and flowers. The pretty, cosy rooms overlook a pleasant, peaceful garden. Exposed beams, thick stone walls and a huge fireplace add character to the dining room in the converted barn. Relax on the shaded terrace and admire the beautiful countryside of hills and meadows where the owners' horses graze.

Access : Not far from the centre of the village

AUVERGNE

FONTANGES - 15140

13 AUBERGE DE L'ASPRE
M. Landau

15140 Fontanges
Tel. 04 71 40 75 76
Fax 04 71 40 75 27
auberge-aspre@wanadoo.fr
www.auberge-aspre.com

Closed 17 Nov to 4 Feb; Sun and Wed evenings and Mon from Oct to May • 8 rooms, one of which has disabled access. All have unusual split-level bathrooms and television • €50 to €55; breakfast €8; half-board available • Menus €17 to €34 • Terrace, garden, car park • Outdoor swimming pool

We most liked
The tinkling of the cow-bells.

This old farmhouse with its beautiful stone-shingled roof lies in a secluded hamlet of the Aspre Valley not far from the village of Salers. The modern, brightly-coloured bedrooms, each of which has an unusual split-level bathroom, are situated in the old barn. Savour the traditional, tasty Auvergne menu in the rustic-style dining room, the veranda or on the pleasant terrace overlooking the garden.

Access : 5km southbound from Salers on the D 35

GIOU-DE-MAMOU - 15130

14 DE BARATHE
M. et Mme Breton

15130 Giou-de-Mamou
Tel. 04 71 64 61 72
barathe@wanadoo.fr

Open all year • 5 rooms • €48, breakfast included • Table d'hôte €13 (evenings only except Sun) • Garden, car park. Credit cards not accepted, dogs not admitted

We most liked
The authentic character of this country setting.

If you like the idea of waking to the sound of the cow-bells from the Salers cattle grazing in the lush, green meadows, then make a beeline for this place! Simple, yet comfortable rooms, ideal for families. Exposed stonework, old furniture, a fireplace, wood benches and a sink set the scene of the authentic dining room. Meals are, of course, prepared using produce grown and reared on the farm.

Access : 7km eastbound from Aurillac on the N 122 then the D 58

AUVERGNE

LANAU - 15260

15 AUBERGE DU PONT DE LANAU
M. et Mme Kergoat

15260 Lanau
Tel. 04 71 23 57 76
Fax 04 71 23 53 84
aubergedupontdelanau@wanadoo.fr
auberge-du-pont-de-lanau.fr

Closed Jan; Mon and Tue lunchtime from early Nov to Easter • 8 rooms on 2 floors, all have bath/WC or shower/WC • €55 to €60; breakfast €9; half-board available • Menus €25 (weekdays) to €50 (by reservation only) • Terrace, garden, car park

The endless meanders of the River Truyère.

This former coaching house, built in 1821, spans one of the rare crossing-places over the Truyère. Good, solid furniture adorns the well-maintained rooms. The typical, Auvergne-style decoration of the dining room with its well-worn panelling, exposed beams and huge stone fireplaces, has been preserved by successive owners over the years. Guests have the run of a small garden and a pleasant, shaded terrace.

Access: 4.5km from Chaudes-Aigues on the D 921 (Saint-Flour road)

LASCELLE - 15590

16 LAC DES GRAVES
M. Barbério

Jaulhac
15590 Lascelle
Tel. 04 71 47 94 06
Fax 04 71 47 96 55
lac.des.graves@wanadoo.fr
www.lacdesgraves.com

Open all year, closed Tue and Wed out of season • 24 rooms, 5 of which are non-smoking, 2 of which have disabled access; all have bath/WC or shower/WC and television • €62 (€50 low season); breakfast €6; half-board available • Menus €15 to €38 • Private car park, park, terrace • Swimming pool, fishing in the lake, horse riding

Ever fancied a spot of fly fishing?

The Canadian-inspired architecture of this hotel blends in perfectly with the superb landscape of the Jordanne Valley. Several wood chalets built on the edge of the lake house brand new rooms, which are both simple and welcoming, and a panoramic restaurant. Sweeping views of the water or the Cantal mountains are available from all the rooms. Horse-lovers will be enchanted by the riding center in extensive 90 acre grounds.

Access: 12km north of Aurillac towards Puy-Mary and Saint-Simon

AUVERGNE

LOUBARESSE - 15320

17 LA PAGNOUNE
Mme et Mlle Coutarel

Valadour
15320 Loubaresse
Tel. 04 71 73 74 69
auberge-lapagnoune@wanadoo.fr
www.auberge-lapagnoune.com

Closed in Jan and Feb, Sun evening and Mon from 1 Sep to 1 Jul • 7 rooms, 1 with disabled access, all have bathrooms • €50 (€44 low season); breakfast €8 • Menus €11 (weekdays) to €20

We most liked: A visit to the Pierre Allègre Farm, a farming museum in the heart of the village.

Farewell calves, cows and pigs! This former farm, built in 1877, is now home to an inviting hostelry whose simplicity and authenticity are irresistible. Exposed beams and rough stone walls, impressive fireplaces, an old grandfather clock, farming tools and rustic furniture grace the country-style dining room, whose cuisine is of course equally regional. The rooms may not be luxurious, but they are comfortable, well kept and fitted out in a similar rustic spirit.

Access : 5km southbound from the Viaduc du Garabit on the D 909, head towards Charmensac

MURAT - 15300

18 HOSTELLERIE LES BREUILS
M. et Mme Rochès

34 avenue Docteur Mallet
15300 Murat
Tel. 04 71 20 01 25
Fax 04 71 20 33 20
info@hostellerie-les-breuils.com
www.hostellerie-les-breuils.com

Open late May to 15 Oct • 10 rooms, most have bath/WC, some have television • €62 to €78 (€60 to €76 low season); breakfast €7 • No restaurant • Garden, private car park. No dogs admitted • Indoor swimming pool, sauna, leisure area

We most liked: The friendly, personalised welcome.

All the rooms of this small 19C mansion backing onto the historic town, have recently been treated to a facelift of bright, bold colours and some have retained their Louis XVI furniture. The roomy bathrooms are well fitted-out. Attractive reading room with fireplace and piano. A building to the rear of the garden houses an indoor swimming pool.

Access : Outside the ramparts, by the main road

AUVERGNE
SAINT-ÉTIENNE-DE-CARLAT - 15130   SAINT-JACQUES-DES-BLATS - 15800

19 LOU FERRADOU
M. et Mme Balleux

Caizac
15130 Saint-Étienne-de-Carlat
Tel. 04 71 62 42 37
Fax 04 71 62 42 37
balleux@louferradou.com
www.louferradou.com

Open all year • 6 non-smoking rooms with bathrooms • €44 to €54, breakfast included; half-board available • Table d'hôte €14 (evening only) • Car park, garden, terrace. Credit cards not accepted, no dogs admitted • Games room

Dining and breakfasting in the enchanting garden in fine weather.

The typically austere Auvergne façade of this old farm cannot fail but impress. The eye is also drawn to the recently restored beams, bare stone walls and fireplace indoors. One of the rooms in the main wing has its own sitting room and an outhouse is home to two split-level rooms, all are furnished in a regional style. Large games room. At mealtimes, sample the vegetables fresh from the garden and other local delicacies, such as the famous truffade, a dish of potatoes, cheese, bacon and garlic.

Access : Drive for 4km on a minor road

20 LE GRIOU
M. Troupel

15800 Saint-Jacques-des-Blats
Tel. 04 71 47 06 25
Fax 04 71 47 00 16
hotel.griou@wanadoo.fr
www.hotel-griou.com

Closed 5 to 20 Apr, and 10 Oct to 20 Dec • 16 rooms all with bath/WC or shower/WC, one has disabled access, some have television • €42 to €52; breakfast €7; half-board available • Menus €14 (weekdays) to €31 • Car park, garden

Admiring the natural and architectural wealth of the Regional Volcano Park.

Built in two stages, the hotel offers guests a choice of accommodation; recent rooms, furnished in a Louis-Philippe style or others in more classical vein. All are quite spotless and most have a balcony. If unsure about which of the two dining rooms to choose, we recommend the one with the large bay windows that offers a delightful view over the village steeple and Cantal mountains.

Access : On the way out of the village

AUVERGNE

SALERS - 15140

21 LE BAILLIAGE
M. et Mme Gouzon

Rue Notre-Dame
15140 Salers
Tel. 04 71 40 71 95
Fax 04 71 40 74 90
info@salers-hotel-bailliage.com
www.salers-hotel-bailliage.com

Closed from 15 Nov to 6 Feb • 25 rooms, 4 in a separate wing (La Demeure Jarriges, 300m away), all have bath/WC and television • €55 to €75 (€49 to €70 low season); breakfast €9; half-board available • Menus €14 to €40 • Terrace, garden, garage, car park • Outdoor swimming pool

Strolling past the historic buildings of Salers.

The stone walls of this 1960s farmstead stand in one of the region's most enchanting medieval villages. The spacious, comfortable rooms overlook either the garden, the town or the slopes of the nearby Puy Violent. Soft lighting, cane furniture and red and orange drapes adorn the stylish redecorated restaurant. Gourmets come from miles around to enjoy the cuisine in which the region's famous Salers beef naturally takes pride of place, as does its namesake cheese. Pleasant garden-terrace.

Access: At the entrance to the village next to the large car park

SALERS - 15140

22 CHAMBRE D'HÔTE M. PRUDENT
M. et Mme Prudent

Rue des Nobles
15140 Salers
Tel. 04 71 40 75 36
Fax 04 71 40 75 36
claudine@chezprudent.com
www.chezprudent.com

Open all year • 6 rooms with separate entrances • €42, breakfast included • No table d'hôte • Garden

Contemplating the exceptional panorama of the volcanic peaks of the Cantal.

This 17C house is idyllically situated in the heart of the picturesque medieval village of Salers. All the simply decorated yet comfortable rooms have their own private entrance and some command a fine view over the volcanoes. Treat yourself to breakfast in bed or venture downstairs and admire the attractive Auvergne dining room or the wonderful view from the terrace in fine weather. Souvenir shop in the hotel.

Access: In the town centre

AUVERGNE

TRIZAC - 15400

23 LE COUVENT
M. et Mme Belaiche

Le Bourg
15400 Trizac
Tel. 04 71 78 67 51
Fax 04 71 78 67 51
le-couvent@wanadoo.fr
www.lecouvent.fr

Open from Easter to 31 Oct • 1 room and 3 apartments with bath/WC • €65 to €75; breakfast €10 • No table d'hôte • Park. Credit cards not accepted, dogs admitted on request

We most liked Relaxing in the peaceful garden between the former convent and the village's Romanesque church.

Ask your friendly hosts to tell you the long story of this ancient abode and its slightly forbidding façade. You will find it all the easier to appreciate the efforts deployed since 1995 to turn it into a delightful house, whose comforts are now the antithesis of its former monastic vocation. A fine staircase leads up to the master bedroom and to three suites, each unique, and all comfortably and tastefully decorated and extremely peaceful.

Access : In the centre of the village, on the D 678 between Mauriac and Riom-ès-Montagne

VIC-SUR-CÈRE - 15800

24 AUBERGE DES MONTAGNES
M. et Mme Combourieu

15800 Vic-sur-Cère
Tel. 04 71 47 57 01
Fax 04 71 49 63 83
info@auberge-des-montagnes.com
www.auberge-des-montagnes.com

Closed from 12 Oct to 20 Dec except weekend of 1 Nov • 25 rooms, 10 of which are in a separate wing and one has disabled access. Rooms have bath/WC or shower/WC, some have television • €49 to €56 (€45 to €50 low season); breakfast €7; half-board available • Restaurant closed Tue out of season; menus €15 (weekdays) to €24 • Terrace, car park, garage • 2 swimming pools, mountain bikes

We most liked Visiting the farm where the film "With a friend like Harry" was shot.

The still waters of a pond reflect this picture-book hotel comprised of a handsome old farmstead with a stone-shingled roof, a more recent house flanked by a tower and a spacious stone terrace. The vast rooms are decorated in a rustic or a contemporary style. Swimming pool, mountain bikes, hiking, horse-drawn carts, fishing, skiing: the extensive range of activities illustrates the owners' get-up-and-go personality. Delicious feasts of Auvergne cooking.

Access : At Vic-sur-Cère leave the N 122 (Aurillac-Murat road) and take the D 54 for Pailherols

AUVERGNE

AUREC-SUR-LOIRE - 43110

25 LES CÈDRES BLEUS
M. et Mme Duverney

Route de la Rivière
43110 Aurec-sur-Loire
Tel. 04 77 35 48 48
Fax 04 77 35 37 04
www.lescedresbleus.com

Closed from 2 Jan to 2 Feb, Sun evening and Mon lunchtime • 15 rooms, one has disabled access, most have bath/WC, some have shower/WC, all have television • €58 to €75; breakfast €8; half-board available • Air-conditioned restaurant; menus €18 (weekdays) to €75 • Terrace, garden, car park. No dogs admitted

Most liked: Trying your hand at water-skiing on Lake Grangent.

Even though the site may lack the giant redwood trees, grizzly bears and log cabins of America's national parks, the same spirit reigns in this lakeside spot. The reception and restaurant are installed in the old family house, while three modern "chalets" house functional rooms, all of which overlook the garden and cedars. A well cared-for flowered terrace adds the final touch to this pastoral picture of unspoilt countryside.

Access: To the south-west of Saint-Étienne on the D 46, then at Aurec-sur-Loire towards Bas-en-Basset

CHASPINHAC - 43700

26 LA PARAVENT
M. Jourde

43700 Chaspinhac
Tel. 04 71 03 54 75
michel-jourde@wanadoo.fr

Open all year • 5 rooms • €44 to €48, breakfast included • Table d'hôte €16 • Garden. Credit cards not accepted, no dogs admitted

Most liked: The warm atmosphere of this handsome early-20C house.

The sterling welcome, constant attention to detail and eagerness to please immediately strike the visitor to this country house, just a few minutes' drive from Le Puy-en-Velay. The rustic-style interior decoration is full of character. Some of the cosy rooms have their own small sitting room and all have a private entrance. In the winter the lady of the house runs patchwork courses.

Access: 10km to the north-east of Le Puy on the D 103 towards Retournac, then take the D 71

AUVERGNE

LA CHAISE-DIEU - 43160

27 LA JACQUEROLLE
Mme Chailly

Rue Marchédial
43160 La Chaise-Dieu
Tel. 04 71 00 07 52
lajacquerolle@hotmail.com
www.lajacquerolle.com

Open all year • 4 rooms, one with bathroom • €55 to €58, breakfast included, half-board available • Table d'hôte €22 (evening only) • Car park. Credit cards not accepted, no dogs admitted

We most liked **Going mushrooming for cèps in the surrounding forest.**

Entirely built out of local stone, this characterful house stands in the lower part of town. Countless family heirlooms, including a beautiful Louis-Philippe wardrobe and elegant looking mirrors grace the tastefully decorated, predominantly wood interior. A roaring log fire, lit in the dining room's magnificent stone fireplace, takes the chill off the short autumn and winter days.

Access : In the lower part of town

LA SEAUVE-SUR-SEMÈNE - 43140

28 LOU CHANDEL'AIGUE
M. et Mme Pigat

Les Mazeaux
43140 La Séauve-sur-Semène
Tel. 04 71 66 26 16

Open all year • 4 non-smoking rooms, all with shower/WC • €45, breakfast included • No table d'hôte • Park, car park. Credit cards not accepted, dogs not admitted • Outdoor swimming pool

We most liked **The tranquillity of this secluded spot.**

A small bridge spanning the river provides access to this vast 17C property. Inside are spacious, tastefully decorated rooms, a cosy sitting room and a pleasant dining room where breakfasts are served in winter. The outdoor swimming pool surrounded by greenery and flowers invites guests to relax. The hotel is greatly favoured by trout anglers because of the Semène which borders the grounds.

Access : 500m eastbound from the town on the D 12, then a minor road for 1.5km

AUVERGNE

RETOURNAC - 43130

29 LES REVERS
M. et Mme Chevalier

43130 Retournac
Tel. 04 71 59 42 81
Fax 04 71 59 42 81
jean-pierre.chevalier6@libertysurf.fr
www.lesrevers.fr.st

Closed from Oct to Apr • 4 rooms • €45, breakfast included • Table d'hôte (evenings only and by reservation) €16 • Garden, car park. Credit cards not accepted, dogs not admitted

The unspoilt countryside of this rural hideaway.

Those on a quest for silence, nature and authenticity will swoon at the sight of this extraordinarily secluded spot, wedged in between field and forest. The capacious, well-appointed rooms are furnished with comfortable bedding and all overlook the unspoilt countryside. Two rooms are on split-levels. The owner breeds horses and can organise rides for guests. A perfect hideaway for a relaxed, peaceful break.

Access: 8km to the south-east of Retournac on the D 103, then follow the signs

SAINT-FRONT - 43550

30 L'HERMINETTE
M. Mathieu

Bigorre - Les Maziaux
43550 Saint-Front
Tel. 04 71 59 57 58
Fax 04 71 56 34 91
lherminette@wanadoo.fr

Open all year by reservation except 1 week in Sep and 1 week in Mar • 6 rooms with bathrooms • €64 to €74 (€56 to €60 low season) breakfast included; half-board available • Restaurant closed Sun evening and Mon; menus €12 (weekdays) to €23 • Garden, car park. No dogs admitted • Museum of local life nearby

The change of scenery offered by this hamlet.

An enchanting hamlet of stone farmsteads topped with well-combed thatched roofs forms the backdrop to this typical Auvergne inn. Large, airy bedrooms, two on split-levels, regional-style dining rooms and delicious country cooking at unbeatable prices. If you're interested in finding out more about daily life in years gone by and how thatched roofs are made, stop by the Ecomuseum, and all will be revealed.

Access: 5km to the north-west of Saint-Front on the D 39, then take the lane on the right

AUVERGNE
SAUGUES - 43170   SAUGUES - 43170

31 LES GABALES
M. Gauthier

Route du Puy-en-Velay
43170 Saugues
Tel. 04 71 77 86 92
Fax 04 71 77 86 92
pierrelesgabales@wanadoo.fr
www.lesgabales.com

Closed 1 Dec to late Feb • 5 non-smoking rooms • €45 to €72, breakfast included, half-board available • Park, car park. Credit cards not accepted, no dogs admitted

32 LA TERRASSE
M. Fargier

Cours Dr. Gervais
43170 Saugues
Tel. 04 71 77 83 10
Fax 04 71 77 63 79
laterrasse-saugues@wanadoo.fr
www.chemindecompostelle.com

Closed 30 Nov to 28 Feb, Sun evening and Mon (out of season) • 9 rooms on two floors, all with bath/WC or shower/WC and television • €58; breakfast €8; half-board available • Air-conditioned restaurant; menus €23 (weekdays) to €50 • Garage

Finding out more about the legendary Beast of Gévaudan.

The legend of the Beast of Gévaudan is far from dead as you will find out when you listen to the tales related by the owner of this good-sized 1930s house. His other passion is walking and he is happy to share tips. Once safely back inside the hotel's walls, relax in the cosy sitting room-library; the wood panelling in the dining room is original. In the morning, after a well-earned night's sleep in one of the charmingly "retro" personalised rooms, guests can also enjoy a walk in the park.

Enjoy the thrill of exploring the home of the legendary Beast of Gévaudan.

The Fargier family, inhabitants of Sauges since 1795, welcomes guests in a house originally built for the town's solicitor now restored and turned into a hotel. The cleverly renovated rooms are modern and comfortable and most are quite spacious except for two smaller ones. As you sit down in the welcoming half-rustic, half-contemporary dining room with stone fireplace to feast on the chef's traditional fare, make sure you leave room to sample the impressive array of Auvergne cheeses.

Access : On the road from Le Puy-en-Velay

Access : In the centre of the village

AUVERGNE

TENCE - 43190

VIEILLE-BRIOUDE - 43100

33 LES PRAIRIES
M. et Mme Bourgeois

1 rue du Pré Long - Salettes
43190 Tence
Tel. 04 71 56 35 80
thomas.bourgeois@freesbee.fr
www.lesprairies.com

Open all year (by reservation from 1 Nov to 15 Apr)
• 5 non-smoking rooms, one with disabled access, all have bath/WC or shower/WC • €66, breakfast included
• No table d'hôte • Terrace, garden, car park, television room and library. Credit cards not accepted • Children's play room and table-tennis

We most liked
The owners' faultless hospitality.

This handsome stone property (1850), nestling in a well-tended park planted with century-old trees, is just a stone's throw from the town. It is made up of two wings, one for the owners and one for guests with an independent entrance. On the ground-floor is a room with disabled access equipped with a large bathroom, while four other rooms are available upstairs. All are simply decorated and furnished with handsome pieces picked up in antique fairs and shops.

Access : In the town

34 ERMITAGE SAINT VINCENT
M. et Mme Boyer

Place de l'Église
43100 Vieille-Brioude
Tel. 04 71 50 96 47

Closed Dec and Jan (except for groups with reservations)
• 5 rooms with bathrooms • €50, breakfast included
• Table d'hôte €20 (evenings only by reservation)
• Terrace, garden. Credit cards not accepted, no dogs admitted

We most liked
Enjoy listening to the babble of the river and the birdsong.

This restored former presbytery overlooks the river, commanding a fine view of the Allier Valley. Indoors, guests are immediately impressed by the proportions of the large hall, adorned with old farming tools, the extensive sitting room-library and the great stone staircase leading up to equally sizeable and comfortable bedrooms, fitted with good quality contemporary furnishings. The kind owner bends over backwards to make your stay as pleasant as possible, whatever your fancy.

Access : 4km southbound of Brioude, on the N 102 near l'Allier

AUVERGNE

AUBUSSON- D'AUVERGNE - 63120

35 LE MOULIN DES VERNIÈRES
Mme Hansen

63120 Aubusson-d'Auvergne
Tel. 04 73 53 53 01
Fax 04 73 53 53 01
www.moulindesvernières.com

Closed from 1 Nov to 1 Mar • 6 non-smoking rooms • €65 to €85, breakfast included • Table d'hôte €22 (evenings) • Park, car park. No dogs admitted • Outdoor swimming pool

We most liked **The chef's inventive recipes using delicious local produce.**

It is easy to see why the owner fell in love with this old mill and the artistically laid out garden and cascading stream. The scent of rose and jasmine fills the pretty rooms, named after cottage garden flowers (English rose, Forget-me-not, Poppy). Inside the owner has given free rein to her decorative flair with polished antique furniture, classic black and white photos by Doisneau and naive paintings. The cooking is just as inventive and your host loves rustling up mouth-watering dishes.

Access : 7km eastbound from Coupière on the D 7 and the D 311

BEAUREGARD-VENDON - 63460

36 CHAMBRE D'HÔTE MME BEAUJEARD
Mme Beaujeard

8 rue de la Limagne à Chaptes
63460 Beauregard-Vendon
Tel. 04 73 63 35 62

Open all year, by reservation only from Nov to Mar • 3 non-smoking rooms • €66 to €70, breakfast included • No table d'hôte • Garden. Credit cards not accepted, no dogs admitted

We most liked **The enchanting, old-fashioned decoration.**

This handsome late-18C country seat is the epitome of charm and tranquillity. The tastefully furnished rooms, all non-smoking, are perfect for winding down at the end of the day. The cosy sitting room with its fireplace, lavishly flowered garden in the summer, generous breakfasts, excellent welcome and moderate prices all add to the appeal.

Access : 9km northbound from Riom on the N 144 then the D 122

AUVERGNE

CEILLOUX - 63520

37 DOMAINE DE GAUDON
M. et Mme Bozzo

63520 Ceilloux
Tel. 04 73 70 76 25
Fax 04 73 70 74 04
domainedegaudon@wanadoo.fr
www.domainedegaudon.fr

Open all year • 5 non-smoking rooms, all have bath/WC or shower/WC and telephone • €90, breakfast included • No table d'hôte • Terrace, park, garage. No dogs admitted

We most liked: Being welcomed as if you were a friend of the family.

Park and woodland surround this handsome 19C property. A splendid wooden staircase leads up to superb rooms, each of which is poetically named: "Esther's dressing-table", "Garden of Love" or "Birds' Nest". Breakfasts are served in a lovely wood-panelled room or on the terrace in fine weather with the Puy de Dôme mountain range in the distance. Private fishing possible on the estate.

Access: From Saint-Dier-d'Auvergne, head towards Domaize. 3km further on at "Les Palles", turn right towards Ceilloux, Gaudon is 1km away

CHATELGUYON - 63140

38 RÉGENCE
M. et Mme Porte

31 avenue des États-Unis
63140 Chatelguyon
Tel. 04 73 86 02 60
Fax 04 73 86 02 49
hotel-regence3@wanadoo.fr
www.hotel-regence-central.com

Closed from 1 Jan to 15 Mar and 1 to 18 Dec; Mon and Sun evening • 26 rooms with bath/WC or shower/WC, some have television • €50; breakfast €8; half-board available • Menus from €24 to €39 • Garden, private car park. No dogs admitted in the restaurant • Free shuttle bus to the spa

We most liked: The architecture of this quaint old resort.

A splendid carved wooden fireplace, well-worn, polished antique furniture and an upright piano contribute to maintaining the delicious 1900s atmosphere of the Régence. The ground floor has however been entirely renovated with a fresh coat of paint, double-glazing and a smart red and gold facelift for the sitting and dining rooms; the bedrooms are next in line. Lush green garden.

Access: At the entrance to the resort, on the main road

AUVERGNE

DAVAYAT - 63200

39 LA MAISON DE LA TREILLE
M. et Mme Honnorat

25 rue de l'Église
63200 Davayat
Tel. 04 73 63 58 20
honnorat.la.treille@wanadoo.fr
http://honnorat.la.treille.free.fr

Open all year • 4 rooms including one family apartment, all with bath/WC or shower/WC • €70 to €85, breakfast included • No table d'hôte • Park, car park. Credit cards not accepted, no dogs admitted

We most liked **Tucking into the jams made with fruit from the orchard at breakfast time.**

Italian Neoclassicism clearly inspired this smart bourgeois property built in 1810. A pleasant sitting room with piano and breakfast room, lit by a stone fireplace, make up the ground floor. Guests are accommodated in the orangery, an elegant outhouse which stands in the enchanting garden. The names of the trim, well-tended rooms give guests an idea of each room's decorative style: wheat, birds, grapes and beehive (for four people).

Access : 7km northbound from Riom on the N 144

GLAINE-MONTAIGUT - 63160

40 AUBERGE DE LA FORGE
M. et Mme Zuk

Place de l'Église
63160 Glaine-Montaigut
Tel. 04 73 73 41 80
Fax 04 73 73 33 83
a.delaforge@wanadoo.fr
www.aubergedelaforge.com

Closed from 1 to 20 Sep • 4 rooms with showers/WC • €39 to €50 (€28 to €39 low season); breakfast €6; half-board available • Restaurant closed Sun evening and Tue; menus €12 to €30 • Terrace

We most liked **Wholesome country snacks served all day long.**

Situated opposite a beautiful Romanesque 11C-12C church, the village café and forge have been successfully converted into a pleasant country inn. A smart façade with pale blue shutters, traditional old walls, simple yet appealing rooms and a restaurant, with a reconstruction of the former blacksmith's workshop complete with hearth, bellows and anvil, serving yummy country cooking. A renovation which marries authenticity with intelligence.

Access : Around 5km to the north-east of Billom, towards Thiers on the D 229 and the D 212

AUVERGNE

LAQUEUILLE - 63820

41 AUBERGE DE FONDAIN
Mme Demossier

Lieu-dit Fondain
63820 Laqueuille
Tel. 04 73 22 01 35
Fax 04 73 22 06 13
auberge.de.fondain@wanadoo.fr
www.auberge-fondain.com

Closed for 10 days early Mar, Nov, Wed lunchtime during school holidays; Sun evening and Mon • 6 rooms with bath/WC or shower/WC • €70 (€60 low season); breakfast €8; half-board available • Menus €12 (weekdays) to €23 • Terrace, garden, car park • Fitness room with sauna, hiking, mountain biking

Signposted footpaths on themes such as fauna, flora and crater lakes.

This elegant 19C country house lost among fields and meadows is said to have belonged to the inventor of a local blue cheese: Laqueuille. The recently renovated rooms, named after flowers, combine a light, airy colour scheme with contrasting dark timbers, discreetly modern fittings and in some cases, a view of the Banne d'Ordanche. A fitness room, sauna and a dozen or so mountain bikes will make sure you work up an appetite for the tasty Auvergne cooking served in a welcoming rustic dining room.

Access: 2km to the north-east of Laqueuille, on the D 922 then a minor road

LE MONT-DORE - 63240

42 LA CLOSERIE DE MANOU
Mme Larcher

Au Genestoux - BP 30
63240 Le Mont-Dore
Tel. 04 73 65 26 81
Fax 04 73 65 58 34
lacloseriedemanou@club-internet.fr
www.lacloseriedemanou.com

Closed from 15 Oct to 15 Mar; open Sat-Sun early Mar • 5 non-smoking rooms • €75, breakfast included • No table d'hôte • Garden, car park. Credit cards not accepted, dogs not admitted

The wealth of information about the region.

Nestling in the countryside, this traditional 18C Auvergne house with its stone walls and white shutters is quite enchanting. The decoration of the spacious rooms wavers between modern-uncluttered and snug; all are non-smoking. The sitting and dining rooms, furnished with antiques, provide a wonderful backdrop to the delicious breakfasts. The charm and attention of your hostess will be another reason why you won't want to leave.

Access: 3km westbound from Mont-Dore, take the Avenue des Belges D 996 towards Murat-le-Quaire on the A 89

AUVERGNE

MAZAYE - 63230

43 AUBERGE DE MAZAYES
M. Michy

à Mazayes-Basses
63230 Mazaye
Tel. 04 73 88 93 30
Fax 04 73 88 93 80
www.restolit-auvergne.com

Closed from 12 Dec to 20 Jan, Mon out of season and Tue lunchtime • 15 rooms, one of which has disabled access, with shower/WC, all have television • €56 to €69; breakfast €9; half-board available • Menus €16 (weekdays) to €38 • Terrace, car park

We most liked The farm's ideal situation for exploring the Monts Dôme.

This attractive Auvergne farmhouse built out of solid basalt stone is located just near the popular tourist site of the Puy de Dôme (1 465m). Bold colours, carefully chosen fabrics and a few old pieces of furniture adorn the rooms which are a stylish blend of rustic and modern. The stables have been converted into a dining room full of character with a lava stone floor and a low ceiling supported by dark timber rafters. Wholesome regional cooking.

Access: South of Pontgibaud, 6km on the D 986, cross the Sioule at St Pierre-le-Chastel and drive to Mazayes

MONTPEYROUX - 63114

44 CHAMBRE D'HÔTE MME BOISSIÈRE
Mme Boissière

Rue de la Poterne
63114 Montpeyroux
Tel. 04 73 96 69 42
Fax 04 73 96 95 39
jules.boissiere@wanadoo.fr

Open all year • 5 non-smoking rooms • €53 to €59, breakfast included • No table d'hôte • Car park. Credit cards not accepted

We most liked Exploring this historic village overlooking the Allier River.

Set at the foot of a 13C keep, this pretty sandstone house is well worth the short climb up the hill from the town car park; there are a few parking spaces in front of the house if needed. Each of the bedrooms boasts its own little extra bonus: terrace, fireplace, canopied bed or jacuzzi bath. After taking refreshments in the vaulted dining room, set off round the narrow lanes and meet the painters and potters who have replaced the wine-growers of yesteryear.

Access: 8km to the south-west of Vic-le-Comte on the A 75, exit no 7

AUVERGNE

MONTPEYROUX - 63114

45 LES PRADETS
Edith Grenot

Les Pradets
63114 Montpeyroux
Tel. 04 73 96 63 40
Fax 04 73 96 63 40
grenot@maison-hotes.com
www.auvergne.maison-hotes.com

Open all year • 3 rooms with bathrooms • €68, breakfast included • No table d'hôte • Garden. Credit cards not accepted

We most liked
Edith Grenot's faultless welcome.

This delightful house lies in a secluded lane of the picturesque fortified village of Montpeyroux. Relax in the cosy ground floor sitting room strewn with well-used furniture, a piano and books on the Auvergne region. In fine weather, you will no doubt make a beeline for the inner courtyard garden where breakfast is served. Parquet floors, rugs, paintings by local artists and rustic furniture add character to the well-decorated rooms.

Access : In the heart of the village

NÉBOUZAT - 63210

46 LES GRANGES
Mme Gauthier

Recoleine
63210 Nébouzat
Tel. 04 73 87 10 34
Fax 04 73 87 10 34
gauthier.jocelyne@free.fr

Closed from 15 Nov to 1 Feb • 3 rooms • €44 to €48, breakfast included; half-board available • Table d'hôte €16 • Credit cards not accepted, dogs not admitted

We most liked
The pastoral scene just two minutes from the Dôme mountain range.

A warm welcome awaits visitors inside this old barn, beautifully renovated by a farming couple. The comfortable, tasteful rooms all enjoy views of the surrounding countryside. An immense living-sitting room and spacious sofa are most appreciated. Your charming, talkative hostess will be more than happy to point out walks and hikes. Ideal for nature lovers.

Access : 3km from Randanne on the N 89

AUVERGNE

ORCINES - 63870   ORCINES - 63870

47 DOMAINE DE TERNANT
Mme Piollet

Ternant
63870 Orcines
Tel. 04 73 62 11 20
Fax 04 73 62 29 96
domaine.ternant@free.fr
http://domaine.ternant.free.fr

Closed from 15 Nov to 15 Mar • 5 non-smoking rooms • €72 to €86, breakfast included • No table d'hôte • Sitting room, park, car park. Credit cards not accepted, no dogs admitted • Tennis, billiard room

We most liked The sheltered environment of this old building.

This elegant 19C property stands in 25 acres of grounds at the foot of the Dôme mountain range. A profusion of family heirlooms scattered throughout the bedrooms, sitting room, library and games room creates a warm, lived-in feel. The personal touch and taste of the lady of the house, a patchwork artist, can be felt everywhere. Tennis court in the grounds and other sports facilities nearby, including Vulcania, the Regional Volcano Park.

Access: 11km north-west of Clermont-Ferrand on the D 941A and the D 90

48 HOSTELLERIE LES HIRONDELLES
M. Amblard

Route de Limoges
63870 Orcines
Tel. 04 73 62 22 43
Fax 04 73 62 19 12
info@hotel-leshirondelles.com
www.hotel-leshirondelles.com

Closed from 30 Nov to 4 Feb, Sun evening, Mon and Tue lunchtime from Oct to Apr • 18 rooms, one of which has disabled access. Rooms have bath/WC or shower/WC, all have television • €62 to €70; breakfast €8; half-board available • Restaurant closed Mon and Tue lunchtimes (May, Jun, Sep); menus €17 (weekdays) to €42 • Terrace, car park

We most liked The fascinating Monts Dôme.

This old grey-stone family farmstead, recently converted into an inn, nestles at the foot of the Monts Dôme. The rooms situated in the converted barn are practical before all else; those overlooking the street are larger and lighter. The vaulted dining room located in the former cow-shed offers more character; the swallows' nests, from which the inn takes its name, complete the rural picture.

Access: Westbound from Clermont-Ferrand, take the D 941A then the D 941B (Limoges road) to Orcines

AUVERGNE

PERRIER - 63500　　　　　　　　　　**ROCHEFORT-MONTAGNE - 63210**

49 CHAMBRE D'HÔTE PAUL GEBRILLAT
M. Gebrillat

Chemin de Siorac
63500 Perrier
Tel. 04 73 89 15 02
Fax 04 73 55 08 85
lgebrillat@club.fr
www.maison-gebrillat.com

Closed 1 Dec to 31 Jan • 3 rooms and one apartment • €48 to €55, breakfast included • No table d'hôte • Garden, car park. Credit cards not accepted, dogs welcome on request

Most liked: Strolling in the park bounded by the Couze de Pavin River.

This handsome 18C country house is perfect for those wishing to get to know the Dore Mountains a little better. The tastefully decorated rooms marry charm and comfort. As soon as the first rays of sun appear, the breakfast table is laid outdoors under a heated awning which overlooks a delightful inner courtyard; warm sweaters advisable. Your host, Paul, is a gold mine of useful tourist tips.

Access: 3km westbound from Issoire on the D 996

50 CHÂTEAU DE VOISSIEUX
M. et Mme Phillips

Saint-Bonnet-d'Orcival
63210 Rochefort-Montagne
Tel. 04 73 65 81 02
Fax 04 73 65 81 27

Closed from Nov to Jan • 4 rooms with bathrooms • €52 to €60, breakfast included • No table d'hôte • Terrace, park, car park. Credit cards not accepted • Mountain biking, horse-riding, swimming, golf, paragliding, hot-air ballooning and skiing nearby

Most liked: Being treated like the lord or lady of the manor in the heart of the Auvergne Regional Park.

Volcanic stone was of course used to build this 13C castle, it was also used to restore it to its present-day state. In the park a 400-year-old lime tree keeps watch over the estate's quiet solitude. You have a choice between two soberly furnished rooms or a more exuberant rococo style in the third. Breakfasts are served in the kitchen by the fireside or on the flowered terrace overlooking the park. It isn't possible to lunch or dine in the castle, but restaurants are hardly in short supply.

Access: 4km to the north-east of Orcival on the D 27

AUVERGNE

ROYAT - 63130

SAINT-ANTHÈME - 63660

51 CHÂTEAU DE CHARADE
M. et Mme Gaba

63130 Royat
Tel. 04 73 35 91 67
Fax 04 73 29 92 09
gaba@chateau-de-charade.com
www.chateau-de-charade.com

Closed from early Nov to late Mar • 5 rooms with bathrooms • €74 to €83, breakfast included • No table d'hôte • Park, car park. Credit cards not accepted, no dogs admitted

We most liked **The country house feel of this whimsical castle just two minutes from the regional capital.**

This castle which borders the Royat golf course extends a majestic welcome. High ceilings, a stone staircase and the antique furniture in the bedrooms and bathrooms all bear witness to an illustrious past. As for the present, guests are invariably charmed by the appeal of the lady of the house's gracious welcome, the tinkling of the piano playing in the sitting room or the click of billiard balls. If you don't feel like visiting the town, head for the nearby Dôme mountains.

Access: 6km to the south-west of Royat on the D 941C and the D 5, towards the racing track and golf course

52 AU PONT DE RAFFINY
M. et Mme Beaudoux

Raffiny
63660 Saint-Anthème
Tel. 04 73 95 49 10
Fax 04 73 95 80 21
hotel.pont.raffiny@wanadoo.fr
www.hotel-pont-raffiny.com

Closed from 2 Jan to 5 Mar, Sun evening and Mon (except Jul-Aug),Tue to Thu from 6 to 31 Mar • 11 rooms and 2 small wooden chalets with private gardens. All rooms have bath/WC or shower/WC, television • €39 to €45; breakfast €7; half-board available • Menus €16 to €30 • Car park • Swimming pool, sauna, Jacuzzi, billiards, hiking, mountain bike rental

We most liked **A ride in the panoramic "Livradois-Forez" train.**

Two chalets designed for families, complete with kitchenette and private gardens, have recently been added to the hotel's amenities. The bedrooms in the main wing – a former village café – are more simply furnished, even if those on the second floor, lined in wood, do have a certain alpine charm. A rockery fountain lends an amusing touch to the rustic dining room. All in all, we were quite won over by the charm of this country hotel.

Access: Leave Saint-Anthème southbound on the D 261 and drive for 5.5km

AUVERGNE

SAINT-GERVAIS-D'AUVERGNE - 63390

53 CASTEL HÔTEL 1904
M. Mouty

Rue du Castel
63390 Saint-Gervais-d'Auvergne
Tel. 04 73 85 70 42
Fax 04 73 85 84 39
castel.hotel.1904@wanadoo.fr
www.castel-hotel-1904.com

Open from Mar to Dec • 17 rooms with bath/WC or shower/WC, all have television • €65 to €75; breakfast €8; half-board available • Restaurant closed Mon, Tue and Wed; menus €15 to €55 • Garden, car park. No dogs admitted

We most liked: The rather quaint old-fashioned atmosphere.

The carved "1616" over the fireplace bears witness to the age of these walls. This private residence, built for the Marquis of Maintenon, passed into the hands of a religious community in the 19C before it became a coaching inn at the turn of the 20th Century. Beams, creaky floorboards, well-worn furniture, gleaming silver and 1900 statuettes and lights bestow an almost nostalgic feel to this "castel". Sample the excellent home cooking of the Comptoir à Moustaches, a nearby country bistro.

Access: In the centre of the village

SAINT-GERVAIS-D'AUVERGNE - 63390

54 MONTARLET
M. et Mme Pelletier

Lieu-dit Montarlet
63390 Saint-Gervais-d'Auvergne
Tel. 04 73 85 87 10
Fax 04 73 85 75 79
montarlet@libertysurf.fr
www.montarlet-chambresdhotes.com

Closed 1 Jan to 29 Feb • 3 rooms with bathrooms • €46, breakfast included • No table d'hôte • Park, car park. Credit cards not accepted

We most liked: The enchanting natural site of this farmhouse.

Guests are often in raptures over the charm and tranquillity of this renovated farmhouse in the middle of the countryside. The rooms illustrate how much the owners have their guests' welfare at heart, from the sponge-painted walls and antique furniture gleaned in local flea markets to the matching bed-linen and curtains and roomy bathrooms. The sitting room is graced with a fireplace and floor made out of Volvic stone and the landscaped parkland commands a fine view over the Auvergne mountains.

Access: 3km westbound from St-Gervais-d'Auvergne on the D 532 towards Espinasse and take the lane on the left

AUVERGNE

SAINT-RÉMY-DE-CHARGNAT - 63500   SAINT-RÉMY-DE-CHARGNAT - 63500

55 CHÂTEAU DE LA VERNÈDE
M. et Mme Chauve

63500 Saint-Rémy-de-Chargnat
Tel. 04 73 71 07 03
Fax 04 73 71 07 03
chateauvernede@aol.com
www.chateauvernedeauvergne.com

Open all year • 5 non-smoking rooms, all have bath/WC or shower/WC • €60 to €75, breakfast included • No table d'hôte • Park, garage. Dogs admitted on request • Sitting room with billiards

Discovering the charm of the "Tuscany of Auvergne".

This enchanting castle restored in the 19C in a Neo-Gothic style was originally a hunting lodge which belonged to Queen Margot. The interior still bears the trace of its splendid heritage: wainscoting, fireplaces, antique furniture, lovely sitting and dining rooms and elegant bedrooms. The park which boasts a stream, an old mill, a dovecote, well-tended flower beds and shady paths is equally inviting. A must at excellent value for money.

Access: 6km southeast of Issoire on the D 996, then the D 125 for 1km

56 CHÂTEAU DE PASREDON
Mme Marchand

63500 Saint-Rémy-de-Chargnat
Tel. 04 73 71 00 67
Fax 04 73 71 08 72

Closed from 16 Oct to 14 Apr • 5 non-smoking rooms, all have bathrooms • €70 to €90, breakfast included • No table d'hôte • Park, library, garage. No dogs admitted • Tennis

Sleeping in a castle steeped in history.

This 17C and 19C castle stands in a handsome park facing the Puy mountain range. The interior is equally appealing with spacious personalised bedrooms (Louis Philippe furniture or the "Polish" bed in the middle of one of the rooms, etc.), a splendid sitting room complete with coffered ceiling and wainscoting and the richly stocked library. But let us not forget the mouth-watering breakfasts...

Access: 8km southeast of Issoire on the D 996 and D 999

AUVERGNE

THIERS - 63300

VARENNES-SUR-USSON - 63500

57 LE PARC DE GEOFFROY
M. Brugere

49 avenue du Général-de-Gaulle
63300 Thiers
Tel. 04 73 80 87 00
Fax 04 73 80 87 01
reservation@parc-de-geoffroy.com
www.parc-de-geoffroy.com

Open all year • 31 rooms on 3 floors. Rooms have bath/WC and television • €67 to €85; breakfast €8; half-board available • Menus €11 (weekdays) to €38 • Terrace, garden, car park

We most liked: Enjoying a cutting-edge visit to the House of Cutlery-makers.

A luxurious walled garden protects the residence from the bustle of the nearby busy shopping centre. The comfortable reception and dining rooms decorated with frescoes are housed in a former cutlery workshop. The rooms, located in a quiet, modern wing, are light, airy and practical. The well-provisioned breakfast table provides guests with the energy necessary to embark on the "ascent" of the upper town.

Access: 5km along the N 89 towards Clermont-Ferrand

58 LES BAUDARTS
Mme Verdier

63500 Varennes-sur-Usson
Tel. 04 73 89 05 51
Fax 04 73 89 05 51

Closed from 1 Oct to 1 May • 3 rooms • €65 to €75 (€62 to €72 low season), breakfast included • No table d'hôte • Garden, car park. Credit cards not accepted, dogs not admitted

We most liked: The unadulterated sophistication of every room.

Tucked away in the countryside, this establishment may not be easy to find, but it is well worth persevering because its dusty pink walls contain a marvel of sophistication, calm and comfort. The superb, spacious rooms are exquisitely decorated in light, warm tones. The sitting room, lit in the winter by a roaring log fire, is crammed with books. Who could resist Mrs Baudart's delightful welcome?

Access: On leaving Varennes take the first right (D 123), then turn into the wooded drive at the first bend

BURGUNDY

A visit to Burgundy takes travellers back through time to an era when its mighty Dukes rivalled even the kings of France. Born of an uncompromising desire for perfection, their stately castles and rich abbeys bear witness to a golden age of ostentation and prestige. As we look back now, it is difficult to reproach them for the flamboyance which has made Dijon a world-renowned city of art. And who would dispute Burgundy's claim to the "best wines in Christendom" when one sees how the hordes of today continue to lay siege to the region's cellars, where cool and canny wine-growers guard the secret of their finest vintages? This dedication to time-honoured traditions also rules the region's steadfast homage to the culinary arts, from strong-smelling époisses cheese to gingerbread dripping with honey. After sinning so extravagantly, you may be tempted to make amends and take a barge trip down the region's canals and rivers to digest in peace amidst the unspoilt countryside.

- Côte-d'Or (21)
- Nièvre (58)
- Saône-et-Loire (71)
- Yonne (89)

BURGUNDY

AIGNAY-LE-DUC - 21510

1 MANOIR DE TARPERON
M. de Champsavin

Route de Saint-Marc
21510 Aignay-le-Duc
Tel. 03 80 93 83 74
Fax 03 80 93 83 74
manoir-de-tarperon@wanadoo.fr

Closed from Nov to Mar • 5 rooms with bathrooms • €65, breakfast included • Table d'hôte €25 (evenings) • Terrace, garden. Credit cards not accepted, no dogs admitted • Stabling, concerts, exhibitions

We most liked The beautiful "Wind in the Willows" feel to this location.

A unique charm emanates from this manor and its superb riverside setting on the banks of the Coquille. The bedrooms, of varying sizes, are colourfully and tastefully furnished. The sitting room, complete with library, leads onto a pleasant veranda overlooking the garden. Fly fishing enthusiasts are in for a treat with a private stream all of their own. Those otherwise inclined will enjoy boat trips and an excursion to the source of the Seine.

Access: Take the small road towards Saint-Marc

BEAUNE - 21200

2 GRILLON
M. et Mme Grillon

21 route de Seurre
21200 Beaune
Tel. 03 80 22 44 25
Fax 03 80 24 94 89
joel.GRILLON@wanadoo.fr
www.hotel-grillon.fr

Closed from 30 Jan to 3 Mar • 18 air-conditioned rooms, most of which have bath/WC and television. Several are non-smoking • €52 to €65; breakfast €9 • No restaurant • Garden, terrace, private car park • Swimming pool

We most liked A haven of greenery close to the Hospices de Beaune.

This spruce pink house with light-green shutters is almost hidden in the summer by a thick curtain of chestnut trees, but we highly recommend venturing past the wrought-iron gate and inside the comfortable 19C mansion. The rooms vary between light and airy or cosy and some feature interesting old pieces of furniture picked up in local antique shops. The vaulted cellar has been turned into a sitting room and bar. Breakfast is served on a pretty flowered terrace.

Access: At the entrance to Beaune, from Seurre (D 973, Dôle road)

BURGUNDY

BEAUNE - 21200

3 VILLA FLEURIE
Mme Chartier

19 place Colbert
21200 Beaune
Tel. 03 80 22 66 00
Fax 03 80 22 45 46
la.villa.fleurie@wanadoo.fr
www.lavillafleurie.fr

Open from 1 Jan to 1 Feb • 10 rooms, most have bath/WC, all have television • €68 to €78; breakfast €8 • No restaurant • Garden, private car park

We most liked
The friendly, family atmosphere.

This small 1900 villa is entwined in the sweet-scented branches of an old wisteria bush. It offers three styles of room: contemporary, bourgeois and split-level family on the top floor. Chintz curtains, a fireplace and mouldings give the breakfast room a distinctly English feel, while the deck-chairs on the garden-terrace invite guests to relax and unwind.

Access : Set back from the lane, on a small square near the swimming pool

CHÂTEAUNEUF - 21320

4 CHAMBRE D'HÔTE MME BAGATELLE
Mme Bagatelle

Rue des Moutons
21320 Châteauneuf
Tel. 03 80 49 21 00
Fax 03 80 49 21 49
jean-michel.bagatelle@wanadoo.fr

Closed during the February holidays • 4 rooms with shower/WC • €50 to €60, breakfast included • Table d'hôte €23 • Garden, car park. Credit cards not accepted, no dogs admitted

We most liked
Wandering through the narrow streets of this lovely fortified village.

This old stone sheepfold stands in the centre of the medieval village on the banks of the Burgundy Canal. Stone and wood take pride of place in this tastefully decorated house. Guests immediately feel at home in the welcoming bedrooms, one of which has a fireplace, while the split-level rooms are perfectly suited to families.

Access : In the village

BURGUNDY

CHÂTEAUNEUF - 21320

5 HOSTELLERIE DU CHÂTEAU
M. Dusoulier

Rue du Centre
21320 Châteauneuf
Tel. 03 80 49 22 00
Fax 03 80 49 21 27
hdc@hostellerie-chateauneuf.com
www.hostellerie-chateauneuf.com

Closed from Dec to Feb, Mon and Tue except in Jul and Aug • 17 rooms, 8 of which are in a separate wing (4 are split-level for families) and one has disabled access. Rooms have bath/WC or shower/WC • €45 to €70; breakfast €8; half-board available • Menus €23 to €40 • Terrace, garden. No dogs admitted in restaurant

We most liked
Contemplating the medieval castle over a refreshing glass of kir.

The fortified town, perched high above France's "motorway to the south", formerly controlled the entire plain below. Today its heavy doors swing open to reveal a pleasant stopping place. The hostelry is just an arrow's distance from the majestic medieval castle which can be seen from the garden. The main building and annex, a 17C house, are home to a few rooms decorated with original old beams and stonework. Warm medieval-style sitting room.

Access: In the centre of the village next to the castle

COUCHEY - 21160

6 CHAMBRE D'HÔTE LES BRUGÈRES
M. et Mme Brugère

7 rue Jean-Jaurès
21160 Couchey
Tel. 03 80 52 13 05
Fax 03 80 52 93 20
brugeref@aol.com
www.francoisbrugere.com

Closed from Dec to Mar • 4 rooms with shower/WC • €58 to €66, breakfast included • No table d'hôte • Car park. No dogs admitted

We most liked
Soak up the atmosphere of a wine estate.

This charming 17C establishment, the property of a Marsannay wine-grower, provides a perfect opportunity to get to know more about the region's wine. The attractively restored rooms are decorated with exposed beams and prize finds from the local antique dealers: one bedroom even has a piano. In the winter, roaring log fires light up the breakfast room, hung with tapestries. The cellar is open for visits and wine-tastings.

Access: 2km southbound from Marsannay on the D 122

BURGUNDY

DIJON - 21000

7 WILSON
Mmes Descaillot et Etievant

1 rue Longvic
21000 Dijon
Tel. 03 80 66 82 50
Fax 03 80 36 41 54
hotelwilson@wanadoo.fr
www.wilson-hotel.com

Open all year • 27 rooms, 18 of which have bath/WC, 9 have shower/WC, all have television • €65 to €91; breakfast €11 • No restaurant • Garage

Snug as a bug in this house of character.

Lovingly and tastefully restored, this 17C coaching inn has now added the bonus of modern comforts to its beautifully preserved Burgundian architecture. The exposed beams and cosy, lived-in feel of the well-soundproofed rooms, laid out round an inner courtyard, never fail to win over guests. Breakfast is served by an open fire in winter.

Access: From the town centre, drive to Place du Théâtre and then along Rue Chabot-Charny

GEVREY-CHAMBERTIN - 21220

8 LES GRANDS CRUS
Mme Farnier

Rue de Lavaux
21220 Gevrey-Chambertin
Tel. 03 80 34 34 15
Fax 03 80 51 89 07
hotel.lesgrandscrus@ipac.fr
www.hoteldesgrandscrus.com

Closed Dec to Mar • 24 air-conditioned rooms on 2 floors, all have bath/WC and television • €70 to €80; breakfast €10 to €12 • No restaurant • Garden, private car park

Burgundy's amply justified pride in its wine.

Treat yourself to a night in this village, also known as the kingdom of wine and celebrated by hosts of wine lovers and writers: one of the authors, Gaston Roupnel, even tried his hand at wine-making. The plush bourgeois or rustic-style rooms command fine views over the vineyards. In wintertime, snuggle up in the deep armchairs next to a log fire and wax lyrical over the merits of this or that vintage year. Pleasant flowered garden and summer terrace.

Access: On the corner of Route des Grand Crus and Rue de Lavaux

BURGUNDY

LEVERNOIS - 21200

9 PARC
M. et Mme Oudot

13 rue du Golf
21200 Levernois
Tel. 03 80 24 63 00
Fax 03 80 24 21 19
hotel.le.parc@wanadoo.fr
www.hotelleparc.fr

Closed from 26 Nov to 26 Jan • 25 rooms, all of which have bath/WC or shower/WC and television • €52 to €92; breakfast €8 • No restaurant • Car park, park. Dogs not admitted

We most liked **Listening to the wind rustling the leaves of the hundred-year-old trees in the park.**

A lovely flowered courtyard separates these two buildings, whose distinctive Burgundy-style façades are covered in Virginia creeper. The eye is drawn to the tall trees standing in the pleasant grounds. A cosy family atmosphere reigns throughout the rooms decorated with old furniture, retro lamps and flowered drapes. All are equally impeccably looked after and those in the second building are slightly larger. Most attentive family welcome.

Access : 5km south-east of Beaune on the Verdun-sur-le-Doubs road, D 970 and D 111

LUSIGNY-SUR-OUCHE - 21360

10 LA SAURA
M. et Mme Berthaud

Route de Beaune
21360 Lusigny-sur-Ouche
Tel. 03 80 20 17 46
Fax 03 80 20 07 73
la-saura@wanadoo.fr
www.douix.com/la-saura

Open all year • 6 rooms with shower/WC • €60 to €80, breakfast included • No table d'hôte • Garden, car park. Credit cards not accepted, no dogs admitted in dining room • Outdoor swimming pool, horse-riding, tennis, golf and boating on the canal nearby

We most liked **The fine collection of contemporary art.**

The owner, a painter in his spare time, has acquired a fine collection of contemporary works, including several abstracts which blend in beautifully with the original fireplace, beams and stone floors. The rooms are decorated in a variety of eclectic styles, marrying parquet floor and antiques in one and a wrought-iron bed, terracotta tiles and painted furniture in another; all overlook the terraced garden. An art gallery and a swimming pool have recently been built in the outbuildings.

Access : 2km southbound from Bligny-sur-Ouche on the D 970

BURGUNDY

MEURSAULT - 21190

11 DOMAINE DU MOULIN AUX MOINES
M. Hanique

Auxey-Duresses
21190 Meursault
Tel. 03 80 21 60 79
Fax 03 80 21 60 79
contact @ laterrasse.fr
www.laterrasse.fr

Open all year • 3 rooms and 1 gîte at the mill, 3 rooms 500m away at Meursault, all have bathrooms • €72 to €115; breakfast €7 • No restaurant • Garden, car park

We most liked — Its unique location in the heart of the prestigious Meursault vineyard.

This handsome property surrounded by vineyards once belonged to the Abbey of Cluny. Stone walls, beams, tiled floors and a fireplace add a great deal of cachet to the tastefully-appointed rooms; ask for the one in the mill. The inner courtyard, right on a riverbank, is also very pleasant. A wealth of activities awaits guests, including tastings of the estate's wine and visits to the dovecote and to the small wine-growing museum with an interesting 15C wine press.

Access : In the middle of the estate's vineyards

MONTAGNY-LÈS-BEAUNE - 21200

12 LE CLOS
M. Oudot

22 rue des Gravières
21200 Montagny-lès-Beaune
Tel. 03 80 25 97 98
Fax 03 80 25 94 70
hotelleclos @ wanadoo.fr
www.hotelleclos.com

Closed from 25 Nov to 15 Jan • 19 rooms and 5 apartments, 2 rooms have disabled access, with bath/WC or shower/WC and television • €65 to €110; breakfast €9 • No restaurant • Car park, park. Dogs not admitted

We most liked — A quiet night's sleep just five minutes from the heart of Beaune, France's prestigious city of wine.

An ancient wine press stands proudly in the centre of the large courtyard of this lovely 18C property, formerly home to wine-growing estate. Entirely restored, it now offers well-proportioned rooms furnished in a rustic style and fitted with good quality linen: rest and relaxation guaranteed.

Access : 3km southbound from Beaune on Avenue Charles-de-Gaulle and the D 113

BURGUNDY

NOLAY - 21340

ROUGEMONT - 21500

13 AU TEMPS D'AUTREFOIS
M. Pocheron

Place Monge
21340 Nolay
Tel. 03 80 21 76 37
Fax 03 80 21 76 37
noellepocheron@wanadoo.fr
www.terroirs-b.com/gite

Open all year • 4 rooms, one of which is an apartment • €60, breakfast included • No table d'hôte • Credit cards not accepted

The well-preserved charm of yesteryear.

A deliciously faded atmosphere emanates from this attractive 14C half-timbered house, standing on a little square opposite a fountain. The warm, welcoming interior features exposed beams, antique furniture, chequered curtains and tiled floors. The quiet, pretty rooms are adorned with old black and white photos of Nolay. In the summer, breakfast is served on the terrace of the inn, on the opposite side of the square.

Access : In the village

14 CHAMBRE D'HÔTE MME BACCHIERI
Mme Bacchieri

La Forge, bord du Canal de Bourgogne
21500 Rougemont
Tel. 03 80 92 35 99
Fax 03 80 92 35 99

Closed from Christmas to 1 Jan • 3 rooms with bath/WC • €50, breakfast included • No table d'hôte • Car park. Credit cards not accepted • Boating

Boating on the untroubled waters of the Burgundy Canal.

This delightful little house on the banks of the Burgundy Canal in the Armançon Valley lives up to its promise of peace and quiet. The welcoming, well-kept rooms are full of character and above all very peaceful; all have a fireplace. The manicured garden near the lock and the bicycle towpath along the banks of the canal further enhance its charm. Lavish breakfasts and gracious welcome.

Access : 10km to the north-west of Montbard on the D 905

BURGUNDY

SEMUR-EN-AUXOIS - 21140

15 LES CYMAISES
M. et Mme Faidide

7 rue Renaudot
21140 Semur-en-Auxois
Tel. 03 80 97 21 44
Fax 03 80 97 18 23
hotel.cymaises@libertysurf.fr
www.hotelcymaises.com

Closed 3 Nov to 4 Dec • 18 rooms, one of which has disabled access, most have bath/WC, some have shower/WC, all have television • €62; breakfast €7 • No restaurant • Garden, private car park

We most liked: A leisurely stroll on the ramparts of Semur.

The small capital of Auxois is within "cannonball" distance of some of the most noted jewels of Burgundy, including the Abbey of Fontenay, the fortified village of Flavigny and the Gallo-roman excavations at Alésia. A street near the Porte Sauvigny leads to this imposing 18C townhouse. The rooms are well soundproofed and furnished in a practical country style, while a comfortable sitting room plus conservatory makes a perfect setting for breakfast. Pleasant, peaceful garden to the rear.

Access : On a side street in the medieval city

TALANT - 21240

16 LA BONBONNIÈRE
M. Kreis

24 rue des Orfèvres
21240 Talant
Tel. 03 80 57 31 95
Fax 03 80 57 23 92
labonbonniere@wanadoo.fr
www.labonbonnierehotel.fr

Closed 23 Dec to 9 Jan, 30 Jul to 15 Aug, Sat and Sun in Jan and Feb • 20 rooms, all of which have bath/WC or shower/WC and television • €65 to €90; breakfast €8 • No restaurant • Private car park. Dogs not admitted

We most liked: Savouring the tranquillity of this lovely flowered garden just a few kilometres from Dijon.

This private house transformed into a hotel, almost on the doorstep of a 13C church, stands in a fetching little village overlooking Lake Kir. The interior decoration fully justifies the establishment's name and the pastel colours and stylish furniture definitely lend it a bijou feel. Quiet, spacious rooms, plush bourgeois sitting room and welcoming breakfast room. Even better, the patrons can't do enough to make their guests feel welcome.

Access : In the centre of the village near the church

BURGUNDY

CERCY-LA-TOUR - 58340

17 LE VAL D'ARON
M. Terrier

5 rue des Écoles
58340 Cercy-la-Tour
Tel. 03 86 50 59 66
Fax 03 86 50 04 24
val.aron@wanadoo.fr
www.hotelrestaurant-aron.com

Closed 20 Dec to 10 Jan, Sat and Sun from Oct to May • 12 rooms with bath/WC and television • €64 to €74 (€56 to €64 low season); breakfast €9; half-board available • Menus €19 (weekdays) to €46 • Terrace, garden, car park • Outdoor swimming pool

Whiling away a few hours on the Nivernais Canal.

This 19C mansion formerly housed the local police station before it was turned into a hotel. The attic rooms feature exposed beams and timbers, while those on the ground floor open onto the garden: take your pick when you book – all are spacious and cool. In the winter, meals are served in the rustic dining room with fireplace, and in the summer on a "terrace" under the rafters of a reconstructed farmhouse.

Access : Midway between Decize and Saint-Honoré-les-Bains

CHAULGNES - 58400

18 BEAUMONDE
Mme Trinquard

Le Margat
58400 Chaulgnes
Tel. 03 86 37 86 16
Fax 03 86 37 86 16
cheryl.jj.trinquard@wanadoo.fr

Open all year (reservations only in winter) • 4 non-smoking rooms with bathrooms, 2 have power showers, all have television • €60 to €75, breakfast included • Table d'hôte €22, drinks included • Park, private car park. Credit cards not accepted, dogs not admitted • Outdoor swimming pool, fitness room, fishing in pond

The discreet but friendly welcome.

This handsome characterful house (1960), set in 7ha of grounds in the heart of the Burgundy countryside, invites guests to enjoy the overflow swimming pool, fitness room or fireside, depending on the season. The tastefully decorated and pleasantly understated rooms, are very well equipped. Meals are a happy blend of French and Australian influences, birthplace of the welcoming owner.

Access : 7km north of Pougues-les-Eaux, by the D 138 and D 267

BURGUNDY

CORVOL-D'EMBERNARD - 58210

19 LE COLOMBIER DE CORVOL
M. et Mme Collet

58210 Corvol-d'Embernard
Tel. 03 86 29 79 60
Fax 03 86 29 79 33
robert.collet1@wanadoo.fr
www.lecolombierdecorvol.com

Closed Nov to Jan; open for Christmas and New Year • 4 non-smoking rooms; all have bath/WC or shower/WC • €85 to €95, breakfast included • Table d'hôte €25 to €35 • Park, car park. Dogs not admitted • Outdoor heated swimming pool, badminton court, bicycles

Admiring the works of art on display in each room.

Belgian-born Robert Collet assuages his two passions in this farmhouse (1812) nestling in the Nivernais countryside: art and cooking. The dining room, sitting room and bedrooms are crammed with paintings, sculpture, photos, etc, which are either his own work or that of artists chosen by him. Contemporary furniture adorns the rooms decorated on an animal theme (cockerel, pheasant, boar). There is no lack of outdoor activities either, including a heated swimming pool, badminton, bicycles, walking.

Access: By the D 977 towards Nevers, between Varzy and Prémery

COSNE-COURS-SUR-LOIRE - 58200

20 LES FORGES
M. Marcellot

21 rue Saint-Agnan
58200 Cosne-Cours-sur-Loire
Tel. 03 86 28 23 50
Fax 03 86 28 91 60
denis.cathye@wanadoo.fr
www.lesforges58.com

Closed one week early Jul and one week at Christmas • 7 rooms with bath/WC, television and internet access • €45 to €60; breakfast €7 • Air-conditioned restaurant, closed Sun evening and Mon; menus €18 to €60 • Mountain bike rentals

The discreet charm of this beautifully renovated establishment.

Colour greets the eye right from the lovely green façade of this well-renovated traditional house, encouraging guests to cross its threshold. The small spruce rooms sport yellow and white striped wallpaper, pastel shades and matching fabrics. Ochre takes pride of place in the restaurant, while in the welcoming dining room, burgundy-coloured tablecloths and white mats provide the setting for deliciously up-to-date cuisine.

Access: In the town centre

BURGUNDY

LA CHARITÉ-SUR-LOIRE - 58400

21 LE BON LABOUREUR
M. Boulin

Quai Romain Mollot
58400 La Charité-sur-Loire
Tel. 03 86 70 22 85
Fax 03 86 70 23 64
lebonlaboureur@wanadoo.fr
www.lebonlaboureur.com

Open all year • 16 rooms with bath/WC or shower/WC, all with television • €45 to €72; breakfast €6 • Menus €15 • Garden. No dogs admitted in rooms • Reading room

We most liked: Killing time in the peaceful garden on a summer's day.

This former coaching inn, complete with a barn formerly used by bargees, is located on an island on the Loire. The gracious proprietors take great pleasure in welcoming their guests in style. All the rooms are renovated, light and airy and perfectly kept. The breakfast room with a veranda section overlooking a charming garden is another high spot of this address.

Access: Near the town centre on the Loire, on the D 955 towards Sancerre

LORMES - 58140

22 PERREAU
M. et Mme Girbal

8 route d'Avallon
58140 Lormes
Tel. 03 86 22 53 21
Fax 03 86 22 82 15

Closed from 25 Dec to 31 Jan, Sun evening and Mon from Oct to Apr • 17 rooms, 9 of which are in a separate wing, with bath/WC or shower/WC, all have television • €44 to €50; breakfast €6; half-board available • Menus €16 to €35 • Private car park. Dogs not admitted • Hiking, horse-riding and mountain biking

We most liked: The fine views of the Morvan from Lormes and the Mount of Justice.

This traditional hostelry stands on the road through a picturesque Morvan town. Behind its recently spruced up façade lie pleasant bedrooms, while those in the other wing are quieter and more modern. The exposed stone, dark timbers and stained-glass lights make the dining room most inviting.

Access: In the centre of the village, 29km southbound from Avallon on the D 944

BURGUNDY

NEVERS - 58000

23 CLOS SAINTE-MARIE
M. et Mme F. Vincent

25 rue du Petit Mouësse
58000 Nevers
Tel. 03 86 71 94 50
Fax 03 86 71 94 69
clos.ste.marie@wanadoo.fr
www.clos-sainte-marie.fr

Closed 24 Dec to 2 Jan • 17 rooms with bath/WC or shower/WC, all with television; 8 are non-smoking • €62 to €78; breakfast €9 • No restaurant • Garden, car park. No dogs admitted

We most liked: Relaxing to the sound of the pools in the hotel's inner courtyard.

Some of the rooms of this hotel near a busy street overlook the road but are well soundproofed to ensure a good night's sleep; most are however laid out around a lush green, peaceful patio whose ornamental pools are home to goldfish. The bedrooms, most of which are spacious, are all excellently looked after and furnished with antiques picked up in local markets; some have been recently renovated.

Access: 2km from the town centre on the N 81 towards Dijon

NEVERS - 58000

24 VERDUN
M. et Mme Prat

4 rue de Lourdes
58000 Nevers
Tel. 03 86 61 30 07
Fax 03 86 57 75 61
hotel.de.verdun@wanadoo.fr
www.hoteldeverdun-nevers.com

Closed from 31 Jul to 20 Aug and 26 Dec to 8 Jan • 21 rooms around a patio or in a separate wing, with bathrooms with or without WC and television, 1 has disabled access • €32 to €54; breakfast €6 • No restaurant • No dogs admitted • Two minutes from the historic centre

We most liked: Strolling through Roger Salengro Park opposite the hotel.

This town centre hotel has been treated to a well-needed makeover. The determination and commitment of the new owners have transformed the establishment into a very pleasant port of call in this ancient city. Bright colours, new fabrics, modern bedding and renovated bathrooms give the unpretentious bedrooms an inviting appeal. The breakfast buffet is served in a pleasant country-style dining room and, in summer, on a pleasant patio.

Access: In the town centre, opposite the town park

BURGUNDY

SAINT-PÈRE - 58200

25 L'ORÉE DES VIGNES
Mme Kandin

Croquant
58200 Saint-Père
Tel. 03 86 28 12 50
Fax 03 86 28 12 50
loreedesvignes@wanadoo.fr
www.loreedesvignes.com

Open all year • 5 non-smoking rooms, all have bathrooms. Smoking area available in house • €50 to €52, breakfast included; half-board available • Table d'hôte €22 (by reservation only) • Terrace, garden, car park. Credit cards not accepted, no dogs admitted

The well-stocked information corner in the hall.

This pretty stone-walled farmhouse topped with a traditional tiled roof has a number of assets. First and foremost, its spacious, tastefully decorated rooms with sloping ceilings. Next, the pleasure of eating in the handsome dining room complete with Burgundy and Spanish Renaissance furniture. Finally the sitting room with its old bread oven and the terrace where you can sit back and contemplate the beautiful garden.

Access: 3.2km eastbound from Cosne-sur-Loire on the D 33 and the D 168

SAUVIGNY-LES-BOIS - 58160

26 CHÂTEAU DE MARIGNY
M. et Mme Belz

58160 Sauvigny-les-Bois
Tel. 03 86 90 98 49
Fax 03 86 90 98 45
belz.marigny@wanadoo.fr
http://perso.wanadoo.fr/marigny

Open all year • 3 non-smoking rooms upstairs all with bath/WC or shower/WC • €85 to €99, breakfast included • No table d'hôte • Terrace, park, car park, television room with piano. Credit cards not accepted, dogs not admitted

Admiring the view of the Loire Valley.

Guests must first show their credentials by announcing themselves at the electric gate before they can venture into this handsome Napoleon III castle which belonged to Alain Prost at one time. Its current owners, of German origins, are delightful. He is a keen gardener and tends the grounds, while she takes excellent care of guests. After a restful night's sleep in one of the characterful rooms, guests are treated to a hearty breakfast of cold meats, cheese, cereals, etc.

Access: 8km from Nevers by the N 81

BURGUNDY

BOURBON-LANCY - 71140 **BOURBON-LANCY - 71140**

27 LE GRAND HOTEL
M. Monssus

Parc Thermal
71140 Bourbon-Lancy
Tel. 03 85 89 08 87
Fax 03 85 89 32 23
bourbon.thermal@wanadoo.fr
www.grand-hotel-thermal.com

Open Apr to Oct • 29 rooms with bath/WC or shower/WC, all have television and 8 have a kitchenette • €54 to €76; breakfast €6; half-board available • Menus €13 to €33 • Terrace, inner courtyard, park, car park. No dogs admitted in restaurant

We most liked A leisurely stroll along the ramparts of this spa town.

This hotel, a former convent, lies on the edge of the spa centre's woody park. The gradually renovated and spacious rooms feature a variety of functional or more old-fashioned furniture and all benefit from the pervading restful atmosphere. Light floods in through the dining room's large bay windows but on fine days many guests prefer the terrace in the cloisters.

Access: In the town centre, next to the spa and park

28 VILLA DU VIEUX PUITS
M. et Mme Perraudin

7 rue de Bel-Air
71140 Bourbon-Lancy
Tel. 03 85 89 04 04
Fax 03 85 89 13 87

Closed from Dec 23 to Jan 3 and mid-Feb to mid-Mar, Sun evening and Mon • 7 rooms upstairs with bath/WC or shower/WC, all have television • €45 to €52; breakfast €9; half-board available • Menus €18 to €50 • Terrace, garden, car park. Dogs not admitted in restaurant

We most liked The landscaped garden complete with pond.

The walls of a former tannery now house this smart country inn. The rooms of variable size are both cosy and modern; those on the garden side are quieter and enjoy a better view. A countrified dining room, pleasant outdoor terrace and a slightly threadbare sitting room, its piano still in good tone, complete the picture of this unpretentious, excellent family establishment where guests can always be sure of a warm welcome.

Access: Near Place d'Aligre and the spa

BURGUNDY

BOURGVILAIN - 71520

29 LE MOULIN DES ARBILLONS
M. et Mme Dubois-Favre

71520 Bourgvilain
Tel. 03 85 50 82 83
Fax 03 85 50 86 32
arbillon@club-internet.fr
www.club-internet.fr/perso/arbillon

Open 15 Apr to 15 Oct • 5 rooms • €58 to €79, breakfast included • No table d'hôte • Terrace, garden, park. Credit cards not accepted, no dogs admitted • Wine cellar, tasting and sales

We most liked: The rural setting of this group of 18C, 19C and 20C buildings.

The 18C mill is flanked by a handsome 19C country house and set in a park which boasts a river and a pond. Beautiful period wardrobes grace the generally well-proportioned rooms, all of which overlook the valley and village. A bold blue and white colour scheme and vaulted ceiling make the smallest room our favourite. Breakfast is served in the 20C orangery which features frescoes, iron furniture and a porcelain stove.

Access: 8km southbound from Cluny on the D 980 then the D 22

CHARDONNAY - 71700

30 LE TINAILLER DU MANOIR DE CHAMPVENT
Mme Rullière

Lieu-dit Champvent
71700 Chardonnay
Tel. 03 85 40 50 23
Fax 03 85 40 50 18

Closed from 1 Nov to 1 Mar • 5 rooms • €55 to €60, breakfast included • No table d'hôte • Garden, park, car park. Credit cards not accepted, dogs admitted by request • Art gallery

We most liked: The regular drama performances.

Venture past the porch and you will discover a lovely stone manor house. The rooms are in the outbuildings and furnished with antiques, still-lifes and abstract works by a family ancestor. A room is set aside for regular drama performances and exhibitions of sculpture. The gardens are equally attractive and children generally love romping through the meadow. Flowered courtyard.

Access: 11km to the south-west of Tournus on the D 56 then the D 463

BURGUNDY

CHARNAY-LÈS-MÂCON - 71850　　　CHARolles - 71120

31 LE MOULIN DU GASTRONOME
M. et Mme Goineau

540 route de Cluny
71850 Charnay-lès-Mâcon
Tel. 03 85 34 16 68
Fax 03 85 34 37 25

Closed 15 Feb to 1 Mar, 25 Jul to 9 Aug, Sun evenings and Mon except public holidays • 8 rooms, 1 with disabled access, all with bathrooms • €58 to €72; breakfast €10 • Menus €23 to €54, drinks included • Terrace, park, meeting room, car park • Outdoor swimming pool

Authenticity and good wine on the menu.

This delightful hotel opposite the rock of Solutré boasts a garden with swimming pool and eight supremely comfortable bedrooms. The establishment's main claim to fame however resides in its restaurant where a young and energetic team takes great pleasure in concocting tasty traditional dishes made with home-grown and local market produce. The extensive wine list features a mouth-watering selection of Burgundies and Clarets, which the jovial owner will happily recommend.

Access: Near the town centre overlooking the town of Macon

32 LA POSTE
M. et Mme Doucet

2 avenue de la Libération
71120 Charolles
Tel. 03 85 24 11 32
Fax 03 85 24 05 74
hotel-de-la-liberation-doucet@wanadoo.fr
www.la-poste-hotel.com

Closed fortnight late Nov and fortnight beginning of the year, Sun evening and Mon • 14 rooms, 3 of which have a terrace, all have bath/WC and television • €48 to €120; breakfast €10; half-board available • Menus €23 (week-days) to €70 • Terrace, garage

The festive atmosphere of the cattle markets.

The comfortable bedrooms of this traditional well-kept Burgundian house are equally classical with their chocolate box patterns. Alcove statues, ornaments, period furniture and Charolles porcelain tableware abound in the refined bourgeois décor of the dining room. Burgundy's legendary generosity and hospitality are done full justice in the delicious menu, where the local Charolais beef, of course, has pride of place. Meals are served in the flowered courtyard in fine weather.

Access: On a street corner, opposite the church in the town centre

BURGUNDY

HURIGNY - 71870

33 CHÂTEAU DE SALORNAY
M. Guérin

71870 Hurigny
Tel. 03 85 34 25 73
Fax 03 85 20 11 43

Open all year • 4 rooms • €45 to €52, breakfast included • No table d'hôte • Garden, car park. Credit cards not accepted

The sweeping view over Mâcon from the castle terrace.

The towers, thick walls and guard posts of this 11C and 15C castle cannot fail to attract admiring glances. The antique furnished rooms were built along the same grand lines and overlook the fields. The room in the keep has retained its original terracotta flooring and mullioned windows. Not to be outdone, the dining room boasts beams, flagstones and a fireplace. Children are always welcome to visit the barnyard animals in the nearby farm. Two gîtes are also available.

Access : 6km westbound from Mâcon on the D 82 then a minor road

LOUHANS - 71500

34 MOULIN DE BOURGCHÂTEAU
M. Donatelli

Rue du Guidon
71500 Louhans
Tel. 03 85 75 37 12
Fax 03 85 75 45 11
bourgchateau@netcourrier.com
www.bourgchateau.com

Open all year • 19 rooms with bath/WC or shower/WC, all have television • €54 to €85; breakfast €9; half-board available • Restaurant closed Mon out of season, menus €24 (weekdays) to €60 • Park, car park • 2 pedalos available, local wines sold

Relaxing amidst the cogs and gears of the old mill's machinery.

This enchanting 1778 mill spanning the Seille River was in use up until 1973. The modern, immaculate rooms on the upper floors enjoy a wonderful view of the woodland and river. A millstone and its hopper, leftovers from the mill's working days, lend the dining room a great deal of character. Local wines are on sale in one of the outbuildings. Two pedalos are available for the use of guests who fancy a spin on the river.

Access : Leave Louhans towards Chalon on Rue du 11-Nov-1918, then Rue du Guidon, turn right into the lane towards Bourgchâteau

BURGUNDY

POISSON - 71600   ST-MAURICE-LÈS-CHÂTEAUNEUF - 71740

35 CHAMBRE D'HÔTE M. MATHIEU
M. et Mme Mathieu

Sermaize
71600 Poisson
Tel. 03 85 81 06 10
Fax 03 85 81 06 10
mp.mathieu@laposte.net

Closed from 1 Nov to 15 Mar • 5 rooms with shower/WC • €48 to €58, breakfast included • Table d'hôte €20 • Garden, parking. Credit cards not accepted, no dogs admitted

We most liked: The library's excellent collection of works about the region.

This former 14C hunting lodge with its impressive circular tower and flower-filled courtyard forms a very pleasing picture. An original spiral staircase winds up to a few personalised rooms, two of them have bathrooms in the tower. The suite boasts immense beams, cosy armchairs and walls lined with prints of 19C paintings and old photos by Doisneau. The garden overlooking the open countryside is very pleasant in the summer.

Access: 12.5km south-east of Paray-le-Monial on the D 34 then the D 458, towards Saint-Julien-de-Civry

36 LA VIOLETTERIE
Mme Chartier

71740 Saint-Maurice-lès-Châteauneuf
Tel. 03 85 26 26 60
Fax 03 85 26 26 60
madeleinechartier@yahoo.fr

Closed from 11 Nov to 15 Mar • 3 rooms, one of which is under the eaves, all have bath/WC • €55, breakfast included • Table d'hôte €18 (evenings only and by reservation only) • Garden, car park. Credit cards not accepted, no dogs admitted

We most liked: The sophisticated 19C ambience.

A wrought-iron gate takes you into the courtyard and garden and a flight of steps leads into this 19C mansion. The former holiday home of architect Roux-Spitz, it is now a hotel with light, airy rooms. Those in the attic with painted furniture have retained their original tiled floors and beams. The elegant wood panelling and the fireplace in the sitting and dining room further add to the establishment's appeal.

Access: 10km to the north-east of Charlieu on the D 487, then the D 987 towards La Clayette

BURGUNDY

VERZÉ - 71960

37 LE CHÂTEAU D'ESCOLLES
M. et Mme de Potter

71960 Verzé
Tel. 03 85 33 44 52
Fax 03 85 33 34 80
info@gite-escolles.com

Open all year • 4 rooms with bathrooms • €70, breakfast included • No table d'hôte • Park, car park. Credit cards not accepted, no dogs admitted

We most liked: The faultless decoration of this elegant house.

Guests are always welcomed warmly to this outbuilding of a 17C castle, standing on the edge of a 12-acre park with a pond and surrounded by vineyards and woodland. The sloping ceilings of the bedrooms add a cosy touch, further enhanced by thick carpets, beams and old furniture. Breakfasts, a chance to feast on home-made jams and fresh fruit juice, are served in a beautiful room graced with a dresser, old kneading machine and wrought-iron light. Delightful terrace.

Access: 2km to the north of Roche-Vineuse by D 85

ANCY-LE-FRANC - 89160

38 AU MOULIN D'ANCY LE FRANC
M. et Mme Guiennot

Chemin de Halage
89160 Ancy-le-franc
Tel. 03 86 75 02 65
info@moulin-ancy.com
www.moulin-ancy.com

Open from Apr to Oct, rest of the year by reservation • 5 non-smoking rooms, including 4 apartments upstairs, all have bath or shower/WC • €61 to €130, breakfast included • No table d'hôte • Park, private car park. Credit cards not accepted, dogs not admitted • Mountain bike rentals

We most liked: The idyllic setting.

The Guiennot couple renovated this most impressive (5 floors and over 400m^2) 17C mill. Today one room and four apartments are available for guests. Marie-Pierre, an artist, has turned one floor into painter's studio, while Jean-Louis has converted an old sawmill into an art gallery for local artists. The bucolic site – a 2ha-island poised between canal and river – cannot fail but appeal!

Access: On the way out of Ancy-le-Franc, head towards Montbard, over the Bourgogne canal and turn left before the Armançon bridge

BURGUNDY

APPOIGNY - 89380

39 LE PUITS D'ATHIE
Mme Siad et M. Fèvre

1 rue de l'Abreuvoir
89380 Appoigny
Tel. 03 86 53 10 59
bnbpuitsd'athie@wanadoo.fr
www.puitsdathie.com

Open all year • 4 rooms, including 3 non-smoking apartments, all have bathrooms • €69 to €115, breakfast included • Table d'hôte €45 • Park. Credit cards not accepted • Games room with billiards and pinball machine

We most liked
The happy marriage of old and new.

This handsome Burgundian property should not be missed. Two rooms are located in the main wing, while the others, including the "Porte d'Orient" apartment, a magnificent room with king size bed, balneo bathtub and dressing-room, are reached via the orangery, in an independent wing. At breakfast time, dig in to homemade jams made from a variety of creative recipes; at dinner time, guests are invited to taste up-to-date recipes served with regional wines.

Access: In the village 50m from the Yonne

AUXERRE - 89000

40 MAXIME
M. et Mme Leclerc

2 quai de la Marine
89000 Auxerre
Tel. 03 86 52 14 19
Fax 03 86 52 21 70
hotel-maxime@wanadoo.fr
www.lemaxime.com

Open all year • 25 rooms with bath/WC and television • €75 to €120; breakfast €10; half-board available • Terrace, private car park

We most liked
Trying to learn how to pronounce "Ausserre" like the locals.

This hotel is in the midst of Auxerre's marine district, surrounded by the barge owners half-timbered houses and the Horse-Drawn Barge Museum. The rooms facing the quay with a view of the Yonne are being gradually renovated, but those to the rear are quieter. The typically Burgundian restaurant and the vaulted bistro have, over the years, become the haunt of Auxerre's successful football team. The sounds of liberally washed-down post match celebrations still echo round the walls.

Access: On the road on the left bank of the Yonne

BURGUNDY

AUXERRE - 89000   AUXERRE - 89000

41 NORMANDIE
M. Ramisse

41 boulevard Vauban
89000 Auxerre
Tel. 03 86 52 57 80
Fax 03 86 51 54 33
reception@hotelnormandie.fr
www.hotelnormandie.fr

Open all year • 47 air-conditioned rooms, most at the rear of the building. All rooms have bath/WC or shower/WC and television, 4 are non-smoking • €58 to €80; breakfast €8 • No restaurant • Terrace, garage • Billiards

Endless discussions over a game of billiards.

Virginia creeper has covered the pretty redbrick and white stone façade of this comfortable 19C townhouse with a pleasant gravel forecourt where breakfasts are served in the summer. Most of the rooms, which are in the process of being renovated, are situated in a more recent, quieter wing. The rooms are comfortable and some have power showers. Guests' welfare is the prime concern of this pleasant establishment - they even provide room service.

Access: On the ring-road round town, turn right at the roundabout coming from the A 6 (Paris) and the N 6 (Sens)

42 LE PARC DES MARÉCHAUX
M. et Mme Leclerc

6 avenue Foch
89000 Auxerre
Tel. 03 86 51 43 77
Fax 03 86 51 31 72
contact@hotel-parcmarechaux.com
www.hotel-parcmarechaux.com

Open all year • 14 air-conditioned rooms on 2 levels, all have bath/WC and television • €79 to €110; breakfast €12; half-board available • No restaurant but room service or terrace service available from €18.50 to €29.50 • Terrace, park, car park • Swimming pool

The recently sunk swimming pool which blends into the abundant foliage.

A Parisian judge had this elegant mansion built in 1854 in a style favoured by Napoleon III. When it was converted into a hotel in 1980, the owners were astute enough to retain as much of its original character as possible. The Empire bedrooms are named after Marshals of the French army, while the sitting rooms and breakfast room are reminiscent of Victorian parlours. The superb park and its hundred-year-old trees add a certain hint of romanticism to the mansion.

Access: From the A 6 (Paris) or N 6 (Sens) turn right at Boulevard Vauban roundabout, then right past the Natural History museum

BURGUNDY

CHABLIS - 89800

CHEVANNES - 89240

43 HOSTELLERIE DES CLOS
M. et Mme Vignaud

18 rue Jules-Rathier
89800 Chablis
Tel. 03 86 42 10 63
Fax 03 86 42 17 11
host.clos@wanadoo.fr
www.hostellerie-des-clos.fr

Closed from 20 Dec to 16 Jan • 32 rooms and 4 apartments with bath/WC and television • €60 to €110; breakfast €10; half-board available • Menus €38 to €73 • Garden, car park

44 CHÂTEAU DE RIBOURDIN
M. et Mme Brodard

89240 Chevannes
Tel. 03 86 41 23 16
Fax 03 86 41 23 16
château.de.ribourdin@wanadoo.fr

Open all year • 5 rooms, one of which is on the ground floor and has disabled access • €60 to €70, breakfast included • No table d'hôte • Garden. Credit cards not accepted, no dogs admitted • Outdoor swimming pool

We most liked Savouring a Havana cigar in the smoking room instead of being banished to the garden.

We most liked The select atmosphere of this wonderful little castle.

This former hospital, which still has its original 14C chapel, used to own numerous vineyards. The beautiful vaulted cellar bears witness to the house's wine-growing heritage and has a choice of over 30 Chablis. Rich fabrics and modern comforts adorn the recently renovated rooms. The bow windows of the restaurant open onto a patio where drinks are served in the evenings and breakfast in the morning, the cooking is generous and full of flavour and the wine-list is quite simply out of this world!

The 16C dovecote and castle stand at the foot of the village in the midst of wheat fields. Patience and care lavished over the years have resulted in the beautiful restoration visible today. The 18C barn now houses the bedrooms, each of which is named after a local castle and the spacious breakfast room has a fireplace. The overall look is rustic, mirroring the countryside views from the windows.

Access : In the centre of the village

Access : 9km to the south-west of Auxerre on the N 151 then the D 1, then a minor road

BURGUNDY

COLLAN - 89700

45 LA MARMOTTE
M. et Mme Lecolle

2 rue de l'École
89700 Collan
Tel. 03 86 55 26 44
Fax 03 86 55 00 08
lamarmotte.glecolle@wanadoo.fr
www.bonadresse.com/bourgogne/collan.htm

Open all year • 3 non-smoking rooms with bathrooms • €45, breakfast included • No table d'hôte • Garden, car park. Credit cards not accepted, no dogs admitted • Horse-drawn carriage rides, boating on the Burgundy canal and fishing nearby

We most liked
The footpaths through the Chablis vineyards.

This beautiful old stone house lies in the heart of one of the Yonne's picturesque little villages. All the personalised rooms are named after a colour chosen for the interior decoration. The "Blue" room has cane furniture, while open beams and a wrought-iron four-poster bed grace the "Pink" room. Breakfast is served in the winter garden to the tinkling sound of the fountain.

Access : 7.5km to the north-east of Chablis on the D 150 then the D 35

ESCOLIVES-SAINTE-CAMILLE - 89290

46 DOMAINE BORGNAT LE COLOMBIER
Mme Borgnat

1 rue de l'Église
89290 Escolives-Sainte-Camille
Tel. 03 86 53 35 28
Fax 03 86 53 65 00
regine@domaineborgnat.com
www.domaineborgnat.com

Open all year • 5 rooms, 3 of which have shower/WC, the other 2 have bath/WC • €50 to €60, breakfast included; half-board available • Table d'hôte €23 to €35 • Garden, car park. No dogs admitted in restaurant • Outdoor swimming pool, tours of the wine cellars

We most liked
Visiting the superb cellars.

This fortified 17C farmhouse presides over a superb wine-growing estate. On the accommodation side, guests can choose between the simple comfort of B&B rooms or the self-catering cottage in the former dovecote. Bistro tables, a piano and a terrace around the swimming pool set the scene for breakfasts. Meals are invariably served with a choice of "home-grown" wines. Don't miss the chance to visit the splendid 12C and 17C cellars for further tasting sessions.

Access : 9.5km southbound from Auxerre on the D 239

BURGUNDY

LÉZINNES - 89160

47 CHAMBRE D'HÔTE M. PIEDALLU
M. et Mme Piedallu

5 avenue de la Gare
89160 Lézinnes
Tel. 03 86 75 68 23

Open all year • 3 rooms • €43, breakfast included • No table d'hôte • Garden, car park. Credit cards not accepted, no dogs admitted

The immaculate upkeep of this contemporary house.

This brand-new house has been built in keeping with local styles and even has a square stone tower. The interior is equally pleasing and the spacious, well-appointed rooms with sloping ceilings are furnished with antiques. The breakfast room leads onto a pleasant veranda and guests have the run of a private sitting room for a quiet read.

Access: 11km to the south-east of Tonnerre on the D 905

LIGNY-LE-CHATEL - 89144

48 LE RELAIS SAINT VINCENT
Mme Vuillemin

14 Grande-rue
89144 Ligny-le-Chatel
Tel. 03 86 47 53 38
Fax 03 86 47 54 16
relais.saint.vincent@libertysurf.fr

Closed from 16 Dec to 8 Jan • 15 rooms in 2 buildings, one room has disabled access, all have bath/WC and television • €43 to €70; breakfast €8; half-board available • Menus €13 to €27 • Terrace, inner courtyard, private car park • Ideally located to visit the vineyards and abbeys

The Chablis white wines.

Precious historic clues narrate the illustrious past of these 17C walls, formerly the home of the bailiffs of Ligny. The slightly faded rooms are spacious and calm. The Renaissance era of the restaurant is apparent in the monumental fireplace, open beams and old tapestries. When the weather is fine, meals are served in the inner courtyard surrounded by stone walls or traditional timber frames. The magnificent Abbey of Pontigny is 4km away.

Access: Leave Auxerre on the N 77 towards St-Florentin, turn right between Montigny-la-Resle and Pontigny (D 8)

BURGUNDY

L'ISLE-SUR-SEREIN - 89440

49 AUBERGE LE POT D'ÉTAIN
M. et Mme Pechery

24 rue Bouchardat
89440 L'Isle-sur-Serein
Tel. 03 86 33 88 10
Fax 03 86 33 90 93
potdetain@ipoint.fr
www.potdetain.com

Closed in Feb, the last week of Oct, Sun evening and Mon (except Jul and Aug) and Tue lunchtime • 9 rooms, all rooms have bath/WC or shower/WC and television • €56 to €75; breakfast €8; half-board available • Menus €23 (weekdays) to €49 • Terrace, garage

We most liked: Meals are served in the flowered inner courtyard in the summer.

Who could possibly want to remain stuck to the boiling tarmac of the A6 when the enchanting valley of Serein is so close at hand? Particularly as we've found "the" place that will capture your heart for ever. Nothing quite matches the unparalleled desire to please as that of this 18C coaching inn. Choose your room from the inn's web-site. All display the same faultless style and character as that present in the tasty Burgundian dishes and the fine selection of Chablis vintages.

Access : In the village, on the D 86: leave Avallon north-east bound on the D 957 then left 2km after Montréal

MOLAY - 89310

50 LE CALOUNIER
M. et Mme Collin

5 rue de la Fontaine Hameau de Arton
89310 Molay
Tel. 03 86 82 67 81
Fax 03 86 82 67 81
info@lecalounier.fr
www.lecalounier.fr

Open all year • 5 non-smoking rooms, 2 of which are on the ground floor and have disabled access. All rooms have bathrooms with WC • €58, breakfast included; half-board available • Table d'hôte €23 • Library, garden, car park. Credit cards not accepted, no dogs admitted

We most liked: The cookery courses run by the owner, a cordon-bleu chef.

It is impossible to resist the charm of this lavishly restored Burgundian farm, named after the walnut trees on the estate. The rooms are situated in two wings and are decorated in a hybrid mixture of "colonial" and rustic styles, with bold colour schemes, old furniture picked up in local antique shops and works by local artists. The barn, graced with two large windows, is home to the dining and sitting rooms. Local produce has pride of place on the dining table.

Access : 8km northbound from Noyers on the D 86, and then a minor road

BURGUNDY

NEUVY-SAUTOUR - 89570   QUARRÉ-LES-TOMBES - 89630

51 LA GRANGE DE BOULAY
M. et Mme Gron

Lieu-dit Boulay
89570 Neuvy-Sautour
Tel. 03 86 56 43 52
Fax 03 86 56 43 98
christiane-laurent@wanadoo.fr
www.lagrangedeboulay.com

Open all year • 5 non-smoking rooms with bathrooms, one has a jacuzzi • €70 to €90, breakfast included • Table d'hôte €20 • Terrace, park, car park, barbecues, kitchenette. Credit cards not accepted, dogs not admitted • 2 outdoor swimming pools, bicycle and mountain bike rentals, petanque, table tennis and billiards

We most liked: The variety of types of accommodation available.

This recently restored old house can accommodate up to 42 people in three gîtes and 5 guestrooms. The latter are located in a building known as the "Palombière" (wood-pigeon), and each is in a different style. The "Colonial" for example exhibits a distinctly exotic flavour with an Indonesian-type bed. Also worthy of mention is the "Forge" gîte which boasts a large medieval style room and a mezzanine with billiards table. Swimming pools, table tennis and mountain bikes also available on site.

Access : At Neuvy-Sautour, take the D 12 for 2km towards Chailley then Boulay

52 AUBERGE DES BRIZARDS
M. Besancenot

Les Brizards
89630 Quarré-les-Tombes
Tel. 03 86 32 20 12
Fax 03 86 32 27 40
lesbrizards@free.fr
www.aubergedesbrizards.com

Closed from 5 Jan to 18 Feb and on Mon and Tue • 20 rooms, 7 of which are in the annex, most have bath/WC, some have television • €39 to €115; breakfast €9; half-board available • Menus €23 (weekdays) to €30 • Terrace, garden, park, car park • Tennis, ponds

We most liked: The forest path leading to the Abbey of Pierre qui Vire.

The position of this inn in the heart of the Morvan region would be hard to beat, surrounded by lakes, ponds, forests, unspoilt countryside and utter peace and quiet. A group of outbuildings, including two dolls' houses hidden in the park, make up the hotel; most of the snug rooms have been freshly renovated. The sophisticated restaurant, overlooking the flowered garden, serves generous country cooking. Ideal for nature lovers who enjoy the good things in life.

Access : South-east of Quarré-les-Tombes, 10km on the D 55 and the D 355, after Moulin Colas and Trinquelin

BURGUNDY

SACY - 89270

53 LES VIEILLES FONTAINES
M. et Mme Moine

89270 Sacy
Tel. 03 86 81 51 62
Fax 03 86 81 54 86
vf.cm@free.fr
http://lesvieillesfontaines.free.fr

Closed in Jan and Feb • 4 rooms • €58, breakfast included • Table d'hôte €27 (evenings only) • Garden, car park. Credit cards not accepted, no dogs admitted

Putting your feet up with a good book in the magnificent vaulted cellar-sitting room.

This delightful stone house in the heart of an old Burgundy village used to belong to a local wine-grower. The simple but comfortable rooms have parquet floors. The sitting room and kitchen, fitted out in the old vaulted wine cellar, are definitely worth a look. Meals are served in the owners' dining room, graced with a fireplace and a beautiful wrought-iron light, or on the covered terrace, weather permitting.

Access : 6km eastbound from Vermenton on the D 11

TANNERRE-EN-PUISAYE - 89350

54 LE MOULIN DE LA FORGE
M. et Mme Gagnot

89350 Tannerre-en-Puisaye
Tel. 03 86 45 40 25
renegagnot@aol.com

Open all year • 5 rooms, 3 of which are on the ground floor, all have bath/WC • €52, breakfast included • No table d'hôte • Terrace, garden, car park. Credit cards not accepted • Outdoor swimming pool

Fishing in the estate's river.

It is impossible not to admire the careful restoration of this 14C mill. The wheel has been rebuilt and the old sawmill turned into a pleasing rustic room with a kitchenette for the sole use of guests. Bare beams and 1930s furniture grace the comfortable rooms. Venture out into the landscaped parkland and explore the river, waterfall and pond teeming with fish.

Access : 11km to the north-east of Saint-Fargeau on the D 18 then the D 160

BURGUNDY

VENOY - 89290

VERMENTON - 89270

55 LE MOULIN DE LA COUDRE
M. et Mme Vaury

2 rue des Gravottes
89290 Venoy
Tel. 03 86 40 23 79
Fax 03 86 40 23 55
lemoulin89@wanadoo.fr
www.moulin-de-la-coudre.com

Closed 1 week in Nov and last 3 weeks in Jan • 14 rooms, 5 of which are in a house at the other side of the garden. Rooms have bath/WC or shower/WC and television • €60 to €100; breakfast €9; half-board available • Restaurant closed Sun eve and Mon; menus €22 to €55 • Terrace, garden, car park

We most liked: The peace and quiet just a giant's step from a slip-road off the A6 motorway.

The gardener-handyman clearly has his work cut out here amid the pools full of croaking frogs, borders of primroses and pansies and well-tended paths. This 19C mill on the banks of the Sinotte is perfect for a relaxing night's sleep on your journey southwards. The countrified rooms are a haven of peace and quiet and, in the summer, meals are served in the shade of dense foliage. Staff will happily give the lovingly restored millwheel a spin if so requested, to the delight of young and old alike.

Access : Leave Auxerre on the N 65 towards Chablis, turn left past the A 6 (Auxerre-Sud interchange)

56 LE MOULINOT
M. et Mme Wootton

Route d'Auxerre - RN 6
89270 Vermenton
Tel. 03 86 81 60 42
Fax 03 86 81 62 25
lemoulinot@aol.com
www.moulinot.com

Closed 20 Dec to 10 Jan • 6 rooms with bathrooms • €55 to €80, breakfast included • No table d'hôte • Garden, park, car park. Credit cards not accepted, no dogs admitted • Outdoor swimming pool

We most liked: The wealth of water activities.

Guests have to cross a narrow bridge over the rapid waters of the Cure to reach the idyllic site of this 18C mill. A fine wood staircase leads up to pretty, spacious rooms each of which is individually decorated. Cane furniture, beams, fireplaces and reproduction Impressionist paintings adorn the dining and sitting rooms overlooking the pond. Swimming, fishing, canoeing and mountain biking are just a few of the countless outdoor activities close at hand and the port is just five minutes away.

Access : Take the small private bridge spanning the Cure

BURGUNDY

VÉZELAY - 89450

57 **LES AQUARELLES**
Mme Basseporte

Fontette, 6 ruelle des Grands Prés
89450 Vézelay
Tel. 03 86 33 34 35
Fax 03 86 33 29 82

Closed from 19 Dec to 15 Mar, 12 Nov to 5 Dec, Tue and Wed • 10 rooms, one of which has disabled access, each has bath/WC • €46 to €52; breakfast €6; half-board available • Menu à la carte €12 to €34 • Terrace, car park. Dogs not admitted in restaurant

We most liked **The path winding its way through the fields to Vézelay.**

When this old farmstead was turned into a hotel, the owners were determined to preserve its original character and cachet. The stables now house a sitting room, while the oak furnished bedrooms have been installed in the former hayloft. Meals are served on two enormous farm tables. In the summertime, Mrs Basseporte insists that dinner be taken outside to benefit from the warmth of the beautiful old limestone walls.

Access : 5km eastbound from Vézelay on the D 957 (Avallon road)

VÉZELAY - 89450

58 **CABALUS, L'ANCIENNE HÔTELLERIE DE L'ABBAYE**
Albert Schmidij

Rue Saint-Pierre
89450 Vézelay
Tel. 03 86 33 20 66
Fax 03 86 33 38 03
contact@cabalus.com
www.cabalus.com

Closed Mon and Tue • 4 rooms • €38 to €56; breakfast €9 • A la carte menu €18 • Terrace

We most liked **The art gallery exhibiting contemporary pottery, sculpture and paintings.**

The magic of this inn and its amazing location just 100yds from the basilica lend it a quite unique charm. It was built as the hostelry of the Abbey of Vézelay and its magnificent 12C vaulted room is now home to a tea-room and an art gallery. The extremely well-proportioned and comfortable rooms are imaginatively decorated. Generous breakfasts are served on an enchanting terrace shaded by a scent-laden wisteria.

Access : Near the abbey

BURGUNDY
VÉZELAY - 89450   VÉZELAY - 89450

59 CRISPOL
Mme Schori

Fontette
89450 Vézelay
Tel. 03 86 33 26 25
Fax 03 86 33 33 10
crispol@wanadoo.fr
www.crispol.com

Closed Jan and Feb, Tue lunchtime and Mon • 12 rooms in a separate wing, one of which has disabled access. All rooms have bath/WC and television • €72 to €90; breakfast €9-10; half-board available • Menus €21 to €50 • Terrace, garden, car park

The impeccable upkeep of this establishment.

A number of surprises await visitors inside the thick stone walls of this building in the heart of a hamlet. Firstly, the unexpected contemporary style of the rooms' decoration with sharp corners, lacquered ceilings and works by the owner-artist. Next, the peaceful garden sheltered from the hairpin bend in the road. Finally, the elegant restaurant which surveys the Cure Valley, with the hilltop basilica in the background.

Access : Leave Vézelay on the D 957 towards Avallon and drive 5km; the hotel is on the roadside

60 LA PALOMBIÈRE
Mme Danguy-Pandel

Place du Champ-de-Foire
89450 Vézelay
Tel. 03 86 33 28 50
Fax 03 86 32 35 61
lapalomberie-host@wanadoo.fr

Closed from Jan to Feb • 10 rooms with bathrooms • €55 to €79; breakfast €9 • No table d'hôte • Garden, car park

The pleasant blend of styles and periods.

Situated in the lower part of town, this elegant 18C mansion swamped in Virginia creeper is not lacking in character. The spacious, snug rooms feature an eclectic mixture of styles and periods ranging from Louis XIII, Louis XIV and Empire to satin bedspreads and "retro" bathrooms. Breakfasts, which are lavishly accompanied with home-made jams, are served on the veranda which opens onto the surrounding countryside. The flowered garden is at its best in full bloom in early summer.

Access : In the lower part of town

BURGUNDY

VILLIERS-SAINT-BENOÎT - 89130

61 LE RELAIS SAINT BENOÎT
M. et Mme Roche

89130 Villiers-Saint-Benoît
Tel. 03 86 45 73 42
Fax 03 86 45 77 90
micheline.roche@wanadoo.fr
www.relais-saintbenoit.fr

Closed from 3 to 16 Feb, from 25 to 30 Dec and on Sun evening and Mon • 6 rooms with shower/WC and television • €42 to €62; breakfast €8; half-board available • Menus €19 to €37 • Terrace, garden • Second-hand/antique "shop" at the bottom of the garden

Picking up bargains in the back room of this hotel-cum-restaurant-cum-antique shop.

Those who have read Colette, a local author born in the nearby town of St Sauveur, will immediately recognise Claudine's surroundings. Indeed the village even boasts an Art and History Museum just a step from the hotel to further steep yourself in local traditions. The hotel features renovated rooms, a sandstone collection from the region in the restaurant and a tiny shaded terrace. A country inn which lives up to the best local traditions.

Access : Leave the Auxerre-Saint-Fargeau road (N 965) at Toucy to take the D 950 for 8.5km

VOUTENAY-SUR-CURE - 89270

62 AUBERGE LE VOUTENAY
M. et Mme Poirier

89270 Voutenay-sur-Cure
Tel. 03 86 33 51 92
Fax 03 86 33 51 91
auberge.voutenay@wanadoo.fr
www.monsite.wanadoo.fr/auberge.voutena

Closed three weeks in Jan, one week in Jun and in Nov, Sun eve, Mon and Tue • 8 rooms with bath/WC, and a suite opening onto the garden • €45 to €65; breakfast €7; half-board available • Menus €24 to €42 (limited seating so it is necessary to book) • Garden, car park. No dogs admitted

The mountain bikes and canoes available for use by guests.

The inn's canine mascot, Lafayette, happily does the honours of this handsome 18C mansion which is little by little undergoing a facelift. The bedrooms are being renovated, a spacious 45sq metre flat has just been installed and the restaurant boasts a handsome fireplace with a carved wooden mantelpiece. The slightly unruly walled garden planted with hundred-year-old trees and extending down as far as the River Cure, is sheer bliss. A hiking path runs alongside the establishment.

Access : On the N 6 from Auxerre to Avallon

BRITTANY

Brittany – Breizh to its inhabitants – is a region of harsh granite coastlines, dense, mysterious forests and pretty ports tightly packed with brightly painted fishing boats. Its charm lies in its brisk sea breeze, its incredibly varied landscapes, its countless legends and the people themselves, born, so they say, with a drop of salt water in their blood. Proud of the customs and language handed down from distant Celtic ancestors, today's Bretons nurture their identity throughout the year with a calendar of events, in which modern-day bards and minstrels exalt their folklore and traditions. Of course, such devotion to culture requires plenty of good, wholesome nourishment: sweet and savoury pancakes, thick slices of *kouign-aman* (pronounced "queen-aman") dripping in caramelised sugar and salted butter and mugs of cold cider. However, Brittany's gastronomic reputation extends far beyond such tasty titbits and gourmets can feast on the oysters, lobster, crab and other seafood delicacies for which this rocky peninsula is renowned.

- Côte-d'Armor (22)
- Finistère (29)
- Ille-et-Vilaine (35)
- Morbihan (56)

BRITTANY

DINAN - 22100

1. ARVOR
M. Renault

5 rue A. Pavie
22100 Dinan
Tel. 02 96 39 21 22
Fax 02 96 39 83 09
hote-arvor@wanadoo.fr
www.hotel-arvor-dinan.com

Open all year • 24 rooms, one of which has disabled access, all have bath/WC or shower/WC and television • €48 to €63; breakfast €6 • No restaurant • Private car park

We most liked Dinan's streets lined with lovely old half-timbered houses.

Guests are often struck by the amazing contrast between the old 18C walls of this former convent and the distinctly modern flavour of the bedrooms. A handsome Renaissance porchway leads into the reception and functional, well-equipped identical rooms. A few parking spaces near a ruined chapel are most welcome in the heart of the old town.

Access : In the old town almost opposite the theatre

KERBORS - 22610

2. MANOIR DE TROÉZEL VRAS
M. et Mme Maynier

22610 Kerbors
Tel. 02 96 22 89 68
Fax 02 96 22 90 56
troezel.vras@free.fr
http://troezel.vras.free.fr

Closed 20 Oct to 1 Apr • 5 rooms • €66 (€59 low season), breakfast included • Table d'hôte €19 (except Sun) • Garden, car park. Credit cards not accepted, no dogs admitted

We most liked The numerous walking and biking opportunities.

This pretty 17C manor house surrounded by rambling peaceful countryside has everything the travel-weary visitor could wish for. Terracotta tiled floors, apricot painted walls, antique wardrobes and prints of local landscapes adorn the bedrooms. The equally agreeable dining room features white-painted beams and a stone fireplace. Depending on the season, meals are served in the garden or near a log fire: seafood is a speciality all year round.

Access : 9km to the north-east of Tréguier on the Paimpol road towards Pleumeur-Gautier, then Kerbors

BRITTANY

MORIEUX - 22400

PLÉNEUF-VAL-ANDRÉ - 22370

3 LE MANOIR DE LA VILLE GOURIO
M. et Mme Guihot

22400 Morieux
Tel. 02 96 32 72 60
Fax 02 96 32 75 68
golf @ lacriniere.fr
www.lacriniere.fr

Closed late Dec • 5 rooms with bath/WC and television • €58 to €107; breakfast €9 • Table d'hôte €11 to €15 • Terrace, garden, park, car park. No dogs admitted

4 VILLA MARGUERITE
M. et Mme Campion-Levive

34 rue des Garennes
22370 Pléneuf-Val-André
Tel. 02 96 72 85 88
Fax 02 96 72 85 88

Open Apr to Sep (by reservation in low season) • 4 rooms on 2 floors • €58 to €63, breakfast included • No table d'hôte • Garden. Credit cards not accepted, no dogs admitted

We most liked Taking a golf lesson with a pro.

We most liked Strolling along the pedestrian coast path alongside Val-André beach.

This 17C Brittany manor house overlooks a 9-hole golf course surrounded by trees which are almost as old as the house. The rustic rooms upstairs all overlook the garden, fairways and ponds. On the ground floor, guests have the run of a reading room, a billiards table and a breakfast room where a fire takes the chill out of those brisk autumn mornings. The former stables house a bar, restaurant, night club and the clubhouse – ask here for expert tips and private coaching.

This pretty villa, quite in keeping with the architectural style of this quaint 19C seaside resort, enjoys a fine view over the Bay of St-Brieuc. Sea-lovers will adore the rooms, most of which have sea-facing balconies. All are decorated in a sober yet fetching style with floorboards, colourful walls and two have four-poster beds. Peaceful nights guaranteed thanks to the large garden surrounding the house. Note the interesting antique furniture which adorns the breakfast room.

Access : 11km southbound from Val-André on the D 786 and the D 34

Access : 300m from the town centre, on the sea front

BRITTANY

PLOUËR-SUR-RANCE - 22490

5 MANOIR DE RIGOURDAINE
M. Van Valenberg

Route de Langrolay
22490 Plouër-sur-Rance
Tel. 02 96 86 89 96
Fax 02 96 86 92 46
hotel.rigourdaine@wanadoo.fr
www.hotel-rigourdaine.fr

Closed from 13 Nov to 31 Dec • 19 rooms, 5 of which are split-level, 2 have disabled access. Rooms have bath/WC or shower/WC and television • €66 to €82 (€58 to €74 low season); breakfast €7 • No restaurant • Park, private car park. No dogs admitted • Games room with billiards, private fishing

The countless paths around the Rance estuary.

A narrow lane leads up to this picturesque farmstead, which is almost as old as the River Rance itself. Its secluded position overlooking the estuary ensures guests a peaceful night's sleep, awakened only by the calls of the seagulls overhead. Good old country furniture and brightly coloured fabrics grace the bedrooms, while old beams, bare stone walls and a gigantic family table adorn the breakfast room. Full of character.

Access : 3km northbound from Plouer-sur-Rance on the D 12 towards Langrolay, then right at a private road

QUINTIN - 22800

6 COMMERCE
M. Gourdin

2 rue Rochonen
22800 Quintin
Tel. 02 96 74 94 67
Fax 02 96 74 00 94
hotelducommerce@cegetel.net
http://www.hotelducommerce.fr.st

Closed from 1 to 4 Jan, 22 to 28 Mar and 23 to 29 Aug and on Mon, Fri eve and Sun eve (except by reservation) • 11 rooms, all have shower/WC and television; non-smokers only • €54 to €66 (€49 to €60 low season); breakfast €7; half-board available • Menus €13 (weekdays except evenings in season) to €40

Walking along the banks of the Gouët.

The origins of this impressive granite house covered in Virginia creeper have been traced back to the 18C. The modern, personalised rooms have been recently renovated and each is named after an appetising spice or condiment, such as Fleur de sel, paprika or cinnamon. A beautiful period fireplace with a carved wooden mantelpiece is the centrepiece of the rustic wainscoted dining room.

Access : In the centre of the village, on the D 790 between Saint-Brieuc and Rostrenen

BRITTANY

SABLES-D'OR-LES-PINS - 22240

7 MANOIR SAINT-MICHEL
M. et Mme Fournel-Besnier

La Carquois
22240 Sables-d'Or-les-Pins
Tel. 02 96 41 48 87
Fax 02 96 41 41 55
manoir-st-michel@fournel.de
www.fournel.de

Closed 2 Nov to 14 Apr • 20 rooms on 2 floors, all have bath/WC or shower/WC and television • €44 to €106; breakfast €8 • No restaurant • Car park, garden. Dogs not admitted • Fishing in the lake

In fine weather, breakfast overlooking the garden with the ocean in the background.

What better spot for a romantic stay than this 16C and 17C manor? The little lane leading up to the property is quickly forgotten as you are greeted by the lovely stone walls of the building and the immense garden and pond. You may even catch a glimpse of the breathtaking Sables-d'Or-les-Pins beach. An old-fashioned charm pervades the rooms which are appointed with splendid old wardrobes and furnished in a variety of styles ranging from rustic to Louis XIII and Louis XV. Attentive staff.

Access : 1.5km eastbound on the D 34

ARZANO - 29300

8 CHÂTEAU DE KERLAREC
M. et Mme Bellin

Kerlarec
29300 Arzano
Tel. 02 98 71 75 06
Fax 02 98 71 74 55
château-de-kerlarec@wanadoo.fr
www.chateau-de-kerlarec.com

Open all year • 6 rooms • €78 to €110, breakfast included; half-board available • No table d'hôte • Park, car park. Credit cards not accepted • Outdoor swimming pool, tennis, exhibitions. 18-hole golf course and horse-riding nearby

The well-preserved Second Empire style.

It is easy to see why the current owners fell in love with this 1830 mansion set in a park complete with ornamental pool. The Second Empire reigns supreme amid the period frescoes, antique furniture and objets d'art gleaned from local antique shops and flea markets or brought back from voyages overseas. Relax in the peace and quiet of the spacious, individually decorated bedrooms. Don't leave without a look at the Jeanne d'Arc room.

Access : 6km eastbound from Quimperlé on the D 765 Lorient road, and left onto the Arzano road (D 22)

BRITTANY

BERRIEN - 29690

9 LA FERME DE PORZ KLOZ
M. et Mme Berthou

Trédudon-le-Moine
29690 Berrien
Tel. 02 98 99 61 65
Fax 02 98 99 67 36
yvberthou@wanadoo.fr
http://monsite.wanadoo.fr/porzkloz

Open Mar to Nov • 5 rooms and 1 apartment with bath/WC • €45 to €90 (€39 to €80 low season); breakfast €7 • Restaurant €20 (by reservation only) • Car park. Credit cards not accepted, no dogs admitted • Horse-riding, swimming pool, tennis and golf nearby

We most liked — Finding out more about Brittany's less well-known hinterland.

Time seems to have stood still in this cluster of 17C farmhouses, formerly outbuildings of the Abbey of Releq, where only the best locally-grown produce is good enough for the dinner table. The bedrooms, decorated with family heirlooms, are particularly delightful and most are large enough to sleep entire families. Admire the photos relating aspects of daily life in 19C Brittany in the reception.

Access: 11km to north-west of Huelgoat on the D 14, take the Berrien road and the D 42 on the left

CLÉDER - 29233

10 COS-MILIN
Mme Moysan

29233 Cléder
Tel. 02 98 69 42 16
Fax 02 98 69 42 16
www.gites-finistere.com/gites/cozmilin

Open all year • 3 non-smoking rooms, all have bathrooms • €50, breakfast included • No table d'hôte • Sitting room, garden, car park. Credit cards not accepted, no dogs admitted

We most liked — Traditional Breton favourites at breakfast.

The seaside and coastal footpaths are not far from this stone-built house with slate roof. Individually decorated bedrooms combine old and new in an imaginative blend and, on the ground floor, the elegant sitting and breakfast rooms are furnished in the same eclectic style. Tuck into a delicious spread of pancakes, "far", a local rum and raisin flan and other traditional Breton delicacies at breakfast, before relaxing on a deck chair in the flowered garden.

Access: 3km westbound from Saint-Pol, take the D 10 and at Lléder follow signs to "les plages"

BRITTANY

ROSPORDEN - 29140

11 LE MANOIR DE COAT CANTON
M. et Mme Simon

Grandbois
29140 Rosporden
Tel. 02 98 66 31 24

Open all year • 4 rooms, 2 of which are on the ground floor, all have bathrooms • €40 to €45, breakfast included • No table d'hôte • Car park. Credit cards not accepted, no dogs admitted • Horse-riding in the grounds

Going hacking around the lush, green Breton countryside.

The construction of this pleasing manor house full of character took place from the 13C to the 17C. The rooms, located in a converted farmhouse, are decorated in a variety of styles, including medieval, Breton and English. The antique furnished breakfast room is very pleasant. The owners, who also run a riding stable nearby, will be only too happy to introduce you to the joys of riding.

Access : 13km north-east of Concarneau on the Pont-l'Abbé road (D 783), and right on the Rosporden road (D 70)

FOUESNANT - 29170

12 LA POINTE DU CAP COZ
M. et Mme Le Torc'h

153 avenue de la Pointe - Cap Coz
29170 Fouesnant
Tel. 02 98 56 01 63
Fax 02 98 56 53 20
bienvenue@hotel-capcoz.com
www.hotel-capcoz.com

Closed 1 Jan to 10 Feb and 20 to 27 Nov; Sun evening and Mon lunchtime from 15 Sep to 15 Jun and Wed • 16 rooms with bath/WC or shower/WC and television • €63 to €88; breakfast €8 • Menus €22 to €42 (disabled access) • Terrace • Billiards; nearby: golf, beach, water sports

The site which is quite as exotic as other more far-flung destinations.

The hotel is built on a stretch of sandy beach bounded on one side by the ocean and on the other by a small bay whose waters are crystal-clear. The rooms are low-key and discreet, as if to do full justice to the beauty of the coast. All are peaceful and some enjoy terraces from which to contemplate the superb vista. Both dining rooms, recently renovated and non-smoking only, specialise in fresh local produce mainly from the sea. Enchanting sitting room-bar.

Access : 2.5km south-east from Fouesnant on minor road

BRITTANY

ÎLE-DE-BATZ - 29253

13 TI VA ZADOU
M. et Mme Prigent

Le bourg
29253 Île-de-Batz
Tel. 02 98 61 76 91
Fax 02 98 61 76 91

Closed from 15 Nov to 1 Feb • 4 rooms on 2 floors, all have bathrooms, except for one family room with a bathroom on the landing • €60, breakfast included • No table d'hôte • Credit cards not accepted, no dogs admitted

We most liked Cycling around on the lanes of this tiny island village.

A sense of humour and a love of life set the tone in this blue-shuttered residence, whose name means "house of my fathers" in Breton. Old and new mingle happily in the cosy, welcoming bedrooms and all have a splendid view of the port, the cluster of islets and the mainland. Family heirlooms take pride of place in the sitting and breakfast rooms, both with fireplace. Bicycles can be rented nearby.

Access : Near the harbour

ÎLE-DE-SEIN - 29990

14 AR-MEN
M. Fouquet-Portais

Route du Phare
29990 Île-de-Sein
Tel. 02 98 70 90 77
Fax 02 98 70 93 25
hotel.armen@wanadoo.fr
www.hotel-armen.com

Closed 2 to 25 Jan and 2 to 25 Oct • 10 rooms with sea view, all have shower/WC • €50 to €65; breakfast €8; half-board available • Restaurant closed Sun evening and Wed (in season); menus from €18 • Sitting room-library

We most liked Tasting the charm of island life.

Forget the hurly-burly of urban life for a few days and head for the island of Sein! After a short crossing, pass through the village and head towards the lighthouse to reach the imposing pink façade of this house. The modestly-sized, relatively simple rooms are painted bright colours and all enjoy a sea view. The meals are equally simple and rich in sea flavours; try the island's speciality, lobster stew. Sitting room-cum-library with fireplace and friendly welcome.

Access : On the way out of the village towards the lighthouse

BRITTANY

LOC-EGUINER-ST-THÉGONNEC - 29410

15 TY-DREUX
Mme Martin

29410 Loc-Eguiner-Saint-Thégonnec
Tel. 02 98 78 08 21
Fax 02 98 78 01 69
ty-dreux@club-internet.fr
gites-peche-saint-thegonnec.com

Open all year • 7 rooms with shower/WC and 3 gîtes • €46 to €56, breakfast included • Table d'hôte €19 • Garden. Credit cards not accepted, no dogs admitted

It is worthwhile remembering that home-made cider is pretty potent!

The name of this dairy farm, more than worth a trip, in the heart of the countryside means "weaver's house" in testimony to its textile heritage. Period furniture, a huge 18C granite fireplace and a permanent exhibition of costumes belonging to former generations set the scene for this establishment which upholds local traditions. Modern canopied beds add character to the renovated rooms. Meals are a chance to sample the succulently prepared farm-grown produce.

Access : 3.5km to the south-east of Guimiliau on the Plouneour-Menez road (D 111)

PLOGOFF - 29770

16 AN TIEZ BIHAN
M. et Mme Ganne

Kerhuret
29770 Plogoff
Tel. 02 98 70 34 85
www.fumoir-2lapointeduraz.com

Closed 15 Nov to 1 Jan • 4 rooms • €40, breakfast included • Table d'hôte €18 by reservation (except Wed and Sun) • Car park, garden. Credit cards not accepted

Tucking into homemade pancakes and jams at breakfast time.

A recent restoration has breathed a new lease of life into this old farmhouse, whose new owners wisely chose to retain the original proportions and materials. Several little houses, formerly stables and barns, are now home to simply furnished rooms and a gîte is also available. The main building houses the dining room where you can sample delicious local seafood. Hikers will enjoy the chance to set off along the coast path as far as the Pointe du Raz.

Access : 2.5km along the D 784 towards the Pointe du Raz

BRITTANY

PLOGOFF - 29770

17. DE LESCOFF
M. et Mme Le Corre

29 rue des Hirondelles - Lieu-dit "Lescoff"
29770 Plogoff
Tel. 02 98 70 38 24

Open all year • 3 rooms with bath/WC • €40 (€38 low season), breakfast included • No table d'hôte • Car park, garden, terrace. Credit cards not accepted

We most liked: A bracing walk along the cliffs to the Pointe du Raz during rough weather.

The little town of Lescoff is home to the last cluster of houses before you reach the unspoilt, windswept site of the Pointe du Raz. Laid out around a little courtyard, the buildings of this former working farm offer a highly inviting picture. The rooms make up in charm what they may lack in size with rustic furniture and bare stone or white roughcast walls. Guests have the use of a practical kitchenette in the breakfast room with a sloping ceiling on the first floor.

Access: 300m from the Pointe du Raz car park

PLOMODIERN - 29550

18. PORZ-MORVAN
M. Nicolas

Route de Lescuz
29550 Plomodiern
Tel. 02 98 81 53 23
Fax 02 98 81 28 61
christian.nicolas19@wanadoo.fr

Closed 10 Jan to late Feb • 12 rooms, 4 upstairs, 8 are in a separate wing. All have bath/WC or shower/WC and television • €48 to €50; breakfast €6 • Crêperie in an old barn • Terrace, garden, car park • Tennis

We most liked: Feasting on pancakes!

Those in search of peace and quiet will adore this delightful stone farmhouse built in 1830 just next door – as the seagull flies – from the famous viewpoint of Ménez-Hom (330 m), which overlooks the region. Most of the gradually-renovated rooms are on the garden level in the former cow-shed. The barn has been converted into a friendly crêperie where the old rafters and timbers have been preserved. Large garden with pond and warm welcome guaranteed.

Access: 3km eastbound from Plomodiern on a minor road

BRITTANY

PLOUIGNEAU - 29610

19 MANOIR DE LANLEYA
M. Marrec

Au bourg de Lanleya
29610 Plouigneau
Tel. 02 98 79 94 15
Fax 02 98 79 94 15
manoir.lanleya@wanadoo.fr
www.manoir-lanleya.com

Open all year • 5 non-smoking rooms with shower/WC • €66, breakfast included • No table d'hôte • Garden, car park. Credit cards not accepted, no dogs admitted

The manor's legend, related by the lord of the house.

The quality of the restoration is such that it is difficult to believe that this 16C manor house and its adjoining 18C malouinière were saved from ruin in the nick of time. The stunning interior features Breton furniture, old beams, slate floors, exposed stone walls, a beautiful spiral staircase, pink granite fireplace and rich fabrics. The Louis XV room is particularly splendid, but the others, which are smaller, display the same exquisite taste. Lovely riverside garden.

Access: 5km to the north-east of Morlaix on the D 712, then take the D 64 towards Lanmeur

PONT-AVEN - 29930

20 LE MOULIN DE ROSMADEC
M. et Mme Sébilleau

Venelle de Rosmadec
29930 Pont-Aven
Tel. 02 98 06 00 22
Fax 02 98 06 18 00

Closed during the February holidays, from 14 to 30 Oct, Sun evening out of season and Wed • 4 rooms in a separate wing with bath/WC and television • €85 to €100; breakfast €10 • Menus €32 to €74; limited seating so book in advance

Breakfasting on the delightful veranda overlooking the river.

This bucolic mill was built in 1456. According to a local proverb, "Pont Aven, a town of standing, boasts fourteen mills and fifteen houses". The town no doubt owes at least part of its celebrity to the millers who settled by its fast-flowing river, but the town's renowned pancakes and the painters who endowed it with worldwide posterity, also played their part. The traditional Breton restaurant is decorated with artwork from the local school. Spacious, modern bedrooms.

Access: In the town centre, near the bridge

BRITTANY

SAINT-THÉGONNEC - 29410

21 AR PRESBITAL KOZ
Mme Prigent

18 rue Lividic
29410 Saint-Thégonnec
Tel. 02 98 79 45 62
Fax 02 98 79 48 47
andre.prigent@wanadoo.fr

Open all year • 6 rooms on 2 floors, 4 of which have bath/WC, the other 2 have shower/WC • €47 to €50, breakfast included • Table d'hôte €20 (evenings only) • Garden, car park. Credit cards not accepted, no dogs admitted

We most liked
The nearby "enclos paroissiaux".

This former 18C presbytery, hidden by a curtain of cypress trees, is home to comfortable, well-dimensioned rooms, each of which is decorated in a different colour and furnished with antiques. The largest has a fireplace. Admire the collection of ducks from all over the world in the smoking and sitting rooms. In the summer, wander round the garden and vegetable plot or rent a bicycle (from the hotel) and venture further afield.

Access: Near the Saint Bernadette Retirement Home

TRÉGUNC - 29910

22 AUBERGE LES GRANDES ROCHES
M. Raday

Les Grandes-Roches
29910 Trégunc
Tel. 02 98 97 62 97
Fax 02 98 50 29 19
hrlesgrandesroches@club-internet.fr
www.hotel-lesgrandesroches.com

Closed from 20 Dec to 1 Feb • 17 rooms located in several houses and cottages, all have bath/WC or shower/WC • €75 to €130; breakfast €12; half-board available • Menus €41 • Park with dolmen and standing stone, car park. No dogs admitted

We most liked
The 100 % "Breizh" - Breton - character of this establishment.

This delightful hamlet of old farms and two-hundred-year-old cottages nestles in the semi wilderness of five acres of parkland where a giant dolmen and sacred menhir still stand. The stylish, tastefully decorated and regularly refurbished rooms resound to the immense silence all around. The restaurant boasts all the authentic character of traditional Breton houses with huge fireplaces and thick stone walls.

Access: 0.6km to the north-east of Trégunc on a minor road

BRITTANY

CANCALE - 35260

CANCALE - 35260

23 LE CHATELLIER
Mme Lescarmure

Route de Saint-Malo
35260 Cancale
Tel. 02 99 89 81 84
Fax 02 99 89 61 69
hotelchatel@aol.com
www.hotellechatellier.com

Open all year • 13 rooms, one of which has disabled access, with bath/WC or shower/WC and television • €55 to €73; breakfast €8 • No restaurant • Garden, car park

24 LA POINTE DU GROUIN
Mme Simon

À la Pointe-du-Grouin
35260 Cancale
Tel. 02 99 89 60 55
Fax 02 99 89 92 22
hotel-pointe-du-grouin@wanadoo.fr
www.hotelpointedugrouin.com

Open all year • 16 rooms on 2 floors with bath/WC or shower/WC, all have television • €78 to €98; breakfast €8; half-board available • Restaurant closed Tue and Thu lunchtime in low season; menus €20 to €61 • Car park • 400m from the beach

The untamed landscape of the rocky Pointe du Grouin just a stone's throw away.

This comfortable stone house, a former farm turned into a hotel, makes an ideal base camp to explore the region in fine weather and get away from the bustling seaside resort. Four rooms are brand new; the others are relatively generously sized, decorated in a rustic style and spotlessly clean. A log fire heats the sitting room during the cold winter nights.

Venturing onto the outcrop at sunset.

In the summer, things can get a bit frantic here. What's more, the iconic landmark of the Pointe du Grouin is also the starting point of the famous Route du Rhum sailing race which takes place every four years (2006). Come sunset, however, the view from this stone house, perched on a cliff in a far corner of Brittany, is breathtaking. The cosy, comfortable rooms and panoramic restaurant all enjoy a splendid vista over the Island of Landes, sanctuary to countless seabirds, and St Michel Bay.

Access: 2km westbound on the D 355 towards Saint-Malo

Access: 5km northbound from Cancale on the D 201

BRITTANY

CESSON-SÉVIGNÉ - 35510

25 GERMINAL
M. et Mme Goualin

9 cours de la Vilaine
35510 Cesson-Sévigné
Tel. 02 99 83 11 01
Fax 02 99 83 45 16
le-germinal@wanadoo.fr
www.legerminal.com

Closed during the Christmas school holidays • 20 rooms on 3 floors, all have bath/WC and television • €70 to €90; breakfast €9 • Restaurant closed Sun (except summer) and Mon; menus €17 to €43 • Terrace, car park.

We most liked: The terrace overlooking the river.

An unusual spot, to say the least: this 19C mill stands on an islet of the River Vilaine. Another little island has a car park and guests reach the hotel over a footbridge. The new owners are determined to add a new lease of life to their establishment and both the restaurant and the rooms are being renovated. The views and idyllic location are gradually re-establishing this unique building as one of the unexpected delights of the Rennes area.

Access: 6km eastbound from Rennes, on a small island in the Vilaine

CHÂTEAUBOURG - 35220

26 AR MILIN'
M. Burel

30 rue de Paris
35220 Châteaubourg
Tel. 02 99 00 30 91
Fax 02 99 00 37 56
resa.armilin@wanadoo.fr
www.armilin.com

Closed 1 to 4 Jan • 32 rooms in the Moulin and Résidence du Parc, with bath and shower/WC and television • €85 (€79 low season); breakfast €11; half-board available • Menus €27 to €44 • Park and arboretum, terrace, car park • Tennis court

We most liked: The superb 12.5-acre park complete with arboretum and sculptures.

Welcome to Ar Milin', an inviting flour mill built in the 19C on the banks of the Vilaine. The building is home to two restaurants: a comfortable dining room with exposed rafters and a veranda overlooking the river and a pleasantly contemporary-style bistro. A few rooms full of character are available in the mill, but the majority of the accommodation is located in a pavilion surrounded by greenery which is calmer and more modern in spirit.

Access: 16km west of Rennes on the N 157, Châteaubourg exit, 900m from the exit in the heart of the village

BRITTANY

LE RHEU - 35650

27 MANOIR DU PLESSIS
M. Desmots

Route de Lorient
35650 Le Rheu
Tel. 02 99 14 79 79
Fax 02 99 14 69 60
info@manoirduplessis.fr
www.manoirduplessis.fr

Closed 26 Dec to 3 Jan and 15 to 20 Feb • 5 rooms with bath/WC and television • €95; breakfast €9 • Menus €16 to €27 • Terrace, park, car park • Billiard room

Indulge in a game of billiards before sitting down to the chef's tasty cooking.

A six-acre park protects this lovely old manor house from the busy Lorient road. The manor is well known for its excellent up-to-date cooking, stylish dining rooms, with parquet floors, wainscoting, fireplaces and Louis XVI-style furniture and its lush green terrace. The spacious bedrooms, all of which overlook the park, are equally worthy of praise and equipped with all the modern comforts in a pleasantly old-fashioned style.

Access : 6km westbound of Rennes on the Lorient road

PAIMPONT - 35380

28 LA CORNE DE CERF
Mme Morvan

Le Cannée
35380 Paimpont
Tel. 02 99 07 84 19

Closed in Jan • 3 rooms with bathroom • €50, breakfast included • No table d'hôte • Library, garden. Credit cards not accepted, no dogs admitted

The epitome of sophistication.

This lovely old home is hidden deep in the heart of the forest of Brocéliande, a land steeped in legends of wizards and magic. A profusion of paintings, tapestries and painted furniture set the tone for the tasteful, elegant interior decoration. The light, airy rooms open onto a delightful, well cared-for garden. There is absolutely no shortage of leisure activities in the vicinity including many footpaths, and water sports on the village lake.

Access : 2km southbound from Paimpont on the D 71

BRITTANY
QUEDILLAC - 35290   SAINT-COULOMB - 35350

29 RELAIS DE LA RANCE
M. Guitton-Chevrier

6 rue de Rennes
35290 Quedillac
Tel. 02 99 06 20 20
Fax 02 99 06 24 01
relaisdelarance@21s.fr

Closed from 20 Dec to 20 Jan, Fri and Sun evenings • 13 rooms with bath/WC or shower/WC, all with television • €49 to €64; breakfast €9; half-board available • Menus from €20 to €70 • Car park

We most liked **The faultless welcome extended by the Guitton family since 1946.**

This house has quietly and steadfastly remained true to its founding spirit, to the delight of its regulars who grow in number each year. What lures them back time after time? The pleasant family atmosphere that reigns throughout this regional-style residence, the tasty traditional cuisine supplemented by local produce and the recently renovated, comfortable rooms, each of which is personalised and equipped with a modern bathroom.

Access : On the edge of the département, between Rennes and Saint-Brieuc, on the N 12 and D 220, in the centre of the village

30 AUBERGE DE LA MOTTE JEAN
M. et Mme Simon

35350 Saint-Coulomb
Tel. 02 99 89 41 99
Fax 02 99 89 92 22
hotel-pointe-du-grouin@wanadoo.fr
www.hotelpointedugrouin.com

Open all year • 11 rooms located in 2 modern buildings. Rooms have bath/WC or shower/WC, all have television • €78 to €130 (€65 to €110 low season); breakfast €7; half-board available • Menus €20 to €61 • Garden, car park. Dogs not admitted in rooms • Duck pond

We most liked **Breakfasts are served by the fireside in winter and opposite the garden in summer.**

The headlands, bluffs and capes carved by the ocean and the island of Guesclin, whose fort belongs to singer-songwriter Léo Ferré, are just two minutes away from this secluded farmhouse which dates from 1707. The good taste of the lady of the house can be seen in the cosy style and old furniture in the rooms, particularly those in the former stables. Gardeners will adore the rose bushes in the beautiful garden "à la française".

Access : On leaving Cancale, take the D 355 towards Saint-Malo

BRITTANY

SAINT-MALO - 35400

31 QUIC-EN-GROIGNE
Mme Roualec

8 rue d'Estrées
35400 Saint-Malo
Tel. 02 99 20 22 20
Fax 02 99 20 22 30
rozenn.roualec@wanadoo.fr
www.quic-en-groigne.com

Closed 5 to 19 Jan and 23 to 25 Dec • 15 rooms on 2 levels, all have bath/WC or shower/WC and television • €58 to €64 (€54 to €59 low season); breakfast €7 • No restaurant • Garage. No dogs admitted

We most liked: The peace and quiet of this hotel located in the heart of St Malo.

The name, taken from the tower next to the castle, is a reminder of Anne of Brittany's haughty reply to the townspeople of St Malo who took a very poor view of the ramparts erected round their town. The duchess dismissed them with the words: "Grumble as you will ('qui qu'en groigne'), so I decide". The hotel is in an old stone house near the beaches. The rooms are modern and gradually being redone. Breakfasts can be taken in the cane-furnished veranda or the pleasant garden.

Access: In the old town, take Rue de Toulouse from Porte Saint-Louis, at the end turn right twice

SAINT-SULIAC - 35430

32 LES MOUETTES
Mme Rouvrais

17 Grande-Rue
35430 Saint-Suliac
Tel. 02 99 58 30 41
contact@les-mouettes-saint-suliac.com
http://www.les-mouettes-saint-suliac.com

Open all year • 5 rooms, one of which has disabled access, all have bathrooms • €48 (€43 low season), breakfast included • No table d'hôte • Garden. Credit cards not accepted, no dogs admitted

We most liked: The sincerity of the warm welcome.

Formerly the village grocery store and pork butchers, this stone house built in 1870 stands on the main road leading to the banks of the River Rance. Today it features snug rooms painted in pastel colours and decorated with old paintings and furniture picked up in second-hand antique shops. One of the rooms is equipped for disabled guests. The breakfast room, complete with library, as well as the small garden in the rear, are both very pleasant.

Access: In the heart of the village

BRITTANY

BADEN - 56870

CARNAC - 56340

33 GAVRINIS
M. et Mme Lignières

Toulbroch
56870 Baden
Tel. 02 97 57 00 82
Fax 02 97 57 09 47
gavrinis@wanadoo.fr
www.gavrinis.com

Closed from 16 Jan to 2 Feb, 16 Feb to 5 Mar, Sat lunchtime, Mon lunchtime (in season), Sun evening and Mon • 18 rooms, 4 non-smoking, with bath/WC or shower/WC and television • €72 to €89; breakfast €11; half-board available • Menus €20 to €46 • Terrace, garden, car park • Nearby: mountain biking and walking, fishing, sailing

A perfect HQ to explore the Gulf of Morbihan and its islands.

The classical neo-Breton architecture of this house and garden is home to a highly welcoming family establishment. A few of the comfortable, exquisitely kept rooms boast a small balcony. But for many guests, the real draw is the establishment's cooking: the owner, assisted by his son, tirelessly scours the region for good local produce which he lovingly transforms into dishes which reveal a mouth-watering blend of traditional and regional.

Access: From Baden, head towards Vannes as far as the hamlet of Toulbroch

34 L'ALCYONE
Mme Balsan

Impasse de Beaumer - Carnac-plage
56340 Carnac
Tel. 02 97 52 78 11

Closed 10 days in Jan and fortnight in Nov • 5 rooms with bathrooms • €62 (€57 low season), breakfast included • No table d'hôte • Garden, car park. Credit cards not accepted, dogs admitted on request

Scrumptious breakfasts.

Whitewashed walls, parquet floors and tasteful fabrics await behind the creeper-clad façade of this 1870 farmhouse. The soft, inviting sofas in the sitting room and the deck chairs in the garden overlooking the fields make it impossible not to take things easy. The sea and menhirs are within easy reach, as is one of the most beautiful beaches of the bay of Carnac.

Access: On leaving Carnac Plage drive towards Trinité-sur-Mer

BRITTANY

CARNAC - 56340

35 AUBERGE LE RÂTELIER
M. Bouvart

4 chemin du Douet
56340 Carnac
Tel. 02 97 52 05 04
Fax 02 97 52 76 11
bouvart@infonie.fr
www.le-ratelier.com

Closed from 13 to 30 Nov, Tue and Wed out of season • 8 rooms, some have shower/WC and television • €46 to €55 (€38 to €43 low season); breakfast €7; half-board available • Menus €17 to €40 • Courtyard, car park

The superb view of Carnac's famous menhirs without risking wrack and ruin!

This stone farmhouse on a quiet side street of the old village was built by a soldier returning from Napoleon's Grande Armée, or so the story goes. Its granite façade, swamped by Virginia creeper, hides a welcoming, country interior: the unfussy rustic charm of the bedrooms makes up for their small size. The beams and manger in the former cow-shed, converted into a dining room, are original and the pretty flowered fabrics add a cheerful touch.

Access: In the old village, a short distance from the church

CARNAC - 56340

36 TY ME MAMM
Mme Daniel

Quelvezin
56340 Carnac
Tel. 02 97 52 45 87

Open all year • 4 rooms, one of which is on the ground floor • €50, breakfast included • No table d'hôte • Garden, car park. Credit cards not accepted

Your hosts' hospitality and spontaneity.

Off the beaten track, this handsome farmhouse, built in 1900 and entirely restored, stands in a large garden, bordered by a pond on one side. Each of the immaculate rooms, named after one of Carnac's beaches, is decorated in a mixture of rustic and modern styles. Breakfast time by the side of the huge granite fireplace is always pleasant. Guests have the use of a fridge and a microwave.

Access: 5km northbound from Carnac on the D 768 and then the Quelvezin road (C 202)

BRITTANY

ÉTEL - 56410

37 LE TRIANON
Mme Guezel

14 rue du Général-Leclerc
56410 Étel
Tel. 02 97 55 32 41
Fax 02 97 55 44 71
hotel.letrianon@wanadoo.fr
www.hotel-le-trianon.com

Closed in Jan; Mon and Sat lunchtimes and Sun eve from Nov to Mar • 24 rooms with bath/WC or shower/WC and television • €60 to €100 (€48 to €65 low season); breakfast €9; half-board available • Menus €19 to €42 • Garden, car park

The awe-inspiring sight of the Barre d'Étel during bad weather.

Don't be put off by the somewhat ordinary façade of this building in the heart of the little fishing port, the interior has a few surprises up its sleeve. The bedrooms, decorated in a chocolate-box style, vary in size and comfort; some still have original hip baths – ask for one in the villa at the end of the peaceful garden. Attractive rustic and homely dining room and very warm welcome.

Access : In the centre of the village, near the church

GUILLIERS - 56490

38 RELAIS DU PORHOËT
M. et Mme Courtel

11 place de l'Église
56490 Guilliers
Tel. 02 97 74 40 17
Fax 02 97 74 45 65
aurelaisduporhoet@wanadoo.fr
www.aurelaisduporhoet.com

Closed from 1 to 22 Jan, 1 to 8 Oct, 1 to 8 Jul, Sun evening and Mon (out of season) • 12 rooms with bath/WC or shower/WC and television • €40 to €49; breakfast €7; half-board available • Menus €10 (weekdays) to €36 • Garden, private car park. No dogs admitted in rooms

The delightful young owners so in love with their region.

Let's not beat about the bush: this handsome country inn, adorned with flowers in the summer, is a very special place. Peaceful nights of refreshing sleep in rustic-style bedrooms more than large enough to swing a cat and delicious, generous helpings of good local recipes served in a pretty dining room complete with a huge fireplace. Children can romp to their heart's content in the garden.

Access : In the centre of the village, opposite the church

BRITTANY

ILE DE GROIX - 56590

39 LA GREK
M. et Mme Le Touze

3 place du Leurhé
56590 Île de Groix
Tel. 02 97 86 89 85
Fax 02 97 86 58 28
groe@infonie.fr
www.groix.com

Closed in Feb • 4 non-smoking rooms, with bath/WC • €50 (€38 to €45 low season), breakfast included • No table d'hôte • Garden, car park. Credit cards not accepted, no dogs admitted

We most liked **Hoping a storm would blow up and cut us off for days.**

The name of this Art Deco-style property, formerly the home of a tuna boat owner, is the nickname given to the inhabitants of this windswept island. Restored in 1993 and 1997, the hotel has retained its appealing insular charm. One of the best things about the elegant, comfortable bedrooms is the enormous bathrooms. Antique furniture adorns the sitting rooms, one of which has a fine collection of old coffee pots. Laze about in the large walled garden.

Access : In the village

ÎLE DE GROIX - 56590

40 LA MARINE
Mme Hubert

7 rue du Général-de-Gaulle
56590 Île de Groix
Tel. 02 97 86 80 05
Fax 02 97 86 56 37
hotel.dela.marine@wanadoo.fr
www.hoteldelamarine.com

Closed in Jan, Sun evening and Mon out of season except in the school holidays • 22 rooms with bath/WC or shower with or without WC • €42 to €90 (€36 to €80 low season); breakfast €8; half-board available • Menus €16 to €25 • Terrace, garden

We most liked **Sailing round the island on an old pirate ship.**

The short walk from the landing stage to the main town is enough to work up a healthy appetite and ensure you do full justice to the hearty, varied dishes rustled up in the kitchen of this plush bourgeois 19C home. Don't worry about the calories, the best way to explore the Island of Groix is on foot or by bicycle! Simple, spotless rooms, a terrace shaded by tall pine trees and a walled garden will make you wish you had planned to stay longer...

Access : In the town, 5min walk from the port

BRITTANY

LA TRINITÉ-SUR-MER - 56470

41 STIREN AR MOR
M. et Mme Hans

1 clos du Poulbert
56470 La Trinité-sur-Mer
Tel. 02 97 30 15 28
Fax 02 97 30 15 28
danchant@libertysurf.fr
www.stiren-ar-mor.fr.st

Open from Easter to 15 Oct • 4 rooms (2 with private sitting rooms), with bath/WC or shower/WC and television • €48 to €63, breakfast included • No table d'hôte • Car park, terrace. Credit cards not accepted, no dogs admitted

Parking the car and setting off for the beach and coastal paths on foot.

This modern Breton-style house and garden is ideally located near the beach in a quiet residential neighbourhood. The blue, salmon, yellow and green rooms are all comfortable, recently fitted out and furnished in a rustic or more classical style. The largest are on the first floor and have their own sitting room, but those on the second floor with sloping ceilings and beams are just as appealing. Family heirlooms and knick-knacks brighten up the ground floor.

Access : 300m from the beach

NOYAL-MUZILLAC - 56190

42 MANOIR DE BODREVAN
M. et Mme Rüfenacht

56190 Noyal-Muzillac
Tel. 02 97 45 62 26
Fax 02 97 45 61 40
www.pour-les-vacances.com

Closed 7 Jan to 1 Apr and 2 Nov to 20 Dec • 6 rooms, 1 of which has disabled access; all have bath/WC or shower/WC and television • €74 to €96 (€65 to €84 low season); breakfast €10; half-board available • Menus €21 (evenings only for guests) • Private car park, garden. No dogs admitted in restaurant

The delightful flower garden noted for its roses.

If in need from a break from the stress of urban life, this former 16C hunting lodge set in the heart of Brittany's peaceful countryside, will suit you to a T. The "prestige boarding house" atmosphere announced on the sign outside the manor is more than amply justified. An eclectic taste in interior decoration, bordering on the baroque at times, sets the tone for the spacious rooms. Only house guests are invited to partake of the appetising set menu.

Access : 2km north-east on the D 153 and a minor road

BRITTANY

PLOEMEL - 56400

43 CHAMBRE D'HÔTE M. MALHERBE
M. et Mme Malherbe

Kerimel
56400 Ploemel
Tel. 02 97 56 84 72
Fax 02 97 56 84 72
elisabeth.malherbe@wanadoo.fr
http://kerimel.free.fr

Closed 14 Nov to 3 Feb • 4 non-smoking rooms, with bathrooms and television • €65 to €70, breakfast included • No table d'hôte • Garden, car park. Credit cards not accepted, no dogs admitted

We most liked: The enveloping warmth of the wood stove after a day in the open air.

This cluster of 17C cottages laid out around a large lawn complete with flower-beds is definitely worth a photo or two. Inside, the stylish renovation of the attic rooms with period furniture, comfortable bedding and well-fitted bathrooms leaves nothing to be desired. Tuck into the profusion of Breton delicacies at breakfast time (croissants, "far", pancakes, home-made jams), served in front of the huge granite fireplace in winter. Guests also have the run of a pleasant sitting room and library.

Access: 8km northbound from Carnac on the D 119, go through the town towards Erdeven, after 1.5km turn right towards Kerimel

PLOËRMEL - 56800

44 LE THY
M. et Mme Dinael

19 rue de la Gare
56800 Ploërmel
Tel. 02 97 74 05 21
Fax 02 97 74 02 97
info@lethy.com
www.le-thy.com

Open all year • 7 rooms with bath/WC or shower/WC and television • €50 to €60; breakfast €5 • No restaurant but the bar serves sandwiches • Small car park. No dogs admitted • Concerts and theatre at weekends

We most liked: The 3km-long path lined with 220 species of hydrangea on the banks of the lac au Duc.

This unusual hotel has absolutely nothing in common with your run-of-the-mill establishments. As the web-site proudly proclaims, the imaginative rooms are named after and decorated in the style of artists from all periods: "Tapies", "Hopper", "Bonnard", "Hugo Pratt", "Klimt", "Van Gogh" and a "Flemish artist's studio". A cabaret room, decorated with three hundred drawers, stages "rock" concerts at the weekends. Trendy, personalised and immaculate – definitely worth a visit!

Access: In the town centre

BRITTANY
PLOUGOUMELEN - 56400　　　PLOUGOUMELEN - 56400

45　LES CHAUMIÈRES DE CAHIRE
M. et Mme Hermellin

56400 Plougoumelen
Tel. 02 97 57 84 83

- 3 rooms with shower/WC • €63 to €70, breakfast included • No table d'hôte • Garden, car park. Credit cards not accepted, no dogs admitted • Tennis and horse-riding nearby

46　FERME DE GUERLAN
M. Le Douaran

À Guerlan
56400 Plougoumelen
Tel. 02 97 57 65 50
Fax 02 97 57 65 50
ledouaran@aol.com
www.bedbreak.com/guerlan

Closed from 15 Nov to 1 Mar • 5 rooms, one of which is a family room and one has disabled access • €36 to €50, breakfast included • No table d'hôte • Garden, car park. Credit cards not accepted

We most liked
The manicured lawns and flowerbeds.

We most liked
The rapturous smiles of toddlers visiting the farm.

Three instantly likeable 17C cottages stand clustered together in a listed hamlet. Beautiful antiques and contemporary works of art adorn the sophisticated, well-dimensioned rooms. Two are in the converted press-house, another is in the old bakery and the last is in the main wing. Fortifying breakfasts are served in the wonderful kitchen before an open fire.

This impressive 18C country seat makes an ideal base for exploring the Gulf of Morbihan. The spotless rooms are a happy marriage of old and new. One is designed for families and another for disabled guests. A fireplace graces the enormous dining room and guests have the use of a kitchen and a shaded garden. The owners are very happy to show you round the farm.

Access : 7km on the Vannes road, Plougoumelen exit, then drive towards Cahire

Access : 12km westbound from Vannes on the N 165, Plougoumelen exit, towards Meriadec

BRITTANY

PLOUHINEC - 56680

47 HÔTEL DE KERLON
M. et Mme Coeffic

56680 Plouhinec
Tel. 02 97 36 77 03
Fax 02 97 85 81 14
hotel-de-kerlon@wanadoo.fr
www.auberge-de-kerlon.com

Open from late Mar to early Nov • 16 rooms, some of which have bath/WC, the others have shower/WC, all have television • €52 to €61; breakfast €8; half-board available • Restaurant open in the evening only; menus €16 • Garden, car park. Dogs not admitted

The spectacle of the sea crashing against the Ria d'Étel.

This stone-built 19C farmstead, cradled in a peaceful Morbihan hamlet, commands a wonderful view of the Ria d'Étel. The bedrooms are somewhat outdated and hardly enormous but very well cared for and at delightfully reasonable prices. All overlook the peaceful, flowered garden. Traces of the establishment's farming past can be seen in the restaurant, which serves home-reared poultry and lamb. The sea is just 10min away.

Access : 1.5km to the north-east of Plouhinec, on the D 158 then a minor road

QUELVEN - 56310

48 AUBERGE DE QUELVEN
SCI de la Lande

À la Chapelle
56310 Quelven
Tel. 02 97 27 77 50
Fax 02 97 27 77 50

Closed on Wed • 7 rooms have shower/WC and television • €55; breakfast €6 • Menus €10 to €12 • Car park

"Napoléonville" or Pontivy: a geometric town laid out by the Emperor himself.

The long granite façade of this inn is in the heart of this secluded hamlet in the Morbihan countryside. Practical, spotless bedrooms, some of which overlook the pretty 16C chapel and a traditional-style crêperie full of character with stone walls and a beautiful old fireplace. A very pleasant establishment noted for its warm welcome.

Access : 10km to the south-west of Pontivy on the Plouay road. Opposite the chapel

BRITTANY

RIANTEC - 56670

49 LA CHAUMIÈRE DE KERVASSAL
M. et Mme Watine

Lieu-dit Kervassal
56670 Riantec
Tel. 02 97 33 58 66
Fax 02 97 33 58 66
gonzague.watine@wanadoo.fr
http://pro.wanadoo.fr/chaumiere.kervassal

Open all year • 3 non-smoking rooms under the eaves with bathrooms • €64, breakfast included • No table d'hôte • Sitting room, garden, car park. Credit cards not accepted, no dogs admitted • Beach nearby

The faultless taste of this delightful home.

It is difficult not to fall head over heels in love with this beautifully restored 17C cottage. It has everything from an impeccable thatched roof, exposed beams and stone walls, period furniture and tasteful fabrics down to abundant bouquets of flowers. Inside and out it is a delight for the eyes. The tranquil bedrooms have high ceilings and ultra-modern bathrooms. Exquisite breakfasts are served in the garden in the summer.

Access: 8km eastbound from Port-Louis on the D 781, then the D 33, Merlevenez road

ROCHEFORT-EN-TERRE - 56220

50 LE PÉLICAN
M. Nays

Place des Halles
56220 Rochefort-en-Terre
Tel. 02 97 43 38 48
Fax 02 97 43 42 01

Closed from 15 Jan to 15 Feb and Mon • 7 rooms with bath/WC or shower/WC and television • €42 to €48; breakfast €7; half-board available • Menus €13 (lunchtime weekdays) to €37

A picturesque site worthy of a watercolour or, for the less artistic among us, a photo!

A charming Breton town is home to this delightful 16C-18C house whose window-boxes are adorned with brightly coloured geraniums in the summer. The spruce, modern rooms are decorated with modern furniture, with one exception, which boasts an old wardrobe and bed. The high rafters of the dining room add a rustic air, further enhanced by a handsome fireplace.

Access: On the main square, next to the town hall and tourist office

BRITTANY

SAINTE-ANNE-D'AURAY - 56400

51 **L'AUBERGE**
M. et Mme Larvoir

56 route de Vannes
56400 Sainte-Anne-d'Auray
Tel. 02 97 57 61 55
Fax 02 97 57 69 10
auberge-jl-larvoir@wanadoo.fr
www.auberge-larvoir.com

Closed from 24 Feb to 13 Mar, from mid-Nov to mid-Dec, Tue (except Jul-Aug) and Wed • 17 rooms with bath/WC or shower/WC, all have television • €60 to €110; breakfast €8; half-board available • Air-conditioned restaurant; menus from €20 (weekdays) to €67 • Car park

We most liked The pilgrimages or "pardons" of Saint Ann are a sight to behold.

The impressive basilica, the house of Nicolazic and the pilgrimages in honour of Saint Ann, the patron saint of Brittany, offer an authentic insight into Breton tradition at is most fervent and picturesque. This spruce, flower-decked inn offers modern rooms in bright fabrics, decorated with regional or Art Deco-style furniture. Admire the elegant Quimper tableware as you eat in the traditionally-furnished Breton dining room, which is clearly, and justifiably, proud of its local produce.

Access: At the entrance to the village, on the main street

SAINT-PHILIBERT - 56470

52 **CHAMBRE D'HÔTE MADAME GOUZER**
Mme Gouzer

17 route de Quéhan (C 203)
56470 Saint-Philibert
Tel. 02 97 55 17 78
Fax 02 97 30 04 11
fgouzer@club-internet.fr
http://chrisgouzer.free.fr

Open all year • 3 rooms • €60 to €65, breakfast included • No table d'hôte • Garden, car park. Credit cards not accepted

We most liked The sweeping view over the River Crach and the oyster beds.

Lovers of seafood, oysters in particular, and Brittany in general will adore this place. This charming oyster farmhouse enjoys an exceptional situation, in the midst of pine trees, overlooking the River Crach and opposite the busy port of Trinité sur Mer. Guests are always welcomed warmly. The light, airy rooms all command a view of this fascinating coastal scenery. Two rooms are equipped with a kitchenette and the largest also boasts a balcony.

Access: 2km on the Auray road, turn left at the first set of traffic lights (after Kérisper bridge)

CENTRE AND UPPER LOIRE VALLEY

Sleeping Beauty is said to slumber still within the thick walls of one of the Loire's fairy-tale castles, like Chambord, Azay-le-Rideau or Chenonceau. A list of the region's architectural wonders and glorious gardens would be endless; but its treasures are shown to full effect in a season of 'son et lumière' shows depicting the fabled deeds of brave and courtly knights and the thwarted love of fair demoiselles. The landscape has inspired any number of writers, from Pierre de Ronsard, "the Prince of Poets", to Balzac and Georges Sand. All succumbed to the charm of this valley of kings, without forgetting to give the game-rich woodlands their due. To savour the region's two-fold talent for storytelling and culinary arts, first tuck into a delicious chicken stew, then curl up by the fireside to hear your hosts' age-old local legends.

- Cher (18)
- Eure-et-Loir (28)
- Indre (36)
- Indre-et-Loire (37)
- Loir-et-Cher (41)
- Loiret (45)

CENTRE AND UPPER LOIRE VALLEY

ARCAY - 18340

1 CHÂTEAU DE BEL AIR
M. et Mme Maginiau

Lieu-dit le Grand-Chemin
18340 Arcay
Tel. 02 48 25 36 72
Fax 02 48 25 36 72

Open all year • 6 rooms with bath/WC • €45, breakfast included • No table d'hôte • Park, car park. Credit cards not accepted

We most liked
Unbeatable value for money.

This 19C castle stands in a 10-acre parkland whose trees and grounds afford calm and comfort. Most of the large rooms are furnished in a Louis XVI style. One also features a private sitting room with fireplace, while another connects with a room which can accommodate two child-sized beds. The stately dining room, complete with monumental fireplace, is equally characterful. Bicycle rentals and golf practice in the grounds.

Access: 11km northbound from Châteauneuf on the D 73

BERRY-BOUY - 18500

2 DOMAINE DE L'ERMITAGE
M. et Mme De La Farge

L'Ermitage
18500 Berry-Bouy
Tel. 02 48 26 87 46
Fax 02 48 26 03 28
domaine-ermitage@wanadoo.fr

Closed 20 to 31 Dec • 5 rooms with bathrooms • €57 to €60, breakfast included • No table d'hôte • Car park. Credit cards not accepted, no dogs admitted

We most liked
The tranquillity of the park disturbed only by the twittering of birds.

This handsome property, formerly the priory of the Abbey of Saint Sulpice of Bourges, owes its name to a hermit who stayed here for a while. The nearby paper mill dates back to 1495. Nowadays, the well-proportioned, tastefully decorated rooms are situated in two buildings, each as quiet as the next. Take a pleasant stroll through the grounds and admire the ancient trees, venturing perhaps into the wine cellars to taste the estate's own production of Menetou-Salon.

Access: 6km to the north-west of Bourges on the D 60

CENTRE AND UPPER LOIRE VALLEY

BRINON-SUR-SAULDRE - 18410

3 LA SOLOGNOTE
M. et Mme De Passos

34 Grande-Rue
18410 Brinon-sur-Sauldre
Tel. 02 48 58 50 29
Fax 02 48 58 56 00
lasolognote@wanadoo.fr
www.lasolognote.com

Closed from 15 Feb to 31 Mar • 13 rooms with bath/WC or shower/WC and television • €58 to €78; breakfast €10; half-board available • Air-conditioned restaurant; menus €26 to €45 (closed Tue and Wed from 12 Nov to 15 Mar) • Garden, car park. No dogs admitted in rooms

A glimpse of village life in France.

Anyone who has read Alain-Fournier will instantly recognise the inimitable soul of this old country village full of French character and charm. The unpretentious hotel stands in the main street where it blends in perfectly with the other redbrick houses. Cosy or more contemporary rooms are laid out around a delightful courtyard-garden. The red floor tiles, stained-glass and period furniture are all synonymous with local styles and the fine porcelain bears the hallmark of Gien.

Access : Leave the N 20 at Lamotte-Beuvron onto the D 923

CHÂTEAUMEILLANT - 18370

4 AUBERGE DU PIET À TERRE
M. Finet et Mme Piet

21 rue du Château
18370 Châteaumeillant
Tel. 02 48 61 41 74
Fax 02 48 61 41 88
TFINET@wanadoo.fr
http://le.piet.a.terre.free.fr

Open from Mar to 30 Nov, closed Sun evening, Mon and Tue lunchtime (except Jul-Aug) • 5 rooms with bath/WC or shower/WC, all have television • €46 to €78; breakfast €15 • Air-conditioned restaurant; menus €40 (weekdays) to €120; limited seating • Dogs not admitted

The parents' suite with a proper child's room.

Hear ye, hear ye, good folk! Here is a pleasant inn where every weary traveller should rest awhile! Entrust your faithful steed to the groom, have no fear, the stables, sorry the car park, is next door to the mounted constabulary, and rest your tired feet in this country haven. The rooms are as pretty as a picture and the tavern replete with good victuals to tickle even the finest palate. The chef's devotion has won the establishment a well-earned Michelin star.

Access : Next to the gendarmerie (police station)

CENTRE AND UPPER LOIRE VALLEY

VIGNOUX-SUR-BARANGEON - 18500

5 VILLEMENARD
M. et Mme Gréaud

18500 Vignoux-sur-Barangeon
Tel. 02 48 51 53 40
Fax 02 48 51 58 77
villemenard@wanadoo.fr
www.villemenard.com

Open all year • 6 rooms • €50 to €55, breakfast included • No table d'hôte • Park, terrace, car park. Credit cards not accepted, dogs not admitted • River and pond on the property. Billiards room

We most liked
An afternoon stroll through ancient woodland.

The lane, lined with ponds, crosses a river before entering this wonderful 19C country house which is still the hub of a thriving agricultural business. The interior decoration is particularly worthy of note: beautiful azulejos tiles grace the entrance and dining room, weapons and prints adorn the staircase and a superb varnished wooden bar stands in the billiards room. All the well-dimensioned, quiet rooms overlook the peaceful Berry countryside.

Access: 6km northbound from Méhun on the D 79 towards Vouzeron

VIGNOUX-SUR-BARANGEON - 18500

6 LE PRIEURÉ
Famille Ribail

2 route de Saint-Laurent
18500 Vignoux-sur-Barangeon
Tel. 02 48 51 58 80
Fax 02 48 51 56 01
prieurehotel@wanadoo.fr
www.leprieurehotel.com

Open Jun to Sep • 7 rooms upstairs with shower/WC and television • €54 to €66 (€49 to €60 low season); breakfast €7; half-board available • Menus €27 (weekdays) to €67. Restaurant closed Tue and Wed • Terrace, garden, car park • Outdoor swimming pool

We most liked
A religious devotion to guests' welfare.

Built in 1860 for the village priest, the ogival windows immediately evoke this priory's religious roots. The establishment's former spiritual vocation has given way to a more down-to-earth, but equally committed desire for hospitality. The intimate, bright rooms are named after flowers. Traditional dishes and flavourful Berry wines are consumed with gusto on the pleasant terrace. Connoisseurs will immediately recognise the beautiful tableware as Foëcy porcelain!

Access: Set back from the lane, on the D 30 (towards Neuvy-sur-Barangeon), near the church

CENTRE AND UPPER LOIRE VALLEY

BAILLEAU-L'ÉVÊQUE - 28300

7 LA FERME DU CHÂTEAU
M. et Mme Vasseur

À Lévesville
28300 Bailleau-l'Évêque
Tel. 02 37 22 97 02
Fax 02 37 22 97 02

Open all year • 3 rooms • €55, breakfast included • Table d'hôte €18 • Garden, car park. Credit cards not accepted, dogs not admitted

We most liked: The overwhelming peace and quiet of this country spot.

A pretty manor farm laid out around a spacious inner courtyard next door to a small castle. The good-sized rooms are cheerful, well equipped and all are peaceful. The simple, unaffected welcome, reasonable prices, pretty garden and its location only 15km from Chartres are among the most noteworthy of this establishment's many charms.

Access: 8km to the north-west of Chartres on the N 154 then the D 134

CHERVILLE - 28700

8 CHAMBRES D'HÔTES
Mme Lethuillier

2 rue des Prunus
28700 Cherville
Tel. 02 37 31 72 80
Fax 02 37 31 38 56
info@cherville.com
www.cherville.com

Open all year • 4 non-smoking rooms, all have bath/WC or shower/WC • €44 to €55, breakfast included • No table d'hôte • Garden, car park, kitchenette

We most liked: The authenticity of this old farmhouse.

The owners of this country estate, still a working farm, have tastefully renovated one of the old outhouses to create four refreshing and charming bedrooms (three have sloping ceilings). Breakfasts, served in a room which sports bare stone walls and the original manger, are an opportunity to taste specialities from the garden and pancakes stuffed with home-made jams made by the lady of the house.

Access: N 10 towards Chartres, 13km from the roundabout, head towards Umpeau, go through the village, on the right at Cherville

CENTRE AND UPPER LOIRE VALLEY

ÉCROSNES - 28320

9 CHÂTEAU DE JONVILLIERS
M. et Mme Thompson

17 rue L.-Petit-Jonvilliers
28320 Écrosnes
Tel. 02 37 31 41 26
Fax 02 37 31 56 74
info@chateaudejonvilliers.com
www.chateaudejonvilliers.com

Open all year • 5 non-smoking rooms with shower/WC • €65 to €75, breakfast included • No table d'hôte • Garden, car park. Dogs not admitted

The sheer elegance of this majestic property.

A pleasant drive leads up to this elegant 18C castle which stands in private grounds next to thick woodland. Peace and quiet reign in all the spacious, tastefully decorated rooms. Delicious and generous helpings of breakfast fare are served in a huge antique furnished dining room. Note that the establishment is entirely non-smoking.

Access: 4km to the north-east of Gallardon on the D 32

MONTIGNY-SUR-AVRE - 28270

10 LE MOULIN DES PLANCHES
Mme Maï

28270 Montigny-sur-Avre
Tel. 02 37 48 25 97
Fax 02 37 48 35 63
moulin.des.planches@wanadoo.fr
www.moulin-des-planches.fr

Closed in Jan, Sun evening and Mon • 18 rooms, most have bath/WC, all have television • €49 to €100; breakfast €9; half-board available • Menus €26 (weekdays) to €55 • Terrace, park, car park. No dogs admitted in rooms • Board games, billiards

The total seclusion of this riverside mill.

However hard you listen, the only sounds you will hear are those of the countryside, but those who know the embattled history of the borderlands between France and Normandy may think they can still make out the distant echo of battle cries over the river. Nowadays the mill is a perfect haven of tranquillity, to which is added the pleasure of rooms decorated in period furniture and overlooking the river or the park. Beams, red floor tiles and open brickwork further enhance the rustic ambience.

Access: 1km to the north-east on the D 102 (towards Tillières-sur-Avre)

CENTRE AND UPPER LOIRE VALLEY

NOGENT-LE-ROTROU - 28400

11 L'AULNAYE
M. et Mme Dumas

Route d'Alençon
28400 Nogent-le-Rotrou
Tel. 02 37 52 02 11
http://laulnaye-accueil-France.com

Open all year • 3 rooms with bath/shower and WC • €65 to €68, breakfast included • No table d'hôte • Park, car park. Credit cards not accepted, no dogs admitted

We most liked The tranquillity of the park so close to the town centre.

The main appeal of this almost Victorian-looking 19C mansion is its priceless position in the heart of a park full of countless species of trees and plants. The plush interior decoration is also worthy of note: a handsome wooden staircase leads up to the rooms, all of which boast parquet floors, period furniture and marble fireplaces. Delicious breakfasts are served in the wainscoted dining room in winter and in the delightful wrought-iron conservatory in the summer.

Access: 3.5km westbound from Nogent-le Rotrou towards Alençon

SAINT-AUBIN-DES-BOIS - 28300

12 L'ERABLAIS
M. et Mme Guinard

38 rue Jean-Moulin à Chazay
28300 Saint-Aubin-des-Bois
jmguinard@aol.com
www.erablais.com

Open all year • 3 non-smoking rooms, all have shower/WC • €33 to €45, breakfast included • No table d'hôte • Garden, private car park, kitchenette, library. Dogs not admitted • Bicycles rented

We most liked The peace and quiet of the countryside.

The 19C farmhouse, tucked away in a hamlet near Chartres, is made up of five buildings built from traditional materials. The former stables are now home to three attractive guest rooms (two of which have sloping ceilings) individually decorated on a flower theme. Home-made jams are served at breakfast which is taken on the terrace or in a room overlooking the fields of crops. Bicycles available on request; water-skiing and angling nearby.

Access: D 24 towards Senonches, at Saint-Aubin-des-Bois, left towards Chazay. On rue Jean Moulin, on the right.

CENTRE AND UPPER LOIRE VALLEY

SAINT-LAURENT-LA-GÂTINE - 28210

13 CLOS SAINT-LAURENT
M. et Mme James

Chemin départemental 113
28210 Saint-Laurent-la-Gâtine
Tel. 02 37 38 24 02
clos-st-laurent@fr.st
www.clos-st-laurent.fr.st

Closed 23 Dec to 2 Jan • 3 non-smoking rooms, all have bath/WC or shower/WC • €53 to €63, breakfast included • No table d'hôte • Garden, private car park. Dogs not admitted

We most liked: The tranquil location of this old farmhouse.

The Clos is a fine example of a successful conversion. The owners of this old farmhouse have created three spacious airy bedrooms, tastefully decorating them in a smart country style with bare beams, white walls and tiled floors. The bathrooms are equally praiseworthy. If you then add the delightful breakfast room complete with fireplace and the garden-terrace, you will agree that it is excellent value for money.

Access: By the N 154 head towards Dreux, Nogent-le-Roi exit by the D 26, then D 21 towards Anet. House opposite the church.

VILLIERS-LE-MORHIER - 28130

14 LES CHANDELLES
M. et Mme Simon

19 rue des Sablons, village les Chandelles
28130 Villiers-le-Morhier
Tel. 02 37 82 71 59
Fax 02 37 82 71 59
info@chandelles-golf.com
www.chandelles-golf.com

Open all year • 5 non-smoking rooms with bath/WC and television • €60 to €80, breakfast included • No table d'hôte • Garden, car park. No dogs admitted

We most liked: A wealth of leisure activities so close at hand.

An impressive wooden porch leads into this renovated 1840 farmhouse set in grounds where horses graze peacefully. The barn has been converted into a guest wing which features bold colour schemes and excellent bathrooms. Interesting old furniture picked up from antique dealers and flea markets adds character to the breakfast room. On the leisure side, you can choose between golf and horse-riding (the owner's twin passions – he is a golf pro) or try your hand at fishing.

Access: 8km northbound from Maintenon on the D 116, towards Coulomb

CENTRE AND UPPER LOIRE VALLEY

ARGENTON-SUR-CREUSE - 36200

15 MANOIR DE BOISVILLERS
M. et Mme Fournal

11 rue du Moulin-de-Bord
36200 Argenton-sur-Creuse
Tel. 02 54 24 13 88
Fax 02 54 24 27 83
manoir.de.boisvilliers@wanadoo.fr
www.manoir-de-boisvillers.com

Closed Jan • 16 rooms located in 2 buildings, all have bath/WC or shower/WC and television • €58 to €105 (€57 to €97 low season); breakfast €8 • No restaurant • Garden, private car park. No dogs admitted • Outdoor swimming pool, sun deck

Diving into the pool after a hot day's sight-seeing.

The Boisvilliers went into exile during the Revolution, but their manor house in old Argenton continues to honour their memory. Cheerful Jouy tapestries and antique furniture set the tone in the main wing which overlooks the valley, while the other wing is more modern. All the hotel's bedrooms have been lovingly renovated by the current owners, but the sitting room is resolutely modern with luxurious designer sofas, high-tech TV and striking modern works of art. Delightful garden.

Access : In the town centre, drive towards Gargilesse, turn right at Rue Paul Bert, left at Rue d'Orion then a sharp right

BOUESSE - 36200

16 CHÂTEAU DE BOUESSE
M. et Mme Lorry

36200 Bouesse
Tel. 02 54 25 12 20
Fax 02 54 25 12 30
château.bouesse@wanadoo.frf
www.chateau-bouesse.de

Closed Jan-Mar, Mon and Tue from Apr 1 to May 15 and from Oct 1 to end Dec • 12 rooms, all with WC/bath, 6 with television • €85 to €110, breakfast €10; half-board available • Menus €23 (weekdays) to €36 • Terrace, park, car park

The bedroom in the dungeon and raftered ceiling.

Joan of Arc, Charles VII, Louis XI and Charles VIII are just a few of the famous names to have stayed in this small fortified 13C castle. Today the charm of yesteryear can still be felt in the spacious bedrooms, some medieval-style with four-poster beds and fireplaces, others with a more intimate appeal, and in the elegant restaurant which boasts a 15C fresco on the ceiling and a lovely terrace overlooking the garden à la française. Wouldn't it be easy to get used to a life of luxury?

Access : In the centre of the village, 11km from Argenton-sur-Creuse by N 20

CENTRE AND UPPER LOIRE VALLEY

SAINT-BENOÎT-DU-SAULT - 36170

17 LE PORTAIL
Mme Boyer

Rue Émile-Surun
36170 Saint-Benoît-du-Sault
Tel. 02 54 47 57 20
Fax 02 54 47 57 20

Open all year • 3 rooms, one of which is a studio • €43 to €58, breakfast included • No table d'hôte • Credit cards not accepted, dogs admitted on request

Wandering around the historic medieval city.

A fortified gate, carved stone cross and spiral staircase bear witness to the venerable age of this beautiful 14C-15C former property of the Knights Templar. Character and authenticity emanate from the old beams and medieval or Renaissance inspired furniture in the bedrooms and apartment. The breakfast room is equally appealing and the lady of the house's gracious welcome is quite faultless.

Access : In the medieval city

SARZAY - 36230

18 MONTGARNI
M. et Mme Labaurie

36230 Sarzay
Tel. 02 54 31 31 05
Fax 02 54 31 30 10

Open all year • 5 non-smoking rooms • €43, breakfast included; half-board available • Table d'hôte €17 • Park, car park. Dogs not admitted • Outdoor swimming pool. Farm-grown produce

The gourmet owner-chef's inspired culinary talents.

This farming couple have been extending their friendly hospitality to guests in search of tranquillity and the good things in life for over 15 years. The rooms in the 19C mansion, half-hidden by greenery, are extremely comfortable. Only 100 % local produce crosses the threshold of the kitchen to become healthy, mouth-watering dishes. If you feel like some gentle exercise, the immense parkland which extends into the unspoilt Berry countryside offers some great walks.

Access : 1.5km southbound from Sarzay on the D 41 towards Chassignolles

CENTRE AND UPPER LOIRE VALLEY

AMBOISE - 37400

19 LE BLASON
M. Varin

11 place Richelieu
37400 Amboise
Tel. 02 47 23 22 41
Fax 02 47 57 56 18
leblason@wanadoo.fr
www.leblason.fr

Closed from 10 Jan to 10 Feb • 25 rooms, 2 of which have disabled access, all have shower/WC and television • €49 to €56; breakfast €7 • Terrace, garage

We most liked
The easy-going atmosphere.

Leonardo da Vinci ended his days in this town, now home to a family inn offering appealing attic rooms with a dash of local character. If you're feeling downhearted, ask for one of the rooms facing the street, which overlook the "Rue Joyeuse". A discreetly rustic atmosphere reigns in the dining room and the terrace-veranda in the rear courtyard, where good home cooking can be savoured.

Access : On a square in the town centre

AZAY-LE-RIDEAU - 37190

20 DE BIENCOURT
Mme Marioton

7 rue Balzac
37190 Azay-le-Rideau
Tel. 02 47 45 20 75
Fax 02 47 45 91 73
biencourt@infonie.fr
www.hotelbiencourt.com

Open from 1 Mar to 15 Nov • 16 rooms located in the main building and the old school, with bath/WC or shower/WC, some have television • €47 to €53; breakfast €7 • No restaurant • Inner courtyard. No dogs admitted

We most liked
Being on the doorstep of a famous castle and parkland.

This elegant 18C property is tucked away in a semi-pedestrian street which leads to one of France's most beautiful Renaissance castles. Space and rustic furniture characterise the rooms, which have sloping ceilings on the top floor. A number of rooms decorated in Directoire style are also available in a building in the rear of the courtyard. Attractive cane-furnished sitting room, comfortable 19C-style dining room with a winter garden conservatory where breakfast is served.

Access : In the town centre (near the post office), on the semi-pedestrian street leading to the castle

CENTRE AND UPPER LOIRE VALLEY

CANGEY - 37530　　　　　　　　　　　**CHAMBOURG-SUR-INDRE - 37310**

21 LE FLEURAY
M. et Mme Newington

37530 Cangey
Tel. 02 47 56 09 25
Fax 02 47 56 93 97
lefleurayhotel@wanadoo.fr
www.lefleurayhotel.com

Open all year • 14 rooms with bath/WC or shower/WC and television, 6 with disabled access • €78 to €115; breakfast €11; half-board available • Non-smoking restaurant open only in evenings and by reservation; menus €28 to €48 • Terrace, garden, garage • Heated swimming pool

We most liked: Sauntering round the garden between fruit trees and the small pond.

The charm of the countryside, unmitigated peace and quiet and a matchless welcome explain the appeal of this beautifully restored farmhouse. Guests can choose between the comfortably cosy rooms in the main wing or those in the barn, which are more spacious and which open out directly onto the handsome swimming pool. The dining room aims for a Country Chic style and in summer, meals are served on a lovely terrace overlooking the countryside. The only drawback is having to say goodbye!

Access: 15km from Amboise on the N 152 to Blois and D 74 towards Cangey and Dame-Marie-des-Bois

22 LE CLOS DU PETIT MARRAY
M. et Mme Plantin

37310 Chambourg-sur-Indre
Tel. 02 47 92 50 67
Fax 02 47 92 50 67
serge.plantin@wanadoo.fr
www.opencom.fr/petitmarray

Open all year • 4 rooms with bathrooms • €52 to €62, breakfast included • Table d'hôte €26 (evenings only and by reservation) • Garden, car park. Credit cards not accepted, no dogs admitted in restaurant • Play area and fishing for children

We most liked: Walking along the banks of the Indre.

Children will enjoy fishing in the pond in the grounds of this handsome 19C farmhouse in the heart of the countryside. Names evocative of well-being and freedom have been given to each of the generously-sized and tastefully decorated rooms. A library and the nearby forest will keep you busy throughout your stay.

Access: 5km northbound from Loches on the N 143, towards Tours

CENTRE AND UPPER LOIRE VALLEY
CHINON - 37500 CINQ-MARS-LA-PILE - 37130

23 DIDEROT
M. et Mme Dutheil

4 rue de Buffon - 7 rue Diderot
37500 Chinon
Tel. 02 47 93 18 87
Fax 02 47 93 37 10
hoteldiderot@hoteldiderot.com
www.hoteldiderot.com

Closed fortnight early Jan • 27 rooms, 1 with disabled access, all have bath/WC or shower/WC, some have television • €51 to €71; breakfast €7 • No restaurant • Inner courtyard, private car park. No dogs admitted

Home-made lavender jam made with home-grown lavender!

Olive, banana, lemon, mandarin and medlar trees form a spectacularly exotic curtain of greenery to this 18C hotel acquired in the 1970s by the Cypriot owner. A classical accent is being given to the gradually renovated rooms, the quietest overlooking the courtyard. Home-made jams figure prominently on the breakfast table, served next to a crackling log fire in winter or out on the terrace whenever the weather permits.

Access : A short distance from the town centre, on a quiet street between Place Jeanne d'Arc and Rue Diderot

24 LA MEULIÈRE
M. et Mme Manier

10 rue de la Gare
37130 Cinq-Mars-la-Pile
Tel. 02 47 96 53 63
Fax 02 47 96 53 63
cgmanier-lameuliere@planetis.com
www.lameuliere.free.fr

Open all year • 3 rooms with bathrooms • €44 to €52, breakfast included • No table d'hôte • Garden, car park. Credit cards not accepted, no dogs admitted

The tranquillity of this establishment within walking distance of the station.

The uncontested bonus of this handsome 19C mansion is its situation close to the station without any of the noise or fuss you might expect. A fine wooden staircase takes you up to colourful, well-soundproofed rooms furnished with antiques. A comfortable dining room provides the backdrop to breakfasts. In the summer, deck chairs can be found in the garden for a quiet afternoon nap.

Access : Near the railway station

CENTRE AND UPPER LOIRE VALLEY

CIVRAY-DE-TOURAINE - 37150

25 CHAMBRE D'HÔTE LA MARMITTIÈRE
M. et Mme Boblet

22 Vallée-de-Mesvres
37150 Civray-de-Touraine
Tel. 02 47 23 51 04
marmittiere@libertysurf.fr
http://perso.libertysurf.fr/marmittiere

Open from 16 Mar to 14 Nov • 3 non-smoking rooms • €56, breakfast included • Table d'hôte €22 (closed Sat-Sun and by reservation only) • Terrace, garden, car park. Credit cards not accepted, no dogs admitted

We most liked: Breakfasts and dinners are prepared with 100 % organic produce.

The breakfast room and table d'hôte are located in a 17C wine-growers home, while the rooms have been fitted out in an early 20C stone villa. The interior decoration, although contemporary and highly colourful, blends in wonderfully with the old walls. To wind up this enticing picture, take a stroll round the garden and be ready to encounter some of its residents – the estate's donkeys and chickens – roaming freely.

Access : 4km westbound of Chenonceaux on the D 40 then a minor road

CONTINVOIR - 37340

26 LA BUTTE DE L'ÉPINE
M. Bodet

37340 Continvoir
Tel. 02 47 96 62 25
Fax 02 47 96 07 36
mibodet@wanadoo.fr
www.labutte delepine.com

Closed from 15 Dec to 15 Jan • 3 non-smoking rooms, one of which is upstairs • €60, breakfast included • No table d'hôte • Park. Credit cards not accepted, no dogs admitted

We most liked: The amazing care taken to restore this period house to its former glory.

The owners have spent years faithfully restoring this delightful residence of 16C-17C origins using only authentic materials. The sitting-breakfast room is imaginatively strewn with period furniture and features a huge fireplace. The spotless rooms are genuine boudoirs, the most romantic of which is upstairs. Well-tended flower-beds grace the park behind the house.

Access : 2km eastbound from Gizeux on the D 15

CENTRE AND UPPER LOIRE VALLEY
HUISMES - 37420   LANGEAIS - 37130

27 LA PILLETERIE
Mme Prunier

37420 Huismes
Tel. 02 47 95 58 07
Fax 02 47 95 58 07
www.lapilletrie.com

Open all year • 4 rooms • €57 to €65, breakfast included • No table d'hôte • Garden, car park. Credit cards not accepted, no dogs admitted • Nearby: Châteaux of Azay le Rideau, Villandry, etc.

The convenient situation near the castles of Azay and Villandry.

If in dire need of a break from the stress of urban life, this 19C farm in the middle of the countryside is just what the doctor ordered. Original red floor tiles add character to the rustic rooms, the quietest of which are located in an independent cottage. Young children adore the sheep, geese and other farmyard animals all of whom happily cohabit in a single pen. Relaxed and friendly hosts will make you feel at home the moment you arrive.

Access : 6km northbound from Chinon on the D 16

28 MAISON ERRARD
M. et Mme Errard

2 rue Gambetta
37130 Langeais
Tel. 02 47 96 82 12
Fax 02 47 96 56 72
info@errard.com
www.errard.com

Closed Dec, Jan, Mon and Tue lunchtime and Sun evening from Oct to Apr • 10 rooms with bath/WC and television • €67 to €94; breakfast €12 • Air-conditioned restaurant; menus €29 to €49 • Terrace, garage

The gargantuan hospitality of this provincial inn.

This hostelry is surrounded by some of Touraine's most beautiful castles and within walking distance of Langeais. Guests can choose between plush 19C or contemporary rooms, but those overlooking the street are noisier, even though the traffic can hardly be called "busy" after nightfall. Any doubts you may still have that you are in the birthplace of Rabelais' Gargantua, epic trencherman, will immediately vanish at the sight of the Brobdingnagian dishes liberally washed down with Loire wines.

Access : In the town centre, opposite the tourist office

CENTRE AND UPPER LOIRE VALLEY

LIGRÉ - 37500

29 LA MILAUDIÈRE
M. Marolleau

5 rue St-Martin
37500 Ligré
Tel. 02 47 98 37 53
Fax 02 47 98 37 52
milaudiere@club-internet.fr
www.milaudiere.com

Open all year • 6 rooms, one of which is on the ground floor and 3 are upstairs • €43 to €60, breakfast included • No table d'hôte • Car park. Credit cards not accepted, no dogs admitted

We most liked: The owners' exquisite charm and hospitality.

The walls of this original old 18C house are built out of "tuffeau", a soft local chalk. The owners dug in and undertook the majority of the restoration work themselves and can rightly be proud of the result. The rooms under the eaves are extremely pleasant and those on the ground floor with their old tiled floors, net curtains and rustic furniture are full of character. The breakfast room which boasts an old bread oven is also something of an eye-opener.

Access: 8km to the south-east of Chinon, towards Île-Bouchard on the D 749, then take the D 29

PANZOULT - 37220

30 DOMAINE DE BEAUSÉJOUR
M. et Mme Chauveau

37220 Panzoult
Tel. 02 47 58 64 64
Fax 02 47 95 27 13
info@domainedebeausejour.com
www.domaine.de.beausejour.com

Open all year • 3 rooms • €75 to €90 (€70 to €80 low season), breakfast included • No table d'hôte • Car park. Credit cards not accepted, no dogs admitted • Outdoor swimming pool

We most liked: Relaxing on a genuine wine-growing estate in Gargantua's homeland: in vino veritas!

This delightful house was built in 1978 from old materials gleaned in the region, some said to be three centuries old! The slate floors of the carefully decorated rooms contrast beautifully with the choice antique furniture. The superb view over Rabelais' beloved Chinon vineyards bodes well for a pleasant stay; those who so desire can taste some of the estate's best vintages in the company of the proprietress.

Access: 5km north-west of Bouchard on the D 757, then drive towards Chinon on the D 21

CENTRE AND UPPER LOIRE VALLEY

SAINT-BRANCHS - 37320

31 LE LOGIS DE LA PAQUERAIE
M. et Mme Binet

La Paqueraie
37320 Saint-Branchs
Tel. 02 47 26 31 51
Fax 02 47 26 39 15
monique.binet@wanadoo.fr
http://perso.wanadoo.fr/lapaqueraie/

Open all year • 4 rooms with bathrooms and one gîte • €85, breakfast included; half-board available • Table d'hôte €26 (beverages included) • Garden, car park. Credit cards not accepted • Outdoor swimming pool. Fishing, hiking, tennis, 18-hole golf course and riding nearby

The delightful landscaped garden and swimming pool.

The traditional regional architectural style, rampant curtain of Virginia creeper and the venerable old oaks in the park all combine to lend this recently built house a much older feel! The rooms display an excellent blend of practicality, comfort and sophistication. Mirrors, antiques and an original fireplace grace the sitting room. At mealtimes, you will sample classic French cooking made with local produce. If still not convinced, the peace and quiet of the grounds are bound to win you over.

Access : On leaving Cormery (coming from Tours) take the D 32 and turn right after the level-crossing

VERNOU-SUR-BRENNE - 37210

32 LES PERCE-NEIGE
M. et Mme Chartier

13 rue Anatole-France
37210 Vernou-sur-Brenne
Tel. 02 47 52 10 04
Fax 02 47 52 19 08
perceneige@perceneige.com
www.perceneige.com

Closed Nov • 5 rooms, with bath/WC or shower/WC • €50 to €70; breakfast €5 • No restaurant • Terrace, garden, private car park. Credit cards not accepted

The peaceful village encircled by the vineyards of Vouvray.

This modest 19C mansion formerly served as the offices of the solicitor of Vernou. An "old world" aura still pervades the rooms, which vary in comfort: book one which overlooks the spacious gardens and the old well. Local Loire dishes and wines are served in two elegant dining rooms and on the terrace to a backdrop of greenery and flowers.

Access : In the centre of the village, 4km eastbound from Vouvray (D 46)

CENTRE AND UPPER LOIRE VALLEY

BOURRÉ - 41400

33 MANOIR DE LA SALLE DU ROC
M. et Mme Boussard

69 route de Vierzon
41400 Bourré
Tel. 02 54 32 73 54
Fax 02 54 32 47 09
boussard.patricia@wanadoo.fr
www.manoirdelasalleduroc.monsite.wanadoo.fr

Open all year • 4 rooms • €70 to €110, (€70 to €100 low season), breakfast included • No table d'hôte • Park, car park. American Express cards not accepted, no dogs admitted • Tennis

We most liked **Luxury, calm and voluptuousness, a stone's throw from the troglodyte village of Bourré.**

A handsome tree-lined drive leads up to this pretty manor built against a rock face. The eye is naturally drawn to the welcoming façade, but also to the lovely park surrounding it, whose features include pools, old stone staircases, clipped boxwood hedges, statues, flowerbeds and over 500 rosebushes. The charm of the interior also greets the eye, whether in the ground-floor sitting rooms and the lovely library or upstairs in the comfortably furnished, plush bedrooms.

Access: 2km northbound of Montrichard on the D 62

CONTRES - 41700

34 LA RABOULLIÈRE
Mme Thimonnier

Chemin de Marçon
41700 Contres
Tel. 02 54 79 05 14
Fax 02 54 79 59 39
raboullière@wanadoo.fr
www.laraboullere.com

Open all year • 6 rooms, one of which is upstairs • €60 to €90, breakfast included • No table d'hôte • Park, car park. No dogs admitted

We most liked **The sophisticated decorative flair.**

The half-timbered walls of this Sologne farmhouse look so authentic it is hard to believe they were entirely built from materials found in neighbouring farms. The sumptuously furnished rooms all have exposed beams. Breakfasts are served by the fireside in winter and in the garden in summer. The gentle countryside is perfect for long country rambles.

Access: 10km southbound from Cheverny on the D 102, then a minor road

CENTRE AND UPPER LOIRE VALLEY

COUR-CHEVERNY - 41700

35 LE BÉGUINAGE
M. et Mme Deloison

41700 Cour-Cheverny
Tel. 02 54 79 29 92
Fax 02 54 79 94 59
le.beguinage@wanadoo.fr
www.lebeguinage.fr.st

Open all year • 6 rooms, 4 of which are in a separate wing • €50 to €95, breakfast included • No table d'hôte • Park, car park • Hot-air ballooning, golf, hiking

Flying over the Loire châteaux in a hot-air balloon.

The manicured park and pond are not the only treasures of this stone property covered in Virginia creeper. Parquet or tiled floors, exposed beams, fireplaces, king-size beds and generous dimensions all grace the sophisticated bedrooms: with the smallest measuring 20sq m, this is truly "the great indoors". For a quite matchless view of some of France's architectural gems, forget the cost and treat yourself to a flight over the Loire châteaux in a hot-air balloon piloted by the proprietor.

Access : In a park

LA VILLE-AUX-CLERCS - 41160

36 LE MANOIR DE LA FORÊT
M. et Mme Redon

Fort Girard
41160 La Ville-aux-Clercs
Tel. 02 54 80 62 83
Fax 02 54 80 66 03
manoirdelaforet@wanadoo.fr
www.manoirdelaforet.fr

Closed 2 weeks in Jan • 18 rooms on 2 floors, all have bath/WC or shower/WC and television • €51 to €90; breakfast €10; half-board available • Restaurant closed Sun evening and Mon from Oct to Easter; menus €27 to €48 • Terrace, park, car park

The suite with a terrace overlooking the park (sadly the most expensive!).

This redbrick and stone hunting lodge was built in the heart of the countryside on the edge of the forest of Fréteval. The slightly faded rooms are furnished with antiques and all overlook the immense 8-acre park. The tall French windows of the stately dining room are thrown open to the terrace and flowered garden. Two sitting rooms, also furnished with antiques, are perfect for a quiet after-dinner drink or coffee.

Access : 1.5km eastbound on a minor road

CENTRE AND UPPER LOIRE VALLEY

MONDOUBLEAU - 41170

37 CHAMBRE D'HÔTE PEYRON-GAUBERT
M. et Mme Peyron-Gaubert

Carrefour de l'Ormeau
41170 Mondoubleau
Tel. 02 54 80 93 76
Fax 02 54 80 93 76
i.peyron1@tiscali.fr
www.carrefour-de-lormeau.com

Open all year • 5 rooms with bathrooms • €43 to €48, breakfast included • Table d'hôte €22 (evening only, by reservation only) • Garden, car park. Credit cards not accepted, no dogs admitted • Exhibition and concert room

This one-off address, also a cabinetmaker's workshop.

The least you can say about this 17C redbrick house is that it is unusual, home to both a B&B establishment and exhibition hall for the cabinetmaker-owner's imaginative furniture. The rooms, of varying sizes, house some of the finished articles; simple, elegant waxed furniture made out of elm, ash and acacia wood. Concerts are sometimes held on the top floor. The garden to the rear is also very pleasant.

Access : In the town, opposite the Ford garage

PONTLEVOY - 41400

38 HÔTEL DE L'ÉCOLE
M. et Mme Preteseille

12 route de Montrichard
41400 Pontlevoy
Tel. 02 54 32 50 30
Fax 02 54 32 33 58

Closed from 20 Feb to 21 Mar, from 14 Nov to 6 Dec, Sun evening and Mon (except Jul-Aug and public holidays) • 11 rooms with bath/WC or shower/WC, some have television • €51 to €70; breakfast €10; half-board available • Menus €21 to €51 • Terrace, garden, private car park. No dogs admitted

The delightful flowered garden and murmuring fountain.

You'll immediately reach for your camera when you catch sight of this adorable house covered in variegated vine and surrounded by masses of brightly coloured geraniums. A distinctly old-fashioned feel in the rooms is compensated for by their size and spotless upkeep. Tables are prettily laid out in one of two rustic dining rooms or on the pleasing shaded terrace. What better invitation to enjoy finely judged dishes which make the most of local produce!

Access : In the town centre, on the D 764 between Montrichard and Blois

CENTRE AND UPPER LOIRE VALLEY

SAINT-DYÉ-SUR-LOIRE - 41500

39 MANOIR DE BEL AIR
M. Abel

1 route d'Orléans
41500 Saint-Dyé-sur-Loire
Tel. 02 54 81 60 10
Fax 02 54 81 65 34
manoirbelair@free.fr
www.manoirbelair.com

Closed 15 Jan to 20 Feb • 43 rooms located in 3 wings, with bath/WC (3 shower/WC) and television • €60 to €89 (€54 to €75 low season); breakfast €7; half-board available • Menus €24 to €46 • Inner courtyard, park, private car park. Dogs not admitted in restaurant

We most liked
Ambling down the old towpath which skirts the hotel.

A wine merchant and governor of Guadeloupe was among the proprietors of this elegant 17C manor house made out of "tuffeau", the chalky local stone. Most of the rooms have been renovated as has the restaurant which features a fine stone fireplace and regional furniture. All command fine views of the Loire. Pleasant leafy park.

Access : 15km from Blois towards Orléans, on the D 951 bordering the Loire

SAINT-GEORGES-SUR-CHER - 41400

40 LE PRIEURÉ DE LA CHAISE
Mme Duret-Therizols

8 rue du Prieuré - Lieu-dit la Chaise
41400 Saint-Georges-sur-Cher
Tel. 02 54 32 59 77
Fax 02 54 32 69 49
prieuredelachaise@yahoo.fr
http://www.prieuredelachaise.com

Open all year • 4 non-smoking rooms • €60 to €115, breakfast included • No table d'hôte • Garden, car park, park. Credit cards not accepted, no dogs admitted • Outdoor swimming pool

We most liked
Tasting the estate's wines.

A chance to stay in this former priory built in the heart of a wine-growing estate should not be missed. Next door to a magnificent 13C chapel (Mass is still celebrated here once a year), the 16C manor and its rooms are all equally elegant: soft stone walls, red-brick tiles, beams, fireplace and antique furniture and tapestries. The 17C outhouses have been converted into a wine-growing museum which you will come upon as you stroll around the tree-lined grounds.

Access : 2km southbound of St-Georges-sur-Cher on the D 27A

CENTRE AND UPPER LOIRE VALLEY

SELLES-SAINT-DENIS - 41300

41 LES ATELLERIES
Mme Quintin

41300 Selles-Saint-Denis
Tel. 02 54 96 13 84
Fax 02 54 96 13 78
caroline.quintin@wanadoo.fr
www.lesatelleries.com

Closed during Feb school holidays • 4 rooms with bath/WC • €52, breakfast included • No table d'hôte • Sitting room, park. Credit cards not accepted, no dogs admitted

We most liked — The beautiful Sologne countryside surrounding this farm.

Set in a 150-acre estate of woodland, moors and ponds, this old Sologne farm is sure to appeal to small-game hunters. Dog kennels are available and guests can go out hunting for the day with locals who know all the best coverts. As for the accommodation, the rooms are soberly decorated and well kept, two are installed in the former bakery where the old bread oven is still visible. Bicycles can be rented from the estate.

Access: 16km to the north-east of Romorantin-Lanthenay on the D 123 between Selles-Saint-Denis and Marcilly.

THÉSÉE - 41140

42 LE MOULIN DE LA RENNE
M. Suraud

11 Route de Vierzon
41140 Thésée
Tel. 02 54 71 41 56
Fax 02 54 71 75 09
contact@moulindelarenne.com
www.moulindelarenne.com

Closed from mid-Jan to mid-Mar Tue lunchtime (high season) Sun evening and Mon • 15 rooms on 2 floors, almost all have bath/WC or shower/WC • €46 to €51; breakfast €8; half-board available • Menus €16 (weekdays) to €39 • Terrace, garden, car park • Children's play area

We most liked — Walking next to the peaceful river as far as the first of the ponds of Sologne.

Once upon a time, there lived an old mill surrounded by a shaded garden through which passed the River Renne. Nearly all the simply decorated rooms have been renovated mirroring the dining room's bright, bold colours. An aquarium, a fireplace and children's games are most appreciated in the spacious sitting room, while the terrace on the banks of the millpond adds the finishing touch.

Access: Between Montrichard and Noyers-sur-Cher on the D 176, on the banks of the Renne.

CENTRE AND UPPER LOIRE VALLEY

AMILLY - 45200

43 BELVÉDÈRE
M. Massicard

192 rue Jules Ferry
45200 Amilly
Tel. 02 38 85 41 09
Fax 02 38 98 75 63
h.belvedere@wanadoo.fr
http://perso.wanadoo.fr/hbelvedere

Closed 16 Dec to 2 Jan and 13 to 31 Aug • 24 rooms (12 non-smoking) with bath/WC or shower/WC, all with television • €51 (€43 Fri and Sat from 14 Oct to 30 Apr) • No restaurant • Private car park, garages, garden. No dogs admitted in breakfast room

We most liked The calm which prevails in this family-run establishment.

Trees and flowers abound in the garden which takes visitors into the house hidden in a quiet neighbourhood on the outskirts of Montargis. Its countrified charm is enhanced by the rooms, which while they are not enormous, are stylishly and individually decorated with colourful wallpaper, pretty fabrics, antique furniture, knickknacks and potted plants. Non-smoking rooms are available for those that wish (enquire on booking).

Access: 4km southbound of Montargis, on the D 943 towards Auxerre, then follow Centre Ville, opposite the school

BRIARE - 45250

44 DOMAINE DE LA THIAU
Mme Bénédicte François Ducluzeau

Route de Gien
45250 Briare
Tel. 02 38 38 20 92
Fax 02 38 38 06 20
lathiau@club-internet.fr
http://lathiau.club.fr

Open all year • 4 non-smoking rooms upstairs • €46 to €59, breakfast included; half-board available • No table d'hôte • Garden, car park. Credit cards not accepted • Tennis, bicycle rentals

We most liked The private lane through the estate that leads down to the banks of the Loire.

It is impossible not to miss the ancient old trees, one of which is over two hundred years old, that have taken root in the extensive grounds around this graceful 18C house. The rooms have a pleasantly old-fashioned appeal with flowered wallpaper and period-style patterns on the walls and family heirlooms and antiques picked up in the region. Tennis courts, table tennis and bicycle rentals on the estate.

Access: 300m from the Loire

CENTRE AND UPPER LOIRE VALLEY

CHAILLY-EN-GÂTINAIS - 45260

45 LA FERME DU GRAND CHESNOY
M. Chevalier

45260 Chailly-en-Gâtinais
Tel. 02 38 96 27 67
Fax 02 38 96 27 67
bclechesnoy@yahoo.fr

Closed from 1 Dec to 31 Mar • 4 non-smoking rooms with bathrooms • €60, breakfast included • No table d'hôte • Sitting room, garden, car park. Credit cards not accepted, no dogs admitted in rooms • Tennis, billiards

We most liked: The country spirit of the decoration.

This immense two-hundred-acre estate of woodland, fields and ponds surrounds an immense property built on the banks of the Orléans Canal. Luckily, the owners retained the original parquet floors, family heirlooms, antiques and tapestries in the rooms installed in the 1896 tower. The extremely generously-sized bathrooms are very well fitted-out. A charming dovecote, tennis courts and countless footpaths into the immense forest complete the picture.

Access : 8.5km northbound from Lorris on the D 44, take the Bellegarde road and then the minor road on the right

CHÉCY - 45430

46 LES COURTILS
Mme Monthel

Rue de l'Avé
45430 Chécy
Tel. 02 38 91 32 02
Fax 02 38 91 48 20
les-courtils@wanadoo.fr
www.france-bonjour.com/les-courtils/

Open all year • 4 rooms with bathrooms • €50, breakfast included • No table d'hôte • Garden. Credit cards not accepted, no dogs admitted

We most liked: The owners' loving care and attention is visible in every tiniest detail.

The moment you cross the threshold, you begin to feel at home! The view of the Loire is quite exceptional and the interior decoration rises to the challenge. Flowered fabrics, a tasteful blend of beiges and creams, antique and modern furniture, tiled floors. Each room is named after a local plant – let's see whether you can match the English to the French: "Bitter Apple", "Morning Glory", "Honeysuckle" and "Nasturtium". The friezes in the bathrooms were hand-stencilled.

Access : 10km eastbound from Orléans on the N 460

CENTRE AND UPPER LOIRE VALLEY

LA FERTÉ-SAINT-AUBIN - 45240

47 LA VIEILLE FORÊT
Mme Ravenel

Route de Jouy-le-Potier
45240 La Ferté-Saint-Aubin
Tel. 02 38 76 57 20
Fax 02 38 64 82 80
www.vieilleforetra@aol.com

Closed during the February school holidays • 2 rooms • €48, breakfast included • No table d'hôte • Garden, car park. Credit cards not accepted, no dogs admitted

The beautiful Sologne scenery surrounding this handsome 20-acre property.

This brick farmhouse, which stands at the end of a forest path frequented by deer, is equally popular with families, walkers, anglers (there's a pond) and those who've had enough of towns in general, at least for a little while. The converted stables are now home to mainly modern looking rooms, with one exception, which has a beautiful tiled floor and fireplace.

Access: 5.5km to the north-west of Ferté-Saint-Aubin on the D 18, and take the lane on the right

MARIGNY-LES-USAGES - 45760

48 LES USSES
M. Marin

145 rue du Courtasaule
45760 Marigny-les-Usages
Tel. 02 38 75 14 77
Fax 02 38 75 90 65
kris.marin@wanadoo.fr
www.france-bonjour.com/marigny

Closed from 20 to 29 Dec • 3 rooms with bath/WC, television and telephone • €55, breakfast included • No table d'hôte • Garden, car park. Credit cards not accepted, no dogs admitted • Children's play area, badminton court, mountain biking

The encroaching silence of the Forest of Orléans.

After two years of titanic work, this modest 1850 farmhouse has been brought back to life. The beautiful stone walls are inviting and the interior makes you want to stay forever. Period furniture graces the bedrooms, equipped with excellent bathrooms. Breakfast is served in the old stables, complete with manger. The silence of the vast garden is interrupted only by the leaves rustling in the dense forest.

Access: 12km to the north-east of Orléans, towards Pithiviers on the N 152

CENTRE AND UPPER LOIRE VALLEY

NEVOY - 45500

49 LE DOMAINE DE SAINTE-BARBE
Mme Le Lay

45500 Nevoy
Tel. 02 38 67 59 53
Fax 02 38 67 28 96
annielelay@aol.com
www.france-bonjour.com/sainte-barbe/

Closed from 20 Dec to 6 Jan and 10 to 28 Aug • 4 rooms, 3 of which have bathrooms, and one gîte 25m from the house • €65, breakfast included • No table d'hôte • Garden, car park. Credit cards not accepted, no dogs admitted • Outdoor swimming pool, jacuzzi, tennis

We most liked
The easy-going personality of the hospitable lady of the house.

This house is imbued with the charm of homes which have belonged to the same family for generations. A few decorative touches from the lady of the house have lent the interior chintz fabrics, tiled floors, ornaments and old furniture. The rooms, some of which have a canopied bed, overlook the garden. Breakfast is served on the terrace overlooking fields and woods in the summer. For those who can't tear themselves away, there's also an independent self-catering holiday cottage.

Access : 4km north-west of Gien towards Lorris, after the level-crossing take the second road on the left and follow the signs

POILLY-LEZ-GIEN 45500

50 VILLA HÔTEL
M. et Mme Petit

Z. A. Le Clair Ruisseau
45500 Poilly-lez-Gien
Tel. 02 38 27 03 30
Fax 02 38 27 03 43

Open all year • 24 rooms with shower/WC and television, 2 rooms have disabled access, 10 rooms are non-smoking • €33, breakfast €5; half-board available • Restaurant closed Fri, Sat and Sun, day before national holidays and national holidays, evenings only; menus €11 to €14 • Car park

We most liked
A visit to the delightful museums of Gien, one devoted to porcelain, the other to hunting.

Book your room well in advance because this hotel is often full. Its success can be explained by its quiet neighbourhood location, friendly welcome, modern comforts and immaculate upkeep, though the delightful rooms are not exactly enormous. In the kitchen, the lady of the house rustles up a different main dish every evening and starters and desserts are available from a buffet. Gien porcelain plates adorn the restaurant walls.

Access : 2km south-west of Gien on the D 940 towards Bourges

CHAMPAGNE-ARDENNE

It is easy to spot visitors bound for Champagne-Ardenne by the sparkle in their eyes and a sudden, irrepressible delight when they finally come face to face with mile upon mile of vineyards: in their minds' eye, they are already uncorking a bottle of the famous delicacy which was known as "devil's wine" before a monk discovered the secret of Champagne's divine bubbles. As they continue their voyage, the beautiful cathedral of Reims rises up before them and they remember the delicious taste of its sweet pink biscuits delicately dipped in a glass of demi-sec. At Troyes, their eyes drink in the sight of tiny lanes lined with half-timbered houses while their palate thrills to the flavour of andouillettes, the local chitterling sausages. After such indulgence, our pilgrims welcome the sanctuary of the dense Ardennes forests, bordered by the meandering Meuse. But far from fasting and penitence, this woodland retreat offers a host of undreamt-of delights: the graceful flight of the crane over an unruffled lake or the prospect of sampling the famous Ardennes wild boar.

- Ardennes (08)
- Aube (10)
- Marne (51)
- Haute-Marne (52)

CHAMPAGNE ARDENNE

CHÂTEL-CHÉHÉRY - 08250

RUMIGNY - 08290

1 CHÂTEAU DE CHÂTEL
M. et Mme Huet

08250 Châtel-Chéhéry
Tel. 03 24 30 78 54
Fax 03 24 30 25 51
jacques.huet9@wanadoo.fr
http://perso.fr/chateaudechatel

Closed Sun evenings • 3 rooms • €70 to €80 (€60 to €70 low season), breakfast included; half-board available • Table d'hôte €22 (evening only) • Park, car park. Credit cards not accepted, dogs not admitted • Outdoor swimming pool

2 LA COUR DES PRÉS
M. Avril

08290 Rumigny
Tel. 03 24 35 52 66
Fax 03 24 35 52 66
la-cour-des-pres@laposte.net

Closed from Nov to Mar • 2 rooms • €65 to €70, breakfast included • No table d'hôte • Park, car park. Credit cards not accepted, dogs not admitted • Castle visits (except Tue), dinner-concerts in the summer

A glass of champagne is offered to guests on the "Gastronomic" package.

This 18C hillside castle and park dominating the Aire Valley has charm in abundance. Despite major renovation work, numerous traces of the apartments' former glorious days are still visible, including a superb staircase, huge fireplaces and period furniture. All the well-dimensioned rooms have excellent bathrooms. A wide choice of leisure activities is also available with swimming pool, tennis courts on request and walking or cycling trails.

The lady of the house's spontaneity and warmth.

It would be difficult to find somewhere more authentic than this moated stronghold, built in 1546 by the provost of Rumigny. The present owner, a direct descendant, is clearly proud of her roots and only too happy to relate her family's history. The wood panelling and period furniture in the rooms are original, as is the magnificent dining room in what was formerly the guard room. Stroll round the park and admire the ancestral beeches.

Access: 9km to the north-west of Varennes-en-Argonne on the D 38A and then the D 42

Access: On the D 877, entering the village from the east, on the corner of the D 27

CHAMPAGNE ARDENNE

BRÉVONNES - 10220

③ AU VIEUX LOGIS
M. et Mme Baudesson

1 rue de Piney
10220 Brévonnes
Tel. 03 25 46 30 17
Fax 03 25 46 37 20
logisbrevonnes@wanadoo.fr
www.auvieuxlogis.com

Closed from 6 to 30 Mar, Sun eve and Mon • 5 rooms with shower/WC and television • €42 to €52; breakfast €7; half-board available • Menus €16 (weekdays) to €40 • Terrace, garden, private car park • At the edge of the regional park of Forêt d'Orient

We most liked: 140km of signposted footpaths through the Forêt d'Orient.

Fishing, water sports, or just walking along the shore: the lakes of Orient and Temple, names which recall the medieval religious orders who once owned the land, offer a wide range of activities. Right on the doorstep stands this recently spruced up "old abode", whose delightfully old-fashioned interior preserves the charm of times past. Country furniture, ornaments and flowered paper set the scene for this unostentatious and unpretentious establishment with a singularly friendly atmosphere.

Access: To the north-east of Troyes, drive 25km on the D 960, then at Piney take the D11

COURTERON - 10250

④ FERME DE LA GLOIRE DIEU
M. Ruelle

10250 Courteron
Tel. 03 25 38 20 67
Fax 03 25 38 21 78

Closed in Jan • 3 rooms • €37, breakfast included • Park, terrace, car park. Credit cards not accepted

We most liked: The delicious farm-grown produce which can be tasted there and/or taken home.

The sign "Farm to the Glory of God" rather gives the game away, even before you've had a chance to glimpse the fascinating architectural remains of the 13C monastery. This immense 16C fortified farm nestles at the foot of a valley; its pretty, well-kept rooms still have their original exposed stone walls. The profusion of patés, cooked meats and poultry, fresh from the farm, will entice even the most delicate of palates. Warm, friendly and very reasonably priced.

Access: 10km eastbound from Riceys on the D 70 then the N 71

CHAMPAGNE ARDENNE

ESTISSAC - 10190

ESTISSAC - 10190

5 DOMAINE DU VOIRLOUP
M. et Mme Hulo

3 place Betty-Dié
10190 Estissac
Tel. 03 25 43 14 27
le.voirloup@free.fr
www.vrlp.com

Open all year • 3 non-smoking rooms, all have bathrooms, television and telephone • €60, breakfast included • Table d'hôte €19 to €25 • Terrace, garden, car park. Credit cards not accepted, dogs not admitted • Internet available

6 LE MOULIN D'EGUEBAUDE
M. Mesley

10190 Estissac
Tel. 03 25 40 42 18
Fax 03 25 40 40 92
eguebaude@aol.com

Open all year • 8 non-smoking rooms, 3 of which in a separate wing, all have bath/WC and television • €49 to €70, breakfast included • Table d'hôte €20 (evenings only) • Terrace, garden, car park, small kitchen. Credit cards not accepted, dogs not admitted • Sauna, fish farm

We most liked: The decoration of this immense bourgeois home built in 1904.

We most liked: Tasting the specialities of the Aubois region.

This comfortable bourgeois home, built in the early 20C in the middle of 8000m^2 of grounds, sports a smart tasteful interior. The simply decorated rooms are functional, furnished in a contemporary style and equipped with Wifi internet access, etc. Homemade cakes, bread and jams take pride of place on the breakfast table. The table d'hôte for its part offers family and regional dishes and when the weather is fine, meals are served out of doors beneath an arbour.

This old mill welcomes guests for a peaceful relaxing stay between woodlands and fish-farming ponds. In a regional Champagne-style building, three impeccably fitted and warmly decorated rooms have recently been added to the five already located in the mill itself. When she is not rustling up a local speciality or two (fillet of salmon with herb sauce), the owner can be found in her shop which specialises in regional delicacies.

Access : In the centre of the village

Access : In the town

CHAMPAGNE ARDENNE

LAUBRESSEL - 10270

7 LES COLOMBAGES CHAMPENOIS
Mme Jeanne

33 rue du Haut
10270 Laubressel
Tel. 03 25 80 27 37
Fax 03 25 80 80 67

Open all year • 6 rooms with shower/WC • €42, breakfast included • No table d'hôte • Garden, car park. Credit cards not accepted, dogs not admitted • Outdoor swimming pool

We most liked **Gazing over the meadows stretching over the horizon.**

Although built only 10 years ago from old materials gleaned from neighbouring ruins, these two enchanting half-timbered houses look as if they've always been here. The ingenious owner has even managed to rebuild a dovecote! The stylish rooms are a tasteful mixture of old beams and modern furniture. The kitchen serves mainly farm-grown produce.

Access : 7km to the north-east of Lusigny-sur-Barse on the N 19 and then the D 186

MOUSSEY - 10800

8 DOMAINE DE LA CREUSE
M. Le Borgne

10800 Moussey
Tel. 03 25 41 74 01
Fax 03 25 73 13 87
contact@domainedelacreuse.com
www.domainedelacreuse.com

Open all year • 3 non-smoking rooms on ground-floor, all have bath/WC • €85 to €95, breakfast included • No table d'hôte • Terrace, garden, garage. Credit cards not accepted, dogs not admitted

We most liked **The peace and quiet of the countryside – on the doorstep of Troyes.**

This traditional 18C timber-framed building stands in a small park planted with trees and flowers, set off from the main road. The brick outhouses are home to three spacious, good quality rooms, each with its own individual style. Breakfasts, served on flower-decked tables, are fully worthy of those of a luxury hotel. While the welcoming owner does not offer table d'hôte facilities, he can however make any number of recommendations to local establishments.

Access : 2km east of Moussey on the D 25 and the D 444

CHAMPAGNE ARDENNE

BOURSAULT - 51480

9 LA BOURSAULTIÈRE
Mme De Coninck

44 rue de la Duchesse-d'Uzès
51480 Boursault
Tel. 03 26 58 47 76
Fax 03 26 58 47 76

Open all year • 4 rooms • €60, breakfast included • No table d'hôte • Garden, car park. Credit cards not accepted

The mammoth breakfasts, liberally served with smiles.

Bordered by Champagne vineyards on all sides, this attractive stone house provides enchanting rooms lined with medieval or Renaissance-style printed fabrics. The luxurious bathrooms are lightened by beautiful Italian tiles. As soon as the sun shines, you will appreciate the refreshing cool of the paved courtyard, strewn with succulent green plants. Exemplary welcome.

Access: 9km westbound from Épernay on the N 3 and then the D 222

MAREUIL-SUR-AY - 51160

10 LA FAMILLE GUY CHARBAUT
M. et Mme Charbaut

12 rue du Pont
51160 Mareuil-sur-Ay
Tel. 03 26 52 60 59
Fax 03 26 51 91 49
champagne.guy.charbaut@wanadoo.fr
www.champagne-guy-charbaut.com

Open all year except Christmas and New Year's Day • 6 rooms with bath/WC • €65, breakfast included • Table d'hôte €40 (evening only) • Car park. No dogs admitted in restaurant • Visits to the family's vineyards and the wine cellars

The tour of the family estate's vineyard, cellars and grape presses.

Wine growers from father to son since 1930, the Charbauts bend over backwards to make your stay as pleasant as possible in their beautiful old house. They relish taking guests round the grape presses and cellars and introducing them to some of the best white and rosé vintage champagnes. All the airy, spacious rooms have their own sitting room and are decorated with period furniture. In the evenings, dinner is served in the superb wine cellar where the champagne, of course, flows freely!

Access: In the wine estate

CHAMPAGNE ARDENNE

MATOUGUES - 51510

11 LA GROSSE HAIE
M. et Mme Songy

Chemin de Saint-Pierre
51510 Matougues
Tel. 03 26 70 97 12
Fax 03 26 70 12 42
songy.chambre@wanadoo.fr

Closed 24 and 25 Dec • 3 non-smoking rooms upstairs • €42 to €45, breakfast included • Table d'hôte €18 to €27 (closed Sun) • Garden, park, car park. Credit cards not accepted, no dogs admitted • Farm visits

Breathing in the rich, evocative scents of the orchard.

A stone's throw from a farm which rears splendid Charolais cattle, this hospitable house knows how to tempt its guests into the out-of-doors. The children can romp unfettered in the orchard and the strawberries, artichokes and other cottage-garden delights are just waiting to be plucked, and, it comes as no surprise to discover, figure prominently on the menu. Pink, white and blue adorn the simply decorated rooms and the traffic on the nearby road will have almost disappeared by nightfall.

Access: 12km westbound from Châlons-en-Champagne on the D 3, towards Épernay

REIMS - 51100

12 CRYSTAL
Mme Jantet

86 place Drouet-d'Erlon
51100 Reims
Tel. 03 26 88 44 44
Fax 03 26 47 49 28
hotelcrystal@wanadoo.fr
www.hotel-crystal.fr

Closed 24 Dec to 3 Jan • 31 rooms, 23 of which have shower/WC, 8 have bath/WC, all have television • €50 to €68; breakfast €9 • No restaurant • Garden

The fully original lift shaft.

This 1920s house provides a welcome and unexpected haven of greenery and calm in the heart of busy Reims, sheltered from the bustle of Place Drouet-d'Erlon by a curtain of buildings. The rooms have recently been treated to good quality furniture and new bedding and the bathrooms are spruce and practical. In the summer, breakfast is served in the charming flowered courtyard-garden.

Access: In the town centre near the railway station

CHAMPAGNE ARDENNE

REIMS - 51100

SAINT-EUPHRAISE-ET-CLAIRIZET - 51390

13 UNIVERS
M. Bombaron

41 boulevard Foch
51100 Reims
Tel. 03 26 88 68 08
Fax 03 26 40 95 61
contact@hotel-univers-reims.com
www.hotel-univers-reims.com

Open all year • 42 rooms, 36 of which have bath/WC, 6 have shower/WC, all have television • €78 to €88 (€70 to €76 low season); breakfast €11 • Menus €18 (weekdays) to €40 • Public car park nearby

Sipping a glass of champagne at the hotel bar.

The Art Deco origins of this corner building built in 1932 opposite Colbert Square are betrayed by a number of architectural features. Excellent soundproofing, king size beds, wifi internet access, burr walnut furniture and beautiful bathrooms: the comfortable rooms are regularly spruced up. The stylish lounge-bar is snug and cosy and the restaurant is panelled in dark wood.

Access : Near the railway station, opposite Colbert Gardens

14 CHAMBRE D'HÔTE DELONG
M. et Mme Delong

24 rue des Tilleuls
51390 Saint-Euphraise-et-Clairizet
Tel. 03 26 49 20 86
Fax 03 26 49 24 90
jdscom@wanadoo.fr
www.domainedelong.com

Open all year • 4 rooms, with bath/WC • €56, breakfast included • No table d'hôte • Car park. Dogs not admitted • Visits to the wine cellar and press. Hiking, mountain biking

Opening a bottle of champagne after visiting the estate's cellars.

This former cowshed has stylishly been given a new lease of life in the heart of a thriving family wine business. Exposed stone walls, beams and rafters add character while good quality bedding and furniture and pleasant bathrooms add comfort to the rooms. The equally attractive breakfast room boasts brick walls and a huge country dining table. The owner, a descendant of a long line of "vignerons", happily does the honours of his cellar and grape press.

Access : In the heart of the village

CHAMPAGNE ARDENNE

SAINT-RÉMY-EN-BOUZEMONT - 51290

15 AU BROCHET DU LAC
M. Gringuillard

15-17 Grande-Rue
51290 Saint-Rémy-en-Bouzemont
Tel. 03 26 72 51 06
Fax 03 26 73 06 95
info @ au-brochet-du-lac.com
www.au-brochet-du-lac.com

Closed from Christmas to New Year • 5 rooms • €45, breakfast included; half-board available • Table d'hôte €19 (evening only) • Sitting room, terrace, car park. Dogs not admitted in restaurant • Mountain bike rental and canoeing

Awaiting the arrival of the migratory birds over the nearby Lake Der.

This enchanting wood-framed house is the ideal spot to explore Lake Der-Chantecoq and try some of its countless leisure activities – boating, water-skiing, fishing, swimming. The house is very well-equipped and rents out mountain bikes and canoes. Pristine bedrooms are decorated with good country furnishings and wood features prominently in the red-tiled living room where a roaring fire is most welcome in winter.

Access : 6km westbound from Arrigny on the D 57 and the D 58, in the centre of the village and not far from the lake

CHAMOUILLEY - 52100

16 LE MOULIN
M. et Mme Forêt

52100 Chamouilley
Tel. 03 25 55 81 93
Fax 03 25 55 81 93

Open all year • 5 non-smoking rooms, all have bath/WC, power shower, satellite television • €53 to €57, breakfast included • Table d'hôte €27 (evenings only by reservation) • Garden, park, car park. Credit cards not accepted, dogs not admitted in dining room • Outdoor swimming pool, children's play area

The owner's warm welcome.

Close your eyes and imagine yourself transported to a haven of peace and quiet on an island between the tail race of this former mill and the River Marne, just a few steps from the town. A park and swimming pool await you outside, while indoors is a lovely sitting-cum-reading room. The rooms, furnished in a contemporary style, are tasteful and welcomingly understated; all boast faultless facilities (bathrooms with balneo showers, bath robes, etc). What's more, the owner's delightful smile and unaffected welcome cannot fail but appeal.

Access : Near the town centre, take small lane for 500m between Marne canal and river

CHAMPAGNE ARDENNE

LANGRES - 52200

17 LE CHEVAL BLANC
M. et Mme Chevalier

4 rue de l'Estres
52200 Langres
Tel. 03 25 87 07 00
Fax 03 25 87 23 13
info@hotel-langres.com
www.hotel-langres.com

Closed from 10 to 30 Nov • 22 rooms, 11 of which are in a separate wing and one has disabled access. All have bath/WC or shower/WC and television • €65 to €84; breakfast €9; half-board available • Restaurant closed Wed lunchtime; menus €27 to €75 • Garage

We most liked
A past which dates back to 834.

First an abbey, then a parish church, the White Horse became an inn during the Revolution and its walls could date from any time between the 9C to the 16C. One thing is sure though, they provide excellent natural soundproofing! The rooms in the "Diderot pavilion", a stone house opposite the main hotel, have been recently renovated and their vaulted ceilings and arches are full of character. Paintings and contemporary light fittings set the scene for the restaurant.

Access: In the town centre

PRANGEY - 52190

18 L'ORANGERIE
M. et Mme Trinquesse

Place Adrien-Guillaume
52190 Prangey
Tel. 03 25 87 54 85

Open all year • 3 rooms • €58 to €63, breakfast included • No table d'hôte • Credit cards not accepted, dogs not admitted

We most liked
The graceful feminine touch.

Gentility and the romantic reign supreme in this ivy-covered house, next door to the castle and church in a pleasantly secluded village, set in Champagne's unspoilt countryside. Charm fills the bright, cosy rooms, one of which, decorated in shades of blue, commands a view of the stately abode and its 12C tower. Best of all, though, is the lady of the house's exquisite welcome.

Access: 16km southbound from Langres on the N 74 and then the D 26

CHAMPAGNE ARDENNE
PRAUTHOY - 52190

19 **CHÂTEAU DE PRAUTHOY**
MM. Bugnod et Berchard

22 Grand'Rue
52190 Prauthoy
Tel. 03 25 84 95 70
Fax 03 25 87 37 19
ch.prauthoy@infonie.fr
www.chateaudeprauthoy.com

Closed 2 Jan to late Mar and Dec • 4 non-smoking rooms, including 2 apartments, with bath/WC or shower/WC • €99, breakfast included • No table d'hôte • Terrace, park, car park, satellite television, pianos • Outdoor heated swimming pool with sun deck

We most liked
A taste of the good life.

This fully restored 18C and 19C castle is set in extensive 5ha grounds complete with woodland, hundred-year-old trees, a swimming pool and sun deck. The two engaging owners welcome guests in a splendid Louis XV sitting room. Each of the rooms is furnished with pieces from different periods: Louis XVI, Napoleon III, etc. Make sure you admire the cave which links the inner courtyard to the former kitchens, now a genuine ecomuseum with objects and souvenirs from daily 19C life.

Access : In the centre of the village

CORSICA

Corsica catches the eye like a jewel glinting in the bright Mediterranean sun. Its citadels perched up high on the island's rocky flanks will amply reward you for your perseverance and courage as you embark upon the twisting mountain roads. Enjoy spectacular views and breathe in the fragrance of wild rosemary as you slowly make your way up the rugged, maquis-covered mountains. The sudden sight of a secluded chapel, the discovery of a timeless village or an encounter with a herd of mountain sheep are just a few of the prizes that travellers to the Île de Beauté take home in their memories. Corsicans are as proud of their natural heritage as they are of their history and traditions. Years of experience have taught them how to revive the weary traveller with platters piled high with cooked meats, cheese and home-made pastries. After exploring the island's wild interior, you will probably be ready to plunge into the clear turquoise waters and recharge your solar batteries as you bask on the warm sand of a deserted bay.

- Corse-du-Sud (2A)
- Haute-Corse (2B)

CORSE

CAP CORSE

Rogliano

Bastia

S.t Florent

I'Ile Rousse
Belgodère
Calvi
N 197
89
N 193
68
Vescovato
N 1197
Ponte-Leccia
N 198
D 81
2
70
Cervione
2706 △
M.te Cinto
Corte
Évisa
M.te Rotondo
△ 2622
48
N 200
Porto
159
Vizzavona
Aléria
D 81
Cargèse
84
Ghisonaccia

Ajaccio
N 193
St.e Marie-Sicché
N 198
Solenzara

N 196
8
100
5
13
Olmeto
Zonza
140
Propriano
11
Porto-Vecchio
Sartène
N 196 D 859

Bonifacio

CORSICA

FELICETO - 20225

1 MARE E MONTI
M. et Mme Renucci

20225 Feliceto
Tel. 04 95 63 02 00
Fax 04 95 63 02 01

Closed from 1 Nov to 30 Mar • 16 air-conditioned rooms with bath/WC or shower/WC • €81 to €114 (€58 to €77 low season); breakfast €7 • No restaurant • Car park. No dogs admitted • Swimming pool

The sweet scent of Corsica's wild flowers wafting over the sun-drenched terrace.

Exquisitely set between sea and mountains ("mare e monti" in Corsican), this is one of the rare "American palaces" of Balagne, of which there are many more around the coast of Cap Corse. After striking it rich in sugar cane, this family's ancestors returned from Puerto Rico in the 19C to build this elegant blue-shuttered white house. Character overflows from the slightly monastic rooms offset with brass beds, red floor tiles, fireplaces, etc. Delightful little chapel and exuberant garden.

Access : 20km southbound from Île-Rousse

GALÉRIA - 20245

2 A MARTINELLA
Mme Corteggiani

Route du Port
20245 Galéria
Tel. 04 95 62 00 44

Closed from late Oct to 15 Mar • 5 rooms on the first floor with private terraces • €63 (€52 low season), breakfast included • No table d'hôte • Garden, car park. Credit cards not accepted, dogs not admitted • Beach and the Scandola Nature Reserve nearby

Exploring the under-water treasures of the Nature Reserve of Scandola.

An unpretentious, excellently kept place, to which you should add the priceless location just 150m from a large pebble beach and the nature reserve of Scandola. It is easy to see why the place is so popular. The simple rooms all have their own private terrace, while the tranquillity of the garden and the owner's genuinely warm welcome all contribute to its charm.

Access : 150m from the beach

CORSICA

L'ÎLE-ROUSSE - 20220

3 FUNTANA MARINA
M. et Mme Khaldi

Route de Monticello
20220 L'Île-Rousse
Tel. 04 95 60 16 12
Fax 04 95 60 35 44
hotel-funtana-marina@wanadoo.fr
www.hotel-funtana.com

Open all year • 29 rooms with bath or shower • €85 to €91 (€49 to €62 low season); breakfast €9 • No restaurant • Car park. No dogs admitted • Outdoor swimming pool

We most liked
The site dominating the harbour of Île Rousse.

The narrow mountain lane that leads up to this recent house hidden by luxuriant vegetation is worth taking, if only to enjoy the super view of the sea and the harbour of Île Rousse. Comfortable renovated rooms all have matching bathrooms, but it's the panoramic swimming pool and your hosts' wonderful welcome that make this place so memorable.

Access: In the upper part of Île-Rousse, 1km drive

LURI - 20228

4 LI FUNDALI
M. et Mme Gabelle-Crescioni

Spergane
20228 Luri
Tel. 04 95 35 06 15

Closed from Nov to Mar • 16 rooms • €40 to €45, breakfast included; half-board available • Table d'hôte €14 • Terrace, garden, car park. Credit cards not accepted, dogs not admitted

We most liked
The owners' boundless hospitality.

This charming house, drenched in sunshine and encircled by foliage, nestles in a hollow (fundali) of the lush green valley of Luri. After trekking along the countless paths around the estate, you will happily return to a simple, yet immaculate room for a well-earned rest. Afterwards you can sit down around the large communal table and sample the delicious family recipes, under your host's attentive eye.

Access: In the valley

CORSICA

OLMETO - 20113

5 SANTA MARIA
M. et Mme Ettori

Place de l'Église
20113 Olmeto
Tel. 04 95 74 65 59
Fax 04 95 74 60 33
ettorinathalie @ aol.com
www.hotel-restaurant-santa-maria.com

Closed in Nov and Dec • 12 air-conditioned rooms with shower/WC and television • €53 (€40 to €48 low season); breakfast €6; half-board available • Menus €16 to €23 • Terrace

We most liked Realising how out of place the word "stress" seems on the Island of Beauty.

This old granite house which stands opposite the church has been gazing down on the Gulf of Valinco for over a century. A steep staircase leads up to practical, well-kept rooms, rather lacking in charm however. The vaulted dining room, the only remains of an old oil mill, is pleasant enough, but the highlight of the establishment has got to be the wonderful flowered terrace where you can sample Mimi's delicious cooking.

Access : In the centre of the village, 8km northbound from Propriano on the N 196

PIGNA - 20220

6 LA CASA MUSICALE
M. et Mme Casalonga

Fondu di u paese
20220 Pigna
Tel. 04 95 61 77 31
Fax 04 95 61 74 28
infos @ casa-musicale.org
www.casa-musicale.org

Closed from 7 Jan to 10 Feb and Mon from Nov to Mar • 7 rooms with bath/WC or shower/WC • €65 to €92 (€48 to €68 low season); breakfast €6; half-board available • À la carte €17 to €30 • Dogs not admitted • Live music (Corsican polyphonic concerts)

We most liked The "Terza" room with its tiny sun terrace reached by a ladder!

Keep it under your hat! This priceless gem can only be reached on foot through the lanes of its delightful high-perched village laden with the scent of bougainvillaea. The frescoes on the walls of the rooms are a work of art in themselves and all overlook the sea or Corsica's mountainous slopes. The restaurant can be found in a converted olive oil press and the idyllic terrace and concert room are regularly the scene of lively traditional Corsican musical evenings.

Access : Drive from Île-Rousse towards Calvi on the N 197, after 2km turn left onto the D 151 (8km); park on the square (pedestrian village)

CORSICA

PIOGGIOLA - 20259

7 A TRAMULA
M. Giovanetti

20259 Pioggiola
Tel. 04 95 61 93 54

Open all year • 7 rooms • €70 (€52 to €60 low season); breakfast €7 • No restaurant • Park, car park. Credit cards not accepted

We most liked **The warm welcome from the native Corsican owner who loves to talk about his country.**

The bedrooms on the first floor of this handsome stone-built house all display the same tasteful blend of salmon-coloured walls, terracotta floor tiles, new furniture and modern bathrooms. The bar and sitting room, heated by a stove and fireplace, are most welcoming. Pull on your walking boots and hike round the grounds on the slopes of the mountainside. The honey, lavishly served at breakfast time, is made by the owner himself.

Access: 1.9km westbound from Olmi-Cappella towards Tartagine forest

PORTICCIO - 20166

8 PIAGGIOLA
M. et Mme Paolini

20166 Porticcio
Tel. 04 95 24 23 79

Closed from late Jan to 15 Apr • 6 rooms • €62, breakfast included • Table d'hôte €20 • Car park. Credit cards not accepted, dogs not admitted • Swimming pool

We most liked **The vast estate surrounding the house, full of things to see.**

A warm welcome, innate sense of hospitality and tasty home-cooking are just a few of the many attractions of this neat granite house cradled in the heart of superb grounds. Admire the sweeping view of the Gulf of Valinco or the forest from the windows. The rooms are furnished with fine wardrobes. If you can tear yourself away from the beach, venture out into the grounds which are rich in surprises.

Access: 13km to the south-east of Agosta beach on the D 255A (towards Pietrosella), then right on the D 255

CORSICA

SAN-MARTINO-DI-LOTA - 20200

9 CHÂTEAU CAGNINACCI
Famille Cagninacci

20200 San-Martino-di-Lota
Tel. 06 78 29 03 94
Fax 06 76 43 01 44
www.chateaucagninacci.com

Closed from 1 Oct to 14 May • 4 rooms, 2 of which air-conditioned, overlooking the island of Elba • €92 to €97 (€76 to €81 low season), breakfast included • No table d'hôte • Terrace. Credit cards not accepted, dogs not admitted

We most liked: The utter peace and quiet of this spot hidden in greenery.

This lovely 17C Capuchin convent, remodelled in the 19C style of a Tuscan villa, is built on a steep mountain hillside. Tastefully renovated, it offers spacious rooms furnished with antiques, and immaculate bathrooms. Wherever you look, you are met with the superb view of the island of Elba and the sea. Taking breakfast on the terrace surrounded by greenery and warmed by the sun's first rays is a moment of sheer bliss.

Access: 10km to the north-west of Bastia on the D 80 (towards Cap Corse), then the D 131 at Pietranera

SAN-MARTINO-DI-LOTA - 20200

10 LA CORNICHE
M. Anziani

20200 San-Martino-di-Lota
Tel. 04 95 31 40 98
Fax 04 95 32 37 69
info@hotel-lacorniche.com
www.hotel-lacorniche.com

Closed in Jan • 19 rooms with bath/WC and television • €69 to €99 (€48 to €62 low season); breakfast €8; half-board available • Restaurant closed Mon and Tue lunchtime; menus €25 to €46 • Terrace, car park • Outdoor swimming pool

We most liked: The swimming pool on the flanks of the mountain, sheltered by a chestnut grove.

The shaded terrace of this establishment perched up high above Bastia is a feast for the eyes. Look out and savour the view of the two-storey bell tower and the houses of the old village cut into the rock face in sharp contrast with the deep blue water stretching out in the background. The practical rooms are gradually being individualised with terracotta tiles and hand-painted walls; they too command a view of the sea. The restaurant is known and appreciated for its excellent Corsican menu.

Access: 13km northbound from Bastia on the D 80, then turn left on the D 131

CORSICA

SARTÈNE - 20100

11 DOMAINE DE CROCCANO
M. et Mme Perrier

Route de Granace
20100 Sartène
Tel. 04 95 77 11 37
Fax 04 95 77 11 37
christian.perrier@wanadoo.fr
www.corsenature.com

Closed in Dec • 4 non-smoking rooms • €78 (€64 low season), breakfast included; half-board available • Non-smoking restaurant for half-board guests only • Terrace, park, car park. Dogs not admitted • Horse-riding on the estate

Waking up to the sight of horses cantering through the maquis.

Travellers in search of nature, silence and peace and quiet will fall in love with this solid granite house peeping out from behind a wilderness of cork oaks and olive trees. Beautiful old stone walls and vitrified cork floor tiles add style to the snug, cosy rooms. The lovely owners organise horse-rides through the fragrant Corsican shrub, or for those otherwise inclined, walking and botanic trails.

Access : 3.5km to the north-east of Sartène on the D 148

SPELONCATO - 20226

12 A SPELUNCA
Mme Princivalle

Place de l'Église
20226 Speloncato
Tel. 04 95 61 50 38
Fax 04 95 61 53 14
hotel.a.spelunca@wanadoo.fr

Closed from 1 Nov to 31 Mar • 17 rooms • €60 to €70 (€50 to €60 low season); breakfast €6 • No restaurant • Terrace

The sweeping view of the region of upper Balagne.

The stately architectural masterpiece you see before you is none other than the former palace of Cardinal Savelli, Minister of Police to Pope Pius IX. The vast halls, sitting rooms rich in period furniture, old light fixtures and turret still remain from its glorious past. The discreetly luxurious bedrooms are bathed in an aura of gentility; three command an enchanting view of the valley and village. Highly recommended.

Access : In the heart of the village

CORSICA

ZONZA - 20124

13 L'AIGLON
Mlle Quilichini

20124 Zonza
Tel. 04 95 78 67 79
Fax 04 95 78 63 62
info@aiglonhotel.com
www.aiglonhotel.com

Closed 15 Jan to 15 Apr and Mon out of season • 10 rooms • €60 to €70 (€51 to €54 low season); breakfast €7; half-board available • Menus €16 to €25 • Terrace, car park

We most liked **The regularly organised Corsican musical evenings.**

This venerable granite house standing in the heart of the village has committed itself to upholding the soul of Corsica. Much love and time has been poured into the stylish interior decoration where collections of old objects such as coffee grinders and irons are proudly displayed. Each of the small but delightful rooms is decorated in a different colour and two have sloping ceilings. The restaurant takes you on a gastronomic tour of Corsica's many local specialities.

Access : In the heart of the village

FRANCHE-COMTÉ

Once upon a time in a land called Franche-Comté... So begin many of France's tales and legends, inspired by the secret wilderness of this secluded region on the Swiss border. The Jura's peaks and dales are clad in a dark cloak of fragrant conifers, casting its magic charm over unwitting explorers of the range's grottoes and gorges. The spell is also woven by a multitude of torrents, waterfalls and deep, mysterious lakes, their dark blue waters reflecting the surrounding hills. The nimble fingers of local woodworkers transform its wood into clocks, toys and pipes which will delight anyone with a love of fine craftsmanship. Hungry travellers will be only too happy to give in to temptation and savour the rich hazelnut tang of Comté cheese, made to a recipe passed down through the generations. But beware, the delicate aroma of smoked and salted meats, in which you can almost taste the pine and juniper, together with the tempting bouquet of the region's subtle, fruity wines may well lure you back for more.

- Doubs (25)
- Jura (39)
- Haute-Saône (70)
- Ter.-de-Belfort (90)

FRANCHE COMTÉ

BAUME-LES-DAMES - 25110

1 HOSTELLERIE DU CHÂTEAU D'AS
MM. Patrick et Laurent Cachot

24 rue du Château-Gaillard
25110 Baume-les-Dames
Tel. 03 81 84 00 66
Fax 03 81 84 39 67
chateau.das@wanadoo.fr
www.château-das.fr

Closed from 24 Jan to 7 Feb, from 21 Nov to 4 Dec, Sun evening and Mon • 6 rooms with bath/WC or shower/WC and television • €57 to €74; breakfast €10; half-board available • Menus €19 to €68 • Terrace, car park

You either love or hate the local cheese speciality: Cancoillotte!

This comfortable house, which would blend in perfectly in any number of German or Swiss towns, was built on the heights of this little town in the 1930s. The light, airy and well-equipped rooms have recently been treated to a facelift. The dining room has however retained the grandeur of its bygone days with original light fixtures and grandfather clock. Classic cuisine.

Access: In the upper part of town, on the outskirts

CHALEZEULE - 25220

2 A L'HÔTEL DES TROIS ÎLES
M. Thierry

1 rue des vergers
25220 Chalezeule
Tel. 03 81 61 00 66
Fax 03 81 61 73 09
hotel.3iles@wanadoo.fr
www.hoteldes3iles.com

Closed from 26 Dec to 6 Jan • 17 rooms, two of which are non-smoking, all with bath/WC or shower/WC and television • €46 to €80; breakfast €7; half-board available • Menus €20 (evenings) • Terrace, car park, no dogs admitted in the restaurant

The tranquillity of this village nestling on the right bank of the Doubs.

Guests inevitably fall in love with the peaceful, pastoral setting of this large house with its steep roofline. The rooms are not really spacious but are well renovated and adorned with pleasantly rustic looking furniture. In the kitchen, the chef rustles up a new set menu every day solely for the benefit of his hotel guests. The dining room is equally appealing with its large bay windows, massive pine beams and gaily coloured tablecloths.

Access: 4km north-east of Besançon, in the heart of the village

FRANCHE COMTÉ

GOUMOIS - 25470

HAUTERIVE - 25650

3 TAILLARD
M. Taillard

3 route de la Corniche
25470 Goumois
Tel. 03 81 44 20 75
Fax 03 81 44 26 15
hotel.taillard@wanadoo.fr
www.hoteltaillard.com

Open from mid-Mar to mid-Nov • 21 rooms, 1 with disabled access, all have bath/WC or shower/WC and television • €60 to €110; breakfast €11; half-board available • Menus €30 to €70 • Terrace, garden, car park • Reading room, outdoor swimming pool, fitness room

An enchanting traditional hostelry nestled in greenery.

The Taillard family has been perfecting the art of hospitality since 1874 within the walls of this lovely hotel overlooking the Doubs Valley. The rooms in the annex, larger and more comfortable, are often preferred to those in the main wing which are due for a spot of sprucing up. In the predominantly warm wood finishings of the restaurant, classical dishes are spiced up with regional accents and accompanied by a fine wine list. Look out for the paintings by the master of the house.

Access: Overlooking the village

4 CHEZ LES COLIN
Mme Colin

25650 Hauterive-la-Fresse
chezlescolin@wanadoo.fr
www.chezlescolin.fr

Open all year • 6 rooms with washbasins • €80, full board • Car park. Credit cards not accepted, dogs not admitted

The sumptuous setting between meadows and fir trees.

This former customs house perched on a ridge of the Franco-Swiss Jura range is ideal for those in search of a 100 % nature and country stay. Each of the six rooms, furnished with regional pine, has its own wash-basin and shared showers and toilets on the landing. The mistress of the house takes great pleasure in whipping up tasty regionally-inspired dishes. Courses organised: yoga, watercolour painting, golf, cross-country skiing, etc.

Access: 10km southeast of Pontarlier, follow the D 47 between Pontarlier and Les Gras

FRANCHE COMTÉ

LA LONGEVILLE - 25650

5 LE CRÊT L'AGNEAU
M. et Mme Jacquet-Pierroulet

Les auberges
25650 La Longeville
Tel. 03 81 38 12 51
lecret.lagneau@wanadoo.fr
www.lecret-lagneau.com

Closed from 1 to 31 Jul • 7 rooms • €76 to €90, breakfast included • Table d'hôte €21 to €24 • Car park. Credit cards not accepted, no dogs admitted • Snowshoe trekking and cross-country skiing

We most liked **The countless excursions organised by the owner, a cross-country ski instructor.**

This superb 17C farmhouse, tucked away between fir trees and meadows has been offering accommodation and sustenance to all those "in the know" for over twenty years. Wood prevails in the cosy bedrooms. However the main reason for its lasting success is two-fold: first the generous helpings of locally-sourced food cooked by the lady of the house, and second the variety of outings on foot, mountain bikes, snowshoes or skis organised by the owner.

Access: 5.5km northbound from Montbenoît on the D 131 as far as La Longeville-Auberge

MALBUISSON - 25160

6 LE BON ACCUEIL
M. et Mme Faivre

Rue de la Source
25160 Malbuisson
Tel. 03 81 69 30 58
Fax 03 81 69 37 60
lebonaccueilfaivre@wanadoo.fr

Closed 24 Apr to 3 May, 30 Oct to 8 Nov, 18 Dec to 17 Jan, Sun evening, Mon and Tue lunchtime • 12 rooms, most of which have shower/WC, some have bath/WC, all have television • €60 to €75; breakfast €9; half-board available • Menus €26 to €47 • Garden, garage, car park. No dogs admitted

We most liked **The breakfast table laden with brioche, jams, home-made yoghurt and fresh fruit juice.**

On the edge of a forest of fir trees, this manicured, hospitable village inn is the sort of place you want to tell your friends about. Immaculate, modern, spacious rooms. Beautiful spruce wood rafters, brightly coloured blinds and large windows overlooking the forest set the scene for the recently extended dining room. The cherry on the cake is without doubt the deliciously inventive cooking.

Access: In the village, on a bend by the side of the road

FRANCHE COMTÉ

MONTBÉLIARD - 25200

7 LA BALANCE
M. et Mme Receveur

40 rue de Belfort
25200 Montbéliard
Tel. 03 81 96 77 41
Fax 03 81 91 47 16
hotelbalance@wanadoo.fr
www.hotel-la-balance.com

Closed at Christmas • 44 rooms with bath/WC and television; 2 rooms have disabled access and 5 are non-smoking • €79 to €100; breakfast €9; half-board available • Menus €14 to €22 • Terrace, private car park

We most liked
The Peugeot Adventure Museum.

At the foot of the castle, this 16C abode was the HQ of one of France's best-known Second World War generals, Marshal De Lattre de Tassigny. A beautiful old wooden staircase leads up to renovated, practical rooms of varying sizes. The warm old-fashioned style and light-wood panelling of the dining room is still visible. We loved the veranda where breakfast is served.

Access: In the main shopping street, at the foot of the castle

MOUTHIER-HAUTE-PIERRE - 25920

8 LA CASCADE
M. et Mme Savonet

4 route des Gorges-de-Noailles
25920 Mouthier-Haute-Pierre
Tel. 03 81 60 95 30
Fax 03 81 60 94 55
hotellacascade@wanadoo.fr

Closed from 1 Jan to 13 Mar • 17 rooms, one of which has disabled access, most have bath/WC, some have shower/WC, all have television • €48 to €61; breakfast €8; half-board available • Restaurant non-smoking only; menus €19 to €44 • Car park. No dogs admitted • Trout fishing and canoeing on the Loue

We most liked
Canoeing down the beautiful gorges of the River Loue.

The valley of the Loue is what you will see when you throw open the windows of the recently spruced-up rooms of this traditional old hostelry. Excellent family cooking is served in a non-smoking atmosphere, while huge bay windows provide guests with a restful view of the green landscape.

Access: On the main road, in the centre of the village

FRANCHE COMTÉ

ORNANS - 25290

9 LE JARDIN DE GUSTAVE
M. Rigoulot

28 rue Édouard-Bastide
25290 Ornans
Tel. 03 81 62 21 47
Fax 03 81 62 21 47
www.louelison.com

Open all year • 3 rooms, all with bath/WC or shower/WC • €60 to €78, breakfast included • Table d'hôte €20, drinks included • Terrace, television room, garage. Credit cards not accepted

We most liked
The owner's kind welcome.

This town house stands on the main street of Ornans alongside of which runs the Loue. Two of the rooms overlook the garden and river, while the third overlooks the street but is well sound-proofed. The personalised pleasant rooms were decorated by the owner herself; the "Jungle" room, for example, sports a distinctly exotic African inspiration... At mealtimes you will be treated to regional specialities in winter and lighter dishes, served in the garden, in the summer.

Access : In the town

PONT-LES-MOULINS - 25110

10 L'AUBERGE DES MOULINS
M. et Mme Porru

Route de Pontarlier
25110 Pont-les-Moulins
Tel. 03 81 84 09 99
Fax 03 81 84 04 44
auberge.desmoulins@wanadoo.fr

Closed from 22 Dec to 20 Jan, Sun evenings from Sep to Jun (except holidays) Sat lunchtime and fri • 14 rooms with bath/WC or shower/WC, all have television • €50; breakfast €7; half-board available • Menus €18 (weekdays) to €20 • Park, car park • Private fishing

We most liked
The wealth of magnificent natural sites: grottoes, nature reserves and unforgettable views.

Jura is renowned for its excellent trout and this place is bound to appeal to those bitten by the fishing bug: the country house stands in a park which boasts its very own private stream. Back at the hotel, relax in rooms of varying sizes and styles and dream of the one that got away. A cosy restaurant serves tasty regional dishes.

Access : Southbound from Baume-les-Dames, drive for 6km on the D 50

FRANCHE COMTÉ

VAUCLUSE - 25380

VERRIÈRES-DE-JOUX - 25300

11 LE MOULIN
M. et Mme Malavaux

Le Moulin du Milieu, Route de Consolation
25380 Vaucluse
Tel. 03 81 44 35 18

Closed from 15 Oct to 1 Mar and Wed • 6 rooms, some with terrace, all have bath/WC or shower/WC and television • €42 to €65; breakfast €7; half-board available • Menus €29 • Garden, car park. Dogs not admitted in restaurant • Private fishing

12 AUBERGE LE TILLAU
M. Parent

Le Mont-des-Verrières
25300 Verrières-de-Joux
Tel. 03 81 69 46 72
Fax 03 81 69 49 20
luc.parent@wanadoo.fr
www.letillau.com

Closed from 15 Nov to 15 Dec, April school holidays, Sun evening and Mon • 12 rooms • €40 to €52; breakfast €7; half-board available • Menus €17 to €33 • Terrace • Sauna, games room, hiking and mountain biking

We most liked The spectacular natural site of the Cirque de Consolation.

We most liked Toast your toes in front of a roaring log fire after a day in the open air.

This unusual 1930s villa, complete with turret and a colonnaded terrace, was built by a miller from the valley. Subsequent owners have lovingly preserved the superb Art Deco decoration – including a Le Corbusier chaise longue in the hall which would be the envy of any collector. The windows of the dining room open onto a shaded garden which leads down to the banks of the Dessoubre.

This enchanting mountain inn, 1200m up, is ideal to clear your lungs of urban pollution as you breathe in the crisp, fresh scent of meadows and fir trees. The rooms are appealingly decorated in an alpine style and you can relax in the reading room or soothe your muscles in the Jacuzzi and sauna. The mountain air is guaranteed to work up a healthy appetite for the profusion of local delicacies, including cooked meats and cheeses, sometimes accompanied by more eclectic creations.

Access : From Montbéliard leave the D 437 at St-Hippolyte, take the D 39 and at Pont Neuf turn left towards Consolation

Access : 7km eastbound from La Cluse-et-Mijoux on the D 67bis and a minor road

FRANCHE COMTÉ

ARBOIS - 39600

13 MESSAGERIES
M. et Mme Ricoux

2 rue de Courcelles
39600 Arbois
Tel. 03 84 66 15 45
Fax 03 84 37 41 09
hotel.lesmessageries@wanadoo.fr
www.hoteldesmessageries.com

Closed in Dec, Jan and Wed • 26 rooms with bath or shower, 8 do not have WC in the room, most have television • €54 to €80; breakfast €8 • No restaurant • Arbois wine tasting and the Pasteur museum nearby

We most liked Tasting the local vintages in the numerous wine cellars dotted round the village.

Wine lovers should make a point of stopping at Arbois, highlight of Jura's vineyards, a delightful village off the beaten track simply bursting with treasures. This former ivy-covered coaching inn offers modest comfort, at equally modest prices, which is all the more appreciated if you are there during the Biou procession, a traditional "grape parade" that takes place in early September. Book one of the rooms at the back which have bathrooms.

Access : In the town centre

BERSAILLIN - 39800

14 LA FERME DU CHÂTEAU
Association E. de Villeneuve-Bargemont

Rue de la Poste
39800 Bersaillin
Tel. 03 84 25 91 31
Fax 03 84 25 93 62

Closed in Jan • 9 rooms, one of which has disabled access • €60 to €62; breakfast €8 • No table d'hôte • Car park • Painting exhibitions, concerts in the summer

We most liked Just two minutes from Jura's vineyards and the "Route du Comté".

Many of the original features of this admirably restored 18C farmhouse have been preserved, including the wonderful vaults and columns of the main chamber, where exhibitions and concerts are held in the summer. The sober, yet elegant bedrooms command a view of the countryside and one has been specially equipped for disabled guests. Guests also have the use of a well-equipped kitchen.

Access : 9km westbound from Poligny on the N 83 and then the D 22

FRANCHE COMTÉ

BONLIEU - 39130

CHAREZIER - 39130

15 L'ALPAGE
M. Lerch

1 chemin de la Madone
39130 Bonlieu
Tel. 03 84 25 57 53
Fax 03 84 25 50 74
reservation@alpage-hotel.com
www.alpage-hotel.com

Closed from 15 Nov to 15 Dec, Mon and Tue lunchtime except during the school holidays • 9 rooms • €55 to €63; breakfast €8; half-board available • Menus €22 (weekdays) to €35 • Terrace, car park. No dogs admitted in rooms

We most liked · The sweeping view over the entire valley of lakes.

A narrow road winds up to this delightful chalet built in the upper reaches of Bonlieu. The valley of lakes and its wooded hillsides are visible from almost all the comfortable bedrooms. Plants and immense bay windows bathe the dining room in dappled light and the sheltered terrace also commands the same sweeping view. Tasty local dishes.

Access: On the N 78 drive towards Saint-Laurent-en-Grandvaux.

16 CHAMBRE D'HÔTE MME DEVENAT
Mme Devenat

17 rue du Vieux-Lavoir
39130 Charezier
Tel. 03 84 48 35 79

Open all year • 4 rooms • €40, breakfast included; half-board available • Table d'hôte €11 • Garden, car park. Credit cards not accepted, no dogs admitted in restaurant

We most liked · The wide range of regional delicacies on offer.

Guests immediately feel at home in this large, welcoming family house cradled in a tiny village halfway between Clairvaux les Lacs and Lake Chalain. The rooms in the little house near the thicket are more independent and a handsome wooden staircase leads up to the others in the main house. The memory of the delicious local specialities, a different one each day, will have you planning your return trip the moment you arrive home.

Access: 13km to the south-west of Lake Chalain on the D 27

FRANCHE COMTÉ

CHÂTEAU-CHALON - 39210

17 LE RELAIS DES ABBESSES
M. Vidal

Rue de la Roche
39210 Château-Chalon
Tel. 03 84 44 98 56
Fax 03 84 44 68 58
relaisdesabbesses@wanadoo.fr
www.chambres-hotes-jura.com

Open all year • 4 non-smoking rooms, all with shower/WC • €60, breakfast included • Table d'hôte €20, drinks included • Garden, car park. Credit cards not accepted

Breakfasts served on the terrace overlooking the valley in summer.

This village house located in a superb medieval city is home to tastefully decorated and furnished rooms, all of which enjoy lovely views of the Côtes de Beaune and Voiteur. The table d'hôte, whose reputation is more than well established, features a fine menu of classical French cuisine made with fresh produce (terrine of boar, tenderloin of pork in pastry). In summer, breakfast is served in the garden and terrace which overlook the valley.

Access: In the town

CHÂTENOIS - 39700

18 À LA THUILERIE DES FONTAINES
M. et Mme Meunier

2 rue des Fontaines
39700 Châtenois
Tel. 03 84 70 51 79
Fax 03 84 70 57 79
michel.meunier2@wanadoo.fr

Open all year • 4 rooms • €50, breakfast included • No table d'hôte • Terrace, park, car park. Credit cards not accepted, dogs not admitted • Outdoor swimming pool

Pick your owners' brains about their beloved region.

Hospitality and attention to detail are the hallmarks of this 18C country house located between the extensive Serre forest and the lower Doubs valley. A flight of stone stairs leads up to well-cared for, very "comfy" and totally peaceful rooms. Stroll round the attractive park or laze on the deck chairs round the swimming pool near the old stables.

Access: 7.5km to the north-east of Dole on the N73 towards Besançon, then take the D 10 and the D 79 to Châtenois

FRANCHE COMTÉ

DOUCIER - 39130

19 LE COMTOIS
M. Menozzi

806 route des 3 lacs
39130 Doucier
Tel. 03 84 25 71 21
Fax 03 84 25 71 21
restaurant.comtois@wanadoo.fr

Closed from 19 Dec to 11 Feb, Tue evening, Wed and Sun evening • 8 rooms with showers, some have WC • €50; breakfast €7; half-board available • Menus €20 to €37 • Terrace

We most liked **The wonderful footpath to Hérisson Falls just a few kilometres away.**

Le Comtois offers an ideal introduction to this fascinating region. The heart of a remote Jura village is home to this spruce auberge offering a few rooms and above all a menu worthy of the most demanding traveller. A warm neo-rustic setting provides the backdrop to delicious recipes with a modern slant prepared with a strong focus on local products. The owner, who is also President of Jura's Association of Wine Waiters, will wax lyrical about wine and food for as long as you'll listen...

Access : In the centre of the village, opposite the post office

LA CURE - 39220

20 ARBEZ FRANCO-SUISSE
M. Arbez

39220 La Cure
Tel. 03 84 60 02 20
Fax 03 84 60 08 59
hotelarbez@netgdi.com
www.hotelarbez.fr.st

Open all year • 10 rooms, half are in France and half are in Switzerland. Rooms have bath/WC or shower/WC, all have television • €59 (€53 low season); breakfast €7; half-board available • Menus €15 to €33 • Car park. Dogs not admitted in restaurant

We most liked **Testing your balance on the "commando course" at nearby Fort Rousses!**

Make sure you take your passport when you go to the bathroom and also remember to decide which half of you will sleep in Switzerland and which in France! This Swiss-French inn, quite literally on the border, offers modern rooms lined in pine and has a choice of classic restaurant fare or quick brasserie snacks and dishes, all within easy reach of alpine ski slopes, cross-country ski trails, snowshoe paths and Rousses Lake. Is there anything else to declare?

Access : On the Swiss border, to the south-east of Rousses, drive 2.5km on the N 5 (towards Geneva)

FRANCHE COMTÉ

LE FRASNOIS - 39130

21 LES CINQ LACS
M. et Mme Colombato

66 route des Lacs
39130 Le Frasnois
Tel. 03 84 25 51 32
Fax 03 84 25 51 32
pcolomba@club-internet.fr
http://auberge.5.lacs.free.fr

Open all year (by reservation) • 5 non-smoking rooms, one of which has disabled access. 2 chalets have been converted into gîtes • €50, breakfast included; half-board available • Table d'hôte €17 • Terrace. Credit cards not accepted, no dogs admitted • Excursions around the lakes

The owners' useful tips about the area.

Hikers have held this old Jura farmstead in great esteem ever since it opened; it nestles in the heart of a lush green landscape of lakes, waterfalls and forest. The comfortable rooms were individually decorated by the lady of the house and each is named after one of the region's innumerable lakes. Don't miss the opportunity to taste the many local specialities on the dining table, served before a roaring fire in winter or on the sheltered terrace in the summer.

Access : 3.5km northbound from Illay on the D 75

PONT-D'HÉRY - 39110

22 MOULIN CHANTEPIERRE
M. et Mme Godin

Route du Val-Cercennes, Moutaine
39110 Pont-d'Héry
Tel. 03 84 73 29 90
Fax 03 84 37 97 06
chante-pierre@tele2.fr
www.chantepierre.com

Closed Jan • 3 non-smoking rooms, all with shower/WC • €57, breakfast included • No table d'hôte • Garden, car park. Credit cards not accepted, dogs not admitted

The owners' graceful hospitality.

In this former 19C watermill on the banks of the Furieuse stream, the owners offer three exquisite guestrooms: "Ingrid" in white and blue, "Ornella", wrought-iron furniture and "Romy" furnished with lovely little armchairs. Depending on the weather, the breakfasts, comprised of home-made products – pastries, bread, yoghurts, and fruit in summer, are served in a pleasant breakfast room or teak furnished terrace.

Access : 7km south of Salins-les-Bains on the D 467 towards a place known as "Moutaine"

FRANCHE COMTÉ
SAINT-GERMAIN-LES-ARLAY - 39210   CULT - 70150

23 HOSTELLERIE SAINT-GERMAIN
M. et Mme Tupin

39210 Saint-Germain-les-Arlay
Tel. 03 84 44 60 91
Fax 03 84 44 63 64

Closed 15 Jan to mid-Feb • 6 rooms, most have bath/WC, some have shower/WC, all have television • €50 to €70; breakfast €7; half-board available • Menus €17 to €50 • Terrace, car park

The homemade foie gras with morels and vin jaune!

Should you want to find out more about this region's rich store of traditions and legends, the Hostellerie St Germain, right in the heart of Jura's vineyards, is the ideal place to start. A refreshing night's sleep in the spotless rooms will leave you eager to begin exploring, and after a hard day's touring, you will be able to tuck into the delicious traditional recipes served in one of two vaulted dining rooms, complete with exposed beams and stonework.

Access : At the crossroads in the centre of the village, opposite the church

24 CHAMBRE D'HÔTE LES ÉGRIGNES
Mme Lego-Deiber

Le Château - Route d'Hugier
70150 Cult
Tel. 03 84 31 92 06
Fax 03 84 31 92 06
lesegrignes@wanadoo.fr
www.les-egrignes.com

Open all year • 3 non-smoking rooms, all with bath/WC • €80, breakfast included • Table d'hôte €25 (evenings only by reservation) • Sitting room, park, car park. Credit cards not accepted, no dogs admitted

Forget about your diet and do justice to the lady of the house's delicious cooking.

This 19C mansion stands proudly in grounds lined with trees and flowers. A tasteful, well-thought out interior restoration has enhanced the original moulded ceilings, stucco work, staircase and trompe-l'oeil marble. Louis-Philippe, Directoire and Napoleon III furniture graces the elegant rooms all of which enjoy the same pastoral view. In the dining room, note the lovely old porcelain stove which dates from 1805.

Access : 4km north-east of Marnay

FRANCHE COMTÉ

PESMES - 70140

PUSY-ET-ÉPENOUX - 70000

25 LA MAISON ROYALE
M. Hoyet

70140 Pesmes
Tel. 03 84 31 23 23
Fax 03 84 31 23 23

Closed from 15 Oct to 15 Mar • 7 rooms • €70, breakfast included • No table d'hôte • Garden, car park. Credit cards not accepted, dogs not admitted • Library, billiards, organ, art exhibitions and cultural events

26 CHÂTEAU D'ÉPENOUX
M. Klufts

5 rue Ruffier
70000 Pusy-et-Épenoux
Tel. 03 84 75 19 60
Fax 03 84 74 45 05
fernand.klufts@wanadoo.fr
www.chateau-epenoux.com

Open all year • 4 non-smoking rooms, all have bath/WC or shower/WC • €70 to €80, breakfast included • Table d'hôte €23, drinks included • Park, car park

We most liked Living like royalty without blowing the family fortune!

We most liked Walking through the park and admiring the ancient trees.

The quality of the restoration and the sheer beauty of this superb 15C stronghold always draw gasps of admiration. The hospitable owners have filled this aptly named establishment with objects from their countless trips around the world. Most of the highly individualised rooms enjoy an exceptional view over the village rooftops and the countryside. Relax in style with a game of billiards, play a few notes on the organ and if the weather is fine, take time to enjoy the pretty flowered garden.

This handsome 18C château, surrounded by a wooded park, welcomes guests into an elegant setting. At mealtimes, the friendly owner invites her guests to taste traditional dishes, prepared only for castle guests, served on a beautifully laid table complete with fine china, silverware and crystal glasses. Upstairs, four spacious rooms furnished with antiques and tastefully decorated, are the epitome of comfort.

Access : In the town centre, near a service station

Access : At Vesoul, take the N 19, then the D 10 towards Saint-Loup-sur-Vesoul

FRANCHE COMTÉ
BELFORT - 90000

27 **VAUBAN**
M. Lorange

4 rue du Magasin
90000 Belfort
Tel. 03 84 21 59 37
Fax 03 84 21 41 67
hotel.vauban@wanadoo.fr
www-hotel-vauban.com

Closed from Christmas to New Year, Feb holidays and Sun • 14 rooms with bath/WC or shower/WC, all have television • €70 to €74; breakfast €8 • No restaurant • Garden. Dogs not admitted

The easy-going family atmosphere.

You will feel more like a friend of the family than a paying guest behind the colourful façade of this inviting hotel where hundreds of paintings by the owner and his artist friends adorn the walls. The rooms, gradually being renovated, are pretty and well soundproofed; ask for one in the rear from which you will enjoy a view of the pretty flowered garden stretching down to the banks of the Savoureuse.

Access : Near the tourist office, on the street running alongside the Savoureuse

ILE-DE-FRANCE AND PARIS

Historic Paris, the City of Light, is the first name to spring to mind at the mention of the île de France. The slender outline of the Eiffel Tower dominates France's chic and cosmopolitan capital, where former royal palaces are brazenly adorned with glass pyramids, railway stations become museums and close-set alleyways of bohemian houses lead off broad, plane-planted boulevards. Paris is a never-ending kaleidoscope of contrasts: the sleepy village side street decked in flowers and the bustle of the big department stores; the artists' studios of Montmartre and the crowded cafés where screen celebrities sit side by side with star-struck fans; a view of Paris by night from a bateau-mouche and the whirlwind glitz of a cabaret. But the fertile land along the Seine is not content to stay in the shadows of France's illustrious first city; the region is also home to secluded châteaux set in formal gardens, the magic of Disneyland and the turn-of-the-century gaiety of the summer cafés along the banks of the Marne. And who could forget the sheer splendour of Versailles, home to the 'most beautiful palace in the world'?

- Seine (Paris) (75)
- Seine-et-Marne (77)
- Yvelines (78)
- Essonne (91)
- Hauts-de-Seine (92)
- Seine-Saint-Denis (93)
- Val-de-Marne (94)
- Val-d'Oise (95)

PARIS

ÎLE DE FRANCE

ÎLE DE FRANCE AND PARIS

PARIS - 75005

1 PIERRE NICOLE
M. Dayot

39 rue Pierre-Nicole
75005 Paris
Tel. 01 43 54 76 86
Fax 01 43 54 22 45
hotelpierre-nicole@voila.fr

Closed 1 to 21 Aug • 33 rooms, most have bath/WC or shower/WC, all have television • €80 to €95; breakfast €6 • No restaurant • No dogs admitted

We most liked Ambling round the deliciously romantic Jardin de Luxembourg.

This hotel, in a handsome Haussmann building, pays homage to a controversial 17C theologian of Paris's Port-Royal Abbey. Many more recent celebrities, such as novelist Gabriel García Márquez and Patrick Modiano have stayed in these compact, practical and well-kept rooms, which maybe lack a little Parisian chic. The comparative calm of this side street, close to the busy restaurants of the Boulevard Montparnasse, should ensure a good night's sleep.

Access : Coming from Bd du Montparnasse, continue onto Bd de Port-Royal and take the third street on the left

PARIS - 75006

2 SÈVRES-AZUR
M. Baguès

22 rue de l'Abbé-Grégoire
75006 Paris
Tel. 01 45 48 84 07
Fax 01 42 84 01 55
sevres.azur@wanadoo.fr
www.sevres-azur.com

Open all year • 31 rooms with bath/WC or shower/WC and television • €85 to €110; breakfast €8 • No restaurant

We most liked The unusual chapel of the Miraculous Medal on Rue du Bac.

A 19C stone building near the smart Bon Marché department store: well-soundproofed rooms, some of which have brass beds, are decked out with colourful fabrics. Plants adorn the light breakfast room. The preferential rates in the nearby car park for hotel guests are a definite bonus.

Access : Go up Rue de Vaugirard and take the second left past Bd du Montparnasse

ÎLE DE FRANCE AND PARIS

PARIS - 75013

3 RESIDENCE VERT GALANT
M. et Mme Laborde

43 rue Croulebarbe
75013 Paris
Tel. 01 44 08 83 50
Fax 01 44 08 83 69
www.vertgalant.com

Open all year • 15 rooms, 11 of which have bath/WC, 4 have shower/WC, all have television • €90 to €100; breakfast €7 • Restaurant closed 6 to 21 Aug; menus €25 to €32 • No dogs admitted in rooms

The village ambience, just two minutes from the Place d'Italie.

This hotel in the Gobelins area is welcome proof that it is still possible to find quiet accommodation in the heart of Paris at a reasonable price. All the functional, neatly kept rooms are sheltered by a restful curtain of greenery. Depending on the weather, breakfast is served in the small garden lined by vines or in a winter-garden dining room. The owners of the Vert Galant also run the cheerful Basque restaurant next door.

Access: From Place d'Italie, go along Avenue des Gobelins and turn left

PARIS - 75014

4 APOLLON MONTPARNASSE
M. Prigent

91 rue de l'Ouest
75014 Paris
Tel. 01 43 95 62 00
Fax 01 43 95 62 10
apollonm@wanadoo.fr
www.apollon-montparnasse.com

Open all year • 33 rooms, 22 of which have shower/WC, 11 have bath/WC, all have television • €79 to €95; breakfast €7 • No restaurant • Nearby car park • Near Montparnasse railway station

A pleasant welcome in the heart of Montparnasse.

This small hotel is ideally placed for those intending to spend a few days in the French capital, close to the Montparnasse railway station and Air France's shuttle buses, the Rue de la Gaîté and cinemas for evenings out and Ricardo Bofill's amazing architectural feats. The bedrooms, in fairness, are more practical than charming, but look all the better for their recent makeover. Vaulted breakfast room.

Access: From Place de Catalogne go along Rue du Château and turn right

ÎLE DE FRANCE AND PARIS

PARIS - 75016

[5] BOILEAU
M. Fabrice Royer

81 rue Boileau
75016 Paris
Tel. 01 42 88 83 74
Fax 01 45 27 62 98
info@hotel-boileau.com
www.hotel-boileau.com

Open all year • 31 rooms with bath/WC or shower/WC and television, 1 of which has disabled access • €77 to €90 (€65 to €72 low season); breakfast €9 • No restaurant

We most liked The cheerful welcome from Oscar, the hotel parrot.

Situated in a smart street of what used to be the "village of Auteuil" until 1860, a distinctly un-Parisian atmosphere continues to reign in this hotel. Paintings and ornaments picked up in antique shops relate tales from Brittany and North Africa, the owner's twin passions. The statues in alcoves and wainscoting in the lobby lend it a resolutely classical air. Ask for one of the renovated Eastern-styled rooms. Breakfast is served in a room flooded with sunlight overlooking a flowered patio.

Access: From Place de la Porte de Saint-Cloud take Rue Michel-Ange, then first right and second left

PARIS - 75019

[6] HOTEL LAUMIÈRE
Mme Desprat

4 rue Petit
75019 Paris
Tel. 01 42 06 10 77
Fax 01 42 06 72 50
le-laumiere@wanadoo.fr
www.hotel-lelaumiere.com

Open all year • 54 rooms with bath/WC or shower/WC and television • €54 to €74; breakfast €8 • No restaurant

We most liked A (well-needed) breath of fresh air in the picturesque Buttes Chaumont Park.

This charming small hotel, run by the same family since 1931, makes up for its distance from Paris' main monuments with a whole host of other advantages: the attractive modern flavour of the renovated interior, a leafy corner where breakfast is served on sunny days and the nearby Laumière métro station. If you prefer more space and calm, book one of the rooms overlooking the cheerful garden.

Access: From Place de Stalingrad take Av J Jaurès, turn right into Rue A Carrel, take the second on the left and the second on the right

ÎLE DE FRANCE AND PARIS

BARBIZON - 77630

7 HOSTELLERIE LA CLÉ D'OR
M. Gayer

73 Grande-Rue
77630 Barbizon
Tel. 01 60 66 40 96
Fax 01 60 66 42 71
cle.dor@wanadoo.fr
www.hotelcledor.com

• 16 rooms, all with bathrooms • €56 to €83; breakfast €11 • Restaurant closed Nov to Apr; menus €29 to €39, drinks included • Terrace, garden, car park, meeting room

most liked The canvases hanging in the bedrooms.

This former post house, whose façade is a riot of flowering wisteria in springtime, is located just opposite the Auberge Ganne, much favoured by the artists of the Barbizon School in the 19C. The personalised bedrooms of the "Golden Key" overlook the garden-terrace. The delicious up-to-date cuisine made from seasonal produce is served in a plush dining room (parquet floor, beams and fireplace).

Access: In the centre of the village

BRÉAU - 77720

8 LA FERME DU COUVENT
M. et Mme Legrand

Rue de la Chapelle-Gauthier
77720 Bréau
Tel. 01 64 38 75 15
Fax 01 64 38 75 15
ferme.couvent@wanadoo.fr
www.lafermeducouvent.fr

Open all year • 13 rooms • €55, breakfast included • Table d'hôte €18 to €20 (weekdays, by reservation only) • Garden, park. Credit cards not accepted • Tennis, hot-air ballooning

most liked Flying over the Brie region in a hot-air balloon.

What better place to relax than this handsome 18C farmhouse planted in the middle of nearly 20 acres of parkland in the countryside. Attractive modern furniture graces the bedrooms, freshly painted in shades of cream with sloping ceilings. If you fancy something different, climb aboard the experienced owners' multicoloured hot-air balloon for a proper bird's eye view of the Brie region.

Access: 14.5km eastbound from Vaux-le-Vicomte on the Provins road (D 408) and then the D 227 on the left

ÎLE DE FRANCE AND PARIS

CHARTRETTES - 77590

CHÂTRES - 77610

9 CHÂTEAU DE ROUILLON
Mme Morize-Thévenin

41 avenue Charles-de-Gaulle
77590 Chartrettes
Tel. 01 60 69 64 40
Fax 01 60 69 64 50
château.de.rouillon@club-internet.fr
www.chateauderouillon.net

Open all year • 5 non-smoking rooms, including 1 apartment, all with bathrooms • €73 to €95, breakfast included • No table d'hôte • Terrace, park, private car park • Table tennis, mountain bike rentals

We most liked **The choice of leisure activities (angling, water skiing, mountain bikes, etc).**

A gracious French-style park extending down to the banks of the Seine and a sophisticated interior, in which every chair and object seems to tell a story, set the scene for your stay in this 17C castle. Each bedroom overlooks the river and is decorated individually and equipped with spacious, light bathrooms. Breakfasts are served in an elegant dining room or on the terrace.

Access: In the centre of the village on the banks of the Seine

10 LE PORTAIL BLEU
M. et Mme Laurent

2 route de Fontenay
77610 Châtres
Tel. 01 64 25 84 94
Fax 01 64 25 84 94
leportailbleu@voila.fr
www.leportailbleu.com

Open all year • 4 rooms, including 3 apartments, all with shower/WC and television • €57, breakfast included • Table d'hôte €20 • Terrace, garden, car park. Credit cards not accepted, dogs not admitted • Library

We most liked **Ideal for a relaxing country retreat.**

The owners of this restored farmhouse never fail to treat their guests to a warm welcome. The rooms, located in two buildings surrounded by an attractive garden, are a picture of cosy comfort. The welcoming dining room features a large communal table, handsome wooden fireplace and countless paintings on the wall: quiches, pies and other house specialities often made from home-grown produce.

Access: In the village centre

ÎLE DE FRANCE AND PARIS

ÉCHOUBOULAINS - 77830

11 FERME DE LA RECETTE
Famille Dufour

Au hameau d'Échou
77830 Échouboulains
Tel. 01 64 31 81 09
Fax 01 64 31 89 42
fermedelarecette@aol.com
www.fermedelarecette.com

Closed during the Feb holidays • 3 rooms with bath/WC and television • €55, breakfast included • Table d'hôte €22 to €29 • Dogs not admitted in rooms

We most liked The farmer-owner's friendly, genuine welcome.

The origins of this farm, formerly the property of the Cistercian abbey of Preuilly, have been traced back to the 12C. It now houses cosy rooms with snug, inviting duvets. Meals are served in a dining room where stone and wood feature prominently. Remember to reserve one of the tables near the windows so that you can enjoy the view of the pond, meadows and contented grazing cows.

Access : 11km to the north of Montereau-Fault-Yonne on the N 105 Melun road then on the D 107 at Valence-en-Brie

GRISY-SUR-SEINE - 77480

12 LA FERME DE TOUSSACQ
Mme Colas

Hameau de Toussacq
77480 Grisy-sur-Seine
Tel. 01 64 01 82 90
Fax 01 64 01 82 90
toussacq@wanadoo.fr
www.hameau-de-toussacq.com

Open all year • 5 non-smoking rooms with bathrooms • €50, breakfast included • Table d'hôte €15 to €18 (only by reservation) • Garden, park, car park • Chapel and dovecote visits

We most liked The country atmosphere on the banks of the Seine.

Don't be put off by the somewhat forbidding aspect of this 17C farmhouse: you will, in any case, be sleeping in the castle outbuildings, whose loving restoration has taken more than 25 years. Bedrooms are simply styled with sloping ceilings and the breakfast room is a pleasant blend of rustic and modern. A fountain, chapel and dovecote together with a few sheep can be seen in the park. Appetising home cooking with a sprinkling of home-grown produce.

Access : 20km southbound from Provins on the Nogent-sur-Seine road (N 19), then the D 78 and the D 411

ÎLE DE FRANCE AND PARIS

LÉSIGNY - 77150

LIZINES - 77650

13 HÔTEL DU GOLF
Mme Kranz-Groslein

Ferme des Hyverneaux
77150 Lésigny
Tel. 01 60 02 25 26
Fax 01 60 02 03 84
reservation@parisgolfhotel.com
www.parisgolfhotel.com

Open all year • 48 rooms, 2 of which have disabled access, all have bath/WC and television • €75 to €110; breakfast €10 • Private car park • Golf course

We most liked **The excellent soundproofing which masks the noise of Paris' busy outer ring road.**

The remains of a 12C abbey can still be seen in this hotel, where the addition of huge skylights and glass walls add a light, modern touch. The practical rooms and timbered restaurant command a view of an 18-hole golf course of nearly 250 acres. The terrace of the clubhouse is practically on the green.

Access: Drive to Lésigny on the "Francilienne" or on the A 4 (exit no 19), then head for the golf course

14 CHAMBRE D'HÔTE M. DORMION
M. et Mme Dormion

2 rue des Glycines
77650 Lizines
Tel. 01 60 67 32 56
Fax 01 60 67 32 56

Open all year • 5 non-smoking rooms, all are in the attic with kitchenettes • €45, breakfast included • No table d'hôte • Garden, park. Credit cards not accepted, no dogs admitted

We most liked **The immaculate bedrooms.**

This three-century-old building, still a working farm, has offered accommodation and sustenance to visitors for over a decade. The spotless rooms with sloping ceilings are decorated with rustic furniture and each one has its own kitchenette. An old barn has been converted into a light, airy breakfast room with an enormous bay window. Venture out of doors and admire the lawn and orchard in the garden.

Access: 15km to the south-west of Provins on the N 19 and the D 209

ÎLE DE FRANCE AND PARIS

NEUFMOUTIERS-EN-BRIE - 77610

15 BELLEVUE
M. et Mme Galpin

77610 Neufmoutiers-en-Brie
Tel. 01 64 07 11 05
Fax 01 64 07 19 27
bellevue@fr.st
www.bellevue.fr.st

Open all year • 7 rooms, 5 of which are in a separate wing, all have bath/WC and television • €57 to €76, breakfast included • No table d'hôte • Garden, car park

The elegant setting of this 19C manor house.

Don't be put off by the sight of the surrounding residential suburbia, because the garden of this fine 19C manor house commands a view of open fields which stretch as far as the eye can see. All the split-level bedrooms have a few personal touches. Two lodges with private garden and deck chairs are the most pleasant. A superb dining room with beams, old flagstones and a beautiful wood table set an elegant tone for mealtimes.

Access: 10km south of Disneyland-Paris, on the A 4 take exit no 13, the D 231 then the D 96

ORMEAUX - 77540

16 LA FERME DU VIEUX CHÂTEAU
Mme Maegerlein

Chemin du Pont-Levis
77540 Ormeaux
Tel. 06 78 02 25 17
BandB77@wanadoo.fr
www.chambres-table-hotes.com

Open all year by reservation • 4 non-smoking rooms, all have television • €48 to €65, breakfast included • Table d'hôte €13 to €55 • Garden, car park. Credit cards not accepted, no dogs admitted in rooms

Guests and their horses are received warmly.

The "old castle" is no longer visible, but the exquisitely restored 18C farmhouse is guaranteed to satisfy even the most demanding visitor. The owners' decorative flair has combined rich materials and period furniture with collections of old tools and popular arts. The bathrooms of the cosy rooms are all fitted with power showers. The high ceilinged lounge is graced with a huge Louis XIII fireplace. You are welcome to try your hand at carriage riding in the company of the farm's mare, Ivoire.

Access: In the town

ÎLE DE FRANCE AND PARIS

POMMEUSE - 77515

PROVINS - 77160

17 LE MOULIN DE POMMEUSE
M. et Mme Thomas

32 avenue du Général-Huerne
77515 Pommeuse
Tel. 01 64 75 29 45
Fax 01 64 75 29 45
info@le-moulin-de-pommeuse.com
www.le-moulin-de-pommeuse.com

Open all year • 5 non-smoking rooms • €58, breakfast included • Table d'hôte €25 to €35 • Park, car park. Dogs not admitted • Hammam, sauna

We most liked **As soon as you've crossed the threshold, you'll start to feel at home.**

The lady of the house certainly knows how to receive her guests in style, offering them a drink on arrival, the traditional sprig of lily of the valley on May 1 and gifts at Christmas. The setting of the 14C water mill is quite delightful, as are the rooms, which have suitably agricultural names such as Sowing, Harvesting, Threshing. Relax in the small sitting room in the old machine room or in the park which hides its very own island!

Access: 5km westbound from Coulommiers on the N 34, then a minor road

18 FERME DU CHATEL
M. Lebel

5 rue de la Chapelle-Saint-Jean
77160 Provins
Tel. 01 64 00 10 73
Fax 01 64 00 10 99
fermeduchatel@wanadoo.fr

Open all year • 5 non-smoking rooms, all have bathrooms • €44 to €46 • No table d'hôte • Garden, car park. Credit cards not accepted, no dogs admitted

We most liked **"Wasting" time in the orchard garden.**

This old house, built and rebuilt from the 12C to the 18C, enjoys a superb position in the heart of the medieval town. The bedrooms, under exposed rafters, are peaceful and spotless with well-equipped bathrooms. Breakfast is served in a rustic dining room full of character; afterwards head for the huge garden and wander between the fruit trees.

Access: In the medieval city

ÎLE DE FRANCE AND PARIS

SAINT-DENIS-LÈS-REBAIS - 77510

19 CHAMBRE D'HÔTE BRIE CHAMPAGNE
M. et Mme Bodin

22 Chantareine
77510 Saint-Denis-lès-Rebais
Tel. 01 64 65 46 45
Fax 01 64 65 46 45
contact@chambres-brie-champagne.com
www.chambres-brie-champagne.com

Open all year • 3 non-smoking rooms, 1 has a kitchenette, all have bath/WC or shower/WC • €60, breakfast included • No table d'hôte • Terrace, park, private car park. Credit cards not accepted, no dogs admitted

We most liked
Breakfasting under the arbour.

This old farmhouse covered in Virginia creeper and wisteria extends a warm country welcome to guests. The half-timbered walls and family heirlooms in the dining room are just a foretaste of the authentic character of this guesthouse whose cosy bedrooms are located in a converted corn loft. Generously served meals are served in the shady garden or by a roaring fire indoors depending on the season.

Access : Take exit 16 off the A 4, then the N 34 towards Coulommiers and D 222 towards Rebais. Beyond Mazagran, left onto the D 19 towards "Chantareine" on the D 22

SAINT-GERMAIN-SUR-MORIN - 77860

20 LES HAUTS DE MONTGUILLON
M. et Mme Legendre

22 rue de Saint-Quentin, Hameau de Montguillon
77860 Saint-Germain-sur-Morin
Tel. 01 60 04 45 53
Fax 01 60 42 28 59
chantal.legendre@wanadoo.fr

Open all year • 3 rooms, 2 of which are upstairs, all have bathrooms • €66 to €80, breakfast included • Garden, car park. Credit cards not accepted, no dogs admitted • Disneyland Paris nearby

We most liked
The cheerful decoration.

This lovingly restored farmhouse is conveniently located near Disneyland-Paris. A tasteful contrast of pastel shades and dark timbered beams prevails in the bedrooms which have large beds, old wardrobes and chest of drawers picked up in second-hand shops and brand new bathrooms. This creative mixture of old and new continues in the rest of the establishment, particularly in the hall with its old bread oven. The shaded, well-manicured garden is the place to be on sunny days.

Access : Southbound from St-Germain sur Morin, in the upper part of Montguillon

ÎLE DE FRANCE AND PARIS

SAINTS - 77120

VARREDDES - 77910

21 LA BASTIDE DE L'AUBETIN
M. et Mme Pyla

3 rue du Chardon
77120 Saints
Tel. 01 64 03 27 86
Fax 01 64 03 27 86
evelyne.pyla@free.fr
http://evelyne.pyla.free.fr

Open all year • 3 rooms, all with bath/WC or shower/WC • €59, breakfast included • Table d'hôte €20 to €25, drinks included • Terrace, park, car park. Credit cards not accepted, dogs not admitted

22 AUBERGE DU CHEVAL BLANC
Mme Cousin

55 rue Victor-Clairet
77910 Varreddes
Tel. 01 64 33 18 03
Fax 01 60 23 29 68
r.cousin2@libertysurf.fr
www.auberge-cheval-blanc.fr

Closed from 1 to 24 Aug, Sun evening, Mon and Tue lunchtime • 8 rooms with bath/WC and television • €77 to €96; breakfast €10 • Menus €33 to €49 • Garden, private car park

The faultless decoration of this Parisian "bastide".

A lane then a dirt track lead to this delightful country house tucked away in a flower-decked garden lined in trees. The owners have three guestrooms, one of which on the ground-floor, all of which are decorated in bright Spanish tiles and colours. At mealtimes, savour the mouth-watering dishes made with home-grown vegetables and produce from local farms.

The terrace decked in flowers and shaded by trees.

This former staging inn houses recently redone "chocolate-box" bedrooms featuring designer fabrics, pine and wrought-iron furniture and teak-floored bathrooms. In the plush dining room hung with still-lifes, the accent is on creativity and healthy local produce. Don't even think about leaving without tasting the inimitable Brie de Meaux cheese!

Access : From Saints, exit eastbound on the D 15

Access : On the main road in the village

ÎLE DE FRANCE AND PARIS

VOSVES - 77190

23 LA FERME DE VOSVES
Mme Lemarchand

155 rue de Boissise
77190 Vosves
Tel. 01 64 39 22 28
Fax 01 64 79 17 26
contact@fermedevosves.com
www.fermedevosves.com

Closed from 21 Dec to 3 Jan • 3 rooms • €55 to €65, breakfast included • No table d'hôte • Garden, car park. Credit cards not accepted, no dogs admitted

The simple, unpretentious welcome and setting.

This green-shuttered old farmhouse is bordered by two attractive gardens full of fruit trees and flowers and complete with a well. The unostentatious, tranquil bedrooms, spread throughout the buildings and the warm, unaffected welcome from the lady of the house are reason enough to stay, but the sitting room with piano and dining room with fireplace and watercolours by the owner are also delightful.

Access : 10km northbound from Barbizon on the N 7 and the D 372, then take Rue de la Gare

LA BOISSIÈRE-ÉCOLE - 78125

24 LA GÂTINE
M. Chauzy

15 route de Faverolles
78125 La Boissière-École
Tel. 01 34 94 32 79
Fax 01 34 94 32 79
marion.gatine@wanadoo.fr
www.lagatine.com

Closed from 15 Jan to 15 Feb • 6 non-smoking rooms, 1 with disabled access, all have bathrooms • €72 to €95, breakfast included • Table d'hôte €32 (by reservation) • Terrace, park, car park. Credit cards not accepted, no dogs admitted • Possibility of access to Country Spa facilities

Winding down in a spa resort in the heart of the countryside just one hour from Paris.

This estate on the edge of the Rambouillet forest boasts a country spa resort with a host of beauty treatments, massages and keep-fit programmes to boost the spirits flagging urbanites. Each of the bedrooms, located in a thatched cottage, is decorated differently on a travel theme. The lobby is the scene of temporary art exhibitions which change each month. In season, don't miss the chance to sample the local game.

Access : From Faverolles, turn left on the D 152 towards la Boissière-École. 3km further on, La Gâtine is on your left

ÎLE DE FRANCE AND PARIS

MOISSON - 78840

25 LE PRIEURÉ MAÏALEN
M. et Mme Lévi

4 allée du Jamboree
78840 Moisson
Tel. 01 34 79 37 20
Fax 01 34 79 37 58
blevi@free.fr

Open all year • 4 rooms with bathrooms • €65 (€59 low season), breakfast included • Table d'hôte €20 (only by reservation) • Garden, car park. Credit cards not accepted, no dogs admitted • Outdoor swimming pool. Golf, horse-riding, tennis and leisure park nearby

We most liked: A spin in one of the owner's vintage cars.

A former 16C priory is an excellent place to spend a night in the heart of this village so dear to Monet. Time and care have clearly been lavished on the interior and each room is a delight to behold. The "Boat" room contains an 18C model sailing boat, "Scheherazade" is steeped in mystery and "Provence" bathed in bright, cheerful colours. Antique furniture, ornaments and a collection of LPs add a personal touch to the sitting room and the flowered garden is perfect to relax in.

Access: 3km to the south-east of Roche-Guyon

MONTAINVILLE - 78124

26 LA FAUCONNERIE DU ROY
M. et Mme Oger

1 rue de l'Ormoir
78124 Montainville
Tel. 01 34 75 17 24
oger@lafauconnerie.com
www.lafauconnerie.com

Closed 24 and 25 Dec • 2 rooms and one gîte • €75 to €80, breakfast included • No table d'hôte • Car park. Credit cards not accepted, no dogs admitted • Outdoor swimming pool

We most liked: The history behind these beautifully preserved buildings.

History and character meet your eye wherever you turn in this falconry built in 1680 for Louis XIV. Everything is authentic from the original wooden carved staircase and doors, tiled floors and period furniture down to the piano in the breakfast room. Excellent mattresses, canopy and four-poster beds and good quality bathrooms have been chosen for the bedrooms. Swimming pool, children's play area in the park and bicycle rental available.

Access: 6km eastbound from Thoiry on the D 45, take the Maule road and turn right

ÎLE DE FRANCE AND PARIS

MOIGNY-SUR-ÉCOLE - 91490

27 CHAMBRE D'HÔTE
CLOS DE LA CROIX BLANCHE
M. Lenoir

9 rue du Souvenir
91490 Moigny-sur-École
Tel. 01 64 98 47 84
lenoir@aol.com
www.compagnie-des-clos.com

Open all year • 4 rooms, one of which is on the ground floor • €55 to €60, breakfast included • Table d'hôte €16 • Garden. Credit cards not accepted

We most liked **The sheltered landscaped garden.**

High walls protect this handsome stone house and its beautifully laid-out garden from prying eyes. The tastefully decorated rooms are totally tranquil and the one on split-levels is very practical for families. If you listen quietly you may still hear the clucking of the former inhabitants of the breakfast room, where the chicken roosts can still be seen. A pleasant stay and cordial welcome assured.

Access: 3.5km northbound from Milly-la-Forêt

NAINVILLE-LES-ROCHES - 91750

28 LE CLOS DES FONTAINES
Mme Soton

3 rue de l'Église
91750 Nainville-les-Roches
Tel. 01 64 98 40 56
Fax 01 64 98 40 56
soton@closdesfontaines.com
www.closdesfontaines.com

Open all year • 5 non-smoking rooms, 1 with disabled access, all have bath/WC or shower/WC, television and Internet access • €100 (€84 low season); breakfast €7 • No table d'hôte • Park, car park. No dogs admitted • Outdoor swimming pool, tennis, petanque, theme weekends

We most liked **The timeless peace and quiet.**

Nestling between the tiny church and town houses, this former presbytery is set in pleasant park planted with trees. The attractive contemporary rooms are tastefully decorated on the theme of spices after which they are named (Saffron, Cinnamon, Nutmeg, etc.). Home-made pastries and jams are served at breakfast time in a modern room which leads into the veranda-sitting room. Tennis, pétanque, fitness room and sauna on site.

Access: In the heart of the village

ÎLE DE FRANCE AND PARIS

CHÉRENCE - 95510

29 **CHAMBRE D'HÔTE LE SAINT-DENIS**
Mme Pernelle

1 rue des Cabarets
95510 Chérence
Tel. 01 34 78 15 02

Open all year (by reservation) • 5 rooms with bathrooms • €60 to €65, breakfast included • No table d'hôte • Garden, car park. Credit cards not accepted, no dogs admitted

The lavish breakfasts.

This appealing stone house in the lovely medieval village of Chérence was formerly a traditional hotel-restaurant. It was turned into a B&B establishment in 1996, offering simple, compact rooms in all shapes and sizes. The ground floor, full of nooks and crannies, houses the dining and sitting room complete with fireplace. Spending or wasting time in the delightful garden is definitely a high point. Faultless welcome.

Access : 4km to the north-east of Roche-Guyon on the D 100

PARMAIN - 95620

30 **CHAMBRE D'HÔTE MONSIEUR DELALEU**
M. Delaleu

131 rue du Maréchal-Foch
95620 Parmain
Tel. 01 34 73 02 92
Fax 01 34 08 80 76
chambresdhotes.parmain@wanadoo.fr

Open all year • 4 rooms • €51, breakfast included • No table d'hôte • Garden, car park. Credit cards not accepted, no dogs admitted

The unusual bathrooms.

By the time you have opened your suitcase, you will feel that you have come home. Each of the spacious, colourful rooms is named after a playing card; Spade, Heart, Diamond and Club. However the highly unusual bathrooms, all are different, are what guests always rave about. Children are in heaven over the vaulted cellar turned into a games room, the mini football pitch and the visit to the working farm.

Access : 1km westbound from Isle-Adam on the D 64

LANGUEDOC-ROUSSILLON

Languedoc-Roussillon is home to a diverse collage of landscape and culture: the feverish rhythm of its festivals, the dizzying beauty of the Tarn Gorges, the haughty splendour of the Pyrenees, the bewitching spell of its caves and stone statues, the seclusion of its clifftop Cathar citadels which witnessed one of the bloodiest chapters of France's history, the heady perfumes of its sunburnt garrigue, the nonchalance of the pink flamingos on its long salt flats, the splendour of Carcassonne's ramparts, the ornamental exuberance of Catalan altarpieces, the quietly flowing waters of the Midi Canal and the harsh majesty of the Cévennes mountains. Taking in so many contrasts is likely to exhaust more than a few explorers, but effective remedies are close at hand: a steaming plate of *aligot* – mashed potato, garlic and cheese – and a simmering cassoulet, the famously rich combination of duck, sausage, beans and herbs, followed by a delectable slice of Roquefort cheese, all washed down with a glass of ruby-red wine.

- Aude (11)
- Gard (30)
- Hérault (34)
- Lozère (48)
- Pyrénées-Orientales (66)

LANGUEDOC ROUSSILLON
BIZANET - 11200   BOUTENAC - 11200

1 DOMAINE DE SAINT-JEAN
M. et Mme Delbourg

11200 Bizanet
Tel. 04 68 45 17 31
Fax 04 68 45 17 31
didierdelbourgbizanet@yahoo.fr

Open all year • 4 upstairs rooms, all have bathrooms • €55 to €70, breakfast included • No table d'hôte • Garden. Credit cards not accepted, dogs not admitted

We most liked: Whiling away time in the former wine cellar converted into a sitting room.

This rambling 19C wine-growing property stands amid vineyards and pine trees, ready to welcome travellers in search of quiet authenticity. Hand-stencilled furniture and walls adorn the accommodation in the converted vat house: each room is named after one of the family's ancestors; the one with a private terrace enjoys a particularly lovely view of the Fontfroide massif. The well-tended garden is Mr Delbourg's pride and joy.

Access: 2.5km to the north-west of the abbey on the D 613 towards Lagrasse, then on a minor road

2 LA BASTIDE DES CORBIÈRES
M. et Mme Camel

17 rue de la Révolution
11200 Boutenac
Tel. 04 68 27 20 61
Fax 04 68 27 62 71
bastide.corbières@wanadoo.fr
www.bastide-corbieres.com

Closed from 10 Jan to 15 Feb and 15 Nov to 26 Dec • 5 rooms with bath/WC • €79 to €84 (€70 to €75 low season), breakfast included • Table d'hôte €30 (evenings only except Tue and Fri) • Terrace, garden. Dogs not admitted • Outdoor swimming pool, reading room, table-tennis, mountain bike rental

We most liked: The apéritif offered to guests on arrival.

This late 19C mansion features a wonderful mixture of modern comforts and period atmosphere. The rooms, generously sized, brightly coloured and decorated with antiques are named after the grapes used to produce rich, full-bodied Corbières wines. The sweet scent of roses, irises, peonies and acacia fills the garden where meals are served.

Access: 7.5km southbound from Lézignan on the D 61 towards Luc-sur-Orbieu

LANGUEDOC ROUSSILLON

CARCASSONNE - 11000 | CARCASSONNE - 11000

3 LA MAISON SUR LA COLLINE
Mme Galinier

Lieu-dit Sainte-Croix
11000 Carcassonne
Tel. 04 68 47 57 94
Fax 04 68 47 58 67
contact@lamaisonsurlacolline.com
www.lamaisonsurlacolline.com

Closed from 10 Dec to 14 Feb • 6 rooms with bathrooms and television • €65 to €85, breakfast included • Table d'hôte €30 (evenings only by reservation) • Garden, car park. Credit cards not accepted • Outdoor swimming pool

We most liked: **As soon as you hear the chirping of the cicadas you know you're in the south.**

Broom, cypress trees, thyme and wild mint lend a wonderfully relaxing atmosphere to this hillside farmstead overlooking the historic city of Carcassonne. Old red floor tiles, antiques and knick-knacks adorn the spacious rooms. Each has its own colour scheme, beige, blue, yellow – the "white" room has a private garden. Breakfast is served by the pool in the summer.

Access : 1km southbound from the historic town on the Sainte-Croix road

4 MONTSÉGUR
M. Faugeras

27 allée d'Iéna
11000 Carcassonne
Tel. 04 68 25 31 41
Fax 04 68 47 13 22
info@hotelmontsegur.com
www.hotelmontsegur.com

Closed from 20 Dec to 1 Feb • 21 rooms on 3 floors, all have air-conditioning, bath/WC or shower/WC and television • €73 to €96; breakfast €9; half-board available • Menus €24 to €44 • Private car park

We most liked: **The unforgettable tour of the historic city ramparts.**

A late-19C mansion on the doorstep of the lower town. An undeniable faded charm emanates from these gradually spruced-up rooms filled with the scent of beeswax. Herringbone parquet floors, "retro" lights and a marble fireplace are among the features of the classic period sitting room. The breakfast room is graced with a beautiful old dresser.

Access : From Castelnaudary on the N 113 (av du Prés F Roosevelt), turn right at the Artigues Bridge

LANGUEDOC ROUSSILLON

CASTELNAUDARY - 11400

5 HÔTEL DU CANAL
Mme Geli

2 ter avenue Arnaut-Vidal
11400 Castelnaudary
Tel. 04 68 94 05 05
Fax 04 68 94 05 06
hotelducanal@wanadoo.fr
www.hotelducanal.com

Open all year • 38 rooms, 2 have disabled access. All have bath/WC, television (and broadband internet access for €5/night) • €56 to €60; breakfast €7 • No restaurant • Garden, car park • Billiards room

We most liked: Stepping out of the hotel onto the banks of the Canal du Midi.

These handsome ochre walls housed a quicklime factory back in the 19C. The quiet if ordinary rooms overlook the garden or the canal and in the summer, you will want to linger over breakfast for hours as you gaze at the canal's quietly flowing waters. It would be a crime to leave town without sampling its world-renowned cassoulet!

Access : Towards Pamiers on the banks of the Midi canal

CUCUGNAN - 11350

6 AUBERGE DE CUCUGNAN
M. Villa

2 place de la Fontaine
11350 Cucugnan
Tel. 04 68 45 40 84
Fax 04 68 45 01 52

Closed Jan to 15 Mar and Wed • 6 air-conditioned rooms upstairs with bath/WC or shower/WC and television • €45 to €60; breakfast €7; half-board available • Restaurant closed Wed; menus €17 to €44 • Terrace, car park

We most liked: Exploring the narrow, winding roads that border the lovely Corbières vineyards.

For several years now the reputation of this inn, nestled in a picturesque village of the Corbières, has been steadily growing thanks to the quality of its country cooking, served in a converted barn and at deliciously reasonable prices. Guests can now also enjoy the prospect of getting to know the region better by booking (recommended) one of the inn's recently fitted-out comfortable rooms whose immaculate walls are set off by wrought-iron furniture and bright fabrics.

Access : In a lane in the heart of the village

LANGUEDOC ROUSSILLON

GINCLA - 11140

7 HOSTELLERIE DU GRAND DUC
M. et Mme Bruchet

2 route de Boucheville
11140 Gincla
Tel. 04 68 20 55 02
Fax 04 68 20 61 22
host-du-grand-duc@ataraxie.fr
www.host-du-grand-duc.com

Closed from 3 Nov to late Mar • 12 rooms, all have bath/WC or shower/WC and television • €65 to €70; breakfast €9; half-board available • Restaurant closed on Wed lunchtime except in Jul and Aug; menus €30 to €59 • Terrace, garden, garage, private car park • Ideal for exploring the upper Aude Valley

Candle-lit dining overlooking the garden and its ornamental pool.

This grand old mansion built in 1780 stand proudly in one of Cathar country's many remote villages, perfect for long walks in the nearby forest. The accommodation may be a tad old-fashioned, but certainly can't be faulted for character; a second wing has just been finished with three delightful rooms. An elegant rustic dining room opens onto a terrace shaded by a thick canopy of lime trees.

Access: At Lapradelle, leave the D 117 (Quillan to Perpignan road) and take the D 22 alongside the Bouizane

LA POMARÈDE - 11400

8 HOST. DU CHÂTEAU DE LA POMARÈDE
M. Garcia

Place du Château
11400 La Pomarède
Tel. 04 68 60 49 69
Fax 04 68 60 49 71
www.hostellerie-lapomarede.fr

Closed fortnight after Feb holidays, Nov, Sun evening out of season and Mon and Tue all year • 6 rooms and 1 apartment with bath/WC and television • €75 to €110; breakfast €12; half-board available • Menus €16 (weekdays) to €80 • Terrace, car park

Wouldn't it be easy to get used to living in luxury?

An enthusiastic young couple are at the head of this wonderful establishment tucked away in a hamlet of the Montagne Noire. The outbuildings of a medieval fortress have recently been converted into a likeable hostelry: tastefully decorated rooms, an elegant dining room with exposed timbers and wrought-iron furniture, a terrace overlooking the valley and, above all, the mouth-watering, confident and inventive cuisine, which earned it a Michelin star, no less, in 2002.

Access: Set back from the D 624 from Castelnaudary to Revel

LANGUEDOC ROUSSILLON
NARBONNE - 11100　　　　　　　　　　PORTEL-DES-CORBIERES - 11490

9　LA RÉSIDENCE
La Résidence SA

6 rue du 1er-Mai
11100 Narbonne
Tel. 04 68 32 19 41
Fax 04 68 65 51 82
hotellaresidence@free.fr
http://hotelresidence.fr

Closed from 15 Jan to 15 Feb • 25 air-conditioned rooms on 2 floors with bath/WC or shower/WC and television • €68 to €96 (€58 to €86 low season); breakfast €8 • No restaurant • Small garage • Near the historic centre

We most liked: Stepping back in time to the turn of the 20C.

This gracious late-19C residence was converted into a hotel in the 1950s: the atmosphere of old provincial France can still be felt in its lovingly preserved decoration. Some of the rooms overlook the Archbishops' Palace and the cathedral. The hotel has enjoyed the patronage of a whole host of famous politicians, sportsmen and artists, as a peep inside the Visitor's Book will reveal.

Access: Take the Narbonne-Sud exit and head for the town centre, cross the Robine canal, turn right at Rue J Jaurès and then the 2nd left

10　DOMAINE DE LA PIERRE CHAUDE
M. et Mme Pasternak

Les Campets
11490 Portel-des-Corbières
Tel. 04 68 48 89 79
Fax 04 68 48 89 79
lescampets@aol.com
www.lapierrechaude.com

Closed from 1 Jan to 15 Feb • 4 rooms with bath/WC • €72 to €80, breakfast included • No table d'hôte • Terrace, garden, car park. Credit cards not accepted, no dogs admitted

We most liked: Everything!

This 18C former wine and spirit house nestled in a hamlet amid vineyards and pinewoods, was beautifully restored in 1960 by a pupil of the architect Gaudi. Since then, constant improvements have turned the estate into a pleasant getaway with splendid bedrooms (terracotta tiles, wrought iron, worn wooden furniture, warm fabrics, etc.), a lovely Andalusian-style patio-cum-sitting room, a terrace shaded by fig trees and a garden rich with the sweet scents of southern France. Unforgettable!

Access: In a place known as Les Campets, 6km from the Wildlife Park on the D 611A towards Durban-Corbières

LANGUEDOC ROUSSILLON

SAINT-MARTIN-LE-VIEIL - 11170   **BARJAC - 30430**

11 ABBAYE DE VILLELONGUE
M. Eloffe

11170 Saint-Martin-le-Vieil
Tel. 04 68 76 92 58
Fax 04 68 76 92 58

Closed 10 days in Nov and 10 days at Christmas • 4 rooms • €60, breakfast included • No table d'hôte • Car park, park, garden. Credit cards not accepted, no dogs admitted • Guided and non-guided visits of the abbey daily

Quietly meditating in the abbey gardens, before or after the throngs of daily visitors.

Stand still and drink in the silence and solemnity of the former Cistercian abbey built in the 12C. Be reassured, however, the comfort on offer is far from monastic and old furniture, canopy beds and private bathrooms now set the scene in the rooms. All the rooms gaze down on the lovely cloisters and garden, where breakfast is served in the summer. In the winter, they are served in the monks' storeroom, restored in 1998.

Access : 5km to the north-west on the D 64

12 LA SÉRÉNITÉ
Mme L'Helgoualch

Place de la Mairie
30430 Barjac
Tel. 04 66 24 54 63
Fax 04 66 24 54 63
catherine@la-serenite.fr
www.la-serenite.fr

Closed from 11 Nov to 20 Mar • 3 rooms with bath/WC or shower/WC • €70 to €115, breakfast included • No table d'hôte • Terrace. Credit cards not accepted, no dogs admitted

Snuggling up in the book-lined bedroom or in front of the fire.

Fragrant lavender and beeswax greet you as you cross the threshold of this 17C country home. Afterwards, feast your eyes on the sophisticated good taste of the ochre-coloured walls, hand-stencilled friezes, rich fabrics, antiques and ornaments picked up by the antique dealer-owner and on the personalised rooms decorated with fine linen and lace. Settle down and relax as you savour the delicious breakfasts served by the fireside or on the flowered terrace in the summer.

Access : 6km westbound from Aven d'Orgnac on the D 317 and then the D 176

LANGUEDOC ROUSSILLON

CASTILLON-DU-GARD - 30210

13 VIC
M. Vic

Mas de Raffin
30210 Castillon-du-Gard
Tel. 04 66 37 13 28
Fax 04 66 37 62 55
viccastillon4@aol.com
www.chambresdhotes-vic.com

Open all year • 5 rooms • €70 to €90, breakfast included • No table d'hôte • Garden, car park. Credit cards not accepted • Outdoor swimming pool, spa, hammam

The happy marriage of old and new.

It would be difficult to find a more idyllic spot for this former wine-growing farm set amidst the unspoilt landscape of fragrant scrub, vines and hundred-year-old olive trees. Red and yellow features predominantly in the bright rooms where modern amenities blend in wonderfully with old stones and antique furniture; some are vaulted while others are split-level. Savour breakfast served under the refreshing shade of a mulberry tree.

Access: 4km to the north-east of Pont-du-Gard on the D 19 and then the D 228

LA ROQUE-SUR-CÈZE - 30200

14 LA TONNELLE
M. et Mme Rigaud

Place des Marronniers
30200 La Roque-sur-Cèze
Tel. 04 66 82 79 37
Fax 04 66 82 79 37
latonnelle30@aol.com

Open all year • 6 rooms • €72, breakfast included • No table d'hôte • Car park. No dogs admitted

Row, row, row your boat, gently down the Cèze!

Merrily, merrily, merrily, merrily, life is but a dream! The infectious good humour of the owner is impossible to resist as she guides you round her lovely country house that can't be missed on the way into the village. Each of the sober, immaculate rooms is named after a flower. In the summer, treat yourself to breakfast in the shade of an arbour while you gaze down on the village and its girdle of cypress trees.

Access: 17km to the north-west of Bagnols-sur-Cèze on the N 86 then the D 298 towards Barjac, and the D 166

LANGUEDOC ROUSSILLON

LE VIGAN - 30570

15 CHÂTEAU DU REY
Mme Cazalis de Fondouce

Le Rey
30570 Le Vigan
Tel. 04 67 82 40 06
Fax 04 67 82 47 79
abeura@club-internet.fr
www.château-du-rey.com

Closed 30 Sep to 1 Apr • 13 rooms, all have bath/WC and television • €70 to €97; breakfast €8; half-board available • Restaurant closed on Sun evening and Mon except in Jul and Aug; menus €20 to €42 • Terrace, riverside park, car park • Outdoor swimming pool, private fishing

Eight centuries of family history.

This lovely 13C fortress, remodelled by the tireless Viollet-le-Duc, Napoleon's architect, has been in the same family for over eight centuries! The rooms, some with fireplace, are furnished with elegant period furniture. The former sheep pen is now the dining room and its vaulted ceiling makes it pleasantly cool in summer. The view from the terrace extends over the immense parkland and river, much prized by anglers.

Access: 5km eastbound on the D 999 (towards Ganges), turn left just before Pont d'Hérault

MONTCLUS - 30630

16 LA MAGNANERIE DE BERNAS
M. et Mme Keller

Le Hameau de Bernas
30630 Montclus
Tel. 04 66 82 37 36
Fax 04 66 82 37 41
lamagnanerie@wanadoo.fr
www.magnanerie-de-bernas.com

Open from Easter to 28 Oct • 15 rooms, two are split-level, one has disabled access, all have bath/WC and television • €65 to €105; breakfast €10; half-board available • Restaurant closed Tue, Wed in Mar, Apr and Oct; menus €20 to €46 • Terrace, garden, car park • Outdoor swimming pool

Treasure hunting in this 13C Knights Templar stronghold.

Patrick and Katrin, a young Swiss couple with energy to spare, have recently finished their patient, flawless restoration of this medieval former command post. Beautiful stone walls, exposed beams and rich, warm fabrics adorn the tasteful rooms, most of which look down over the Cèze valley. Character abounds in the vaulted dining room, but the highlight is perhaps the shaded courtyard-terrace and south-facing garden, designed by a professional landscape gardener, none other than Patrick himself.

Access: Between Barjac and Bagnols-sur-Cèze, then 2km eastbound from Monclus

LANGUEDOC ROUSSILLON
PORT-CAMARGUE - 30240   **SAINT-MAMERT-DU-GARD - 30730**

17 RELAIS DE L'OUSTAU CAMARGUEN
M. Daweritz

3 route des Marines
30240 Port-Camargue
Tel. 04 66 51 51 65
Fax 04 66 53 06 65
oustaucamarguen@wanadoo.fr
www.chateauxhotels.com/camarguen

Open from 24 Mar to 4 Nov and Fri, Sat evening in Feb, Mar and Nov • 39 air-conditioned rooms, most on ground-floor, with bath/WC or shower/WC and television • €99; breakfast €11; half-board available • Air-conditioned restaurant; menus €27 to €31 (evenings only) • Terrace, garden, private car park • Outdoor swimming pool

We most liked
Winding down in the peaceful atmosphere of this small mas.

This recently-built hotel has adopted a traditional Camargue style as its name suggests. All the rooms are spacious and on the ground-floor and some have small, flower-decked terraces overlooking the pleasant garden. The tasteful interior decoration was clearly inspired by neighbouring Provence. A country style with exposed beams in the restaurant, a pleasant pool-side terrace and a select traditional menu comprise the establishment's other appeals.

Access : On Route des Marines

18 LA MAZADE
Mme Couston

In the village
30730 Saint-Mamert-du-Gard
Tel. 04 66 81 17 56
Fax 04 66 81 17 56
www.bbfrance.com/couston.html

Open all year • 3 rooms with bathrooms • €55 to €60, breakfast included • Table d'hôte €20 (by reservation) • Garden, car park. Credit cards not accepted, no dogs admitted

We most liked
Mrs Couston's highly personal approach to interior decoration.

This beautiful country mas, set in the heart of a sleepy village, reveals the talents of its owner's flair for interior decoration. An almost staggering collection of antique and contemporary furniture, rugs and modern and folk art blends surprisingly well in the plant-filled rooms: the result is truly unique. All the rooms overlook the garden and arbour, where dinner is served in the long summer evenings.

Access : 17km westbound from Nîmes on the D 999 and then the D 1

LANGUEDOC ROUSSILLON

SAINT-QUENTIN-LA-POTERIE - 30700 SAINT-VICTOR-DE-MALCAP - 30500

19 LE MAS DU CAROUBIER
Mme Charpentier

684 route de Vallabrix
30700 Saint-Quentin-la-Poterie
Tel. 04 66 22 12 72
Fax 04 66 22 12 72
contact@mas-caroubier.com
www.mas-caroubier.com

Closed in Jan • 4 rooms, non-smokers only, with bath/shower and WC • €70 to €85, breakfast included • No table d'hôte • Garden. Credit cards not accepted, no dogs admitted • Outdoor swimming pool

We most liked
A secret hideaway.

The traditional ochre walls and sky-blue shutters of this 18C mas suddenly appear when you reach the end of a country lane. Inside, the guests' welfare is clearly the only thing that counts, from the gracious greeting and rooms filled with old furniture to the delicious home-made jams at breakfast time. Outside, the turquoise water of the swimming pool and quiet garden encourage you to idle away long summer afternoons, unless of course you would prefer to do a pottery, painting, cookery course.

Access : 5km to the north-east of Saint-Quentin-la-Poterie on the D 982 and then the D 5

20 LA BASTIDE DES SENTEURS
M. Subileau

30500 Saint-Victor-de-Malcap
Tel. 04 66 60 24 45
Fax 04 66 60 26 10
subileau@bastide-senteurs.com
www.bastide-senteurs.com

Open from Mar to Oct • 14 rooms, one of which has disabled access, all have bath/WC and television • €72 to €85; breakfast €9; half-board available • Menus €37 to €100 • Private car park, terrace • Swimming pool

We most liked
Choosing which local wine to drink with the chef's cuisine.

This 19C stronghold is built against the walls of a delightful village dominated by the shadow of a medieval castle. The fully renovated abode offers pleasant, colourful rooms decked out in antique and wrought iron furniture. Some enjoy a fine view of the Cèze Valley and all are equally tranquil. Gourmets will love sitting down in the stylish Southern-flavoured dining room or on the terrace opening onto the overflow swimming pool.

Access : In the village

LANGUEDOC ROUSSILLON

SOMMIÈRES - 30250 **TAVEL - 30126**

21 MAS FONTCLAIRE
Mme Labbé

8 rue Émile-Jamais
30250 Sommières
Tel. 04 66 77 78 69
Fax 04 66 77 78 69

Open all year • 3 rooms • €67 to €80, breakfast included • No table d'hôte • Garden, car park. Credit cards not accepted • Outdoor swimming pool

22 LE PONT DU ROY
M. Schorgeré

Route de Nîmes - D 976
30126 Tavel
Tel. 04 66 50 22 03
Fax 04 66 50 10 14
contact@hotelpontduroy.fr
www.hotelpontduroy.fr

Open from 14 Apr to 30 Sep • 14 air-conditioned rooms with bath/WC or shower/WC and television • €73 to €79 (€59 to €65 low season); breakfast €7; half-board available • Menus €25 to €45 (evenings only for hotel guests) • Terrace, garden, private car park. No dogs admitted in restaurant • Outdoor swimming pool, petanque, play area

We most liked
Speech may be silver, but silence is golden!

We most liked
Never make the mistake of thinking that pétanque is "just a game"!

Imagine waking up to blue, cloudless skies and tucking into delicious home-made jams and freshly squeezed orange juice, served on the patio in the summer or by the fireside in winter. You only need to put one foot over the threshold of this former wine-grower's house to know you're in for a treat. The three rooms in the converted outbuildings are decorated in different styles: Provençal, modern and Louis XVI. The quality of the silence is such that you may even find yourself whispering!

You can always dive into the swimming pool for a refreshing dip if things get too hot on the pétanque ground! Built in the style of a Provençal mas, this house was turned into a hotel in 1986. The pastel coloured rooms overlook either the shaded garden or the legendary vineyards of Tavel. A fresh country look prevails in the restaurant and in the summer tables are laid outside on the terrace. The self-taught owner-chef rustles up regional dishes depending on what he finds in the market.

Access : In the village

Access : 3km to the south-east of Tavel, on the D 4 then the D 976 (Roquemaure-Remoulins road)

LANGUEDOC ROUSSILLON

VILLENEUVE-LÈS-AVIGNON - 30400

23 L'ATELIER
M. Burret

5 rue de la Foire
30400 Villeneuve-lès-Avignon
Tel. 04 90 25 01 84
Fax 04 90 25 80 06
hotel-latelier@libertysurf.fr
www.hoteldelatelier.com

Closed from 2 Jan to 20 Feb • 23 rooms, all have bath/WC or shower/WC and television • €61 to €91 (€49 to €81 low season); breakfast €9 • No restaurant • Garden, garage • Exhibition of painting and sculpture, tea room

We most liked: The view of Avignon from the patio and tiny terrace.

This 16C "workshop" in the heart of a picturesque town has just been creatively redesigned by a film set decorator. Tasteful ornaments, antique furniture, rush matting, elegant bathrooms, exposed beams, fireplaces and a lovely staircase are combined in this masterful renovation which has retained the character of the abode's ancestral walls. Mediterranean-style breakfast room, exhibitions of painting and sculpture.

Access: In the old town

ARGELLIERS - 34380

24 AUBERGE DE SAUGRAS
M. et Mme Aurelle

Domaine Saugras
34380 Argelliers
Tel. 04 67 55 08 71
Fax 04 67 55 04 65
auberge.saugras@wanadoo.fr

Closed from 9 to 25 Aug, 20 Dec to 20 Jan, Mon, Tue and wed except evenings in Jul-Aug • 7 air-conditioned rooms, with bath/WC and television • €42 to €85; breakfast €8; half-board available • Menus €18 to €49 • Terrace, car park • Swimming pool

We most liked: Feeling like you've left the everyday world behind - even though Montpellier is close by.

Finding your way to the inn is something of a treasure hunt, but once there, your efforts will be more than rewarded. The bare stone walls of this old mas which dates back to the 12C are splendidly isolated and surrounded by sweet-smelling garrigue and wooded hills. The appetising local fare, served in a rustic dining room or on the panoramic terrace, also tempts visitors to return. Finally, lovers of peaceful nights will appreciate the recently renovated comfortable bedrooms.

Access: 21km southbound of St-Martin-de-Londres on the D 32, D 127 and D 127E

LANGUEDOC ROUSSILLON

CAPESTANG - 34310

25 LA BASTIDE VIEILLE
Mme Fouissac

La Bastide Vieille
34310 Capestang
Tel. 04 67 93 46 23
Fax 04 67 93 46 56

Closed from 1 Nov to 1 Mar • 3 rooms • €54, breakfast included • Terrace, garden, car park. Credit cards not accepted, dogs not admitted

Whether by bicycle, carriage or barge (on request), the Canal du Midi is a joy to explore.

These old walls flanked by a 12C tower lie amid vineyards in a totally secluded spot, well off the beaten track. The spacious rooms installed in the former outbuildings are decorated with appealing Provençal prints and colours. The dining table is in the former bread-making room. On the leisure side, get to grips with a good book in the delightful sitting room-library or in the small garden.

Access : 13km westbound from Béziers, Castres road on the D 39

LE CAYLAR - 34520

26 LE BARRY DU GRAND CHEMIN
M. et Mme Vandenbroucke

88 faubourg Saint-Martin
34520 Le Caylar
Tel. 04 67 44 50 19
Fax 04 67 44 52 36
lebarry34@aol.com
www.le-barry.fr

Open all year • 5 rooms • €50 to €55, breakfast included; half-board available • Table d'hôte €20 • Car park. Credit cards not accepted, dogs not admitted in dining room

The secretive, silent countryside – the "causse" – surrounding this stone farmstead.

Built in 1850, the immaculate stone walls of this house stand at the foot of the strange, tormented Roc Castel in the heart of the unspoilt Larzac limestone plateau. The ground floor rooms are quiet and very well-maintained if not vast. Tuck into the delicious chargrilled fare cooked over an open fire in the delightful vaulted dining room, which remains refreshingly cool in the height of summer.

Access : In the village

LANGUEDOC ROUSSILLON

MONTAGNAC - 34530

27 CHAMBRE D'HÔTE MONSIEUR GENER
M. et Mme Gener

34 avenue Pierre-Sirven
34530 Montagnac
Tel. 04 67 24 03 21
Fax 04 67 24 03 21
valexboyer@aol.com

Open all year • 4 rooms with shower/WC, all air-conditioned • €48, breakfast included • No table d'hôte • Terrace, garden, car park. Credit cards not accepted

We most liked Pézenas and its wealth of craft stalls within easy reach.

In 1750, the buildings laid out around the well-sheltered, spacious inner courtyard belonged to the mounted constabulary. Nowadays, the stables have been converted into large, calm, well-appointed rooms, in some of which the old oak partitions between the loose-boxes can still be seen. In the summer, breakfast is served on a pleasant upstairs terrace.

Access : 6.5km to the north-west of Pézenas on the N 9 then the N 113

MONTPELLIER - 34000

28 PARC
Mme Jacquin

8 rue Achille-Bège
34000 Montpellier
Tel. 04 67 41 16 49
Fax 04 67 54 10 05
hotelduparcmtp@wanadoo.fr
www.hotelduparc-montpellier.com

Open all year • 19 rooms, most have shower/WC, some have bath/WC or shower without WC, all have air-conditioning and television • €48 to €75; breakfast €9 • No restaurant • Car park. Dogs not admitted

We most liked Being treated like a regular.

Despite the fact that the park has been sold off, the noble walls of this 18C mansion are as smart as ever and the plush bourgeois rooms are being gradually and tastefully renovated. The regulars of this establishment, located in a quiet side street, appreciate its calm just two minutes away from the town centre and the nearest tram stop; they generally leave their cars in the private car park in the courtyard. In the summer, breakfast is sometimes served on the terrace.

Access : Drive up Rue Proudhon (towards the zoo), and at the ECAT, take a left at Rue Turgot

LANGUEDOC ROUSSILLON

SAINT-SATURNIN-DE-LUCIAN - 34725

29 MIMOSA
M. et Mme Pugh

10 place de la Fontaine
34725 Saint-Saturnin-de-Lucian
Tel. 04 67 88 62 62
Fax 04 67 88 62 82
ostalaria.cardabela @ wanadoo.fr

Closed from 1 Jan to 9 Mar and 30 Oct to 31 Dec • 7 rooms on 2 floors with bath/WC • €68 to €95; breakfast €10 • No restaurant at the hotel, but the owners also run Le Mimosa at St-Guiraud • Dogs not admitted

Ostalaria's authenticity.

The only clue that this delightful village house is a hotel is the tiny sign almost absentmindedly posted outside. The recently spruced up rooms have plenty of style with brightly coloured quilts, elegant lights and Provençal furniture blending in perfectly with the lovely exposed stone walls, polished floor tiles, well-worn beams and original fireplaces. Some overlook the quite exquisite little square of St-Saturnin. Breakfast is served on a large friendly dining table. Delightful.

Access : On the village square near the church

AUMONT-AUBRAC - 48130

30 GRAND HÔTEL PROUHÈZE
M. et Mme Roudgé-Joly

2 route du Languedoc
48130 Aumont-Aubrac
Tel. 04 66 42 80 07
Fax 04 66 42 87 78
prouheze @ prouheze.com
www.prouheze.com

Closed first fortnight of Jan and 3 to 30 Nov • 24 rooms with bath/WC and television • €50 to €90; breakfast €10; half-board available • Restaurant closed Mon; menus €33 to €58; at the Compostelle (bistro) €18 to €27 • Terrace, car park

Mr and Mrs Prouhèze's spontaneity and warmth.

This traditional hostelry was founded in 1891 by the current owners' great-grandmother. Snug rooms are decorated with painted wood or Louis Philippe-style furniture. Brightly coloured fabrics are a recent addition to the main dining room which specialises in large helpings of good regional cooking. A country bistro caters to pilgrims on the way to St James of Compostela who pass by on the GR footpath through the village. Chinaware and home-made preserves on sale.

Access : In the village, opposite the railway station

LANGUEDOC ROUSSILLON

COCURÈS - 48400 | LA GARDE-GUÉRIN - 48800

31 LA LOZERETTE
Mme Agulhon

48400 Cocurès
Tel. 04 66 45 06 04
Fax 04 66 45 12 93
lalozerette@wanadoo.fr

Open from Easter to 1 Nov • 21 rooms, one of which has disabled access, all have bath/WC or shower/WC and television • €52 to €76 (€51 to €74 low season); breakfast €8; half-board available • Restaurant closed Tue and Wed lunchtime except in Jul-Aug. Menus €16 (weekdays) to €46 • Car park, garden. No dogs admitted in restaurant

Oleander bushes planted in the lovely glazed Anduze vases in the garden.

This inn is both a hamlet on the doorstep of the National Park of Cévennes and a genuine family home because the young owner was born here and the auberge was opened by her grandmother. Feast your eyes on the renovated rooms with matching bedspreads, lace curtains and flowered balconies overlooking the village and the countryside. Admire the carved ceiling in the "country chic" dining room. The extensive wine-list is further proof of the owner-sommelier's many talents.

Access: 5.5km to the north-east of Florac on the N 106, then right onto the D 998

32 AUBERGE RÉGORDANE
M. Nogier

48800 La Garde-Guérin
Tel. 04 66 46 82 88
Fax 04 66 46 90 29
pierre.nogier@free.fr
www.regordane.com

Closed from 1 Jan to 15 Apr and 15 Oct to 31 Dec • 15 rooms with bath/WC or shower/WC, some have television • €51 to €62; breakfast €8; half-board available • Menus €17 to €33 • Terrace in an inner courtyard

The head-spinning view of the gorges of Chassezac from the village.

This fortified village was founded by the bishops of Mende along the old Roman road linking Auvergne with the Languedoc in an effort to eradicate highway robbery. An order of knights from La Garde Guérin were entrusted with the task of escorting voyagers. The stronghold of one of these knights is now a characterful inn with small rooms and mullioned windows, a restaurant with vaulted ceiling and a beautiful terrace-courtyard of granite flagstones.

Access: In the heart of the village

LANGUEDOC ROUSSILLON

MEYRUEIS - 48150

33 LE SAINT-SAUVEUR
M. Bourguet

Place Jean-Séquier
48150 Meyrueis
Tel. 04 66 45 40 42
Fax 04 66 45 40 43
saint-sauveur@demeures.de.lozere.com
www.demeures-de-lozere.com

Closed 15 Nov to 1 Apr • 10 rooms, all have bath/WC and television • €40 to €45 (€39 to €43 low season); breakfast €6; half-board available • Menus €16 to €32 • Terrace

We most liked
The stone terrace shaded by a lovely old sycamore tree.

This elegant 18C mansion, full of character and very reasonably priced, stands in the heart of a region that abounds in magnificent natural sites: Aven Armand, Dargilan Cave and the Gorges de La Jonte. Well-appointed rooms are decorated with cherry wood furniture and well protected by double-glazing. Both dining rooms have been entirely refurbished.

Access: In the town centre

CÉRET - 66400

34 LES ARCADES
M. Astrou

1 place Picasso
66400 Céret
Tel. 04 68 87 12 30
Fax 04 68 87 49 44
hotelarcades.ceret@wanadoo.fr
www.hotel-arcades-ceret.com

Open all year • 30 rooms, on 4 levels with lift, with bath/WC or shower/WC, 7 are air-conditioned and 12 have a kitchenette • €42 to €57; breakfast €7 • No restaurant • Garage. No dogs admitted

We most liked
The superb collections of Céret's Museum of Modern Art are definitely worth a visit.

To reach the entrance to this well-located establishment opposite the ramparts of the small Catalan town, guests must cross a large café terrace shaded by colourful parasols and plane trees. Admire the paintings, posters and lithographs in tribute to painters of the Céret School in the hall, staircase and corridors on your way up to your room. The excellent upkeep, dark country furniture and comfortable family atmosphere all contribute to the hotel's appeal.

Access: In the heart of the town near the archaeological museum

LANGUEDOC ROUSSILLON

ELNE - 66200

LAS ILLAS - 66480

35 CAN OLIBA
M. Boisard et Mme Le Corre

24 rue de la Paix
66200 Elne
Tel. 04 68 22 11 09
elna @ club-internet.fr
www.can-oliba.com

Open all year • 6 non-smoking rooms with bath/WC • €60, breakfast included • Table d'hôte €22 (by reservation and evenings only) • Garden. Credit cards not accepted, no dogs admitted • Swimming pool

36 HOSTAL DELS TRABUCAYRES
M. Davesne

66480 Las Illas
Tel. 04 68 83 07 56
Fax 04 68 83 07 56

Closed from 6 Jan to 15 Mar, from 25 to 30 Oct, Tue and Wed out of season • 5 rooms upstairs, 3 of which have a terrace • €29 to €33; breakfast €5; half-board available • Menus €12 (weekdays) to €42 • Terrace, car park. Dogs not admitted in the rooms • Hiking

---

The owner's experience as interior decorator can be seen everywhere.

Visitors inevitably fall head over heels in love with this attractive 17C Catalan abode not far from the cathedral. A fine stone staircase and delightful sitting room strewn with antique furniture immediately set the tone and visitors cannot help but be spellbound. In the unusual rooms, the colours, furniture, curios and paintings vie with each other to incite guests to return and try them all... Don't miss the tiny walled garden complete with swimming pool. Irresistible!

Long walks in the silent forest of cork oaks surrounding the hotel.

Don't give up! The winding hairpin bends of this tiny mountain road may seem endless but your efforts will be repaid tenfold. This tiny hamlet in the middle of nowhere is home to an old inn which provided accommodation to the exiled officers of Spain's Republican Army in 1936. Admire the view from the simple but pleasant rooms. The restaurant in a converted barn serves typically Catalan dishes.

Access : In the historic centre of the town, near Sainte-Eulalie Cathedral

Access : Take the D 618 between Céret and Le Boulou; at Maureillas take the D 13 and drive south-west for 11km

LANGUEDOC ROUSSILLON

LATOUR-DE-CAROL - 66760

37 AUBERGE CATALANE
Mme Ernst

10 avenue du Puymorens
66760 Latour-de-Carol
Tel. 04 68 04 80 66
Fax 04 68 04 95 25
auberge-catalane@club-internet.fr
www.auberge-catalane.fr

Closed 2 to 10 Apr, 12 Nov to 22 Dec, Sun evening and Mon except during school holidays • 10 rooms with shower/WC and television • €52 (€48 low season); breakfast €6; half-board available • Menus €15 to €32 • Terrace, car park

Taking a ride on the little canary-yellow train through the picturesque Cerdagne region.

This inn, built in 1929, returned to the family when the original owner's grandchildren bought it back a few years ago and today the great-grandson, Benoît, presides over the kitchens. The rooms have been renovated and modernised, but the original Art Deco-inspired furniture has been retained; some bedrooms have balconies overlooking the village rooftops. Dining room-veranda.

Access : On the main road of the village (N 20) between Bourg-Madame and the Puymorens Pass

PERPIGNAN - 66100

38 DOMAINE DU MAS BOLUIX
M. et Mme Ceilles

chemin du Pou de les Colobres
66100 Perpignan
Tel. 04 68 08 17 70
Fax 04 68 08 17 71
www.domaine-de-boluix.com

Open all year • 7 rooms with bath/WC • €82, breakfast included • No table d'hôte • Terrace, garden, car park. Credit cards not accepted, dogs not admitted • Swimming pool and tennis nearby

The secluded situation on the doorstep of Perpignan.

An easy-going atmosphere reigns throughout this 18C mas set in the midst of Cabestany's vineyards and orchards. Restored in 1998, the interior is comfortable, roomy and spotlessly clean. Each of the personalised rooms, whose immaculate walls are hung with bright regional fabrics, is named after a famous Catalan: Dali, Rigaud, Maillol, Picasso, Casals. The sweeping view over Roussillon, the coast and that emblem of Catalonia, the mighty Canigou mountain, is definitely worth a trip.

Access : 5km southbound from Perpignan towards Argelès

LANGUEDOC ROUSSILLON

PRUGNANES - 66220

THUIR - 66300

39 DOMAINE DE COUSSÈRES
Joo et Ann Maes

66220 Prugnanes
Tel. 04 68 59 23 55
Fax 04 68 59 23 55
www.cousseres.com

Open from 16 Mar to 31 Oct • 6 rooms • €75, breakfast included • Table d'hôte €23 (evenings only) • Car park, park. Credit cards not accepted, no dogs admitted • Swimming pool

Basking in the silence disturbed only by the twittering of birds.

The setting will take your breath away: perched on a hillock surrounded by vineyards, this superb fortified house dominates the impressive landscape of mountains and sweet-scented scrub. The spacious, tastefully and individually decorated rooms and the welcoming dining room and massive table within all live up to expectations. A lovely garden, swimming pool and maze of terraces around the house enhance the matchless calm and tranquillity of this spot.

Access : 5km to the north-west of Saint-Paul-de-Fenouillet on the D 117 and D 20

40 CASA DEL ARTE
Mme Toubert

Mas Petit
66300 Thuir
Tel. 04 68 53 44 78
Fax 04 68 53 44 78
casadelarte@wanadoo.fr
www.casadelarte.fr.fm

Open all year • 5 rooms • €75 to €100, breakfast included • Meals €25 including beverages • Garden, car park • Outdoor swimming pool, sun deck

The arty feel to the individually decorated rooms.

The owner-painter has converted this 11C and 14C mas into a real art gallery. The walls of the often well proportioned rooms and bathrooms are covered in colourful paintings; the one devoted to ancient Rome is particularly lovely. Works by local artists adorn the walls of the sitting room, whose centrepiece is a medieval fireplace. The sun deck overlooking the swimming pool, the hundred-year-old oaks in the park and the small bamboo grove invite guests to take life easy.

Access : 17km westbound from Perpignan, towards Thuir and Ille-sur-Têt

LANGUEDOC ROUSSILLON
VALCEBOLLÈRE - 66340

41 AUBERGE LES ÉCUREUILS
M. et Mme Laffitte

66340 Valcebollère
Tel. 04 68 04 52 03
Fax 04 68 04 52 34
auberge-ecureuils@wanadoo.fr
www.aubergeecureuils.com

Closed from 5 to 20 May and 3 Nov to 4 Dec • 15 rooms with bath/WC, some have television • €70 to €90; breakfast €9 to €11; half-board available • Menus €19 (weekdays) to €52 • Terrace, fitness room • Indoor swimming pool, balneo, hammam, cross-country skiing, snowshoe trekking

Whether it be smuggler's footpaths or secluded fishing spots, the owner is a treasure-trove of tips.

Only twenty-or-so souls still live in this half-abandoned village, perched at an altitude of 1 500m on a dead-end road in the remote Pyrenees. Should you decide to join them for a day or so, you won't regret it! The genuine warmth and solicitude of the owners of this former 18C sheep-fold, full of character, are quite captivating. Comfortable rooms, with bathrooms done out in Spanish marble, and an elegant rustic dining room complete the picture.

Access : 9km to the south-east of Bourg-Madame on the D 70, then at Osséja take the D 30

LIMOUSIN

Life in Limousin is lived as it should be: tired Parisians in need of greenery flock here to taste the simple joys of country life, breathe in the bracing air of its high plateaux, stroll along the banks of rivers alive with fish and wander through its woodlands in search of mushrooms and chestnuts. The sight of peaceful cattle grazing in utter contentment or lambs frolicking in the meadows in spring is enough to rejuvenate even the most jaded city-dweller. By late October, the forests are swathed in a cloak of autumn colours and the ground becomes a soft carpet of russet leaves. A perfect backdrop to the granite walls and soft sandstone façades of sleepy hamlets and peaceful cities, where ancestral crafts, such as Limoges porcelain and Aubusson tapestries, combine a love of tradition with a whole-hearted desire to embrace the best in contemporary art. The food is as wholesome as the region: savoury bacon soup, steaming Limousin stew and, as any proud local will tell you, the most tender, succulent beef in the world.

- Corrèze (19)
- Creuse (23)
- Haute-Vienne (87)

LIMOUSIN

AUBAZINE - 19190

1 LA TOUR
M. Lachaud

Place de l'Église
19190 Aubazine
Tel. 05 55 25 71 17
Fax 05 55 84 61 83

Closed 2 to 24 Jan • 19 rooms with bath/WC or shower/WC and television • €49; breakfast €7; half-board available • Menus €16 (weekdays) to €37

Amble alongside the pretty Canal des Moines dug in the 12C.

On the village square, opposite the Cistercian Abbey stand two characterful houses, the older one flanked by the tower from which the hotel takes its name. Bright wallpaper livens up the bedrooms, while the main dining room and smaller rooms for families or business lunches feature a rustic flavour in keeping with the array of regional delicacies on the menu. Apéritifs and after-dinner coffee are served on the terrace.

Access : On the main square in the village, opposite the abbey

BEAULIEU-SUR-DORDOGNE - 19120

2 LA MAISON
M. Henriet

11 rue de la Gendarmerie
19120 Beaulieu-sur-Dordogne
Tel. 05 55 91 24 97
Fax 05 55 91 51 27

Closed from Oct to Mar • 6 rooms, 4 overlooking a patio, all have bath/WC • €52 to €62, breakfast included • No table d'hôte • Credit cards not accepted, no dogs admitted • Terraced garden, outdoor swimming pool

More hacienda than country farmhouse.

The arcades, ruddy ochre walls and profusion of hydrangeas, rose bushes and lemon trees in the patio are more reminiscent of an exotic hacienda than a French country farmhouse: all becomes clear when you learn that this astonishing 19C house was built by one of Napoleon's generals, homesick for Mexico. The adorable, unusually named rooms – "The Bride", "The Indians", "The Caricatures" – are quite unique; two overlook the sumptuous hanging garden and swimming pool.

Access : In the village

LIMOUSIN
BEAULIEU-SUR-DORDOGNE - 19120   COLLONGES-LA-ROUGE - 19500

3 LE MANOIR DE BEAULIEU
M. Landrein

4 place du Champ-de-Mars
19120 Beaulieu-sur-Dordogne
Tel. 05 55 91 01 34
Fax 05 55 91 23 57
reservation@manoirdebeaulieu.com
www.manoirdebeaulieu.com

Closed from 1 Jan to 1 Mar • 25 rooms with bath/WC or shower/WC, some have television • €55 to €90 (€36 to €70 low season); breakfast €8; half-board available • Menus €24 (weekdays) to €50 • Terrace, private car park • Outdoor swimming pool

Take a compass to explore the labyrinth of narrow lanes in the historic town.

The central location of this sturdy hotel, founded in 1912 by Amélie Fournié, does full justice to its name. When booking, ask for one of the restored rooms. The house's excellent reputation is also due to the generous helpings of wholesome country cooking served in an attractive dining room or on the terrace where you can enjoy the warm breeze.

Access : On the main square in the centre of the village

4 LA RAZE
Mme Tatien

19500 Collonges-la-Rouge
Tel. 05 55 25 48 16
domainedelaraze@yahoo.fr
http://chambrelaraze.free.fr

Open all year • 5 rooms • €45, breakfast included • No table d'hôte • Car park, garden. Credit cards not accepted, no dogs admitted

Throw open your windows and feast your eyes on the countryside.

This 18C farmstead lies just 800m outside the crimson sandstone village: serenity reigns, broken only by the high-pitched calls of the peacock in the mating season. The lady of the house's artistic talents can be admired in the hand-stencilled patterns on the walls of the comfortable bedrooms. The breakfast room, adorned with family furniture and heirlooms and the park "à l'anglaise" overflowing with fruit trees and roses, are magnificent.

Access : 5.5km to the south-west of Collonges on the D 38 and the D 19, then follow the La Raze signs

LIMOUSIN

DONZENAC - 19270

NAVES - 19460

5 LE RELAIS DU BAS LIMOUSIN
M. et Mme Delavier

Sadroc
19270 Donzenac
Tel. 05 55 84 52 06
Fax 05 55 84 51 41
relais-du-bas-limousin@wanadoo.fr
www.relaisbaslimousin.fr

Closed from 15 to 25 Feb and 23 Oct to 5 Nov • 22 rooms with bath/WC or shower/WC and television • €42 to €67; breakfast €8; half-board available • Restaurant closed Sun evening except Jul-Aug and Mon lunchtime; menus €16 (weekdays) to €47 • Terrace, garden, garage, car park • Outdoor swimming pool

We most liked A visit to the disused slate quarries – if you're not afraid of heights!

This solid construction inspired by regional styles dates from the 1960s and was clearly built to last a few centuries. The stylish personalised rooms have matching fabrics, bedspreads and lampshades and those facing the rear look out over a peaceful Limousin landscape. Welcoming family dining rooms, a veranda flooded with light and a terrace opening onto the garden complete with swimming pool and play area.

Access : 6km on the D 920 towards Uzerche

6 CHEZ MONSIEUR ET MADAME PERROT
M. et Mme Perrot

Gourdinot
19460 Naves
Tel. 05 55 27 08 93
brunhild.perrot@wanadoo.fr
www.hotes-naves-correze.com

Open all year • 3 rooms upstairs, one of which has a loggia • €38 to €41, breakfast included; half-board available • Table d'hôte €15 • Car park. Credit cards not accepted, dogs not admitted

We most liked The sense of being right in the middle of nowhere.

This old Corrèze farmhouse built out of rough-hewn stone and nestling in a wooded valley is ideal for touring the region: Millevaches – literally "Thousand cows" plateau, Lake Seilhac and Uzerche. Soak up the peaceful atmosphere of the cosy bedrooms and relax by the fireside in the company of your lively young hosts. In the morning, you will awake to the enticing smell of fresh-baked bread, steaming coffee and a breakfast table piled high with a profusion of home-made gingerbreads and preserves.

Access : 5km northbound from Naves on the N 20, then take a minor road

LIMOUSIN
NESPOULS - 19600　　　　　　　　　　　SAINT-MARTIN-LA-MÉANNE - 19320

7　À LA TABLE DE LA BERGÈRE
Mme Verlhac

Belveyre
19600 Nespouls
Tel. 05 55 85 82 58

Open all year • 5 rooms • €40, breakfast included; half-board available • No table d'hôte • Garden, car park. Credit cards not accepted, no dogs admitted

If this farm wins any more awards, it may well run out of space to display them.

This sturdily built farmstead in the midst of oaks, meadows and dry stone huts is very well placed to explore the region's wealth of tourist sights. The rooms, furnished with family heirlooms, are very inviting, particularly those on the second floor, while the flavourful regional cooking, friendly atmosphere and Madame's ability to make you feel at home are unparalleled.

Access : Nespouls exit no 53, at the roundabout, turn right, then 1st right and 1st left

8　LES VOYAGEURS
M. et Mme Chaumeil

Place de la Mairie
19320 Saint-Martin-la-Méanne
Tel. 05 55 29 11 53
Fax 05 55 29 27 70
info@hotellesvoyageurs.com
www.hotellesvoyageurs.com

Open late Mar to 2 Nov; closed Sun evening and Mon out of season • 8 rooms upstairs with bath/WC or shower/WC, some have television • €40 to €51; breakfast €6; half-board available • Menus €16 to €34 • Terrace, garden, car park • Private pond for anglers

The lady of the house's warm greeting.

This establishment, which has been run by the same family for five generations, is ideal to get away from it all and take things easy. Within its solid stone walls, built in 1853, you'll find simple, but well cared-for bedrooms. Admire the wood carving in the rustic dining room, if you can tear yourself away from the traditional cuisine prepared by the chef-owner for a minute. After lunch or dinner, venture out into the garden as far as the pond and watch the carp and pike.

Access : On a square in the centre of the village

LIMOUSIN

TURENNE - 19500

SAINT-PARDOUX-LE-NEUF- 23200

9 LA MAISON DES CHANOINES
M. et Mme Cheyroux

Chemin de l'Église
19500 Turenne
Tel. 05 55 85 93 43
Fax 05 55 85 93 43
www.maison-des-chanoines.com

Open from Easter to late Sep • 6 rooms located in 2 buildings, with bath/WC or shower/WC • €65 to €90; breakfast €9; half-board available • Menus €30 to €40 (evenings only by reservation) • Terrace. Dogs not admitted in rooms

We most liked: The terrace overlooking a manicured herb garden.

It is well worth venturing past the late-Gothic door and into this lovely 16C house set in the heart of a picturesque village. There is as much character inside as out from the vaulted dining room, fireplace to the spiral staircase up to the rooms, which are furnished with the results of forays to local antiques dealers. At mealtimes, roll up your sleeves and dig into the chef's creative recipes prepared with the best local produce (including Périgord truffles). Limited seating only.

Access: In the centre of the village

10 CHAMBRE D'HÔTE M. DUMONTANT
M. et Mme Dumontant

Les Vergnes
23200 Saint-Pardoux-le-Neuf
Tel. 05 55 66 23 74
Fax 05 55 67 74 16
sylvie.dumontant@freesbee.fr
www.lesvergnes.com

Closed from late Oct to early Apr • 6 rooms with bathrooms and separate WC • €56, breakfast included • Table d'hôte €17 to €25 • Terrace, car park. Credit cards not accepted • Fishing

We most liked: Fishing in the nearby pond.

If in desperate need of a break from city life, your prayers will be answered in this 18C farmhouse, set in the heart of the countryside and surrounded by a prosperous working farm, only 7km from the tapestry capital of France. All the spacious, fully renovated rooms overlook the pond and nearby woodland. Original exposed stone walls and a huge fireplace add character to the dining room.

Access: 7km eastbound from Aubusson on the N 141

LIMOUSIN
COUSSAC-BONNEVAL - 87500   SAINT-PRIEST-TAURION - 87480

11 LE MOULIN DE MARSAGUET
M. Gizardin

87500 Coussac-Bonneval
Tel. 05 55 75 28 29
Fax 05 55 75 28 29
www.tourismorama-moulindemarsaguet.com

Closed from late Sep to mid-Apr • 3 rooms • €45, breakfast included • Table d'hôte €20 • Garden, terrace, car park. Credit cards not accepted, dogs not admitted • Cookery courses. Fishing, boating and swimming

Finding out how tasty farm delicacies are made.

The hospitality of this farming family will make you want to return to their rambling 18C farmstead and its immense 30-acre fishpond. Anglers will love catching pike while the others can go swimming or boating. The light, airy rooms are simply decorated and every evening brings an excellent opportunity to wine and dine on the succulent home-made delicacies in lively company.

Access: 3.6km northbound from Coussac on the D 17 towards La Roche-l'Abeille, then take the D 57

12 LE RELAIS DU TAURION
M. Roger

2 chemin des Contamines
87480 Saint-Priest-Taurion
Tel. 05 55 39 70 14
Fax 05 55 39 67 63

Closed from 15 Dec to 15 Jan • 8 rooms with bath/WC or shower/WC, almost all have television • €49 to €69; breakfast €8 • Restaurant closed Sun evening and Mon; menus €20 (weekdays) to €38 • Terrace, garden, car park. No dogs admitted in rooms • Swimming, fishing, canoeing nearby

The delightful owners.

This grand hundred-year-old mansion covered in Virginia creeper is home to immaculate little rooms, some of which have old marble fireplaces. Old beams and rustic furniture add charm to the sitting room. In the fine weather, tables are laid amid the luxuriant foliage of the flowered garden. Traditional cuisine.

Access: 11km to the north-east of Limoges on the D 29

LIMOUSIN

SOLIGNAC - 87110

13 SAINT-ÉLOI
Mme Ashton

66 avenue Saint-Éloi
87110 Solignac
Tel. 05 55 00 44 52
Fax 05 55 00 55 56
lesaint.eloi@wanadoo.fr
www.lesainteloi.fr

Closed 3 weeks in Jan, 1 week in Jun, 2 weeks in Sep, Mon, Sat lunchtime and Sun evening • 15 rooms with bath/WC and television, one room has disabled access • €46 to €65; breakfast €9; half-board available • Menus €16 (weekdays) to €45 • Terrace. No dogs admitted • Tea room with painting and sculpture exhibitions

The blessed union of medieval and modern.

Opposite the abbey founded by St Éloi, this half-timbered house in local stone welcomes guests in a spirit of peace and quiet. Spacious, well-soundproofed rooms are adorned with bright sunny fabrics and paintings. From his stained-glass window, good King Dagobert's treasurer, the patron saint of goldsmiths, gazes benignly down on diners as they savour the owner's flavoured cooking in a 12C dining room complete with granite fireplace.

Access: 10km southbound from Limoges on the D 704 (towards St-Yrieix), then right on the D 32

THOURON - 87140

14 LA POMME DE PIN
M. Mounier

Étang de Tricherie
87140 Thouron
Tel. 05 55 53 43 43
Fax 05 55 53 35 33

Closed during the February holidays, Sep, Mon and Tue, Wed and Sat lunchtimes • 7 rooms with bath/WC and television • €59 to €61; breakfast €7; half-board available • Menus €27 (weekdays) to €32 • Terrace, garden. No dogs admitted in rooms

Feast your eyes on a landscape of ponds, lakes and forest.

All the quiet, spacious rooms in the former spinning mill enjoy a view of the river, while the old mill on the banks of the millpond houses two dining rooms. The first offers an authentically rustic setting with rough stone walls and a huge fireplace where meat is roasted; the second is airier and overlooks the wonderful Limousin countryside.

Access: Northbound from Limoges on the A 20, take exit no 26, then take the D 5 towards Nantiat

LORRAINE

If you are planning a trip to Lorraine and want to do justice to the region's wealth of wonderful sights, make sure you pack your walking boots. However, before you set off for the distant reaches of its lofty slopes, pause for a moment in Nancy and take in its splendid artistic heritage, without forgetting to admire the lights of Metz. You can then move on through a string of tiny spa resorts, renowned for the slimming properties of their water, and the famous centres of craftsmanship which produce the legendary Baccarat crystal, enamels of Longwy and porcelain of Lunéville, before you reach the poignant silence of the dormant mines and quarries at Domrémy and Colombey. The deep lakes, thick forests and wild animals of the Vosges Regional Park will keep you entranced as you make your way down through the gentle hillsides, dotted with plum-laden orchards. Stop for a little 'light' refreshment in a *marcairerie*, one of the region's old farm-inns, and sample the famous quiches and tarts, before finishing with a slab of pungent Munster cheese or a kirsch-flavoured dessert for the sweet-toothed among us.

- Meurthe-et-Moselle (54)
- Meuse (55)
- Moselle (57)
- Vosges (88)

LORRAINE

ANCEMONT - 55320

1 CHÂTEAU DE LABESSIÈRE
M. Eichenauer

9 rue du Four
55320 Ancemont
Tel. 03 29 85 70 21
Fax 03 29 87 61 60
rene.eichenauer@wanadoo.fr
www.labessiere.com

- 4 rooms with bath/WC • €74, breakfast included; half-board available • Table d'hôte €28 • Garden, car park. Credit cards not accepted, dogs are welcome on demand. • Outdoor swimming pool

We most liked: A mite outdated but full of charm.

Midway between Argonne and the Côtes de Meuse, this unassuming 18C castle makes an ideal base camp to explore the region. Pastel wallpaper, canopied beds and old furniture all add to rather than detract from the rooms' appeal. The same pleasantly outmoded atmosphere prevails in the sitting room, remarkably well stocked with guides, brochures and works on the Meuse. The table d'hôte, open every evening, shaded garden and attractive outdoor swimming pool further enhance the establishment's allure.

Access : 15km southbound from Verdun on the D 34 (Saint-Mihiel road)

GORZE - 57680

2 HOSTELLERIE DU LION D'OR
M. Erman

105 rue du Commerce
57680 Gorze
Tel. 03 87 52 00 90
Fax 03 87 52 09 62

Closed Sun evening and Mon • 15 rooms located in 2 buildings, with bath/WC or shower/WC, all have television • €55 to €60; breakfast €8; half-board available • Menus €18 to €59 • Terrace, garden, car park • Children's play area

We most liked: The dense foliage shading the terrace.

Run by the same family for over fifty years, this 19C coaching inn has moved with the times without losing sight of its roots. The rooms have been gradually updated and we recommend those opening onto the lovely patio with a trout aquarium and splendid rafters. Back in the restaurant, a huge stone fireplace, fine enough to grace any castle banquet hall, holds its own among the distinctly contemporary-style furniture.

Access : To the south-west of Metz, on the D 6

LORRAINE

MANDEREN - 57480

3. AU RELAIS DU CHÂTEAU DE MENSBERG
M. Schneider

15 rue du Château
57480 Manderen
Tel. 03 82 83 73 16
Fax 03 82 83 23 37
aurelaismensberg@aol.com
www.relais-mensberg.com

Closed 26 Dec to 21 Jan, Mon from Jan to 15 Mar and Tue • 13 rooms, one of which has disabled access, almost all have shower/WC (2 have bath/WC), all have television • €60 (€51 low season); breakfast €8; half-board available • Menus €19 to €44 • Terrace, garden, car park

We most liked: The castle forms a handsome backdrop to a wide variety of performances.

"Malbrouck" was the name the French soldiers gave to one of their most redoutable enemies, the Duke of Marlborough. The duke set up his HQ here at Mensberg (also called Marlborough) Castle in 1705 but was unable to do battle, giving rise to a nursery rhyme still sung today. Three rooms overlook the beautifully restored castle. In addition to a rustic dining room graced by a huge stone fireplace, the inn has two split-level sitting rooms and a quiet terrace in the rear.

Access: From Sierck-les-Bains take the N 153 northbound for 2km, then at Apach turn right on the D 64

MEISENTHAL - 57960

4. AUBERGE DES MÉSANGES
M. et Mme Walter

2 rue du Tiseur
57960 Meisenthal
Tel. 03 87 96 92 28
Fax 03 87 96 99 14
hotel-restaurant.auberge-mesanges@wanadoo.fr
www.aubergedesmesanges.com

Closed from 18 Feb to 7 Mar, from 1 to 9 Jul and from 23 Dec to 2 Jan • 22 rooms with shower/WC, half of the rooms have television • €45 to €51 (€32 to €44 low season); breakfast €7; half-board available • Restaurant closed Sun evening and Mon; menus €10 (weekdays) to €17 • Terrace, car park

We most liked: Need to get back in touch with the things that really matter?

This inn, on the edge of the Nature Reserve of the Northern Vosges, is ideally located in calm surroundings and close to a whole range of leisure pursuits, including walking, golf, museums and castles. Good-sized, practically-equipped rooms in excellent order. Meals are served in a dining room whose uncluttered rustic style perfectly complements the simple, regional fare.

Access: Near the centre of the village

LORRAINE

METZ - 57000

5 LA CATHÉDRALE
M. Hocine

25 place de la Chambre
57000 Metz
Tel. 03 87 75 00 02
Fax 03 87 75 40 75
hotelcathedrale-metz@wanadoo.fr
www.hotelcathedrale-metz.fr

Open all year • 19 rooms and 1 apartment on 3 floors, most have bath/WC, some have shower/WC, all have television • €68 to €95; breakfast €11 • No restaurant

The splendid view of St Étienne Cathedral from most of the rooms.

The passing of time seems to have left no traces on the fine façade of this former coaching inn, which first opened its doors in 1627. Inside, however, the owners have really gone to town: individually styled rooms are adorned with wrought-iron furniture, bright fabrics or old pieces of furniture picked up in auctions and antique shops. The timber frames, fireplaces and parquet all bear witness to the establishment's four-hundred-year commitment to hostelry.

Access: In the town centre, near Saint-Étienne Cathedral

AUTREVILLE - 88300

6 LE RELAIS ROSE
M. Loëffler

24 rue de Neufchâteau
88300 Autreville
Tel. 03 83 52 04 98
Fax 03 83 52 06 03

Open all year • 16 rooms located in 3 buildings, most have bath/WC or shower/WC, all have television, some are non-smoking • €48 to €75; breakfast €9; half-board available • Menus €12 to €35 • Terrace, garden, garage, car park

The whole family bends over backwards to please its guests.

A prayer-stool, a handsome wardrobe, a well-worn leather armchair, an unusual patchwork of wallpapers from every age and era, some adorned with wonderfully garish flowers: the list is endless and the result a higgledy-piggledy mixture which proudly refuses to toe the line to any theme or age, and will strike a chord with your secret nonconformist side! For all their casually eclectic style, the renovated rooms are most appealing and the restaurant tables are laid with elegant china from Limoges.

Access: In the village, on the N 74 between Colombey-les-Belles and Neufchâteau

LORRAINE

BULGNÉVILLE - 88140

7 CHAMBRES D'HÔTES M. BRETON
M. Breton

74 rue des Récollets
88140 Bulgnéville
Tel. 03 29 09 21 72
Fax 03 29 09 21 72
benoit.breton@wanadoo.fr

Open all year, in winter by reservation only • 4 rooms • €68, breakfast included • No table d'hôte • Garden, car park. Credit cards not accepted. Dogs not admitted

A faultlessly decorated country home.

This unostentatious country house dating from 1720 was entirely redecorated by the owner-antique dealer. The result invites the admiration of everyone who sees it: spacious, comfortable rooms decorated with a tasteful blend of period furniture and modern décor. The sandstone bathrooms are particularly lovely and the garden behind the house is also worthy of note.

Access : 7.5km westbound from Contrexéville on the D 164

CONTREXÉVILLE - 88140

8 LA SOUVERAINE
M. Paris

Parc Thermal
88140 Contrexéville
Tel. 03 29 08 09 59
Fax 03 29 08 16 39
contact@hotel-souveraine.com
www.hotel-souveraine.com

Closed 25 Sep to late Mar • 31 rooms, half overlook the park, all have bath/WC or shower/WC and television • €85; breakfast €9; half-board available • Menus €26 to €34 • Car park. No dogs admitted in restaurant

The branches laden with crows do have a slightly Hitchcockian air to them.

Contrexéville was "the" place to take the waters at the height of the Belle Époque. The glass awning and friezes which embellish the graceful pink and white façade of this elegant home, leave one in no doubt about its allegiance to a former illustrious guest, the Grand Duchess Vladimir, aunt of Czar Nicholas II. Marble fireplaces, moulded ceilings and brass beds continue to grace the recently renovated bedrooms, some of which overlook the resort park.

Access : In the spa resort

LORRAINE

GÉRARDMER - 88400

9 LE CHALET DU LAC
M. Bernier

97 chemin de la Droite du Lac
88400 Gérardmer
Tel. 03 29 63 38 76
Fax 03 29 60 91 63

Closed from 1 to 31 Oct • 11 rooms, 4 of which are in a separate chalet, with shower/WC and television • €57; breakfast €8; half-board available • Menus €22 to €41 • Garden, car park • Table-tennis

Time seems to stand still on the shores of the lake.

This trim, traditional Vosges chalet built in 1866 is one of the few holiday homes of this sort, so popular round Lake Gérardmer in the 19C, to have made it through to the present day. The sober, immaculate rooms are sometimes furnished with family heirlooms; ask for a renovated room. Alsace tableware and cut-crystal glasses adorn the tables in the "winstub" styled restaurant with a sweeping view. The garden tumbles down to the lake and it is a real pleasure to wander round its paths.

Access : On the Épinal road, 1km to the west, opposite the lake

GÉRARDMER - 88400

10 JAMAGNE
Famille Jeanselme

2 boulevard Jamagne
88400 Gérardmer
Tel. 03 29 63 36 86
Fax 03 29 60 05 87
hotel.jamagne@wanadoo.fr
www.jamagne.com

Closed from 5 to 31 Mar and from 12 Nov to 22 Dec • 48 rooms with bath/WC or shower/WC, all have television • €80 to €90 (€70 to €85 low season); breakfast €10; half-board available • Menus €13 to €40 • Terrace, private car park. No dogs admitted in restaurant • Indoor swimming pool, fitness room, sauna, hammam, jacuzzi, hiking, water sports

Upholding traditions since 1905.

It is impossible to miss this impressive building on a street corner. Its owners endeavour to cater to families, offering several partitioned rooms, and to those with fewer family worries, with a cosy bar and sitting rooms. Guests eager to sample the region's delicious recipes can head for two lovely dining rooms, while those who have come for the region's sporting pursuits will not be disappointed by the hotel's excellent keep-fit facilities, indoor swimming pool and the countless forest paths.

Access : In the town centre

LORRAINE

GIRMONT-VAL-D'AJOL - 88340

11 AUBERGE DE LA VIGOTTE
M. et Mme Bouguerne

88340 Girmont-Val-d'Ajol
Tel. 03 29 61 06 32
Fax 03 29 61 07 88
courrier@lavigotte.com
www.lavigotte.com

Closed from 15 Oct to 15 Dec • 15 rooms and 1 apartment, most have bath/WC, some have shower/WC • €55 to €100; breakfast €7; half-board available • Restaurant closed Tue and Wed; menus €25 to €38 • Terrace, garden, car park • Tennis, fishing and swimming in private ponds, play area, hiking, cross-country skiing

It is impossible to find a fault with this Vosgian inn.

A quick glimpse at the web site of the "via gotta" – "way of springs" – will give you an idea of the new owners' energetic, up-to-date approach since buying the inn in 2000. In no time at all, this old farmhouse, perched at a height of 700m in a forest of fir trees and ponds, has become a very pleasant and popular hostelry thanks to its delightful rooms and "country chic" restaurant. The chef's inventive recipes are a feast for the eyes as well as the mouth.

Access : Between the Ajol Valley and Remiremont (D 23), at Faymon take the D 83 for 5km

LA CHAPELLE-AUX-BOIS - 88240

12 LES GRANDS PRÉS
Mme Chassard

9 les Grands-Prés
88240 La Chapelle-aux-Bois
Tel. 03 29 36 31 00
Fax 03 29 36 31 00

Open all year • 3 rooms and 2 gîtes • €40, breakfast included; half-board available • Table d'hôte €15 • Garden, car park. Credit cards not accepted, dogs not admitted in restaurant

Fishing in the garden.

This immense 19C house encircled by lush green countryside lies just a few minutes from the spa resort of Bains-les-Bains. Spotless, soberly styled rooms overlook a garden through which a fishing stream gurgles and babbles. Home-grown vegetables from the cottage garden and fresh poultry and rabbit reared on the premises are among the specialities on the dinner table.

Access : 3.5km to the south-east of Bains-les-Bains towards Saint-Loup, then take a minor road

LORRAINE

LA PETITE-FOSSE - 88490

13 AUBERGE DU SPITZEMBERG
M. et Mme Calba

88490 La Petite-Fosse
Tel. 03 29 51 20 46
Fax 03 29 51 10 12

Closed Jan • 10 rooms upstairs with bath/WC or shower/WC, some have television • €48 to €61; breakfast €7; half-board available • Restaurant closed Mon evening and Tue evening out of season; menus €16 (weekdays) to €25 • Garden, garage, car park • Mini-golf and walks in the forest

We most liked: Swathed in a curtain of greenery.

Step inside this haven of tranquillity in the remote forest of the Vosges and forget your troubles for a while. The comfortable rooms are pleasantly homely and welcoming and the tasty, unfussy cooking, made with rigorously selected regional produce, is served in a rustic dining room. All you have to decide now is which direction to head off for your long walk in the country. No need to leave that trail of breadcrumbs, though; all the paths are well signposted.

Access : 3.5km from Provenchères-sur-Fave on the D 45, then take a forest road

LE VAL-D'AJOL - 88340

14 LA RÉSIDENCE
Mme Bongeot

5 rue des Mousses
88340 Le Val-d'Ajol
Tel. 03 29 30 68 52
Fax 03 29 66 53 00
contact@la-residence.com
www.la-residence.com

Closed from 26 Nov to 26 Dec • 49 rooms located in 3 buildings with bath/WC or shower/WC and television • €58 to €85; breakfast €9; half-board available • Restaurant closed Sun eve from 1 Nov to 30 Apr; menus €17 (weekdays) to €53 • Park, car park • Swimming pool with a retractable roof, tennis

We most liked: Waking up to a dawn chorus.

Contemporary and Louis XV rooms are spread over three buildings backing onto the forest which make up the Residence: a 19C country house, an "orangery" which can be reached by a glass-covered gallery, and a former coaching inn, 50m away. A fireplace is the centrepiece of a light, airy dining room. As for leisure, the hotel offers a swimming pool with removable roof, tennis courts and a mature wooded park for pre-dinner strolls.

Access : On leaving the village take the lane leading to Hamanxard

LORRAINE

LE VALTIN - 88230   XONRUPT-LONGEMER - 88400

15 LE VAL JOLI
M. et Mme Laruelle

12 bis Le Village
88230 Le Valtin
Tel. 03 29 60 91 37
Fax 03 29 60 81 73
le-val-joli@wanadoo.fr
www.levaljoli.com

Closed from 13 Nov to 6 Dec, Sun evening, Mon evening and Tue lunchtime (except school holidays) • 7 rooms and 3 apartments, with bath or shower/WC • €75 to €80; breakfast €12; half-board available • Restaurant closed Mon lunchtime; menus €16 (weekdays) to €70 • Terrace, garden, car park • Tennis, hiking

That sound, unlike anything else you have ever heard, is that of a rutting buck!

This appealing country inn almost on the doorstep of the superb Route des Crêtes (Peak Road) has a number of renovated rooms; and all the accommodation overlooks the dense pine forests and mountains. A strong emphasis is given to local produce on the menu and meals are served in the rustic dining room – yes, the 19C carved wooden ceiling is original – or in the more modern veranda. The owner-mayor is a mine of helpful tips about the "panoramic path" around the village, dotted with viewpoints.

Access : In the village, drive along the D 23 from Fraize to the Schlucht Pass

16 LE COLLET
M. et Mme Lapôtre

Col de la Schlucht
88400 Xonrupt-Longemer
Tel. 03 29 60 09 57
Fax 03 29 60 08 77
hotcollet@aol.com
www.chalethotel-lecollet.com

Closed from 5 Nov to 4 Dec • 25 rooms, all have bath/WC or shower/WC and television • €72 to €92; breakfast €10; half-board available • Menus €15 (lunchtime weekdays) to €26 • Terrace, car park. No dogs admitted in restaurant • Skiing and hiking trails nearby

A perfect base camp to explore the breathtaking Route des Crêtes (Peak Route).

The walls of this hotel chalet, lost in a forest of fir trees, make it impossible to guess what is inside. For the hospitable owners, entertaining guests does not simply mean providing a cheerful mountain décor with pretty fabrics and painted furniture or a deliciously tempting regional menu: it is above all, a state of mind. Their attention to detail can be felt in the smell of warm brioche in the morning, the wealth of useful tips for walkers or the magic shows for children.

Access : 2km from the Schlucht Pass on the Gérardmer road, by the D 417

MIDI-PYRÉNÉES

Lourdes may be famous as the site of miracles, but some would say that the whole of the Midi-Pyrénées has been uniquely blessed. The region is home to a rich and varied plant and animal life, with the remoter parts of the Pyrenees still supporting a population of brown bears. A great rampart guarding the border with Spain, these breathtaking mountains are riven by spectacularly deep clefts and are drained by rushing torrents. At sunset, the towers of medieval cities and fortresses glow in the evening light; forbidding Cathar castles are stained a bloody red, Albi and its famous fortified cathedral turn crimson while Toulouse is veiled in dusty pink. Deep beneath the surface of the earth at Lascaux and elsewhere are equally extraordinary sights, the vivid cave-paintings of our gifted prehistoric ancestors. To this list of regional marvels must be added the bounteous lands along the River Garonne, a fertile land famous for its cereal crops, vegetables fruit and wine, which has given rise to a host of culinary traditions; it would be a crime to leave without sampling a sumptuous cassoulet, confit de canard or foie gras.

- Ariège (09)
- Aveyron (12)
- Haute-Garonne (31)
- Gers (32)
- Lot (46)
- Hautes-Pyrénées (65)
- Tarn (81)
- Tarn-et-Garonne (82)

MIDI PYRÉNÉES

AULUS-LES-BAINS - 09140

1 LES OUSSAILLÈS
Mme Charrue

09140 Aulus-les-Bains
Tel. 05 61 96 03 68
Fax 05 61 96 03 70
jcharrue@free.fr

Open all year • 12 rooms on two floors, with bath/WC or shower/WC and television • €47 to €53; breakfast €7; half-board available • Menus €10 to €14 • Terrace, garden, garage. No dogs admitted

We most liked
So friendly, you'll think you're at home.

This 1920s stone house is flanked by a turret. The bedrooms overlooking the garden, by far the most pleasant, enjoy a lovely view of the flourishing green valley. Even better, you can ask for breakfast to be served on your own private balcony. In fine weather, the welcoming restaurant opens onto a shaded terrace.

Access : In the heart of the village, 33km to the south-east of Saint Girons

FOIX - 09000

2 AUBERGE LES MYRTILLES
M. et Mme Blazy

Col des Marrous
09000 Foix
Tel. 05 61 65 16 46
Fax 05 61 65 16 46
aubergelesmyrtilles@wanadoo.fr
http://perso.wanadoo.fr/auberge.les.myrtilles

Closed from 1 Jan to 10 Feb, Nov and Dec, Wed lunchtime (low season) and Mon and Tue • 7 rooms, 5 with shower/WC, 2 with bath/WC, all have television • €66 to €72; breakfast €7; half-board available • Menus €17 to €25 • Terrace, garden, car park. No dogs admitted in restaurant • Swimming pool, sauna, jacuzzi

We most liked
The two rooms recently renovated in an alpine spirit.

Dig into a piece of blueberry pie, choose a vintage Bordeaux from the wine-list, dive into the swimming pool, walk along the signposted footpath through a beech forest, gaze down on Arget Valley from the terrace, listen to the bucks rutting or just soak up the priceless serenity. Shake them all up and voilà: a delicious "sport and leisure" cocktail! You can of course simply do absolutely nothing from dawn until dusk!

Access : 19km westbound from Foix on the D 17

MIDI PYRÉNÉES

SAINT-GIRONS - 09200

3 EYCHENNE
Famille Bordeau

8 avenue Paul-Laffont
09200 Saint-Girons
Tel. 05 61 04 04 50
Fax 05 61 96 07 20
eychen@club-internet.fr
www.ariege.com/hotel-eychenne

Closed from Dec to Jan, Sun evening and Mon from Nov to Mar (except public holidays) • 43 rooms, all have bath/WC or shower/WC and television • €53 to €190 (€45 to €165 low season); breakfast €10; half-board available • Menus €25 to €55 • Private car park • Swimming pool

The banks of the Salat shaded by a long line of plane trees - how beautifully, typically French!

The Bordeau family has been running this coaching inn for seven generations. This lasting dedication probably explains the quality of the welcome and the deliciously old-fashioned atmosphere that reigns throughout the establishment. The stamp of a family business can be felt everywhere from the scent of beeswax in the bedrooms or the tad outdated wallpaper down to the lovely "retro" lamps. Classic cuisine and full-bodied wines from south-western France take pride of place on the table.

Access : Leave Bd du Général de Gaulle to take Av d'Aulot, then Rue F. Arnaud and turn right

SALSEIN - 09800

4 MAISON DE LA GRANDE OURSE
Mme Roux

09800 Salsein
Tel. 05 61 96 06 25

Open weekends in winter • 3 rooms, one of which is self-contained. One room has a shower and 1 a private sitting room and bathroom • €45, breakfast included • Table d'hôte €15 (evenings only) • Car park. Credit cards not accepted

The sophistication of this mountain dwelling.

This old village house has been beautifully restored. The rooms are tastefully decorated and the one under the eaves boasts a bathroom with a magnificent claw-footed bathtub and an enormous aquarium. Breakfast and meals are taken in the delightful flagstoned kitchen decorated with old furniture. Highly recommended.

Access : 3km westbound from Castillon-en-Couserans

MIDI PYRÉNÉES

AUBRAC - 12470

5 HÔTEL - RESTAURANT LA DÔMERIE
Mme Augny

12470 Aubrac
Tel. 05 65 44 28 42
Fax 05 65 44 21 47
david.mc@wanadoo.fr
www.hoteldomerie.com

Closed from 10 Oct to 15 Apr • 28 rooms on 2 floors with bath/WC or shower/WC, some have television • €57 to €80; breakfast €9; half-board available • Restaurant closed Wed, Thu and Fri lunchtimes (low season); menus €19 to €39 • Garden, car park • Walking

We most liked **Don't miss your chance to taste a real "aligot" – mashed potato with garlic and local cheese!**

Aubrac is justly renowned for its exceptional wild flora, sprawling fields dotted with peacefully grazing light-brown cows and "burons", or cowherds' huts, its vast beech forests and its old Roman road. Countless footpaths criss-cross the region and the owner is more than happy to advise and point you in the right direction! His large house, built in 1870 out of local basalt, offers well-maintained rooms with sturdy farmhouse furniture and a timbered dining room in pale wood.

Access : In the centre of the village

BELCASTEL - 12390

6 HÔTEL DU VIEUX PONT
Mmes Fagegaltier

12390 Belcastel
Tel. 05 65 64 52 29
Fax 05 65 64 44 32
hotel-du-vieux-pont@wanadoo.fr
www.hotelbelcastel.com

Closed from 1 Jan to 15 Mar, Sun evening, Mon and Tue lunchtime • 7 rooms in a converted barn, one of which has disabled access, all have bath/WC and television • €75 to €90; breakfast €12; half-board available • Menus €27 (weekdays) to €78 • Car park

We most liked **The village of Belcastel, voted one of the most beautiful in Aveyron.**

Two old stone houses stand on either side of the beautiful 15C arched bridge which spans the River Aveyron. The hotel, on the left bank, is home to small rooms with parquet floors, most of which overlook the river. In the summer, breakfast is served in the garden. The restaurant, on the right bank, is an elegant blend of rustic and modern styles; its gourmet dishes do full justice to the excellent local produce and have earned the house "star" status in the Michelin Red Guide since 1991.

Access : In the heart of the village, opposite the old bridge

MIDI PYRÉNÉES

BOZOULS - 12340

7 À LA ROUTE D'ARGENT
M. Catusse

La Rotonde
12340 Bozouls
Tel. 05 65 44 92 27
Fax 05 65 48 81 40
yves.catusse@wanadoo.fr

Closed in Jan, Feb, Sun evening and Mon except evenings in Jul-Aug • 21 rooms with bath/WC or shower/WC and television, 6 in a separate wing, 1 with disabled access • €40 to €56; breakfast €6; half-board available • Air-conditioned restaurant; menus €15 (weekdays) to €38 • Car park, garage • Outdoor swimming pool

Tasty traditional fare lovingly prepared by the owner-chef.

The unassuming façade of this family hostelry hides a contemporary interior. Unpolished metal, modern light fixtures, warm woodwork and light fabrics set the scene in the lobby and restaurant. The bar-sitting room lit by a veranda window is equally unusual in style with a fresco and map of the region engraved on a sheet of glass. The rooms are cheerful and comfortable; those in the annex are more spacious with balconies overlooking a small garden.

Access : On the way into Bozouls, at the crossroads between the D 988 and the D 920

ENTRAYGUES-SUR-TRUYÈRE - 12140

8 AUBERGE DU FEL
Mme Albespy

Le Fel
12140 Entraygues-sur-Truyère
Tel. 05 65 44 52 30
Fax 05 65 48 64 96
info@auberge-du-fel.com
auberge-du-fel.com

Open from 8 Apr to 3 Nov • 10 rooms with bath/WC or shower/WC and television, 1 with disabled access • €54 to €60; breakfast €7; half-board available • Restaurant closed lunchtimes except Sat, Sun, national and school holidays; menus €18 to €33 • Terrace, garden

This hamlet overlooking the Lot Valley feels like the middle of nowhere.

This stone house, veiled in Virginia creeper and nestling in a peaceful hamlet, is perfect for those in search of ultimate quietude. The owner however takes nothing for granted and is devoted to the upkeep of her inn, from the pretty personalised bedrooms, each named after a vine, to the delicious dining room, part of which overlooks the Lot Valley. Pounti, charcuterie, truffade and other local dishes are just a few of the delicacies you can taste, all washed down with a Fel wine perhaps.

Access : 10km westbound of Entraygues-sur-Truyère, take the D 107, turn right on the D 573

MIDI PYRÉNÉES

ESTAING - 12190

9 AUBERGE SAINT-FLEURET
Mme Moreau

19 rue François d'Estaing
12190 Estaing
Tel. 05 65 44 01 44
Fax 05 65 44 72 19
auberge.st.fleuret@wanadoo.fr
http://perso.wanadoo.fr/auberge.st.fleuret

Open from 15 Mar to 15 Nov, closed Sun evening and Mon out of season • 14 rooms with shower/WC, some have television • €47 to €51; breakfast €7; half-board available • Menus €17 to €55 • Garden, garage

Savouring the full-flavoured cuisine in front of the fire or overlooking the garden depending on the season.

"A good meal and a good night's sleep" is the self-declared motto of this welcoming inn, a staging post in its former life. The rooms may not be enormous, but are renovated, colourful and well soundproofed, with a view either of the village or the garden. Don't forget to book a table in the restaurant. The chef gets up before dawn to select the best produce of the season which he skilfully assembles into a host of tasty regional dishes.

Access : In the heart of the village

MILLAU - 12100

10 CHÂTEAU DE CREISSELS
M. et Mme Austruy

Route de Saint-Affrique - Creissels
12100 Millau
Tel. 05 65 60 16 59
Fax 05 65 61 24 63
www.château-de-creissels.com

Closed Jan and Feb • 30 rooms, 2 of which have disabled access, 12 are in the old castle. Most rooms have bath/WC, some have shower/WC, all have television • €58 to €88; breakfast €9; half-board available • Restaurant closed Sun evening and Mon lunchtime; menus €24 to €52 • Terrace, garden, car park

View of the village and valley.

Chequered parquet floors, wainscoting, a marble fireplace and period furniture: the "Bishop's Room" in the medieval castle can hardly be said to lack character. The others, more everyday, are located in the 1970s wing and have balconies. A vaulted 12C hall houses the restaurant. On fine days, tables are laid outdoors under the arcades of a gallery overlooking the village rooftops.

Access : In a small village above Millau, on the road to Albi

MIDI PYRÉNÉES

NANT - 12230

11 L'HERMITAGE SAINT-PIERRE
M. et Mme Macq

Lieu-dit Saint-Pierre-de-Revens
12230 Nant
Tel. 05 65 62 27 99
madeleine.macq@wanadoo.fr
http://hermitage.st.pierre.site.voila.fr

Open all year • 5 rooms • €69 to €79, breakfast included • Table d'hôte €20 to €25 (by reservation from 15 Oct to 15 Apr) • Credit cards not accepted, dogs not admitted • Swimming in the river nearby

The laughter of the children swimming in the crystal-clear waters of the Dourbie.

You can't blame the owners for falling head over heels with this spot steeped in history which was originally a chapel (10C and 11C), then a Knights Templar post and a parish church. Now a B&B establishment, it offers beautifully decorated rooms whose heritage can still be seen in any number of details, such as the stone vaults, period furniture, four-poster beds or a 17C altarpiece. The garden at the foothills of the Causse Noir and on the banks of the Dourbie is equally delightful.

Access : 11km to the north-west of Nant towards Millau on the D 991

SAINT-JEAN-DU-BRUEL - 12230

12 MIDI-PAPILLON
M. et Mme Papillon

12230 Saint-Jean-du-Bruel
Tel. 05 65 62 26 04
Fax 05 65 62 12 97

Open from Palm Sunday to 11 Nov • 18 rooms with bath/WC, some have shower/WC • €33 to €59; breakfast €5; half-board available • Menus €14 (weekdays) to €37 • Garden, car park, garage • Outdoor swimming pool

A hotel committed to upholding country traditions.

Ten pigs fatted up each year by a local farmer, a full-time gardener supplying fresh fruit and vegetables to the kitchen table, a farmyard full of barn animals and mushrooms picked by shepherds: since 1850 the Papillon family has been a perfect illustration of the fierce local desire to remain close to its roots. Personalised bedrooms, without the modern distraction of television, and a pleasant restaurant whose bay windows overlook the Dourbie and its lovely 15C arched bridge.

Access : In the village, on the D 999, next to the stone bridge

MIDI PYRÉNÉES

SAINT-SERNIN-SUR-RANCE - 12380

13 CARAYON
M. Carayon

Place du Fort
12380 Saint-Sernin-sur-Rance
Tel. 05 65 98 19 19
Fax 05 65 99 69 26
carayon.hotel@wanadoo.fr
www.hotel-carayon.com

Closed Sun evening, Mon and Tue lunchtime (except Jul-Aug) • 74 rooms, 4 of which with disabled access, with bath/WC or shower/WC and television • €41 to €89; breakfast €8; half-board available • Menus €14 to €54 • Garage, private car park, park, terrace • Tennis, mini-golf, keep-fit rooms, sauna, swimming pools

We most liked
The countless leisure activities dotted around the tree-lined park.

Since 1876, this coaching inn has been the hub of this peaceful Aveyron village standing on the banks of the Rance. The Carayon family has been perfecting the art of receiving guests here for four generations. You will sleep either in the original building, a more recent wing or in one of the little houses in the park. The rooms are comfortable and practically fitted out; we recommend those opening onto the woodland. The spacious dining room leads onto a terrace overlooking the open fields.

Access : In the heart of the village

ALAN - 31420

14 LE POUPAT
Mme Marnay

Route de Bachas
31420 Alan
Tel. 05 61 98 98 14
Fax 05 61 98 71 45
michelle.bechard@wanadoo.fr

Open all year • 3 rooms with bath/WC • €50, breakfast included • Table d'hôte €20 • Play area, park, garden, car park • Outdoor swimming pool, horses

We most liked
Riding round the countryside on one of the three horses available to guests.

This sprawling 16C building, nestling within extensive parkland lost in the countryside, is ideal for weary travellers in need of a peaceful night's rest. On the ground-floor, the sitting and dining rooms boast impressive period fireplaces and are furnished with Louis XV-style pieces. Upstairs, bare beams, rustic furniture, colourful walls and knickknacks adorn the sober rooms. Guests appreciate the pleasant homely atmosphere.

Access : 1km from Alan on the Bachas road

MIDI PYRÉNÉES

AUTERIVE - 31190

15 LA MANUFACTURE
Mme Balansa

2 rue des Docteurs-Basset
31190 Auterive
Tel. 05 61 50 08 50
Fax 05 61 50 08 50
manufacture@manufacture-royale.net
www.manufacture-royale.net

Closed Nov to Mar • 5 non-smoking rooms and 1 gîte, all with bath/WC or shower/WC and internet access • €75 to €80, breakfast included • No table d'hôte • Park, terrace, car park. Credit cards not accepted, dogs not admitted • Outdoor swimming pool, table tennis, bicycles

Admire the period furniture and objects.

This royal bed-linen factory (18C), converted into living accommodation around 1880 by Dr Jules Basset, has retained many traces of its rich past: the swimming pool is located in the former rinsing pool, family portraits adorn the staircase and the spacious bedrooms are furnished with family heirlooms. An ideal chance to take a step back in time while continuing to enjoy modern comforts and a pleasantly relaxed youthful welcome.

Access: In the village on the banks of the Ariège

AYGUESVIVES - 31450

16 LA PRADASSE
M. et Mme Antoine

39 chemin de Toulouse
31450 Ayguesvives
Tel. 05 61 81 55 96
Fax 05 61 81 89 76
contact@lapradasse.com
www.lapradasse.com

Open all year • 5 rooms with bath/WC or shower/WC, 1 with disabled access • €65 to €80, breakfast included; half-board available • Table d'hôte €25 • Park, car park. No dogs admitted • Outdoor swimming pool

The exquisite interior decoration is worthy of the cover of any Home and Garden magazine.

The brochure of La Pradasse mentions "characterful rooms set in a haven of peace and quiet". Which is totally misleading, because the reality is much better! The superbly restored, early-19C house boasts rooms, each more charming than the last, to such an extent that you will want to try them all. Light floods into the dining-sitting room through an enormous glass window and outside an extensive park, flower garden, vegetable plot and swimming pool are just waiting to be discovered.

Access: 15km south-east of Toulouse on the N 113, then the D 16 for 1.1km

MIDI PYRÉNÉES

BAGNÈRES-DE-LUCHON - 31110

17 PAVILLON SÉVIGNÉ
Mme Seiter

2 avenue Jacques-Barrau
31110 Bagnères-de-Luchon
Tel. 05 61 79 31 50
seiter@pavillonsevigne.com
http://www.pavillonsevigne.com

Open all year • 5 non-smoking rooms on 2 floors, all with bath/WC or shower/WC and modem access • €80, breakfast included; half-board available • Table d'hôte €20 • Credit cards not accepted, dogs not admitted

Exquisite antique furniture.

This 19C manor house is home to pleasant airy rooms decorated with carefully selected fabrics and furnished with some quite remarkable antiques. At weekends, meals are served in the dining room overlooking the garden and in a neighbouring restaurant the rest of the week (half-board). Lovely sitting room-library with piano. Antique lovers will make a beeline for this address, particularly as it is equally well appointed in modern comforts.

Access: In the town centre

BALMA - 31130

18 LE MANOIR SAINT-CLAIR
M. Bourdoncle

20 chemin de Sironis
31130 Balma
Tel. 05 61 24 36 98
manoirsaintclair@cegetel.net
www.manoirsaintclair.com

Open all year • 3 non-smoking rooms upstairs, all with bath/WC or shower/WC, air-conditioning and television • €73 to €83, breakfast included • No table d'hôte • Terrace, garden, car park. Credit cards not accepted

Savouring the calm of the countryside just two minutes from Toulouse.

An immaculately groomed park with well-tended paths and lovely roses surrounds this authentic 17C pink brick manor house. Breakfasts are served on the veranda, which leads up to the personalised simple but well-cared for rooms, whose names evoke local historic events: "Cathare", "Pastel" and "Aeropostale", the latter is the most spacious and overlooks Saint-Clair Lake. Delightfully welcoming owners.

Access: 4km east of Toulouse on the D 50

MIDI PYRÉNÉES

CABANAC-SEGUENVILLE - 31480

19 CHÂTEAU DE SÉGUENVILLE
M. Lareng

Séguenville
31480 Cabanac-Séguenville
Tel. 05 62 13 42 67
Fax 05 62 13 42 68
info@chateau-de-seguenville.com
www.chateau-de-seguenville.com

Closed from 15 Dec to 15 Jan • 5 rooms with bath/WC or shower/WC • €95 to €115, breakfast included • Table d'hôte €22 • Park, car park. Credit cards not accepted, no dogs admitted • Outdoor swimming pool

We most liked: Exploring the park and its hundred-year-old trees with the Pyrenees in the background.

The origins of this château, set in a secluded park, date back to 1271, but its current architecture bears more resemblance to the 19C because it was rebuilt after the French Revolution. The guestrooms, reached by a lovely staircase, are full of charm with old parquet floors or tiles, handsome fireplaces, antique furniture, bright colours, curios and immaculate bathrooms. On the ground-floor, two inviting sitting rooms add to the establishment's appeal.

Access: 5km from Cox on the D 1 north-west of l'Isle-Jourdain

JUZET-DE-LUCHON - 31110

20 LE POUJASTOU
M. Cottereau

Rue du Sabotier
31110 Juzet-de-Luchon
Tel. 05 61 94 32 88
Fax 05 61 94 32 88
info@lepoujastou.com
www.lepoujastou.com

Open all year • 5 rooms upstairs, all have bath/WC or shower/WC • €47, breakfast included; half-board available • Table d'hôte €16 • Terrace, garden, car park. Credit cards not accepted, no dogs admitted

We most liked: Your host, an alpine guide, organises snowshoe excursions in winter and mountain biking in summer.

This large south-facing house, which commands fine views of the Luchonnais peaks, began life as the village's concert hall in the 18C. Stylishly renovated, it now offers brand new ochre-coloured bedrooms, some sizeable, others more compact. A warm sitting room lined with works on the region's fauna and flora and a Pyrenean-style dining room are on the ground floor. A terrace, garden and finely-flavoured home cooking round off the picture of an excellent establishment.

Access: Near the church

MIDI PYRÉNÉES

MONTESQUIEU-VOLVESTRE - 31310

21 LA HALTE DU TEMPS
Mme Garcin

72 rue Mage
31310 Montesquieu-Volvestre
Tel. 05 61 97 56 10
Fax 05 61 90 49 03
lahaltedutemps@free.fr

Open all year • 5 rooms with bathrooms • €54 to €64, breakfast included; half-board available • Table d'hôte €22 (evening only by reservation) • Garden. Credit cards not accepted • Outdoor swimming pool, jacuzzi, sauna

We most liked: Madame's exceptional story-telling talents.

Cross the charming inner courtyard to reach this elegant 17C mansion in the heart of town: the façade may not seem inspiring but the fully original staircases, floors and furniture make it well worth a stay. Superb, exquisitely decorated bedrooms with alcove bathrooms. The lovely dining room with a huge fireplace is quite the equal of the delicious cuisine.

Access: In the town centre

RAMONVILLE-SAINT-AGNE - 31250

22 LA PÉNICHE SOLEÏADO
Mme Roussel

Pont-de-Mange-Pomme
31250 Ramonville-Saint-Agne
Tel. 06 86 27 83 19
Fax 05 62 19 07 71

Open all year • 3 non-smoking rooms, all with bathrooms • €80, breakfast included; half-board available • Table d'hôte €30 • Terrace. Credit cards not accepted, dogs not admitted

We most liked: The irresistible charm of this barge on the Midi canal.

There is of course no point in expecting to enjoy the same space you would find in castles or manor houses, but this barge moored along the Midi canal shaded by plane trees is nonetheless full of character. The wooden interior is both warm and simple with a pleasant sitting-dining room area and pretty bedrooms with private bathrooms. The friendly welcome and the meals served on deck also add to the appeal of this unusual form of accommodation.

Access: At the roundabout at the south port (Port Sud), take the road behind the pharmacy, towards "Ferme Cinquante"

MIDI PYRÉNÉES

REVEL-SAINT-FERRÉOL - 31250

23 HÔTELLERIE DU LAC
M. Maréchal

Avenue Pierre-Paul Riquet
31250 Revel-Saint-Ferréol
Tel. 05 62 18 70 80
Fax 05 62 18 71 13
contact @ hotellerie-du-lac.com
www.hotellerie-du-lac.com

Open all year • 25 rooms, 4 of which are split-level (with kitchenettes), one has disabled access, all have bath/WC and television • €62; breakfast €8; half-board available • Menu €12 to €35 • Terrace, garden, car park. No dogs admitted in rooms • Heated outdoor swimming pool overlooking the lake

The view of the lake from the striking terraced swimming pool

If the locals are to be believed, Saint Ferréol, the local patron saint, continues to watch over the tranquillity of this elegant lakeside house surrounded by greenery. A masterful renovation has left the original character of the place intact: most of the rooms share a splendid view of the lake with the exquisite swimming pool. When it comes to relaxing, the warm sitting room-bar, sauna, fitness room and quaint garden are also worthy of mention. Classic dishes on a traditional menu.

Access : Overlooking the lake, 3km to the south-east of Revel on the D 629

RIEUMES - 31370

24 AUBERGE LES PALMIERS
M. Vallès

13 place du Foirail
31370 Rieumes
Tel. 05 61 91 81 01
Fax 05 61 91 56 36
infos @ auberge-lespalmiers.com
www.auberge-lespalmiers.com

Closed one week in Jan and late Aug to early Sep • 7 rooms, one of which has disabled access, with bath/WC or shower/WC and television • €58 to €75; breakfast €7; half-board available • Restaurant closed Sun evening and Mon; menus €14 to €35 • Garden, terrace. Dogs not admitted in rooms • Outdoor swimming pool

The friendly, down-to-earth owners.

Several palm trees adorn the garden behind this picturesque inn. Built in the 19C, it was recently extended, and borders the pretty village square. The spacious, comfortable rooms feature a happy marriage of rustic furniture, parquet floors and contemporary touches. Fancy a snack or a full three-course meal? Sit down under the beams in the dining room and build up your strength with generous helpings of traditional cuisine.

Access : In the heart of the village

MIDI PYRÉNÉES

ST-BERTRAND-DE-COMMINGES - 31150

25 HÔTEL DU COMMINGES
Mme Alaphilippe

Place de la Basilique
31510 Saint-Bertrand-de-Comminges
Tel. 05 61 88 31 43
Fax 05 61 94 98 22

Open from Apr to Oct • 14 rooms, most have bath/WC or showers, with or without WC • €30 to €52; breakfast €6 • No restaurant • Small car park. No dogs admitted

The peace and quiet of a convent.

Overlooking the forecourt of the fascinating Cathédrale Ste-Marie, this hotel was once a convent and it cannot be faulted for its peace and quiet, particularly in the summer, when the square is entirely free of cars. The guests' quarters and rooms are all fitted with handsome country furniture. During the long summer months, a pleasant terrace is laid under an arbour behind the main building. Run by the same family for three generations, it is a place you will remember.

Access: In the centre of the village, opposite the cathedral

SAINT-FÉLIX-LAURAGAIS - 31540

26 AUBERGE DU POIDS PUBLIC
M. Taffarello

Rue St-Roch
31540 Saint-Félix-Lauragais
Tel. 05 62 18 85 00
Fax 05 62 18 85 05
poidspublic@wanadoo.fr
www.auberge-du-poidspublic.com

Closed Jan and 1 week in Nov • 11 rooms and 1 apartment with bath/WC or shower/WC and television, 4 are air-conditioned • €65 to €98; breakfast €11; half-board available • Menus €27 to €68 • Terrace, garage

The unusual and historic public weighing-scales next door to this charming inn.

This inn is the talk of the town and the region! Some vaunt the quality of the cooking which is a creative blend of classical cuisine and local produce, while others sing the praises of the country-style restaurant with its pleasant terrace overlooking the countryside. Finally, the comfortable, low-key rooms have been gradually renovated and are immaculately cared for. All in all, this attractive village inn is a treat, as much for the eye as for the palate.

Access: In the village

MIDI PYRÉNÉES

SAINT-PAUL-D'OUEIL - 31110

27 MAISON JEANNE
Mme Guerre

au bourg
31110 Saint-Paul-d'Oueil
Tel. 05 61 79 81 63
Fax 05 61 79 81 63
www.maison-jeanne-luchon.com

Open all year • 3 non-smoking rooms, all with bath/WC or shower/WC • €67, breakfast included • No table d'hôte • Garden. Credit cards not accepted, dogs not admitted

Getting back to grass roots.

The shingled terrace, stone walls and marble floors of this handsome sun-drenched house are typical of the Oueil valley. Guests appreciate the comfortable and stylish bedrooms furnished with antiques and pretty fabrics, all of which command fine views of the Pyrenean peaks. The lady of the house did the delicate stencil-work on the walls and floors herself. Home from home!

Access : 8km northwest of Bagnères-de-Luchon on the D 51 and D 618

VACQUIERS - 31340

28 VILLA LES PINS
Mme Daigre

Route de Bouloc
31340 Vacquiers
Tel. 05 61 84 96 04
Fax 05 61 84 28 54
www.villa-les-pins.com

Open all year (by reservation only) • 15 rooms with bath/WC or shower/WC and television • €60 to €65; breakfast €7 • Menus €16 to €35 (evenings only) • Car park, terrace, garden

Summer evenings on the charming terrace overlooking the park.

To the north of busy Toulouse, this pleasant halt is beautifully quiet. A pine forest surrounds this extensive villa with a pleasant guesthouse atmosphere. The rooms, more spacious on the first floor, have a plush bourgeois flavour created by antique furniture, chandeliers and thick curtains. The same ambience extends to the dining room and its impressive fireplace.

Access : 2km westbound on the D 30

MIDI PYRÉNÉES

VARENNES - 31450

29 CHÂTEAU DES VARENNES
M. et Mme Mericq

31450 Varennes
Tel. 05 61 81 69 24
Fax 05 61 81 69 24
j.mericq@wanadoo.fr

Open all year • 5 rooms with bath/WC • €100 to €135, breakfast included • Table d'hôte €35 • Terrace, garden, park, car park • Outdoor swimming pool. Tennis and horse-riding nearby

We most liked: The view of the slopes of Lauragais from the swimming pool.

The magic begins from the moment you set foot in the park of this 16C castle next to the church. Push open the iron gate, venture into the wonderful courtyard and through a heavy wooden door into the main pink brick building, where you will find yourself gazing up at a double flight of stairs. Superbly exotic colours adorn the "Bédouin" room on the ground floor and those upstairs are equally elegant and opulent. The sitting rooms and vaulted cellars add the finishing touch.

Access: 15km westbound from Saint-Félix on the Toulouse road (D 2)

CAUSSENS - 32100

30 AU VIEUX PRESSOIR
M. Martin

Saint-Fort
32100 Caussens
Tel. 05 62 68 21 32
Fax 05 62 68 21 32
auvieuxpressoir@wanadoo.fr
http://perso.wanadoo.fr/vieuxpressoir

Closed for a fortnight in February • 3 rooms • €49, breakfast included; half-board available • Meals at l'Auberge: €16 to €26 • Terrace, garden, park, car park. No dogs admitted in rooms • Outdoor swimming pool, jacuzzi

We most liked: The lively atmosphere at the weekends.

This lovely old 17C stone house commands a fine view over the vineyards, countryside and the flocks of ducks reared on the property. The rooms, furnished with old pieces, are comfortable and well looked after. The family suite in the attic has been thoughtfully equipped with a games room and a VHS recorder. Farm produce takes pride of place on the dinner table and connoisseurs in search of fine foie gras will not be disappointed.

Access: 11km from Caussens on the D 7 and take a lane on the right

MIDI PYRÉNÉES

EAUZE - 32800

31 CHAMBRE D'HÔTE HOURCAZET
Mme Lejeunne

Hourcazet
32800 Eauze
Tel. 05 62 09 99 53
Fax 05 62 09 99 53
claude.lejeunne@mageos.com

Open all year • 4 rooms • €65, breakfast included • No table d'hôte • Terrace, park, car park. Credit cards not accepted

Soaking up the vineyard ambience.

An air of tranquillity reigns in these two houses standing side by side in the midst of Armagnac's vineyards. The rooms are tastefully decorated with beautiful fabrics and furniture and equipped with fine bathrooms. The largest are under the massive beams up in the converted attic, the other two open directly onto the garden. Meals are served in a traditionally decorated dining room or on one of two terraces. Forty winks can be had in the garden complete with pond.

Access: 7km westbound from Eauze on the D 626, then the N 524 towards Cazaubon, and a lane "chemin Espajos" 500m on the right

JUILLAC - 32230

32 AU CHÂTEAU
M. et Mme de Rességuier

32230 Juillac
Tel. 05 62 09 37 93
deresseguier@marciac.net

Closed for one week in October • 4 rooms with bathrooms • €50, breakfast included • Table d'hôte €16 • Terrace, garden, park, car park. Credit cards not accepted, no dogs admitted • Fishing

Lie on your back and gaze up into the branches of the ancient trees.

Fie, fair visitor! What you see is no castle, but an 18C charterhouse, now the headquarters of a thriving farming business. The rooms, in a separate wing, are vast and tastefully decorated and the bathrooms boast all the modern comforts. As you would expect, a generously spread table d'hôte showcases the wealth of produce grown and reared on the farm. Bicycling, walking and fishing feature among the possible leisure activities, and the owner and mayor of Juillac is a wonderful source of advice.

Access: 5km westbound from Marciac, towards Juillac on the D 255

MIDI PYRÉNÉES
LECTOURE - 32700   MIRANDE - 32300

33 DE BASTARD
M. et Mme Arnaud

Rue Lagrange
32700 Lectoure
Tel. 05 62 68 82 44
Fax 05 62 68 76 81
hoteldebastard@wanadoo.fr

Closed from 20 Dec to 1 Feb, Sun evening, Mon and Tue lunchtime • 29 rooms on 2 floors, all have bath/WC or shower/WC and television • €45 to €68; breakfast €10; half-board available • Menus €15 (weekdays) to €56 • Terrace, garden, garage • Outdoor swimming pool

We most liked
One for all and all for one.

Your quest for a harbour in Gascony is over! Despite its name, the pedigree of this 18C house is flawless. Elegance and opulence reign throughout. Progressively renovated rooms, a string of sophisticated sitting and dining rooms with parquet floors, moulded ceilings and fireplaces, a pleasant garden terrace, a cottage with a sitting room-bar for lovers of good cigars and Armagnac and succulent cooking worthy of the most demanding musketeers among you.

Access : From Agen, follow rue d'Alsace-Lorraine, turn left at the post office, then right on rue Subervie, then left again

34 AU PRÉSIDENT
M. Piquemil

Route d'Auch
32300 Mirande
Tel. 05 62 66 64 06
Fax 05 62 66 64 06
jacques.piquemil@wanadoo.fr
www.chez.com/aupresident

Open all year • 4 rooms, 2 of which are on garden level, with bathrooms • €50, breakfast included • No table d'hôte • Terrace, garden, car park. Credit cards not accepted, no dogs admitted • Billiards, children's play area

We most liked
Trying your luck on the billiards table in the elegant sitting room.

This lovely abode flanked with turrets belonged to the president of Mirande's law courts during the first half of the 20C, hence its name. The bedrooms with sloping ceilings all have brand new bathrooms. Those on the ground floor are enormous and adorned with family heirlooms. In the winter, breakfast is served by the fireside in the huge dining room and in a sheltered courtyard in the summer. Pretty garden.

Access : 3km northbound from Mirande on the N 21 route d'Auch

MIDI PYRÉNÉES

SAINT-CLAR - 32380

35 LA GARLANDE
M. et Mme Cournot

Place de la Mairie
32380 Saint-Clar
Tel. 05 62 66 47 31
Fax 05 62 66 47 70
nicole.cournot@wanadoo.fr
www.lagarlande.com

Closed from 6 Nov to 23 Feb • 3 rooms with bathrooms • €54 to €65, breakfast included • No table d'hôte • Garden. Credit cards not accepted, no dogs admitted

We most liked
Harmony abounds in all the rooms.

Standing firmly four-square on its arcades, this beautiful, rambling house with an ochre façade is in the heart of the village opposite a 16C hall. The rooms, decorated with tapestries and well-polished antiques, have retained their original parquet or tiled floors. The bathrooms have been renovated. The reading room and walled herb garden are perfect places to relax. Guests have the use of a summer kitchen.

Access : Opposite the covered market

SAINT-MAUR - 32300

36 DOMAINE DE LORAN
M. et Mme Nédellec

32300 Saint-Maur
Tel. 05 62 66 51 55
Fax 05 62 66 78 58

Open from 30 Apr to 30 Oct (by reservation the rest of the year) • 2 rooms and 2 apartments with bathrooms • €45 to €50, breakfast included • No table d'hôte • Park, car park. Credit cards not accepted • Billiards

We most liked
Fishing in the lake hidden in the park.

Two towers, a long colonnade of plane trees and parkland graced with huge old trees make this old Gascony farm look more like a castle. A lovely old wooden staircase will take you up to the spacious rooms fitted out with old furniture; the two suites are particularly worth a look. The immense dining room on the ground floor with dark wainscoting is furnished with lovely antiques. Fishing, billiards and table-tennis will keep you amused for hours.

Access : From the N 21 take the long lane that leads to the Domaine de Loran

MIDI PYRÉNÉES

SAINT-MÉZARD - 32700

37 CHAMBRES D'HÔTES LE SABATHÉ
M. et Mme Barreteau

Le Sabathé
32700 Saint-Mézard
Tel. 05 62 28 84 26
barreteau.sabathe@wanadoo.fr
http://perso-wanadoo.fr/barreteau.sabathe

Open all year • 4 rooms • €43, breakfast included; half-board available • Table d'hôte €10 to €15 • Terrace, car park. Credit cards not accepted

We most liked
Take refuge in this sanctuary of meditation.

Tai Chi sessions are organised every morning in this unaffected, almost monastic abode. The old farm on the doorstep of the town aims to provide sanctuary to those in search of a place for meditation. The rooms, spread throughout the outbuildings, are all fully independent. Depending on the weather, meals are served by the fireside in the dining room or on a tiny walled terrace in front of the main hall, overlooking the chapel of Notre-Dame-d'Esclaux.

Access: 12km northbound on the D 36

BÉLAYE - 46140

38 MARLIAC
Mme Stroobant

46140 Bélaye
Tel. 05 65 36 95 50
Fax 05 65 31 99 04

Closed from early Nov to early Apr • 5 rooms • €61 to €66, breakfast included • Table d'hôte €15 to €17 • Park, car park. Credit cards not accepted, no dogs admitted • Outdoor swimming pool

We most liked
Close your eyes and listen to the sound of silence.

A long, winding lane leads to this 18C farmhouse, a haven of peace and quiet in the midst of over 10 acres of woods and fields. You will want to unpack your cases and spend time in the tastefully decorated utterly calm rooms; two of which are on split levels. The breakfast room has preserved its beams, stonework and the old oven. Engaging welcome.

Access: 15km westbound from Luzech on the D 8 and the D 50

MIDI PYRÉNÉES

FIGEAC - 46100

GOURDON - 46300

39 LE PONT D'OR
M. et Mme Bonnaud

2 avenue Jean-Jaurès
46100 Figeac
Tel. 05 65 50 95 00
Fax 05 65 50 95 39
contact@hotelpontdor.com
www.hotelpontdor.com

Open all year • 35 rooms on three levels, all with bathrooms, television and air-conditioning; 2 have disabled access and 7 are non-smoking • €75 to €100; breakfast €10; half-board available • Menus €12 to €15 • Terrace, garden, car park • Billiards, overflow swimming pool, fitness room with sauna

most liked The Champollion Museum, located in the birthplace of the famous Egyptologist.

This welcoming stone house, ideally located on the banks of the Célé at the foot of a medieval bridge, reopened in 2001 after major renovation work. A yellow and orange colour scheme, contemporary furniture, new bedding and immaculate bathrooms characterise the rooms, some of which have a balcony. In addition the hotel boasts a fitness room, and a swimming pool on the roof of the house. In summer, breakfast is served on the riverside terrace.

Access : On the way into the historic centre, near the medieval bridge

40 DOMAINE DU BERTHIOL
Famille Dubreuil

Route de Cahors
46300 Gourdon
Tel. 05 65 41 33 33
Fax 05 65 41 14 52
domaine-du-berthiol@wanadoo.fr
www.hotelperigord.com

Open from Apr to late Dec • 29 rooms with bath/WC or shower/WC and television • €77 to €84 (€67 to €75 low season); breakfast €11; half-board available • Air-conditioned restaurant; menus €24 to €48 • Park, car park. No dogs admitted • Outdoor swimming pool, tennis

most liked Lush green countryside.

On the outskirts of the town in the middle of a beautifully maintained park, this impressive country house offers identical rooms with fully equipped bathrooms. Tennis courts, swimming pool and children's play area. The contemporary dining room opens onto the pleasant greenery. The menu shows a marked preference for local produce. Immense banquet hall in another wing.

Access : 1km eastbound from Gourdon on the D 704

MIDI PYRÉNÉES

GRAMAT - 46500

41 MOULIN DE FRESQUET
M. et Mme Ramelot

46500 Gramat
Tel. 05 65 38 70 60
Fax 05 65 33 60 13
moulindefresquet@ifrance.com
www.moulindefresquet.com

Closed from 1 Nov to 1 Apr • 5 non-smoking rooms with bathrooms • €57 to €82, breakfast included; half-board available • Table d'hôte €21 including beverages (evenings only) • Park, car park. Credit cards not accepted, no dogs admitted

We most liked Wining and dining by candlelight on Périgord's succulent fare.

The good life at its best! This authentic 17C water mill stands in an idyllic rural spot, just 800m from the centre of Gramat. Lovely furniture and tapestries, exposed stonework and beams and a profusion of good books set the scene for the interior. The comfortable, elegant rooms have been recently restored and most enjoy a view of the enchanting shaded garden and the stream, much prized by fishermen. Gracious hosts and wonderful food.

Access : On the way into Gramat

GRÉZELS - 46700

42 CHÂTEAU DE LA COSTE
M. Coppé

46700 Grézels
Tel. 05 65 21 38 28
Fax 05 65 21 38 28
gervais.coppe@wanadoo.fr

Open in Jul and Aug • 3 rooms • €75 to €105, breakfast included • No table d'hôte • Credit cards not accepted, no dogs admitted

We most liked The Cahors Wine Museum within the walls of this fortified castle.

If you're passing through, this medieval fortress dominating the Lot Valley is definitely worth a visit. Character abounds in the rooms which have been given evocative names such as "Study of the setting sun", "Lookout tower" and "Squire's abode" – all are furnished with lovely period pieces. In addition, the striking dining room commands an exceptional view. Don't leave without visiting the Wine Museum.

Access : 16km westbound from Luzech on the D 8

MIDI PYRÉNÉES

LACAPELLE-MARIVAL - 46120

43 LA TERRASSE
M. Amalric

Le Bourg
46120 Lacapelle-Marival
Tel. 05 65 40 80 07
Fax 05 65 40 99 45
hotel-restaurant-la-terrasse@wanadoo.fr
hotel-restaurant-la-terrasse-lot.fr

Closed Jan and Feb, Sun evening, Mon except evenings in summer, Tue lunchtime • 13 rooms, all have bath/WC or shower/WC and television • €45 to €65; breakfast €7; half-board available • Menus €19 (weekdays) to €55 • Garden • Fishing

Forty winks in the flower garden.

The hotel is next door to the massive square keep, flanked by the towers of the castle of Lacapelle. Practical, recently renovated rooms and a light, airy veranda-dining room whose bay windows overlook the pretty garden on the banks of a stream, with the Francès Valley in the background. Park and private fishing 2km away.

Access: Near the castle

LOUBRESSAC - 46130

44 CHÂTEAU DE GAMOT
M. et Mme Belières

46130 Loubressac
Tel. 05 65 10 92 03
Fax 01 48 83 01 91
annie-belieres@wanadoo.fr
www.domaine-de-gamot.com

Closed from 1 Oct and 1 May • 7 rooms, some have bathrooms • €45 to €60, breakfast included • No table d'hôte • Garden, car park. Credit cards not accepted, no dogs admitted

Conveniently located near Quercy's main tourist attractions.

The allure of this rambling 17C stately home and its pastoral setting opposite the castle of Castelnau never fails to weave its magic spell. The comfortable rooms are well proportioned. Guests who visit in June and September enjoy the run of the owners' private swimming pool. Other leisure activities in the vicinity include a 9-hole golf course, tennis courts and horse-riding.

Access: 5km westbound from St-Céré on the D 673 and the D 30

MIDI PYRÉNÉES
MARCILHAC-SUR-CÉLÉ - 46160   MARTEL - 46600

45 LES TILLEULS
Mme Ménassol

46160 Marcilhac-sur-Célé
Tel. 05 65 40 62 68
Fax 05 65 40 74 01
michelle.menassol@wanadoo.fr
www.les-tilleuls.fr.st

Closed from 16 Nov to 16 Dec • 4 rooms • €40 to €42, breakfast included • No table d'hôte • Park, car park. Credit cards not accepted

We most liked
Meeting the enchanting owner.

Cradled in the heart of the village, this 19C stately home owes its success to the lady of the house's efforts to make guests feel truly welcome: she is always well informed about life in the region and is happy to suggest local activities. The rooms are comfortable and unfussy and the breakfasts copious to say the least: prepare to delve into a memorable array of up to 50 home-made jams. The garden, complete with barbecue and hammock, is slightly unruly and instantly likeable.

Access: In the village

46 LA COUR AU TILLEUL
Mme Jouvet

Avenue du Capitani
46600 Martel
Tel. 05 65 37 34 08
www.la-cour-au-tilleul.com

Open all year • 3 rooms with shower/WC • €55 (€50 low season), breakfast included • No table d'hôte • Credit cards not accepted

We most liked
A bright, well cared-for interior behind very old walls.

The walls of this enchanting stone house bedecked in flowers date back to the 12C no less! A great deal of time has clearly been lavished on the decoration of the tranquil, spacious rooms which are located to the rear of the house. Depending on the season, breakfast is served in the brightly coloured blue and orange dining room or in the inner courtyard under the shade of a linden tree. The welcome is as friendly as you could wish.

Access: In the village

MIDI PYRÉNÉES

MAUROUX - 46700

47 HOSTELLERIE LE VERT
M. Philippe

Lieu-dit Le-Vert
46700 Mauroux
Tel. 05 65 36 51 36
Fax 05 65 36 56 84
info@hotellevert.com
www.hotellevert.com

Closed from 1 Nov to 31 Mar • 7 rooms with bath/WC or shower/WC and television • €60 to €110 (€55 to €90 low season); breakfast €9; half-board available • Restaurant closed lunchtime; menus €40 • Terrace, garden, car park. No dogs admitted in rooms • Outdoor swimming pool, bicycle and mountain bike rental in the summer

Most liked: Signposted footpaths weaving in and out of vineyards and old farms.

An ideal opportunity to get back to grass roots! This former wine estate, which lies in the remote countryside, is surrounded by a garden planted with cedar trees and a timeless silence. The hotel does its utmost to welcome you in style with its character-filled dining room with exposed beams, stonework and old furniture and personalised rooms in the same vein. The most unusual room is in the converted pantry with a lovely stone vaulted ceiling and tiny windows to keep it cool in the summer.

Access : 12km to the south-west of Puy-L'Évêque on the D 8 then the D 5

ROCAMADOUR - 46500

48 LE BEAU SITE
M. Menot

Cité Médiévale
46500 Rocamadour
Tel. 05 65 33 63 08
Fax 05 65 33 65 23
info@bestwestern-beausite.com
www.bestwestern-beausite.com

Closed from 15 Nov to 1 Feb • 39 rooms located in 2 buildings on each side of the street. Rooms have bath/WC or shower/WC and television, 21 are air-conditioned • €65 to €98 (€49 to €74 low season); breakfast €11; half-board available • Menus €23 to €52 • Terrace, garage, car park (access by a pedestrian road)

Most liked: The mountain village of Rocamadour – words fail us!

Old beams blackened by the centuries, a massive wooden staircase, stone walls and beautiful worn flagstones: the hall of this 15C bastion in the heart of the city is definitely worth a look. The rooms in the wing, of variable sizes, are more up-to-date and enjoy a fine view. The elegant restaurant-veranda and its flowered terrace overlook the Alzou canyon. 2km from the hotel, a swimming pool has been sunk in a lovely park of oak trees.

Access : Main road of the medieval city (pedestrian road) between Porte Salmon and Porte du Figuier

MIDI PYRÉNÉES
ROCAMADOUR - 46500 | ROCAMADOUR - 46500

49 LE TROUBADOUR
M. Menot

Route de Brive
46500 Rocamadour
Tel. 05 65 33 70 27
Fax 05 65 33 71 99
troubadour@rocamadour.com
www.hotel-troubadour.com

Open from 15 Feb to 15 Nov • 10 rooms and 2 apartments with bath/WC or shower/WC and television • €60 to €85 (€55 to €70 low season); breakfast €10; half-board available • Air-conditioned restaurant; menus €26 to €36 • Car park, garden, terrace. • Swimming pool, billiards

We most liked Lazing around the swimming pool after a hard day's sightseeing.

A handsome flowered and tree-lined garden protects the peace and quiet of this tastefully renovated old farmhouse. Forget the size of the rooms and admire the rustic furniture and floorboards of the pristine bedrooms. Some enjoy a view of the swimming pool with the countryside in the distance. The restaurant, which is only open out of season, doesn't believe in fussy, elaborate cuisine. Friendly, family welcome.

Access: 2.5km to the north-east on the D 673

50 LES VIEILLES TOURS
M. Brousse

Lieu-dit Lafage
46500 Rocamadour
Tel. 05 65 33 68 01
Fax 05 65 33 68 59
les.vieillestours@wanadoo.fr
www.chateauxhotels.com/vieillestours

Closed from 16 Nov to 26 Mar • 17 rooms located in 2 buildings, almost all are on garden level, with bath/WC and television • €60 to €110; breakfast €12; half-board available • Menus €25 (weekdays) to €62 • Terrace, garden, car park • Outdoor swimming pool

We most liked Sleeping in a 13C falconry!

The construction of this secluded hunting lodge took place over several centuries from the 13C to the 17C. Most of the rooms in the outhouses open directly onto the garden and enjoy a splendid view of the countryside. Diners can choose between a welcoming country-style restaurant and a quiet, shaded terrace to sample a sophisticated regional repertoire.

Access: 4km westbound from Rocamadour on the D 673 towards Payrac, then take a minor road

MIDI PYRÉNÉES

SAINT-SIMON - 46320   ARCIZANS-AVANT - 65400

51 LES MOYNES
Mme Le Cerf-Arets

Les Moynes de Saint-Simon
46320 Saint-Simon
Tel. 05 65 40 48 90
Fax 05 65 40 48 90
les.moynes@free.fr
http://les.moynes.free.fr

Open from 15 Apr to 14 Nov • 5 rooms, one of which has disabled access, with bath/WC or shower/WC and television • €50 to €60, breakfast included; half-board available • Table d'hôte €19 • Terrace, car park, park. Credit cards not accepted • Outdoor swimming pool, table-tennis, mountain biking

We most liked
A guided tour of the duck farm in the company of the owner.

This recently renovated Quercy house, which dates back to 1885, is located in a nearly 30-acre working farm. Bright colours, timber beams and stone walls, new parquet flooring and well-fitted bathrooms depict the snug rooms, all with names which reflect the region. Breakfasts and dinners are served in a delightful dining room complete with old mangers and a fireplace big enough to sit in.

Access : 7km north-west of Assier on the D 11 and D 25, towards Flaujac

52 CHAMBRE D'HÔTE MADAME VERMEIL
Mme Vermeil

3 rue du Château
65400 Arcizans-Avant
Tel. 05 62 97 55 96
Fax 05 62 97 55 96

Open all year • 3 rooms with valley or mountain view • €43, breakfast included • No table d'hôte • Credit cards not accepted, dogs not admitted

We most liked
A panoramic wide-screen view of the valley.

This handsome 19C house boasts a wealth of attractions. Wood prevails in the attic rooms – walls, floors and furniture – which afford a fine view of the valley or the mountains. Guests have the run of a kitchen, a pleasant garden and a dining room with a relief map of the Pyrenees: plan your next expedition over a coffee and feel free to ask for advice from the owner, a mountain guide who speaks from experience.

Access : 5km southbound from Argèles on the D10, then on the D13.

MIDI PYRÉNÉES

ARREAU - 65240

BEAUCENS - 65400

53 ANGLETERRE
Mme Aubiban

Route de Luchon
65240 Arreau
Tel. 05 62 98 63 30
Fax 05 62 98 69 66
hotel-angleterre@oreka.com
www.hotel-angleterre-arreau.com

In winter open Sat-Sun and school holidays; closed 1 Apr to 15 May and 10 Oct to 25 Dec • 20 rooms with bath/WC or shower/WC and television • €62 to €92; breakfast €8; half-board available • Restaurant closed Mon and Tue lunchtime; menus €19 to €38 • Car park, garden. No dogs admitted • Heated swimming pool

The friendly welcome and the family atmosphere.

A little village typical of the Aure Valley is the site of this former coaching inn. All the rooms have been recently renovated. The stylish dining room sports country furniture, old utensils dotted about here and there and bright, contemporary colours. Meals are also served in the veranda facing the garden where a swimming pool and play area will keep the children busy.

Access: On leaving Arreau, take the D 618 towards Luchon

54 ETH BÉRYÈ PETIT
M. et Mme Vielle

15 route de Vielle
65400 Beaucens
Tel. 05 62 97 90 02
Fax 05 62 97 90 02
contact@beryepetit.com
www.beryepetit.com

Open all year • 3 rooms with bathrooms • €45 to €54; breakfast included • Table d'hôte €18, including beverages (evenings only from 1 Nov to 30 Apr) • Terrace, garden, car park. Credit cards not accepted, dogs not admitted

The lady of the house's gracious welcome.

This country house, whose name means "little orchard" in Occitan, was built in 1790 in the purest traditions of regional architecture. Tastefully decorated rooms overlook the Lavedan and the Pyrenean peaks, the one upstairs is the most spacious and leads out onto a balcony which runs along the entire length of the façade. There are two others under the eaves. Breakfast is always a delight by the fireside or on the terrace.

Access: 8.5km to the south-east of Argelès on the D 100, then take a minor road

MIDI PYRÉNÉES

CAMPARAN - 65170

55 LA COUETTE DE BIÉOU
Mme Moreilhon

65170 Camparan
Tel. 05 62 39 41 10
Fax 05 62 39 41 10

Open all year • 3 rooms • €42, breakfast included • No table d'hôte • Car park. Credit cards not accepted, no dogs admitted

Stupendous view of the valley and the Pyrenean peaks.

Right in the heart of town, this attractive stone farm with flower-decked balconies commands a matchless view of the valley and the Pyrenees. Wood sets the tone in the cosy rooms which enjoy exceptional views, one of which overlooks Saint-Lary-Soulan. The hospitable owners are both genial souls and if you're lucky, you'll be able to see how the local "gâteau à la broche" is made, even lending a welcome helping hand in the four hours of spit-roasting in front of the fire.

Access : 4km northbound, on the Arreau road and then turn right

CASTELNAU - MAGNOAC - 65230

56 CHAMBRE D'HÔTE LE MOULIN D'ARIES
M. Dorit Weimer

À Aries-Espenan
65230 Castelnau-Magnoac
Tel. 05 62 39 81 85
Fax 05 62 39 81 82
moulindaries@aol.com
www.poterie.fr

Open from 15 May to 31 Dec • 5 rooms with bathrooms and separate WC • €56, breakfast included • Table d'hôte €20 (evenings) • Reading room. No dogs admitted in restaurant

Open the door and breathe in the perfume of yesteryear.

Time and care have clearly been lavished over the restoration of this 14C mill next door to an attractive manor whose stylish interior reveals original wood floors, an ancient staircase and latched doors. White prevails in the spacious rooms with king-size beds and well-equipped bathrooms. In the mill are a reading and television room and a small bar, all set against the backdrop of the old millstones. Forget about your diet and treat yourself to Gascony's delicacies!

Access : 4km to the south-east of Castelnau-Magnoac on the D 623 towards Boulogne, then turn right towards Aries-Espenan

MIDI PYRÉNÉES

MONTGAILLARD - 65200

NESTIER - 65150

57 MAISON BURRET
M. Cazaux

67 le Cap-de-la-Vielle
65200 Montgaillard
Tel. 05 62 91 54 29
Fax 05 62 91 52 42
jlcazaux@tiscali.fr

Open all year • 3 rooms, one of which is an apartment • €45 to €50, breakfast included • Table d'hôte €16 • Garden, car park. Credit cards not accepted, dogs not admitted

Authentic and delightfully anachronistic.

Countless original architectural features are still visible in this lovely farmhouse, dating from 1791, such as the dovecote, bakery, stables, cowshed, handsome carved staircase and collection of old agricultural machinery. The comfortable rooms have been decorated with some fine antique pieces and in the winter a fire is lit in the one on the ground floor. Meals are served in a friendly dining room.

Access: 5km northbound from Pouzac on the D 935

58 LE RELAIS DU CASTERA
M. Latour

Place du Calvaire
65150 Nestier
Tel. 05 62 39 77 37
Fax 05 62 39 77 29
sarl.sergelatour@wanadoo.fr
www.hotel-lecastera.com

Closed from 1 to 8 Jun, 3 to 21 Jan, Sun evening, Mon, Tue evening (out of season) • 7 rooms upstairs, all have shower/WC, some have television • €42 to €65; breakfast €8; half-board available • Menus €23 to €44 • Terrace. No dogs admitted

The delicious cassoulet simmering on the stove

The village in the Comminges region is dominated by Mount Arès and its unusual calvary of twelve shrines on the slope. The inn offers recently renovated rooms in an up-to-date style and a welcoming restaurant renowned for its generous traditional cooking which makes the most of local ingredients. The almost sophisticated rustic interior makes it a pleasant stopping place near the attractive walled town of Montréjeau.

Access: Westbound from Montréjeau, take the D 638 then the D 938 as far as Saint-Laurent-de-Neste and turn left

MIDI PYRÉNÉES

OMEX - 65100

59 LES ROCAILLES
M. Fanlou

65100 Omex
Tel. 05 62 94 46 19
Fax 05 62 94 33 35
muriellefanlou@aol.com
www.lesrocailles.com

Closed from 1 Nov to Easter • 3 rooms • €65, breakfast included • Garden, car park. Credit cards not accepted, dogs not admitted • Outdoor swimming pool

We most liked: The discreet luxury of this snug little nest.

It is impossible not to be won over by the charm of this small stone house with comfortably modern rooms. One of the rooms, named "The Seamstress" by the owner and former wardrobe mistress of the Paris Opera House, is home to an old sewing machine and a mannequin; it also has a private terrace. Those under the eaves are air-conditioned and command a fine view of the valley. A fireplace and old furniture set the scene in the dining room and the flowered garden and swimming pool are most welcome.

Access: 4.5km to the south-west of Lourdes on the D 13 then the D 213

PINAS - 65300

60 DOMAINE DE JEAN-PIERRE
Mme Colombier

20 route de Villeneuve
65300 Pinas
Tel. 05 62 98 15 08
Fax 05 62 98 15 08
marie@domainedejeanpierre.com
www.domainedejeanpierre.com

Open all year, by reservation only in winter • 3 rooms upstairs • €50, breakfast included • No table d'hôte • Park. Credit cards not accepted • Tennis and golf nearby

We most liked: Long walks in the country.

This handsome house covered in Virginia creeper stands at an altitude of 600m on the plateau of Lannemezan, looking south towards the Pyrenees. Old furniture and pretty fabrics adorn the spacious, quiet rooms, all of which overlook the beautifully cared-for grounds. The distant notes of a piano being played in the sitting room can sometimes be heard. In the summer, breakfast is served on the terrace. Simple, cordial welcome.

Access: 200m eastbound from the town on the D 158

MIDI PYRÉNÉES

SAINT-ARROMAN - 65250

61 DOMAINE VÉGA
M. et Mme Mun

65250 Saint-Arroman
Tel. 05 62 98 96 77
Fax 05 62 98 96 77

Open from Jun to Sep • 5 rooms with bath/WC or shower/WC • €58, breakfast included; half-board available • Table d'hôte €18 (weekdays) to €25 • Park, car park. Credit cards not accepted, dogs not admitted • Landscaped swimming pool

most liked Lovely landscaped garden and grounds.

Originally built in the 16C, this manor house was the property of a Russian prince in the Belle Époque and a Buddhist centre in the 1970s. Now a B&B, it offers pleasant rooms named after flowers, with unusual carved headboards. All overlook the cedars, giant thuja and linden trees in the park and the countryside beyond. In the kitchen, the chef prepares imaginative recipes based on regional produce.

Access: 11km northbound from Sarrancolin on the D 929 then the D 26

SAINT-LARY-SOULAN - 65170

62 LA FERME DE SOULAN
M. et Mme Amelot

Soulan
65170 Saint-Lary-Soulan
Tel. 05 62 98 43 21
fermedesoulan@tiscali.fr
www.fermedesoulan.free.fr

Closed Nov • 4 rooms with bathrooms and television • €80 to €85 (€70 to €75 low season), breakfast included; half-board available • Menus €21 (evenings only, including beverages) • Garden. Credit cards not accepted, dogs not admitted • Sauna, hammam

most liked The superb view overlooking the Aure valley from this mountain village at an altitude of 1280m.

Utter peace and quiet and pure mountain air (no smoking please!) pervade this old farmhouse located in the heart of a high-perched village whose name means sun in the local dialect. The buildings, set around a paved courtyard, are home to a ground-floor rustically-decorated dining room with a fireplace and two comfortable bedrooms with exposed beams and wainscoting. Upstairs are two other rooms with sloping ceilings and a panoramic sitting room with a south-facing bay window.

Access: North-west of St-Lary-Soulan; go to Vieille-Aure, then turn left onto the D 123

MIDI PYRÉNÉES

SAINT-PÉ-DE-BIGORRE - 65270

63 LE GRAND CÈDRE
M. et Mme Peters

6 rue du Barry
65270 Saint-Pé-de-Bigorre
Tel. 05 62 41 82 04
christian@grandcedre.com
www.grandcedre.com

Open all year • 4 rooms with bathrooms • €65, breakfast included • Table d'hôte €22 including beverages (by reservation) • Terrace, park, car park. Internet access. Credit cards not accepted • Sauna, spa

Botanical walks in the park.

This 17C country seat owes its name to the three-hundred-year-old cedar planted in the centre of the park, which casts a welcome shade over a few deckchairs. Each of the personalised rooms, linked by an outdoor gallery, is in a different style: Art Deco, Louis-Philippe, Henry II and Louis XV. The music room and piano, classical dining room, greenhouse with orchids, geraniums and cacti, pergola of roses and delightful cottage garden are a feast for the eye.

Access : In the village

SALLES - 65400

64 LE BELVÉDÈRE
Mme Crampe

6 rue de l'Église
65400 Salles
Tel. 05 62 97 23 68
Fax 05 62 97 23 68
www.argeles-pyrenees.com

Closed in Nov • 3 rooms with shower/WC • €60, breakfast included; half-board available • Table d'hôte (evenings for half-board guests only except Sun) • Park, car park. Credit cards not accepted, no dogs admitted • Excursions to the mountains, swimming pool

The enchanting perspective from this 18C abode.

The sweeping view of the valleys of Luz, Cauterets and Arrens with the Pyrenean peaks in the distance from this handsome manor house does full justice to its name. The rooms under the eaves are modern in flavour while those on the first floor are decorated with lovely old furniture and a fireplace; all enjoy the same view. In the winter, meals are served by the fireside and in the summer under an arbour.

Access : 12.5km southbound from Lourdes on the N 21 then the D 102

MIDI PYRÉNÉES

VISCOS - 65120 | ALBI - 81000

65 LA GRANGE AUX MARMOTTES
M. et Mme Senac

Au village
65120 Viscos
Tel. 05 62 92 91 13
Fax 05 62 92 93 75
hotel@grangeauxmarmottes.com
www.grangeauxmarmottes.com

Closed from 20 Nov to 20 Dec • 6 rooms with bath/WC or shower/WC and television • €69 to €79 (€55 to €67 low season); breakfast €10; half-board available • Menus €19 (weekdays) to €45 • Terrace, garden • Outdoor swimming pool

Heaven for sleepyheads and marmots.

The region is so untamed and rich in spectacular natural sights that you will spend all your days out exploring until the mountain cows come home! This old stone barn, with its cosy rooms and perfect peace and quiet are just what you need when your head finally does touch the pillow. The sun will already be high in the sky before you're ready to get up and feast your eyes on the sumptuous view of the valley, hemmed in all sides by peaks and summits.

Access : To the north-west of Luz-Saint-Sauveur towards Pierrefitte-Nestalas

66 GEORGE V
Mme Selles

29 avenue du Maréchal-Joffre
81000 Albi
Tel. 05 63 54 24 16
Fax 05 63 49 90 78
info@hotelgeorgev.com
www.hotelgeorgev.com

Open all year • 9 rooms, all have showers with or without WC, television, some have fireplaces • €33 to €44; breakfast €6 • No restaurant • Inner courtyard

Basking in the first rays of morning sunshine.

Although not as luxurious as its famous Parisian namesake, this establishment is fully worthy of notice and most definitely less expensive than your average palace! The recently spruced up, spacious rooms are quiet despite the nearby railway station and decorated in pastel shades with good quality furniture; some have fireplaces. In the rear, a small shaded courtyard is perfect for open-air breakfasts.

Access : On one of the roads to the railway station

MIDI PYRÉNÉES

BOUT-DU-PONT-DE-LARN - 81660

67 LA MÉTAIRIE NEUVE
M. Tournier

Bout-du-Pont-de-L'Arn
81660 Pont-de-Larn
Tel. 05 63 97 73 50
Fax 05 63 61 94 75
metairieneuve@wanadoo.fr
www.metairieneuve.com

Closed from 15 Dec to 25 Jan • 14 rooms, most have bath/WC, some have shower/WC, all have television • €73 to €86; breakfast €10; half-board available • Restaurant closed Sun evening and Mon (Oct to Easter) and Sat lunchtime; menus €18 (weekdays) to €25 • Terrace, garden, car park • Outdoor swimming pool

After a refreshing night's sleep, dig into a delicious breakfast.

We recommend booking one of the rooms recently renovated in a "country chic" style, which are not without character, overlooking the garden of this 18C family farmhouse converted into an inn in the 1980s. There are two pleasantly decorated rustic indoor dining rooms, but most guests prefer the rafters of the old barn which is now a delightful summer terrace.

Access: 2km eastbound from Mazamet: leave on the N 112 towards Saint-Pons and turn left at La Richarde

BURLATS - 81100

68 LE CASTEL DE BURLATS
M. et Mme Dauphin

8 place du 8-Mai-1945
81100 Burlats
Tel. 05 63 35 29 20
Fax 05 63 51 14 69
le.castel.de-burlats@wanadoo.fr
www.lecasteldeburlats.fr.st

Closed from 1 to 15 Mar and Nov half-term holidays • 10 non-smoking rooms, all have bath/WC or shower/WC and television • €61 to €100; breakfast €9 • Menus €20 (evenings only) • Park with garden, private car park • Billiards room, reading room, hiking trails nearby

Savouring a whisky in the Renaissance salon.

You cannot miss this lovely 14C and 16C "castel" at the entrance to this medieval village in the gorges of the Agout. Spacious rooms, individually decorated with furniture picked up in antique shops, overlook a park where Mother Nature appears to have been given a free rein. Try your hand at billiards or catch up on the region's art and history in the Renaissance room complete with fireplace, wainscoting and beams. Even if it's your first stay, you will be greeted like a friend of the family.

Access: 9km north-east of Castres on the D 89, then take the D 58 that runs alongside the Agout

MIDI PYRÉNÉES

CASTRES - 81100

69 EUROPE
M. Vialar

5 rue Victor-Hugo
81100 Castres
Tel. 05 63 59 00 33
Fax 05 63 59 21 38
hotelrenaissanceeurope@wanadoo.fr
www.hotelrenaissance.fr

Open all year • 38 rooms, all have bath/WC or shower/WC and television • €60 to €90 (€50 to €90 low season); breakfast €8; half-board available • Menus €10, from Mon to Sat • Patio • Piano bar on Fri and Sat

We most liked The unusual interior decoration.

Right in the heart of the historic town of Castres, these three 17C houses linked by a patio have been embellished with a lovely hotchpotch of objets trouvés, sculpture, paintings of cherubs and plants. The owners' originality and flair is also visible in the rooms' brick walls, timbers and open-plan bathrooms. The sitting rooms double as dining rooms and there is live music at the weekends.

Access : In the town centre, in a quiet street that links Bd des Lices and Place Jean-Jaurès

CORDES-SUR-CIEL - 81170

70 AURIFAT
Mme Wanklyn

81170 Cordes-sur-Ciel
Tel. 05 63 56 07 03
Fax 05 63 56 07 03
aurifat@wanadoo.fr
www.aurifat.com

Closed from mid-Dec to mid-Feb • 4 non-smoking rooms • €70 (€62 low season), breakfast included • No table d'hôte • Garden, car park. Credit cards not accepted, dogs not admitted • Outdoor swimming pool

We most liked A magical place steeped in history.

The superb restoration of this 13C half-timbered brick watchtower is most impressive. Its name, which means "path of gold" was inspired by the Aurosse stream which runs down below. All the cane-furnished rooms have a balcony overlooking the fields and valley. Make sure you have a peep in the suite in the 17C dovecote. The terraced gardens are also worth exploring. The tower's situation, just a few minutes walk from the medieval heart of Cordes, is one of its greatest assets.

Access : 600m from the city on the St-Jean road

MIDI PYRÉNÉES

CORDES-SUR-CIEL - 81170

CORDES-SUR-CIEL - 81170

71 HOSTELLERIE DU VIEUX CORDES
M. et Mme Thuriès

Haut de la Cité
81170 Cordes-sur-Ciel
Tel. 05 63 53 79 20
Fax 05 63 56 02 47
vieux.cordes@thuries.fr
www.thuries.fr

Closed in Jan • 20 rooms at the Hostellerie, 8 are in a separate wing: La Cité. All rooms have bath/WC or shower/WC and television • €49 to €130; breakfast €9; half-board available • Restaurant closed Sun eve, Tue lunchtime and Mon out of season, menus €18 to €36 (no restaurant in separate wing) • Terrace

Exploring the countless secrets of the medieval city of Cordes.

The tasteful bedrooms might lack the character of the main building, an old monastery with an original spiral staircase, but they do allow visitors to explore and enjoy the heart of this medieval Gothic town, "the city of a hundred arches". The windows overlook the valley of Cérou and command picturesque views of the tiny paved streets or of the old wisteria whose perfume lingers on the exquisite patio terrace. Salmon and duck take pride of place on the menu.

Access : In the town centre, between the covered market and the church

72 MAISON BAKEA
M. et Mme Aguirre

28 Le Planol
81170 Cordes-sur-Ciel
Tel. 05 63 56 29 54
Fax 05 63 56 29 54
lamaison.bakea@tiscali.fr
www.maisonbakea.chez.tiscali.fr

Closed 15 Nov to 15 Mar • 5 non-smoking rooms • €55 to €75, breakfast included • No table d'hôte • Credit cards accepted in high season, no dogs admitted

A serene atmosphere reigns throughout this establishment run by two opera singers.

This beautiful 13C house blends perfectly into the picturesque medieval town. A delightfully restored inner courtyard enhances the appeal of the covered passages, brickwork and timbers. Bright colours, antique furniture, stained-glass windows, bare flagstones and beams set the tone for the personalised bedrooms, each of which has a modern bathroom. The terrace overlooking the hilly countryside is impossible to resist. A dream come true!

Access : 800m from Cordes on the Planol in the medieval city

MIDI PYRÉNÉES

LACABARÈDE - 81240

73 DEMEURE DE FLORE
M. Di Bari

106 route Nationale
81240 Lacabarède
Tel. 05 63 98 32 32
Fax 05 63 98 47 56
demeure.de.flore@hotelrama.com
www.hotelrama.com

Closed from 2 Jan to 30 Jan and Mon out of season • 10 rooms (3 in a detached house) and one apartment, one of which has disabled access, with bath/WC and television • €79 to €100; breakfast €10; half-board available • Menus €26 to €34 • Terrace, garden, private car park. Dogs not admitted in restaurant • Outdoor swimming pool

We most liked: Wandering around the delightfully unruly garden.

From the moment you set foot (or wheel) on the drive lined by majestic linden trees, you will fall under the spell of this charming manor-villa, built back in 1882. The rooms are decorated with elegant Louis XVI furniture and three open directly onto the swimming pool with the Montagne Noire in the background. The meals demonstrate a distinctly Italian-Provençal influence but the establishment also serves an excellent cup of tea – even by British standards!

Access: In Lacabarède, leave the N 112 and drive along a lane bordered with lime trees

ROUAIROUX - 81240

74 LA RANQUIÈRE
M. et Mme Lecoutre

La Ranquière
81240 Rouairoux
Tel. 05 63 98 87 50
ranquiere@aol.com

Closed Jan to Mar • 4 rooms with bath/WC or shower/WC • €60 to €70 (€50 to €60 low season), breakfast included • Table d'hôte €20 (evenings only by reservation) • Terrace, garden, park, car park. Credit cards not accepted, dogs not admitted • Swimming pool

We most liked: This smart trim farmhouse would be at home in any interior decorating magazine.

Blue, yellow, green or pink - which room of this splendid 17C farmhouse set on a 5-acre estate will you be lucky enough to sleep in? Whatever the colour, they are all brimming with charm and delightfully appointed with bare beams, polished red tiles, worn wooden doors, colourful fabrics and antique furniture. The warm welcome, inviting garden and orchard, handsome pool and terrace overlooking the Montagne Noire all add to the appeal of this maison d'hôte.

Access: At Lacabarède take the D 52 towards Rouairoux, 800m further on turn left towards La Ranquière

MIDI PYRÉNÉES

ESCATALENS - 82700

75 MAISON DES CHEVALIERS
M. et Mme Choux

Place de la Mairie
82700 Escatalens
Tel. 05 63 68 71 23
Fax 05 63 30 25 90
claude.choux@wanadoo.fr
www.maisondeschevaliers.com

Open all year • 6 rooms with bathrooms • €70, breakfast included; half-board available • Table d'hôte €20 • Terrace, garden, park, car park. Credit cards not accepted • Outdoor swimming pool

We most liked
The imaginative cooking of the lady of the house, originally from southern Portugal.

Good taste and a certain daring distinguish the restoration of this lovely 18C manor house. Warm, sunny colours adorn the immense bedrooms complete with four-poster beds and period furniture, while the bathrooms boast lovely old bathtubs and washbasins in Portuguese marble. A games room and a music room have been installed in the outbuildings. Delightful courtyard and a swimming pool set in the middle of a meadow.

Access : 14km eastbound from Montauban on the N 113

LAFRANÇAISE - 82130

76 LE PLATANE
Mme Horf

Coques-Lunel
82130 Lafrançaise
Tel. 05 63 65 92 18
Fax 05 63 65 88 18
leplatane@wanadoo.fr
www.leplatane.fr.tt

Open all year • 4 rooms • €60 to €65, breakfast included; half-board available • Table d'hôte €20 • Garden, car park. Credit cards not accepted • Outdoor swimming pool, horse-riding

We most liked
The quintessence of comfort.

This lovely brick country house, flanked by stables and a dovecote, dates from 1904. Comfort was clearly high on the priority list of the restoration and the rooms are spacious and decorated in a modern or Neo-rustic style. Sunbathe around the oval swimming pool or head for the shade of the park's magnificent old planes, lindens and weeping willows. Horse-riding and bicycling available for those in need of more exercise.

Access : 10km eastbound from Moissac on the D 927, the D 2 and then the D 68

MIDI PYRÉNÉES

LAMOTHE-CAPDEVILLE - 82130

77 LA MAISON DE MANON
M. et Mme Pico

122 chemin Antoine-Cadillac
82130 Lamothe-Capdeville
Tel. 05 63 31 36 29
Fax 05 63 31 36 29
manon.pico@wanadoo.fr
http://www.lamaisondemanon.com

Closed Nov • 3 rooms and 1 apartment, all with bath/WC or shower/WC • €70, breakfast included • No table d'hôte • Terrace, garden, car park. Credit cards not accepted, dogs not admitted • Outdoor swimming pool

The faultless welcome.

From this secluded house on a small hill, the view stretches over the hilly countryside, the rooftops of Montauban, and on a fine day, as far as the Pyrenean mountains. The understated decoration of the well-groomed bedrooms was inspired by the evocative towns whose names they bear (Madras, Venice, Asmara); all open onto the partially covered terrace, which overlooks the park and swimming pool.

Access : 1.5km north-east of Lamothe-Capdeville on the D 78 and D 69 Mirabel road then a lane to the left

LAUZERTE - 82110

78 LE QUERCY
M. Bacou

Faubourg d'Auriac
82110 Lauzerte
Tel. 05 63 94 66 36
Fax 05 63 39 06 56
hotel.du.quercy@wanadoo.fr

Open all year except Feb school holidays • 10 rooms, 4 have a view over the countryside, with bath/WC or shower/WC • €32 to €42; breakfast €6; half-board available • Restaurant closed Mon and Sun evening (low season); menus €10 to €28 • Small car park

Following in the footsteps of the pilgrims on the road to St James of Compostela.

The GR65 footpath runs alongside this late 19C house in the heart of a village, perched high on an outcrop, whose lovely timber framed medieval houses nestle around a pretty covered square. The small rooms have been fully renovated and four, in the rear of the house, overlook the valley of the Barguelonne. The restaurant has also been tastefully and simply redone. Very friendly.

Access : In the heart of the medieval village by the D 953, between Montcuq and Valence-d'Agen

MIDI PYRÉNÉES

MEAUZAC - 82290

79 MANOIR DES CHANTERELLES
M. et Mme Brard

Bernon-Boutonnelle
82290 Meauzac
Tel. 05 63 24 60 70
Fax 05 63 24 60 71
Nathalie@manoirdeschanterelles.com
www.manoirdeschanterelles.com

Open all year • 4 non-smoking rooms on 2 floors, all with bathrooms, air-conditioning and modem access • €70 to €100, breakfast included • Table d'hôte €25 to €30 • Terrace, park, car park. Credit cards not accepted • Outdoor swimming pool, billiards

We most liked: **The unusual decoration of the rooms.**

This delightful manor is home to personalised rooms decorated in a variety of themes: "Louis XVI" has period furniture, "Savane" is African in spirit and the "Orientale" apartment of North African inspiration. Countless leisure activities available including a billiards table, swimming pool, tennis court and pleasant grounds complete with apple orchard. The owners' warm welcome adds the finishing touch to this delightful establishment.

Access : 2.5km north-west from Meauzac on the D 45 to Bernon-Boutounelle

MOISSAC - 82200

80 LE MOULIN DE MOISSAC
M. Barthélémy

Esplanade du Moulin
82200 Moissac
Tel. 05 63 32 88 99
Fax 05 63 32 02 08
hotel@lemoulindemoissac.com
www.lemoulindemoissac.com

Open all year • 35 air-conditioned rooms with bath/WC and television, lift, 2 with disabled access, 26 non-smoking rooms • €50 to €100; breakfast €8; half-board available • Air-conditioned restaurant closed Sat lunch-time and Sun; menus €15 to €32 • Private car park • In the heart of the historic centre

We most liked: **Gazing at the Tarn from the windows of this lovely mill before visiting the former abbey of Moissac.**

After a former vocation as a flour mill, this establishment is now devoted to the well-being of its guests. The origins of the mill, anchored on the right bank of the Tarn, date back to 1474. Countless transformations and several fortunes later, a serious rejuvenation programme has endowed the impressive building with great charm, from the comfortable theme rooms (country, alpine or seafaring) to the cosy piano-bar and delightful restaurant with a contemporary bistro atmosphere.

Access : From the A 62 motorway, take exit 9 towards Moissac Centre, turn right after Napoléon Bridge

MIDI PYRÉNÉES

MONTPEZAT-DE-QUERCY - 82270 | SAINT-ANTONIN-NOBLE-VAL - 82140

81 DOMAINE DE LAFON
M. et Mme Perrone

Pech de Lafon
82270 Montpezat-de-Quercy
Tel. 05 63 02 05 09
Fax 05 63 27 60 69
micheline.perrone@domainedelafon.com
www.domainedelafon.com

Closed 15 Feb to 15 Mar and a fortnight in Nov • 3 rooms with bathrooms • €65 to €72 (€65 low season), breakfast included; half-board available • Table d'hôte €22 to €50 (evenings by reservation) • Terrace, garden, car park. Credit cards not accepted, no dogs admitted in dining room

We most liked
Taking a course in trompe l'œil painting.

Perched on a green hillside, this 19C square manor house enjoys a sweeping view of the surrounding countryside. Admire the immense rooms decorated by the owner, an artist and a former theatre set designer. The "Indian" is cloaked in oriental fabrics, marble and architectural trompe-l'œil scenes, azulejos tiles adorn the "Parrots" and "Baldaquin" features a pretty yellow and grey foliage pattern. Not to be missed!

Access: 2km on the D 20 towards Molières, then turn left towards Mirabel for 2km

82 LA RÉSIDENCE
M. et Mme Weijers

37 rue Droite
82140 Saint-Antonin-Noble-Val
Tel. 05 63 67 37 56
Fax 05 63 67 37 56
info@laresidence-france.com
www.laresidence-France.com

Open all year • 5 non-smoking rooms overlooking the garden or the terrace, all have bath/WC • €65 to €80, breakfast included; half-board available • Table d'hôte €22 (evening only) • Garden. Credit cards not accepted, dogs not admitted

We most liked
Idyllically situated in the heart of the medieval village.

The different cultures and backgrounds of the Franco-British husband and wife team that runs this 18C manor house are reflected in its interior decoration. Most of the spacious, tastefully decorated rooms overlook the Roc d'Anglars; book the one with a private terrace if possible. In the summer, linger in the beautiful garden, unless of course you would prefer the more energetic appeal of the nearby climbing centre.

Access: In the heart of the medieval village

MIDI PYRÉNÉES

SAINT-PORQUIER - 82700

83 LES HORTENSIAS
M. et Mme Barthe

82700 Saint-Porquier
Tel. 05 63 68 73 62
Fax 05 63 68 73 62

Open all year • 3 non-smoking rooms, all with bath/WC or shower/WC and modem access • €60, breakfast included • No table d'hôte • Garden, car park. Credit cards not accepted, dogs not admitted • Outdoor swimming pool

The unaffected friendly welcome.

This typical pink brick house simply overflows with charm. The three attractive bedrooms, recently renovated and named after flowers, are furnished with family heirlooms. The old wine house is now home to the dining room and an exquisite covered terrace overlooking the vegetable and flower gardens. The enticing swimming pool offers guests the chance of a refreshing dip after basking in the hot southern sun.

Access : In the town

NORD-PAS-DE-CALAIS

This region of northern France has everything to warm the soul. According to a local saying, "the hearts of the men of the north are warm enough to thaw the coldest climate." Just watch these northerners as they throw themselves body and soul into the traditional 'Dance of the Giants', re-enacted everywhere in countless fairs, fêtes and carnivals. Several tons of chips and mussels – and who knows how many litres of beer! – are needed to sustain thousands of stall-holders and over one million visitors to Lille's annual Grande Braderie, just one of many huge street markets. The influence of Flanders can be seen not only in the names of many of the towns and inhabitants and the wealth of Gothic architectural treasures, but also in filling local dishes such as *carbonade* of beef, braised in amber beer, and *potjevleesch*, a chicken or rabbit stew with potatoes. Slender belfries, neat rows of former miners' houses and the distant outline of windmills further remind visitors that they are on the border of Belgium, or, as a glance over the Channel on a sunny day will prove, just a pebble's throw from the white cliffs of Dover!

- Nord (59)
- Pas-de-Calais (62)

NORD PAS DE CALAIS

ARTRES - 59269

1 LA GENTILHOMMIÈRE
Mme Fournier

2 place de l'Église
59269 Artres
Tel. 03 27 28 18 80
Fax 03 27 28 18 81
la.gentilhommiere@wanadoo.fr
www.hotel-lagentilhommiere.com

Closed from 2 to 25 Aug, Sun evenings • 10 rooms with bath/WC and television • €80; breakfast €10 • Menus €29 to €39 • Garden, private car park • Horse-riding treks (by reservation), hiking, mountain biking, horse-drawn carriage rides

The Fine Arts Museum of Valenciennes – the "Athens of the North".

This redbrick farmstead on the doorstep of Valenciennes was built in 1746: its surprisingly airy, well-proportioned rooms overlook a quiet inner courtyard or the manicured garden. Sample delicious regional dishes in the light restaurant installed in the converted cow-shed, complete with vaulted ceiling and old mangers. The hotel can arrange horse-riding excursions and outings in a horse-drawn carriage if you book ahead.

Access : Southbound from Valenciennes on the D 958 (towards Le Cateau), take a left on the D 400 after Famars

BANTEUX - 59266

2 FERME DE BONAVIS
Mme Delcambre

59266 Banteux
Tel. 03 27 78 55 08
Fax 03 27 78 55 08
contact@bonavis.fr
www.bonavis.fr

Open all year • 3 rooms with bathrooms • €47 to €62, breakfast included • No table d'hôte • Credit cards not accepted, no dogs admitted

Children adore exploring the ins and outs of this working farm.

You can't help but be impressed by the handsome scale of this former coaching inn, turned into a farm at the end of the Second World War. High ceilings and parquet floors set the scene for the well-decorated and well-soundproofed rooms. Countless leisure activities on the farm or nearby, including boules, table-tennis, table-football, cycling and walking trails; gliding and aerodrome 9km away.

Access : 11km southbound from Cambrai on the N 44

NORD PAS DE CALAIS

BEAUCAMPS-LIGNY - 59134

3 CHEZ JULIE
M. et Mme Tilmant

8 rue Radinghem
59134 Beaucamps-Ligny
Tel. 03 20 50 33 82
Fax 03 20 50 34 35
ctilmant@wanadoo.fr
http://perso.wanadoo.fr/chezjulie

Open all year • 3 rooms with shower/WC and telephone • €44, breakfast included • No table d'hôte • Car park. Credit cards not accepted, no dogs admitted

Simple and unaffected.

Guests immediately feel at home and welcome in this comfy farmstead, built in Flanders brick on the threshold of a village near Lille. Pastel shades of yellow or beige adorn the immaculate rooms, two of which are upstairs under the eaves. A piano, wood stove, two traditional Flemish games and pleasant light wooden furniture adorn the breakfast room. Stretch out in inviting deep armchairs in the sitting room.

Access: 12km westbound from Lille on the A 25, exit no 7, then take the road to Radinghem (D 62)

BOURBOURG - 59630

4 LE WITHOF
Mme Battais

Chemin du Château
59630 Bourbourg
Tel. 03 28 22 16 17
Fax 03 28 62 38 88

Closed early Aug • 5 non-smoking rooms with bathrooms • €52, breakfast included • No table d'hôte • Garden, car park. No dogs admitted

The magnificent architecture of this 16C farm.

This fortified 16C farmhouse seems to float on its moat which, combined with its turrets and an imposing entrance reminiscent of a drawbridge, gives it the allure of a full-blown castle. This stately atmosphere extends through handsome doors into spacious bedrooms, all with immense bathrooms. On sunny days, breakfast is served in the courtyard. Excellent value for money.

Access: 14km to the south-west of Dunkerque on the A 16 towards Calais (exit no 23)

NORD PAS DE CALAIS

JENLAIN - 59144

5 CHÂTEAU D'EN HAUT
M. Demarcq

59144 Jenlain
Tel. 03 27 49 71 80
Fax 03 27 35 90 17
chateaudenhaut@fr.st
www.chateaudenhaut.fr.st

Open all year • 6 rooms with bathrooms • €48 to €75, breakfast included • No table d'hôte • Park, car park. Credit cards not accepted, no dogs admitted

A castle literally crammed with antiques.

A long paved drive leads up to this magnificent 18C château and dovecote, set in the middle of pleasant parkland. The remarkable interior, rich in marquetry, antiques and period paintings is certainly worthy of the grand approach and is beautifully cared for by the charming hosts. Four-poster beds adorn the comfortable bedrooms and guests have the run of a light, airy breakfast room, library and even a small chapel.

Access: 6km to the south-east of Valenciennes on the D 934 and the D 59

LIESSIES - 59740

6 CHÂTEAU DE LA MOTTE
M. Plateau

59740 Liessies
Tel. 03 27 61 81 94
Fax 03 27 61 83 57
contact@chateaudelamotte.fr
www.chateaudelamotte.fr

Closed from 18 Dec to 9 Feb and Sun evening and Mon lunchtime out of season • 9 rooms in 2 wings, most have bath/WC, some have shower/WC, all have television • €65; breakfast €8; half-board available • Menus €21 to €37 • Park, car park • Mountain-bike rentals

Sampling a little slice of the very, er,… "robust" local Boulette d'Avesnes cheese.

This delightful pink-brick edifice was built in the 18C on the edge of the forest of l'Abbé Val Joly for the Benedictine brotherhood of Liessies; the monks may have gone, but the peace and quiet remains. The wide bay windows of the restaurant, reminiscent of an orangery, overlook a leafy park and the rooms, furnished with rustic or period pieces, and the bathrooms have just been treated to a new lease of life. Guests can look forward to exploring the paths of the Avesnes Nature Reserve.

Access: Leave Liessies southbound on the D 133 or the D 963 and take the minor road to Motte

NORD PAS DE CALAIS
LILLE - 59000

LILLE - 59000

7 BRUEGHEL
Mme Lhermie

3-5 parvis Saint-Maurice
59000 Lille
Tel. 03 20 06 06 69
Fax 03 20 63 25 27
hotel.brueghel@wanadoo.fr
www.hotel-brueghel.com

Open all year • 65 rooms with bath/WC or shower/WC, all have television • €75 to €83; breakfast €8 • No restaurant • Public car park nearby

8 PAIX
M. et Mme Trénaux

46 bis rue de Paris
59000 Lille
Tel. 03 20 54 63 93
Fax 03 20 63 98 97
hotelpaixlille@aol.com
www.hotel-la-paix.com

Open all year • 35 rooms with bath/WC or shower/WC, all have television • €80 to €105; breakfast €9 • No restaurant • Public car park nearby

The lively historic centre of Lille and its convivial atmosphere.

This unpretentious establishment is rarely empty and it's not hard to see why. There's the typically Flemish first impression of its redbrick and chalk-white façade, then its pleasing old-fashioned interior with dark wainscoting and a period lift shaft in wood and wrought-iron, not to mention the fresh, pastel-coloured rooms, most of which overlook the Gothic church of St Maurice. Best of all is its practical location in the heart of Lille, just two minutes from the Grand'Place.

The arty feel to this reasonably priced hotel.

The delightfully askew frontage of the Hôtel de la Paix, which in fact dates back to 1782, hides a collection of 250 reproduction works of art worthy of an art gallery. The rooms, corridors and staircases each has its own "old master", exhibited on yellow, dusty pink or light green walls. This "Who's Who" of fine art is curated by the owner, whose own creations can be admired on the walls of the breakfast room. A friendly establishment which has earned itself a loyal clientele.

Access: Opposite St Maurice Church

Access: In the town centre, near the Grand'Place, theatre and opera house

NORD PAS DE CALAIS

LOMPRET - 59840　　　　　　　**ROUBAIX - 59100**

9 · LA FERME BLANCHE
Mme Deleval

Rue Pasteur
59840 Lompret
Tel. 03 20 92 99 12
Fax 03 20 54 29 82
dadeleval@nordnet.fr

Open all year • 3 rooms with bath/WC • €50, breakfast included • No table d'hôte • Park, car park. Credit cards not accepted • Outdoor swimming pool

10 · ABRI DU PASSANT
M. Renart

14 rue Vauban
59100 Roubaix
Tel. 03 20 11 07 62
Fax 03 20 11 07 62
jean-françois.renart@wanadoo.fr
www.ifrance.com/abri-du-passant

Closed in Aug • 5 rooms with bathrooms • €37; breakfast €5; half-board available • Table d'hôte €11 (evening only during the week, by reservation) • Garden. Credit cards not accepted

We most liked **Cycling around the countryside.**

A stony lane leads to this pretty farm whose whitewashed buildings form a rectangle behind the large iron gate, watched over by the vigilant eye of a security camera. The old barn has been converted into simple, comfortable rooms; one of which features a lovely mixture of crimson, pink and white. The exposed beams and pastel shades in the breakfast room are also very pleasant. A small swimming pool lies in the inner courtyard.

We most liked **Contemporary works of art adorn the whole house.**

You will not be disappointed by the restful mood of this late-19C property next door to Barbieux park. Many original architectural features, such as the tiled mosaic floor in the hall, impressive high ceilings and lovely light wood staircase, still reveal an almost Victorian love of discreet home comforts. The bedrooms and bathrooms are all generously proportioned. The sitting and dining room provide the setting for an exhibition of works of art by a young local painter.

Access : 7km to the north-west of Lille exit no 6, then take the lane on the right

Access : To the south-west of town, near the park

NORD PAS DE CALAIS

SAINT-PIERRE-BROUCK - 59630 | SARS-POTERIES - 59216

11 CHÂTEAU DE SAINT-PIERRE-BROUCK
M. et Mme Duvivier-Alba

287 route de la Bistade
59630 Saint-Pierre-Brouck
Tel. 03 28 27 50 05
Fax 03 28 27 50 05
contact @ lechateau.net
www.lechateau.net

Open all year by reservation • 5 non-smoking rooms with bathrooms • €65 to €70, breakfast included • Table d'hôte €25 (except Tue and Thu) • Park, car park. Credit cards not accepted, no dogs admitted

Cosily comfortable.

Nestling in a five-acre park, this impressive château built in 1905 is home to richly furnished rooms complete with moulded ceilings and marble fireplaces, and named after flowers. Make sure you taste the mistress of the house's tasty Flemish-flavoured cooking, served in the plush dining room or in the lovely winter garden-cum-conservatory overlooking the countryside.

Access: 8km northbound from Éperlecques National Forest, on the D 1

12 HÔTEL DU MARQUAIS
Mmes Carrié et Guinot

65 rue du Général-de-Gaulle
59216 Sars-Poteries
Tel. 03 27 61 62 72
Fax 03 27 57 47 35
hoteldumarquais @ aol.com
www.hoteldumarquais.com

Closed from 1 to 15 Feb • 11 non-smoking rooms with bath/WC or shower/WC • €50; breakfast €7 • No restaurant • Garden, car park • Tennis

Picking out a treasure in the stone pottery workshops of Sars, still in working order.

Painted brick walls and old furniture grace the bedrooms of this former farmhouse, converted into a hotel. Depending on the weather, breakfast is served on the large communal table in the hall or on the terrace overlooking the garden. Guests can choose between tennis or a visit to the Museum-Workshop of Glass in the rambling house of the former director of the glassworks.

Access: On the main road through town, on the outskirts

NORD PAS DE CALAIS

ARRAS - 62000

13 LES 3 LUPPARS
M. Libouton

49 Grand'Place
62000 Arras
Tel. 03 21 60 02 03
Fax 03 21 24 24 80
contact.3luppars@wanadoo.fr
www.ostel-les-3luppars.com

Open all year • 42 rooms, one of which has disabled access, all have shower/WC and television • €60 to €65; breakfast €7 • No restaurant • Sauna

We most liked: Strolling underneath the arcades of the magnificent Grand'Place.

We must admit that the simple, practical accommodation is nothing special in itself and the quieter rooms to the rear don't overlook the square. But surely this is a small price to pay for the luxury of staying in the oldest house in Arras. Built in 1467, its lovely Gothic façade, richly worked with gables, watchtower and ogival windows, fully deserves its place on the meticulously restored Grand'Place, one of the marvels of Flemish architecture.

Access: In the town centre, on the Grand'Place

BEUSSENT - 62170

14 LA HAUTE CHAMBRE
M. Barsby

124 route d'Hucqueliers Hameau le Ménage
62170 Beussent
Tel. 03 21 90 91 92
Fax 03 21 86 38 24

Closed from 1 to 15 Sep and from 15 Dec to 15 Jan • 5 rooms upstairs • €90, breakfast included • No table d'hôte • Garden, park, car park. Credit cards not accepted, dogs admitted by request • Visit to the owner's sculpture studio

We most liked: A delightful 19C manor nestling behind a curtain of greenery.

Sumptuous! If we only had one word to describe this mid-19C country house and its idyllic park, that would be it. A collection of the sculptor-owner's works is dotted around the grounds. The comfortable, exquisitely furnished rooms are a feast for the eyes and the breakfasts generous enough to satisfy the most demanding appetites. Exploring the park, home to some 300 animals, is always a hit with children.

Access: 10km northbound from Montreuil on the N 1 then the D 127

NORD PAS DE CALAIS

CALAIS - 62100 | DUISANS - 62161

15 MEURICE
M. et Mme Cossart

5 rue Edmond-Roche
62100 Calais
Tel. 03 21 34 57 03
Fax 03 21 34 14 71
meurice@hotel-meurice.fr
www.hotel-meurice.fr

Open all year • 41 rooms on 3 floors, most of which have bath/WC, some have shower/WC, all have television • €60 to €130; breakfast €12; half-board available • Restaurant closed Sat lunchtime; menus €12 (weekdays) to €70 • Garage

The Lace Museum next door to the hotel.

Although a coaching inn had stood here since before the Revolution, its old walls were unable to survive the air raids of the Second World War. Rebuilt in a style reminiscent of a miniature palace, this period-piece has the evocative look of a 1950s film set. Crystal chandeliers, a fireplace and antique furniture adorn the vast classical hall, the rooms have a charmingly old-fashioned feel and the restaurant has kept its period-style wood panelling.

Access : Behind the Lace Museum, in a small quiet street, near Rue Royale and Richelieu Park

16 LE CLOS GRINCOURT
Mme Annie Senlis

18 rue du Château
62161 Duisans
Tel. 03 21 48 68 33
Fax 03 21 48 68 33
patrick.senlis@wanadoo.fr

Closed from Nov to Mar, except by reservation • 1 room and 1 apartment (non-smoking) • €49, breakfast included • No table d'hôte • Park, car park. Credit cards not accepted, no dogs admitted

The Clos believes in pampering its guests.

As you drive up the paved lane to this delightful manor house, get ready to be coddled and indulged. A lovely white spiral staircase leads up to rooms, more akin to suites, all of which overlook the park, which becomes a carpet of daffodils in the spring. Family photos adorn the walls of this lovely building begun in the reign of Louis XIV but only finished in the Second Empire.

Access : 9km westbound from Arras on the N 39

NORD PAS DE CALAIS

ESCALLES - 62179

17 LA GRAND'MAISON
M. Boutroy

Hameau de la Haute-Escalles
62179 Escalles
Tel. 03 21 85 27 75
Fax 03 21 85 27 75
www.lagrandmaison.chez.tiscali.fr

Open all year • 6 rooms, all have bath/WC or shower/WC and television • €45 to €55, breakfast included • No table d'hôte • Garden, car park. Credit cards not accepted, dogs admitted on request

We most liked
Poised between land and sea.

Wedged between two headlands and almost in sight of the white cliffs of Dover, this lovely 18C flower-decked farm has a spacious inner courtyard whose centrepiece is a dovecote. The spacious rooms overflow with antiques, the "prestige" rooms are the most comfortable. Children can romp to their heart's content in their very own play area and in the garden, which is home to a few animals. Walking, mountain biking and windsurfing less than 2km away.

Access : 2km eastbound from Cap-Blanc-Nez on the D 243

FILLIÈVRES - 62770

18 LE MOULIN
M. et Mme Legrand

16 rue de Saint-Pol
62770 Fillièvres
Tel. 03 21 41 13 20
Fax 03 21 04 32 41
aufildeleau@free.fr
http://aufildeleau.free.fr

Open all year • 5 non-smoking rooms with bathrooms • €48 to €52, breakfast included • Table d'hôte €19 (evenings) • Garden, park, car park. Credit cards not accepted, dogs admitted by request • Fishing, canoeing, mountain bike rental

We most liked
The idyllic country setting of this mill.

This 18C mill, which boasts its original wheel and mechanism, lies on the road of the Field of the Cloth of Gold, where François I and Henry VIII's diplomatic summit once indulged their shared passion for power politics and full-blown pageantry. The well-restored mill is home to spacious rooms furnished with old pieces, where only the murmur of the Canche flowing beneath the windows will disturb the quiet. Magnificent park with two ponds, one for fishing.

Access : 7km to the south-east of Vieil-Hesdin on the D 340

NORD PAS DE CALAIS

LOISON-SUR-CRÉQUOISE - 62990   MARCK - 62730

19 LA COMMANDERIE
Mme Flament

Allée des Templiers
62990 Loison-sur-Créquoise
Tel. 03 21 86 49 87

Closed in Feb • 3 non-smoking rooms • €62 to €70, breakfast included • No table d'hôte • Garden, car park. Credit cards not accepted, no dogs admitted

20 LE MANOIR DU MELDICK
M. et Mme Houzet

2528 avenue du Général-de-Gaulle -
Le Fort-Vert
62730 Marck
Tel. 03 21 85 74 34
Fax 03 21 85 74 34
jeandaniele.houzet@free.fr
www.manoir-du-meldick.com

Closed 24 Dec to 6 Jan • 5 rooms • €60, breakfast included • No table d'hôte • Car park. Credit cards not accepted, no dogs admitted

---

The atmosphere, dripping with character and history.

The wonderful architecture of this former Knights' Templar command post, said to date back to the 12C, has been beautifully restored. Each of the refined rooms is named after one of the family's ancestors: Alice, Maria, Mancienne and Tantise. An agreeable clutter of old objects adorns the ground floor including pewter pots, a classically-French zinc bar and a set of forge bellows turned into a coffee table. The gurgling waters of the Créquoise add to the appeal of the park.

The owners' attentive care.

So close to the port of Calais and yet so far, this lovingly restored manor house is a little gem of a find. Each of the spacious, individually decorated rooms is named after a flower: "Daisy", "Cornflower", "Rose" and "Poppy" – "Hyacinth" has a king-sized bed. All are equipped with coffee and tea making facilities and biscuits. Even better than home!

Access : Take the long drive near the river

Access : 6km eastbound from Calais on the D 940 and the D 119

NORD PAS DE CALAIS

MARLES-SUR-CANCHE - 62170
NOEUX-LES-MINES - 62290

21 MANOIR FRANCIS
Mme Leroy

1 rue de l'Église
62170 Marles-sur-Canche
Tel. 03 21 81 38 80
Fax 03 21 81 38 56
manoir.francis@wanadoo.fr

Open all year • 3 rooms with bath/WC • €60, breakfast included • No table d'hôte • Garden. Credit cards not accepted, dogs admitted by request

We most liked — The lady of the house's attention to detail.

You have to go under the immense porch and through the garden, home to a host of farmyard animals, to reach this 17C fortified farmhouse. We loved the interior, particularly the ground floor with its lovely chalk vaults upheld by diagonal beams. Old furniture, a private sitting room and unusual bathrooms complement the spacious rooms. The terrace under the shade of an apple tree is enchanting.

Access: 5.5km to the south-east of Montreuil-sur-Mer on the D 113

22 LES TOURTERELLES
M. et Mme Verbrugge

374 rue Nationale
62290 Noeux-les-Mines
Tel. 03 21 61 65 65
Fax 03 21 61 65 75
les.tourterelles@wanadoo.fr
www.lestourterelles.fr

Open all year • 22 rooms on 3 floors, with bath/WC or shower/WC and television • €50 to €75; breakfast €8; half-board available • Menus €20 to €45 • Terrace, garden, private car park. No dogs admitted in rooms • Loisinord Park nearby: year-round skiing, water sports

We most liked — Skiing down the slag heap ski slope of Loisinord!

This redbrick house was the headquarters a coal mining company over a century ago. The modest rooms are more than compensated for by the elegant restaurant installed in the muted atmosphere of the former boardroom with dark wainscoting, marble fireplace and Louis XVI cane chairs. Terrace in the garden in fine weather.

Access: Between Arras and Béthune, by the main road going through the town

NORD PAS DE CALAIS
SAULTY - 62158　　　　　　　　TIGNY-NOYELLE - 62180

23 CHÂTEAU DE SAULTY
Mme Dalle

82 rue de la Gare
62158 Saulty
Tel. 03 21 48 24 76
Fax 03 21 48 18 32
chateaudesaulty@nordnet.fr

Closed in Jan • 4 rooms with bathrooms • €50, breakfast included • No table d'hôte • Park, car park. Credit cards not accepted, no dogs admitted

We most liked: A glass of home-grown apple or pear juice at breakfast time.

This splendid castle, built in 1835, lies opposite a superb park and a fruit orchard. The rooms, of varying sizes, have parquet floors and are decorated with old or pine furniture; all have a decorative marble fireplace. An assortment of home-made jams and fruit juices are served at breakfast in the ancestral dining room. Library and table-tennis.

Access : 19km to the south-west of Arras towards Doullens on the N 25

24 LE PRIEURÉ
M. Delbecque

Impasse de l'Église
62180 Tigny-Noyelle
Tel. 03 21 86 04 38
Fax 03 21 81 39 95
r.delbecque@wanadoo.fr
www.leprieure-tigny.com

Open all year • 5 rooms with bath/WC and television • €64 to €92, breakfast included • Table d'hôte €25 (evenings only) • Garden, park

We most liked: Stylish interior decoration.

The owner-antique dealer has lovingly restored his pretty turquoise-shuttered house, set in a small park. The rooms are stylish and feature exposed beams and antiques; the split-level room is most praiseworthy, as is the suite with sitting room and fireplace. The breakfast room and the superb regional fireplace are also worth a look. Golfers will adore the prospect of trying out the 36-hole golf course of Nampont, only 3km away.

Access : Behind the church

NORD PAS DE CALAIS

VERTON - 62180

WIERRE-EFFROY - 62720

25 LA CHAUMIÈRE
Mme Terrien

19 rue du Bihen
62180 Verton
Tel. 03 21 84 27 10
genevieve.terrien@free.fr
www.alachaumiere.com

Open all year • 4 non-smoking rooms • €57; breakfast included • No table d'hôte • Garden, car park. Credit cards not accepted, no dogs admitted

The charm of a doll's house.

This quaint cottage with its thatched roof and flowered garden is just 4km from the sea. An atmosphere of refined elegance and warmth pervades the place. Each of the non-smoking rooms has its own individual personality. Stay for a few days and you'll notice that breakfast is served on different tableware each morning, thanks to the lady of the house's wonderful collection. Golf nearby.

Access: 4km eastbound from Berck on the D 303

26 LA FERME DU VERT
M. Bernard

62720 Wierre-Effroy
Tel. 03 21 87 67 00
Fax 03 21 83 22 62
ferme.du.vert@wanadoo.fr
www.fermeduvert.com

Closed from 15 Dec to 20 Jan and Sun from Nov to Mar • 16 rooms with shower/WC • €60 to €85; breakfast €9; half-board available • Menus €22 to €39 • Garden, park, car park. Dogs not admitted in restaurant

Visiting the cheese-makers, also run by your hosts.

A perfect invitation to get back to grass roots. You won't be disappointed by the comfortable, quiet rooms, decorated simply and tastefully; the largest are full of amusing nooks and crannies. Sample the delicious home cooking made with local produce. Before leaving, make sure you stop by the next door cheese-makers and stock up on fresh and matured cheeses.

Access: 10km to the north-east of Boulogne on the N 42 and the D 234

NORD PAS DE CALAIS
WIMEREUX - 62930

27 LA GOÉLETTE
Mme Avot

13 Digue de Mer
62930 Wimereux
Tel. 03 21 32 62 44
Fax 03 21 33 77 54
lagoelette@nordnet.fr
www.lagoelette.com

Open all year • 4 rooms with bath/WC and television • €77 to €130 (€77 to €90 low season), breakfast included • No table d'hôte • Credit cards not accepted, no dogs admitted

We most liked **Gulping down the fresh sea air when you open your shutters in the morning.**

Who could resist the charm of this 1900 villa so well located on the dyke-promenade of Wimereux? The perfectly restored interior has remained authentic and the rooms now reveal their original harmonious shades, moulded ceilings and warm sea-faring pine furniture. The Blue and Yellow rooms offer a wonderful view of the sea, while the others overlook the inner garden. Ask your hosts for walking tips.

Access : On the seafront

NORMANDY

Hormandy, the muse of poets and artists from the world over, offers an ever-changing vision of rural pleasures. Take a bracing walk along the miles of coastline and admire her string of elegant seaside resorts. You will be left breathless when you first catch sight of Mont Saint-Michel rising from the sands or look down over Étretat's chalky cliffs into the sea crashing on the rocks below. It is impossible not to be moved by the memory of the men who died on Normandy's beaches in June 1944 or to be captivated by the cottage-garden charm of Guernsey and Jersey. Further inland, acres of neat'hedge-lined fields meet the eye, home to thoroughbred horses and herds of dairy cows. Breathe in the scent of the apple orchards in spring and admire the half-timbered cottages and smart manor houses, before wandering down to the Seine, following its meanders past medieval cities, daunting castles and venerable abbeys. No description would be complete, however, without Normandy's culinary classics: fresh fish and seafood, creamy, ivory-white Camembert, cider and, last but not least, the famous oak-aged apple brandy, Calvados.

- Calvados (14)
- Eure (27)
- Manche (50)
- Orne (61)
- Seine-Maritime (76)

N C H E

Cap de la Hague

Cherbourg-Octeville 40

32 Barfleur

Beaumont-Hague

42 46 45 41
35 St Vaast-la-Hougue
les Pieux Valognes 44
54

33 43

Barneville-Carteret Ste Mère-Eglise 17
11 St Laurent-sur-Mer 1 7
78 10 19 8
la Haye-du-Puits Carentan Bayeux 2
Isigny 20 40 15 Courseulles 4
Lessay 18 28 Ouistreham Houlga
D2 Vire St Lô 3 N 13 Caen Cabo
D 572 Troa
34 38 D 972 27 25 9 52 A 84 13 Moult
Coutances Torigni 61 14 Thury-Harcourt N 158
D 971
30 Villers-Bocage 57 59
Granville Villedieu-les-Poêles 19 Vire D 517 Condé-sur-Noireau Orne Fala
34 39 47 Tinchebray D 524 Flers Argentan
St Malo Cancale 56 37 39 D 962 D 924 51
Dinard le Mont-St Michel 31 Mortain 21 la Ferré-Macé
16 36 St Hilaire-du-Harcouet Domfront 49
D 188 N 175 Bagnoles-de-l'Orne Carrouges
Plancoët D 766 Dol-de-Bretagne 15 19 N 176 39
N 176 31 Pontorson 28 Landivy Gorron 35 63 Pré-en-Pail
Antrain D 177 Lassay
Dinan Combourg 34 A 84 Ambrières-les-Vallées
77 D 175 8 Fougères 44 Ernée N 12 63 Bais
100 N 166 55 D 178
Caulnes N 137 Hédé 58 Mayenne N 162 Fre s-S
Montauban-de-Bretagne 39 St Aubin-du-Cormier 31 Si
St Méen-le-G. 43 N 12 Châteaubourg Vilaine Vitré 75 A 81 147 24 le-Gu
Mordelles Evron St Denis-d'Orques
N 24 **Rennes** N 157 75 N 157 72 N 12 72

NORMANDIE

NORMANDY

ARROMANCHES-LES-BAINS - 14117

1 LA MARINE
M. Durand

1 quai du Canada
14117 Arromanches-les-Bains
Tel. 02 31 22 34 19
Fax 02 31 22 98 80
hotel.de.la.marine@wanadoo.fr
www.hotel-de-la-marine.fr

Closed from 27 Nov to 1 Mar • 28 rooms with bath/WC or shower/WC and television • €61 to €87; breakfast €10; half-board available • Menus €22 to €49 • Car park

Imagine the Allied Forces landing on D-Day.

The discreet, practical rooms of this rambling white hotel resemble the cabins of a luxury liner. Taking pride of place on the menu are lobster – choose your own in the tank – fish and shellfish, served in the turquoise dining room and bar-brasserie. All the windows overlook the Channel and the horizon out of which the Allied forces emerged, before landing at dawn on "the longest day", 6th June 1944.

Access : At the port

BANVILLE - 14480

2 FERME LE PETIT VAL
M. Gérard Lesage

24 rue du Camp-Romain
14480 Banville
Tel. 02 31 37 92 18
Fax 02 31 37 92 18

Closed from 1 Nov until the spring holidays • 5 rooms, 2 of which are on the ground floor and 3 are upstairs, all have bathrooms • €50 to €56, breakfast included • No table d'hôte • Garden, car park. Credit cards not accepted, no dogs admitted

Watch the cows grazing in the meadows.

This characteristic farmhouse, thought to date from the 17C, is ideal to get back to grass roots. Its snug, quietly elegant rooms are spread over two wings around a central courtyard. Family heirlooms adorn the pleasant breakfast room. In the summer, the flowered garden is particularly inviting.

Access : In the town

NORMANDY

BAYEUX - 14400

3 D'ARGOUGES
M. et Mme Ropartz

21 rue Saint-Patrice
14400 Bayeux
Tel. 02 31 92 88 86
Fax 02 31 92 69 16
dargouges@aol.com

Closed 24 and 25 Dec • 28 rooms, most have bath/WC, some have shower/WC, all have television • €68 to €100 (€52 to €84 low season); breakfast €8 • No restaurant • Garden, garage, car park. No dogs admitted

A quiet garden in the heart of the town.

It is more than worthwhile venturing past the rather austere façade of this 18C house to catch a glimpse of the lovely garden in the rear. The house's glorious past can still be seen in the intricate patterns of the parquet floors, old doors and worn beams in some of the rooms. A number of the most spacious bedrooms are perfect for families: new bedding, fabrics and wallpaper are on the agenda for the bedrooms.

Access : On the road from the town centre to the N 13, Cherbourg road

CABOURG - 14390

4 LE COTTAGE
Mme Rival

24 avenue du Général-Leclerc
14390 Cabourg
Tel. 02 31 91 65 61
Fax 02 31 28 78 82
www.hotellecottage.com

Closed 5 to 31 Jan • 14 rooms on 2 floors, with bath/WC or shower/WC and television • €66 to €89 (€60 to €86 low season); breakfast €8 • No restaurant • Garden • Fitness room, sauna

As pretty as a picture.

This lovely 1900 half-timbered cottage lies at the rear of a pretty garden. A staircase winds its way up to snug rooms all of which are individually decorated and regularly smartened up. Those on the upper floor are the least roomy. Family breakfast room, billiards and a small fitness room. Home from home!

Access : Opposite the church, on the avenue that extends from the D 514, from Ouistreham

NORMANDY

CAMBREMER - 14340

5 MANOIR DE CANTEPIE
Mme Gherrak

Le Cadran
14340 Cambremer
Tel. 02 31 62 87 27
Fax 02 31 62 87 27

Closed from 15 Nov to 1 Mar • 3 rooms upstairs, with bathrooms • €60, breakfast included • No table d'hôte • Garden, park, car park. Credit cards not accepted, no dogs admitted

Normandy at its best!

This splendid early 17C manor house will weave its magic spell the minute you set foot within its elegant, tasteful walls. A superb oak staircase takes you up to immense, well-appointed rooms; the old-fashioned bathrooms are particularly stunning. Family heirlooms grace the sitting room and the flowered grounds are clearly the work of a devoted gardener. Not to be missed!

Access : 11km westbound from Lisieux on the N 13 then the D 50

CAMBREMER - 14340

6 LES MARRONNIERS
M. et Mme Darondel

Les Marronniers
14340 Cambremer
Tel. 02 31 63 08 28
Fax 02 31 63 92 54
chantal.darondel@wanadoo.fr
www.les-marronniers.com

Open all year • 5 rooms • €50 to €58, breakfast included • No table d'hôte • Park. Credit cards not accepted, no dogs admitted

Time and care have clearly been lavished over the rooms.

This pleasant 17C edifice set in the middle of a flowered park enjoys a lovely view over the Dive Valley, with the sea in the distance. Each of the personalised rooms has been named after a goddess: "Venus", is full of light, "Diane" is smaller but much more romantic. Tuck into the ample breakfasts served on a pretty patio.

Access : 5km on a by-road

NORMANDY

CRÉPON - 14480

7 LA FERME DE LA RANÇONNIÈRE
Famille Sileghem et Vereecke

Route d'Arromanches-les-Bains
14480 Crépon
Tel. 02 31 22 21 73
Fax 02 31 22 98 39
ranconniere@wanadoo.fr
www.ranconniere.com

Open all year • 35 rooms, 1 of which has disabled access, with bath/WC or shower/WC and television • €52 to €110; breakfast €11; half-board available • Menus €16 (weekdays) to €45 • Garden, car park

A stay in these farms is like reading a page of a history book.

High ceilings upheld by worn beams, vaults, monumental fireplaces, exposed stone walls and flagstones are just some of the original decorative features of this 13C fortified farmhouse. The furniture and ornaments showcased in the rooms were found in local second-hand and antique shops. For a few euros extra, treat yourself to the luxury of added space and calm in the 18C Ferme de Mathan just 800m away.

Access: Westbound from Bayeux, take the D 12 towards Douvres-la-Délivrande for 12km, turn left onto the D 65

CRÉPON - 14480

8 LE MANOIR DE CRÉPON
Mme Poisson

14480 Crépon
Tel. 02 31 22 21 27
Fax 02 31 22 88 80
manoirdecrepon@wanadoo.fr
www.manoirdecrepon.com

Closed from 10 Jan to 10 Feb • 4 rooms with bath/WC • €75 to €110, breakfast included • No table d'hôte • Garden, car park • Mountain biking

A faultlessly decorated home.

Towering trees grace an immense park surrounding this 18C manor house whose blood-red façade is characteristic of the region. Once inside the well-dimensioned, comfortable rooms, the owner-antique dealer's flair is visible in the beautiful choice of furniture. On cold winter days, a log fire burns in the breakfast room, formerly the kitchen. Bicycles rented on the estate.

Access: In the village

NORMANDY

DAMPIERRE - 14350

FORMIGNY - 14710

9 CHÂTEAU DE DAMPIERRE
MM. Cherrier et Jouvin

Le Château
14350 Dampierre
Tel. 02 31 67 31 81
Fax 02 31 67 02 06
www.chateau-de-dampierre.com

Open all year • 5 rooms with a view of the dovecote • €60 to €90, breakfast included • No table d'hôte • Credit cards not accepted, dogs not admitted • Receptions organised

The sight of the impressive corner watchtowers at the end of the drive invariably takes one's breath away.

In the heart of the Normandy countryside on the borders of Calvados and Manche, this splendid 16C manor house, is the work of François Gabriel who also built the château of Carrouges. The rooms are more functional than you might expect in a castle, and are comfortably equipped and well cared for. They look down onto the deep moat, former Henry IV-style gatehouse and superbly restored pigeon coop, whose 2200 nesting alcoves bear witness to the prestige of the lords of Dampierre.

Access : 9km from Thorigny-sur-Vire on the D 13, then right on the D 53

10 LA FERME DU MOUCHEL
Mme Lenourichel

Lieu-dit Le Mouchel
14710 Formigny
Tel. 02 31 22 53 79
Fax 02 31 21 56 55
odile.lenourichel@liberty.surf.fr

Open all year • 4 rooms with bathrooms, some non-smoking • €45 to €47, breakfast included • No table d'hôte • Garden, car park. Credit cards not accepted, dogs not admitted • Near the D-Day Landing Beaches

The spontaneity and quality of Odile's welcome.

This inviting manor farmhouse which dates back to the 16C stands at the end of a tiny country lane. Three delightful rooms are located upstairs in the main wing, while another room complete with an adjoining small room, is situated in the wing next door, on the ground-floor of which breakfast is served. The welcoming owners, who also raise dairy cows, might even introduce you to the pleasures of milking if you're lucky!

Access : Leave the Carentan-Bayeux N 13 road at Formigny on the D 517, turn right, then left onto a minor road

NORMANDY

GÉFOSSE-FONTENAY - 14230

11 MANOIR DE L'HERMEREL
M. et Mme Lemarié

14230 Géfosse-Fontenay
Tel. 02 31 22 64 12
Fax 02 31 22 76 37
lemariehermerel@aol.com
www.manoir-hermerel.com

Closed from 15 Nov to 15 Feb • 4 rooms with bathrooms • €60, breakfast included • No table d'hôte • Car park. No dogs admitted

A guided visit of the manor and the farm.

Surrounded by meadows, this 17C fortified manor-farm with its proud aspect, handsome porch, regular lines and elegant dovecote could easily pass for a castle. The rooms in the manor are a subtle blend of comfort and charm. The sitting room in a 15C Gothic chapel is supremely restful and your hosts' unaffected welcome quite captivating.

Access : 8km northbound from Isigny on the D 514 then take the D 200 to Osmanville

GONNEVILLE-SUR-MER - 14510

12 FERME DES GLYCINES
M. et Mme Exmelin

Carrefour Malernes
14510 Gonneville-sur-Mer
Tel. 02 31 28 01 15

Closed from Jan to Mar, Nov to late Dec and Mon to Thu in low season • 3 rooms • €50, breakfast included • No table d'hôte • Garden, car park. Credit cards not accepted, no dogs admitted

"Old Macdonald had a farm!"

Children love the horses, sheep, hens and ducks who live in the grounds of this timber-framed farm which dates from 1780 and is surrounded by over 40 acres of orchards and park. The colour schemes render the rooms most pleasant and one has a private terrace. Farm produce features prominently on the breakfast table, served by the fireside in winter. Delightful garden.

Access : At Houlgate take the D 24 for 4km, turn left at the crossroads between the D 24 and D 142

NORMANDY

LONGVILLERS - 14310

13 MANOIR DE MATHAN
M. et Mme de Mathan

14310 Longvillers
Tel. 02 31 77 10 37
Fax 02 31 77 49 13
mathan.normandie@caramail.com

Open from late Mar to 15 Nov • 4 rooms on 3 levels with bathrooms, non-smokers only • €43 to €50, breakfast included • No table d'hôte • Garden-orchard, car park. Credit cards not accepted, no dogs admitted • Horse riding 500m away.

The owners' faultless hospitality.

Half-way between Aunay-sur-Odon and Villers-Bocage, surrounded by fields and orchards, an imposing manor farmhouse founded in the 15C but reworked several times. A spiral staircase with its own entrance leads up to a sitting room, a small kitchen and three fine rooms all of which are most comfortable. A courtyard shaded by a chestnut tree is lined with barns and outhouses for farm equipment. The former bakery now houses a delightful gîte. Riding centre nearby.

Access : 3km northbound of Aunay-sur-Odon on the D 6, half-way from Longvillers

LONGVILLERS - 14310

14 LA NOUVELLE FRANCE
Mme Godey

Lieu-dit La Nouvelle France
14310 Longvillers
Tel. 02 31 77 63 36
Fax 02 31 77 63 36
courrier@la-nouvelle-france.com
www.la-nouvelle-france.com

Open all year • 3 rooms on ground-floor and 2 in another wing, with bath/WC • €42, breakfast included • No table d'hôte on Sun; menu €16 • Terrace, garden. Credit cards not accepted, no dogs admitted • Swings, table-tennis.

This little gem is Normandy through and through - but keep it to yourself.

On the edge of a country lane in a little grove stands a delightful stone farmhouse behind a former barn, now home to three bright, cheery rooms and a sitting room. Sober, tasteful interior decoration, a restful garden, a drive lined with birch trees and superb country views from the moment you wake up. Delicious breakfasts and a 100 % Norman table d'hôte served in the owners' home.

Access : 4km northbound of Aunay-sur-Odon on the D 6, then D 216 towards Longvillers

NORMANDY

MEUVAINES - 14960

15 L'ANCIENNE ÉCOLE
M. Darthenay

Route d'Arromanches
14960 Meuvaines
Tel. 02 31 22 39 59
Fax 02 31 22 39 11
françoise.georges@ancienne-ecole.net
www.ancienne-ecole.net

Closed late Dec • 3 rooms with bath/WC • €45, breakfast included; half-board available • Table d'hôte €20 (evenings only) • Terrace, car park. No dogs admitted

Betwixt land and sea.

As the name suggests, this building which dates from 1741 was formerly the village school. Now a B&B establishment, it offers rustic rooms under the eaves, all of which overlook the countryside. Regional specialities feature prominently on the table, set by the fireside in the pleasant dining room. Nearby are the D-Day Landing beaches and the delightful inland villages of Bessin.

Access : 8km to the south-east of Arromanches on the D 65

ORBEC - 14290

16 LE MANOIR DE L'ENGAGISTE
Mme Dubois

15 rue de Reny
14290 Orbec
Tel. 02 31 32 57 22
Fax 02 31 32 55 58

Open all year • 5 rooms, all with disabled access • €75 to €82, breakfast included • No table d'hôte • Garden

An immaculately decorated half-timbered manor house.

Right in the heart of town, this beautifully restored 16C mansion is definitely worth staying a day or two. You will want to snuggle up in the thoughtfully decorated bedrooms with terracotta tiled floors, wood panelling and old tapestries. In the winter, a huge fire burns in the exquisite sitting room whose centrepiece is a mezzanine with exhibitions of paintings and sculpture. An old carriage takes pride of place in the vast inner courtyard. Not to be missed!

Access : In the heart of the town

NORMANDY

SAINT-PIERRE-DU-MONT - 14450

17 LE CLOS FLEURI
Mme Weidner

Hameau Lefèvre
14450 Saint-Pierre-du-Mont
Tel. 02 31 22 96 22
Fax 02 31 22 96 22

Open all year • 3 rooms with bathrooms • €50, breakfast included • Table d'hôte €23 (including beverages) • Garden, car park. Credit cards not accepted, no dogs admitted

A garden large enough to accommodate everyone.

No sooner have you settled in than you will feel as if you've always lived in this comfortable house. Old furniture embellishes the spacious, cosy rooms and the family cooking never fails to draw a compliment or two. The enormous garden is big enough to be able to host boisterous children's games, more sedate naps for the less energetic and barbecue lunches for everyone. Even better, you're only a little way from the sea. What more could you want?

Access: 2.5km to the south-east of Pointe du Hoc on the road to Vierville

SUBLES - 14400

18 LE MOULIN DE HARD
Mme Fichot

Lieu-dit Le Moulin-de-Hard
14400 Subles
Tel. 02 31 21 37 17
www.gites-de-france-calvados.fr

Open all year • 3 non-smoking rooms • €70 to €85, breakfast included • No table d'hôte • Garden, car park. Credit cards not accepted, no dogs admitted • Fishing in the Drôme

The care taken with the indoor and outdoor fittings.

This handsome 18C watermill stands deep in the country in a landscaped garden through which runs the Drôme, a little river where anglers can savour the pleasure of catching gudgeon in the private fishing waters. Modern fittings add comfort to the rooms which combine old and new decorative elements in the same style found in the communal rooms. Snug sitting room with fireplace and generous breakfasts served in a bright, panoramic kitchen-cum-dining-room.

Access: 6km south-west of Bayeux on the D 572, then D 99 left after Subles

NORMANDY

VAUX-SUR-AURE - 14400

19 LE GRAND FUMICHON
M. et Mme Duyck

14400 Vaux-sur-Aure
Tel. 02 31 21 78 51
Fax 02 31 21 78 51
duyckja@wanadoo.fr

Open all year • 4 rooms, one of which is in a separate house • €40 to €42, breakfast included • No table d'hôte • Car park. Credit cards not accepted, no dogs admitted • Fresh produce made with apples from the orchard

An apple a day keeps the doctor away!

A former outbuilding of the abbey of Longues-sur-mer, this fortified farmstead with square courtyard, porch and press is clearly proud of its early 17C origins. Today it is a working dairy and cider farm and also offers simple, rustic rooms overlooking the orchard. The quietest is in a small independent house. Before leaving, stock up on farm-grown cider, Calvados – apple brandy – apple juice and preserves.

Access : 3km northbound from Bayeux on the D 104

VOUILLY - 14230

20 CHÂTEAU DE VOUILLY
M. et Mme Hamel

14230 Vouilly
Tel. 02 31 22 08 59
Fax 02 31 22 90 58
château.vouilly@wanadoo.fr
www.chateau-vouilly.com

Closed from Dec to Feb • 5 rooms with bathrooms • €65 to €80, breakfast included • No table d'hôte • Garden, car park. No dogs admitted

A step back in time.

This 18C château surrounded by a moat and carefully tended gardens was commandeered as the American press HQ during the landings in June 1944. Beautifully restored by the owner himself, the rooms are spacious and comfortable and some have old furniture. On the ground floor, guests have the run of a string of impressive sitting rooms, one of which doubles as a breakfast room, with lovely old two-tone tiled floors.

Access : 8km to the south-east of Isigny on the D 5

NORMANDY

AIZIER - 27500

21 LES SOURCES BLEUES
M. et Mme Laurent

Route du Vieux-Port
27500 Aizier
Tel. 02 32 57 26 68
Fax 02 32 57 42 25

Open all year • 4 non-smoking rooms on 2 floors, with baths, showers and separate WC • €54, breakfast included • Table d'hôte €20 (evening only) • Garden, car park. Credit cards not accepted

Exploring the wooded park on the banks of the Seine.

Nestled in a delightfully untrammelled park, this lovely Norman house built in 1854 enjoys a wonderful view over the Seine and the boats plying their course to and from Le Havre. Wood, old tiles and parquet floors prevail in the welcoming interior. The rooms are comfortably uncluttered and the most pleasant have sloping ceilings. On the leisure side, you can choose from tennis, horse-riding and canoeing.

Access : 5km northbound from Bourneville on the D 139

BEUZEVILLE - 27210

22 PETIT CASTEL
M. Martin

32 rue Constant-Fouché
27210 Beuzeville
Tel. 02 32 57 76 08
Fax 02 32 42 25 70
auberge-du-cochon-dor@wanadoo.fr
www.le-cochon-dor.fr

Closed from 15 Dec to 15 Jan • 16 rooms with bath/WC and television • €45 to €56; breakfast €7; half-board available • Menus €14 to €40 • Private car park, garden. No dogs admitted in rooms

The quiet rooms facing the flowered garden.

Guests arriving at the Petit Castel may have to announce themselves at the nearby Auberge du Cochon d'Or, also run by the Martin family. In the time it takes to drop off your cases, you will already feel at home in this large house in the centre of the village. Tasteful mural fabrics, white-leaded wooden furniture, recent bedding, spotless premises further will reinforce your pleasant first impression. Some rooms overlook the pleasant flowered garden, where breakfast is served in fine weather.

Access : In the heart of the village

NORMANDY

BRIONNE - 27800

23 L'AUBERGE DU VIEUX DONJON
M. et Mme Chauvigny

19 rue de la Soie
27800 Brionne
Tel. 02 32 44 80 62
Fax 02 32 45 83 23
auberge.vieuxdonjon@wanadoo.fr
www.auberge-vieux-donjon.com

Closed 9 Feb to 18 Mar, 19 to 26 Aug, 13 Oct to 4 Nov, Sun eve (Oct to late Jun), Thu eve and Mon • 7 rooms with bath/WC or shower/WC and television • €50 to €56; breakfast €7; half-board available • Menus €14 (weekdays) to €45 • Terrace, private car park

"Trou normand"? a) A hole in Normandy, b) A mid-dinner drink, c) Authentically Norman.

The blue timbers and chequered decoration of this 18C Norman house, its view of the ruined 11C keep and its shady patio terrace make up for the modest comfort of the rooms. Old porcelain, gleaming copper, worn tiles and dark-timbered beams set the scene for the characteristically rustic dining room, which would not seem out of place in a short story by Maupassant! Shaded patio terrace. This is the place to try the famous "trou normand", a brisk, mid-meal shot of Calvados, the local apple brandy.

Access: Opposite the market square

CONTEVILLE - 27210

24 LE VIEUX PRESSOIR
Mme Anfrey

Hameau le Clos-Potier
27210 Conteville
Tel. 02 32 57 60 79
Fax 02 32 57 60 79
www.la-ferme-du-pressoir.com

Open all year • 5 rooms with bathrooms • €60, breakfast included • No table d'hôte • Car park. Credit cards not accepted, no dogs admitted

Delightfully old-fashioned.

Lovers of calm and authenticity will immediately fall head over heels for this attractive 18C timber-framed farm set in the midst of Normandy's green fields. The picture-perfect interior features a wealth of 19C and 20C objects and furniture picked up in second-hand and antique shops. Rooms which make up in charm what they lack in size, a garden that can hardly be seen for flowers, ducks paddling on the pond and a three-hundred-year-old press add the finishing touches to this rural landscape.

Access: 13.5km from Honfleur on the Pont-Audemer road (D 580), then take the D 312 on the left

NORMANDY

FOURGES - 27630

LES PRÉAUX - 27500

25 CHAMBRE D'HÔTE M. STEKELORUM
M. et Mme Stekelorum

24 rue du Moulin
27630 Fourges
Tel. 02 32 52 12 51
Fax 02 32 52 13 12
www.giverny.org/hotels/stekelorum.htm

Closed from 1 Nov to 1 Mar • 3 non-smoking rooms • €52, breakfast included • No table d'hôte • Garden, car park. Credit cards not accepted, no dogs admitted

26 LE PRIEURÉ DES FONTAINES
M. et Mme Decarsin

Route de Lisieux
27500 Les Préaux
Tel. 02 32 56 07 78
Fax 02 32 57 45 83
jacques.decarsin@wanadoo.fr
www.prieure-des-fontaines.fr

Open all year • 5 non-smoking rooms, with bathrooms and telephone • €86 to €90, breakfast included • No table d'hôte • Garden, car park. Credit cards not accepted, no dogs admitted • Outdoor swimming pool, mountain biking, table-tennis

We most liked **Less than 10km from Claude Monet's house and gardens in Giverny.**

This old farmhouse stands close to the old mill of Fourges, whose picturesque site has prompted more than one budding Monet to reach for palette and canvas. The rooms are located in a separate wing, two are in the former attic and all feature a rustic flavour, which also extends to the raftered breakfast room, old bread oven, family heirlooms and the beautifully landscaped garden. We wished we could stay for ever!

We most liked **Bicycling in the nearby forest.**

This 17C priory cradled in the valley of La Risles has been so well restored, you would be forgiven for thinking that it's new. The well-dimensioned, comfortable rooms are graced with old furniture, beams and tiled floors; all are non-smoking and equipped with telephones. A sitting room with fireplace, hall with piano and lovely garden are perfect to relax in.

Access: In the town

Access: 5km to the south-west of Pont-Audemer on the D 139

NORMANDY

PONT-DE-L'ARCHE - 27340

27 LA TOUR
M. Hélouard

41 quai Foch
27340 Pont-de-l'Arche
Tel. 02 35 23 00 99
Fax 02 35 23 46 22
hotel-de-la-tour@wanadoo.fr
www.hoteldelatour.net

Open all year • 18 non-smoking rooms with bath/WC or shower/WC and television • €60; breakfast €6 • No restaurant • Garden. No dogs admitted

We most liked: Walking between the Seine and the Eure Rivers.

In the shade of the church and opposite the Eure, two semi-detached houses have been turned into a hotel. The elegant, personalised rooms are stylishly furnished and tastefully decorated in bright colours; those on the second floor have sloping ceilings. In the summer, breakfasts are served on the terrace, nestling up against the old town ramparts and leading into the garden.

Access: In the town centre

SAINT-MACLOU - 27210

28 LE PRESSOIR DU MONT
M. Baumann

Hameau Le Mont
27210 Saint-Maclou
Tel. 02 32 41 42 55
Fax 02 32 41 42 55
www.location-honfleur.com/baumann.htm

Open all year • 4 non-smoking rooms, all have bathrooms • €52 to €60, breakfast included • No table d'hôte • Garden, car park, tennis, terrace. Dogs not admitted

We most liked: The stunning quality of the peace and quiet.

7000m^2 of wooded parkland surround this delightful cottage built in a regional style and now the home of a charming couple of Belgians. The pretty personalised rooms are located in the main wing ("Blue" with balcony) and the outhouses ("Yellow" and "Green" both have a private terrace). Before heading off for a game of tennis on the clay court or a bicycle ride, tuck into a breakfast of home-made bread and jam.

Access: A 13 exit no 28 Beuzeville, head towards Pont-Audemer for 1.8km, turn right before the roundabout

NORMANDY

VERNEUIL-SUR-AVRE - 27130

29 HÔTEL DU SAUMON
M. Simon

89 place de la Madeleine
27130 Verneuil-sur-Avre
Tel. 02 32 32 02 36
Fax 02 32 37 55 80
hotel.saumon@wanadoo.fr
www.hoteldusaumon.fr

Closed from 1 to 10 Jan, 19 to 31 Dec and Sun evenings from Nov to Mar • 29 rooms located in the main building on the street and in 2 separate wings in the courtyard, all have bath/WC or shower/WC and television • €43 to €64; breakfast €7 • Menus €11 (weekdays) to €49 • Courtyard

most liked **Verneuil's streets lined with half-timbered façades and smart townhouses.**

This elegant late-18C coaching inn stands in the heart of this pretty town, opposite the church of La Madeleine flanked by a 56m-high tower, an ideal starting point for a tour of the countryside which inspired Dorothy Sayers' short story "The Bibulous Business of a Matter of Taste". The rooms of varying sizes are in the main and side wings, around a flower-filled courtyard; ask for one of the renovated rooms and sample the house speciality, salmon, in the tasteful restaurant.

Access : On the main square, near the church

VERNON - 27200

30 HÔTEL D'ÉVREUX
M. Elbaze

11 place d'Évreux
27200 Vernon
Tel. 02 32 21 16 12
Fax 02 32 21 32 73
contact@hoteldevreux.fr
www.hoteldevreux.fr

Open all year • 12 rooms upstairs with bath/WC or shower/WC and television • €38 to €59; breakfast €6 • Restaurant closed Sun; menus €21 to €27 • Terrace, private car park

most liked **Two kilometres from Claude Monet's lovely house and exquisite garden.**

The rooms of this half-timbered 17C house – former home of the Count of Évreux and later a coaching inn – have recently been renovated. Exposed beams, timber-framed walls, hunting trophies and a stone fireplace set the rustic scene for the dining room. In fine weather, tables are laid in the inner courtyard. An excellent wine-list includes a grand cru or two.

Access : In the town centre, opposite the post office

NORMANDY

AVRANCHES - 50300

31 LA CROIX D'OR
M. Bertheaume

83 rue de la Constitution
50300 Avranches
Tel. 02 33 58 04 88
Fax 02 33 58 06 75
www.hoteldelacroixdor.fr

Closed in Jan and Sun evenings from 15 Oct to 1 Apr • 27 rooms located in several buildings around a courtyard. Rooms have bath/WC or shower/WC and television • €60 to €90; breakfast €8; half-board available • Menus €16 (weekdays) to €53 • Garden, private car park

We most liked
Daydreaming in the delightful garden.

This 17C coaching inn stands near the Patton Memorial which commemorates the "Avranches Breakthrough". Its half-timbered façade borders a pretty garden planted with apple trees and hydrangeas. Quiet rooms, some of which have been renovated. A countrified dining room whose collections of gleaming clocks, well-worn wardrobes, porcelain and copper pots, exposed beams and stonework would almost be worthy of a museum.

Access : From the Mont-Saint-Michel, at Place du Général Patton, turn left onto Rue de la Constitution towards the town centre

BARFLEUR - 50760

32 LE CONQUÉRANT
M. et Mme Delomenede

16/18 rue Saint-Thomas-Becket
50760 Barfleur
Tel. 02 33 54 00 82
Fax 02 33 54 65 25

Open from 15 Mar to 15 Nov • 13 rooms, most with bath/WC or shower/WC, and television • €60 to €83; breakfast €6 to €10 • No restaurant, but there is a crêperie open in the evening for hotel guests; menus €15 to €25 • Garden, small private car park. No dogs admitted

We most liked
Drinking in the atmosphere of this tiny fishing harbour in a quayside café.

This handsome 17C granite house is just two minutes from the port: back in 1066, its shipyard built the vessel which carried William the Conqueror to the shores of England and victory. Twisting corridors, proof of the house's long past, lead to rustic, immaculate rooms, some of which boast beautiful Norman wardrobes. Breakfasts and supper banquets of sweet and savoury pancakes are served outdoors in the garden.

Access : In the street at right-angles to the seaside, between the harbour and Rue de la Poste

NORMANDY

BARNEVILLE-CARTERET - 50270

33 LES ISLES
M. de Mello

9 boulevard Maritime
50270 Barneville-Carteret
Tel. 02 33 04 90 76
Fax 02 33 94 53 83
hotel-des-isles@wanadoo.fr
www.hoteldesisles.fr

Closed Jan and 13 days in Feb • 34 rooms with television, some are non-smoking • €65 to €75 (€45 to €65 low season); breakfast €10; half-board available • Menus €15 to €30 • Terrace, garden, patio • Heated swimming pool, jacuzzi, reading room

We most liked: In fine weather, the eye can see as far as Alderney, Guernsey, Herm, Sark and Jersey.

This seaside villa, opposite the Channel Islands, is perfect for a bracing holiday break. There are plans to give the rooms, already spruced up in 2004, something of a makeover, and to add a patio, while the communal parts of the house will retain their nautical flavour. Pleasant bar, reading room and panoramic breakfast room where a superb buffet is served. A number of paintings by Brazilian artists dotted about the place add a touch of exoticism.

Access : Overlooking the beach

BLAINVILLE-SUR-MER - 50560

34 VILLAGE GROUCHY
M. Sebire

11 rue du Vieux-Lavoir
50560 Blainville-sur-Mer
Tel. 02 33 47 20 31
Fax 02 33 47 20 31
jr.sebire@free.fr
jr.sebire.free.fr

Closed from Jan to Mar • 5 rooms • €40, breakfast included • No table d'hôte • Garden, car park. Credit cards not accepted, no dogs admitted

We most liked: The rustic modern flavour of this fishermen's house.

Village Grouchy is the name of an old fishing village that formerly stood here. Nowadays the granite walls of this old fishermen's house offer spacious rooms lined in wood from floor to ceiling. In the morning, take a seat on the wooden benches around a large table and toast yourself by the fireside. Summer kitchen in the immense garden in the rear. Warm and welcoming.

Access : 2km northbound from Blainville-sur-Mer on the D 72

NORMANDY

FLAMANVILLE - 50340

35 BEL AIR
M. et Mme Morel

2 rue du Château
50340 Flamanville
Tel. 02 33 04 48 00
Fax 02 33 04 49 56
hotelbelair@aol.com
www.hotelbelair-normandie.com

Closed from 20 Dec to 31 Jan • 12 rooms, 6 of which are non-smoking, all have bath/WC or shower/WC and television • €65 to €110 (€55 to €75 low season); breakfast €10 • No restaurant • Garden, car park. No dogs admitted • Piano bar

We most liked: The excisemen's cliff path.

The windows of the cosy rooms overlook the neat fields of the Cotentin ("little coast") region of north-western Normandy. The breakfast room is set in a light, airy conservatory, the old-fashioned lounge-bar has a marble fireplace and piano; palm trees adorn the lovely garden. All this awaits you in the thick granite walls of this house, formerly the home of the steward of the castle farms, just a few fields from the beaches overlooking the Atlantic.

Access : By the D 4 that goes through the village, near the château

HUISNES-SUR-MER - 50170

36 LE MOULIN DE LA BUTTE
Mme Rabasté

11 rue du Moulin-de-la-Butte
50170 Huisnes-sur-Mer
Tel. 02 33 58 52 62
Fax 02 33 58 52 62
beatrice.rabaste@club-internet.fr
www.bedandbreakfastineurope.com/lemoulindelabutte

Open all year • 5 rooms on 2 levels, with bath/WC and television, 1 with disabled access • €35, breakfast included • No table d'hôte • Terrace. Credit cards not accepted, no dogs admitted • Bicycles available

We most liked: Recharging your batteries in this splendid landscape.

Located at the gates of this traditional village in the bay of Mont-Saint-Michel, this recent villa offers quiet accommodation in spacious rooms decorated in a personalised, low-key style; all enjoy the stunning prospect of the famous abbey and rocky island. Breakfast is served in the panoramic sitting room. The owners and staff extend a warm welcome and tourist tips to guests, when they aren't caring for their immaculate and very functional establishment. Guests can borrow bicycles.

Access : Between Avranches and Mont-St-Michel (D 275), head towards Huisnes-sur-Mer, then towards the German Military Cemetery, then turn left on a minor road

NORMANDY

JUVIGNY-LE-TERTRE - 50520

37 LE LOGIS
M. et Mme Fillâtre

50520 Juvigny-le-Tertre
Tel. 02 33 59 38 20
Fax 02 33 59 38 20
fillatre.claude@wanadoo.fr
http://www.gitefillatre.free.fr

Closed from 15 Nov to 15 Mar • 3 rooms • €38 to €42, breakfast included; half-board available • Table d'hôte €15 (except Sat evening) • Car park. Credit cards not accepted, no dogs admitted in dining room

What is so wonderful about France is that you can taste everything!

Old stones and good local produce are the hallmark of this 17C farm. The rooms in the former dovecote are contemporary in style while the one in the main wing, with granite fireplace and beams carved with the royal fleur-de-lys insignia, has more character. Tennis courts and water sports nearby. The farm organises visits and tasting sessions, so save space in the boot to stock up on farm produce, cider and home-made preserves.

Access : 12km westbound from Mortain on the D 977 and the D 5, then take the D 55 towards Saint-Hilaire

MONTCHATON - 50660

38 LE QUESNOT
M. Germanicus

3 rue du Mont-César
50660 Montchaton
Tel. 02 33 45 05 88

Closed from 15 Nov to Easter • 3 rooms • €45, breakfast included • No table d'hôte • Garden, car park. Credit cards not accepted, no dogs admitted

Cradled in a leafy nest of flowers.

Built out of local stone, this 18C house is surrounded by a curtain of foliage and flowers. All the stylish, well-kept rooms are upstairs. On the ground floor is a vast country living-room for the sole use of guests. From the terrace and small garden, you will be able to see the village church perched on an outcrop. Extremely friendly and welcoming.

Access : 6.5km to the south-west of Coutances on the D 20 then the D 72

NORMANDY

MONTVIRON - 50530

39 MANOIR DE LA CROIX
Mme Wagner

La Croix du Gros Chêne
50530 Montviron
Tel. 02 33 60 68 30
Fax 02 33 60 69 21
contact@manoirdelacroix.com
www.manoirdelacroix.com

Open all year (by reservation) • 2 rooms and 2 apartments (non-smoking only) • €62 (room), €79 (apartment), breakfast included • No table d'hôte • Garden, car park. Credit cards not accepted, no dogs admitted

We most liked: Gulp down the fresh air – inside and out of this non-smoking establishment.

If your lungs have had enough of urban pollution, head for this bubble of atmospheric purity. This 19C Anglo-Norman-style manor house overlooks a lovely garden, home to palms and other rare trees. The Empire and Louis-Philippe suites are immense and adorned with antiques, the other rooms and bathrooms are invariably spotless. The breakfast table is laden with cooked meats, cheeses and home-made jams and preserves.

Access: 8km to the north-west of Avranches towards Granville (D 973), then the D 41 (1km after Montviron).

OMONVILLE-LA-PETITE - 50440

40 LA FOSSARDIÈRE
M. Fossard

Hameau de la Fosse
50440 Omonville-la-Petite
Tel. 02 33 52 19 83
Fax 02 33 52 73 49

Closed from 15 Nov to 15 Mar • 10 rooms dotted around a hamlet, 9 have bath/WC, one has shower/WC • €40 to €64; breakfast €9 • No restaurant • Car park • Sauna, thalassotherapy, pond with picnic terrace

We most liked: Nothing could be more pastoral than this hamlet.

This hamlet-cum-hotel is on the doorstep of Omonville, the last resting place of Jacques Prévert, poet-screenwriter and counter-cultural icon. The rooms, which vary in size and comfort, are spread over several sandstone houses. Breakfast is served in the hamlet's former bakery. Young and old always find plenty to do in or around the private pond, 300m away, whether rowing, picnicking or simply making daisy chains.

Access: Near Cap de la Hague, between Saint-Germain-des-Vaux and Omonville-la-Rogue, opposite Anse Saint-Martin

NORMANDY

RÉVILLE - 50760

41 LA FERME DE CABOURG
Mme Marie

50760 Réville
Tel. 02 33 54 48 42
Fax 02 33 54 48 42

Open all year • 3 rooms • €45 to €50, breakfast included • No table d'hôte • Garden, car park. Credit cards not accepted, no dogs admitted

Perfectly located, just 150m from the beach.

A lovely drive lined in poplar trees leads up to this 15C fortified farm just two minutes from the Saire Valley and the seaside. The white walls of the rooms are dotted with the occasional block of granite and mullioned windows, loopholes and arrow slits, now glazed, you'll be glad to hear. Toast your toes in front of the roaring log fire lit in the sitting room in winter after trekking round the region's countless marvels of Romanesque architecture. Charming welcome.

Access : 3.5km northbound from Saint-Vaast on the D 1, 150m from the seashore

SAINTE-GENEVIÈVE - 50760

42 MANOIR DE LA FÉVRERIE
Mme Caillet

4 route d'Arville
50760 Sainte-Geneviève
Tel. 02 33 54 33 53
Fax 02 33 22 12 50
caillet.manoirlafevrerie@wanadoo.fr

Open all year • 3 rooms • €62 to €70, breakfast included • No table d'hôte • Car park. Credit cards not accepted, no dogs admitted

A matchless attention to detail.

The sea and Barfleur's picturesque harbour are only three kilometres from this charming 16C and 17C manor house. The snug bedrooms, reached by a granite staircase, were undoubtedly the work of a romantic at heart, as the pastel wallpaper, old furniture and striped or floral fabrics confirm. Breakfasts, served by the fireside in winter, are a feast for the eyes and the palate. We defy you to resist the temptation to curl up in the soft, inviting sofas and deep armchairs in the sitting room.

Access : 3km westbound from Barfleur on the D 25 and the D 525 Sainte-Geneviève road

NORMANDY

SAINTE-MÈRE-ÉGLISE - 50480

SAINT-VAAST-LA-HOUGUE - 50550

43 FERME MUSÉE DU COTENTIN
Mme Guillotte

1 chemin de Beauvais
50480 Sainte-Mère-Église
Tel. 02 33 95 40 20
Fax 02 33 95 40 24
musee.sainte-mere@wanadoo.fr

Closed in Dec and Jan • 4 rooms • €36, breakfast included • No table d'hôte • Car park • Visit to the museum

Spend a night in a museum!

This farm-museum offers guests the chance to get a real feel for life on the land. The rooms of this 17C and 18C stone farmhouse are an integral part of the museum and their decoration, pastel shades and furniture – including four-poster or alcove beds – is characteristic of the region. Guests can also visit the press, the granite tower where the apples were crushed, the collection of ploughs and the bakery. Highly unusual and well worth a look.

Access : Northbound exit out of Sainte-Mère-Église, on the Valognes road

44 FRANCE ET FUCHSIAS
Famille Brix

20 rue du Maréchal-Foch
50550 Saint-Vaast-la-Hougue
Tel. 02 33 54 42 26
Fax 02 33 43 46 79
reception@france-fuchsias.com
www.france-fuchsias.com

Closed from 3 Jan to 24 Feb, Mon lunchtime in Jul-Aug, Mon and Tue from Nov to Mar • 36 rooms with bath/WC or shower/WC and television • €44 to €106; breakfast €8 to €10; half-board available • Air-conditioned restaurant, menus €26 to €48 • Terrace, garden • In August recitals of chamber music

That inimitable feminine touch in the design of the bedrooms.

The façade, adorned with magnificent hundred-year-old fuchsias, of this old coaching inn hides the house's masterpiece, an extraordinary walled garden home to palms, mimosa, eucalyptus, banana trees and other exotic specimens. Who said that the Cotentin's "micro-climate" was a myth? In the summer, regional dishes are served in the midst of this lush green setting. Four rooms have been recently added, two on the ground-floor; those in the annex are more spacious than those in the main wing.

Access : In the town centre, not far from the port

NORMANDY

TAMERVILLE - 50700

45 MANOIR DE BELLAUNEY
Mme Allix-Desfauteaux

11 route de Quettehou
50700 Tamerville
Tel. 02 33 40 10 62
Fax 02 33 40 10 62
bellauney@wanadoo.fr
www.bellauney.com

Closed from 1 Nov to Easter • 3 rooms upstairs • €50 to €70, breakfast included • No table d'hôte • Garden, car park. Credit cards not accepted, no dogs admitted

History oozes from every crevice of this old manor house.

This 16C manor house, flanked by a tower and three handsome Romanesque arches is set in a lovely, tended mature garden. An impressive staircase leads up to the individually decorated rooms, each of which evokes a significant period in the domain's history. "Medieval" on the ground floor, "Louis XV" and "19C Norman" upstairs. The original wainscoting in the breakfast room adds the final touch to this historic abode.

Access : 3km to the north-east of Valognes towards Quettehou

TOURLAVILLE - 50110

46 MANOIR SAINT-JEAN
M. et Mme Guérard

Le hameau Saint-Jean
50110 Tourlaville
Tel. 02 33 22 00 86

Open all year • 3 non-smoking rooms • €47 to €52, breakfast included • No table d'hôte • Car park. Credit cards not accepted, no dogs admitted

It would be difficult to find a more amiable ambassador for the region.

This warm, welcoming 18C manor lies on the edge of the park of the Château des Ravalets. The view from the windows over Trottebec, Cherbourg and the coast is quite superb. The immaculate rooms are adorned with family heirlooms, as are the sitting rooms. Your graceful hostess could talk until the cows come home about her region's immense natural and cultural heritage.

Access : 1km past the castle on the D 322, then head for the "centre aéré" (play centre) and the Brix road

NORMANDY

VILLEDIEU-LES-POÊLES - 50800

47 MANOIR DE L'ACHERIE
M. Cahu

L'Acherie - Ste-Cécile
50800 Villedieu-les-Poêles
Tel. 02 33 51 13 87
Fax 02 33 51 33 69
manoir@manoir-acherie.fr
www.manoir-acherie.fr

Closed 20 Feb to 8 Mar and 13 to 30 Nov • 19 rooms located in 3 buildings around a courtyard, one has disabled access, all have bath/WC or shower/WC and television • €45 to €100; breakfast €7; half-board available • Menus €16 to €38 • Garden, car park. No dogs admitted • Children's play area

We most liked: The peace and quiet of Normandy.

The practical, well-kept rooms have less character than the spot itself, which is comprised of a manor built in 1660, a small 18C chapel and a beautifully manicured flower garden. The restaurant serves copious regional dishes and chargrilled specialities and is extremely popular with locals who come from far and near – always a good sign. Shop selling local produce.

Access: 3.5km eastbound from Villedieu-les-Poêles on the D 554

ALENÇON - 61000

48 LE GRAND CERF
M. Bouvet

21 rue Saint-Blaise
61000 Alençon
Tel. 02 33 26 00 51
Fax 02 33 26 63 07
legrandcerf-alencon@wanadoo.fr
www.hotelgrandcerf-61.com

Closed Sun and public holidays • 22 rooms, all have bath/WC or shower/WC and television • €59 to €83; breakfast €7; half-board available • Restaurant closed Sun; menus €14 to €27 • Terrace

We most liked: Whether made out of wrought-iron or threads as fine as human hair, lace is everywhere.

The ornate wrought-iron adorning the façade of this hotel, built in 1843, has withstood the passing of time and lives up to Alençon's reputation as the capital of lace. The hotel has recently been treated to a facelift, but the hall is still adorned with the establishment's namesake, a stag's head and the restaurant and most of the rooms have retained their original dimensions and moulded ceilings. In the summer, meals are served in a delightful inner walled courtyard.

Access: From Place du Général de Gaulle, drive towards the town centre, the hotel is on the right past the préfecture

NORMANDY

BAGNOLES-DE-L'ORNE - 61140

LONGNY-AU-PERCHE - 61290

49 L'ERMITAGE
M. Planché

24 boulevard Paul-Chalvet
61140 Bagnoles-de-l'Orne
Tel. 02 33 37 96 22
Fax 02 33 38 59 22
ermitagemc@aol.com
www.hotel-de-l-ermitage.com

Closed from Nov to late Mar • 38 rooms with bath/WC or shower/WC and television • €39 to €70; breakfast €8 • No restaurant • Garage, car park, garden.

Discovering the villas and tree-lined gardens of the resort's Belle Époque district.

This stylish property was built in 1886 in the Belle Époque style, typical of this smart Bagnoles neighbourhood. Soberly, rustic furnishings garnish the rooms, all of which have balconies, as does the breakfast room, overlooking the quiet garden. The cosy sitting room is adorned with a fresco. The charming owner adores pampering and cosseting her guests.

Access : In the Belle Époque neighbourhood

50 L'ORANGERIE
M. et Mme Desailly

9 rue du Docteur-Vivares
61290 Longny-au-Perche
Tel. 02 33 25 11 78
Fax 02 33 73 67 19
desailly-fondeur@tele2.fr
http://lorangerie.free.fr

Open all year • 3 rooms with bath/WC • €47, breakfast included • Table d'hôte (only by reservation) €14 • Garden. Credit cards not accepted, no dogs admitted

Settle down for a quiet evening in front of the fire after a day in the open air.

This attractive former orangery is now home to three lovely rooms, each of which is named after a wild flower: honeysuckle, buttercup and bluebell; the last of these is perfect for families. A large sitting room is ideal for long autumn evenings, grilling chestnuts or sizzling mushrooms over a crackling log fire. Ducks and fish have taken up residence in an old wash house hidden in the garden.

Access : In the village

NORMANDY

RÂNES - 61150

51 SAINT-PIERRE
M. et Mme Delaunay

6 rue de la Libération
61150 Rânes
Tel. 02 33 39 75 14
Fax 02 33 35 49 23
info@hotelsaintpierreranes.com
www.hotelsaintpierreranes.com

Open all year • 12 rooms with bath/WC or shower/WC and television • €43 to €62; breakfast €7; half-board available • Restaurant closed Fri evening; menus €15 to €42 • Terrace

The pleasant family welcome of this village inn.

Two minutes from an old castle now a gendarmerie, this stone-built house stands in the centre of the village, a stone's throw from the old castle. Parquet flooring, stylish wallpaper, exquisite wardrobes and rustic furniture adorn the appealing little rooms which are exceedingly reasonably priced. You will also appreciate the warm dining room; as well as the traditional recipes (frog's legs) made with local produce; make sure you sample the chef's speciality: tripe.

Access: In the centre of the village near the main square

AUMALE - 76390

52 VILLA DES HOUX
M. Mauconduit

6 av. du Général-de-Gaulle
76390 Aumale
Tel. 02 35 93 93 30
Fax 02 35 93 03 94
villa.des.houx@wanadoo.fr
www.villa-des-houx.com

Closed 1 to 27 Jan, Sun evening from 9 Oct to 15 Apr • 22 rooms, 2 have disabled access, with bath/WC or shower/WC and television • €60 to €80; breakfast €8; half-board available • Menus €23 to €39 • Private car park, garden

Tucking into the tasty home cooking on the terrace overlooking the garden.

This handsome half-timbered house used to be the village police station, but the cooking, comfort and welcome have improved since then! The generously proportioned rustically furnished rooms, tasty traditional cuisine enriched by delicious dishes of local produce and the charming dining room will all want to make you come back. The lovingly tended garden full of flowers adds to the villa's charm.

Access: Near the town centre, not far from the N 29

NORMANDY

DIEPPE - 76200

53 CHAMBRE D'HÔTE LA VILLA-FLORIDA
M. et Mme Noël

24 chemin du Golf
76200 Dieppe
Tel. 02 35 84 40 37
Fax 01 72 74 33 76
villa-florida@wanadoo.fr
www.lavillaflorida.com

Open all year • 4 rooms, one with mezzanine, with bath/WC or shower/WC • €66, breakfast included • No table d'hôte • Garden, car park. Credit cards not accepted, dogs not admitted

The faultlessly kind welcome.

This imaginatively designed slate covered house nestles in a delightful garden that opens onto the Dieppe golf course. Serenity and light fill the handsome interior proportions. Sober, contemporary rooms, each with a small private terrace, ensure total peace and quiet for all. Breakfasts are taken in the sitting room or garden, depending on the weather.

Access : 2km eastbound of Dieppe, towards Pourville on the D 75, before the Gulf

DUCLAIR - 76480

54 LE PANORAMA
M. et Mme Lemercier

282 chemin du Panorama
76480 Duclair
Tel. 02 35 37 68 84
Fax 02 35 37 68 84

Open all year • 5 rooms • €52, breakfast included • No table d'hôte • Garden, car park. Credit cards not accepted, no dogs admitted

An exceptional view of the Seine.

This 1930s villa built in the upper part of town lives up to its name, thanks to its idyllic view of the meanders of the Seine down below. The rooms are colourful and attractive; those under the eaves are perhaps the most inviting. The panoramic breakfast room and its tiny sitting room and fireplace are most appreciated, as is the delightful terraced garden.

Access : In the town centre, head towards Maromme, take the 1st turning on the right onto the chemin du Catel

NORMANDY

EU - 76260 **FÉCAMP - 76400**

55 MANOIR DE BEAUMONT
Mme Demarquet

Route de Beaumont
76260 Eu
Tel. 02 35 50 91 91
catherine@demarquet.com
www.demarquet.com

Open all year • 3 rooms • €47 to €55, breakfast included • No table d'hôte • Garden, car park. Credit cards not accepted, no dogs admitted

We most liked **Guests are offered a welcome drink on arrival.**

On the edge of the forest, this former hunting lodge of the château of Eu enjoys a matchless view of the valley. The comfortable, tastefully decorated rooms overlook the park and the countryside; the family room has been thoughtfully equipped with a kitchenette. Relax in the sitting room and library and delve into the numerous books – in French and English – on the area. Bicycles and horse loose-boxes are also available for guests and their four-legged companions.

Access: 2km eastbound from Eu on the D 49 towards the forest

56 LA FERME DE LA CHAPELLE
M. Buchy

Côte de la Vierge
76400 Fécamp
Tel. 02 35 10 12 12
Fax 02 35 10 12 13
fermedelachapelle@wanadoo.fr
www.fermedelachapelle.fr

Open all year • 22 rooms, 5 of which are self-contained with kitchenettes, 2 have disabled access, all have bath/WC and television • €75; breakfast €10; half-board available • Restaurant closed on Mon lunchtime; menu €20 • Garden, car park • Outdoor swimming pool

We most liked **The Museum of Newfoundland Fishermen in Fécamp.**

This old farm next door to a fishermen's chapel enjoys a wonderful position on the cliff, surveying the Channel and the port of Fécamp, from where French fishing sloops once set sail for the icy waters of Newfoundland. Inside the hotel can hardly be called luxurious, but it offers simple rooms, decorated with pine furniture and roughcast walls, laid out around a large square courtyard. We'll happily exchange luxury for authenticity any day!

Access: From the town centre, drive towards Dieppe along the harbour, then left towards Notre-Dame du-Salut

NORMANDY

FORGES-LES-EAUX - 76440

57 AUBERGE DU BEAU LIEU
M. et Mme Ramelet

Route de Paris - Le Fossé
76440 Forges-les-Eaux
Tel. 02 35 90 50 36
Fax 02 35 90 35 98
aubeaulieu@aol.com
www.auberge-du-beau-lieu.com

Closed from 16 Jan to 10 Feb • 3 rooms, with bath/WC and television • €56 to €76; breakfast €6 to €11 • Menus €18 (weekdays) to €54 • Terrace, garden, car park

What could be more symbolic of Normandy than apple trees and dairy cows?

Two minutes from the tiny spa-resort of Forges, this attractive country inn is home to cosy rooms which open directly onto the garden and a snug rustic restaurant complete with beams and a stone fireplace. The tableware is a reminder of the town's illustrious porcelain industry. The warmth of your hosts' welcome is such that you will even forget you're in a hotel.

Access: 2km on the D 915, towards Gournay

JUMIÈGES - 76480

58 LE RELAIS DE L'ABBAYE
M. et Mme Chatel

798 rue du Quesney
76480 Jumièges
Tel. 02 35 37 24 98
Fax 02 35 37 24 98

Open all year • 4 rooms • €42, breakfast included • No table d'hôte • Garden, car park. Credit cards not accepted

Roman Polanski's "Tess" could well have been shot near here!

Nestling in the shadow of the famous abbey, this pretty Norman slate-roofed house has everything you could wish for in a B&B establishment. A sophisticated rustic interior with beams, timbers, enormous fireplace, ornaments and antique plates. The rooms under the eaves upstairs are the most pleasant and the bathrooms merit a special prize. In the summer, breakfast is served in the garden.

Access: Near the abbey

NORMANDY

LE HAVRE - 76600

59 VENT D'OUEST
M. Lassarat

4 rue Caligny
76600 Le Havre
Tel. 02 35 42 50 69
Fax 02 35 42 58 00
contact@ventdouest.fr
www.ventdouest.fr

Open all year • 35 rooms, all have bath/WC or shower/WC and television • €85 to €110; breakfast €10 • No restaurant (room service available) • Tea room

We most liked **Visiting the port of Le Havre in a launch.**

Betwixt land and sea, the "Westerly" is a haven of charm in the heart of Le Havre's Modern Quarter designed by 20C architect Auguste Perret. A stone's throw from the harbour, the interior decoration has a distinctly briny flavour. The guest-rooms, on the other hand, are more adventurous and guests can choose between "country", "meditation" or "mountain" rooms, among others. Knick-knacks, snug quilts and a host of tiny details make all the difference.

Access : Drive along Quai Colbert past Vauban docks, turn right at Quai George V (Commerce docks) and continue straight on as far as St Joseph's Church

LE TRÉPORT - 76470

60 GOLF HÔTEL
Evergreen SARL

102 route de Dieppe
76470 Le Tréport
Tel. 02 27 28 01 52
Fax 02 27 28 01 51
evergreen2@wanadoo.fr
www.treport-hotels.com

Closed Christmas weekend • 10 non-smoking rooms, all have television • €46 to €69; breakfast €7 • No restaurant • Park, car park. No dogs admitted

We most liked **Extremely well-equipped rooms.**

In front of the entrance to Tréport's campsite, turn left onto the tree-lined drive which will take you up to this lovely late-19C half-timbered property set in the grounds of an immense park. All the non-smoking rooms are generously sized, well-equipped and personalised; all have a fridge. Friendly and excellent value for money.

Access : Near Tréport campsite

NORMANDY

LE TRÉPORT - 76470

61 LE PRIEURÉ SAINTE-CROIX
M. et Mme Carton

76470 Le Tréport
Tel. 02 35 86 14 77
Fax 02 35 86 14 77
carton.nicole@wanadoo.fr
http://prieuresaintecroix.free.fr

Open all year • 5 rooms with bathrooms • €45 to €57, breakfast included • No table d'hôte • Garden, car park. Credit cards not accepted, no dogs admitted

We most liked
Listening to the silence all around.

This farmhouse built in the reign of Louis-Philippe was formerly part of the castle of Eu's estate and is still a working cattle-farm. All the rooms, located in a separate wing, have been decorated in the same spirit with parquet floors, period furniture and recent bathrooms. The breakfast area, although entirely revamped, has retained its rustic appeal. Take a seat under the hundred-year-old flowering cherry trees in the garden.

Access: 2km eastbound from Tréport on the D 925 (Abbeville-Dieppe road)

MANNEVILLE-LA-GOUPIL - 76110

62 CHAMBRE D'HÔTE FERME D'ÉCOSSE
M. et Mme Loisel

1216 route des jonquilles
76110 Manneville-la-Goupil
Tel. 02 35 27 77 21
loisel.nicole@wanadoo.fr
http://ferme-ecosse.site-voila.fr

Open all year • 2 rooms upstairs • €50, breakfast included; half-board available • Table d'hôte €22 including beverages (evenings only and by reservation, closed Sun) • Garden, car park. Credit cards not accepted, no dogs admitted

We most liked
Delicious farm produce takes pride of place in the tasty home cooking.

The eye is immediately drawn to the fetching red-brick façade of this handsome 18C mansion. The establishment's rooms are comfortable and soberly decorated. Musically-minded guests have the use of a piano, while others will enjoy strolling through the garden and vegetable plot past the henhouse and sheepfold and children inevitably fall for the adorable donkeys. Try a glass of homemade cider as an aperitif before dinner.

Access: 4.5km on the D 10

NORMANDY

QUIBERVILLE - 76860

63 LES VERGERS
M. Auclert

Rue des Vergers
76860 Quiberville
Tel. 02 35 83 16 10
Fax 02 35 83 36 46
christianaucler@aol.com

Closed from Nov to Feb • 3 rooms with bath/WC • €60, breakfast included • No table d'hôte • Garden, car park. No dogs admitted

We most liked: A beautifully decorated period residence.

Guests can be sure of a pleasant welcome in this early 20C property. The spacious, comfortable rooms show a distinct preference for a discreetly classical opulence with pastel shades, floral fabrics and period furniture. Guests can relax in the lovely landscaped garden. Within easy reach of the sea, it is ideally situated to explore the region.

Access: 7km eastbound from Veules-les-Roses on the D 68 then the D 75

ROUEN - 76000

64 LE CLOS JOUVENET
Mme de Witte

42 rue Hyacinthe-Langlois
76000 Rouen
cdewitte@club-internet.fr
www.leclosjouvenet.com

Closed Christmas holidays • 4 non-smoking rooms, all with bath/WC or shower/WC • €75 to €82, breakfast included • No table d'hôte • Terrace, library, private car park. Credit cards not accepted

We most liked: The delightful view of the town and its steeples.

This enchanting 19C manor house perched on the hillside overlooking the town from the quiet of its immense garden is within wonderfully easy reach of Rouen. The energetic lady of the house enthusiastically welcomes guests to her cosy, elegant, immaculately kept rooms, which survey either the orchard or the town's steeples. In the morning, she prepares the excellent breakfasts herself, which are served in the kitchen, plush dining room or garden, depending on the season.

Access: In the town centre

NORMANDY

ROUEN - 76000

65 LE VIEUX CARRÉ
M. Beaumont

34 rue Ganterie
76000 Rouen
Tel. 02 35 71 67 70
Fax 02 35 71 19 17
vieux-carre@mcom.fr
www.vieux-carre.fr

Open all year • 12 rooms, one of which has disabled access, with bath/WC or shower/WC and television • €55 to €60; breakfast €7 • Menus €12 (lunchtime only)

There was nothing we didn't love!

The handsome walls of this house built in 1715, in the company of other august façades of the same vintage, line a street which is typical of Rouen and makes an ideal base camp from which to explore this "museum town". The interior is equally faultless and the rooms are decorated with frescoes and old wardrobes straight out of a boarding school dorm. The sitting room is snug and welcoming and the hotel boasts a courtyard terrace where mouth-watering pastries and a few choice dishes are served.

Access: In the heart of the old town, between the Palais de Justice and the Musée des Beaux Arts

ROUEN - 76000

66 HÔTEL DE LA CATHÉDRALE
M. Delaunay

12 rue Saint-Romain
76000 Rouen
Tel. 02 35 71 57 95
Fax 02 35 70 15 54
contact@hotel-de-la-cathedrale.fr
www.hotel-de-la-cathedrale.fr

Open all year • 26 rooms with bath/WC or shower/WC, all have television • €62 to €85; breakfast €8 • No restaurant

Breakfasting on the delightful patio which doubles as a tearoom in the afternoons.

This enchanting 17C establishment, located on one of Rouen's most beautiful old streets just a two minute walk from the cathedral, is proof that it is still possible to find good, well-priced accommodation in the heart of a tourist neighbourhood. Period furniture of varying styles, half-timbered walls, brightly coloured wallpaper and knick-knacks set the scene of this pleasantly old-fashioned hotel. An immense fireplace takes pride of place in the breakfast room with its raftered ceiling.

Access: In the heart of the old town

NORMANDY

SAINT-AUBIN-SUR-MER - 76740

67 CHAMBRE D'HÔTE MADAME GENTY
Mme Genty

Hameau de Ramouville
76740 Saint-Aubin-sur-Mer
Tel. 02 35 83 47 05
gisele.genty@wanadoo.fr
http://gisele.genty.free.fr

Open all year • 5 rooms, 2 of which are on the ground floor and 3 are under the eaves • €47 to €50, breakfast included • No table d'hôte • Garden, car park. Credit cards not accepted

We most liked
Waking up to the enticing aroma of oven-fresh bread.

After a masterful restoration this 18C regional farmstead is back in its prime. The thatched roof may have disappeared, but the lovely half-timbered walls were rescued and well-worn tiles and a fireplace adorn the rustic, warm sitting room. The rooms echo this rustic spirit and three are under the eaves. In the morning, the delicious smell of bread, freshly baked in the old oven, will entice you down to breakfast.

Access : 4km northbound from Bourg-Dun then towards Quiberville

SOMMERY - 76440

68 FERME DE BRAY
M. et Mme Perrier

76440 Sommery
Tel. 02 35 90 57 27
www.ferme.de.bray.free.fr

Open all year • 5 rooms with bathrooms • €46, breakfast included • No table d'hôte • Garden, car park. Credit cards not accepted, no dogs admitted • Farm visits, fishing

We most liked
The farm continues to uphold local rural traditions.

The land has been farmed by the same family for 18 generations and their 17C and 18C farmhouse, which doubles as a museum and a B&B, is simply astounding. Rural through and through, the furniture and the simplicity of the interior decoration echo this country spirit: each of the rooms, lightened by striped wallpaper, has its own fireplace. Activities abound on the farm, including a visit to the press, mill, dairy parlour, dovecote, not to mention exhibitions and fishing in the pond.

Access : 10km to the north-east of Forges-les-Eaux on the D 915

NORMANDY

VALMONT - 76540　　　　　　　　VARENGEVILLE-SUR-MER - 76119

69 LE CLOS DU VIVIER
Mme Cachera

4 chemin du Vivier
76540 Valmont
Tel. 02 35 29 90 95
Fax 02 35 27 44 49
dc@le-clos-du-vivier.com
www.leclosduvivier.com

Open all year • 2 rooms and 1 apartment • €80 to €100, breakfast included • No table d'hôte • Garden, car park. Credit cards not accepted

We most liked: **Breakfasting by the garden where ducks, swans, chickens and peacocks roam free.**

This large 17C cottage, hidden deep in the countryside, was formerly an outbuilding of the Château de Valmont. Over the years, the current owners have tirelessly transformed it into a pleasant getaway where they take great pleasure in welcoming guests. Exposed beams, bare stonework and fireplaces make interesting architectural features in the sitting rooms. The appealing "cottage" atmosphere of the rooms has been wisely preserved.

Access: 2km eastbound of Valmont on the D 150 towards Ourville

70 LA TERRASSE
M. et Mme Delafontaine

Route de Vasterival
76119 Varengeville-sur-Mer
Tel. 02 35 85 12 54
Fax 02 35 85 11 70
francois.delafontaine@wanadoo.fr
www.hotel-restaurant-la-terrasse.com

Open from 15 Mar to 15 Oct • 22 rooms with bath/WC or shower/WC • €47 to €52; breakfast €7; half-board available • Menus €18 to €30 • Garden, car park. No dogs admitted in restaurant • Tennis

We most liked: **The family donkey grazing in the meadow alongside the path leading down to the beach.**

At the end of a pretty little lane flanked by fir trees, stands an early-20C brick house, which is the family home of the current owners. Nothing opulent or ostentatious deflects from the establishment's quiet charm: the TV has been thankfully banned from the calm rooms, enhanced by colourful fabrics and tartan carpets. Half of the bedrooms enjoy a sea view. Panoramic restaurant and a shaded garden.

Access: 3km to the north-west on the D 75, then take the small minor road lined by fir trees

NORMANDY

VATTEVILLE-LA-RUE - 76940

71 MANOIR DU PLESSIS
M. et Mme Laurent

1175 route de Caudebec
76940 Vatteville-la-Rue
Tel. 02 35 95 79 79
Fax 02 35 95 79 77
aplvatteville@free.fr

Open all year • 4 rooms with bathrooms • €51 to €56, breakfast included; half-board available • Table d'hôte €22 to €43 • Garden, car park

The country flavour of this fine old manor house.

This Napoleonic brick manor-house topped by two high chimney stacks is worth a pause, if only to savour its quiet atmosphere. The rooms with bathrooms boast parquet floors and lovely antique furniture and are full of character; the others are more sober. The rustic dining room, decorated by dark wainscoting and the billiards table in the sitting room further add to the establishment's appeal. If you can tear yourselves away, do you fancy a spot of hunting, or brushing up on your artistic skills?

Access: A 13 motorway, exit 25 or A 29 motorway, exit 8

YVETOT - 76190

72 AUBERGE DU VAL AU CESNE
M. Carel

76190 Yvetot
Tel. 02 35 56 63 06
Fax 02 35 56 92 78
valaucesne@hotmail.com
www.valaucesne.fr

Closed 9 to 29 Jan, 22 Aug to 4 Sep, 28 Nov to 11 Dec, Mon and Tue • 5 rooms, all with bath/WC, television and telephone • €80; breakfast €9 • Menus €25, drinks included • Terrace, garden, car park, function room

The enchanting dining rooms.

A lush green garden complete with aviary surrounds this three-hundred-year-old Normandy inn made up of two delightful half-timbered houses. One sports a "bijou" style decoration with exquisitely kept bedrooms, each of which has its own private terrace. The other cottage is home to the country-style dining rooms, furnished with antiques and handsome fireplaces. A feast of traditional country cooking and a fine selection of wines.

Access: On the D 5 between Duclair and Yvetot

PAYS DE LA LOIRE

First there is the peaceful valley of the Loire, the "Garden of France", renowned for its peaceful ambience, enchanting views, sumptuous manor houses and castles, magnificent floral gardens, lavish orchards, fields of vegetables and acre upon acre of vineyards. Tuck into a slab of rillettes pâté liberally spread on a crunchy baguette, a steaming platter of eels or a slice of goat's cheese while you savour a glass of light Loire wine. Continue westwards towards the sea to Nantes, once a port of entrance for enticing spices brought back from the New World: this is the home of the famous dry Muscadet. Further south, the Vendée still echoes to the cries of the Royalists' tragic last stand. Explore the secrets of its salt marshes, relax in its seaside resorts or head for the spectacular attractions of the Puy du Fou amusement park. Simple, country fare is not lacking, so make sure you taste a delicious dish of *mojettes* (white beans), a piping-hot plate of *chaudrée* (fish stew) or a mouth-watering slice of fresh brioche.

- Loire-Atlantique (44)
- Maine-et-Loire (49)
- Mayenne (53)
- Sarthe (72)
- Vendée (85)

PAYS DE LA LOIRE

GUÉRANDE - 44350

1 LA GUÉRANDIÈRE
Mme Lauvray

5 rue Vannetaise
44350 Guérande
Tel. 02 40 62 17 15
contact@guerandiere.com
www.guerandiere.com

Open all year (by reservation out of season) • 6 non-smoking rooms on two floors, all with bathrooms • €75 to €85 (€55 to €65 low season); breakfast €10 • No table d'hôte • Walled garden, car park. Dogs admitted on request • Bicycle rentals

We most liked The cosy, timeless atmosphere of this handsome property.

This imposing 19C mansion, partly built against the ramparts of the medieval city, is not lacking in charms. The interior decoration has remained faithful to the spirit of houses of this period: furniture belonging to the family or picked up in antique shops and carefully chosen fabrics and knick-knacks combine to create a cosy, elegant interior. A fine period staircase leads up to the bedrooms. English-style breakfasts are served in the garden in summertime.

Access : At the foot of the ramparts in the medieval town

LA BAULE - 44500

2 HOSTELLERIE DU BOIS
M. et Mme Lethuillier

65 avenue Lajarrige
44500 La Baule
Tel. 02 40 60 24 78
Fax 02 40 42 05 88
hostellerie-du-bois@wanadoo.fr
www.hostellerie-du-bois.com

Closed from 15 Nov to 15 Mar • 15 non-smoking rooms on 2 floors, overlooking the garden or the street, all have bath/WC or shower/WC and television • €70 (€60 low season); breakfast €7; half-board available • Restaurant closed Sat, menus €23 to €26 (evenings only) • Terrace, garden

We most liked La Baule les Pins provides a welcome break from the concrete jungle along the coast.

Poised between the ocean and Parc des Dryades, this 1920s seaside hotel has a distinctive green and white half-timbered façade. The well-travelled owners have carefully preserved its pleasantly old-fashioned flavour as a showcase for the countless ornaments and pieces of furniture brought back from their travels in the Far East. The small garden in the back is simply delightful.

Access : At Place des Palmiers head for the railway station

PAYS DE LA LOIRE

LA BAULE - 44500

3 LE MARINI
M. Le Boudec

22 avenue Georges-Clemenceau
44500 La Baule
Tel. 02 40 60 23 29
Fax 02 40 11 16 98
interhotelmarini@wanadoo.fr
www.hotel-marini.com

Open all year • 33 rooms with bath/WC, all have television • €63 to €84 (€53 to €73 low season); breakfast €8; half-board available • Menus €21 • Garage. Dogs not admitted in restaurant • Indoor swimming pool with jacuzzi

We most liked
The globetrotter spirit of this hotel.

Whether on a serious excursion throughout France or simply in search of a mooring spot to visit the region, you're bound to warm to the discreet ambience and the well thought-out attention to detail of this hotel. Off the beaten seaside track, it boasts a covered swimming pool and jacuzzi, a welcoming sitting room-bar with cosy armchairs, a reading corner and trim, practical bedrooms equipped with comfortable bedding. Breakfast and dinner are served around the pool.

Access : In the town centre

LE PALLET - 44330

4 CHÂTEAU DE LA SÉBINIÈRE
Mme Cannaférina

44330 Le Pallet
Tel. 02 40 80 49 25
Fax 02 40 80 49 25
info@chateausebiniere.com
www.chateausebiniere.com

Open all year • 3 non-smoking rooms, one in a wing, all have bathrooms and television on request • €74 to €100, breakfast included • Table d'hôte €30 • Terrace, park, private car park. Dogs admitted on request • Outdoor swimming pool, billiards room

We most liked
Long riverside walks on the banks of the Sèvre.

Clinging to the hills surrounding the village of Le Pallet, this fully restored castle, protected by woodlands and 13 hectares of vineyards, invites guests to take things easy. The enchanting bedrooms, decorated in an old-fashioned style and the sitting rooms (whitewashed walls, tiled floors and comfy furniture) are filled with a timeless aura of peace and quiet. Muscadet wine tasting on the estate.

Access : At Pallet, the castle is past the vine museum. On the way up the hill, take the first private drive on the right

PAYS DE LA LOIRE
PIRIAC-SUR-MER - 44420   PORNIC - 44210

5 POSTE
M. Malnoé

26 rue de la Plage
44420 Piriac-sur-Mer
Tel. 02 40 23 50 90
Fax 02 40 23 68 96
hoteldelaposte.piriac@wanadoo.fr

Open from 1 Apr to 1 Nov • 15 rooms on 2 floors with bath/WC or showers with or without WC, some have television • €42 to €67; breakfast €7; half-board available • Restaurant closed Mon; menus €19 to €39 • No dogs admitted in restaurant

We most liked
The footpath to the Pointe du Castelli.

This appealing 1930s villa lies in the heart of a tiny fishing port surrounded by picturesque 17C houses. Its spacious, well-appointed rooms are looked after by the owner, for whom the term "clean enough to eat off the kitchen floor" is clearly not an empty remark! The family dining room is lit by immense arcades and in the summer, tables are laid outdoors.

Access : In the centre of the village, on the main road opposite the chemist

6 RELAIS SAINT-GILLES
M. et Mme Robineau

7 rue Fernand-de-Mun
44210 Pornic
Tel. 02 40 82 02 25
www.relaissaintgilles.com

Closed 30 Sep to 1 Apr • 25 rooms, including 1 apartment, with bath/WC and television • €50 to €68 (€48 to €55 low season); breakfast €7 • No restaurant • Terrace

We most liked
A castle set in foliage, sandy beaches and a picture-postcard harbour: what more could you wish for?

This mid-19C coaching inn can be found on a quiet side street of this seaside resort. Two wings stand on either side of a terrace shaded by an arbour of climbing vines. Inside are regularly spruced up rooms with fresh wallpaper and paintwork, some with old furniture, and a plush bourgeois dining room. Your host, a former merchant navy officer, can point you towards a whole host of beautiful footpaths.

Access : In the upper part of town, on a quiet street above the castle

PAYS DE LA LOIRE

SAINT-LYPHARD - 44110

7 LES CHAUMIÈRES DU LAC
M. Logodin

Route d'Herbignac
44110 Saint-Lyphard
Tel. 02 40 91 32 32
Fax 02 40 91 30 33
jclogodin@leschaumieresdulac.com
www.leschaumieresdulac.com

Closed from 15 Dec to 10 Feb • 20 rooms, 2 of which have disabled access, all have bath/WC and television • €72 to €93 (€62 to €77 low season); breakfast €9; half-board available • Auberge Les Typhas; menus €18 (weekdays) to €40 • Garden, car park • Swimming in a small lake

France's best chefs and gourmets only use Guérande's "fleur de sel" – find out why.

This recently built hamlet of cottages right in the heart of the Brière Nature Reserve may not be the epitome of authenticity, but it is definitely an excellent way of finding out more about the region's salt marshes. The appeal is further enhanced by the tasteful yellow and white restaurant, pretty terrace and stylish bedrooms with canopy beds. All the more so once you've caught a glimpse of what the inside of a local cottage really looked like, at the reconstructed cottages in Kerhinet.

Access: Outside the village, by the minor road, opposite the lake

SAINT-MALO-DE-GUERSAC - 44550

8 TY GWENN
M. Collard

25 Île-d'Errand
44550 Saint-Malo-de-Guersac
Tel. 02 40 91 15 04

Closed from 1 Oct to 1 Apr • 3 non-smoking rooms, all have shower/WC, television and a small fridge • €54, breakfast included • Table d'hôte €20 (evening only) • Sitting room, garden, car park. Credit cards not accepted, no dogs admitted • Outdoor swimming pool, billiards. Sailing, golf course, horse-riding and angling nearby

Barge excursions along the canals of the Brière (on request).

The whitewashed walls, thatched roof and the leaded windows framed with curtains of this adorable cottage may well find you hunting for your camera. Inside, the romantic, snug rooms are equally appealing. In the sitting room you will be met with a sophisticated picture of exposed beams, a fireplace, lovely fabrics and a billiards table. Guests – non-smokers only – have the run of a delightful garden and swimming pool.

Access: 3km from Saint-Malo

PAYS DE LA LOIRE

SAINT-MOLF - 44350

9 KERVENEL
M. Brasselet

D 252 - Le Pigeon-Blanc
44350 Saint-Molf
Tel. 02 40 42 50 38
Fax 02 40 42 50 55
ybrasselet@aol.com
www.loire-atlantique-tourisme-com

Open from Apr to Sep • 3 rooms with bath/WC • €60, breakfast included • No table d'hôte • Car park, sitting room. Credit cards not accepted, no dogs admitted • Bicycle rentals.

We most liked Lounging in the garden in fine weather.

This former farmhouse restored in the 1970s borders on the Brière Regional Park. A lovely granite façade hides spacious rooms named after the style in which they are furnished: Louis XVI, Louis XVIII and contemporary. Tasteful bed linen, comfortable bathrooms and the tranquillity of the site all contribute to making your stay a pleasant one.

Access : 2.5km on the D 33 towards La Turballe

ANDARD - 49800

10 LE GRAND TALON
Mme Guervilly

3 route des Chapelles
49800 Andard
Tel. 02 41 80 42 85
Fax 02 41 80 42 85

Open all year • 3 rooms • €63, breakfast included • No table d'hôte • Park, car park. Credit cards not accepted

We most liked Mrs Guervilly does her utmost to make your stay as pleasant as possible.

The graceful façade of this elegant 18C abode, covered in russet-red leaves in autumn, overlooks a square courtyard just two minutes from Angers. The peaceful bedrooms are tastefully decorated. If you're lucky with the weather, you can breakfast and picnic in the garden under a parasol.

Access : 11km eastbound from Angers on the N 147, towards Saumur then take the D 113

PAYS DE LA LOIRE

ANGERS - 49100

11 HÔTEL DU MAIL
M. Le-Calvez

8 rue des Ursules
49100 Angers
Tel. 02 41 25 05 25
Fax 02 41 86 91 20
contact@hotel-du-mail.com
www.hotel-du-mail.com

- 26 rooms on 2 floors, most have bath/WC, the others have shower/WC, all have television • €55 to €70; breakfast €8 • No restaurant • Private car park in the inner courtyard

Most liked: Angers is famed for its mild climate and a tradition of gracious living.

This discreet hotel standing in a side street of the historic town was an Ursuline convent in the 17C, before becoming a guesthouse and now boutique hotel. It takes a bit of finding but your efforts will be amply rewarded by the personalised, beautifully decorated rooms awaiting you. The breakfast room is decorated in a classic bourgeois style and guests can also venture onto a lovely mini-terrace in the inner courtyard. Definitely worth mailing home about!

Access: In a quiet street behind the town hall

AUVERSE - 49490

12 DOMAINE DE LA BRÉGELLERIE
M. et Mme Sohn

Route de Chigne
49490 Auverse
Tel. 02 41 82 11 69
Fax 02 41 82 11 87
isabelle.sohn@wanadoo.fr
http://la.bregellerie.free.fr

Open all year • 5 non-smoking rooms, 4 of which are upstairs, all have bathrooms • €55 to €70, breakfast included • No table d'hôte • Garden, car park. Credit cards not accepted • Outdoor swimming pool, fishing in the pond

Most liked: "The Loire" bedroom.

After a full-scale renovation this old farmstead has been elevated to the rank of inn. The names of the individually decorated rooms located in a recent wing reveal their one-off themes: "Forest", "Vines", "Fields", "Pond" and "The Loire", whose curious boat-shaped bathtub is worth a special mention. A breakfast room, elegantly understated, a pool table, a large summer swimming pool in the garden and a pond – fishing possible – add the finishing touches.

Access: 14.5km to the south-west on the D 767, Noyant road and the D 79 on the right

PAYS DE LA LOIRE
FONTEVRAUD-L'ABBAYE - 49590   FONTEVRAUD-L'ABBAYE - 49590

13 LA CROIX BLANCHE
M. et Mme Chabenat

7 place des Plantagenêts
49590 Fontevraud-l'Abbaye
Tel. 02 41 51 71 11
Fax 02 41 38 15 38
info@fontevraud.net
www.fontevraud.net

Closed 1 week in Nov, from 3 to 31 Jan, Sun evening and Mon from Nov to Mar • 25 rooms with bath/WC or shower/WC, all have television • €65 to €117; breakfast €9; half-board available • Menus €20 to €53 • Terrace, private car park • Swimming pool, petanque, table-tennis, billiards, bicycles lent

Guests can borrow bicycles and explore the countryside.

"It all began in 1696, when Mistress Marie Cohier wedded Master Mathieux Blochon and they opened the hostelry." For over three hundred years, this ancient inn has been welcoming travellers from near and far, come to admire the neighbouring monastery. Many of the renovated bedrooms sport raftered ceilings and period fireplaces. Guests also have the run of a sitting-room and billiards room and have the choice of a traditional restaurant (summer terrace) or a crêperie.

Access: In the town centre, opposite the entrance to the Abbaye Royale

14 DOMAINE DE MESTRÉ
M. et Mme Dauge

49590 Fontevraud-l'Abbaye
Tel. 02 41 51 72 32
Fax 02 41 51 71 90
domaine-de-mestre@wanadoo.fr
www.dauge-fontevraud.com

Closed from 20 Dec to 1 Apr • 12 rooms with bathrooms • €60; breakfast €8 • Table d'hôte €24 (evenings only) • Park, car park. Credit cards not accepted, no dogs admitted

Lavender, vetiver, olive oil, thyme, cinnamon, nutmeg and rose-scented soaps.

This farm and its old tithe barn, dating back to the 13C, once belonged to the Royal Abbey of Fontevraud: nowadays, it is home to attractive, individually decorated rooms in which it is easy to feel at home. Breakfast and dinner, made with home-grown ingredients, are served in the former chapel. The estate's woods and gardens are home to ancient cedar and lime-trees and a visit to the estate's craft soap factory is always a pleasure.

Access: 1km northbound from Fontevraud on the D 947, towards Montsoreau

PAYS DE LA LOIRE

FONTEVRAUD-L'ABBAYE - 49590

15 PRIEURÉ-SAINT-LAZARE
M. Haudebault

Abbaye Royale de Fontevraud Rue Saint-Jean-de-l'Hubit
49590 Fontevraud-L'Abbaye
Tel. 02 41 51 73 16
Fax 02 41 51 75 50
contact@hotelfp-fontevraud.com
www.hotelfp-fontevraud.com

Open from 1 Apr to 12 Nov • 52 rooms, 6 are for non-smokers, with bath/WC or shower/WC, all have television • €65 to €112 (€60 to €107 low season); breakfast €11; half-board available • Restaurant closed Tue and Wed lunchtime; menus €12 (weekdays) to €46 • Garden, private car park. Dogs not admitted

Find sanctuary within the walls of the abbey gardens.

The building was indeed a priory and a lazaret before being turned into a hotel. Although rich in history, its ancient walls have an eternal quality that appears to withstand the wear and tear of time: the almost monastical bedroom-cells provide a haven of peace and quiet for busy urban dwellers and the vaulted breakfast room and restaurant tables around the cloisters further extend this invitation to meditate and take stock.

Access : In the abbey grounds

MONTSOREAU - 49730

16 LE BUSSY
Mme Roi

4 rue Jeanne-d'Arc
49730 Montsoreau
Tel. 02 41 38 11 11
Fax 02 41 38 18 10
hotel.lebussy@wanadoo.fr
www.lebussy.com

Closed on Tue and Wed in Feb, Mar, Nov and Dec • 12 rooms, all have bath/WC or shower/WC and television • €50 to €65; breakfast €8 to €9 • No restaurant • Private car park

What better place to curl up with one of Alexander Dumas' novels of romance and action?

The sign outside this 18C house at the top of the village pays homage to one of Dumas' famous heroes, Bussy d'Amboise, sweetheart of the Dame de Monsoreau. Most of the rooms, furnished in a Louis Philippe style and equipped with brand new bathrooms, survey the castle and the Loire. In the summer, breakfast is served in the flower-decked garden and throughout the rest of the year, in a delightful troglodyte room. Friendly and welcoming.

Access : In the upper part of town behind the castle

PAYS DE LA LOIRE

TURQUANT - 49730

17 DEMEURE DE LA VIGNOLE
Mme Bartholeyns

3 impasse Marguerite-d'Anjou
49730 Turquant
Tel. 02 41 53 67 00
Fax 02 41 53 67 09
demeure@demeure-vignole.com
www.demeure-vignole.com

Open from 15 Mar to 15 Nov • 8 rooms, one of which has disabled access, all have bath/WC and television • €74 to €111; breakfast €9; half-board available • Menus €26 (evenings only by reservation) • Terrace, garden, car park. Dogs not admitted

We most liked The troglodyte chamber where the villagers met in the 12C.

This exquisite estate only opened its doors as a hotel in 2000 following several years of major restoration work under the supervision of the architects of France's Listed Monuments. The 15C manor house and 17C outbuildings perched on the cliff have been turned into individually decorated rooms, where every effort has been taken to retain their historic decorative features such as beams, fireplace and bread oven. A terraced garden commands a wonderful view of the valley. Admirable.

Access : 10km from Saumur on the D 947, in the heart of the village

CHÂTEAU-GONTIER - 53200

18 LE CHÂTEAU DE MIRVAULT
M. et Mme d'Ambrières

53200 Château-Gontier
Tel. 02 43 07 10 82
Fax 02 43 07 10 82
château.mirvault@worldonline.fr

Open all year • 4 rooms • €76, breakfast included • No table d'hôte • Park, car park. Credit cards not accepted, no dogs admitted

We most liked Friendly family welcome.

This elegant château on the banks of the Mayenne has been the home of the same family since 1573. The lavish sitting room is furnished with 18C antiques and family portraits, a beautiful tapestry hangs on the wall of the breakfast room and the park is home to warrens of wild rabbits straight out of "Watership Down". The rooms are equally ornate and overlook the river where you can go boating, should you so fancy.

Access : Northbound on the N 162, on the Laval road on the banks of the Mayenne

PAYS DE LA LOIRE

CHAMPFLEUR - 72610

19 LA GARENCIÈRE
M. et Mme Langlais

72610 Champfleur
Tel. 02 33 31 75 84
Fax 02 33 27 42 09
denis.langlais@wanadoo.fr
www.monsite.wanadoo.fr/garenciere

Closed in Jan • 5 rooms • €50, breakfast included • Table d'hôte €20 (evenings only) • Car park. Credit cards not accepted, no dogs admitted • Indoor swimming pool

Green fields as far as the eye can see.

At the time of the crusades, this hamlet, a former stronghold of the Knights of la Garencière, was a stopover point for pilgrims on the way to Compostela. Nowadays, the large 19C farmhouse, built on the site of the old pilgrims' refuge, offers quiet, tastefully decorated rooms; the one in an independent cottage is ideal for families. Sample a generous spread of local produce, before taking a dip in the covered swimming pool overlooking the countryside.

Access: 6.5km south-east of Alençon towards Mamers and Champfleur (D 19), then continue towards Bourg-le-Roi

COULAINES - 72190

20 CHAMBRE D'HÔTE MADAME BORDEAU
Mme Bordeau

Le Monet
72190 Coulaines
Tel. 02 43 82 25 50

Open all year • 4 rooms • €50, breakfast included • No table d'hôte • Garden, car park. Credit cards not accepted, no dogs admitted

A country atmosphere on the doorstep of Le Mans.

Saved from ruin in the nick of time, this small country house has made a spectacular recovery. Madame clearly spends many hours in her garden. Inside, the original character has been preserved and enhanced by a generous sprinkling of modern comforts. The rooms are not enormous but beautifully furnished; those on the ground floor have exposed beams and the others are under the eaves. A log fire is lit in the winter to take the chill off the morning in the breakfast room.

Access: 5km northbound from Le Mans, towards Mamers then Ballon on the D 300

PAYS DE LA LOIRE
LE LUDE - 72800 LUCHÉ-PRINGÉ - 72800

21 CHAMBRE D'HÔTE MADAME PEAN
Mme Pean

5 Grande-Rue
72800 Le Lude
Tel. 02 43 94 63 36

Closed from Oct to Mar • 3 rooms upstairs • €50, breakfast included • No table d'hôte • Garden. Credit cards not accepted

22 L'AUBERGE DU PORT DES ROCHES
M. et Mme Lesiourd

Le Port des Roches
72800 Luché-Pringé
Tel. 02 43 45 44 48
Fax 02 43 45 39 61

Closed in Feb, Sun evening, Mon and Tue lunchtime • 12 rooms with bath/WC or shower/WC, half of them have television • €45 to €55; breakfast €7; half-board available • Menus €22 to €44 • Terrace and riverside garden, private car park

---

We most liked: Ideally situated, two minutes from the castle.

Who could guess that behind the impressive walls of this handsome 17C property lies such a heavenly garden? Spacious, antique-furnished rooms like these, not to mention the delicious breakfasts, are the makings of a good holiday, but it is the atmosphere that will make you want to return: Madame Pean is so genuinely and clearly delighted to meet her guests that visits might well become an annual event.

We most liked: Strolling along the banks of the river Loir.

This smart country inn on the banks of the Loir now enjoys a supremely quiet location: it's hard to imagine, that not so long ago, soft local stone was quarried from the surrounding hillsides and loaded onto boats which would be moored in front of the hotel. Light, airy, colourful rooms, a comfortable dining room with a homely feel and a riverside garden-terrace await guests in search of peace and quiet.

Access : In the village

Access : 2.5km eastbound on the D 13 towards Mancigné, then take the D 214

PAYS DE LA LOIRE

MONCÉ-EN-BELIN - 72230

23 LE PETIT PONT
Mme Brou

3 rue du Petit-Pont
72230 Moncé-en-Belin
Tel. 02 43 42 03 32
Fax 02 43 42 97 95

Open all year • One room in the house and 5 others in a separate wing • €48 to €60, breakfast included • Table d'hôte €13 (weekdays) to €25 • Garden, car park. No dogs admitted

Your tireless hostess did much of the restoration herself.

Over the years, your energetic hostess has painstakingly restored her lovely house, covered in variegated vine and part of a former working farm. Her efforts have resulted in beautifully appointed, individually decorated rooms (non-smokers only). One of the rooms and a self-catering cottage are in the main building, while the others are in an independent wing. Friendly and welcoming.

Access : 11km southbound from Le Mans on the D 147 towards Arnage, then take the D 307

PONCÉ-SUR-LE-LOIR - 72340

24 CHÂTEAU DE LA VOLONIÈRE
M. Becquelin

49 rue Principale
72340 Poncé-sur-le-Loir
Tel. 02 43 79 68 16
Fax 02 43 79 68 18
chateau-de-la-voloniere@wanadoo.fr
http://chateaudelavoloniere.free.fr

Closed in Feb (except by reservation) • 5 rooms • €60 to €80, breakfast included • No table d'hôte • Park, car park • Visits to the Loire chateaux

Bohemian and easy-going.

Guests can depend on a perfect welcome when they arrive in this château, next door to the birthplace of the 16C poet, Pierre Ronsard. A bold colour scheme and antiques set the scene for the bedrooms, each of which is decorated on a the theme of a well-known tale: "Bluebeard", "Arabian Nights", "Merlin" and "Romeo and Juliet". The 15C chapel has been turned into the dining room and exhibitions are held in the former troglodyte kitchen.

Access : In the village

PAYS DE LA LOIRE

SAINT-LÉONARD-DES-BOIS - 72130

25 LE MOULIN DE LINTHE
M. et Mme Rollini

Route de Sougé-le-Ganelon
72130 Saint-Léonard-des-Bois
Tel. 02 43 33 79 22
Fax 02 43 33 79 22
www.moulindelinthe.net

Closed in Jan and Feb • 5 rooms • €60, breakfast included • No table d'hôte • Terrace, garden, car park. Credit cards not accepted, no dogs admitted • Fishing in the River Sarthe

We most liked **Savour the refreshing peace and quiet of this riverside location.**

Get back to grass roots in this three-hundred-year-old mill surrounded by fields. Anglers can try their luck tempting the pike in the Sarthe at the bottom of the garden, others may prefer to go for long bike rides round the countryside or simply relax in the garden. Each of the spacious, airy rooms is furnished in a different style: Norman, Louis XVI, 1930s. The sitting room commands a lovely view of the millwheel.

Access : 400m south of the village towards Sougé-le-Ganelon

BOUIN - 85230

26 HÔTEL DU MARTINET
Mme Huchet

1 bis place de la Croix-Blanche
85230 Bouin
Tel. 02 51 49 08 94
Fax 02 51 49 83 08
hotel.martinet@free.fr
www.lemartinet.com

Open all year • 30 rooms, 7 of which are on the ground floor, with bath/WC or shower/WC and television • €54 to €74; breakfast €7; half-board available • Menus €23 (weekdays) to €26 • Garden, car park. No dogs admitted in restaurant • Outdoor swimming pool, fitness room

We most liked **Breathe in the scent of fresh flowers and beeswax.**

The discreet walls of this 18C house hide a whole host of assets including a quiet garden, a swimming pool and spotless rooms – those on the ground floor with tiled floors and cane furniture are the most pleasant. Come the evening, take your places in the delightful dining room with its painted woodwork, parquet floor and marble fireplace. The owner, ever-active and unfailingly friendly, will often present you with the catch of the day, brought home by one of her sons and cooked by the other!

Access : In the centre of the village

PAYS DE LA LOIRE

CHALLANS - 85300

LA ROCHE-SUR-YON - 85000

27 L'ANTIQUITÉ
M. et Mme Belleville

14 rue Galliéni
85300 Challans
Tel. 02 51 68 02 84
Fax 02 51 35 55 74
antiquitehotel@wanadoo.fr
www.hotelantiquite.com

Open all year • 16 rooms with bath/WC or shower/WC and television • €52 to €78 (€46 to €70 low season); breakfast €7 • No restaurant • Private car park. No dogs admitted • Swimming pool

We most liked **The breakfast room which leads into a lovely veranda.**

Given the establishment's name, you will not be surprised to learn that this family-run establishment is strewn with antiques picked up in local second-hand shops. Most of the rooms, housed in an imposing white-fronted building, are graced with red-brick tiles, period furniture and old engravings and paintings. A recent wing, with four rather more spacious rooms fitted with brand new bathrooms, has been laid out around the outdoor swimming pool.

Access: Near the exhibition hall

28 LOGIS DE LA COUPERIE
Mme Oliveau

85000 La Roche-sur-Yon
Tel. 02 51 24 10 18
Fax 02 51 46 05 59

Open all year • 3 rooms and 1 apartment, all have bath/WC or shower/WC and television • €75 to €106 (€72 to €100 low season); breakfast €9 • No table d'hôte • Park with cottage garden and pond, car park. Credit cards not accepted, no dogs admitted • Library-sitting room, fishing, bicycling

We most liked **Your hostess' faultless attention to detail.**

As soon as your foot crosses the threshold of this delightful country seat, rebuilt after the Revolution, you know you'll never want to leave. Perhaps it is because the lady of the house is so clearly determined to pamper her guests? Perhaps it is the romantic rooms named after fragrant flowers? Or is it the well-tended garden, vegetable plot or pond where swans and ducks paddle? An unforgettable experience.

Access: 5km eastbound, leave on the D 948 towards Niort, then take a left on the D 80

PAYS DE LA LOIRE

LES HERBIERS - 85500

29 LA MÉTAIRIE DU BOURG
M. et Mme Retailleau

85500 Les Herbiers
Tel. 02 51 67 23 97

Open all year • 3 rooms • €50, breakfast included • No table d'hôte • Garden, car park. Credit cards not accepted, no dogs admitted • Working farm (cattle breeding)

Two minutes from the Puy du Fou Theme Park.

This fine old secluded farmhouse is typical of the region with its stone walls and round tiled roof. Still a working cattle farm, it also offers spotless B&B rooms whose generous dimensions include high raftered ceilings. In the sitting room, a conscious effort has been made to maintain a stylish rustic character with tiled floor, exposed beams, old furniture and a fireplace. Copious breakfasts served by the friendly hosts.

Access : 5km to the north-east of Herbiers on the D 755, then the D 11 and a minor road

MAILLEZAIS - 85420

30 CHAMBRE D'HÔTE MADAME BONNET
Mme Bonnet

69 rue de l'Abbaye
85420 Maillezais
Tel. 02 51 87 23 00
Fax 02 51 00 72 44
liliane.bonnet@wanadoo.fr
www.accueilvendee.com

Open all year • 5 rooms with bathrooms • €63 to €66, breakfast included • No table d'hôte • Garden, park, car park. Credit cards not accepted, no dogs admitted • Exhibition of antique tools. Boating available

Boating on the marsh's meandering, and mercifully mosquito-free, irrigation channels.

Ancient yew trees in the park, an orchard and a cottage garden encircle this 19C manor and its orangery. The stylish rooms are pleasant; the one under the eaves has a four-poster bed and the one in the former hen house opens directly onto the park. Boat-lovers will enjoy exploring the marsh's multitude of canals. Before leaving, make sure you take a peek at the collection of old clogs and farming tools.

Access : Near the abbey

PAYS DE LA LOIRE

ROCHESERVIERE - 85620

SAINT-GERVAIS - 85230

31 LE CHÂTEAU DU PAVILLON
M. et Mme Rio

Rue du Gué-Baron
85620 Rocheserviere
Tel. 02 51 06 55 99
Fax 02 51 06 55 99
ggilann@aol.com
www.le-chateau-du-pavillon.com

Closed 16 Oct to 14 Mar • 3 non-smoking rooms on two floors, all with bathrooms and television • €100 to €110 (€80 to €90 low season); breakfast €9 • No table d'hôte • Nursery, terrace, park. Credit cards not accepted, dogs not admitted • Outdoor swimming pool

We most liked: Charm, elegance and comfort are the motto of this house.

Eight hectares of grounds with a small lake and swimming pool flank this château, dating from 1885, which radiates charm and elegance: spacious Louis XIV dining room, Louis XV sitting room, marble fireplace and grand piano. A lovely wooden staircase leads up to inviting romantic bedrooms. Also available are two gîtes and an extremely well appointed nursery for under 10 year olds. Table d'hôte available at weekends, by reservation.

Access : North of the town on the D 937 and rue du Gué-Baron

32 LE PAS-DE-L'ÎLE
M. Pitaud

85230 Saint-Gervais
Tel. 02 51 68 78 51
Fax 02 51 68 42 01

Closed from 1 Nov to 15 Mar • 2 rooms on the ground floor • €45, breakfast included • No table d'hôte • Garden, car park. Credit cards not accepted, no dogs admitted

We most liked: Boating in the salt marshes.

This appealing low house is a fine example of the architectural style favoured in the Breton-Vendée marshes. Laid out around a central lawn, each of the rooms, decorated with lovely regional antiques, has its own private entrance. The most recent, under the exposed rafters, were our favourites. Don't miss the chance to sample the mouth-watering foie gras, made from ducks reared on the premises. Countless bicycling and boating opportunities.

Access : 4km to the south-east of Beauvoir on the D 948, then the D 59 and a minor road

PAYS DE LA LOIRE
TIFFAUGES - 85130

33 **LE MANOIR DE LA BARBACANE**
M. et Mme Baume

2 place de l'Église
85130 Tiffauges
Tel. 02 51 65 75 59
Fax 02 51 65 71 91
manoir@hotel-barbacane.com
www.hotel-barbacane.com

Closed last week in Dec and Sun from Oct to Apr
- 19 rooms with bath/WC or shower/WC and television
- Menus €77 to €100 (€62 to €80 low season); breakfast €10 • No restaurant • Garden, garage. No dogs admitted
- Outdoor swimming pool, billiards

We most liked **The aura of living history.**

A visit to Barbacane Castle is like stepping back in time to the Middle Ages, but the hotel itself, installed in a 19C property, bears a rather striking resemblance to an English manor house! A countrified atmosphere and numerous knick-knacks set the scene inside. Plans are afoot to renovate the rather threadbare rooms, some of which survey the castle of the sinister Gilles de Rais, former Lord of Tiffauges, but better known as Blue Beard...

Access : Half-way between Montaigu and Cholet on the D 753 in the centre of the village

PICARDY

Ready for an action-packed ride over Picardy's fair and historic lands? The birthplace of France itself – the first French king, Clovis, was born in Soissons – Picardy is renowned for its wealthy Cistercian abbeys, splendid Gothic cathedrals, flamboyant town halls, marvellous castles, as well as its poignant reminders of the two World Wars. Those who prefer the pleasures of the countryside can take a boat trip through the floating gardens of Amiens, explore the botanical reserve of Marais de Cessière or observe the thousands of birds in the estuary of the Somme and at the Marquenterre bird sanctuary. Acre upon acre of unspoilt hills, woodland, plateaux, copses, pastures and vineyards welcome you with open arms. Picardy's rich culinary talents have been refined over the centuries and it would be unthinkable to leave without tasting the famous *pré-salé* – lamb fattened on the salt marshes – some smoked eel, duck pâté or a dessert laced with Chantilly cream.

- Aisne (02)
- Oise (60)
- Somme (80)

PICARDY

BRUYÈRES-SUR-FÈRE - 02130

1 VAL-CHRÉTIEN
M. et Mme Sion

Ancienne abbaye du Val Chrétien
02130 Bruyères-sur-Fère
Tel. 03 23 71 66 71
Fax 03 23 71 66 71
val.chretien@wanadoo.fr
http://perso.wanadoo.fr/valchretien/

Open all year • 5 rooms upstairs • €54 to €64, breakfast included; half-board available • Table d'hôte €20 • Park. Credit cards not accepted, no dogs admitted • Tennis

Exceptional location in the heart of the legendary site of the Tardenois.

This building on the banks of the Ourcq and in the heart of the 12C ruins of the Abbey of Val Chrétien is quite remarkable. The rooms are soberly decorated with one striking exception, which is lined in red velvet and complete with a four-poster bed. On the ground floor are a breakfast room with exposed beams and a library where a fire is lit in winter. The covered tennis court is in an outbuilding.

Access : 8km westbound from Fère-en-Tardenois on the D 310, towards Bruyères-sur-Fère, on a by-road

CHAUNY - 02300

2 LA TOQUE BLANCHE
M. et Mme Lequeux

24 avenue Victor-Hugo
02300 Chauny
Tel. 03 23 39 98 98
Fax 03 23 52 32 79
info@toque.blanche.fr
www.toque-blanche.fr

Closed from 1 to 26 Feb, 2 to 20 Aug, Sat lunchtime, Sun evening and Mon • 6 rooms on 2 floors with bath/WC or shower/WC, 3 have television, 2 are for non-smokers • €72 to €87; breakfast €12; half-board available • Air-conditioned restaurant; menus €32 to €70 • Terrace, park, private car park • Tennis

Duck foie gras is the house speciality.

The Toque Blanche (Chef's hat), a lovely 1920s bourgeois house, not only provides comfortable personalised rooms but also offers cooking renowned for its subtle blends of flavours in either an Art Deco or a more classically-inspired dining room. Don't worry if your waistline seems to have expanded during the meal, you can walk off the extra calories in the immense shaded park.

Access : Near the town centre

PICARDY

CONNIGIS - 02330

ÉTRÉAUPONT - 02580

3 CHAMBRE D'HÔTE M. LECLÈRE
M. et Mme Leclère

1 rue de Launay
02330 Connigis
Tel. 03 23 71 90 51
Fax 03 23 71 48 57

Closed from 20 to 31 Dec • 4 rooms • €40 to €48, breakfast included • Table d'hôte €15 • Park, car park. Dogs not admitted • Bicycle rentals, hiking trails, trout fishing 200m away

Walking or bicycling through vineyards.

This husband and wife team of Champagne producers has been painstakingly restoring this 16C farmhouse, once part of the Château de Connigis estate, for over ten years now. Thanks to their efforts, guests are now welcomed into spacious rooms with original parquet floors overlooking a magnificent park alongside the vineyards; the room in the tower, slightly removed from the main wing and decorated in an attractive Flemish style, is the quietest. Children's play area and bicycle rentals.

Access : 12km eastbound from Château-Thierry on the N 3 and the D 4

4 AUBERGE DU VAL DE L'OISE
M. et Mme Trokay

8 rue Albert-Ledent
02580 Étréaupont
Tel. 03 23 97 91 10
Fax 03 23 97 48 92
contact@clos-du-montvinage.fr
www.clos-du-montvinage.fr

Closed Jan and evening of 25 Dec • 20 rooms, one has disabled access, with bath/WC or shower/WC and television • €63 to €83; breakfast €10; half-board available • Menus €21 to €40 • Terrace, garden, private car park. No dogs admitted in rooms • Billiards room

The honeymoon suite and its four-poster bed!

Driving through the village, the eye is drawn to the intricate pattern of the brick walls of this delightful late-19C mansion. A pleasantly old-fashioned atmosphere extends to the well-dimensioned rooms furnished in a Louis-Philippe style, while a recently opened wing is home to the establishment's brand new restaurant, pleasantly decorated and serving traditional French favourites.

Access : On the N 2, between Vervins and La Capelle, in the village

PICARDY

L'ÉPINE-AUX-BOIS - 02540

5 DOMAINE DES PATRUS
Mme Manning-Royol

la Haute Épine
02540 L'Épine-aux-Bois
Tel. 03 23 69 85 85
Fax 03 23 69 30 14
contact@domainedespatrus.com
www.domainedespatrus.com

Closed from Dec to Feb • 5 rooms, 2 of which are in the attic • €70 to €95, breakfast included • Table d'hôte €28 to €34 (including wine) (evening by reservation) • Sitting room-library, park, car park. Dogs not admitted • Gallery devoted to La Fontaine. Wine and champagne tasting

We most liked: The collection of paintings devoted to La Fontaine's fables.

In addition to the comfort it offers, another reason to stop at this handsome farmhouse is the pleasure of waking up in the morning and gazing out onto the peaceful countryside. The individually decorated rooms are furnished in traditional style; those with sloping ceilings have a little private sitting room. The mezzanine in the library is most attractive. Ask to see the owner's collection of works inspired by La Fontaine's fables; she is a fan and is only too happy to explain them.

Access: 8km westbound from Montmirail on the D 933, towards Meaux

RESSONS-LE-LONG - 02290

6 FERME DE LA MONTAGNE
M. Ferté

02290 Ressons-le-Long
Tel. 03 23 74 23 71
Fax 03 23 74 24 82
lafermedelamontagne@free.fr
http://www.lafermedelamontagne.free.fr

Closed Jan and Feb • 5 rooms with bathrooms • €50, breakfast included • No table d'hôte • Garden, car park. Credit cards not accepted, no dogs admitted • Billiards and piano

We most liked: The sweeping view of the Aisne Valley.

Built on the edge of the plateau, this old farm of the Abbey of Notre-Dame de Soissons whose foundations date back to the 13C, enjoys a superb view of the Aisne Valley. All the generously-sized rooms have independent access and well-equipped bathrooms. A billiards table and piano adorn the sitting room, which also commands a splendid view of the countryside. Warm and welcoming.

Access: 8km westbound from Soissons on the N 31 and the D 1160

PICARDY

REUILLY-SAUVIGNY - 02850

7 AUBERGE LE RELAIS
M. et Mme Berthuit

2 rue de Paris
02850 Reuilly-Sauvigny
Tel. 03 23 70 35 36
Fax 03 23 70 27 76
auberge.relais.de.reuilly@wanadoo.fr
www.relaisreuilly.com

Closed from 29 Jan to 3 Mar, from 20 Aug to 7 Sep, Tue and Wed • 7 rooms with bath/WC or shower/WC, all are air-conditioned and have television • €72 to €90; breakfast €13; half-board available • Air-conditioned restaurant; menus €29 (weekdays) to €76 • Garden, car park. Dogs not admitted in rooms

Most liked: Limousin veal served with green asparagus in truffle sauce.

The flowered walls of this welcoming roadside-inn invite travellers to pause and stay for a while. The interior decoration reveals a masterful grasp of colour and light: the Provençal or contemporary rooms enjoy a superb view over the Champagne vineyards of the Marne Valley. Not to be outdone, the menu is appetising and up-to-date and served on a terrace-veranda or in the muted atmosphere of the dining room.

Access: In the village by the N 3, between Château-Thierry and Dormans

SAINT-QUENTIN - 02100

8 HÔTEL DES CANONNIERS
Mme Michel

15 rue des Canonniers
02100 Saint-Quentin
Tel. 03 23 62 87 87
Fax 03 23 62 87 86
lescanonniers@aol.com
www.hotel-canonniers.com

Closed from 1 to 15 Aug and Sun evening (except by reservation) • 7 rooms, all of which have equipped kitchenettes, with bath/WC or shower/WC and television • €60 to €105; breakfast €8 • No restaurant • Terrace, garden, private car park • Billiards

Most liked: Drop by the Lecuyer Museum and admire the portraits by Quentin de La Tour.

Whether you stay for a night or for two weeks, the Canonniers offers superb personalised suites with a kitchenette at wonderfully reasonable prices. This handsome house, built in 1754, provides the service of a hotel and the charm of a maison d'hôte: guests can play billiards or lounge on the terrace opposite the lush green garden. The establishment also caters to businesses and meetings are held in its handsome old reception rooms.

Access: Drive past the town hall, take a left on Rue de la Comédie, past the theatre, turn right

PICARDY

VILLERS-AGRON-AIGUIZY - 02130

9 MANOIR DE LA SEMOIGNE
M. et Mme Ferry

Chemin de la Ferme
02130 Villers-Agron-Aiguizy
Tel. 03 23 71 60 67
Fax 03 23 69 36 54
manoir.semoigne@club-internet.fr
http://manoirdelasemoigne.online.fr

Open all year • 4 rooms with bathrooms • €68 to €88, breakfast included; half-board available • Table d'hôte €37, beverages included (evenings only during the week) • Park. No dogs admitted • Golf nearby

We most liked
The luxury of an 18-hole golf course right in the grounds.

Golfers will, of course, not be able to resist the prospect of spending a few days in this 18C mansion, whose park and river are home to an attractive golf course. Each of the spacious, quiet bedrooms is named after and decorated in a different colour: beige, blue, yellow, etc. The bathrooms are large and well-equipped. The table d'hôte has laid the accent on wholesome farm produce. If a round of golf doesn't appeal, perhaps tennis or trout fishing will take your fancy.

Access: 15km to the south-east of Fère-en-Tardenois

VILLERS-COTTERETS - 02600

10 LE RÉGENT
M. Brunet

26 rue du Général-Mangin
02600 Villers-Cotterets
Tel. 03 23 96 01 46
Fax 03 23 96 37 57
info@hotel-leregent.com
www.hotel-leregent.com

Open all year • 28 rooms at the front or the back, with bath/WC or shower/WC, all have television • €49 to €76; breakfast €8 • No restaurant • Car park

We most liked
Remember to bring a copy of The Three Musketeers, written by local boy, Alexander Dumas.

The walls of this elegant 18C mansion, just two minutes from the town, are so smart and spruce they could almost be new. Venture past the porch and say hello to the grey cat – the self-appointed master of the house – before you cross the romantic paved courtyard. Inside, classically decorated rooms in keeping with the architecture await you, some of which should soon be treated to a facelift.

Access: Drive into Villers-Cotterets, the hotel is not far from the town centre, near the post office

PICARDY

CAMBRONNE-LÈS-RIBECOURT - 60170

11 LA FERME ANCIENNE DE BELLERIVE
Mme Brunger

492 rue de Bellerive
60170 Cambronne-lès-Ribecourt
Tel. 03 44 75 02 13
Fax 03 44 76 10 34
bellerive@minitel.net
www.bellerive.fr

Open all year • 5 rooms • €50, breakfast included, half-board available • Table d'hôte €15 • Garden, car park. Credit cards not accepted, no dogs admitted

We most liked An authentic two-hundred-year-old farmhouse.

This wonderful old farm, poised between canal and river, is a must for anyone who loves tranquillity and authenticity. An old barn houses simple, appealing rooms with white walls, veil curtains and matching bedspreads, in addition to well-appointed bathrooms. The dining room is decorated in appealing rustic tones and the table d'hôte is open for lunch and dinner, serving appetising farm cooking. Lovely garden.

Access : 7.5km to the south-west of Ourscamps on the N 32 and the D 66

CHELLES - 60350

12 RELAIS BRUNEHAUT
M. et Mme Frenel

3 rue de l'Église
60350 Chelles
Tel. 03 44 42 85 05
Fax 03 44 42 83 30

Open all year • 10 rooms, one of which has a kitchenette, all have bath/WC or shower/WC and television • €48 to €55; breakfast €8; half-board available • Restaurant closed 15 Jan to 13 Feb and Mon and Tue lunchtime; menus €24 (weekdays) to €38 • Inner courtyard, garden, private car park. No dogs admitted in restaurant

We most liked Disneyland's Sleeping Beauty Castle was partly inspired by that of Pierrefonds.

A stay in this delightful coaching inn, actually two buildings set round a flowered courtyard, is the perfect opportunity to discover Pierrefonds, home to a splendid reconstruction of a medieval Gothic castle masterminded by Napoleon's talented architect, Viollet-le-Duc. The inn's mill, still in working order, houses most of the appealing, rustic rooms, filled with the sound of the gurgling stream nearby. The restaurant serves tasty, traditional cooking.

Access : In the centre of the village, 5km eastbound from Pierrefonds on the D 85

PICARDY

CREIL - 60100

13 LA FERME DE VAUX
M. et Mme Joly

11 et 19 route de Vaux
60100 Creil
Tel. 03 44 64 77 00
Fax 03 44 26 81 50
joly.eveline@wanadoo.fr

Open all year except Sat lunchtime and Sun evening • 28 rooms, 10 of which are upstairs, the others are on garden level, all have bath/WC and television • €61 to €67; breakfast €8; half-board available • Menus €17 to €35 • Car park

We most liked **The porcelain of Creil is sought after by collectors from all over the world.**

The owners of this old farm take great pleasure in sharing their "art de vivre" with guests. Each of the bedrooms is individually decorated, but the medieval chapel and its far-reaching gastronomic reputation are what attracts gourmets from all over the region. Savour the traditional French cuisine served in a Gothic dining room complete with arched windows and tapestries, or in the other more classical but equally sophisticated dining room. Some temptations are definitely worth giving in to!

Access : On leaving Creil after the N 16/D 120 crossroads, drive towards Verneuil, on the way into the Vaux Industrial Zone

GOUVIEUX - 60270

14 HOST. DU PAVILLON SAINT-HUBERT
Mme Luck-Bocquet

Avenue de Toutevoie
60270 Gouvieux
Tel. 03 44 57 07 04
Fax 03 44 57 75 42
pavillon.sthubert@wanadoo.fr
www.pavillon-sainthubert.com

Closed 15 Jan to 13 Feb, Sun evening and Mon • 18 rooms, all have bath/WC or shower/WC and television • €55 to €75; breakfast €8; half-board available • Menus €25 (weekdays) to €40 • Riverside terrace, garden, car park

We most liked **Chocolate lovers should not miss the chance to taste a "Crottin de Chantilly"!**

This little gem is hidden at the end of a cul-de-sac, on the banks of the Oise surrounded by acres of peaceful countryside; ask for one of the renovated rooms overlooking the river. In fine weather, let the kids loose in the garden while you linger under the shade of plane trees on the terrace and watch the barges glide gently past. Appetising traditional cuisine.

Access : Leave Chantilly on the D 909 as far as Gouvieux, turn right and at Chaumont take a left into the dead-end road towards the Oise

PICARDY

HANNACHES - 60650

PIERREFONDS - 60350

15 CHAMBRE D'HÔTE M. BRUANDET
M. et Mme Bruandet

13 hameau de Bellefontaine
60650 Hannaches
Tel. 03 44 82 46 63
Fax 03 44 82 26 68
bellefontaine@free.fr
http://bellefontaine.free.fr

Closed in Jan • 3 rooms • €45, breakfast included • No table d'hôte • Garden. Credit cards not accepted

16 DOMAINE DU BOIS D'AUCOURT
M. Clément-Bayard

60350 Pierrefonds
Tel. 03 44 42 80 34
Fax 03 44 42 80 36
bois.d.aucourt@wanadoo.fr
www.boisdaucourt.com

Open all year • 11 rooms with bath/WC • €69 to €110, breakfast €8 • No restaurant • Car park. No dogs admitted • Tennis, walking, mountain biking, horse-riding

The rooms are furnished with unique and quite unusual pieces.

Visitors to this former 19C Picardy farmhouse are often intrigued by both the interior and exterior decoration, all of which is the work of the talented sculptor-owner. Modern furniture adorns the relatively sober rooms, one of which has a mezzanine. The garden is strewn with the owner's metal sculptures, made from salvaged materials such as old farming equipment and everyday scrap. Highly original, to say the least... and most welcoming.

A handsome family property surrounded by foliage.

The peaceful silence of the forest of Compiègne has crept into the walls of this large 19C half-timbered manor house. The rooms, all non-smoking, are decorated individually and all have faultless bathrooms. The only problem is deciding between the "Scottish", "Sevillan", "Tuscan", "Zen" or "Tropical" rooms. Breakfast is served in your hosts' warm, welcoming kitchen.

Access: 5km to the south-west of Gerberoy on the D 930, then the D 104 towards Bellefontaine

Access: 1.6km westbound from Pierrefonds on the D 85

PICARDY

PUITS-LA-VALLÉE - 60480

17 LA FAISANDERIE
M. et Mme Dumetz

8 rue du Château
60480 Puits-la-Vallée
Tel. 03 44 80 70 29
Fax 03 44 80 70 29

Open all year • 4 rooms, all with bath/WC and television • €45 to €70, breakfast included • Table d'hôte €16 • Terrace, garden, private car park. Credit cards not accepted, dogs not admitted • Library, bicycles, table tennis

The lady of the house's faultless welcome.

A gravelled drive leads to this handsome property separated from the rest of the village by wooded parklands. The comfortable "Blue", "Rose", Green" rooms and "Gold" apartment are attractively decorated in a clever mixture of styles. Home-made jams and cakes feature prominently on the breakfast table. Dinner time is a chance to savour tasty dishes in which pheasant, unsurprisingly enough given the property's name, takes pride of place.

Access : In the town centre

DURY - 80480

18 CHAMBRE D'HÔTE DU PETIT CHÂTEAU
M. Saguez

2 rue Grimaux
80480 Dury
Tel. 03 22 95 29 52
Fax 03 22 95 29 52
alainsaguez@libertysurf.fr
http://perso.libertysurf.fr/saguez/dury.html

Open all year • 4 non-smoking rooms, one of which is on ground level, all have bathrooms • €70, breakfast included • No table d'hôte • Garden, park, car park. Credit cards not accepted, no dogs admitted • Horse-drawn carriage rides

The appeal of a countryside setting, just a ten-minute drive from the centre of Amiens.

You will soon forget the nearby road when you see the wonderful country setting of this 19C house and are warmly greeted by the convivial owners. The rooms, non-smoking only, are located in a separate wing and are for the most part spacious, but the smallest of them is also the cosiest. The substantial breakfast, taken in the company of your discreet hosts, will set you up for the day.

Access : 6km southbound from Amiens on the N 1 towards Beauvais

PICARDY

LE CROTOY - 80550

PORT-LE-GRAND - 80132

19 LES TOURELLES
M. et Mme Ferreira Da Silva

2 rue Pierre-Guerlain
80550 Le Crotoy
Tel. 03 22 27 16 33
Fax 03 22 27 11 45
lestourelles@nhgroupe.com
www.lestourelles.com

Closed from 5 to 31 Jan • 27 rooms, most have shower/WC, the others have bath/WC, some have television • €60 to €85; (€57 to €76 low season); breakfast €8; half-board available • Menus €21 to €31 • Children's dormitory

The children's "dorm".

The fairy-tale twin turrets of this 19C red and white brick mansion dominate the tiny seaside resort and the "only south-facing beach of the North" (Pierre Guerlain). Most of the rooms, on a contemporary seafaring theme or in a delightfully clean-lined Swedish style, overlook the bay of the Somme. Delicious mounds of fresh fish and seafood will restore the disconsolate spirits of unlucky "shrimpers".

Access : Overlooking the bay, on the beach road

20 CHAMBRES D'HÔTES DU BOIS DE BONANCE
M. et Mme Maillard

Bois-de-Bonance
80132 Port-le-Grand
Tel. 03 22 24 11 97
Fax 03 22 31 72 01
maillard.chambrehote@bonance.com
www.bonance.com

Closed from Nov to Feb • 5 rooms, 2 of which are in a separate wing, with bath/WC • €73, breakfast included • No table d'hôte • Garden • Swimming pool, keep-fit track, table-tennis, children's play area

The charm of a country garden.

You may be amused to learn that the pink walls and narrow Gothic-style windows of this 19C holiday home, in a secluded spot far from the bustle of traffic, are sometimes described as "English"! Whatever, the antique furnished rooms have been decorated with infinite taste; those in the former servants' quarters open directly onto the beautiful garden, brimming with flowers in the summer. In the winter, a cheerful fire adds warmth to the pleasant breakfast room.

Access : 11km eastbound from Saint-Valery-sur-Somme on the D 940, then the D 40 and a minor road

PICARDY

QUEND - 80120

21 AUBERGE LE FIACRE
M. et Mme Masmonteil

6 rue des Pommiers Hameau
de Routhiauville – 80120 Quend
Tel. 03 22 23 47 30
Fax 03 22 27 19 80
lefiacre@wanadoo.fr
www.aufiacre.fr

Closed mid-Jan to mid-Feb, 1 week at Christmas • 11 rooms, one of which has disabled access, most have bath/WC, some have shower/WC and television • €75 to €79; breakfast €11; half-board available • Restaurant closed Tue and Wed lunchtimes; menus €20 (weekdays) to €42 • Garden, car park. Dogs not admitted in rooms • Golf course

Fancy a quick two-kilometre-run in the dunes?

An old farm has been converted into an appealing inn surrounded in foliage, where the restful, welcoming rooms open onto the lovely garden. In addition, three more modern apartments have recently been created. The restaurant, for its part, has retained a resolutely country style with exposed beams and tiled floors, a perfect setting for its classic repertoire. Character and quality: what more could you want!

Access : Leave the D 940 at Quend, between Berck-sur-Mer and Rue, and take the D 32 towards Fort-Mahon-Plage

SAINT-VALERY-SUR-SOMME - 80230

22 CHAMBRE D'HÔTE MADAME SERVANT
Mme Servant

117 rue Au-Feurre
80230 Saint-Valery-sur-Somme
Tel. 03 22 60 97 56
Fax 03 22 60 97 56

Closed at Christmas • 4 rooms and 2 apartments • €58, breakfast included • No table d'hôte • Garden. Credit cards not accepted, no dogs admitted

The wonderful view of the unspoilt bay of the Somme from the Porte Guillaume.

This country house and neat garden stand in the upper part of town, just round the corner from the elegant 12C Porte Guillaume flanked by two towers. Each of the rooms has been decorated on a different theme: blue and white for the sea and sailors, old posters in the cinema room and shades of green and wrought-iron furniture in the garden room. The breakfast room is light and airy and your hosts unfailingly friendly and welcoming.

Access : In the historic town, near the church and the town hall

PICARDY
SAINT-VALERY-SUR-SOMME - 80230   SAINT-VALERY-SUR-SOMME - 80230

23 LA GRIBANE
M. et Mme Douchet

297 quai Jeanne-d'Arc
80230 Saint-Valery-sur-Somme
Tel. 03 22 60 97 55

Closed 15 Dec to 15 Feb • 4 rooms • €70 to €85, breakfast included • No table d'hôte • Park, car park. Credit cards not accepted, no dogs admitted

We most liked: The garden has been created in a polder opposite the ramparts.

This 1930 house takes its name from the 18C merchant vessel used to navigate the rivers. The rooms of the main wing, painted in tones of blue, white and beige, overlook the bay; the others are in a pavilion in the middle of the garden. The large bay windows of the breakfast room look out onto the wonderful garden, wedged between the land reclaimed from the sea and the old city walls.

Access: In the historic town, near the beach

24 LE RELAIS GUILLAUME DE NORMANDY
MM. Crimet et Dupré

Quai du Romerel
80230 Saint-Valery-sur-Somme
Tel. 03 22 60 82 36
Fax 03 22 60 81 82
relais-guillaume@wanadoo.fr
www.guillaumedenormandy.com

Closed from 19 Dec to 10 Jan and Tue • 14 rooms, all have bath/WC or shower/WC and television • €50 to €65; breakfast €8; half-board available • Air-conditioned restaurant; menus €16 to €42 • Terrace, car park. No dogs admitted in restaurant

We most liked: A trip across the bay of the Somme aboard a real steam train.

Take in the lovely Picardy coast from the windows of this elegant manor house facing the bay and on the outskirts of St-Valery-sur-Somme. None of the rooms are enormous, but half face the Channel, where you will sometimes be able to catch a glimpse of seals. The soberly decorated panoramic dining room also enables diners to enjoy the view while sampling the delicious traditional fare rustled up by the chef.

Access: On the dike, opposite the bay of the Somme

POITOU-CHARENTES

Illustrious names such as Cognac, Angoulême or La Rochelle all echo through France's history, but there is just as much to appreciate in the here and now. Start your journey lazing on the sandy beaches of its unspoilt coastline where the scent of pine trees mingles with the fresh sea air. A stay in a thalassotherapy resort will revive your flagging spirits, further boosted by a platter of oysters and lightly buttered bread. A bicycle is the best way to discover the region's delightfully unhilly coastal islands as you pedal along quaint little country lanes, lined with tiny blue and white cottages and multicoloured hollyhocks. Back on the mainland, embark on a barge and explore the thousand and one canals of the marshy, and mercifully mosquito-free, "Green Venice". You will have earned yourself a taste of vintage Cognac, or perhaps a glass of the less heady local apéritif, the fruity, ice-cold Pineau. If all this seems just too restful, head for Futuroscope, a theme park devoted to the moving image, and enjoy an action-packed day or two of life in the future.

- Charente (16)
- Charente-Maritime (17)
- Deux-Sèvres (79)
- Vienne (86)

POITOU-CHARENTES

POITOU CHARENTES

CHAMPNIERS - 16430

1 LA TEMPLERIE
M. et Mme Richon

Denat
16430 Champniers
Tel. 05 45 68 49 00
Fax 05 45 68 91 18

Open all year • 5 rooms, 2 of which are on the ground floor with disabled access and 1 family room, all have bath/WC • €45, breakfast included • No table d'hôte • Garden, car park. No dogs admitted • Outdoor swimming pool

The windows of this farm have enjoyed the same pastoral view for two hundred years.

Guests are always assured of a warm welcome within this typically regional farmhouse. The rooms, located in the former outbuildings, are colourful and some are furnished with antiques; two open directly onto the garden and the swimming pool. In the winter, a cheerful fire is lit in the immense dining room. The sitting room with a lovely library on a mezzanine particularly caught our fancy.

Access : 9.5km northbound from Angoulême towards Poitiers on the N 10, then Balzac on the D 105

ARCHINGEAY - 17380

2 LES HORTENSIAS
M. et Mme Jacques

16 rue des Sablières
17380 Archingeay
Tel. 05 46 97 85 70
Fax 05 46 97 61 89
jpmt.jacques@wanadoo.fr

Open all year • 3 non-smoking rooms, 1 with disabled access, all with bathrooms • €49 to €54, breakfast included • Table d'hôte €20, drinks included • Garden, private car park. Credit cards not accepted

The tranquillity.

This entirely rebuilt former wine-growers' farmhouse is home to two exquisitely decorated bedrooms and a gîte fitted with regional cherry-wood furniture. The mistress of the house serves breakfast and three times a week, also offers delicious family-style dishes made with local and garden produce.

Access : At Tonnay-Boutonne, take the D 114 towards Archingeay. In the town, head for Les Nouillers and follow the signposts

POITOU CHARENTES

AULNAY - 17470

3 LE DONJON
M. et Mme Imbach

4 rue des Hivers
17470 Aulnay
Tel. 05 46 33 67 67
Fax 05 46 33 67 64
hoteldudonjon@wanadoo.fr
www.hoteldudonjon.com

Closed fortnight in Jan and Feb • 10 rooms, one of which has disabled access, all have bath/WC or shower/WC and television • €61 to €73 (€54 to €64 low season); breakfast €7 • No restaurant

most liked **Long chats around the fire in the sitting room.**

The green shuttered façade of this house stands near the Church of St Pierre, a masterpiece of regional Romanesque architecture. The interior of the house has been carefully restored in order to preserve the lovely old beams and gold-coloured limestone walls. Old furniture graces all the rooms and the bedrooms are further brightened by colourful bedspreads and matching curtains; all have modern bathrooms.

Access : In the heart of the village, near the main square

CLAM - 17500

4 LE VIEUX LOGIS
Mme Brard

3 rue du 8-Mai-1945
17500 Clam
Tel. 05 46 70 20 13
Fax 05 46 70 20 64
info@vieuxlogis.com

Closed 1 to 15 Jan, Sun evening and Mon lunchtime (except in season) • 10 ground-floor rooms with bath/WC or shower/WC and television • €50 to €60; breakfast €7; half-board available • Air-conditioned restaurant; menus €15 to €36 • Terrace, garden, car park. No dogs admitted in rooms • Outdoor swimming pool

most liked **The owners' warm welcome and infectious good nature.**

This 'Old Abode' was formerly home to the village's café-grocer's shop. The tiny cup of piping hot espresso on the bar and the shelves laden with tins and jars have since made way for two country-style dining rooms, the walls of which are adorned by photos taken by the master of the house. His cheerful spouse rustles up tasty local dishes. The modern ground-floor building opens onto the garden and the comfortable, pleasant rooms are equipped with terraces.

Access : 6km northbound of Jonzac on the D 142

POITOU CHARENTES

CRAZANNES - 17350

5 CHÂTEAU DE CRAZANNES
M. et Mme de Rochefort

24 rue du Château
17350 Crazannes
Tel. 06 80 65 40 96
Fax 05 46 91 34 46
crazannes@worldonline.fr
www.crazannes.com

Open all year • 6 rooms, 2 of which are apartments on 2 floors, all with bathrooms • €70 to €190, breakfast included • Table d'hôte €35 • Terrace, garden, car park. Dogs not admitted • Outdoor swimming pool

The sheer luxury of this listed château.

Eight hectares of grounds surround this superb listed 14C château which has been treated to a lavish restoration. It boasts six splendid bedrooms, three of which in the 16C keep noted for their light interior and enormous bathrooms. The regionally inspired cuisine is prepared with fresh market produce and served in the former sheepfold, decorated with old farm tools.

Access : Take Saintes exit no 35, follow RN 137 towards Rochefort, turn right towards Plassay on RN 119 and follow signs to Château de Crazanne

DOMPIERRE-SUR-MER - 17139

6 LOGIS SAINT-LÉONARD
M. et Mme Schwartz

6 rue des Chaumes-l'Abbaye
17139 Dompierre-sur-Mer
Tel. 05 46 35 14 65
Fax 05 46 35 14 65
logis-st-leonard@wanadoo.fr

Open all year • 4 rooms upstairs, all have bath/WC or shower/WC • €65 to €70, breakfast included • No table d'hôte • Park, car park, sitting room-library. Credit cards not accepted • Outdoor swimming pool, billiards, table tennis, jacuzzi, fishing

A haven of peace and quiet just ten minutes from the lively bustle of La Rochelle.

A magnificent tree-lined park surrounds this spacious restored house which offers three personalised guestrooms. The owners have decorated each room personally with objects and furniture brought back from their travels in Polynesia and Africa. The breakfast table is piled high with mouth-watering home-made cakes and jams. On the leisure side, you can choose between table-tennis, a soak in the Jacuzzi or a dip in the swimming pool set amidst trees. Very welcoming and friendly.

Access : In the town centre

POITOU CHARENTES

ILE D'OLERON - 17310

7 LES TRÉMIÈRES
Mme Frat

5 route de Saint-Pierre
17310 La Cotinière
Tel. 05 46 47 44 25
www.chambres-lestremieres.com

Open all year • 4 rooms, 2 of which are apartments • €56 to €74 (€50 to €58 low season); breakfast €7 • No table d'hôte • Garden, car park. Credit cards not accepted, no dogs admitted

Just two minutes from the port and its brightly-coloured fishing boats.

This early 20C house with sandy-coloured walls and blue shutters is only a short walk from the port of La Cotinière and its shops. All the rooms and suites are personalised and immaculately cared for. Take things easy in the comfortable leather sofas and armchairs by the fireside in the sitting room. In the summertime, breakfast is served under the chestnut tree.

Access : 600m from the entrance to the village coming from Maisonneuve

ILE D'OLÉRON - 17310

8 MADAME MICHELINE DENIEAU
Mme Denieau

20 rue de la Legère, la Menounière
17310 Saint-Pierre-d'Oléron
Tel. 05 46 47 14 34
Fax 05 46 36 03 15
denieau.jean-pierre@wanadoo.fr

Open all year • 5 rooms • €51, breakfast included • No table d'hôte • Garden, car park. Credit cards not accepted

Bicycling round the island as you explore its oyster beds and farms.

Oléron wines and the famous Pineau - a fortified aperitif - are still produced on the estate of this stone farmhouse which is a fine example of island architecture. The neat and simple rooms are in the outbuildings; the most recent have old furniture and gaily painted green or blue beams; those with a mezzanine are very popular with families. Guests have the run of a kitchen, complete with an old kneading trough and a fireplace.

Access : 3km westbound from Saint-Pierre-d'Oléron

POITOU CHARENTES

PUYRAVAULT - 17700

9 LE CLOS DE LA GARENNE
M. et Mme François

9 rue de la Garenne
17700 Puyravault
Tel. 05 46 35 47 71
Fax 05 46 35 47 91
info@closdelagarenne.com
www.closdelagarenne.com

Open all year • 4 non-smoking rooms, including one studio with disabled access, all with bath/WC or shower/WC • €63 to €123, breakfast included • Table d'hôte €24 • Terrace, park, car park • Billiards, library, board games, children's play area

The authenticity of this regional manor house.

The owners extend a warm welcome to guests to their handsome manor house steeped in history. On the ground-floor, the 17C dining room and 18C sitting room with Louis XV fireplace, etc, overlook the terraces and grounds. The spacious elegant bedrooms are all furnished with antiques, either in the family for years or picked up in antique shops. A cottage and one-room flat are also available. Excellent value for money.

Access : In the town

ROCHEFORT - 17300

10 CHAMBRES D'HÔTES
M. ET MME BLASSELLE

M. et Mme Blasselle

55 rue de la République
17300 Rochefort
Tel. 05 46 99 55 54
palmiersurcour@wanadoo.fr
www.palmiersurcour.com

Open all year • 3 rooms with bath/WC or shower/WC • €55 to €60, breakfast included • No table d'hôte • Patio, sitting-room, library with television and Internet access, kitchenette. Credit cards not accepted, no dogs admitted • Bicycle rentals

A Mediterranean atmosphere in the heart of the Charentes.

This small 19C mansion in the heart of the historic district is now home to enchanting personalised bedrooms. The "Corderie" pays homage to the famous Rochefort monument, "Aziyadé" is a reference to a local boy and writer, Pierre Loti, while "Marine" is tastefully decorated in blue and white. The patio and palm trees invite you to linger over the tasty breakfasts... A genuinely friendly house which sports a distinctly Southern fragrance.

Access : In the town centre

POITOU CHARENTES
SAINT-FORT-SUR-GIRONDE - 17240 SAINT-PALAIS-SUR-MER - 17420

11 LE CHÂTEAU DES SALLES
Mme Couillaud

Carrefour D 125 et D 730
17240 Saint-Fort-sur-Gironde
Tel. 05 46 49 95 10
Fax 05 46 49 02 81
chateaudessalles@wanadoo.fr
www.chateaudessalles.com

Closed 1 Nov to Easter • 5 rooms • €80 to €110; breakfast €9; half-board available • Table d'hôte €35 • Park, garden, car park. No dogs admitted • Cognac and Pineau de Charentes on sale

We most liked The delicious fare on the table d'hôte lit by candles in the evenings.

The owners of the 15C castle, entirely renovated in the 19C, produce their own Pineau, a delicious aperitif, as well as wines and cognac, which can be bought from the estate. The tastefully furnished, south-facing rooms open onto the garden and its sumptuous magnolia tree; the largest room, under the eaves, displays a happy blend of old and contemporary styles. Lovely old furniture, a piano and a games table grace the sitting room. Candle-lit dining in the evenings.

Access: 7.5km south-east of Mortagne by D 145 then at the D 125 and D 730 crossroads

12 MA MAISON DE MER
Mme Hutchinson

21 avenue du Platin
17420 Saint-Palais-sur-Mer
Tel. 05 46 23 64 86
Fax 05 46 23 64 86
reservations@mamaisondemer.com
www.mamaisondemer.com

Open all year • 6 non-smoking rooms, all have bath/WC • €80 to €99, breakfast included • Table d'hôte, evenings only in Jul and Aug; €21 • Terrace, garden, car park, television room

We most liked The cosy atmosphere of this house right on the waterfront.

A row of pine trees along the beach hides this handsome 1920's home from view. It has been recently renovated in a delightful seaside style with cane furniture, a white and grey colour theme and rush mats in the bedrooms. A timeless, slightly "British" atmosphere reigns throughout this English-owned property... On the ground floor are a dining room and bar; Franco-British cuisine.

Access: 200m from the town centre

POITOU CHARENTES

SAINT-SAUVEUR-D'AUNIS - 17540

13 LE LOGIS DE L'AUNIS
Mme Ecarot

8 rue de Ligoure
17540 Saint-Sauveur-d'Aunis
Tel. 05 46 09 02 14
Fax 05 46 09 02 14
jocelyne.ecarot@wanadoo.fr
www.logisdelaunis.com

Open all year • 3 non-smoking rooms, all with bath/WC or shower/WC, television and safe • €80 to €86, breakfast included • Table d'hôte €23 • Terrace, garden, car park • Outdoor swimming pool

We most liked: The delightful walled courtyard complete with flower-decked garden and swimming pool.

This traditional regional property set in the heart of a quiet village has been tastefully restored. It is home to three attractive rooms, one of which on the ground-floor, two sitting rooms (one with fireplace and another opening onto the garden and pool), as well as a dining room in which wood, stone and wrought iron feature prominently. Home-made cakes and jams on the breakfast table, while local produce takes pride of place on the table d'hôte, evenings only.

Access: In the town centre

SAINT-SORNIN - 17600

14 LA CAUSSOLIÈRE
M. Gates

10 rue du Petit-Moulin
17600 Saint-Sornin
Tel. 05 46 85 44 62
Fax 05 46 85 44 62
reservations@caussoliere.com
www.caussoliere.com

Open all year • 4 non-smoking rooms; all have bathrooms • €70 to €85, breakfast included • No table d'hôte • Terrace, garden, television and library room, private car park. Credit cards not accepted • Outdoor swimming pool

We most liked: The splendid location of this house poised between ocean and countryside.

Only birdsong interrupts the peace and quiet of this masterfully restored farmhouse set in an immense garden planted with a riot of fragrant plants. The interior is equally inviting with personalised bedrooms (antique or painted furniture, pastel colour themes, bare stone and timbers) and the breakfast room-veranda facing the greenery is also delightful.

Access: 12.5km southeast of Marennes on the D 728, Saintes road

POITOU CHARENTES
ST-GEORGES-DES-COTEAUX - 17810   COULON - 79510

15 CHAMBRE D'HÔTE M. TROUVÉ
M. et Mme Trouvé

5 rue de l'Église
17810 Saint-Georges-des-Coteaux
Tel. 05 46 92 96 66
Fax 05 46 92 96 66
adtrouve@yahoo.fr

Closed from 15 Nov to 1 Apr • 4 rooms • €47, breakfast included • No table d'hôte • Garden, car park. Credit cards not accepted, no dogs admitted • Tennis and horse-riding centre in the village

Each bedroom pays light-hearted tribute to a famous author.

You will not be disappointed should you decide to spend a night or two in this 18C farmstead, surrounded by a large garden. The cow-shed and barn have been turned into an immense room which serves as a combined lobby, sitting room, library and billiards room. Country furniture adorns the bedrooms, each named after a favourite author – Agatha Christie and Tintin's creator, Hergé are among them. Make sure you take a look at the old wash house or "bujor".

Access: 9km to the north-west of Saintes towards Rochefort on the N 137 then the D 127

16 AU MARAIS
Mme Nerrière

46 quai Louis-Hardy
79510 Coulon
Tel. 05 49 35 90 43
Fax 05 49 35 81 98
information@hotel-aumarais.com
www.hotel-aumarais.com

Closed from 15 Dec to 5 Feb • 18 rooms located in 2 houses, one has disabled access. Rooms have bath/WC or shower/WC, all have television • €70 to €80; breakfast €12 to €14 • No restaurant

Glide over the waters of "Green Venice".

A perfect place to begin exploring the aquatic maze of what is known as "Green Venice". The pale stone walls and blue shutters of this pair of 19C boatmen's houses face the marsh's landing stage. The modern, cheerful rooms are decorated with bold Provençal fabrics and most give onto the toing-and-froing of the boats. In summer, the area is busy during the day but after nightfall, all becomes peaceful and car-free!

Access: Near the landing stage where boat trips leave

POITOU CHARENTES

NUEIL-LES-AUBIERS - 79250

17 LE MOULIN DE LA SORINIÈRE
M. et Mme Froger

79250 Nueil-les-Aubiers
Tel. 05 49 72 39 20
Fax 05 49 72 90 78
moulin-soriniere@wanadoo.fr
www.lemoulindelasoriniere.com

Closed 10 to 26 Apr, 2 weeks in Sep, 25 Dec, 1 Jan, Sun evenings and Mon • 8 rooms, 2 with disabled access, all with bathrooms and television • €42; breakfast €6 • Menus €10 to €27 • Terrace, garden, car park

We most liked
The calm of this old country mill.

This 19C perched on the banks of the Argent has been given a new lease of life since its conversion into a hotel-restaurant. The reception is located in the former machine room, the dining room sports original timber beams and an old fireplace and the four bedrooms sport a rustic style. Four more spacious rooms are available in a separate wing. In the kitchen, the chef rustles up tasty dishes with a modern slant.

Access : 2km southwest of Nueil-les-Aubiers on the D 33 and C 3, Cerizay road

SAINT-LIGUAIRE - 79000

18 LA MAGNOLIÈRE
M. et Mme Marchadier

16 impasse de l'Abbaye
79000 Saint-Liguaire
Tel. 05 49 35 36 06
Fax 05 49 79 14 28
a.marchadier@libertysurf.fr

Open all year • 3 non-smoking rooms, all with bath/WC or shower/WC and television • €75, breakfast included • Table d'hôte by reservation • Garden, car park. Credit cards not accepted, dogs not admitted • Library, outdoor swimming pool

We most liked
The tranquillity and atmosphere which reigns throughout this establishment.

This comfortable bourgeois home, built in the 19C on the site of a former abbey, a few traces of which remain, stands on the threshold of the Marais poitevin. The rooms are named after women artists – Marie Laurencin, Suzanne Valadon, Berthe Morisot, and furnished with lovely antique pieces. All overlook the garden, home to a magnificent several hundred-year-old magnolia tree, which extends down to the river. On the leisure side: sitting room-library, swimming pool, angling, boating, etc.

Access : 4km from Coulon on the D 9

POITOU CHARENTES

VALLANS - 79270

19 LE LOGIS D'ANTAN
Mme Ragouilliaux et M. Di Battista

140 rue Saint-Louis
79270 Vallans
Tel. 05 49 04 86 75
Fax 05 49 32 85 05
info@logisdantant.com
www.logisdantan.com

Open all year • 5 non-smoking rooms, all with bathrooms and television • €62 to €78, breakfast included • Table d'hôte €23, drinks included (evenings only) • Terrace, park, private car park. Credit cards not accepted

We most liked
The well-preserved authenticity of this old property.

A well-tended flowered walled park and woodland encircle this immense stone manor house, which dates from 1850 and is located just a stone's throw from Green Venice. It offers five spacious bedrooms decorated in a style which mixes country and bourgeois styles. At mealtimes you will be invited to taste regional dishes with a modern flavour such as magret of duck with garden figs, chocolate cake, etc. In summertime, dinner is served on the veranda.

Access: In the town centre

ANGLES-SUR-L'ANGLIN - 86260

20 LE RELAIS DU LYON D'OR
M. Thoreau

4 rue d'Enfer
86260 Angles-sur-l'Anglin
Tel. 05 49 48 32 53
Fax 05 49 84 02 28
thoreau@lyondor.com
www.lyondor.com

Closed Dec to Feb • 11 rooms, one of which has disabled access and one is split-level, all have bath/WC or shower/WC and television • €65 to €100 (€56 to €90 low season); breakfast €8; half-board available • Menus €20 to €26 • Terrace, garden, private car park

We most liked
Relaxing in the idyllic garden.

In a picturesque village, perched on a rocky outcrop, this former 15C coaching inn offers personalised rooms furnished with items picked up in antique shops. The owners clearly have their guests' physical and cultural well-being at heart as is shown by the beauty centre (hammam, massages, etc) and the numerous art courses organised in the spring and autumn (patina, sponge or rag painting, plastering, etc).

Access: In the centre of the village

POITOU CHARENTES

CHAUVIGNY - 86300

CHENECHÉ - 86380

21 LA VEAUDEPIERRE
M. de Giafferi

8 rue du Berry
86300 Chauvigny
Tel. 05 49 46 30 81
Fax 05 49 47 64 12
laveaudepierre@club-internet.fr
perso.club-internet.fr/laveaudepierre

Open all year • 5 rooms • €50 to €55, breakfast included • No table d'hôte • Garden, car park. Credit cards not accepted, no dogs admitted

22 CHÂTEAU DE LABAROM
M. et Mme Le Gallais

86380 Cheneché
Tel. 05 49 51 24 22
Fax 05 49 51 47 38
chateau.de.labarom@wanadoo.fr

Closed from 1 Nov to 30 Mar • 3 rooms • €67 to €75, breakfast included • No table d'hôte • Dovecote, park, car park. Credit cards not accepted, no dogs admitted • Outdoor swimming pool

At the foot of the medieval city.

We were charmed by this superb 18C mansion dominated by the ruins of the baronial castle. The interior is particularly rich in wonderful decoration, including woodwork, period furniture, a lovely stone staircase and a collection of antique musical instruments. Bedrooms in stylish fabrics all overlook the walled garden. The hotel is at the foot of steps which lead to the upper town.

Oh la la! Row upon row of books about the region and all in French!

This 16C and 17C château was built in three hundred acres of parkland. It makes an ideal base camp to explore the region. We loved the well-worn aristocratic feel of the creaky floor boards and old furniture. The spacious rooms are lined in fabric and graced with beautiful antiques: the monumental period fireplace in the breakfast room cannot fail to catch the eye. The owner, who dabbles in art in his spare time, will happily talk you through the rudiments of painting on porcelain.

Access : From the town hall, take the first left after the church

Access : 15km to the north-west of the Futuroscope, towards Neuville and Lencloître then the D 15

POITOU CHARENTES

LOUDUN - 86200

23 HÔTEL - RESTAURANT DE LA ROUE D'OR
M. Cuvier

1 avenue d'Anjou
86200 Loudun
Tel. 05 49 98 01 23
Fax 05 49 98 85 45
www.larouedor.com

Closed Sat from Oct to mid-Apr and Sun evening all year • 14 rooms, one of which has disabled access, with bath/WC or shower/WC and television • €43 to €51; breakfast €6; half-board available • Menus €14 (weekdays) to €35 • Private car park, terrace

Sometimes you may even think you can hear the wheels of the horse-drawn carriages of yesteryear!

The stables still visible in the large courtyard are a constant reminder of the house's former vocation as a coaching inn. The establishment's small rooms are so well soundproofed that you probably won't even notice that it is next door to the ring road. Furnished in a Louis Philippe-style, the rooms are regularly smartened up. A plush, bourgeois dining room provides the setting for tasty traditional cuisine, which displays a distinct preference for local produce.

Access: In the town near Amirault Park

POITIERS - 86000

24 CHÂTEAU DE VAUMORET
M. Johnson

Rue du Breuil-Mingot
86000 Poitiers
Tel. 05 49 61 32 11
Fax 05 49 01 04 54
chateau-vaumoret@tiscali.fr

Open all year • 5 rooms with bath/WC • €59 to €69, breakfast €7 • No table d'hôte • Park, car park

A countryside setting on the doorstep of Poitiers.

Nearly 45 acres of green meadows and woodland encircle this beautifully restored 17C mansion. The rooms, in the right wing, boast some fine old furniture, prints and paintings and all have immaculate bathrooms. Enjoy breakfast in a light, airy room, then borrow a bike and start exploring.

Access: 10km north-east of Poitiers towards La Roche-Posay on the D 3, then Sèvres-Anxaumont on the D 18

POITOU CHARENTES

SAINT-BENOÎT - 86280

25 LE CHALET DE VENISE
M. et Mme Mautret

6 rue du Square
86280 Saint-Benoît
Tel. 05 49 88 45 07
Fax 05 49 52 95 44

Closed during Feb school holidays and last week in Aug • 12 rooms, one of which has disabled access, with bath/WC and television • €46 to €58; breakfast €7 • Restaurant closed Sun eve and Mon; menus €20 (weekdays) to €45 • Terrace, garden, car park

A former Benedictine abbey is the site for this sleepy village.

The austere walls conceal a sumptuous interior. The bay windows of the elegant dining room overlook a riverside garden and some of the modern, practical rooms have a balcony. The riverside terrace is quite idyllic in fine weather, while the meals are imaginative enough to tempt even the most discerning palates. Heaven for gourmets!

Access : In the village, 4km southbound from Poitiers on the D 88, near the town hall

PROVENCE, ALPS and the FRENCH RIVIERA

As you listen to the fishmongers hawking their wares under its sunny blue skies, you cannot help but fall in love with the infectious, happy-go-lucky spirit of Marseilles. Elsewhere, the steady chirring of the cicadas is interrupted only by the sheep-bells ringing in the hills as the shepherds bring their flocks home at night. The sun rises early over the ochre walls of hilltop villages which keep a careful watch over the fields of lavender below. Venture into the multitude of tiny hinterland villages and slow down to the gentle pace of the villagers as they leave the shade of the lime trees for the refreshingly cool walls of the café. However, come 2pm, you will soon begin to wonder where everyone is. On hot summer afternoons, everyone exercises their God-given right to a nap, from the fashionable beaches of Saint Tropez and seaside cabins of the Camargue to medieval walled cities surrounded by cypresses or a tiny fishing boat off the coast of Toulon. As the sun begins to set, life starts up again and the players of pétanque emerge; join them as they down a glass of pastis, then feast on bubbling *bouillabaisse*.

- Alpes-de-Haute-Provence (04)
- Hautes-Alpes (05)
- Alpes-Maritimes (06)
- Bouches-du-Rhône (13)
- Var (83)
- Vaucluse (84)

PROVENCE, ALPS AND THE FRENCH RIVIERA

ANNOT - 04240

1 L'AVENUE
M. Génovesi

Avenue de la Gare
04240 Annot
Tel. 04 92 83 22 07
Fax 04 92 83 33 13
hot.avenue@wanadoo.fr

Closed from late Oct to late Mar • 11 rooms with shower/WC, all have television • €54 to €58; breakfast €8; half-board available • Restaurant closed Mon, Wed and Fri lunchtimes; menus €17 (weekdays) to €26 (reservations advised) • No dogs admitted in restaurant

We most liked **Ambling through the pretty village of Annot and admiring its lanes lined with old houses.**

The attractive ochre façade of this regional-style house is impossible to miss as you drive into the village. Excellent soundproofing, practical furnishings and spotless housekeeping are just a few of the appeals of the rooms, all of which sport the warm colours of the south of France. The owner-chef enjoys delving into the region's flavours and scents for his tasty cuisine and the lady of the house is as cheerful as the sunny south itself.

Access: On the way into the village

BARCELONNETTE - 04400

2 AZTECA
M. Chabre

3 rue François-Arnaud
04400 Barcelonnette
Tel. 04 92 81 46 36
Fax 04 92 81 43 92
hotelazteca@wanadoo.fr
www.hotel-azteca.fr.st

Closed from 13 Nov to 5 Dec • 27 rooms, 5 of which are split-level and one has disabled access. Rooms have bath/WC and television • €64 to €97 (€50 to €70 low season); breakfast €4 to €11 • No restaurant • Private car park, private shuttle bus to the ski resorts • Nearby: swimming pool, tennis, golf, horse-riding, climbing

We most liked **The fascinating link between this tiny mountain village and Mexico.**

A wing has recently been added to this "Mexican" villa built in 1888 by one of the many farmers and craftsmen who left the hills of Ubaye to seek their fortune in the New World, and returned to mark their success in grand style. The hotel's Latin American theme, which may surprise at first but is in fact common throughout the valley, features naive "mural" paintings, an Aztec calendar and arts and crafts from Mexico. We were particularly taken with the three "Mexican" bedrooms.

Access: Near the post office

PROVENCE, ALPS AND THE FRENCH RIVIERA

BEVONS - 04200

DIGNE-LES-BAINS - 04000

3 — MAS DU FIGUIER
M. Levrault

La Fontaine
04200 Bevons
Tel. 04 92 62 81 28
Fax 04 92 62 81 28
mas.du.figuier@wanadoo.fr
www.guideprovence.com/gites/masdufigier

Closed Nov to Jan • 3 rooms with bathrooms • €50 to €52, breakfast included; half-board available • Table d'hôte €19 • Park, car park. Credit cards not accepted, dogs not admitted

We most liked **Trekking up to the ridge of the Lure – on donkey-back!**

A field of lavender stretches in front of this remote 17C mas – or Provençal farm – which stands at an altitude of 650m opposite the Lure Mountain. A proudly southern flavour prevails in the welcoming rooms, decorated in warm colours with tiled ceilings and exposed beams. We particularly liked the large bathrooms and their Moorish influence. In the winter, the fireside in the sitting room is definitely the cosiest spot in the house.

Access : 18km westbound from Sisteron on the N 85, the D 946 and the D 553

4 — VILLA GAÏA
M. et Mme Martin

24 route de Nice
04000 Digne-les-Bains
Tel. 04 92 31 21 60
Fax 04 92 31 20 12
hotel.gaia@wanadoo.fr
www.hotelvilla.gaia.fr

Open from Easter to 1 Nov • 10 rooms with bath/WC or shower/WC • €70 to €99; breakfast €9; half-board available • Restaurant closed 1 to 10 Jul, Wed out of season; menus (guests only) €26 • Library, terrace, park, car park. No dogs admitted

We most liked **Listen to the wind rustling through the leaves of the ancient trees in the park as you fall asleep.**

A relaxed family atmosphere reigns throughout this villa built in 1730, reworked in the early 20C and finally turned into a hotel in 1993. The period furniture, knick-knacks, tiles and well-preserved woodwork visible throughout the comfortable rooms, library and sitting rooms bear witness to the villa's past. In the evening, guests of the Villa Gaïa gather in the attractive plush dining room to sample an enticingly simple set menu.

Access : Take the N 85 towards Nice for 2km

PROVENCE, ALPS AND THE FRENCH RIVIERA

FORCALQUIER - 04300

5 AUBERGE CHAREMBEAU
M. Berger

Route de Niozelles
04300 Forcalquier
Tel. 04 92 70 91 70
Fax 04 92 70 91 83
contact@charembeau.com
www.charembeau.com

Open from 15 Feb to 15 Nov • 24 rooms, one of which has disabled access, with bath/WC or shower/WC, all have television, some have a balcony or terrace • €58 to €89 (€52 to €78 low season); breakfast €8 • No restaurant • Park, car park. Dogs not admitted • Swimming pool, tennis, bicycles, horse-riding, mountain-bike rentals

What better way to explore the region than by bicycle or on horse-back (on request)!

This lovely 18C farmhouse, which lies in a secluded landscape of hill and dale, enjoys the patronage of regular, satisfied customers. The lady of the house chose the Provençal fittings and fixtures in the well-proportioned bedrooms herself. The house doesn't have a restaurant but guests are welcome to picnic in the shaded park and perhaps taste the famous local goat's-cheese, known as banon.

Access : Eastbound from Forcalquier, on the N 100 towards Niozelles for 2.5km, then right on a minor road

FORCALQUIER - 04300

6 CAMPAGNE « LE PARADIS »
M. Pourcin

04300 Forcalquier
Tel. 04 92 75 37 33
campagneleparadis@wanadoo.fr
www.campagneleparadis.com

Open all year • 4 rooms • €55, breakfast included • No table d'hôte • Garden, terrace, car park. Credit cards not accepted, no dogs admitted

Horses everywhere – the riding stables are only a horseshoe's throw away!

The old horse mangers and photos on the walls of the vaulted breakfast room bear witness to the establishment's long-standing relations with our four-legged friends. The old farmhouse nestles at the foot of a citadel, overlooking the quiet countryside. The immaculate bare walls of the bedrooms in the old barn add a monastical flavour; two have a mezzanine.

Access : Villeneuve road on the D 16 and the D 216

PROVENCE, ALPS AND THE FRENCH RIVIERA

MÉOLANS-REVEL - 04340

7 MAISON D'HÔTE DES MÉANS
Mme Millet

Les Méans
04340 Méolans-Revel
Tel. 04 92 81 03 91
Fax 04 92 81 03 91
elisabeth@les-means.com
www.les-means.com

Open all year • 4 rooms and one apartment, all have bath/WC • €50 to €85, breakfast included • Table d'hôte €25 to €30, beverages included • Terrace, garden, car park. No dogs admitted in dining room

We most liked
A glimpse of the typical interior of houses in the valley.

Built when this secluded mountain region still swore allegiance to the counts of Savoy, this 16C farmhouse at an altitude of 1 000m is just the place to get away from it all and catch up on your beauty sleep. The spacious, well-appointed rooms all have lovely bathrooms with earthenware tiles; some also have a balcony. In the winter, a roaring log fire takes the chill off the large vaulted room on the ground floor. In the summertime, meals are often served in the garden, near the old bread oven.

Access: 4km from Martinet on the D 900, Gap road

MOUSTIERS-SAINTE-MARIE - 04360

8 LE CLOS DES IRIS
Mlle Dorche-Teissier

Le Pavillon Saint-Michel
04360 Moustiers-Sainte-Marie
Tel. 04 92 74 63 46
Fax 04 92 74 63 59
closdesiris@wanadoo.fr
www.closdesiris.fr

Closed from 1 to 26 Dec • 6 rooms and 2 apartments with shower/WC • €62 to €68; breakfast €9 • No restaurant • Garden, terrace

We most liked
Cat-napping on a deck chair under the trellis.

We fell head over heels for this blue-shuttered mas surrounded by greenery at the foot of the village. All the garden-level rooms and suites have private terraces equipped with garden tables and deck chairs, protected from the sun by a bower of sweet-scented climbing roses. The bathrooms are tiled with the lovely rustic tiles of Salernes, a famous tile village just a short way down the road to Toulon.

Access: 400m from the village, on the Chemin de Quinson

PROVENCE, ALPS AND THE FRENCH RIVIERA

MOUSTIERS-SAINTE-MARIE - 04360   PIERRERUE - 04300

9 MONASTÈRE DE SEGRIÈS
M. et Mme Allègre

04360 Moustiers-Sainte-Marie
Tel. 04 92 74 64 32
Fax 04 92 74 64 22
c.allegre@wanadoo.fr

Closed from Nov to late Mar • 5 rooms with bathrooms • €52, breakfast included; half-board available • Table d'hôte €18 • Terrace, park, car park. Credit cards not accepted, dogs not admitted

10 JAS DES NEVIÈRES
M. Duermael

Route de Saint-Pierre
04300 Pierrerue
Tel. 04 92 75 24 99
Fax 04 92 75 03 75
duermael@wanadoo.fr
http://jas-des-nevieres.com

Closed from 1 Nov to 31 Mar • 4 rooms, 2 of which are on the ground floor with shower/WC, the 2 upstairs have bath/WC • €70 (€65 low season), breakfast included • No table d'hôte • Terrace, car park. Credit cards not accepted • Outdoor swimming pool

Only tell special friends about this enchanting monastery.

The fragrance of lavender and rosemary is all around you as you make your way up the winding lane to this superb monastery surrounded by oak trees. The spacious rooms, which overlook the cloisters and pool or the valley, are so quiet, you may well wonder if the monastery is still cloaked in its vow of silence. Deep sofas and a billiards table set the scene in the sitting room. It's the sort of place you want to tell everyone about and then worry that it might get overcrowded!

"Baa, baa, black sheep have you any wool?"

The thick stone walls of this former sheepfold in the heart of the hamlet hide an undreamt-of haven of style and sophistication. We were unable to find fault with the refined good taste of the lovely bedrooms. Breakfast is served on a delightful inner patio, which echoes to the chirping of cicadas in the summertime. From the pool, you will be able to enjoy an uninterrupted view of mile upon mile of open fields.

Access : 6km to the north-west of Moustiers on the D 952

Access : 6km eastbound from Forcalquier on the D 12 then the D 212

PROVENCE, ALPS AND THE FRENCH RIVIERA

PRA-LOUP - 04400

11 LA FERME DU COUVENT
M. Riehl

Les Molanes
04400 Pra-Loup
Tel. 04 92 84 05 05
Fax 04 92 84 05 05
info@ferme-du-couvent.fr
www.ferme-du-couvent.com

Closed 1 week in Jun • 5 rooms • €38 to €76, breakfast included; half-board available • Table d'hôte €16 to €25 • Garden. No dogs admitted in restaurant • Tennis

We most liked
A 100 %-authentic Ubaye farmhouse.

In the heart of the resort, this 14C farm is a welcome surprise among the string of modern chalets. The farm's venerable age is still visible inside, in its low door-frames, floor made out of larch logs, narrow windows and cool rooms. Each of the simple bedrooms has its own terrace overlooking the valley, Barcelonette and the peaks. We particularly liked the fireside dinners.

Access: In the resort

PRA-LOUP - 04400

12 LE PRIEURÉ DE MOLANES
M. Paradis

Les Molanes
04400 Pra-Loup
Tel. 04 92 84 11 43
Fax 04 92 84 01 88
hotel.leprieure@wanadoo.fr
www.prieure-praloup.com

Closed from 24 Apr to 3 Jun and 20 Sep to 17 Dec • 14 rooms on 2 floors, with bath/WC or shower/WC, all have television • €60 to €80 (€60 to €75 low season); breakfast €8; half-board available • Menus €21 to €49 • Terrace, garden, car park • Summer swimming pool

We most liked
Did you notice the owner's name? What more can we say?

May the devil take you if don't find happiness in this 17C priory! All the more so, as the chairlift of this alpine resort overlooking the lovely valley of Ubaye is on the doorstep of a superb skiing domain which unabashedly claims to be "a top resort for top people"! If the thrill of swooping down a powdery slope doesn't appeal, slap on the sun cream and relax on the south-facing terrace! A cheerful fire burns in the restaurant where you can sample a wide range of tasty dishes.

Access: 8.5km to the south-west of Barcelonnette, on the D 902, then the D 908 and right on the D 109

PROVENCE, ALPS AND THE FRENCH RIVIERA
ROUMOULES - 04500   SAINT-GENIEZ - 04200

13 LE VIEUX CASTEL
M. et Mme Léonardi

1 route des Châteaux
04500 Roumoules
Tel. 04 92 77 75 42
vieuxcastel@free.fr
http://vieuxcastel.free.fr

Closed Jan and Dec • 5 non-smoking rooms, all have bath/WC • €55, breakfast included; half-board available • Table d'hôte €20, beverages included • Garden, sitting room. Credit cards not accepted, dogs not admitted

14 DOMAINE DES RAYES
M. Masure

04200 Saint-Geniez
Tel. 04 92 61 22 76
Fax 04 92 61 06 44
les.rayes@wanadoo.fr
www.lesrayes.fr

Open all year • 5 rooms • €72 to €79 (€65 to €72 low season), breakfast included • Table d'hôte €17 • Car park. Dogs not admitted • Outdoor swimming pool, children's play area

The authenticity of this elegant Provençal property with lavender-coloured shutters.

Blessed with silence.

Planted over three hundred years ago, mature chestnut trees still stand guard over this 17C house, formerly the property of the Clérissy family, inventors of Moustiers porcelain. The bedrooms have coffered ceilings and are decorated with hand-painted stencils; all are non-smoking. Arches, a fireplace and period furniture in the dining-room set off the ornate stone patterned floor.

Exceptional is the only word to describe the location of this 17C sheepfold perched at an altitude of 1 300m and surrounded by open heath. Quiet, often immense bedrooms are decorated in a bold local palette. Wining and dining in the inviting dining room, reading in the superb vaulted sitting rooms or daydreaming on the terrace which commands a stunning view of the Durance Valley; all offer their own particular pleasure.

Access : 4km to the north-east of Riez, Moustiers-Ste-Marie road (D 952), on the way into the village of Roumoules

Access : 17km to the north-east of Sisteron, Saint-Geniez road on the D 3

PROVENCE, ALPS AND THE FRENCH RIVIERA

SAINT-LAURENT-DU-VERDON - 04500

15 MOULIN DU CHÂTEAU
M. et Mme Staempfli-Faoro

Le Village
04500 Saint-Laurent-du-Verdon
Tel. 04 92 74 02 47
Fax 04 92 74 02 97
info@moulin-du-chateau.com
www.moulin-du-chateau.com

Closed early Nov to late Feb • 10 rooms, one with disabled access, with shower/WC, half have television • €85 to €99 (€77 to €88 low season); breakfast €8; half-board available • Restaurant closed Mon, Thu and lunchtime; menus (guests only) €30 • Terrace, garden. Dogs not admitted in the restaurant • Library, billiards

We most liked
The friendly guesthouse atmosphere.

The former oil mill, built in the 17C and nestled in an extensive wooded garden, adjoins the castle of this town located in the heart of the Verdon regional nature reserve. The press and millstone continue to take pride of place in the middle of the spacious sitting room. Immaculate walls, wrought-iron beds, brightly-coloured fabrics and small cane armchairs preside over the deliberately unfussy bedrooms. The set menu is served in a rustic dining room or on the delicious terrace.

Access: Behind the château

ARVIEUX - 05350

16 LA GIRANDOLE
M. Morel

Brunissard
05350 Arvieux
Tel. 04 92 46 84 12
Fax 04 92 46 86 59
lagirandole@tiscali.fr
lagirandole.info

Closed from 15 Nov to 15 Dec • 6 non-smoking rooms with shower/WC and bath/WC and 2 gîtes • €66, breakfast included • No table d'hôte • Garden, car park. Credit cards not accepted, no dogs admitted • Outdoor swimming pool

We most liked
Well-situated on the "Sundial Route" – a themed tour of the villages of Haute-Provence.

Both the architecture and the sundial which adorns the façade of this old farmhouse are typical of the valley of Arvieux. The interior has been tastefully refurbished with old furniture and objects, colourful prints and fabrics, a piano and soft sofas in the sitting room. The rooms display a more uncluttered style with plain white walls and have balconies with a variety of views over the pleasant hilly landscape. Guests have the use of a kitchen.

Access: 3km northbound on the D 902

PROVENCE, ALPS AND THE FRENCH RIVIERA

BARATIER - 05200

17 LES PEUPLIERS
M. Bellot

Chemin de Lesdier
05200 Baratier
Tel. 04 92 43 03 47
Fax 04 92 43 41 49
info@hotel-les-peupliers.com
www.hotel-les-peupliers.com

Closed from 26 mar to 14 Apr, 25 Sep to 26 Oct and Tue and Fri lunchtimes • 24 rooms, 6 of which are non-smoking, with bath/WC or shower/WC and television • €53 to €57; breakfast €7; half-board available • Menus €16 to €34 • Terrace, car park • Outdoor swimming pool, petanque

As welcoming in winter as in summer.

This alpine chalet enjoys a wonderful position surrounded by mountains and overlooking the lake of Serre Ponçon. The rooms are a cheerful mixture of sturdy, hand-painted furniture and bold regional fabrics; those on the second floor with a lake-view balcony were our favourite. Stone and wood feature prominently in the alpine dining room. Put your feet up on the shaded, south-facing terrace after a couple of hours energetic hiking, mountain biking or cross-country skiing, depending on the season!

Access: Leave the N 94 towards Les Orres, then Baratier, in the village, take the second turning on the right

BUISSARD - 05500

18 LES CHEMINS VERTS
Mme Dubois

05500 Buissard
Tel. 04 92 50 57 57
lescheminsverts@free.fr
www.lescheminsverts.com

Open all year • 4 rooms and one gîte • €45, breakfast included; half-board available • Table d'hôte €14 • Terrace, car park. Credit cards not accepted, dogs not admitted

Fill your lungs with fresh mountain air.

At an altitude of 1 200m, this pretty 18C farmhouse, run by amiable, helpful hosts, surveys the Drac valley and the rocky bastion of Dévoluy massif. The tasteful rooms are comfortable; the one called "Fleurette" has the best view. A brand new apartment is also available and the sitting room and panoramic terrace are worthy of note.

Access: 1km eastbound from Saint-Julien-en-Champsaur on the D 15

PROVENCE, ALPS AND THE FRENCH RIVIERA

GAP - 05000

19 LE PARLEMENT
M. et Mme Drouillard

Charance
05000 Gap
Tel. 04 92 53 94 20
Fax 04 92 53 94 20
www.maisondhotes-leparlement.com

Open all year • 5 rooms • €60 to €80, breakfast included • No table d'hôte • Car park. Dogs not admitted • Swimming pool, sauna, billiards, play area, theme weekends

This establishment democratically offers something for everyone!

This appealing 18C house surrounded by greenery was formerly an outbuilding of the castle of Charance. Although only a few minutes from Gap, it is quiet and peaceful and commands a splendid vista of the Gapençais and the Ubaye range. The rooms are spacious, sophisticated and quite spotless; some command a view of the town. A swimming pool, sauna, billiards and children' play area will keep young and old busy. The owner, an alpine and mountain-bike guide, will happily give you ideas for outings.

Access : From Gap, 4km towards Orange and Valence (D 994), at the Rond Point des 3 Cascades, drive towards the Charance domain

LA GRAVE - 05320

20 LES CHALETS DE LA MEIJE
M. et Mme Teyras

Le Nouveau Village
05320 La Grave
Tel. 04 76 79 97 97
Fax 04 76 79 97 98
contact@chalet-meije.com
www.chalet-meije.com

Closed 2 to 14 May and 8 Oct to 17 Dec • 12 rooms, 2 with disabled access, all with bath/WC and television • €60 to €78; breakfast €8 • No restaurant • Garage, sitting room-bar • Outdoor swimming pool, sauna, fitness room, jacuzzi

The exceptional view of the Meije.

This modern construction, ideally located opposite the Meije, offers a variety of types of accommodation. Its chalets are home to rooms, split-level flats and apartments, all comfortable and tastefully decorated with wrought-iron chairs, Indonesian furniture, pretty fabrics, etc. The main wing boasts a relaxation centre with keep-fit facilities, sauna and Jacuzzi, as well as a bar where you can admire the mountains as you sip a drink.

Access : On the N 91 between the Deux-Alpes and Serre-Chevalier

PROVENCE, ALPS AND THE FRENCH RIVIERA
LE MONÊTIER-LES-BAINS - 05220   NÉVACHE - 05100

21 L'ALLIEY
M. et Mme Buisson

11 rue des Écoles
05220 Le Monêtier-les-Bains
Tel. 04 92 24 40 20
Fax 04 92 24 40 60
hotel @ alliey.com
www.alliey.com

Closed 16 Apr to 30 Jun and 1 Sep to 19 Dec • 23 rooms, all with bath/WC and television • €59 to €89; breakfast €10; half-board available in season • Table d'hôte €29 • Terrace, park. Dogs not admitted • Indoor swimming pool

We most liked
The warm mountain atmosphere.

Tucked away in a village, this house is full of charm. Wood is the prevailing feature of the warm atmosphere whether in the lobby area, sitting rooms, dining room or the alpine-style bedrooms, all of which are decorated with handsome larch wood furniture. After a day's skiing or hiking, relax in the balneo centre before heading for the restaurant to sample the tasty regional dishes and make your choice from the fine wine list, which boasts a number of excellent vintages.

Access : In the centre of the village

22 LE CHALET D'EN HÔ
M. et Mme Baudoux

Hameau des Chazals - Le Roubion
05100 Névache
Tel. 04 92 20 12 29
Fax 04 92 20 59 70
chaletdenho @ aol.com
www.chaletdenho.com

Closed from 17 Apr to 2 Jun, 17 Sep to 27 Oct and 5 Nov to 22 Dec • 14 non-smoking rooms with bath/WC or shower/WC and television, most have a balcony • €79 to €117 (€51 to €71 low season); breakfast €9; half-board available • Menu €23 (evenings only) • Car park. No dogs admitted in restaurant • Cross-country skiing, hiking, sauna

We most liked
Breakfast on the terrace overlooking the valley's multitude of wild flowers.

The climb up to this larchwood chalet will reward you with lovely bedrooms named after the mountains and lakes you can see from the balconies. A tasteful marriage of walls lined in pine and local draperies and the dining room is adorned with tools which recall the local tradition of woodworking. The nature-loving owners are always happy to pass on tips and expert advice on exploring the lovely Clarée Valley.

Access : Northbound from Briançon, leave the N 94 for the D 994G that follows the Clarée, turn right at Roubion

PROVENCE, ALPS AND THE FRENCH RIVIERA

POLIGNY - 05500

23 LE CHALET DES ALPAGES
M. et Mme Potut

Les Forestons
05500 Poligny
Tel. 04 92 23 08 95
www.le-chalet-des-alpages.com

Open all year • 6 non-smoking rooms, all with bath/WC
• €55 to €86, breakfast included • Table d'hôte €17
• Garage. Credit cards not accepted, no dogs admitted
• Fitness facilities, sauna, Jacuzzi, hot outdoor tub

Most liked: Taking a dip in the Norwegian bathtub in the heart of winter.

It is easy to see why the owners chose this location for their maison d'hôte. The chalet, set on an immense meadow close to the forest, commands a priceless view of the Noyer pass, the Fararud, Cuchon and Vieux Chaillol mountains. The Alpine spirit of the cosy interior decoration is equally appealing. Each of the attractive well-equipped bedrooms boasts either a balcony or a small garden for those on the ground floor. Regional and Provençal flavoured cuisine.

Access : From Poligny, head towards the Col du Noyer for 2km to the place known as Les Forestons, and turn left onto the small lane

SAINT-CHAFFREY - 05330

24 LES MARMOTTES
M. Lucas

22 rue du Centre - village de Chantemerle
05330 Saint-Chaffrey
Tel. 04 92 24 11 17
lucas.marmottes@wanadoo.fr

Open all year • 5 non-smoking rooms, all with bath/WC and television • €49 to €56, breakfast included • Table d'hôte €19, drinks included • Credit cards not accepted, dogs not admitted

Most liked: Relaxing around the lovely fireplace in the sitting room.

This former barn converted into a guesthouse and set in the heart of the historic village of Chantemerle has retained all its charm of yesteryear. Wood prevails in the spacious personalised bedrooms, sitting room and dining room. An immense oak table, which can seat up to twelve guests, invites the visitor to sit down in the company of other guests and partake of the lady of the house's copious family cooking.

Access : In the village centre

PROVENCE, ALPS AND THE FRENCH RIVIERA

SAINT-DISDIER - 05250

25 AUBERGE LA NEYRETTE
M. et Mme Muzard

05250 Saint-Disdier
Tel. 04 92 58 81 17
Fax 04 92 58 89 95
info@la-neyrette.com
www.la-neyrette.com

Closed from 17 to 30 Apr and from 15 Oct to 15 Dec • 12 rooms with bath/WC or shower/WC, all have television • €64 to €72; breakfast €8; half-board available • Menus €20 to €40 • Terrace, garden, car park • Pond with trout fishing, play area

most liked Fancy a nap under a tree in the company of the local marmots?

This inn lies in a secluded spot on Dévoluy's high plateau at the foot of an arid crest of peaks. The recently renovated rooms are decorated in keeping with their wild flower names. The peaceful garden boasts a pond where you can fish for your own trout, the house speciality. In the summer, meals are served on the terrace overlooking the solitary stone fortress. In the winter, the ski slopes of Superdévoluy are just a short drive away.

Access : On leaving the village, on the Superdévoluy road

CABRIS - 06530

26 CHAMBRE D'HÔTE MADAME FARAUT
Mme Faraut

14 rue de l'Agachon
06530 Cabris
Tel. 04 93 60 52 36
Fax 04 93 60 52 36

Closed from 1 Oct to 31 Mar • 5 rooms • €50 to €60, breakfast included • No table d'hôte • Credit cards not accepted

most liked Wandering around the lanes of this old village so popular with contemporary artists.

The yellow walls of this tiny village house are bound to catch your eye. The restful rooms are painted a spotless white; some of them enjoy a view of the Esterel massif and St-Cassien Lake, as does the sitting room. A light-hearted atmosphere also prevails in the beams and fireplace in the breakfast room and the countryside almost seems to creep in through the large bay window.

Access : In a lane in the village

PROVENCE, ALPS AND THE FRENCH RIVIERA

CAGNES-SUR-MER - 06800

27 LES JARDINS FRAGONARD
M. Mombeck

12 rue Fragonard
06800 Cagnes-sur-Mer
Tel. 04 93 20 07 72
Fax 04 93 20 07 72
jardinsfragonard@hotmail.com

Open all year • 4 rooms with bath/WC • €85 (€55 to €70 low season), breakfast included • Table d'hôte by reservation • Terraces, garden, car park. Credit cards not accepted, no dogs admitted • Outdoor swimming pool, billiards. Tennis and golf nearby

Conveniently located near the Renoir Museum.

Trees indigenous to the south fill the park of this secluded 1925 villa perched on the heights of Cagnes. An equally authentic Provençal look prevails in the brightly coloured rooms, often furnished in cane; all have brand new bathrooms. Depending on the season, breakfast is served on the terrace or inside, at a large communal table. The shaded garden and swimming pool are ideal for quiet, relaxing afternoons.

Access: Near the Renoir Museum

CANNES - 06400

28 VILLA L'ÉGLANTIER
M. et Mme Daran

14 rue Campestra
06400 Cannes
Tel. 04 93 68 22 43
Fax 04 93 38 28 53
www.bnbnet.com

Open all year • 4 rooms with bath/WC • €75 to €100, breakfast included • No table d'hôte • Terrace, garden. Credit cards not accepted

A haven of peace and quiet within walking distance of the Croisette.

This large white villa hidden away on the heights of Cannes is set in a lovely garden planted with palm, orange and other exotic trees. Built in the 1920s, its original Art Deco soul can still be felt. The guestrooms, spacious, quiet and tastefully decorated, all have large bathrooms. The White, Green and Blue rooms upstairs have a balcony or a terrace, while the Red room, on the ground-floor, opens onto the garden.

Access: On the heights of Cannes

PROVENCE, ALPS AND THE FRENCH RIVIERA

CAP-D'ANTIBES - 06160

29 LA JABOTTE
M. April et M. Mora

13 avenue Max-Maurey
06160 Cap-d'Antibes
Tel. 04 93 61 45 89
Fax 04 93 61 07 04
info @ jabotte.com
www.jabotte.com

Closed 3 weeks in Nov and 1 week at Christmas • 10 non-smoking rooms with shower/WC • €78 to €83 (€56 to €61 low season); breakfast €8 • No restaurant • Terrace, garden, car park. No dogs admitted

Superbly located just a stone's throw from a lovely sandy beach.

This establishment, well located in a quiet side street at right angles to Salis Beach, is home to tastefully decorated trim bedrooms. Their tiny terraces all overlook a pleasant gravelled patio adorned with plants. The work of one of the owners, a calligraphist in his spare time, can be seen in some of the rooms and in the smart sitting room where delicious breakfasts are served. Warm, friendly welcome.

Access: 100m from Salis Beach

COARAZE - 06390

30 L'AUBERGE DU SOLEIL
Mme Jacquet

In the village
06390 Coaraze
Tel. 04 93 79 08 11
Fax 04 93 79 37 79
auberge.du.soleil @ wanadoo.fr

Closed from 1 to 15 Jan • 8 rooms with bath/WC • €56 to €84; breakfast €9; half-board available • Menus €23 to €28 • Garden • Outdoor swimming pool

Delicious little Provençal dishes cooked by the lady of the house.

This lovely mansion was built in 1863 and its atmosphere of quiet serenity can only be reached on foot. The immaculate rooms are a happy combination of old and new; four enjoy a view of the valley and the terraced fields. The immense dining room and conservatory also command an impressive vista. Madame uses only fresh produce in her cooking, whose reputation extends throughout the region. As for relaxation, look no further than the billiard table, garden, orchard and pool.

Access: A 8 motorway, Nice-Est exit, then highway towards La Trinité-Drap-Sospel; at La Pointe de Contes, turn left towards Contes-Coaraze

PROVENCE, ALPS AND THE FRENCH RIVIERA

LA BRIGUE - 06430

31 LE MIRVAL
M. et Mme Dellepiane

3 rue Vincent-Ferrier
06430 La Brigue
Tel. 04 93 04 63 71
Fax 04 93 04 79 81
lemirval@club.fr
www.lemirval.com

Open from 1 Apr to 2 Nov • 18 rooms on 2 floors, most have bath/WC, all have television • €45 to €70; (€42 to €62 low season); breakfast €8; half-board available • Restaurant closed Fri lunchtime; menus €19 to €25 • Terrace, garden, car park • Mountain biking, white-water sports

> **Anglers will not be able to resist trying to hook a silver trout in the torrents of the Levense.**

A late-19C alpine inn in a picturesque medieval village close to the Italian border. Nearly all the modern, practical rooms have been renovated. The restaurant-veranda is nothing special in itself, but does offer a superb view over the tiny stone bridge spanning the village's renowned trout-stream. The owner organises excursions in the Vallée des Merveilles (Marvels) either in a four-wheel drive or on foot.

Access : 6.5km southbound from Tende on the D 204, then at St-Dalmas-de-Tendre take a left on the D 143

LA COLLE-SUR-LOUP - 06480

32 LA BASTIDE DE SAINT-DONAT
M. Rosso

Route du Pont-de-Pierre, parc Saint-Donat
06480 La Colle-sur-Loup
Tel. 04 93 32 93 41
Fax 04 93 32 80 61

Open all year • 5 rooms with shower or bath • €65 to €95, breakfast included • No table d'hôte • Terrace, garden. Credit cards not accepted

> **Dawdling on the terrace overlooking the river.**

The stone walls of this sheepfold built in 1850 hide a wealth of ornate interior decoration. The ground floor has been beautifully restored in keeping with local traditions, including arcades, columns, fireplace and terracotta floor tiles. The pastel shades of the bedrooms are a perfect contrast to the old beams and furniture; some have a balcony. As you sit on the terrace, you will be able to listen to the river babbling gently below.

Access : 2km southbound from Saint-Paul on the D 6

PROVENCE, ALPS AND THE FRENCH RIVIERA
LE SUQUET - 06450
MENTON - 06500

33 AUBERGE DU BON PUITS
M. et Mme Corniglion

06450 Le Suquet
Tel. 04 93 03 17 65
Fax 04 93 03 10 48
http://www.logis06.com

Closed from 1 Dec to 15 Apr and Tue except from 15 Jul to 30 Aug • 8 rooms, 2 of which are non-smoking, with bath/WC, air-conditioning and television • €62 to €65; breakfast €9; half-board available • Menus €20 to €32 • Terrace, park, car park. Credit cards not accepted • Animal park, play area, white-water sports and fishing, scenic walks

The joyful shouts of the pony riders in the small animal park.

Children are welcomed with open arms in this old stone coaching inn complete with a play area and a lovely animal park on the banks of the Vésubie. Since 1890, the rooms have been constantly smartened up and embellished by the owners and their forebears. The kitchen is also a family affair and the delicious recipes have been handed down from mother to daughter for generations. Meals are served under the well-polished beams of the gleaming dining room.

Access : On the D 2565, between Plan-du-Var and Bollène-Vésubie

34 PIERROT-PIERRETTE
M. Mitolo

Place de l'Église - Monti
06500 Menton
Tel. 04 93 35 79 76
Fax 04 93 35 79 76
pierrotpierrette@aol.com

Closed from 6 Dec to 15 Jan and Mon except Easter • 7 rooms, 4 of which are in a separate wing, all have shower/WC, no television • €67 to €76; breakfast €8; half-board available • Menus €28 to €39 • Garden • Swimming pool

Your northern pallor will soon turn a lovely golden brown under Menton's bright sun.

This delightful little inn perched in the upper reaches of a peaceful hamlet lies just outside Menton. Most of the family-sized simply-furnished rooms have balconies. The charm of the rustic dining room is further enhanced by delicious homemade specialities (duck foie gras, bouillabaisse), but guests also come back for the luxurious garden, full of exotic southern plants and sweet-scented roses, and the swimming pool overlooking the valley of Carei.

Access : 5km northbound from Menton, on the D 2566 towards Sospel

PROVENCE, ALPS AND THE FRENCH RIVIERA

NICE - 06000

35 ARMENONVILLE
Mme Moreilhon

20 avenue des Fleurs
06000 Nice
Tel. 04 93 96 86 00
Fax 04 93 44 66 53
nice @ hotel-armenonville.com
www.hotel-armenonville.com

Open all year • 13 air-conditioned rooms with bath/WC or shower/WC, all have television • €75 to €100 (€60 to €75 low season); breakfast €10 • No restaurant • Garden, private car park. No dogs admitted

The old "Russian" district of Nice and its Orthodox cathedral.

This 1900 villa stands at the end of a cul-de-sac in the old Russian quarter. A faded charm emanates from the high-ceilinged rooms of varied sizes decorated with "old-fashioned" furniture from the opulent Negresco Hotel. Some overlook the flowers and palm trees in the garden where breakfast is served on sunny days, i.e. almost every day of the year. A pretty iron stove takes pride of place in the sitting room.

Access: From the Promenade des Anglais, take Boulevard Gambetta, then turn left

NICE - 06000

36 DURANTE
Mme Stramigioli

16 avenue Durante
06000 Nice
Tel. 04 93 88 84 40
Fax 04 93 87 77 76
info @ hotel-durante.com
www.hotel-durante.com

Closed Jan • 24 rooms, 19 of which have kitchenettes, all are air-conditioned with bath/WC or shower/WC and television • €69 to €100; breakfast €10 • No restaurant • Garden, car park

Breakfast on the terrace amid the tangy perfume of citrus fruit trees.

The pink façade and mascarons (carved caricatures) over the windows of this elegant abode, in a quiet cul-de-sac near the railway station are a reminder that Italy is just down the road. It is a pleasure to sleep with the window wide open, because all the rooms, recently refurbished in a Mediterranean flavour, overlook a terracotta tiled terrace-garden lined with rows of palm, orange and lemon trees.

Access: From the railway station, take Av Durante and turn left in the cul-de-sac after Rue Alsace-Lorraine

PROVENCE, ALPS AND THE FRENCH RIVIERA
PÉGOMAS - 06580   SAINT-PAUL - 06570

37 LE BOSQUET
M. Cattet

74 chemin des Périssols
06580 Pégomas
Tel. 04 92 60 21 20
Fax 04 92 60 21 49
hotel.lebosquet@wanadoo.fr
www.hotellebosquet.com

Open all year • 16 rooms with bath/WC or shower/WC and television • €45 to €60; breakfast €7 • No restaurant • Private car park, park. No dogs admitted • Swimming pool, tennis

We most liked: The fruit orchards, regularly plundered for the delicious homemade jams served at breakfast.

Bougainvillaea, oleander, lavender, bamboo, lawns and tall trees make up the multicoloured backdrop that encircles this hotel a few kilometres outside Cannes. A clientele of regulars return annually, drawn by the establishment's peaceful atmosphere, friendly, relaxed welcome and swimming pool. A pleasantly subdued Provençal flavour echoes throughout the rooms, located in two buildings. A studio complete with kitchenette is also available for rent.

Access: To the north-east on the Mouans Sartoux road

38 HOSTELLERIE DES REMPARTS
M. Tibaud

72 rue Grande
06570 Saint-Paul
Tel. 04 93 32 09 88
Fax 04 93 32 06 91
h.remparts@wanadoo.fr
www.hotel-les-remparts.net

Closed from mid-Jan to mid-Feb, Sun evening and Mon • 9 rooms with bath/WC or shower/WC • €39 to €80; breakfast €7; half-board available • Restaurant closed evenings in winter (except weekend); menu €12 to €30 • Terrace, car park

We most liked: Saint-Paul and this old hotel are everything you expect Provence to be.

Beautifully preserved stone walls, antique furniture, rustic earthenware tiles, bright colours and a faultless welcome paint the picture of this delightful hotel, hidden in a narrow street in historic St-Paul. Each of the personalised rooms is named after a flower and the largest offer a fine view of the countryside. It is hard to leave the shade of the lovely covered terrace.

Access: In the part of Rue Grande between Rue de l'Étoile and Rue des Pontis

PROVENCE, ALPS AND THE FRENCH RIVIERA

TOURRETTES-SUR-LOUP - 06140

39 MAS DES CIGALES
M. Prieur-Gelis

1673 route des Quenières
06140 Tourrettes-sur-Loup
Tel. 04 93 59 25 73
Fax 04 93 59 25 73
lemasdescigales@free.fr
www.lemasdescigales.com

Open all year • 5 rooms • €92 to €97 (€80 low season), breakfast included • No table d'hôte • Garden, car park. No dogs admitted • Outdoor swimming pool, tennis, mountain bikes, wi-fi internet access

We most liked **The surrounding countryside, perfect for taking a stroll.**

This pleasant villa perched on a hillside of pine trees commands a wonderful view of the Riviera coast. Hand-painted furniture adorns the personalised rooms named after local fauna and flora: Nasturtium, Peony, Butterfly, Violet and Olive. You can choose between a covered veranda overlooking the garden or (in summer) a poolside table for breakfast. If you lean slightly over the terrace, you will catch sight of a small waterfall and the property's tennis courts.

Access : 2km from Tourrettes, Saint-Jean road

VALBERG - 06470

40 BLANCHE NEIGE
M. et Mme Kretchmann

10 avenue de Valbery
06470 Valberg
Tel. 04 93 02 50 04
Fax 04 93 02 61 90

Closed in Nov, Mon evening and Tue in low season • 17 rooms with shower/WC, some have bath/WC, all have television • €76 (€66 low season); breakfast €8 to €10; half-board available • Restaurant closed out of season; menus €18 to €25 • Terrace, garage, car park. No dogs admitted • Skiing, hiking

We most liked **Hey Ho, Hey Ho, it's out to play we go!**

Once upon a time there was a chalet whose green and yellow shutters looked onto a forest of larch trees. Legend has it that these small rooms decorated with hand-quilted bedspreads and painted furniture were formerly the home of seven cheerful dwarves and their guest, Snow White – the hotel's namesake. Nowadays the region's white gold – 50km of slopes between 1 500 and 2 000m – has stolen the limelight from the princesses of yesteryear. Snug restaurant and spacious terrace overlooking the road.

Access : At the entrance to the resort

PROVENCE, ALPS AND THE FRENCH RIVIERA
VAL-DU-TIGNET - 06530   VENCE - 06140

41 MAS DE CLAIREFONTAINE
M. et Mme Lapostat

3196 route de Draguignan
06530 Val-du-Tignet
Tel. 04 93 66 39 69
andre.lapostat@wanadoo.fr
http://masdeclairefontaine.online.fr

Open all year • 3 rooms with bathrooms and television • €80, breakfast included • No table d'hôte • Terrace, park, car park. Credit cards not accepted, no dogs admitted • Outdoor swimming pool. Fishing and sailing on the lake nearby

As you drive up to the mas, wind down your window and listen to the cicadas chirping!

The picture of the stone mas and its terraced garden dotted with umbrella pines and clumps of reeds will make you reach for your camera. The Provençal-style bedrooms and bathrooms are strewn with delightful details such as delicately scented Fragonard soaps, postcards and sweets, that make you feel you were expected. The Iris room has its own private terrace. In the summer months, guests are invited to eat outside in the welcome shade of the oak tree.

Access: 10km to the south-east of Grasse, Draguignan road

42 AUBERGE DES SEIGNEURS
Mme Rodi

Place du Frêne
06140 Vence
Tel. 04 93 58 04 24
Fax 04 93 24 08 01

Open from Mar to Oct • 6 rooms with shower/WC • €70 to €85; breakfast €10; half-board available • Restaurant closed Sun and Mon; menus €31 to €42

Ladies are offered a flower after the meal.

This historic 17C inn next door to the Château de Villeneuve is said to have enjoyed the patronage of famous people such as François 1st, who died in 1547! "But, but", you stammer as you quickly compare dates. However the original decoration of this house has been so skilfully preserved that you would be forgiven for falling into the trap! Whatever the case, a taste of the superb spit-roasted lamb from the open fire is bound to reconcile you with the hotel's miraculous past.

Access: In the grounds of the old town, near the castle

PROVENCE, ALPS AND THE FRENCH RIVIERA

AIX-EN-PROVENCE - 13100

43 QUATRE DAUPHINS
M. et Mme Lafont

54 rue Roux-Alphéran
13100 Aix-en-Provence
Tel. 04 42 38 16 39
Fax 04 42 38 60 19
lesquatredauphins@wanadoo.fr

Open all year • 13 air-conditioned rooms with bath/WC or shower/WC, all have television • €65 to €85; breakfast €9 • No restaurant

You won't regret opting for the romantic rooms under the eaves, however stifling in summer!

The tiny lanes lined with lovely old 17C and 18C mansions, the busy café terraces of the Cours Mirabeau, a multitude of tiny restaurants and colourful street markets – it could only be Aix en Provence! Turn a deaf ear to the noise, steel yourself to the heat and immerse yourself from head to toe in the charm of this hotel's tiled floors and painted furniture, only a step from the graceful little square of the Quatre Dauphins.

Access : In a quiet, small street in the Mazarin area

AIX-EN-PROVENCE - 13100

44 SAINT-CHRISTOPHE
M. Bonnet

2 avenue Victor-Hugo
13100 Aix-en-Provence
Tel. 04 42 26 01 24
Fax 04 42 38 59 17
saintchristophe@francemarket.com
www.hotel-saintchristophe.com

Open all year • 58 air-conditioned rooms, one has disabled access, all have bath/WC and television • €79 to €117; breakfast €10 • Menu €21 to €26 • Garage

Admire the paintings by a local artist on the walls of the comfortable lounge-bar.

The smart pink walls of this small building were home to a garage before the Bonnet family bought the premises in 1936 and turned them into a hotel-restaurant. Most of the rooms echo the establishment's Art Deco origins, but several are more Provençal in inspiration. The restaurant and conservatory-terrace have adopted the spirit of a Parisian brasserie, serving a somewhat eclectic range of dishes, including the house special of choucroute!

Access : In the town centre, near the tourist office and the Cours Mirabeau

PROVENCE, ALPS AND THE FRENCH RIVIERA
ARLES - 13200   ARLES - 13200

45 L'AMPHITHÉATRE
M. Coumet et M. Piras

5-7 rue Diderot
13200 Arles
Tel. 04 90 96 10 30
Fax 04 90 93 98 69
contact@hotelamphitheatre.fr
www.hotelamphitheatre.fr

Open all year • 28 rooms and 3 apartments on 3 floors, most have shower/WC, all have television • €49 to €95; breakfast €7 • No restaurant

Breakfasting on fresh fruit juice, crusty croissants and home-made fruit preserves.

A line of plane trees masks this small 17C house whose façade is adorned with a statue of the Virgin Mary. All the airy, tasteful and well cared-for rooms have just been treated to a facelift with painted and wrought-iron furniture and lovely draperies. The sitting and breakfast room feature the same happy blend of old walls, modern décor and bright southern colours. The hotel is ideally situated to explore Arles' countless treasures.

Access : In the historical centre, near the Roman Theatre and Arena

46 CALENDAL
Mme Jacquemin

5 rue Porte-de-Laure
13200 Arles
Tel. 04 90 96 11 89
Fax 04 90 96 05 84
contact@lecalendal.com
www.lecalendal.com

Closed Jan • 38 rooms, all have bath/WC or shower/WC and television • €45 to €104; breakfast €7 • Restaurant only open at lunchtime in season; buffet €14 • Garden. No dogs admitted

Proof that France also drinks tea!

Teatime, something of an institution in this establishment, means tasty pastries and a wonderful selection of teas from one of France's most famous tea houses, served in a light, airy room with veranda, which also doubles as a breakfast room when the weather is not fine enough to enjoy the shade of the palms on the terrace. The rooms overlook either the garden, the Antique theatre, or, for a lucky few, the Arena; ask for one with a view when booking. All are decorated in bright, warm colours.

Access : Between the Antique theatre and arena

PROVENCE, ALPS AND THE FRENCH RIVIERA

BARBENTANE - 13570

47 CASTEL MOUISSON
Mme Mourgue

Quartier Castel-Mouisson
13570 Barbentane
Tel. 04 90 95 51 17
Fax 04 90 95 67 63
contact@hotel-castelmouisson.com
www.hotel-castelmouisson.com

Closed 1 Mar to 31 Oct • 17 rooms, all with bathrooms and television • €56 to €67; breakfast €8 • No restaurant • Terrace, park, private car park. Dogs not admitted • Outdoor swimming pool, tennis

The utter peace and quiet.

This mas-inspired hotel, built at the foot of the Montagnette, boasts a lovely shady park complete with swimming pool. All the bedrooms, decorated in a rustic, understated Provençal style, overlook the garden. The welcoming lady of the house can suggest any number of leisure activities either in the park (tennis, golf) or nearby (walking, mountain biking, horse riding, jet skis, etc).

Access : Avignon sud motorway exit, follow Chateaurenard, Rognonas and Barbentane

CASSIS - 13260

48 LE CLOS DES ARÔMES
M. et Mme Bonnet

10 rue Abbé Paul-Mouton
13260 Cassis
Tel. 04 42 01 71 84
Fax 04 42 01 31 76

Closed from Jan to Feb • 14 rooms, most have shower/WC, some have bath/WC, all have television • €63 to €73; breakfast €8; half-board available • Menus €24 to €36 • Terrace, garden, garage. No dogs admitted

Epitome of the best of life in Provence.

The doors of this pretty blue-shuttered house lead into a cheerful, flowered garden. Provençal prints and colours adorn the tasteful, well-soundproofed rooms, one of which is perfect for families. The meals, equally southern in flavour, are served in the bright dining room or, in the summer, under the shade of plane trees on the terrace.

Access : From the town centre: on Place de la République, take Rue A Thiers then continue straight on past the church

PROVENCE, ALPS AND THE FRENCH RIVIERA

CHÂTEAUNEUF-LE-ROUGE - 13790

49 LA GALINIÈRE
M. et Mme Gagnières

Route de Saint-Maximin
13790 Châteauneuf-le-Rouge
Tel. 04 42 53 32 55
Fax 04 42 53 33 80
lagaliniere@aol.com
www.lagaliniere.com

Closed Sun evening from Oct to Apr • 18 rooms overlooking the courtyard or the garden, most have bath/WC, all have television • €56 to €82; breakfast €9; half-board available • Menus €26 to €53 • Terrace, garden, two car parks, one of which is private • Swimming pool, horse-riding

We most liked: 45 acres of grounds and a riding centre with horses and ponies for the kids.

Built in the 17C on the ruins of a Templar chicken farm, La Galinière was initially a coaching inn and Pope Pius VII slept here on two occasions, in 1809 and 1814. At the foothills of the Ste-Victoire mountain range, immortalised by Cézanne, the estate's elegant wrought-iron gate, still flanked by the stones designed to protect it from the carriage wheels, leads into the inn, which now offers rooms decorated in a rustic style and a characterful restaurant in an old outhouse with a carriage door.

Access: By the N 7, 2km from Châteauneuf-le-Rouge, towards St-Maximin-la-Sainte-Baume

FONTVIEILLE - 13990

50 VAL MAJOUR
M. Güell

22 avenue d'Arles
13990 Fontvieille
Tel. 04 90 54 62 33
Fax 04 90 54 61 67
contact@valmajour.com
www.valmajour.com

Open all year • 32 rooms with bath/WC or shower/WC and television • €62 to €125 (€50 to €83 low season); breakfast €10 • No restaurant • Park, garage, private car park • Outdoor swimming pool, tennis, table-tennis, petanque

We most liked: The trees in the park are home to dozens of busy squirrels.

A stay in this regional house built on the doorstep of Alphonse Daudet's village is always a pleasant prospect. The spacious, rustic rooms are decorated with cheerful Provençal patterns; some have a terrace, while others have a balcony overlooking the park's many trees. On the leisure side, you can choose between a dip in the superb swimming pool or a friendly tennis match in the cool of the evening.

Access: On leaving the town, by the Arles road

PROVENCE, ALPS AND THE FRENCH RIVIERA

GÉMENOS - 13420

51 PARC
M. et Mme Robin

Vallée de Saint-Pons
13420 Gémenos
Tel. 04 42 32 20 38
Fax 04 42 32 10 26
hotel.parc.gemenos@wanadoo.fr
www.hotel-parc-gemenos.com

Open all year • 13 rooms with bath/WC and television • €58 to €89 (€54 to €77 low season); breakfast €7; half-board available • Menus €17 (weekdays) to €35 • Garden, terrace, private car park

Cool down in the refreshing shade of Saint Pons Park in the summer.

This enchanting Provençal home stands in a haven of greenery just as you leave town. The rooms are modern and appealing; some enjoy a view of the park. The large bay windows of the dining room-conservatory open onto a cheerful flowered garden. The shade of the plane trees is most welcome in the heat of the summer. Friendly and unaffected.

Access: 1km on the Sainte-Baume road (D 2)

GRANS - 13450

52 DOMAINE DU BOIS VERT
M. et Mme Richard

Quartier Montauban
13450 Grans
Tel. 04 90 55 82 98
Fax 04 90 55 82 98
leboisvert@hotmail.com
www.domaineduboisvert.com

Closed from 5 Jan to 15 Feb • 3 rooms • €66 to €73, breakfast included • No table d'hôte • Terrace, park, car park. Credit cards not accepted, no dogs admitted • Outdoor swimming pool, table-tennis

The award-winning friendly owners.

This dry-stone mas is surrounded by a riverside park of oak and pine trees. All the ground floor rooms share a typical local style with terracotta tiles, exposed beams and old furniture; one has a canopied bed. Depending on the season and your inclination, breakfast is served in a large dining-sitting room or on the terrace overlooking the garden. Guests have the use of a library and a refrigerator.

Access: 7km southbound from Salon on the D 16 and then towards Lançon (D 19)

PROVENCE, ALPS AND THE FRENCH RIVIERA

GRAVESON - 13690   LES SAINTES-MARIES-DE-LA-MER - 13460

53 LE CADRAN SOLAIRE
Mme Guilmet

Rue du Cabaret-Neuf
13690 Graveson
Tel. 04 90 95 71 79
Fax 04 90 90 55 04
cadransolaire@wanadoo.fr
www.hotel-en-provence.com

Open all year (by reservation only from Nov to Mar) • 12 rooms with bath/WC or shower/WC • €55 to €80; breakfast €8 • No restaurant • Terrace, garden, locked parking

We most liked: The lady of the house treats her guests like friends of the family.

A glance at the sundial on the façade of this three-hundred-year-old post house will explain the establishment's name. Not content merely to represent the timeless charm of Provence, the energetic lady of the house was determined to breathe a new lease of life into her property, and the result is impressive! Enchanting small rooms are decorated with taste and a profusion of delicate details, the bathrooms have been redone and the wrought-iron terrace surrounded by plants is a joy to behold.

Access: In a residential area, on the way into the village

54 LE MAS DES RIÈGES
M. Ducarre

Route de Cacharel
13460 Les Saintes-Maries-de-la-Mer
Tel. 04 90 97 85 07
Fax 04 90 97 72 26
hoteldesrieges@wanadoo.fr
www.hoteldesrieges.com

Closed from 5 Jan to 5 Feb and 15 Nov to 15 Dec • 20 rooms on the ground floor with bath/WC or shower/WC, all have television • €63 to €78 (€57 to €73 low season); breakfast €7 • No restaurant (snacks available around the pool on sunny days) • Garden, car park • Swimming pool

We most liked: Step out of your ground floor room and straight into the Camargue.

Just a few minutes from the tourist bustle of the town centre and already surrounded by marshes, you won't be able to miss this hacienda-style house set in a large garden full of flowers and trees. The lovely rustic-inspired rooms are adorned with Provençal fabrics and all have a private terrace. Treat yourself to a session in the beauty institute, complete with hammam, balneotherapy and a sun bed. Horse-riding possible.

Access: In the heart of the marshes, 1km from Saintes-Maries-de-la-Mer, on the Cacharel road, then a minor road

PROVENCE, ALPS AND THE FRENCH RIVIERA

MARSEILLE - 13012

55 VILLA MARIE-JEANNE
Mme de Montmirail

4 rue Chicot
13012 Marseille
Tel. 04 91 85 51 31
Fax 04 91 49 55 74

Open all year • 3 rooms, one of which has a terrace • €60 to €75, (€50 to €65 low season), breakfast included • No table d'hôte • Garden, car park. Credit cards not accepted, no dogs admitted • Outdoor swimming pool

Not far from the famous "Stade-Vél", home of Olympique Marseille football club!

A rare pearl in the heart of a residential district that has gradually merged with the village of Saint Barnabé. The interior of this tasteful 19C house features a pleasant blend of traditional Provençal colours, old furniture, wrought-iron and contemporary works of art. The rooms are in the outbuildings and overlook the plane trees in the garden; one has a private terrace. Not to be missed!

Access : From Marseille, take Boulevard de la Blancarde eastbound

SAINT-ANDIOL - 13670

56 LE BERGER DES ABEILLES
Mme Grenier

Route de Cabanes
13670 Saint-Andiol
Tel. 04 90 95 01 91
Fax 04 90 95 48 26
abeilles13@aol.com
berger-abeilles.com

Closed from 1 Nov to Easter • 8 rooms upstairs, with bath/WC or shower/WC, all have television • €72 to €95; breakfast €10; half-board available • Restaurant closed Mon and lunchtimes except Sun; menus €36 to €53 • Terrace, garden, car park

Ask the lady of the house why the house is named "The bee shepherd"…

The authenticity of this peacefully situated mas, off the busy N7, cannot be doubted. The charm is enhanced by a wonderful flowered terrace, shaded by a majestic plane tree. The rooms, some of which are furnished with old pieces, are comfortable and well looked after; three open directly into the garden. The rustic dining room is equally appealing, as is the lady of the house's pleasant welcome.

Access : 2km to the north-west of Saint-Andiol, towards Avignon, leave the N 7 and take the D 74 E towards Cabanes

PROVENCE, ALPS AND THE FRENCH RIVIERA
SAINT-RÉMY-DE-PROVENCE - 13210   SAINT-RÉMY-DE-PROVENCE - 13210

57 L'AMANDIÈRE
M. Fougerolle-Jacquemet

Avenue Théodore Aubanel
13210 Saint-Rémy-de-Provence
Tel. 04 90 92 41 00
Fax 04 90 92 48 38
http://pers.wanadoo.fr/hotel.amandiere

Closed from early Nov to late Mar • 26 rooms, one of which has disabled access, with bath/WC or shower/WC and television • €56 to €66; breakfast €7 • No restaurant • Private car park, garden. No dogs admitted • Swimming pool

We most liked **The owners clearly have their guests' welfare at heart.**

Guests invariably fall in love with this discreet hotel tucked away in a sleepy, residential area. Trees and flowers adorn the garden which surrounds the recently built regional-style house. The rooms' fixtures and fittings are unostentatious and practical as is their sober, rustic style. Depending on the floor you will have either a balcony or a private terrace overlooking the garden. Homemade cakes often find their way onto the generously laden breakfast table. Lovely swimming pool.

Access : Near the town centre, drive down Avenue Mirabeau then Avenue de Lattre de Tassigny

58 CASTELET DES ALPILLES
Mme Canac-Roux

6 place Mireille
13210 Saint-Rémy-de-Provence
Tel. 04 90 92 07 21
Fax 04 90 92 52 03
hotel.castel.alpilles@wanadoo.fr
www.castelet-alpilles.com

Open from late Mar to early Nov • 19 rooms in 2 buildings. Most rooms have bath/WC, all have television • €68 to €92 (€65 to €88 low season); breakfast €9 • No restaurant • Garden, private car park

We most liked **Just a five minute walk from St-Rémy, home to Nostradamus and Van Gogh.**

This handsome early-20C house was built very near the antique site of Glanum. Some of the comfortable rooms possess a loggia and those on the second floor command a fine view of the Alpilles, a lovely chain of limestone hills. The immense sitting and dining rooms are decorated in true local style, but in the summer, guests generally prefer to breakfast in the lovely shaded garden.

Access : On leaving the town drive towards the site of Villa Glanum

PROVENCE, ALPS AND THE FRENCH RIVIERA

SALON-DE-PROVENCE - 13300

59 ANGLETERRE
M. Ferrandino

98 cours Carnot
13300 Salon-de-Provence
Tel. 04 90 56 01 10
Fax 04 90 56 71 75
hoteldangleterre@wanadoo.fr
www.hotel-dangleterre.biz

Closed from 20 Dec to 6 Jan • 26 rooms on 3 levels, 15 of which are air-conditioned, with bath/WC or shower/WC, all have television • €46 to €53; breakfast €7 • No restaurant

We most liked The "Château de l'Empéri": former residence of the archbishops of Arles.

This former convent dates back to the early years of the 20C and enjoys a matchless location in the heart of the old town and close to the museums. The simple, but comfortable rooms, with double-glazing and air-conditioning, lie behind well-restored walls. Breakfasting under a glazed dome has a distinctly "Empire" feel. Attentive, friendly service.

Access : In the town centre, near the pedestrian area

TARASCON - 13150

60 RUE DU CHÂTEAU
M. et Mme Laraison

24 rue du Château
13150 Tarascon
Tel. 04 90 91 09 99
Fax 04 90 91 10 33
ylaraison@wanadoo.fr

Closed from 2 Nov to 25 Dec • 5 rooms • €78 to €85, breakfast included • No table d'hôte • Credit cards not accepted, no dogs admitted

We most liked Faultless, down to the tiniest detail.

A porch and heavy door guard the entrance to this 18C edifice in a quiet side street leading up to the castle of Good King René - a truly great Renaissance man. The beautifully restored rooms are of an extremely high standard; two are reached via a lovely medieval-style staircase. As soon as the sun is warm enough, breakfast is served on a lovely flowered patio with ochre-red walls.

Access : Near the castle

PROVENCE, ALPS AND THE FRENCH RIVIERA

BRAS - 83149

61 DOMAINE LE PEYROURIER
« UNE CAMPAGNE EN PROVENCE »
M. Fussler

Chemin du Petit-Temple
83149 Bras
Tel. 04 98 05 10 20
Fax 04 98 05 10 21
info@provence4u.com
www.provence4u.com

Open all year • 6 non-smoking rooms, all with bath/WC • €75 to €83, breakfast included • Table d'hôte Tue, Thu, Sat and Sun: €19 to €28 • Terrace, park, kitchenette, garage. No dogs admitted • Open-air swimming pool, sauna, hammam, internet

Countless walks around the extensive grounds.

This immense estate bordered by vineyards and meadows is an ideal chance to discover the charm of Provence's countryside. The tastefully decorated apartments and rooms are located in former farm buildings which date back to the Knights Templar; each room is individually decorated and enjoys either a view of the countryside or the garden. Home-made and local produce take pride of place on the table d'hôte.

Access : 3km southeast by the D28, then turn left onto lane to Le Peyrourier

BRIGNOLES - 83170

62 LA CORDELINE
M. Dyens

14 rue des Cordeliers
83170 Brignoles
Tel. 04 94 59 18 66
Fax 04 94 59 00 29
lacordeline@wanadoo.com
www.lacordeline.com

Open all year • 5 rooms with bathrooms • €70 to €105, breakfast included • Table d'hôte €30 (evenings only during the week, by reservation) • Terrace, garden. No dogs admitted • Jacuzzi

Listen to the birds singing and the fountain murmuring in the garden.

A haven of well-being right in the heart of town. This splendid 17C mansion offers immense rooms furnished with family heirlooms; all have new bathrooms and a small private sitting room. As soon as the sun begins to shine, breakfasts are served outside on the terrace under the trellis.

Access : In the town centre

PROVENCE, ALPS AND THE FRENCH RIVIERA

CARQUEIRANNE - 83320   COTIGNAC - 83570

63 L'AUMÔNERIE
M. et Mme Menard

620 avenue de Fontbrun
83320 Carqueiranne
Tel. 04 94 58 53 56
www.guidesdecharme.com

Open all year • 4 rooms • €75 to €110, breakfast included • No table d'hôte • Garden, car park. Credit cards not accepted, no dogs admitted • Direct access to the beach

Take a seat in the garden and dangle your feet in the Mediterranean!

The total lack of signposts, in fact signs of any kind, bears witness to this establishment's desire to preserve the quiet tranquillity that reigns within its walls. The rooms are tastefully appointed and breakfast will be served either in your room or, whenever the weather permits, under the shade of the terrace's tall pine trees. The garden which has a tiny staircase down to the sea, was what we liked best, however. All that now remains is to enjoy the luxury of your very own private beach.

Access: In a park by the seaside; 5km from Hyères

64 DOMAINE DE NESTUBY
M. et Mme Roubaud

Route de Montfort
83570 Cotignac
Tel. 04 94 04 60 02
Fax 04 94 04 79 22
nestuby@wanadoo.fr
www.sejour-en-provence.com

Closed from 15 Nov to 1 Mar • 5 rooms • €70 to €80, breakfast included; half-board available • Table d'hôte €22 (closed weekends) • Car park. Credit cards not accepted • Sauna, fitness centre

Nathalie and Jean-François love introducing guests to their estate's red, white and rosé wines.

You know you're in for a treat as soon as you catch sight of this lovely 19C property surrounded by vineyards. The pastel coloured rooms, furnished with items picked up in second-hand and antique shops, are named after the region's grape varieties. The large country dining table is in the old cow-shed, surrounded by mangers and a fireplace. In the summer, you will appreciate the shade of the plane trees and the cool spring water of the large pond.

Access: 5km southbound from Cotignac towards Brignoles

PROVENCE, ALPS AND THE FRENCH RIVIERA

DRAGUIGNAN - 83300

65 LES OLIVIERS
M. Chaillard

Route de Flayosc
83300 Draguignan
Tel. 04 94 68 25 74
Fax 04 94 68 57 54
hotel-les-oliviers@club-internet.fr
www.hotel-les-oliviers.com

Closed 5 to 20 Jan • 12 ground-floor rooms with shower/WC and television, 1 with disabled access • €57 to €61, (€52 to €56 low season); breakfast €8 • No restaurant • Terrace, garden, car park • Outdoor swimming pool

What better start to a summer's day than breakfast on the terrace overlooking the garden?

The nearby road will vanish as soon as you put down your suitcase in this recently-built hotel inspired by regional architectural traditions. Its cosy rooms are all excellently soundproofed and some sport the warm bright colours of Provence. A few overlook the swimming pool and a well-tended garden, planted, unsurprisingly enough given the establishment's name, with Mediterranean plants including olive trees!

Access : 4km on the road to Flayosc then the D 557

FRÉJUS - 83600

66 LES VERGERS DE MONTOUREY
M. Artaud

Vallée du Reyran
83600 Fréjus
Tel. 04 94 40 85 76
Fax 04 94 40 85 76
arttotof@wanadoo.fr
http://perso.wanadoo.fr/vergers.montourey

Open from Feb to 1 Nov • 6 non-smoking rooms with bath/WC and television • €58, breakfast included • Table d'hôte €20, drinks included (Mon, Wed and Fri) • Terrace, garden, park, car park. Credit cards not accepted, dogs not admitted • Table-tennis, children's bicycles, slide

Getting into the spirit of life on the farm.

This delightful maison d'hôte in the Reyran Valley does full justice to its former farming function. The spacious, beautifully cared-for rooms are named after and decorated in the colours of fruit grown on the estate: strawberry, cherry, plum, peach, almond and fig. Home-grown produce takes pride of place on the great breakfast and dinner table, where owners and guests all sit down together, either in a country-style dining room or on the terrace. Excellent advice for tourists. Children welcome.

Access : In Montourey neighbourhood

PROVENCE, ALPS AND THE FRENCH RIVIERA

GRIMAUD - 83310

67 LA TOSCANE
M. et Mme Leroy

RD 44- quartier de l'Avelan
83310 Grimaud
Tel. 04 94 43 24 11
latoscane @ free.fr
www.la-toscane.com

Open 1 Apr to mid-Oct, closed 1 week in Nov, open in low season on request • 4 non-smoking rooms with bathroom • €75 to €80 (€60 to €65 low season), breakfast included • No table d'hôte • Terrace, garden, car park. Credit cards not accepted, no dogs admitted • Swimming pool

We most liked **The care taken with the outdoor fixtures and interior decoration.**

The roughcast ochre-orange walls, the patio (complete with well) of this lovely villa all bring Tuscany to mind. Relax in one of the exquisitely decorated rooms (stained wood furniture, quilted bedspreads, glazed lava tiles), each one named after a colour: off-white, yellow, orange and lavender. All have a pergola and terrace equipped with deckchair and wrought-iron furniture. Teak sun beds await guests around the pool, and there is a beautifully tended garden. (Well-behaved) children welcome!

Access : 4km north-east of Grimaud on the D 14 and the D 44 towards Plan-de-la-Tour.

LE BEAUSSET - 83330

68 LES CANCADES
M. et Mme Zerbib

1195 chemin de la Fontaine-de-Cinq-Sous
83330 Le Beausset
Tel. 04 94 98 76 93
Fax 04 94 90 24 63
charlotte.zerbib @ wanadoo.fr

Open all year • 4 rooms • €75, breakfast included • No table d'hôte • Garden, car park. Credit cards not accepted, no dogs admitted • Outdoor swimming pool

We most liked **Breathe in the scent of pine, olive and cypress trees.**

A steep, narrow lane takes you up to this Provençal villa surrounded by pine and olive trees in a quiet, wooded residential district. Designed by the owner, a retired architect, the tasteful rooms are of varying sizes; two have a terrace overlooking the sumptuous swimming pool. The summer kitchen is in a cabin in the pleasant garden.

Access : 3km eastbound from Castellet, then opposite the Casino supermarket take chemin de la Fontaine de Cinq-Sous.

PROVENCE, ALPS AND THE FRENCH RIVIERA

LE CANNET-DES-MAURES - 83340

69 LA HAUTE VERRERIE
M. Brun

Route de Saint-Tropez
83340 Le Cannet-des-Maures
Tel. 04 94 47 95 51
Fax 04 94 47 95 51
lahauteverrerie@aol.com

Open all year • 3 rooms • €55 to €60, breakfast included • No table d'hôte • Garden, car park. Credit cards not accepted • Outdoor swimming pool

We most liked Right on the edge of the Forest of Maures.

A stream runs at the foot of this delightful mid-18C house, originally built as a glass-blowing workshop. The outbuildings are now home to individually decorated rooms. We loved the one under the eaves of the old attic, which has its own sun-deck, and the tiny stone cottage in the garden. A fireside adds character to the sitting room and the swimming pool in the small garden is also very welcome.

Access : 6km eastbound from Luc on the D 558, towards Saint-Tropez.

LE LUC - 83340

70 LE HAMEAU DE CHARLES-AUGUSTE
Mme Gaudin

Chemin de Baraouque
83340 Le Luc
Tel. 04 94 60 79 45
Fax 04 94 60 79 45
margaud@wanadoo.fr
www.provenceweb.fr/83/charles-auguste

Open all year • 4 non-smoking rooms • €58 to €84 (€50 to €74 low season), breakfast included • Table d'hôte €25 (by reservation) • Terrace, garden, car park. Credit cards not accepted • Swimming pool

We most liked Listening to the owner's tales of the house.

Not a real hamlet as such, it is more a collection of buildings built over time around the original 18C farmhouse. All have been restored with a great deal of taste and warmth, and the comfortable, individually decorated rooms are most appealing, furnished with old family heirlooms and pieces picked up here and there. In fine weather, breakfast is served by the swimming pool in the shade of plane and chestnut trees. A perfectly charming spot and a faultless welcome.

Access : Southbound of Luc, towards the public swimming pool, turn right before the pool towards the Source de la Pioule.

PROVENCE, ALPS AND THE FRENCH RIVIERA

LES MAYONS - 83340

71 DOMAINE DE LA FOUQUETTE
M. et Mme Aquadro

83340 Les Mayons
Tel. 04 94 60 00 69
Fax 04 94 60 02 91
domaine.fouquette@wanadoo.fr
www.domainedelafouquette.com

Closed from Nov to Feb • 4 non-smoking rooms, 1 with disabled access • €60, breakfast included; half-board available • Table d'hôte €20 (evenings only except Sun) • Terrace, garden, car park

We most liked **Diving into this oasis of tranquillity and recharging our batteries.**

A wine-growing estate surrounds this isolated but welcoming farm on the edge of the Maures mountain range. The quiet bedrooms are simply decorated in a Provençal style and the rustic restaurant sports a fireplace and a terrace commanding a superb view. A number of the aperitifs and some respectable little Côtes de Provence wines are produced on the estate and local delicacies have naturally found pride of place on the table d'hôte. Nearby are Tortoise Village and the Mayons Forest.

Access: 10km south-east of Luc on the D 33 and the D 279 on the edge of the Maures mountains

LORGUES - 83510

72 LES PINS
Mme Perin

3630 route de Saint-Antonin
83510 Lorgues
Tel. 04 94 73 91 97
Fax 04 94 73 91 97
www.ehol.com

Open from 15 Mar to 15 Nov • 5 non-smoking rooms with bath/WC and shower/WC • €42 to €58, breakfast included • Table d'hôte €20 (evenings only except Sun and in summer), beverages included • Terrace, car park. Credit cards not accepted, no dogs admitted • Swimming pool, play area

We most liked **The family atmosphere and bursts of laughter from the children in the pool.**

A grove of pines shades this sprawling villa built in the style of a mas next to a small vineyard. The terraces of the three suites in the annex overlook the swimming pool. The other two rooms, more basic but equally immaculately kept, are located in the main building and also decorated in the same Provençal style as the three suites. Countless leisure activities for children who are made particularly welcome by this establishment.

Access: 4km north-west of Lorgues on the D 50 towards Entrecasteaux

PROVENCE, ALPS AND THE FRENCH RIVIERA

PUGET-VILLE - 83390

73 LE MAS DES OLIVIERS
M. Leroy

Chemin des Grands-Prés
83390 Puget-Ville
Tel. 04 94 48 30 89
Fax 04 94 48 30 89
guy.leroy18 @ wanadoo.fr
www.masdesoliviers.sup.fr

Open all year • 3 rooms • €66, breakfast included • Table d'hôte €24 • Terrace, garden, car park. Credit cards not accepted, no dogs admitted • Fitness room, sauna, outdoor swimming pool, horse-riding, cycling

The unmistakable stamp of Provence.

Situated in the heart of the Vars countryside and in the midst of nearly 10 acres of vineyards and olive groves, this mas will delight travellers in search of peace and quiet. Good-sized, well-kept rooms sport the colours of southern France and the bathrooms are very pleasant. The distinctive flavour of Provence can also be tasted in the ochre colours and terracotta decoration of the sitting rooms. Bicycling and horse-riding can be organised on request.

Access : 2.5km on the N 97 Cuers road

RAMATUELLE - 83350

74 LEÏ SOUCO
Mme Giraud

Le Plan - Plaine de Camarat
83350 Ramatuelle
Tel. 04 94 79 80 22
Fax 04 94 79 88 27
www.leisouco.com

Closed from mid-Oct to late Mar • 6 rooms (2 air-conditioned) with bath/WC and television • €78 to €110 (€70 to €95 low season), breakfast included • No table d'hôte • Terrace, park, car park. Credit cards not accepted • Tennis

A quiet night's sleep, far from the hubbub of the coast.

Olive, pine and other Mediterranean trees surround this Provençal house set in a wine-growing estate off the main road between Ramatuelle and St Tropez. Most of the rooms are on the ground-floor and enjoy private terraces overlooking the vineyards. The interior decoration is pleasantly sober and under-stated with immaculate walls, red tiles, bare beams, rustic furniture and bathrooms which sport Salernes tiles.

Access : 3.5km east of Ramatuelle, on the D 93 towards Saint-Tropez

PROVENCE, ALPS AND THE FRENCH RIVIERA

SALERNES - 83690

75 LA BASTIDE ROSE
M. et Mme Henny

Chemin Haut Gaudran
83690 Salernes
Tel. 04 94 70 63 30
Fax 04 94 70 77 34
labastiderose@wanadoo.fr
www.bastide-rose.com

Closed Oct to mid-Mar • 5 non-smoking rooms • €68 to €92, (€68 to €78 low season), breakfast included • Table d'hôte €23 • Terrace, park, garden, car park. Credit cards not accepted, no dogs admitted

We most liked: The rustic charm of the spot.

A stony path leads up to this delightful farm, deep in a landscape of vineyards, orchards and sweet-smelling hillsides. Enjoy a quiet night or two in its rooms and suites fitted out with bathrooms decorated with Salernes tiles; some of the rooms are split-level and have their own private terrace. The Dutch farming couple extends a warm friendly welcome to all. Delicious home-made produce features prominently on the table d'hôte: chicken, goose, olives, wine, eggs, fish, apricots, plums.

Access: 3km south-west of Salernes on the D 31 towards Entrecasteaux, go through la Bresque towards La Colle or Riforan

SANARY-SUR-MER - 83110

76 VILLA LOU GARDIAN
M. et Mme Castellano

646 route de Bandol
83110 Sanary-sur-Mer
Tel. 04 94 88 05 73
Fax 04 94 88 24 13
www.lougardian.com

Closed from Oct to Mar • 4 rooms, 2 of which are in the garden • €80 (€70 low season), breakfast included • No table d'hôte • Garden, car park. Credit cards not accepted, no dogs admitted • Outdoor swimming pool, tennis

We most liked: Conveniently located near the sandy beach of La Gorguette.

Despite the nearby road, this recent villa surrounded by palm trees and a pleasant garden is quiet and peaceful. The bedrooms are colourful and well-soundproofed and all have lovely bathrooms; we preferred those near the large swimming pool. Meals are served on the patio. Tennis courts and table-tennis available in the grounds.

Access: On the Bandol road

PROVENCE, ALPS AND THE FRENCH RIVIERA

TARADEAU - 83460 | **VINS-SUR-CARAMY - 83170**

77 LA BERGERIE DU MOULIN
M. et Mme Guillot

Chemin du Vieux Moulin
83460 Taradeau
Tel. 04 94 99 91 51
Fax 04 94 99 98 98
bergerie.moulin@wanadoo.fr
www.bergeriedumoulin.com

Open all year • 6 non-smoking rooms, air-conditioned upstairs, with bath/WC or shower/WC, satellite television and mini-bar • €85 to €105, breakfast included • Table d'hôte €35 to €40, drinks included • Terrace, garden, private car park. Credit cards not accepted • Outdoor swimming pool, jacuzzi, billiards

The owners' excellent tourist and gastronomic tips.

This characterful house nestles in a peaceful village not far from Arcs-sur-Argens and Lorgues. Rustic outer stone walls overgrown with climbers, Provençal-style bedrooms, kitchen-cum-dining room in the former sheepfold and a lovely outdoor sitting room overlooking the pool and arbour, where meals are sometimes served in the summer. The chirping of the crickets and murmuring stream which used to turn the millwheel are likely to be the only sounds you will hear!

Access: 6km from Arcs-sur-Argens on the D 10

78 CHÂTEAU DE VINS
M. Bonnet

Les Prés du Château
83170 Vins-sur-Caramy
Tel. 04 94 72 50 40
Fax 04 94 72 50 88
chateau.de.vins@wanadoo.fr
http://perso.wanadoo.fr/chateaudevins/

Closed from Nov to Mar • 5 rooms with bathrooms • €70, breakfast included • No table d'hôte • Garden, car park. Credit cards not accepted • Cultural events organised, music courses and summer concerts

A listed historic castle with an emphasis on culture, music in particular.

Saved from ruin and lovingly restored by its owner, this 16C château, complete with towers on all four corners, now offers moderately sized, but beautifully appointed and utterly peaceful rooms, each of which is named after a musician. The former hunting room is now the dining room. Art exhibitions, concerts and music courses take place throughout the year in the other elegantly restored rooms.

Access: 9km from Brignoles on the D 24, Thoronet road

PROVENCE, ALPS AND THE FRENCH RIVIERA

AVIGNON - 84000

79 DE BLAUVAC
Mme Chapron

11 rue de la Bancasse
84000 Avignon
Tel. 04 90 86 34 11
Fax 04 90 86 27 41
blauvac@aol.com
www.hotel-blauvac.com

Open all year • 16 rooms, most have bath/WC and a mezzanine, some have shower/WC, all have television • €67 to €77 (€57 to €70 low season); breakfast €7 • No restaurant • No dogs admitted

A stay in the heart of Avignon without the fuss of a busy town.

The Marquis de Blauvac built this 17C house in a quiet street near the Palais des Papes, from where Avignon's medieval "antipopes" defied Rome for almost 70 years. Its elegant wrought-iron balustrade and thick stone walls are typical of the period: the breakfast room is decorated in a Louis XV style. Most of the rooms, simply furnished but full of character, have a mezzanine with an extra bed.

Access : In the town centre, in a side street leading to Place de l'Horloge (town hall).

AVIGNON - 84000

80 LA FERME
M. Courtois

Chemin des Bois - Ile de la Barthelasse
84000 Avignon
Tel. 04 90 82 57 53
Fax 04 90 27 15 47
info@hotel-laferme.com
www.hotel-laferme.com

Closed from 15 Nov to 15 Mar • 20 air-conditioned rooms, 3 of which are non-smoking, with bath/WC or shower/WC and television • €78 to €89 (€66 to €71 low season); breakfast €10; half-board available • Restaurant closed Mon and Wed; menus €23 to €38 • Terrace, private car park. Dogs not admitted in rooms • Swimming pool

If you come here, you will have to learn the nursery rhyme "Sur le pont d'Avignon…"

This handsome farm is located near to the Papal City on the Island of Barthelasse, one of the largest in Europe and a haven of greenery in Avignon. The tastefully decorated rooms ensure that the only sounds you will hear are those of the dawn chorus. The dining room features enormous beams, thick stone walls and a huge fireplace, while out on the terrace you can relax in the shade of the ancient plane tree.

Access : 5km northbound, on the Ile de la Barthelasse, by the D 228 then a minor road

PROVENCE, ALPS AND THE FRENCH RIVIERA
AVIGNON - 84000 | AVIGNON - 84000

81 HÔTEL DE GARLANDE
Mme Michelotte

20 rue Galante
84000 Avignon
Tel. 04 90 80 08 85
Fax 04 90 27 16 58
hotel-de-garlande@wanadoo.fr
www.hotelgarlande.com

Closed Jan and Sun evenings from Nov to Mar • 11 rooms, 9 of which are air-conditioned, all with bath/WC or shower/WC, television and telephone • €69 to €109; breakfast €7 • No restaurant • Dogs not admitted

Peace and quiet in the heart of the town.

Eminently well located in a pedestrian street of the historic town, two minutes from Place de l'Horloge and the Palais des Papes, this elegant town house is now a pleasant hotel. The quiet atmosphere, the owner's warm welcome and the cosy comfort of the colourful attractive bedrooms, some of which have retained their original timber frame, all add to the charm of this hotel.

Access: In the town centre, in a pedestrian street

---

82 LE MÉDIÉVAL
M. Philippe Régis

15 rue Petite-Saunerie
84000 Avignon
Tel. 04 90 86 11 06
Fax 04 90 82 08 64
hotel.medieval@wanadoo.fr
www.hotelmedieval.com

Closed from 1 Jan to 4 Feb • 35 rooms, all have bath/WC or shower/WC and television, most have a kitchenette • €55 to €84; breakfast €7 • No restaurant • No dogs admitted • Patio

The kitchenettes in the rooms come in handy for a long stay during the festival.

This late-17C mansion built for a cardinal was formerly linked to the Papal Palace by an underground passage. A statue of the Virgin Mary stands in an alcove of its beautiful stone façade. A period staircase leads up to the rooms, a touch outdated but furnished in a rustic style. We recommend booking one of those overlooking the flowered patio, particularly during the summer. Multilingual staff.

Access: In a side street in the heart of the town, from the Porte St-Lazare, take Rue Carreterie and turn right

PROVENCE, ALPS AND THE FRENCH RIVIERA

BÉDOIN - 84410

83 LA GARANCE
M. et Mme Babinet

Hameau de Sainte-Colombe
84410 Bédoin
Tel. 04 90 12 81 00
Fax 04 90 65 93 05
info@lagarance.fr
www.lagarance.fr

Closed from 15 Nov to 1 Apr • 13 rooms located upstairs and on the ground floor, with bath/WC or shower/WC, all have television • €55 to €70 (€50 to €65 low season); breakfast €8 • No restaurant • Car park • Swimming pool

We most liked **Take on the ascent of Mont Ventoux on foot... or by car!**

It is a pleasure to drive into this pretty hamlet surrounded by vines and orchards and up to the front door of the farmhouse. Inside, the rooms' furnishings are modern and the tiles are old. You will be able to wake up and feast your eyes on Mont Ventoux, before tripping down to breakfast on the terrace or in the brightly-coloured dining room. Afterwards embark on the assault of this "giant of Provence" along signposted footpaths. Well worth writing home about.

Access : Head for Bédoin on the D 19 from Malaucène or the D 974 from Carpentras, then drive towards Mont-Ventoux

CARPENTRAS - 84200

84 LE COMTADIN
M. Van Orshoven

65 boulevard Albin-Durand
84200 Carpentras
Tel. 04 90 67 75 00
Fax 04 90 67 75 01
lreception@le-comtadin.com
www.le-comtadin.com

Closed from 12 to 21 Feb • 19 rooms, 2 of which are non-smoking, one has disabled access. Rooms have bath/WC or shower/WC, all have air-conditioning and television • €74 to €86; breakfast €12 • Menus €20 to €35 • Patio, garage

We most liked **Breakfasting on the patio.**

This late-18C mansion stands on the ring road round the busy capital of the Comtat region. Recently refurbished, it proudly sports wrought-iron furniture, high-quality materials and a contemporary decorative style. Most of the rooms overlook the peaceful patio which echoes to the murmur of the fountain in the centre. The reception is home to orchids, the owners' pride and joy.

Access : On the ring-road

PROVENCE, ALPS AND THE FRENCH RIVIERA

CHÂTEAUNEUF-DE-GADAGNE - 84470

85 LE CLOS DES SAUMANES
M. et Mme Lambert

519 chemin de la Garrigue
84470 Châteauneuf-de-Gadagne
closaumane @ aol.com
www.closaumane.com

Open all year • 6 non-smoking rooms, all with bathrooms • €75 to €100, breakfast included • No table d'hôte • Garden, car park. Credit cards not accepted, dogs not admitted • Outdoor swimming pool

We most liked Nothing is too much trouble for the owners.

This elegant 18C bastide, poised between pine forest and vineyards, is an invitation to wind down and take things easy. Don't even attempt to resist the charm of the bedrooms furnished in an old-fashioned Provençal style; one has a terrace. At the end of the day, head for the swimming pool to admire the sunset. The following morning, breakfast is served under an enormous chestnut tree in a paved courtyard.

Access : 1km along the D 97 Morières road

GORDES - 84220

86 AUBERGE DE CARCARILLE
M. Rambaud

Route d'Apt
84220 Gordes
Tel. 04 90 72 02 63
Fax 04 90 72 05 74
carcaril @ club-internet.fr
www.auberge-carcarille.com

Closed Dec, Jan and Fri (Fri evenings only from Apr to Sep) • 11 rooms with bath/WC or shower/WC and television • €60 to €75; breakfast €10; half-board available • Menus €18 to €42 • Private car park, garden, terrace. No dogs admitted • Swimming pool

We most liked Taking life easy on the private terrace of your room.

The beauty of Gordes is no longer a secret, but this discreet country inn is worth keeping to yourself! Installed in a dry-stone construction on the edge of a garden, painted furniture and an elegant Provençal style set the scene for the impeccably kept rooms. Regional dishes take pride of place on the menu and are served in the light, colourful dining room. The terrace is equally appealing.

Access : Beneath the village towards Apt

PROVENCE, ALPS AND THE FRENCH RIVIERA

GORDES - 84220

87 LA BADELLE
Mme Cortasse

84220 Gordes
Tel. 04 90 72 33 19
Fax 04 90 72 48 74
badelle@club-internet.fr
www.la-badelle.com

Open all year, by reservation in Jan and Feb • 5 rooms • €88 to €104 (€80 to €94 low season), breakfast included • No table d'hôte • Garden, car park. No dogs admitted • Outdoor swimming pool, table-tennis, hiking, petanque

A beautiful combination of old and new.

A tiny country road leads to this ancient farmhouse. The rooms in the outbuildings have been entirely redone and all feature the same whitewashed walls, rustic earthenware tiles, old furniture and excellent bathrooms. Four open onto the swimming pool. In the summer guests are offered the use of a practical kitchen.

Access: 7km southbound from Gordes on the D 104 towards Goult

LA BASTIDE-DES-JOURDANS - 84240

88 AUBERGE DU CHEVAL BLANC
M. Moullet

84240 La Bastide-des-Jourdans
Tel. 04 90 77 81 08
Fax 04 90 77 86 51
provence.luberon@wanadoo.fr

Closed in Feb and on Thu • 4 rooms with bath/WC, air-conditioning and television • €70 to €90; breakfast €10; half-board available • Air-conditioned restaurant; menus €17 (weekdays) to €37 • Terrace, private car park

The Luberon Regional Park is riddled with paths.

In just a few years, this former post house has been elegantly transformed into an up-to-date country inn. Exposed beams, thick stone walls and tiled floors set the scene for the spacious, welcoming rooms, some of which have a small cane-furnished sitting room. Warm, sunny colours adorn the elegant dining room which leads into the dappled shade of a quiet terrace.

Access: On the main road of the village

PROVENCE, ALPS AND THE FRENCH RIVIERA

LAURIS - 84360

89 LA MAISON DES SOURCES
Mme Collart

Chemin des Fraisses
84360 Lauris
Tel. 04 90 08 22 19
Fax 04 90 08 22 19
contact@maison-des-sources.com
www.maison-des-sources.com

Open all year • 4 rooms with bathrooms • €85 to €87, breakfast included • Table d'hôte €25 (evenings) • Garden, car park. Credit cards not accepted • Hiking, horse-riding, mountain biking

Breakfast in the welcome shade of acacia trees.

This old farmhouse, built against a cliff face riddled with caves, is hidden in the midst of vineyards, orchards and olive groves in the Luberon foothills. After some major restoration work it was saved from ruin and now offers brightly coloured rooms, the most curious of which features no less than four four-poster beds. The sitting and dining rooms have fine old vaulted ceilings and the somewhat unruly garden only adds to the appeal.

Access : 4.5km to the south-west of Lourmarin on the D 27

LE BARROUX - 84330

90 LES GÉRANIUMS
M. Awada Huw

Place de la Croux
84330 Le Barroux
Tel. 04 90 62 41 08
Fax 04 90 62 56 48
les.geraniums@wanadoo.fr
www.hotel-lesgeraniums.com

Closed 3 Jan to 19 Mar • 22 rooms located in 2 buildings, with bath/WC or shower/WC • €55 to €60; breakfast €10; half-board available • Air-conditioned restaurant; menus €20 to €35 • Terrace, garden, private car park. No dogs admitted • Llama farm in the village

Hiking through vineyards and olive groves in the foothills of the Montmirail.

This impressive stone house stands in the heart of a fortified village overlooking the Comtat plain. The spotless rooms are furnished in a rustic style; some have balconies facing the valley. The chef's delicious recipes, made with local produce, are definitely worth sampling, either on the spacious terrace which overflows with geraniums or in the dining room decorated with paintings left by an artist and regular visitor to the establishment.

Access : In the centre of the village

PROVENCE, ALPS AND THE FRENCH RIVIERA

LE BARROUX - 84330

91 HOSTELLERIE FRANÇOIS JOSEPH
M. Pochat

Chemin des Rabassières
84330 Le Barroux
Tel. 04 90 62 52 78
Fax 04 90 62 33 54
hotel.f.joseph@wanadoo.fr
www.hotel-francois-joseph.com

Open from 10 Apr to 31 Oct • 12 rooms, 6 are apartments, 5 are studios and one has disabled access. All have bath/WC or shower/WC and television • €75 to €110; breakfast €12; half-board available • Menus €25 (evening only except Sun and Thu) • Park, car park. Dogs not admitted • Outdoor swimming pool

Snoozing under the umbrella pines.

In the heart of the countryside, this group of modern buildings has remained true to local architectural tradition. The modern rooms are brightened up by cheerful fabrics; half have loggias or ground floor terraces and families can book one of two cottages. A happy mixture of unruly bushes cohabit peacefully with perfect lawns in the garden and from the swimming pool, you can admire the view of Mont Ventoux.

Access : 2km from Barrous on the Monastères Ste-Madeleine road

LE BARROUX - 84330

92 MAS DE LA LAUSE
M. et Mme Lonjon

Chemin de Geysset
84330 Le Barroux
Tel. 04 90 62 33 33
Fax 04 90 62 36 36
maslause@provence-gites.com
www.provence-gite.com

Closed from 15 Nov to Mar • 5 rooms with shower/WC • €59, breakfast included • Table d'hôte €18 • Garden, car park

Apricot rooms, apricot trees, apricot jam and nectar of apricot.

Nestled among vineyards and apricot trees, this mas built in 1883 has been renovated in true Provençal fashion. The bright sunny rooms, recently repainted, echo their evocative names. Sunflower and Iris overlook the castle of Barroux and the Comtat plain, while Apricot faces the orchards. How about a quick game of pétanque before sampling the tasty regional cooking under the shade of the arbour or the vaulted ceiling of the dining room?

Access : 800m from Le Barroux, towards Suzette

PROVENCE, ALPS AND THE FRENCH RIVIERA

LE CRESTET - 84110

93 LE MAS DE MAGALI
M. et Mme Bodewes

Quartier Chante-Coucou
84110 Le Crestet
Tel. 04 90 36 39 91
Fax 04 90 28 73 40
masmagali@wanadoo.fr
www.masdemagali.com/formhtml

Open from 28 Mar to 16 Oct • 11 rooms with bath/WC and television • €69 to €75; breakfast €8; half-board available • Restaurant closed Wed; menus €25 to €28 • Terrace, garden, car park. Dogs not admitted in restaurant • Outdoor swimming pool

The heady perfume of Provence's vegetation.

The utter peace and quiet, magnificent view of Mont Ventoux and the remote Vaucluse landscape, colourful blue and yellow dining room and spacious rooms, some with terraces: this modern mas captures all that is best in Provence. Magali, the lady of the house, oversees every aspect of your stay from pétanque and pastis to a quiet afternoon nap.

Access: Leave Vaison-la-Romaine on the D 938 (towards Malaucène) and after 3.5km, turn right (D 76)

LOURMARIN - 84160

94 LE MAS DE GUILLES
M. et Mme Lherm

Route de Vaugines
84160 Lourmarin
Tel. 04 90 68 30 55
Fax 04 90 68 37 41
hotel@guilles.com
www.guilles.com

Open from late Apr to early Nov • 28 rooms with bath/WC and television • €80 to €115; breakfast €13; half-board available • Menu €43 • Terrace, garden, private car park. No dogs admitted in restaurant • Outdoor swimming pool, tennis

The perfect peace and quiet.

A stony, but driveable path, leads to a delightful Provençal mas nestled in the midst of vineyards and orchards. The eye is drawn to the enchanting swimming pool surrounded by lawns where deck-chairs invite visitors to settle back and relax. Lovely old wardrobes, period furniture and warm yellow colours set the tone for the bedrooms. The chef's classical cuisine is served in an attractive, vaulted dining room or - weather permitting - on the sun-drenched terrace.

Access: 2km from Lourmarin

PROVENCE, ALPS AND THE FRENCH RIVIERA

MORNAS - 84550

95 LE MANOIR
M. ou Mme Caillet

Avenue Jean-Moulin
84550 Mornas
Tel. 04 90 37 00 79
Fax 04 90 37 10 34
linfo@lemanoir-mornas.fr
www.hotel-le-manoir.com

Closed 10 Jan to 10 Feb • 25 rooms located in 2 wings with bath/WC or shower/WC, some have air-conditioning and television • €50 to €75; breakfast €7; half-board available • Restaurant closed Mon and Tue lunchtimes from Jun to Sep; Sun evening, Mon and Tue lunchtime from Oct to May; menus €17 (weekdays) to €60 • Terrace, car park, garage

Wining and dining by candlelight on the patio.

This impressive 18C mansion stands at the foot of a steep cliff, dominated by the outline of Mornas fortress. The new owners have so far concentrated their restoration efforts on the restaurant, but they plan to redo the rooms shortly. That said, beautiful old wardrobes and marble fireplaces add a great deal of old-fashioned charm to the rooms. The verdant patio and flowered terrace echo to the light-hearted, sunny disposition of Provence.

Access : Beside the N 7 through the village

MURS - 84220

96 LES HAUTS DE VÉRONCLE
M. et Mme Pouget

84220 Murs
Tel. 04 90 72 60 91
Fax 04 90 72 62 07
hauts.de.veroncle@wanadoo.fr
http://hauts.de.veroncle.free.fr

Closed from 4 Nov to 29 Mar • 3 rooms • €51 to €53, breakfast included • Table d'hôte €21 (evenings) except Sun and Wed • Terrace, garden, car park. Credit cards not accepted, no dogs admitted in dining room

Ever longed to be somewhere no-one could find you?

In the middle of nowhere – there is no other way to describe the peaceful tranquillity of this blue-shuttered mas with its dry stone walls, fragrant garrigue and chirping cicadas. A sophisticated cuisine is served by the fireside in winter or under the wisteria in the summer. If you feel like a walk, ask Mr or Mrs Del Corso to point you towards the path of the seven mills which runs alongside the gorges of the Véroncle.

Access : 8km to the north-east of Sénanque on the D 177, the D 244 then the D 15

PROVENCE, ALPS AND THE FRENCH RIVIERA
ORANGE - 84100   PERNES-LES-FONTAINES - 84210

97 MAS DES AIGRAS
M. et Mme Davi

Chemin des Aigras
84100 Orange
Tel. 04 90 34 81 01
Fax 04 90 34 05 66
masdesaigras@free.fr

Closed from 1 to 12 Jan, 24 Oct to 9 Nov, Tue, Wed and Sat lunchtime from Apr to Sep • 12 non-smoking rooms, 8 of which are air-conditioned, all have bath/WC or shower/WC and television • €70 to €110; breakfast €11; half-board available • Menus €26 (weekdays) to €50 • Terrace, garden, private car park. No dogs admitted • Outdoor swimming pool

We most liked: The amazing botanical garden of a leading 19C entomologist, J-H Fabre.

The stone walls of this mas are hidden amid vineyards and fields on the outskirts of Orange. The cheerful young owners have thrown themselves into the task of rejuvenating their property, adding colourful cotton fabrics and hand-painted walls. Little by little, the rooms are regaining their rightful Provençal colours and are also being treated to air-conditioning. Organic produce figures prominently on the up-to-date menu, served in a dining room or on a teak and wrought-iron furnished terrace.

Access: 4km northbound from Orange on the N 7, then take a minor road (100m from the bypass)

98 L'HERMITAGE
Mme Oury

Route de Carpentras
84210 Pernes-les-Fontaines
Tel. 04 90 66 51 41
Fax 04 90 61 36 41
hotel.lhermitage@libertysurf.fr
www.hotel-lhermitage.com

Closed Dec to Feb • 20 rooms upstairs, most have bath/WC, all have television • €74 to €86 (€60 to €72 low season); breakfast €9 • No restaurant • Park, private car park • Swimming pool

We most liked: A refreshing drink from one of the 36 fountains of the "pearl of the Comtat".

Once the property of a relative of the famous Captain Dreyfus, whose court-martial divided public opinion in 1890s France and inspired Emile Zola's famous counterblast "J'accuse", this 19C house has retained a characteristically Provençal atmosphere. Majestic trees, statues and fountains abound in the immense park, together with a host of shaded corners, perfect for a quiet pastis. The colourful rooms are gradually being refurbished. The sitting rooms are decorated with period furniture.

Access: Set back from the road, 2km northbound from Pernes-les-Fontaines, towards Carpentras on the D 938

PROVENCE, ALPS AND THE FRENCH RIVIERA

ROAIX - 84110

99 LES AUZIÈRES
M. Cuer

84110 Roaix
Tel. 04 90 46 15 54
Fax 04 90 46 12 75
alain@auzieres.fr
www.auzieres.fr

Closed late Oct • 5 rooms with bathrooms, separate WC and television • €77, breakfast included • Table d'hôte €25 including beverages (from Mon to Fri only by reservation) • Car park • Outdoor swimming pool, petanque, table-tennis, billiards

A sweeping view of the valley.

It would be hard to find a more secluded spot than this Provençal farm perched on a hillside in the midst of vineyards, olive groves and lavender fields. The spacious, cool bedrooms are spotless and utterly tranquil. Sample the traditional cooking at a huge wooden table in the dining room or on the terrace, facing Mont Ventoux and the jagged peaks of the Dentelles de Montmirail.

Access: 6km westbound from Vaison on the D 975 towards Orange

ROUSSILLON - 84220

100 LES SABLES D'OCRE
M. Hilario

Les Sablières
84220 Roussillon
Tel. 04 90 05 55 55
Fax 04 90 05 55 50
sablesdocre@free.fr
www.roussillon-hotel.com

Closed from early Nov to late Mar • 22 rooms with balcony, or terrace on the ground floor, 2 have disabled access, all have bath/WC or shower/WC, air-conditioning and television • €62 to €75 (€55 to €65 low season); breakfast €10 • No restaurant • Garden, car park • Outdoor swimming pool

Walk along the "ochre footpath" to the breathtaking Giants' Causeway.

The colourful walls of this modern hotel pay homage to the "red villages" of Roussillon and their picturesque houses. The mas built in 1998 on the outskirts of the village offers rooms which are handsomely equipped and have a balcony or garden-level terrace, even though they do rather lack character; some have brass beds. 400m away, the old Mathieu factory has been turned into a pigment conservatory – tours and courses.

Access: Around 10km from Apt, towards Avignon, leave the N 100 and turn right onto the D 149 for 4.5km

PROVENCE, ALPS AND THE FRENCH RIVIERA

VAISON-LA-ROMAINE - 84110

101 L'ÉVÊCHÉ
M. et Mme Verdier

Rue de l'Évêché
84110 Vaison-la-Romaine
Tel. 04 90 36 13 46
Fax 04 90 36 32 43
eveche@aol.com
http://eveche.free.fr

Closed from 15 Nov to 15 Dec • 3 rooms and 2 apartments • €70 to €80, breakfast included • No table d'hôte • Terrace. Credit cards not accepted, no dogs admitted

A warm country welcome after a hard day's sightseeing.

This former Episcopal palace, dating from the 16C, stands in the medieval part of town. Most of its countless rooms, on a variety of levels, overlook a tiny terrace. The breakfast room is the largest and it offers a wonderful view of the lower town. A lovely spiral staircase winds up to the well-furnished and tasteful rooms. Don't forget to take a look at the interesting collection of prints originally from a treatise on lockmaking.

Access : In the old town

VIOLÈS - 84150

102 LA FARIGOULE
Mme Favrat

Le Plan-de-Dieu
84150 Violès
Tel. 04 90 70 91 78
Fax 04 90 70 91 78
www.la-farigoule.com

Closed from Nov to Mar • 5 rooms, including one studio, with shower/WC • €45 to €55, breakfast included • No table d'hôte • Garden, car park. Credit cards not accepted • Play area, table-tennis

The erudite atmosphere of this characterful house.

This 18C wine-growers' house has lost none of its authenticity over the years. A fine staircase leads up to antique furnished rooms, each of which is named after a writer with Provence connections, including Frédéric Mistral, Alphonse Daudet and Marie Mauron; you won't be surprised to discover that your hosts used to own a book shop. Breakfasts are served in a lovely vaulted room. As for free time, there is a play area for children and the hotel rents out bicycles (including tandems).

Access : 10km westbound from Gigondas on the D 80 towards Orange, then the D 8 and the D 977 towards Violès

PROVENCE, ALPS AND THE FRENCH RIVIERA

VIOLÈS - 84150

103 MAS DE BOUVAU
M. et Mme Hertzog

Route de Cairanne
84150 Violès
Tel. 04 90 70 94 08
Fax 04 90 70 95 99

Closed from 15 Dec to 31 Jan, evenings from Nov to Feb, every lunchtime Jun-Aug, Sat, Sun evenings, Tue lunchtime and Mon • 6 rooms with bath/WC or shower/WC and television • €60 to €70; breakfast €9; half-board available • Menus €26 • Terrace, garden, car park. No dogs admitted in rooms

Daydreaming as you gaze on the jagged peaks of the Dentelles de Montmirail.

This old farmhouse is surrounded by the vineyards of the Plan de Dieu plateau which have been cultivated since the Middle Ages. The sober rooms are furnished with sturdy country pieces. Sample the traditional menu in one of the Provençal dining rooms or on the terraces – our favourite is in the old barn. The wine-list is a credit to the region.

Access : Northbound from Violès, leave the D 977 and turn left towards Cairanne

RHÔNE-ALPES

A land of contrasts and a crossroads of culture, the Rhône-Alpes region offers visitors a thousand different faces. Its lofty peaks are heaven on earth to skiers, climbers and hikers attracted by the sublime beauty of its glittering glaciers, torrential streams and tranquil lakes, while its fashionable resorts, like Chamonix and Courchevel, set the tone in alpine chic. If you can tear yourself away from the roof of Europe, venture down past the herds of cattle grazing on the rich mountain grass and into the intense bustle of the Rhône valley, symbolised by its fast-flowing waters. From Antique Roman roads to high-speed inter-city trains, the main artery between north and south has forged the reputation of this region's economic drive. Rhône-Alpes lies on the route taken by hordes of holidaymakers every summer, and those in the know always make a point of stopping in the region to taste its culinary specialities. The area abounds in restaurants, from three-star trend-setters to Lyon's legendary neighbourhood *bouchons*, whose standards and traditions have made the region the kingdom of cuisine.

- Ain (01)
- Ardèche (07)
- Drôme (26)
- Isère (38)
- Loire (42)
- Rhône (69)
- Savoie (73)
- Haute-Savoie (74)

RHÔNE ALPES

AMBÉRIEUX-EN-DOMBES - 01330

1 AUBERGE DES BICHONNIÈRES
M. Sauvage

Route de Savigneux
01330 Ambérieux-en-Dombes
Tel. 04 74 00 82 07
Fax 04 74 00 89 61
bichonnier@aol.com
www.aubergedesbichonnieres.com

Closed 15 Dec to 15 Jan, Sun eve (Mon and Tue lunchtime in Jul-Aug) • 9 rooms with bath/WC or shower/WC and television • €50; breakfast €8; half-board available • Menus €15 to €32 • Terrace, garden, private car park

The charm of the "Route des étangs" (Pond Route).

Guests are pampered within the cob walls of this old farm, typical of the Dombes region. The rooms overlooking the courtyard, although a little on the small side, are refreshingly quiet. The cuisine draws on local traditions and ingredients and is served in a rustic dining room near an old stove or under a canopy on the terrace. Rows of crimson geraniums brighten up the peaceful garden.

Access : On leaving the town, on the Ars-sur-Formans road

BRENS - 01300

2 FERME DES GRANDS HUTAINS
M. et Mme Veyron

Le Petit Brens
01300 Brens
Tel. 04 79 81 90 95
Fax 04 79 81 90 95

Closed in Nov and on Sun • 4 non-smoking rooms with bath/WC • €45 (€40 low season), breakfast included • Table d'hôte €13 to €15 • Terrace, car park. Credit cards not accepted, dogs not admitted in dining room

Enjoyable meals of beautifully cooked garden-fresh vegetables.

The farmhouse and pergola are delightful. The rooms under the eaves are snugly welcoming, furnished with family heirlooms and decorated in an old-fashioned style; all are non-smoking. The dining table, which shows the chef's preference for home-grown produce, is located in a welcoming room where a fire is lit in winter, or when the weather allows, around a stone table in the garden under the shade of an oak and birch trees.

Access : 3km southbound from Belley on the D 31A

RHÔNE ALPES

CHÂTILLON-LA-PALUD - 01320

3 AUBERGE DE CAMPAGNE DU MOLLARD
M. Decré

01320 Châtillon-la-Palud
Tel. 04 74 35 66 09
Fax 04 37 61 11 72
f.decre@wanadoo.fr
www.aubergedumollard.com

Open all year by reservation • 4 rooms • €65, breakfast included • Menus €17 to €35 • Car park. Credit cards accepted in restaurant, no dogs admitted

We most liked — The religiously preserved rustic appeal.

A tiny country lane will take you up to this attractive farmhouse and courtyard-garden bedecked with flowers – a sight to behold in the spring. The four rooms in an outbuilding have wonderful carved wooden beds, but have a shared bathroom. Meals are served in a country-style dining room with a fireplace and a huge cauldron. The tasty family cooking focuses on local produce.

Access: 14km north-east of Pérouges on the D 984 and the D 904, towards Chalamont, then a lane on the left

CHÂTILLON-SUR-CHALARONNE - 01400

4 L'INATTENDU
M. et Mme Jacquet

150 place du Champ-de-Foire
01400 Châtillon-sur-Chalaronne
Tel. 04 74 55 06 86
Fax 04 74 55 42 56
amrjacquet@inattendu-hotes.fr
www.inattendu-hotes.fr

Closed from 22 Dec to 8 Jan • 5 rooms • €56 to €65, breakfast included • Table d'hôte €22 (by reservation) • Garden, car park. No dogs admitted

We most liked — A breakfast worth getting up for!

Old wardrobes, a wooden staircase, huge beams and floral wallpaper: the stage is set and the curtain can rise on this welcoming home. Bunches of fresh flowers and well-polished wooden furniture greet you in the rooms. Make sure you get up early and have had time to work up an appetite, if you want to do justice to the substantial mounds of croissants, walnut bread, pancakes and no less than thirty home-made jams!

Access: In the town centre

RHÔNE ALPES
ÉVOSGES - 01230   GEX - 01170

5 L'AUBERGE CAMPAGNARDE
Mme Merloz

Le Village
01230 Évosges
Tel. 04 74 38 55 55
Fax 04 74 38 55 62
auberge-campagnarde@wanadoo.fr

Closed from 2 Jan to 2 Feb, 5 to 14 Sep and 14 to 30 Nov • 15 rooms with bath/WC or shower/WC, all have television • €42 to €67; breakfast €8; half-board available • Menus €18 to €50 • Terrace, garden, car park • Outdoor swimming pool, mini golf, table tennis, play area, fishing

Ideal for nature lovers with energetic children.

This old family farmstead in a remote village of Bugey has been turned into a lovely country inn with rustic or modern-style rooms and an inviting restaurant with stone walls and a fireplace. Children however generally prefer the shaded garden with play area, mini-golf and swimming pool.

Access : Leave the N 504 (Ambérieu-Belley) between St Rambert-en-Bugey and Argis and follow the D 34

6 LA MAINAZ
M. Part

Route du col de la Faucille - N 5
01170 Gex
Tel. 04 50 41 31 10
Fax 04 50 41 31 77
mainaz@club-internet.com
www.la-mainaz.com

Closed Sun evening and Mon except during school holidays and from 1 Nov to 10 Dec • 22 rooms with bath/WC and shower/WC and television • €62 to €92; breakfast €12; half-board available • Restaurant closed Sun evening, Mon and Tue lunchtime; menus €20 (weekdays) to €52 • Car park • Swimming pool

Contemplating the view of Lake Geneva and the Alps in the distance.

The same family has been presiding over the destiny of this high-perched chalet leading up to the Col de la Faucille for three generations. Some of the rooms command a superb view of the region, as do the restaurant terrace and swimming pool. Varnished pine panelling and 70s furniture gives an idea of the general decorative style, but some of the rooms were recently spruced up and a few also boast balconies. Fill up your lungs with sweet mountain air!

Access : 1km from the Col de la Faucille, on the N 5, towards Gex

RHÔNE ALPES

MIRIBEL - 01700

7 LA VILLA DU RHÔNE
M. et Mme Cabardi

Chemin de la Lune
01700 Miribel
Tel. 04 78 55 54 16
Fax 04 78 55 54 16
contact@lavilladurhone.com
www.lavilladurhone.com

Open all year • 4 rooms • €80 to €100, breakfast included • Table d'hôte €25 (evening only) • Garden, car park. Credit cards not accepted • Outdoor swimming pool

Peace and quiet on the threshold of Lyons.

This modern villa on the heights of Miribel commands a superb view of the Rhône and the valley. Two of the three rooms overlooking the swimming pool have their own private terrace with a view of the landscape. The redbrick walls of the sitting room on the veranda, complete with indoor garden and fireplace, are full of appeal. Breakfast on the terrace in the summer is a pure joy.

Access : 12km to the north-east of Lyon, A 46, Eastbound round Lyon, Rillieux exit, then D 71 towards the Mas-Rillier and Miribel

NEUVILLE-SUR-AIN - 01160

8 CHAMBRE D'HÔTE DE BOSSERON
Mme Rivoire

325 route de Genève
01160 Neuville-sur-Ain
Tel. 04 74 37 77 06
Fax 04 74 37 77 06
arivoire@free.fr
http://arivoire.free.fr

Closed from 1 Nov to Easter • 4 rooms with bathrooms • €60, breakfast included • No table d'hôte • Park, car park. Credit cards not accepted, no dogs admitted • Fitness room, billiards, bicycles

Immaculately decorated.

You won't regret your decision to stay here when you see the impressive manor house and the five acres of parkland on the banks of the Ain. Good taste and a flair for interior decoration have resulted in comfortable, well-soundproofed rooms. A fitness room and billiards table in the outbuildings are for the sole use of guests. Your gracious hostess certainly knows how to make visitors feel welcome.

Access : 8km to the north-east of Pont-d'Ain on the N 84

RHÔNE ALPES
SAINT-MARTIN-DE-BAVEL - 01510   SERVAS - 01960

9 SNC LES CHARMETTES
Mme Vincent

La Vellaz
01510 Saint-Martin-de-Bavel
Tel. 04 79 87 32 18
Fax 04 79 87 34 51

Open all year • 3 rooms, one of which has disabled access • €44, breakfast included • No table d'hôte • Car park. Credit cards not accepted • Hiking and mountain biking

Mother Nature at her best.

Why not treat yourself to a stay in this lovely farmhouse and enjoy the superb surrounding countryside? The snug, comfortable rooms are in the beautifully restored stables and one is equipped for disabled guests. Visitors have the use of a fitted kitchen and dining and sitting rooms in a separate wing. The owner is extremely knowledgeable about his region's tourist attractions.

Access : 11km northbound from Belley on the N 504 as far as Chazey-Bons, then take the D 31C

10 LE NID À BIBI
Mme Bibus

Lieu-dit Lalleyriat
01960 Servas
Tel. 04 74 21 11 47
Fax 04 74 21 02 83
lenidabibi@wanadoo.fr
www.lenidabibi.com

Open all year • 5 non-smoking rooms, all with bath/WC, 1 with balneo bathtub • €90 to €110, breakfast included • Table d'hôte €20 to €30 • Park. Dogs not admitted • Indoor counter-current swimming pool, fitness facilities, sauna, tennis, table tennis, mountain bikes

The very high standard of facilities.

This carefully restored farmhouse offers comfortable accommodation, furnished in a mixture of old and new. Countless leisure activities available on site including a keep-fit room, sauna, covered swimming pool, table-tennis, tennis courts in the grounds and bicycles for rides in the forest. The generous breakfast (free range eggs, cheese, etc) will give you all the energy you need to throw yourself into one or other of the activities available.

Access : 5km south of N 83, then 2km on the D 22 and minor road to the left

RHÔNE ALPES

ALBA-LA-ROMAINE - 07400

11 LE JEU DU MAIL
M. et Mme Arlaud

07400 Alba-la-Romaine
Tel. 04 75 52 41 59
Fax 04 75 52 41 59
lejeudumail @ free.fr
http://lejeudumail.free.fr

Closed 15 Nov to 15 Mar • 5 rooms • €54 to €75, breakfast included • No table d'hôte • Garden, terrace, car park. Credit cards not accepted, no dogs admitted • Outdoor swimming pool

A lengthy lunch under the trellis or in the shade of the plane tree.

The owners of this former 19C Templar stronghold were among the precursors of the Ardèches chambre d'hôte phenomenon in the 1970s. Since then, they have never stopped taking great pleasure in entertaining guests. All the rooms are very pleasant and each has been given a name which relates to the property's history, including Émilie, Jesuit's suite and Servants Quarters. In the summer, breakfast and lunch, served under a shaded trellis or plane tree, are sheer delight.

Access: In the village

BEAULIEU - 07460

12 LA SANTOLINE
M. et Mme Espenel

07460 Beaulieu
Tel. 04 75 39 01 91
Fax 04 75 39 38 79
info @ lasantoline.com
www.lasantoline.com

Open from 1 May to 20 Sep • 8 rooms (some have a balcony), one of which is an apartment, all have bath/WC, some have air-conditioning • €65 to €110; breakfast €12; half-board available • Terrace, garden, car park. Dogs not admitted in restaurant • Outdoor swimming pool

The lovely view of the Ardèche countryside and the Cévennes foothills.

Farm? Stronghold? Hunting lodge? Whatever the case, these 16C walls now house a hotel in a remote spot of garrigue that will appeal to urbanites in search of authenticity and tranquillity. The cheerful Provençal rooms would be quite at home in a glossy home-decoration magazine. Some have air-conditioning, but to our mind the thick dry-stone walls are more than sufficient to keep the scorching heat firmly outside. Vaulted restaurant, pretty terrace and a swimming pool surrounded by greenery.

Access: To the south-east, 1km along a gravel drive

RHÔNE ALPES
CHANDOLAS - 07230   MERCUER - 07200

13 AUBERGE LES MURETS
M. Rignanese

Lengarnayre
07230 Chandolas
Tel. 04 75 39 08 32
Fax 04 75 39 39 90
dominique.rignanese@wanadoo.fr
www.aubergelesmurets.com

Closed from 3 Jan to 10 Feb, 20 Nov to 10 Dec, Mon and Tue from 15 Nov to 30 Mar • 7 air-conditioned rooms with bath/WC or shower/WC and television • €56; breakfast €7; half-board available • Menus €17 to €28 • Car park, park, terrace. No dogs admitted in rooms • Swimming pool

We most liked: The restful swimming pool overlooking the Ardèche landscape.

Vineyards and 5 acres of grounds provide the setting for this lovely regional farm built in the 18C and recently turned into a family hotel. Attractive warm colours and bamboo furniture grace the majority of the rooms. Depending on the season, meals are served in vaulted dining room or on the terrace under the welcome shade of an old mulberry tree. The cuisine does full justice to the region's renowned culinary reputation and the buffet breakfast makes a perfect way to start the day.

Access : 6km northbound on the D 208, the D 104, then a minor road

14 LE MAS DE MAZAN
M. Croze

07200 Mercuer
Tel. 04 75 35 41 88
Fax 04 75 35 41 88
masdemazan@wanadoo.fr
http://perso.wanadoo.fr/masdemazan

Open all year • 5 rooms • €45 to €47, breakfast included • No table d'hôte • Car park. Credit cards not accepted, no dogs admitted

We most liked: The owner takes guests round his pride and joy, a silk-worm farm.

This typical Cévennes farm has been lovingly restored by a farming couple, who enthusiastically greet all new guests. The spot is stunningly tranquil and the view of the valley, wooded hills and the village is matchless. The rooms are inviting and well restored but all, sadly, do not enjoy the wonderful view. The owner breeds silk worms and loves explaining the finer points of his "hobby".

Access : 5km to the north-west of Aubenas on the D 104 and the D 435

RHÔNE ALPES

SAINT-DÉSIRAT - 07340

15 LA DÉSIRADE
M. et Mme Mennier

07340 Saint-Désirat
Tel. 04 75 34 21 88
contact@desirade-fr.com
www.desirade-fr.com

Closed 25 Dec and 1 Jan • 6 rooms • €45, breakfast included • Table d'hôte €18 • Terrace, garden, car park. Credit cards not accepted

We most liked — **The lady of the house's culinary skills.**

This fully renovated 19C mansion among Saint Joseph's trees and vineyards is a feast for the eyes. The simple, light and airy rooms overlook the magnolia tree in the courtyard, or the park and vineyard. Your cordon-bleu hostess loves surprising her guests with tasty regional recipes. A perfect base camp from which to explore the Ardèche.

Access: 15km eastbound from Annonay on the D 82, towards Andance, then take a minor road

SAINT-JULIEN-DU-SERRE - 07200

16 CHAMBRE D'HÔTE BOURLENC
M. et Mme Ventalon

Route de Saint-Andéol
07200 Saint-Julien-du-Serre
Tel. 04 75 37 69 95
Fax 04 75 37 69 95
bourlenc07@free.fr
www.guidewed.com/ardeche/ch-hote/mas-de-bourlenc

Closed from Nov to Feb (open weekends by reservation) • 5 rooms • €60, breakfast included • Table d'hôte €25 (reservation) • Garden. Credit cards not accepted, no dogs admitted

We most liked — **A chance to taste forgotten varieties of fruit and vegetables.**

It is impossible not to wind down during a stay at this house perched on a rock and surrounded by acacias. Colourful wardrobes, whitewashed walls and earthenware tiles add a delightful southern accent to the interior. The Pass of Lescrinet can be seen from the light, airy and generously proportioned rooms. Farm-grown fruit and vegetables take pride of place on the appetising dining table.

Access: 3.5km from Saint-Julien-du-Serre on the D 218

RHÔNE ALPES

SAINT-PAUL-LE-JEUNE - 07460

17 LA PASSIFLORE
Mme Luypaerts

Sauvas
07460 Saint-Paul-le-Jeune
Tel. 04 75 39 80 74
Fax 04 75 39 80 74
godeliva.luypaerts@wanadoo.fr
www.ardeche.com.lapassiflore

Closed 15 Dec to 15 Jan • 3 rooms • €42, breakfast included • No table d'hôte • Garden, car park. Credit cards not accepted, no dogs admitted

We most liked: The owners bend over backwards to make their guests feel at home.

This Flemish couple clearly care about their guests and want to make sure their stay in the Vans region is memorable. Despite the nearby road, the well-isolated house is a haven of peace. The agreeable rooms are extremely well-soundproofed and guests can choose from countless delightful sitting rooms. As to the breakfasts, served under an arbour near the mulberry tree and aviary, you'll certainly pass your plate for more...

Access : 13km southbound from Vans on the D 901, then the D 104 towards Alès

SAINT-PONS - 07580

18 HOSTELLERIE « MÈRE BIQUETTE »
Mme Bossy

Les Allignols
07580 Saint-Pons
Tel. 04 75 36 72 61
Fax 04 75 36 76 25
merebiquette@wanadoo.fr
www.logis-d-ardeche.com/merebiquette

Closed from 15 Nov to 12 Feb and Sun evening from Oct to Mar • 9 rooms in a separate wing, with bath/WC and television • €57 to €105; breakfast €8 to €9; half-board available • Restaurant closed Mon lunchtime, Wed lunch (except public holidays); menus €19 to €38 • Terrace, garden, car park • Outdoor swimming pool, tennis

We most liked: Tucking into the appetising breakfast buffet.

This old country farm is named after a goat's cheese formerly produced here: "la mère biquette" (a biquette is a kid goat) was sold by the current owners' parents in the local markets. It's a perfect hideaway to build up your strength in well-appointed rooms overlooking the chestnut trees or vineyards, a stone and wood rustic-styled restaurant, a shaded terrace overlooking the valley and a superb swimming pool.

Access : Leave the N 102 between Villeneuve-de-Berg and Le Teil, take the D 293, through Saint-Pons and on for 4km

RHÔNE ALPES

CHÂTILLON-SAINT-JEAN - 26750

19 MAISON FORTE DE CLÉRIVAUX
M. et Mme Josquin

Clérivaux
26750 Châtillon-Saint-Jean
Tel. 04 75 45 32 53
Fax 04 75 71 45 43
pierre.josquin@kyxar.fr
www.clerivaux.kyxar.fr

Closed early Jan to Easter • 4 rooms, all have bath/WC or shower/WC • €53 to €58, breakfast included • No table d'hôte • Terrace, park, car park

We most liked **An ideal spot to recharge your batteries.**

Anne and Pierre Josquin harnessed all their enthusiasm and talent to reviving this estate nestled in a tiny valley of the Drôme. The splendid 13C stronghold is surrounded by outhouses, gardens and 11ha of farming and woodland. Four rooms, located in a 17C farmhouse, combine contemporary comforts with the warmth of yesteryear. In fine weather, breakfasts of fruit from the orchard and home-made jams are served under the trellis, opposite the delightful "garden of Julie".

Access : In Châtillon-Saint-Jean, head towards Parnans. 1km further on, turn left towards Saint-Michel and follow signs

CLIOUSCLAT - 26270

20 LA TREILLE MUSCATE
M. Delaitre

26270 Cliousclat
Tel. 04 75 63 13 10
Fax 04 75 63 10 79
latreillemuscate@wanadoo.fr
www.latreillemuscate.com

Closed from 5 Dec to 11 Feb • 12 rooms with bath/WC or shower/WC, most have television • €60 to €110; breakfast €9; half-board available • Menu €15 to €26 • Terrace, small garden, private car park. No dogs admitted in restaurant

We most liked **The fruit trees in blossom in the spring.**

Midway between Valence and Montélimar just off the A 7 motorway, this village lying in the hills of the Drôme valley is home to an inn, made up of two old stone houses with lilac shutters. Terracotta tiled floors and second-hand furniture adorn the uncluttered, individually styled bedrooms. Sunny Provence can be felt in the dining room and the lovely terrace is hidden in a secret garden. However, if you are unable to resist the temptation of a motorway hotel, then have it your own way...

Access : Leave the Valence-Montélimard road (N 7) between Loriol-sur-Drôme and Saulce-sur-Rhône for a minor road eastbound

RHÔNE ALPES

ÉTOILE-SUR-RHÔNE - 26800

21 LA MARE
Famille Chaix

Route de Montmeyran
26800 Étoile-sur-Rhône
Tel. 04 75 59 33 79
Fax 04 75 59 05 20

Open all year • 4 rooms • €45, breakfast included • No table d'hôte • Garden, car park. Credit cards not accepted, no dogs admitted

The warm-hearted hospitality of this farming family.

On the threshold of the south of France, this lovely stone house run by a farming family is a unique chance to taste the legendary "savoir-vivre" of the region first-hand. The comfortable, appealing rooms are fitted with home-made furniture. Garden-produce features prominently in the delicious, generous helpings of home cooking. We also appreciated the friendly greeting and the modest prices.

Access : 15km to the south-east of Valence on the D 111 and the D 111B

LA CHAPELLE-EN-VERCORS - 26420

22 BELLIER
Mme Bellier

26420 La Chapelle-en-Vercors
Tel. 04 75 48 20 03
Fax 04 75 48 25 31
www.hotel-bellier.fr

Closed Jan 1 to 1 Apr, Tue evening and Wed out of season • 13 rooms with bath/WC and television • €58 to €65 (€46 to €55 low season); breakfast €6; half-board available • Menus €15 to €30 • Terrace, garden, car park • Outdoor swimming pool. In winter, cross-country skiing, snowshoe hiking

Right in the heart of the Vercors, in nearly 450 000 acres of Regional Park.

Air raids and fires took their toll on the village in 1944, which explains why the spruce chalet on a rocky outcrop over the road only dates from 1946. The majority of the spacious, welcoming rooms have a balcony. A mountain flavour adds warmth to the dining room and the fireplace in the sitting room is very welcome after a long day's skiing. In the summer, tables are laid round the swimming pool.

Access : In the village, on a rocky outcrop overlooking the road

RHÔNE ALPES

LA GARDE-ADHÉMAR - 26700

23 GÎTE DU VAL DES NYMPHES
M. et Mme Andruejol

Domaine de Magne
26700 La Garde-Adhémar
Tel. 04 75 04 44 54
Fax 04 75 04 44 45
www.valdesnymphes.com

Open all year • 5 rooms • €48, breakfast included • Table d'hôte €18 (evening only) • Terrace, garden. Credit cards not accepted, dogs not admitted in restaurant • Outdoor swimming pool

We most liked: Filling a basket with fruit from the estate.

This mouth-watering fruit farm is built on a hillside in immense grounds which formerly included the Chapelle des Nymphes. The rooms are located in a small independent house overlooking the orchards. Meals are served in a vaulted dining room where old farm tools and family photos hang on the walls. Music lovers can try the family piano, while others may prefer to lounge in the garden. Before leaving, fill your basket with freshly picked peaches and apricots.

Access: 1km on the Chapelle du Val des Nymphes road

MONTÉLIMAR - 26200

24 SPHINX-HÔTEL
M. et Mme Harnichard

19 boulevard Desmarais
26200 Montélimar
Tel. 04 75 01 86 64
Fax 04 75 52 34 21
reception@sphinx-hotel.fr
www.sphinx-hotel.fr

Closed from 23 Dec to 10 Jan • 24 rooms on 2 floors, all have bath/WC, air-conditioning and television • €52 to €66; breakfast €7 • No restaurant • Inner courtyard, locked car park

We most liked: Mornings in the lovely inner courtyard.

This 17C mansion stands on Montélimar's tree-lined Allées Provençales, now a busy pedestrianised shopping area. Lofty ceilings, parquet floors, wainscoting and huge beams bear witness to the home's stately origins, while individual air-conditioning, greatly appreciated in the summer, is a small concession to modernity. All the rooms will soon have been refurbished.

Access: In the town centre, alongside the Allées Provençales

RHÔNE ALPES

NYONS - 26110

25 LA CARAVELLE
M. et Mme Alignol

8 rue des Antignans
26110 Nyons
Tel. 04 75 26 07 44
Fax 04 75 26 07 40
www.guideweb.com/provence/hotel/caravelle

Closed Nov to Dec • 11 non-smoking rooms with bath/WC or shower/WC and television • €75 to €95; breakfast €9 • No restaurant • Garden, private car park. No dogs admitted

We most liked
A quiet read in the unusual garden.

The sign outside and a series of portholes from the battleship 'Jean-Bart' are the legacy of the former hotel owner who had a reputation as something of an old seadog. If you then add the unusual architecture of this 1900 villa and its curious garden full of Indian bean trees, you will be prepared for a stay in the earthly paradise of the olive kingdom but minus the traditional Provençal style. Quiet, well-cared for rooms.

Access : On the Promenade de la Digue

ALLEMONT - 38114

26 GINIÈS
M. et Mme Giniès

Le Plan
38114 Allemont
Tel. 04 76 80 70 03
Fax 04 76 80 73 13
hotel-ginies@wanadoo.fr
www.hotel-ginies.com

Closed Jan, Apr and Dec, Sun eve and Mon • 15 rooms, one of which has disabled access, all have bath/WC or shower/WC and television • €55; breakfast €7; half-board available • Menu €20 • Terrace, garden, car park. No dogs admitted in restaurant • Mini-golf

We most liked
Ideally located near some of the best skiing domains in the Alps.

A sleepy village in the valley of the Eau d'Olle is home to this inn and its recent wing. The rooms are spacious, practical and well looked-after and some have balconies. You will have a choice of dining rooms, ranging from stones and beams in a rustic room to two more modern rooms with a view of the garden. A recently redone mini-golf course completes the picture.

Access : In the village, 9km northbound from Bourg-d'Oisans on the N 91 then right on the D 526

RHÔNE ALPES

AOSTE - 38490

27 AU COQ EN VELOURS
M. et Mme Bellet

1800 route de Saint-Genix
38490 Aoste
Tel. 04 76 31 60 04
Fax 04 76 31 77 55
contact@au-coq-en-velours.com
www.au-coq-en-velours.com

Closed from 1 to 27 Jan, Sun evening and Mon • 7 rooms with bath/WC or shower/WC, all have television • €65 to €70; breakfast €9 • Menus €28 to €56 • Terrace, park, garden, car park

Ever tasted "rooster in velvet breeches"?

This smart village inn run by the same family since 1900 receives its guests in style. The bedrooms, named after different species of the hotel's namesake (rooster), all overlook the rear; those with a bathtub are the most spacious. Fowl take pride of place in the dining room, as a glance at the menu, paintings and ornaments will quickly confirm: unsurprisingly perhaps, the house speciality is "cockerel"! Pleasant terrace under the tall trees in the garden and near a refreshing ornamental pool.

Access: 2km to the north-east of Aoste on the N 516, at the Gare de l'Est

AVIGNONET - 38650

28 CHÂTEAU DES MARCEAUX
M. et Mme Rocca

38650 Avignonet
Tel. 04 76 34 18 94
Fax 04 76 34 18 94
eric.rocca@wanadoo.fr
http://monsite.wanadoo.fr/chateaudesmarceaux

Closed from Jan to mid-Apr and from Nov to late Dec • 2 rooms • €67 to €74, breakfast included • No table d'hôte • Park, car park. Credit cards not accepted, dogs not admitted

Superbly original rooms.

The diversity of architectural styles in this 18C château is such that the ensuing variety of bedroom styles seems perfectly natural. The first room, in the old dovecote, is most spectacular with a superb staircase and walls adorned with hundreds of roosting places. Original parquet floors and high ceilings set the tone for the second in the square tower, while the third in an independent cottage is simply enormous. Look out for the fresco in the dining room, painted by the owner-artist himself.

Access: From the road, take the lane to the castle gates

RHÔNE ALPES

CHARETTE - 38390

29 AUBERGE DU VERNAY
M. Sallemand

Route d'Optevoz
38390 Charrette
Tel. 04 74 88 57 57
Fax 04 74 88 58 57
reservation@auberge-du-vernay.fr
www.auberge-du-vernay.fr

Open all year • 7 rooms, one of which has disabled access, all have shower/WC and television • €60 to €75 (€60 low season); breakfast €8; half-board available • Restaurant closed Sun evening; menus €15 to €23 • Terrace, car park

We most liked
Halcyon days in the countryside.

The spruce white stone walls of this 18C farmstead have been given a new lease of life. All the delightful rooms are decorated individually. In the restaurant, old flagstones, a huge fireplace large enough to roast a whole cow, sandblasted beams, cheerful paintings and multicoloured modern chairs provide an amusing and appealing mixture of tastes and styles. Outside, the old bread oven can still be seen on the shaded terrace.

Access : After the town hall drive towards Optevoz

CHICHILIANNE - 38930

30 CHÂTEAU DE PASSIÈRES
M. et Mme Perli

38930 Chichilianne
Tel. 04 76 34 45 48
Fax 04 76 34 46 25

Closed from mid-Nov to late Feb and Sun evening and Mon out of season • 23 rooms, all have bath/WC or shower/WC, half have television • €50 to €70; breakfast €7 • Menus €19 to €32 • Terrace, garden, car park. No dogs admitted in restaurant • Outdoor swimming pool, tennis

We most liked
Watch a climbing party make the ascent of Mont Aiguille (3842m) from the comfort of your deck-chair!

The turrets of this small 14C manor house look out onto a hamlet in the shadow of Mount Aiguille. Most of the 23 bedrooms are contemporary in style, but three furnished with old pieces and lined in dark wood have more character. The owner, a professional footballer in his day, is a fan of 19C art as the numerous oils on the restaurant and sitting room walls illustrate.

Access : Leave the N 75 after 12km southbound from Monestier-de-Clermont, at "La Gare" take the D 7

RHÔNE ALPES

CHICHILIANNE - 38930

31 FERME DE RUTHIÈRES
M. Sauze

Lieu-dit Ruthières
38930 Chichilianne
Tel. 04 76 34 45 98
Fax 04 76 34 45 98
fsauze@aol.com
www.fermederuthieres.com

Closed from 20 to 27 Dec • 4 rooms upstairs • €45; breakfast included; half-board available • Meals only by reservation and for guests • Garden, car park. Credit cards not accepted

A strong focus on farm-grown produce.

This young farming couple extends a warm, unaffected welcome to guests to their farmhouse. The cow-shed has been turned into enormous guest bedrooms furnished in a country style; two enjoy a view of the Vercors. Regional art exhibitions are regularly held in the vaulted dining room complete with fireplace and columns: try the delicious home-grown produce.

Access: 4km to the north-west of Chichilianne on a minor road

CHONAS-L'AMBALLAN - 38121

32 LE DOMAINE DE CLAIREFONTAINE
M. et Mme Girardon

Chemin des Fontanettes
38121 Chonas-L'Amballan
Tel. 04 74 58 81 52
Fax 04 74 58 80 93
domainedeclairefontaine@yahoo.fr
www.domaine-de-clairefontaine.fr

Closed from 19 Dec to 19 Jan • 28 rooms, 2 of which have disabled access, with bath/WC and television • €45 to €115; breakfast €13; half-board available • Air-conditioned restaurant; menus €40 to €98 • Terrace, park, private car park. No dogs admitted in restaurant • Tennis

A ten-acre park surrounds this elegant manor house, two minutes from the A 7.

Formerly a convalescent home for the bishops of Lyons, these walls have been standing since 1766. Perhaps it is no surprise that the rooms look a little old-fashioned, but the sophisticated cuisine and the dining room more than compensate. A blend of contemporary 19C styles, the dining room leads onto a terrace overlooking mature parkland. For just a few euros extra, you may be interested to know, there is an exquisitely-decorated room which has been built in the old walnut-drying room.

Access: 9km southbound from Vienne on the N 7

RHÔNE ALPES
ESTRABLIN - 38780　　　　　　　　　　GRESSE-EN-VERCORS - 38650

33 LA GABETIÈRE
M. Neyret

D 502
38780 Estrablin
Tel. 04 74 58 01 31
Fax 04 74 58 08 98

Closed 1 to 10 Jan • 12 rooms with bath/WC or shower/WC and television • €50 to €64; breakfast €8 • No restaurant • Park, private car park • Outdoor swimming pool

34 LE CHÂLET HÔTEL PRAYER
M. Prayer

38650 Gresse-en-Vercors
Tel. 04 76 34 32 08
Fax 04 76 34 31 06
lechalet @ free.fr
http://lechalet.free.fr

Closed from 12 Mar to 6 May, 15 Oct to 23 Dec and Wed except school holidays • 20 rooms and 5 apartments, all have bath/WC or shower/WC and television • €56 to €80; breakfast €9; half-board available • Menus €18 to €49 • Terrace, garage, car park. No dogs admitted • Outdoor swimming pool, tennis, petanque

An easy-going 16C manor.

Botanical walks in the high mountain pastures.

On the outskirts of Vienne, trees and parkland surround this little 16C manor. A stone staircase in the tiny tower leads up to individually decorated boudoir bedrooms, recently equipped with double-glazing which cuts out the noise of the nearby road. Character also abounds in the exposed beams and late 17C fireplace in the breakfast room.

Despite its name and warm atmosphere, this hotel bears more resemblance to a prosperous farm than a chalet. The bedrooms are being progressively renovated and all have a view of the village and the mountains. Take a seat in one of the comfortable dining rooms and tuck into large helpings of traditional cuisine. A glance at the visitors' book reveals a number of famous patrons, including actor Gérard Dépardieu and Albert II of Belgium.

Access : 8km eastbound from Vienne on the D 41, then the D 502

Access : In the centre of the village

RHÔNE ALPES

LANS-EN-VERCORS - 38250

35 LE VAL FLEURI
M. Bonnard

730 avenue Léopold-Fabre
38250 Lans-en-Vercors
Tel. 04 76 95 41 09
Fax 04 76 94 34 69
levalfleuri@aol.com

Open from mid-May to 20 Sep and from 20 Dec to 20 Mar • 14 rooms, all have bath/WC and television • €34 to €60; breakfast €8; half-board available • Menus €23 (weekdays) to €26 • Terrace, garden, garage, car park. No dogs admitted in restaurant

An action-packed resort perfect for energetic children!

The old belfry of the church stands guard over the blue shutters of the Val Fleuri Hotel, built in the 1920s. Almost as if defying time to take its toll of the delightfully old-fashioned interior, the decoration of the dining room is exactly as it was when the establishment opened and some of the beautifully-kept bedrooms still boast their original Art Deco furniture or lamps. The fresh mountain air on the terrace, under the lime trees in the flowered garden, will whet your appetite.

Access : On the main road, behind the church

LE PIN - 38730

36 LES BALCONS DU LAC
M. Ferrard

145 chemin de Béluran Lieu-dit Vers-Ars
38730 Le Pin
Tel. 04 76 06 68 82
Fax 04 76 06 68 82

Closed during Christmas school holidays • 5 rooms with bathrooms • €43, breakfast included • Table d'hôte €15 (evenings only) • Credit cards not accepted

Watch Lake Paladru change colour throughout the day.

Half the windows of this gradually restored old farmhouse face Lake Paladru, while the other half gaze out over fields and woods. The majority of the snug, simple bedrooms enjoy a view of the lake's deep waters; three have a kitchenette and all have spanking-new bathrooms. In the morning, you will breakfast in an enormous living room, in the centre of which stands a pyramidal fireplace. Warm and friendly.

Access : 1km to the south-west of Paladru Lake on the D 50

RHÔNE ALPES

L'ISLE-D'ABEAU - 38080

37 LE RELAIS DU ÇATEY
M. Ducretet

10 rue du Didier - Le Bourg
38080 L'Isle-d'Abeau
Tel. 04 74 18 26 50
Fax 04 74 18 26 59
relaiscatey@aol.com
www.le-relais-du-catey.com

Closed 30 Jul to 22 Aug, 24 Dec to 2 Jan • 7 rooms with bath/WC or shower/WC and television • €54 to €65; breakfast €6; half-board available • Restaurant closed Sun; menus €21 to €50 • Terrace, garden, car park

We most liked **Sample the chef's creative recipes on the terrace.**

This elegant Louis XV house surrounded by trees and flowers lies in a residential district, only 10min from the international airport of Lyons. The cosy comfort of the bedrooms has recently been enhanced following high-quality renovation work. Wrought-iron and tasteful paintings adorn the contemporary restaurant, further set off by the original flagstones. Lime and Indian bean trees shade the pleasant terrace. Excellent, imaginative cuisine.

Access: North-west of Bourgoin-Jallieu

MIZOEN - 38142

38 LE PANORAMIQUE
M. Keesman

Route des Aymes
38142 Mizoen
Tel. 04 76 80 06 25
Fax 04 76 80 25 12
info@hotel-panoramique.com
www.hotel-panoramique.com

Closed from 24 Apr to 24 May and 19 Sep to 23 Dec • 9 rooms, 5 of which are non-smoking, all have bath/WC or shower/WC and television • €60 to €65; breakfast €10; half-board available • Evenings only except weekends, public and school holidays; menus €21 to €25 • Non-smoking establishment, terrace, garden, car park. No dogs admitted • Sauna

We most liked **If you're lucky, you may catch a glimpse of the chamois who live in the mountains.**

In the summer, window boxes laden with geraniums adorn the balconies of this hillside chalet. Recently purchased by a young couple from the Netherlands who speak Dutch, French, English, German and Spanish, the atmosphere is decidedly polyglot. Among the establishment's numerous appeals are the warm mountain-style adopted in the bedrooms, a south-facing terrace, sauna and a superb panoramic view of the town, Oisans Valley and surrounding mountains.

Access: Between Le Freney-d'Oisans and the Barrage du Chambon tunnel, leave the N 91 and take the D 25

RHÔNE ALPES

MOISSIEU-SUR-DOLON - 38270 **SAINT-BAUDILLE-DE-LA-TOUR - 38118**

39 DOMAINE DE LA COLOMBIÈRE
Mme Carle

Château de Moissieu
38270 Moissieu-sur-Dolon
Tel. 04 74 79 50 23
Fax 04 74 79 50 25
colombieremoissieu@hotmail.com
www.lacolombiere.com

Closed from 23 Dec to 1 Jan, Feb school holidays, Sun evening and Mon (except public holidays) • 21 air-conditioned rooms, 2 of which have disabled access, all have bath/WC or shower/WC and television • €76 to €118; breakfast €12; half-board available • Air-conditioned restaurant; menus €29 to €66 • Car park, park, terrace • Swimming pool

Ideal for nature-lovers.

This handsome abode, built in 1820, stands in over 10 acres of well-tended grounds. Cleverly restored and turned into a hotel, the establishment offers spacious, brightly coloured rooms, each of which is named after a famous painter and a copy of each artist's paintings, painted by the lady of the house, hangs on the walls of the rooms. The restaurant, located in the estate's only contemporary construction, has a terrace overlooking the idyllic countryside.

Access : Near the village

40 LES BASSES PORTES
M. et Mme Giroud-Ducaroy

Torjonas
38118 Saint-Baudille-de-la-Tour
Tel. 04 74 95 18 23
mirvinc@wanadoo.fr
www.basses-portes.com

Open all year • 3 rooms • €50, breakfast included • Table d'hôte €17 • Terrace, park, car park. Credit cards not accepted, no dogs admitted • Swimming pool

A happy marriage of past and present.

Extensive renovation work has restored this old farmhouse without removing any of its rustic charm. Whenever possible, the old stones, beams and parquet floors have been preserved. The somewhat surprising style of the bedrooms features a happy blend of old and new, in addition to brand-new bathrooms. A perfect base camp to explore the Île Crémieu.

Access : 2km northbound on the D 52B

RHÔNE ALPES
SAINT-LATTIER - 38840   SAINT-MARTIN-DE-LA-CLUZE - 38650

41 LE LIÈVRE AMOUREUX
M. Lapeyre

La Gare
38840 Saint-Lattier
Tel. 04 76 64 50 67
www.lelievreamoureux.com

Closed Jan • 3 rooms, all have bath/WC or shower/WC • €55 to €75; breakfast €7 • Table d'hôte €25 • Terrace, garden, kitchenette

42 LE CHÂTEAU DE PÂQUIER
M. Rossi

38650 Saint-Martin-de-la-Cluze
Tel. 04 76 72 77 33
Fax 04 76 72 77 33
hrossi@club-internet.fr
http://www.chateau.de.paquier.free.fr

Open all year (by reservation in winter) • 5 rooms • €62 to €80, breakfast included • Table d'hôte €21, beverages included • Garden, car park. Dogs not admitted.

The professionalism of the owner.

This former hunting-lodge and former star establishment has been brought back to life by the renovation works carried out by the welcoming owner. Three spacious and personalised bedrooms and two split-level apartments will ensure that your stay is comfortable. The table d'hôte is a feast of local recipes and savours: fresh local produce (truffles, ravioles, walnuts) served with wines that guests can choose themselves from the cellar, served either in the dining room with an open fire or on the terrace.

Unaffected and welcoming.

The owners have clearly put their body and soul into the restoration of the Renaissance castle and pretty garden and the result happily does justice to their efforts. Countless decorative features have been preserved, such as the exposed beams, wooden ceiling, spiral staircase and mullioned windows. The spacious rooms are beautifully decorated and furnished; one affords you a rare opportunity of sleeping in an old chapel. Garden produce and meat chargrilled on the open fire.

Access : Head towards A 49, exit no 8, Baume d'Hostun, go through Eymeux, beyond the bridge, turn right, at the roundabout, head towards Saint-Lattier

Access : 12km northbound from Monestier-de-Clermont on the N 75 and a minor road

RHÔNE ALPES

TREFFORT - 38650

43 LE CHÂTEAU D'HERBELON
M. Castillan

Lac de Monteynard
38650 Treffort
Tel. 04 76 34 02 03
Fax 04 76 34 05 44
chateaudherbelon@wanadoo.fr
www.chateau-herbelon.fr

Closed from 20 Dec to 4 Mar, Mon and Tue except Jul-Aug • 9 rooms, all have bath/WC and television • €56 to €76; breakfast €8; half-board available • Menus €21 to €36 • Terrace, garden, car park. No dogs admitted in rooms • Ideal for wind-surfing

We most liked The 20km-long lake is renowned for its windsurfing.

This traditional country house covered in Virginia creeper and climbing roses stands on the banks of the Monteynard reservoir lake. A great deal of care and attention has clearly been lavished on the sizeable, usefully equipped rooms. An old stone fireplace adds character to the restaurant, while a lovely vaulted room in the basement is regularly rented out for weddings, communions and other family banquets. Children's play area in the walled garden.

Access : By the lake, 3km on the D 110E

URIAGE-LES-BAINS - 38410

44 LES MÉSANGES
M. Prince

Route de Bouloud
38410 Uriage-les-Bains
Tel. 04 76 89 70 69
Fax 04 76 89 56 97
prince@hotel-les-mesanges.com
www.hotel-les-mesanges.com

Closed from 20 Oct to 1 Feb • 33 rooms with bath/WC or shower/WC and television • €57 to €69; breakfast €8; half-board available • Menus €22 to €52 • Terrace, garden, car park. No dogs admitted • Swimming pool, table-tennis, petanque, play area

We most liked Savouring the utter peace and quiet.

The villa overlooks the spa resort and castle. Ask for one of the renovated, practical rooms with balcony and enjoy the view over the Chamrousse or Vercors mountain ranges. A light, airy dining room in a modern style, pleasant terrace shaded by plane trees, peaceful garden with a play area and swimming pool complete the facilities of this family-run establishment.

Access : Avenue des Thermes, drive along the park, turn left onto the Chamrousse road, then at the spa hospital, turn right on Bouloud road

RHÔNE ALPES
VIGNIEU - 38890   CHAZELLES-SUR-LYON - 42140

45. CHÂTEAU DE CHAPEAU CORNU
M. Regnier

Le Rual
38890 Vignieu
Tel. 04 74 27 79 00
Fax 04 74 92 49 31
chapeau.cornu@wanadoo.fr
www.chateau-chapeau-cornu.fr

Closed from 23 Dec to 3 Jan and Sun evening except in Jul and Aug • 21 rooms (and 2 apartments) with bath/WC or shower/WC and television • €65 to €110; breakfast €9 to €12; half-board available • Menus €22 (weekdays) to €57 • Terrace, park, private car park. No dogs admitted • Outdoor swimming pool

If only a night in this fairy-tale castle could turn our fortunes from rags to riches!

The names of the former owners of this 13C fortified castle, Capella and Cornutti, explain the origins of the castle's amusing name which translates as Battered Hat. The rooms, which are gradually being treated to a new coat of paint, tasteful fabrics and wrought-iron furniture all have antique wardrobes; some also boast a four-poster bed. A stone-vaulted dining room, attractive inner courtyard terrace and a 10-acre park with ornamental pools and tree-lined paths complete the picture.

Access: From Bourgoin-Jallieu take the N 6 (towards Lyon), then right on the D 522 as far as Flosaille, then the D 19 and 5km after Saint-Clef, turn right

46. CHÂTEAU BLANCHARD
M. Bonnidal

36 route de Saint-Galmier
42140 Chazelles-sur-Lyon
Tel. 04 77 54 28 88
Fax 04 77 54 36 03
chateau-blanchard@wanadoo.fr

Closed from 7 to 27 Aug • 12 rooms, all have bath/WC and television • €59 to €82; breakfast €8; half-board available • Restaurant closed Sun evening, Mon and Fri evening; menus €20 to €30 • Garden, car park

The Hat Museum's collection shows off hats and caps of the rich and famous!

This rambling, elegant period house built in a shaded park once belonged to a family of milliners and after extensive renovation, it once again shines with the glow of its former youth. Inside, a marble staircase will take you up to comfortable bedrooms decorated individually in a contemporary flavour. The restaurant has opted for a traditional repertoire.

Access: On the way into the village, on the Saint-Galmier road

RHÔNE ALPES

COMMELLE-VERNAY - 42120

47 CHÂTEAU DE BACHELARD
M. et Mme Noirard

Route de Commelle
42120 Commelle-Vernay
Tel. 04 77 71 93 67
Fax 04 77 78 10 20
bachelard@worldonline.fr
www.chateaubachelard.com

Open all year • 4 non-smoking rooms and 1 apartment, all with bath/WC or shower/WC • €93, breakfast included • Table d'hôte €23 (by reservation) • Park, car park. Credit cards not accepted • Outdoor swimming pool, pond with fishing

The owner's warm hospitality.

A peaceful relaxed atmosphere reigns throughout this elegant 17C manor house on the doorstep of Roanne. The personalised bedrooms, including the most unusual "Peintre" and the apartment which can sleep 6, are full of character and floral frescoes in a particularly immaculate setting. The vast dining room opens onto the park, swimming pool and teak furnished terrace where breakfast is served when the weather permits.

Access : 3km south of Roanne

FEURS - 42110

48 LA BUSSINIÈRE
M. et Mme Perrin

Route de Lyon
42110 Feurs
Tel. 04 77 27 06 36
Fax 04 77 27 06 36
la-bussiniere@wanadoo.fr
www.labussiniere.com

Open all year • 3 rooms • €40, breakfast included • Table d'hôte €15 (evenings only) • Garden, car park. Credit cards not accepted

The lady of the house's ceaseless quest for perfection.

The comfort of this renovated farmhouse leaves nothing to be desired: everything has been designed with the welfare of the guest in mind, from the digicode-access on the main gate and the excellent soundproofing to the high quality bedding. Huge beams and tasteful colours adorn the stylish bedrooms, which have immaculate bathrooms. Meals are taken around the large table in the dining room.

Access : 3km eastbound from Feurs on the D 89, towards Lyon

RHÔNE ALPES
NOAILLY - 42640 | PANISSIÈRES - 42360

49 CHÂTEAU DE LA MOTTE
M. et Mme Froumajou

42640 Noailly
Tel. 04 77 66 64 60
Fax 04 77 66 68 10
chateaudelamotte@wanadoo.fr
www.chateaudelamotte.net

Open all year • 6 non-smoking rooms, all with bath/WC, television and Internet access • €72 to €103, breakfast included • Table d'hôte €24, including beverages • Terrace, park, car park, reading and games room. Dogs not admitted in dining room • Outdoor swimming pool, fitness facilities and sauna

We most liked — **The graceful south façade.**

This stunning 18C château, tucked away in five hectares of grounds with swimming pool, is home to spacious, well cared for rooms, each of which is named after a famous writer. The "George Sand", capable of sleeping four people, is ideal for families, while "Lamartine" with a lovely round bathtub and four-poster bed, is a favourite with newly weds. The owners' friendly welcome cannot be faulted, nor can their authentic cooking in which fresh produce takes pride of place.

Access: In the town

50 LA FERME DES ROSES
M. Barthélémy

Le Clair
42360 Panissières
Tel. 04 77 28 63 63
Fax 04 77 28 63 63
jednostka.arabians@free.fr
www.gites-de-France-loire.com

Open all year • 5 non-smoking rooms, all with bath/WC or shower/WC and television • €50 to €55, breakfast included • Table d'hôte €15 • Terrace, garden, car park. Credit cards not accepted, dogs not admitted • Outdoor swimming pool

We most liked — **The enchanting floral decoration.**

The rooms of this old farmhouse, built in 1813, are all named after roses, the owner's second passion after horses. All are furnished in a contemporary style and two, "Rose des peintres" and "Rose de Resht" can sleep up to five people. Local produce features prominently on the menu and meals are served either by the fireside or on the terrace; don't miss the traditional "Forézien" snack" served at breakfast time.

Access: Go through Feurs, towards Panissières on the D 60

RHÔNE ALPES

RENAISON - 42370

51 PLATELIN
M. et Mme de Bats

42370 Renaison
Tel. 04 77 64 29 12
Fax 04 77 62 14 79
contact@platelin.com
www.platelin.com

Open all year • 2 non-smoking rooms and 1 apartment, all with bath/WC, television and kitchenette • €60 to €75, breakfast included • No table d'hôte • Garden, car park. Credit cards not accepted • Sitting room-library with piano, outdoor swimming pool

The view of the Roannais mountains.

Those in search of peace and quiet will fall in love with this former wine-growers' family estate tucked away in the countryside. The apartment, in the converted henhouse is called "Poules" (hens), while the "Lapins" (rabbits) and "Vaches" (cows) rooms are equally bucolic in inspiration; all are tastefully decorated and each has its own secluded garden area with deckchair and access to the swimming pool. The large sitting room, also home to the reception area, boasts a pleasant library corner and a grand piano.

Access : On the way into the village from Roanne

SAINT-MAURICE-SUR-LOIRE - 42155

52 L'ÉCHAUGUETTE
M. et Mme Alex

Ruelle Guy-de-la-Mûre
42155 Saint-Maurice-sur-Loire
Tel. 04 77 63 15 89
contact@echauguette-alex.com
www.echauguette-alex.com

Open all year • 4 rooms • €62 to €72 breakfast included • Table d'hôte €25 (evening only) • Credit cards not accepted, no dogs admitted

Watch the pleasure boats on the lake.

It is difficult to resist the charm of these three houses hidden in a medieval village opposite the peaceful waters of Lake Villerest. All the tastefully decorated rooms are different: one has a fireplace, the other enjoys a view of the lake encircled by hills, while the last overlooks the keep and church. Breakfasts are served on the terrace or behind the kitchen's bay windows: a feast for the palate, and the eyes.

Access : 12km to the south-west of Roanne on the D 53 and the D 203

RHÔNE ALPES
SAINT-PIERRE-LA-NOAILLE - 42190   SAINT-ROMAIN-LE-PUY - 42610

53 DOMAINE DU CHÂTEAU DE MARCHANGY
Mme Grandeau

42190 Saint-Pierre-la-Noaille
Tel. 04 77 69 96 76
Fax 04 77 60 70 37
contact@marchangy.com
www.marchangy.com

Open all year • 3 rooms with bath/WC and television • €85 to €98, breakfast included • No table d'hôte • Park, car park. Credit cards not accepted • Swimming pool

A life of luxury - for just a few euros!

An oak-lined drive leads up to this idyllic 18C château in front of which is a large courtyard. The rooms, located in the former outhouses of the estate, are quiet and brimming with charm: restored parquet floors, family furniture, rugs, canopy beds, curios and paintings. The park, overlooking the countryside, is home to hundred-year-old trees and a splendid swimming pool. A few rows of vines produce a table wine that can only be tasted on the property.

Access: 5.5km north-west of Charlieu on the D 227 then a minor road

54 SOUS LE PIC - LA PÉROLIÈRE
M. Perol

20 rue Jean-Moulin
42610 Saint-Romain-le-Puy
Tel. 04 77 76 97 10
Fax 04 77 76 97 10
laperoliere@wanadoo.fr
www.laperoliere.com

Closed 5 Jan to 15 Mar • 3 non-smoking rooms, 1 with handicapped access and 1 apartment, all have bath/WC or shower/WC, television and modem access • €50 to €68, breakfast included • No table d'hôte • Terrace, car park. Credit cards not accepted, dogs not admitted • Golf, fishing, tennis nearby

The charming welcome of the mistress of the house.

This tastefully restored farmhouse stands at the foot of an 11C priory, attractively lit up in the evenings. After a restful night's sleep in one of the unpretentious inviting rooms, you will be ready to do full justice to a generous breakfast table laden with fruit salad, home-made cakes and jams, etc, before lingering in the sitting room, whose decoration and book shelves pay homage to the Forez region. There is no table d'hôte, but the owner can recommend a host of excellent restaurants.

Access: 7km from Montbrison on the D 8, then right onto the D 107

RHÔNE ALPES

ST-JULIEN-MOLIN-MOLETTE - 42220

55 LA RIVOIRE
M. et Mme Thiollière

42220 Saint-Julien-Molin-Molette
Tel. 04 77 39 65 44
Fax 04 77 39 67 86
info@larivoire.net
www.larivoire.net

Open all year • 5 rooms • €55, breakfast included, half-board available • Table d'hôte €18 • Terrace, garden, car park. Credit cards not accepted, no dogs admitted

Cottage-garden vegetables and local meats on the menu.

A circular stone tower and enormous kitchen garden contribute to the appeal of this lovely stately home, thought to date from the 15C. It enjoys a lovely position in the Nature Park of Pilat, overlooking the fir trees of the Ardèche hillsides, which is the view you will have from the cheerful rooms. Three sitting rooms, complete with piano, board games and a television, are reserved for the use of guests.

Access : 5km eastbound from Bourg-Argental on the N 82

VILLEMONTAIS - 42155

56 DOMAINE DU FONTENAY
M. et Mme Hawkins

42155 Villemontais
Tel. 04 77 63 12 22
Fax 04 77 63 15 95
hawkins@netsysteme.net
www.domainedufontenay.com

Open all year • 4 non-smoking rooms, all with bath/WC or shower/WC • €65, breakfast included • No table d'hôte • Terrace, car park, kitchenette. Dogs not admitted • Wine tasting

The owners' matchless kindness.

A small lane winding up through the vines leads to this guesthouse set in a 10ha wine-growing estate. All the rooms of the handsome property command stunning views of the vineyards and the Roanne plain. The spacious, light and tastefully decorated rooms look out over the surrounding vineyards. The friendly owners offer wine tasting sessions of their excellent wine, made according to ancient traditions.

Access : Leave Roanne by Clermont, follow the D 53 for 10km, at the roundabout turn left towards the motorway and follow signs to Domaine du Fontenay

RHÔNE ALPES
ANSE - 69480 | FLEURIE - 69820

57 SAINT-ROMAIN
M. et Mme Levet

Route de Graves
69480 Anse
Tel. 04 74 60 24 46
Fax 04 74 67 12 85
hotel-saint-romain@wanadoo.fr
www.hotel-saint-romain.fr

Closed from 9 to 20 Jan and Sun evening from early Nov to late Apr • 24 rooms, most have bath/WC, all have television • €48 to €56; breakfast €7; half-board available • Menus €19 (except Sunday lunchtime) to €46 • Terrace, garden, private car park

Make sure you don't get lost in the labyrinthine passages of the village's 13C castle.

Don't pass up the chance of a visit to this lovely stone farmhouse in the heart of the Beaujolais region, where only the wind whispering through the foliage disturbs the silence. The somewhat faded air of the rooms is balanced by their spotless upkeep, while a welcoming rustic dining room leads onto a summer terrace, always packed in the high season. Your taste-buds may already be watering at the prospect of sampling the inspired meals rustled up by your owner-chef.

Access : Set back from the village, near the gendarmerie (police station)

58 DOMAINE DU CLOS DES GARANDS
Mme Yves

Les Garands
69820 Fleurie
Tel. 04 74 69 80 01
contact@closdesgarands.fr
www.closdesgarands.fr

Open all year • 4 non-smoking rooms, all with bath/WC or shower/WC • €79 to €99, breakfast included • No table d'hôte • Park, car park. Dogs not admitted

The stunning view of Fleurie and the Beaujolais mountains.

A path winding through the vines leads to this superb 6ha fully walled estate. The house and terrace command a striking view of the village and vineyards. Great attention has clearly been lavished on the interior decoration (1930's, Louis XVI and contemporary furniture) and the rooms, named after flowers, are attractively personalised. The owners offer wine tasting sessions in their sumptuous vaulted cellar.

Access : At Romanèche-Thorins, turn right onto the D 32 towards Fleurie. Before the "Fleurie" signpost, turn right and follow the "Gîtes de France" sign

RHÔNE ALPES

JULLIÉ - 69840

59 LE DOMAINE DE LA CHAPELLE DE VÂTRE
M. Capart

Le-Bourbon
69840 Jullié
Tel. 04 74 04 43 57
Fax 04 74 04 40 27
www.vatre.com

Closed during grape harvest • 3 non-smoking rooms, 2 in a different wing, all with bathroom and WC • €60 to €95, breakfast included • No table d'hôte • Terrace, car park. Dogs not admitted • Outdoor swimming pool

The happy marriage between modern interior design and old walls.

This estate, perched on the top of a hill, commands an outstanding panorama over the vineyards and the Saône Valley. A couple of Belgians, who fell in love with the property and bought it on the spot, have restored it and created three characterful rooms which combine old and new, as well as an equally attractive gîte. In the upper part of the estate, an overflow swimming pool looks down on the castle of La Roche.

Access : 3km southbound of Jullié, at Moulin-Aujas, take the Émeringes road and the lane to the right

LANCIÉ - 69220

60 LES PASQUIERS
M. et Mme Gandilhon

69220 Lancié
Tel. 04 74 69 86 33
Fax 04 74 69 86 57
ganpasq @ aol.com
www.lespasquiers.com

Open all year • 4 rooms, 1 with disabled access • €80, breakfast included • Table d'hôte €25 • Garden, car park. Credit cards not accepted • Outdoor swimming pool

A step back in time to Second Empire France.

High walls protect this lovely old house and garden from prying eyes. Many of the decorative features inside are original, such as the moulded ceilings, fireplace, carpets, library and grand piano in the sitting room. The rooms in the main house are furnished with 19C antiques, while those in the outbuilding have been reworked to a more modern design with coconut matting, bathrooms hidden by Japanese screens and children's drawings. The terrace is laid next to the swimming pool.

Access : 2km southbound from Romanèche-Thorins

RHÔNE ALPES
LES ARDILLATS - 69430 | LES HALLES - 69610

61 CHAMBRE D'HÔTE M. ET MME BONNOT
M. et Mme Bonnot

Le Bourg
69430 Les Ardillats
Tel. 04 74 04 80 20
Fax 04 74 04 80 20

Closed in Jan • 5 rooms • €42, breakfast included; half-board available • Table d'hôte €17 • Garden, car park. Credit cards not accepted, no dogs admitted

62 MANOIR DE TOURVILLE
M. et Mme Goubier

69610 Les Halles
Tel. 04 74 26 66 57
Fax 04 74 26 66 57
tourville@manoirdetourville.com
www.manoirdetourville.com

Open all year • 5 non-smoking rooms and apartment, all have bath/WC or shower/WC • €60 to €120, breakfast included • Table d'hôte €20 to €35 (evenings only and by reservation) • Park, car park. Dogs admitted on request

---

Pamper your taste-buds in this lovely Beaujolais home.

This handsome farm on the doorstep of a sleepy country village is the sort of place you dream of. Its thick stone walls and natural wooden shutters immediately catch the eye, which is further treated to the vision of a lovely country interior. Bright colours and thick beams paint the juicy picture of the rooms, each of which is named after a fruit – raspberry, pineapple, plum, grapefruit and mandarin. Sample the delicious home cooking, washed down with a fruity glass of Beaujolais.

The immense 20hectare grounds.

Tree-lined grounds, dotted with small lakes which are home to swans and ducks, surround this mansion which dates back to the 14C. Handsome staircases lead up to the bedrooms and to the apartment fitted out with antiques. French breakfasts and delicious family cooking made with home-grown or local produce are served in a beautiful dining room complete with wood panelling and floors.

Access : 5km to the north-west of Beaujeu on the D 37

Access : On the D 4 between Ste-Foy-l'Argentière and St-Laurent-de-Chamrousset

RHÔNE ALPES

LUCENAY - 69480

63 LES TILLEULS
Mme Vermare Michèle

31 route de Lachassagne
69480 Lucenay
Tel. 04 74 60 28 58
Fax 04 74 60 28 58
vermare@hotmail.com
www.lestilleuls.org

Open all year • 3 non-smoking rooms on two floors, one of which in a separate wing, all have bath/WC or shower/WC • €80 to €100, breakfast included • Table d'hôte €25 • Terrace. Credit cards not accepted, dogs not admitted • Golf, water-sports centre

We most liked: The delightful warm welcome.

This former wine-grower's house, parts of which date from the 17C, stands opposite the village church. The interior decoration is an elegant combination of old and new (bare stone walls, timber beams and modern furniture), both in the dining room and sitting room, as in the three cheerful personalised bedrooms. The owner, a keen cook, adores concocting mouth-watering dishes to the delight of her guests and is planning on running cooking courses taught by a chef.

Access: In the town

LYON - 69002

64 ARTISTES
Mme Lameloise

8 rue Gaspard-André
69002 Lyon
Tel. 04 78 42 04 88
Fax 04 78 42 93 76
hartiste@club-internet.fr
www.hoteldesartistes.fr

Open all year • 45 rooms, all have bath/WC or shower/WC and television • €85 to €115; breakfast €9 • No restaurant • No dogs admitted

We most liked: Old Lyons' giant maze of "traboules" – covered pedestrian passages.

This delightful hotel is located right in the heart of Lyons, on the peninsula opposite Fourvière Hill. The rooms are light and airy and make up in practicality what they lack in luxury; some overlook the Célestins Theatre, hence the hotel's name. The breakfast room is adorned with a fresco inspired by Cocteau. A nearby public car park is also most appreciated.

Access: Near Place Bellecour (and Bellecour car park), opposite the theatre

RHÔNE ALPES
QUINCIÉ-EN-BEAUJOLAIS - 69430

QUINCIÉ-EN-BEAUJOLAIS - 69430

65 CHAMBRE D'HÔTE GÉRARD LAGNEAU
M. et Mme Lagneau

Huire
69430 Quincié-en-Beaujolais
Tel. 04 74 69 20 70
Fax 04 74 04 89 44
jealagneau@wanadoo.fr

Open all year • 4 non-smoking rooms upstairs, all have bathrooms • €58, breakfast included • No table d'hôte • Garden, car park. Credit cards not accepted

A genuine wine-growing atmosphere.

A hamlet encircled by vineyards is the scene for the pleasant stone-built home of this wine-growing family who bend over backwards to make you feel at home with them. The rooms upstairs are simply decorated and spotlessly clean. You will breakfast under the beams of a rustic room. The icing on the cake is, however, the 16C cellar. Where better to sample the house vintages?

Access: In the middle of the vineyards

66 DOMAINE DE ROMARAND
M. et Mme Berthelot

69430 Quincié-en-Beaujolais
Tel. 04 74 04 34 49
Fax 04 74 04 35 92

Closed 25 Dec and Jan 1 • 3 rooms • €55 to €58, breakfast included • Table d'hôte €20 (evenings only by reservation) • Garden, car park • Outdoor swimming pool. Wine tasting and sales

The overwhelming bouquet of fine wines.

This lovely stone house run by a wine-growing couple is set in a U-shaped courtyard overlooking a flowered rock garden, vineyards and the surrounding mountains. All the modern, comfortable rooms enjoy the same panoramic view. The rafters, fireplace, huge wooden table and maps of the Beaujolais region add character to the dining room. A profusion of home-made pastries and jams adds that little extra to breakfast time.

Access: 9km to the south-east of Beaujeu on the D 37 and the D 9, then drive towards Varennes

RHÔNE ALPES

SAINT-LAURENT-DE-MURE - 69720

67 HOSTELLERIE LE SAINT-LAURENT
M. Lavault

8 rue Croix-Blanche
69720 Saint-Laurent-de-Mure
Tel. 04 78 40 91 44
Fax 04 78 40 45 41
le.st.laurent@wanadoo.fr
www.lesaintlaurent.fr

Closed from 26 Dec to 2 Jan, 30 Apr to 8 May, 16 May, 14 to 16 Jul, 30 Jul to 20 Aug, 27 Aug • 30 rooms with bath/WC or shower/WC, all have television • €58 to €110; breakfast €7 • Menus €22 to €56 • Terrace, park, 2 car parks, one of which is private. No dogs admitted in rooms

Entirely devoted to guests' welfare.

This 18C mansion and its flowered park make an ideal stopover for weary travellers. It offers small, comfortable rooms – those in a separate wing are more modern. At mealtimes, you can choose between the warmth of maple wood or immense bay windows overlooking the greenery. In fine weather, the shade of the three-hundred-year-old lime tree is sheer bliss.

Access : 15km from Lyon, set back from the N 6

SAINT-VERAND - 69620

68 AUCHERAND
M. Degottex

69620 - Saint-Vérand
Tel. 04 74 71 85 92
degottex@aol.com

Open all year • 5 non-smoking rooms, all with shower/WC • €92, breakfast included • Table d'hôte €20 • Park, car park. Credit cards not accepted, dogs not admitted • Outdoor swimming pool, tennis court

The table d'hôte and its bistro-style decoration

The owners did all the work inside this delightful traditional Beaujolais house themselves. Monsieur, a former antique dealer, chose the furniture, while Madame, an interior decorator, selected the colours and fabrics of the bedrooms, apartment in the converted stables, and the enchanting sitting room area with fireplace and piano. Relax around the swimming pool or knock a few balls about on the tennis court, both of which are located in the 3ha park.

Access : In the town

RHÔNE ALPES

THIZY - 69240

VAUX-EN-BEAUJOLAIS - 69460

69 LA TERRASSE
M. et Mme Arnette

Le Bourg - Marnand
69240 Thizy
Tel. 04 74 64 19 22
Fax 04 74 64 25 95
francis.arnette@wanadoo.fr
www.laterrasse-marnand.com

Closed during Feb and Nov half-terms, Mon (except the hotel) and Sun evening • 10 rooms, one of which has disabled access, with bath/WC and television • €45; breakfast €6; half-board available • Menus €13 (weekdays) to €63 • Terrace, car park • Children's games room

Just six kilometres from the water-sports of Lake Sapins.

This old textile factory, typical of the Beaujolais region, has been turned into a hotel. The agreeable rooms with terraces open directly onto the garden; each is named after a flower or aromatic plant and the decoration, even the fragrance, matches the theme. Two modern, soberly decorated dining rooms and a spacious terrace overlooking the mountains of the Lyonnais complete the picture: their modern menu features regionally inspired recipes.

Access : 2km to the north-east on the D 94, on the way into Bourg-Marnand, opposite the town hall

70 LES PICORETTES
M. et Mme Blettner

Montrichard
69460 Vaux-en-Beaujolais
Tel. 04 74 02 14 07
Fax 04 74 02 14 21
www.picorettes.com

Open all year • 3 non-smoking rooms and 1 apartment, all with bath/WC and shower/WC • €62 to €90, breakfast included • Table d'hôte €23 • Car park. Dogs not admitted • Outdoor swimming pool

The amiable welcome.

The handsome Beaujolais-style house of Josette and Francis Blettner has three bedrooms and one family apartment. All are treated to fresh flowers every day. On the second floor, the "Vigne" room commands the best view of the village. Extremely generous breakfasts (cheese, eggs, bread, home-made jam) are followed by more traditional dishes in the evenings (blanquette de veau, Bresse chicken).

Access : Take the D 49E for 2km southbound from Vaux-en-Beaujolais to a place known as Montrichard

RHÔNE ALPES

VILLEFRANCHE-SUR-SAÔNE - 69400

71 LA FERME DU POULET
M. et Mme Rongeat

180 rue Georges-Mangin
69400 Villefranche-sur-Saône
Tel. 04 74 62 19 07
Fax 04 74 09 01 89
la.ferme.du.poulet@wanadoo.fr

Closed from 7 to 24 Aug, from 23 Dec to 2 Jan, Sun evening and Mon • 10 rooms, all have bath/WC and television • €80; breakfast €12 • Menus €35 to €60 • Terrace, car park. Dogs not admitted in rooms

A cheerful blend of rustic and contemporary flavours.

A sanctuary of greenery in the heart of an industrial estate, this beautifully-restored 17C fortified farm is protected from the bustle of urban life by a wall. All the spacious, functional rooms have excellent bedding. Multicoloured tableware livens up the magnificent old beams of the dining room. Pleasant inner courtyard terrace.

Access : North-east of Villefranche, in the Industrial Zone (ZI) near the exhibition park

AIX-LES-BAINS - 73100

72 AUBERGE SAINT-SIMOND
M. et Mme Mattana

130 avenue Saint-Simond
73100 Aix-les-Bains
Tel. 04 79 88 35 02
Fax 04 79 88 38 45
auberge@saintsimond.com
www.saintsimond.com

Closed in Jan, Nov school holidays, 22 to 31 Dec and Sun evening • 28 rooms, 2 of which have disabled access, all have bath/WC or shower/WC and television • €50 to €75; breakfast €8; half-board available • Menus €21 to €35 • Car park, terrace, garden. No dogs admitted in restaurant • Swimming pool

The garden lined with trees and flowers.

For over a century, travellers have been resting their weary legs in this former post house then inn, just a few minutes from the Lac du Bourget. Eight rooms have been renovated and treated to soundproofing and new furniture, bedding and decoration. The others are comfortable if a little plain; some have a balcony; we recommend those overlooking the garden. Local dishes are served in the dining room-veranda which extends onto a terrace shaded by lovely old plane trees.

Access : Near the town centre

RHÔNE ALPES
AIX-LES-BAINS - 73100   AUSSOIS - 73500

73 LA CROIX DU SUD
Mme Collot

3 rue du Docteur-Duvernay
73100 Aix-les-Bains
Tel. 04 79 35 05 87
Fax 04 79 35 72 71
lecrire@hotel-lacroixdusud.com
www.hotel-lacroixdusud.com

Closed from 4 Nov to 9 Apr • 16 rooms, some have bath/WC or shower/WC and television • €29 to €40; breakfast €6 • No restaurant • Small courtyard-garden. Credit cards not accepted, no dogs admitted in restaurant • Television room with a small library

The old-fashioned charm of this early 20C bourgeois home.

Could it be to conjure up memories of his trips to distant lands that the former owner built up this collection of hats from the world over? Equally popular with tourists and "patients" come to take the waters, this hotel is renowned for its faultless hospitality. The generously-dimensioned bedrooms sport a stylish old-fashioned blend of moulded ceilings and marble fireplaces.

Access : In the town centre, in a small, quiet street

74 SOLEIL
M. Montaz

15 rue de l'Église
73500 Aussois
Tel. 04 79 20 32 42
Fax 04 79 20 37 78
www.hotel-du-soleil.com

Closed from 21 Apr to 15 Jun and 30 Sep to 17 Dec
• 22 rooms, one of which has disabled access, with bath/WC or shower/WC, all have television • €66 to €84, breakfast included; half-board available • Menus €20 to €22 (evenings only) • Terrace, car park. No dogs admitted in rooms • Cinema room, sauna, hammam, jacuzzi, souvenir shop, billiards, skiing in season

Discover the thrill of the 2 560m Via Ferrata rock-climbing course – the longest in France.

Next door to the church, whose bells are considerate enough to remain silent after nightfall, the walls of this austere chalet hide a warm interior. The rooms enjoy superb views of the village and the Vanoise range; ask for one of the renovated chalet-style rooms with light wood and pretty fabrics. There is no lack of outdoor activities from the roof terrace sun deck, open air jacuzzi, giant chess board and skittles, while indoors, you can sample the sauna, hammam and home cinema facilities.

Access : Near the church

RHÔNE ALPES

BONNEVAL-SUR-ARC - 73480

75 À LA PASTOURELLE
M. Blanc

73480 Bonneval-sur-Arc
Tel. 04 79 05 81 56
Fax 04 79 05 85 44
www.pastourelle.com

Closed one week in May or Jun and Nov half-term • 12 rooms with bath/WC • €56 to €58; breakfast €7; half-board available • Restaurant closed out of season; menus €12 to €18 • Library-sitting room. No dogs admitted • Skiing and hiking nearby

On the doorstep of one of France's most beautiful skiing domains.

The roof of schist tiles and the name, which means cowgirl, both bear witness to the house's dedication to local traditions. Whether a one-night stopover on your journey through the French Alps or a base camp for breathtaking races down the slopes of La Vanoise, it will provide that little extra to make each day just perfect. The rooms are snug and cosy and the dining room is rich with the perfume of savoury cheese raclettes, fondues and sweet pancakes.

Access : In the upper part of the resort

BOURG-SAINT-MAURICE - 73700

76 L'AUTANTIC
Mme Bourgeois

69 route d'Hauteville
73700 Bourg-Saint-Maurice
Tel. 04 79 07 01 70
Fax 04 79 07 51 55
hotel.autantic@wanadoo.fr
www.hotel-autantic.com

Open all year • 29 rooms, 2 of which have disabled access, with bath/WC (2 have shower/WC) and television • €45 to €80; breakfast €8 • No restaurant • Car park • Indoor swimming pool, sauna

Tasting the thrills of white-water rafting on the Bourg.

The stone walls and narrow windows of this sturdy house, in the style of a traditional mountain chalet, were built recently in a quiet district of Bourg St Maurice, near the futuristic funicular railway up to the Arcs resort. The rooms, decorated with roughcast walls and pine furniture, overlook the peaceful valley and four have a balcony. Friendly staff and breakfast on the terrace are among the other perks of this modern chalet.

Access : On the way into the village, a little set back from the road

RHÔNE ALPES
CREST-VOLAND - 73590   LA CÔTE-D'AIME - 73210

77 LE CAPRICE DES NEIGES
Famille Borrel

Route du Col des Saisies
73590 Crest-Voland
Tel. 04 79 31 62 95
Fax 04 79 31 79 30
info@hotel-capricedesneiges.com
www.hotel-capricedesneiges.com

Closed from 15 Apr to 19 Jun and 15 Sep to 20 Dec • 16 rooms with bath/WC, some have television • €78 to €88; breakfast €8; half-board available • Menus €15 to €40 • Terrace, garden, car park. Dogs not admitted • In summer: tennis, fly fishing, mini-golf; in winter: skiing and snowshoe hiking

Little teddy bears adorn some of the rooms of this friendly, family establishment.

The soft warm hues of wood greet the eye wherever you look in this exquisite chalet, just outside the village but at the foot of the slopes. Step into its welcoming doll's house interior and feast your eyes on the lovely fabrics, ornaments and Savoyard furniture. The rooms on the second floor have been renovated and it is planned to refurbish the others in the near future. All offer spectacular views of the Aravis and the mountain pastures. Regional delicacies.

Access : On the road from Col des Saisies, 1km from the resort and 50m from the ski lift

78 CHALET LE PARADOU
M. Hanrard

Pré Bérard
73210 La Côte-d'Aime
Tel. 04 79 55 67 79
Fax 04 79 55 67 79
hanrard@aol.com

Closed from 2 May to 30 Jun and from 4 Sep to 20 Dec • 5 rooms, 4 of which overlook a large terrace • €66, breakfast included; half-board available • Table d'hôte €17 to €22 • Garden, terrace, car park. Credit cards not accepted, dogs not admitted

An impeccably-run mountain chalet.

This superb wooden chalet perched at an altitude of 1 000m commands a stunning view of the Tarentaise Valley and Mount Pourri. The spotlessly clean, comfortable rooms open onto a large terrace. The wood-lined sitting room, complete with piano, matches the alpine spirit that prevails throughout the establishment. Skiing packages are available in the winter, and in the summer, you can laze about in the flowered garden.

Access : 3km to the north-east of Aime on the D 86

RHÔNE ALPES

LA GIETTAZ - 73590

PRALOGNAN-LA-VANOISE - 73710

79 FLOR'ALPES
M. Bibollet

73590 La Giettaz
Tel. 04 79 32 90 88
mary-anne.schouppe@wanadoo.fr

Closed from 15 Apr to 1 May and 3 Nov to 15 Dec
• 11 rooms, with bath/WC or shower/WC • €36 to €43; breakfast €6; half-board available • Menus €13 to €25
• Garden. Dogs not admitted in restaurant

Most liked The authentic Savoyard character of this village.

Tucked away between the village church and school, this welcoming boarding house owes its success to the faultless care and attention that the lady of the house lavishes on all her guests. The rooms, simple but pristine, all have a flower-decked balcony and a wonderful view, which more than compensates for the absence of television! Simple, home cooking with a regional tang is served in a rustic dining room overlooking the garden.

Access : On a small square between the town hall and the school

80 LES AIRELLES
M. Boyer

Rue des Darbelays - BP 25
73710 Pralognan-la-Vanoise
Tel. 04 79 08 70 32
Fax 04 79 08 73 51
hotellesairelles@free.fr
www.hotel-les-airelles.fr

Closed from 22 Apr to 3 Jun and from 17 Sep to 23 Dec
• 22 rooms with bath/WC or shower/WC and television
• €68 to €82; breakfast €8; half-board available • Menus €20 to €24 • Terrace, garage, car park. No dogs admitted
• Swimming pool, sauna, Jacuzzi, billiards, shuttle to the ski lifts

Most liked Pralognan combines the charm of a village with the facilities of a top-class ski resort.

This chalet, built on the outskirts of the resort, is encircled by the ridges and crests of the Vanoise massif. The mountain view from the rooms and balconies never fails to bring gasps of admiration. In the kitchen, the talented young chef's recipes provoke further cries of approval. On the leisure side, the swimming pool is heated, and the owner, an enthusiastic hiker, never tires of indicating paths and trails to eager guests.

Access : In the upper part of the resort, next to the Granges forest

RHÔNE ALPES
SAINT-SORLIN-D'ARVES - 73530   ST-CHRISTOPHE-LA-GROTTE - 73360

81 BEAUSOLEIL
M. et Mme Vermeulen

73530 Saint-Sorlin-d'Arves
Tel. 04 79 59 71 42
Fax 04 79 59 75 25
info@hotel-beausoleil.com
www.hotel-beausoleil.com

Closed from 15 Apr to 30 Jun and 1 Sep to 15 Dec • 20 rooms on 3 floors, all have bath/WC or shower/WC and television • €50 to €64; breakfast €9; half-board available • Menus €13 to €24 • Terrace, garden, car park. No dogs admitted in the restaurant • Sauna, hammam, jacuzzi, walks in the Croix de Fer Pass and mountain sports

We most liked **Sunshine and powdery snow: what more could you want?**

You know you're in for a treat right from the moment you begin to climb the road by the Combe Genin or the Croix de Fer Pass, driving past snowy peaks or pastures of wild mountain flowers up to this remote mountain chalet. Families are welcome in the practical, attractively furnished rooms. After a long day out in the open air, you will be ready to feast on the delicacies rustled up by your cheerful host.

Access : Away from the centre of the resort, towards the Col de la Croix-de-Fer

82 LA FERME BONNE DE LA GROTTE
M. Amayenc

73360 Saint-Christophe-la-Grotte
Tel. 04 79 36 59 05
Fax 04 79 36 59 31
info@ferme-bonne.com
www.gites-savoie.com

Open all year • 5 rooms, some have mezzanines • €66 to €89, breakfast included • Table d'hôte €18 to €27 • Terrace, park, car park. No dogs admitted

We most liked **Irresistibly Savoyard in spirit and flavour.**

In the space of a year, this three-century-old farm at the foot of the Échelles caves has become a must in the region. The renowned cuisine has remained true to its Savoyard roots and the gourmet chef takes great pleasure in watching his guests devour his tasty home cooking. The immense but still cosy rooms are all graced with painted furniture; some also boast a mezzanine.

Access : 4km to the north-east of Échelles on the N 6, Chambéry road

RHÔNE ALPES

VILLARODIN-BOURGET - 73500

83 CHÉ CATRINE
Mme Finas

88 rue Saint-Antoine
73500 Villarodin-Bourget
Tel. 04 79 20 49 32
Fax 04 79 20 48 67
info@che-catrine.com
che-catrine.com

Open all year • 3 rooms and 2 apartments, all have bath/WC • €80 to €107 (€64 to €85 low season), breakfast included; half-board available • Table d'hôte €30 • Garden. Credit cards not accepted • Sauna

Savour the good things of life in this superb mansion.

This country house, built in 1524, and restored in keeping with Savoyard traditions, is a gem of a find. You will immediately feel at home in the rooms and suites, decorated with solid pine furniture. Meals are served in the vaulted stables and the lounge-bar – hewn out of solid rock – is a delight for the eyes. The chef makes it a point of honour to use only garden vegetables and meat from the Maurienne Valley. Definitely worth writing home about, unless you'd rather keep it to yourself!

Access: A 43 motorway, exit Modane, then after Modane 2km on the RN 6 towards the Haute Maurienne

CHAMONIX-MONT-BLANC - 74400

84 L'AIGUILLE DU MIDI
M. et Mme Farini

479 chemin Napoléon - Les Bossons
74400 Chamonix-Mont-Blanc
Tel. 04 50 53 00 65
Fax 04 50 55 93 69
hotel-aiguille-du-midi@wanadoo.fr
www.hotel-aiguilledumidi.com

Closed from 17 Apr to 20 May and 20 Sep to 20 Dec • 40 rooms with bath/WC and television • €69 to €80; breakfast €12; half-board available • Menus €21 (weekdays) to €44 • Terrace, garden, car park. No dogs admitted in restaurant • Outdoor swimming pool, tennis, fitness room, sauna, jacuzzi

The view of the Bossons glacier from the shade of the park.

This impressive old country chalet has been a hotel since 1908. Behind the Tyrolean-style frescoes are wainscoted rooms, most a little faded, but all overlooking the wonderful Mont Blanc range. The circular dining room and the terrace with wooden furniture and a giant parasol give onto a lovely flowery park. Make sure you look up and admire the beautiful carved ceiling in the sitting room. Numerous leisure activities.

Access: 3km southbound from Chamonix-Mont-Blanc

RHÔNE ALPES
CHAMONIX-MONT-BLANC - 74400   CHÂTEL - 74390

85 BEAUSOLEIL
M. et Mme Bossonney

Le Lavancher
74400 Chamonix-Mont-Blanc
Tel. 04 50 54 00 78
Fax 04 50 54 17 34
info@hotelbeausoleilchamonix.com
www.hotelbeausoleilchamonix.com

Closed 9 to 24 May and 20 Sep to 20 Dec • 17 rooms on 2 levels, with bath/WC or shower/WC and television • €86 to €98, (€70 to €80 low season); breakfast €10; half-board available • Menus €14 to €28 • Terrace, garden, car park. No dogs admitted in restaurant • Tennis, table-tennis

The tranquillity of this secluded chalet.

Are you more of a winter- or a summer-mountain type? The Bossonney family, who have run the hotel for three generations, are guaranteed to make you feel at home in their inviting chalet, whatever the season. The small, wainscoted, refreshingly simple rooms are faultlessly kept and a few boast balconies with a view of snow-capped peaks or green pastures. Tasty home cooking and cheese-based specialities are served in a country-style dining room which opens onto the terrace and garden.

Access : 6km on the N 506, towards Argentière, then minor road on the right

86 LE KANDAHAR
Mme Vuarand

Route du Linga
74390 Châtel
Tel. 04 50 73 30 60
Fax 04 50 73 25 17
lekandahar@wanadoo.fr
www.lekandahar.com

Closed from 23 Apr to 23 May, 18 Jun to 5 Jul and 1 Nov to 23 Dec, Tue evening and Wed • 8 rooms, all have bath/WC and television • €70 to €80 (€60 to €70 low season); breakfast €8; half-board available • Menus €13 (weekdays) to €33 • Terrace, garden, car park • Fitness room, sauna

The family atmosphere of this alpine chalet.

This hotel on the border of Switzerland is renowned for the hospitable, welcoming aspect of its rooms. Within easy reach of the ski slopes thanks to frequent, free shuttles to the Linga, it is also surrounded by gentler hillsides for the less energetic, but the breathtaking viewpoints over the Chablais definitely require the efforts of serious walkers. In the kitchen, the chef sets-to with a will, to restore and revive body and soul with delicious local specialities.

Access : 1.5km to the south-west, on the Bechigne road, then left on the Linga road

RHÔNE ALPES

CORDON - 74700

LA CHAPELLE-D'ABONDANCE - 74360

87 LE CORDONANT
M. et Mme Pugnat

Les Darbaillets
74700 Cordon
Tel. 04 50 58 34 56
Fax 04 50 47 95 57
lecordonant@wanadoo.fr

Closed from mid-Apr to mid-May and from Oct to Dec • 16 rooms with bath/WC (2 have shower/WC) and television • €78 to €85; (€74 to €80 low season); breakfast €8; half-board available • Menus €24 (weekdays) to €32 • Terrace, car park. No dogs admitted in restaurant • Fitness room, sauna, jacuzzi

The ear-splitting silence and stunning view from the valley windows.

The pink roughcast walls and creamy coloured woodwork of this smart chalet stand on the heights of the "Mont Blanc balcony". The rooms have been refurbished in a contemporary Savoyard style with wood-lined walls, painted furniture and pretty fabrics. From the dining room, you will be able to enjoy a breathtaking view of the "rooftops of Europe" as you sample the appetising, generous cooking, before settling down for a nap in the sun in the flowered garden.

Access : 4km to the south-west of Sallanches on the D 113

88 LES GENTIANETTES
M. et Mme Trincaz

Route de Chevenne
74360 La Chapelle-d'Abondance
Tel. 04 50 73 56 46
Fax 04 50 73 56 39
bienvenue@gentianettes.fr
www.gentianettes.fr

Closed out of season from Easter to 1 Nov and 20 Sep to 18 Dec • 32 rooms with bath/WC or shower/WC and television, 2 have disabled access • €70 to €95; breakfast €9; half-board available • Menus €19 to €59 • Terrace, car park • Indoor swimming pool, sauna, fitness room, hammam

Sampling the chef's mouth-watering cooking after a day in the open air.

A faultless welcome, well-proportioned cheerful bedrooms with wainscoting and balconies, a pleasant dining room and carnotzets (sitting-rooms), impeccable regional cuisine and generous breakfasts – what more could one ask from this pretty chalet built in 1994? Those lucky enough to come to La Chapelle-d'Abondance in the summertime may catch sight of a gentian flower, the high-altitude herbaceous plant which gave the hotel its name. In winter, alpine sports are more the order of the day!

Access : North of Chapelle-d'Abondance

RHÔNE ALPES

LA BEUNAZ - 74500　　　　　　　　　　　LA CLUSAZ - 74220

89　LE BOIS JOLI
M. et Mme Birraux

74500 La Beunaz
Tel. 04 50 73 60 11
Fax 04 50 73 65 28
hboisjoli @ aol.com
www.hotel-bois-joli.com

Closed from 10 Oct to 20 Dec and mid-Mar to mid-Apr • 29 rooms, 8 of which are in a separate wing, all have bath/WC or shower/WC and television • €74 to €85 (€65 to €75 low season); breakfast €10; half-board available • Restaurant closed Sun evening and Wed; menus €22 (weekdays) to €48 • Terrace, garden, car park • Outdoor swimming pool, tennis, sauna, table-tennis, billiards

We most liked **The country appeal of this panoramic chalet.**

The bedrooms, dining room and terrace all enjoy a view of the Dent d'Oche, Mount Billiat and the summits of the Chablais. In the summer, activities include a swimming pool surrounded by foliage and a tennis court, in the winter the ski slopes are nearby while year-round activities include a children's play area and billiards room with Lake Léman and its prestigious spa resorts just a few kilometres away. Idyllic in any season.

Access : Below the road, 1.5km from Bernex on the D 52

90　FLORALP
Mmes Pollet

79 chemin du Pré-de-Foire
74220 La Clusaz
Tel. 04 50 02 41 46
Fax 04 50 02 63 94
info @ hotel-floralp74.com
www.hotel-floralp74.com

Open from 28 Jun to 15 Sep and from 20 Dec to 14 Apr • 20 rooms, all have bath/WC or shower/WC and television. Front-facing rooms have balconies. • €60 to €90 (€48 to €75 low season); breakfast €8; half-board available • Menus €18 (weekdays) to €26 • Car park. No dogs admitted in restaurant • Billiards room

We most liked **A traditional mountain chalet.**

The simple rooms at the front have an east-facing balcony and are much sought after by all the chalet's numerous regular guests. The region is riddled with beautiful, immaculate peaks, dales covered in rhododendron bushes and high rocky ranges. Tangy Tomme and Reblochon cheeses tempt the palate at lunchtime and dinners enable your hostesses to show off the full scope of their culinary skills. The sitting room with bar, billiard table and fireside is the perfect place for a nightcap.

Access : At the entrance to the resort, coming from Annecy on the D 909, take a right

RHÔNE ALPES

LES CARROZ-D'ARACHES - 74300

91 LA CROIX DE SAVOIE
M. et Mme Tiret

768 route du Pernand
74300 Les Carroz-d'Araches
Tel. 04 50 90 00 26
Fax 04 50 90 00 63
info@lacroixdesavoie.fr
www.lacroixdesavoie.fr

Closed Sun evening and Mon lunchtime • 19 rooms with shower/WC, most have a balcony • €77 to €83 (€49 to €75 low season); breakfast €8; half-board available • Menus €18 to €36 • Terrace, garden, car park

Savour the tranquillity and the view of the Aravis and lose track of time.

This establishment, ideally located in the ski resort, is a haven of friendliness. The rooms, nearly all of which have a balcony, are an excellent combination of simple comfort and warm wood-panelling. Wood is also the predominant feature of the restaurant which serves regional dishes. Winter guests can head for the immense skiing domain and in the summer, walkers set off to explore the mineral kingdom of Platé. If you're lucky, you may catch a glimpse of a wild ibex following your climb.

Access : In the upper part of the resort, 1km from the centre, towards Flaine

LES CONTAMINES-MONTJOIE - 74170

92 GAI SOLEIL
Mme Mermoud

288 chemin des Loyers
74170 Les Contamines-Montjoie
Tel. 04 50 47 02 94
Fax 04 50 47 18 43
gaisoleil2@wanadoo.fr
www.gaisoleil.com

Closed from 20 Apr to 14 Jun and 15 Sep to 20 Dec • 19 rooms with bath/WC or shower/WC, no television • €65 to €72 (€62 to €68 low season); breakfast €10; half-board available • Menus €20 to €27 • Garden, car park. Dogs not admitted in restaurant • Fondue evenings and films on mountain life

Mount Joly and the snowy peaks of the Miage greet you in the morning.

The painting on one of the beams bearing the date 1823, was the work of the chalet's original owner. The Gai Soleil's website joyfully relates this family farm's intriguing history – an English version is in the pipeline, we're told. Ask for one of the rooms refurbished in a mountain style with wood walls and pine furniture. The south-facing terrace is popular in winter and summer alike. Attractive garden.

Access : In the upper part of the resort

RHÔNE ALPES
MENTHON-SAINT-BERNARD - 74290 | MORZINE - 74110

93 BEAU SÉJOUR
M. et Mme Blanc

Allée des Tennis
74290 Menthon-Saint-Bernard
Tel. 04 50 60 12 04
Fax 04 50 60 05 56

Open from 15 Apr to late Sep • 18 rooms, 14 of which have shower/WC, 4 have bath/WC • €65 to €73; breakfast €8 • No restaurant • Garden, private car park. Credit cards not accepted • Table-tennis, reading room. Tennis, golf and water sports nearby

We most liked
Visit the fairy-tale castle of Menthon.

One hundred metres from Lake Annecy, this early-20C villa stands in an enormous park. The bedrooms with balcony, the most spacious, have recently been renovated, doing away with the distinctive hallmarks of the seventies. The bay windows of the breakfast room overlook the flowered garden where meals are served whenever the weather is warm enough. Friendly, family service.

Access : 100m from the lake

94 FLEUR DES NEIGES
M. Archambault

74110 Morzine
Tel. 04 50 79 01 23
Fax 04 50 75 95 75
fleurneige @ aol.com
www.fleurdesneiges.com

Closed from 10 Apr to 1 Jul and 5 Sep to 18 Dec • 32 rooms, all have bath/WC or shower/WC and television • €70 to €90 (€50 to €60 low season); breakfast €10; half-board available • Menu €20 to €25 • Terrace, garden, car park. No dogs admitted in restaurant • Indoor swimming pool, tennis, fitness room, sauna, table-tennis, petanque

We most liked
Soothing your aching muscles in the pool after a day on the slopes.

This chalet-style building is a little out of the centre of Chablais' tourist capital, Morzine. When booking, ask for one of the renovated rooms with wood-lined walls, pine furniture and matching fabrics; plans are afoot to redecorate the rather dour dining room in the near future. The hotel's facilities – fitness room, sauna, tennis court, swimming pool (indoor in winter) – reflect the resort's combination of sport and leisure activities.

Access : Slightly out of the centre, on the Thonon-les-Bains road

RHÔNE ALPES

SALLANCHES - 74700

95 AUBERGE DE L'ORANGERIE
M. Liboureau

3 carrefour de la Charlotte
74700 Sallanches
Tel. 04 50 58 49 16
Fax 04 50 58 54 63
auberge-orangerie@wanadoo.fr

Closed from 19 Jun to 3 Jul • 7 rooms with bath/WC or shower/WC and television • €45 to €60; breakfast €8 • Restaurant closed Sun evening, Mon all day and Tue, Wed and Thu lunchtimes; menus €23 to €43 • Private car park, garden, terrace

Gazing up at the mountains from one of the snug rooms.

In the summertime, the façade of this chalet at the foot of the Côte de Passy is a riot of flowers. The well-renovated rooms guarantee that your nights will be quiet and peaceful: pine-panelling, excellent soundproofing against the noise of the road, big beds piled high with duvets, inviting armchairs and fully tiled bathrooms. Some have a balcony. The owner-chef's cuisine, served in the rustic dining room, displays his creative flair for mixing traditional recipes and local dishes.

Access : Outside the town at the foot of the Côte de Passy

SERVOZ - 74310

96 GORGES DE LA DIOSAZ
M. Fraipont

"Sous le Roc"
74310 Servoz
Tel. 04 50 47 20 97
Fax 04 50 47 21 08
info@hoteldesgorges.com
www.hoteldesgorges.com

Closed from 15 to 30 May and from 15 to 30 Nov • 7 rooms with bath/WC or shower/WC and television • €55 to €65 (€50 to €55 low season); breakfast €7; half-board available • Menus €18 to €44 • Terrace

Francine and Sébastien greet guests energetically and warmly.

This traditional mountain chalet decked in flowers stands on the edge of the gorges of the Diosaz. The restful rooms have been refurbished in a sober, contemporary alpine style and the windows of the inviting rustic dining room overlook the Mont Blanc range. Wood prevails in the sitting room and bar, where you can gratefully relax with a glass of mulled wine after a hard day on the slopes.

Access : In the centre of the village, near the post office

RHÔNE ALPES
SEYTHENEX - 74210   YVOIRE - 74140

97 AU GAY SÉJOUR
M. et Mme Gay

Le Tertenoz
74210 Seythenex
Tel. 04 50 44 52 52
Fax 04 50 44 49 52
hotel-gay-sejour@wanadoo.fr
www.hotel-gay-sejour.com

Closed from 15 Nov to 15 Dec, Sun evening and Mon (except public holidays) • 10 rooms with bath/WC and television • €78 to €110; breakfast €12; half-board available • Menus €26 to €75 • Terrace, car park. No dogs admitted in rooms • Snowshoe hiking and ski slopes nearby

We most liked **A summer vista of lush mountain pastures or a winter picture of fields of snow.**

This 17C farm, nestling in a peaceful medium-altitude hamlet, has been turned into a pleasant family inn where you can be sure of a lung-full of pure mountain air. Though hardly stylish, the rooms are nonetheless wonderfully peaceful and some enjoy a lovely view of the valley. In the restaurant, the focus is on immaculate service and well-judged traditional cooking.

Access : 4km to the south-east of Faverges

98 LE VIEUX LOGIS
M. Jacquier-Durand

Rue des Remparts
74140 Yvoire
Tel. 04 50 72 80 24
Fax 04 50 72 90 76
contact @ levieuxlogis.com
www.levieuxlogis.com

Closed from 1 Jan to 15 Feb • 11 rooms, all have bath/WC and television • €68 to €78; breakfast €8; half-board available • Restaurant closed Sun evening and Mon; menus €20 (weekdays) to €45 • Terrace, private car park

We most liked **The Maze-Garden of the Five Senses in the medieval village.**

This "old abode" of character, run by the same family for four generations, is set right in the ramparts. The rooms are practical and those on the first floor have a balcony; thick 14C walls keep the interior cool, even during the hot summer months. Under the vaulted ceiling and well-worn beams of the dining room, you will be invited to sample the house speciality of fillets of perch. In the summer, meals are also served on the lovely shaded terrace.

Access : On the way into the old town, set in the ramparts

LOW PRICE HOTELS AND MAISONS D'HÔTE

So that you can treat yourself without having to break open your piggy bank, we have selected hotels and chambres d'hôte which offer a warm welcome, pleasant setting and character combined with affordable prices. The coin symbol next to an establishment indicates that it is a hotel or maison d'hôte with rooms at a maximum price of €40 per night for two (breakfast included in the maisons d'hôte, but extra in hotels).

ALSACE
Bas-Rhin
La Bonne Franquette 23
Au Cheval Blanc 19
Le Clos de la Garenne 22
Gimbelhof 16
Klein 13
Krumeich 12
La Maison du Charron 20
Le Vignoble 14
Winzenberg 13
Haut-Rhin
Auberge et Hostellerie Paysanne 29
Au Cerf 36
Aux Deux Clefs 30
Ferme du Busset 31
Maison Thomas 25
Aux Mines d'Argent 34

AQUITAINE
Dordogne
Chambre d'Hôte au Village 59
Ferme des Guezoux 60
Hôtel des Bories 51
Hôtel des Récollets 58

Hôtel du Château 44
Le Panoramique 49
La Touille 45
Gironde
Henri IV 65
La Tour du Vieux Port 67
Landes
Les Arbousiers 76
Capcazal de Pachiou 76
Le Domaine de Paguy 74
Le Poutic 74
Pyrénées-Atlantiques
La Belle Auberge 82
Chambre d'hôte M. et Mme Asnar 86
La Closerie du Guilhat 88
La Ferme aux Sangliers 84
Ferme Etxeberria 84
Hôtel du Chêne 85
Maison Elixondoa 87
Maison Rachou 86
Soubeleta 85

AUVERGNE
Allier
Le Chalet de la Neverdière 97
Manoir Le Plaix 96

LOW PRICE HOTELS AND MAISONS D'HÔTE

Cantal
Auberge des Montagnes 104
Chambre d'Hôte M. Prudent 103
De Barathe 99
Le Griou 102
Lou Ferradou 102
Haute Loire
Les Gabales 108
Lou Chandel'Aigue 106
La Paravent 105
Les Revers 107
Puy de Dôme
Auberge de la Forge 112
Chambre d'Hôte Paul Gebrillat 117
Les Granges 115
Montarlet 119
Au Pont de Raffiny 118

BURGUNDY
Côte-d'Or
Hostellerie du Château 127
Nièvre
Le Bon Laboureur 135
Les Forges 134
Perreau 135
Verdun 136
Saône et Loire
Chambre d'Hôte M. Mathieu 142
Château de Salornay 141
La Poste 140
Villa du Vieux Puits 138
Yonne
Les Aquarelles 153
Auberge des Brizards 150
Auberge le Voutenay 155
Cabalus, l'Ancienne Hôtellerie de l'Abbaye 153
Chambre d'Hôte M. Piedallu 148
La Marmotte 147
Le Relais Saint Benoît 155
Le Relais Saint Vincent 148

BRITTANY
Côtes-d'Armor
Arvor 160
Manoir Saint-Michel 163
Finistère
An Tiez Bihan 167
Ar Presbital Koz 170
De Lescoff 168
La Ferme de Porz Kloz 164
Le Manoir de Coat Canton 165
Porz-Morvan 168
Ty-Dreux 167
Ille-et-Vilaine
Les Mouettes 175
Relais de la Rance 174
Morbihan
Auberge le Râtelier 177
Ferme de Guerlan 182
La Marine 179
Le Pélican 184
Relais du Porhoët 178
Stiren ar Mor 180

CENTRE AND UPPER LOIRE VALLEY
Cher
Auberge du Piet à Terre 190
Château de Bel Air 189
Eure-et-Loir
Chambres d'hôtes 192
L'Erablais 194
Le Moulin des Planches 193
Indre
Montgarni 197
Le Portail 197
Indre-et-Loire
Le Blason 198
De Biencourt 198
La Meulière 200
La Milaudière 203
Loiret
Domaine de la Thiau 210
La Vieille Forêt 212
Villa Hôtel 213
Loir-et-Cher
Chambre d'Hôte Peyron-Gaubert 207
Le Moulin de la Renne 209

CHAMPAGNE ARDENNE
Aube
Au Vieux Logis 218

Les Colombages Champenois	220
Ferme de la Gloire Dieu	218
Le Moulin d'Eguebaude	219
Marne	
Au Brochet du Lac	224
La Grosse Haie	222

CORSICA
Corse
Li Fundali	230

FRANCHE COMTÉ
Doubs
A l'hôtel des Trois îles	239
Auberge le Tillau	244
La Cascade	242
Le Moulin	244

Jura
Chambre d'Hôte Mme Devenat	246

ÎLE DE FRANCE AND PARIS
Seine et Marne
Chambre d'Hôte M. Dormion	261
Ferme du Chatel	263
La Ferme du Vieux Château	262

LANGUEDOC ROUSSILLON
Aude
Auberge de Cucugnan	276

Hérault
Auberge de Saugras	285
Chambre d'Hôte Monsieur Gener	287
Parc	287

Lozère
Le Saint-Sauveur	290

Pyrénées-Orientales
Les Arcades	290
Hostal dels Trabucayres	291

LIMOUSIN
Corrèze
Chez Monsieur et Madame Perrot	299
La Raze	298

Le Relais du Bas Limousin	299
À la Table de la Bergère	300
La Tour	297
Les Voyageurs	300
Haute-Vienne	
Le Moulin de Marsaguet	302
Le Relais du Taurion	302
Saint-Éloi	303

LORRAINE
Moselle
Auberge des Mésanges	308

Vosges
Auberge du Spitzemberg	313
Les Grands Prés	312
Le Relais Rose	309

MIDI PYRÉNÉES
Ariège
Maison de la Grande Ourse	319
Les Oussaillès	318

Aveyron
Auberge Saint-Fleuret	322
Carayon	324
Midi-papillon	323
À la Route d'Argent	321

Gers
Au Vieux Pressoir	332
De Bastard	334
Chambres d'Hôtes le Sabathé	336
Domaine de Loran	335

Haute-Garonne
Hôtel du Comminges	330
Le Poujastou	327

Hautes-Pyrénées
Chambre d'hôte Madame Vermeil	343
La Couette de Biéou	345
Eth Béryè Petit	344
Maison Burret	346
Le Relais du Castera	346

Lot
Château de Gamot	339
La Terrasse	339
Les Tilleuls	340

LOW PRICE HOTELS AND MAISONS D'HÔTE

Tarn
- George V 350
- Hostellerie du Vieux Cordes .. 353

Tarn-et-Garonne
- Le Quercy 356

NORD PAS DE CALAIS
Nord
- Abri du Passant 367
- Château d'En Haut 365
- Ferme de Bonavis 363
- Chez Julie 364

Pas-de-Calais
- Le Clos Grincourt 370
- La Grand'Maison 371
- Le Moulin 371

NORMANDY
Calvados
- L'Ancienne École 387
- La Ferme du Mouchel 384
- Le Grand Fumichon 389
- Manoir de Mathan 386
- La Nouvelle France 386

Eure
- Hôtel d'Évreux 394
- Hôtel du Saumon 394
- Petit Castel 390

Manche
- La Ferme de Cabourg 400
- Ferme Musée du Cotentin 401
- La Fossardière 399
- France et Fuchsias 401
- Le Logis 398
- Manoir de l'Acherie 403
- Manoir Saint-jean 402
- Le Moulin de la Butte 397
- Le Quesnot 398
- Village Grouchy 396

Orne
- L'Ermitage 404
- L'Orangerie 404
- Saint-Pierre 405

Seine-Maritime
- Chambre d'Hôte Madame Genty 413
- Ferme de Bray 413

- Golf Hôtel 409
- Manoir de Beaumont 407
- Le Prieuré Sainte-Croix 410
- Le Relais de l'Abbaye 408
- La Terrasse 414

PAYS DE LA LOIRE
Loire-Atlantique
- Poste 422

Sarthe
- L'Auberge du Port des Roches 430
- Le Petit Pont 431

Vendée
- Le Pas-de-l'Île 435

PICARDY
Aisne
- Chambre d'Hôte M. Leclère .. 440
- Le Régent 443

Oise
- Chambre d'Hôte M. Bruandet 446
- La Faisanderie 447
- Relais Brunehaut 444

POITOU CHARENTES
Charente
- La Templerie 453

Charente-Maritime
- Chambre d'Hôte M. Trouvé .. 460
- Les Hortensias 453

Deux-Sèvres
- Le Moulin de la Sorinière .. 461

Vienne
- Le Chalet de Venise 465
- Hôtel - restaurant de la Roue d'Or 464

PROVENCE, ALPS AND THE FRENCH RIVIERA
Alpes-de-Haute-Provence
- La Ferme du Couvent 475

Alpes-Maritimes
- Le Bosquet 488
- Hostellerie des Remparts .. 488
- Le Mirval 485

Bouches-du-Rhône
L'Amphithéatre ... 492
Angleterre ... 499
Calendal ... 492
Hautes-Alpes
Les Chemins Verts ... 478
Les Marmottes ... 481
Var
Les Pins ... 505
Vaucluse
La Farigoule ... 520

RHÔNE ALPES
Ain
L'Auberge Campagnarde ... 528
Ferme des Grands Hutains ... 526
SNC les Charmettes ... 530
Ardèche
La Désirade ... 533
Le Mas de Mazan ... 532
La Passiflore ... 534

Drôme
Gîte du Val des Nymphes ... 537
La Mare ... 536
Haute-Savoie
Auberge de l'Orangerie ... 573
Isère
Les Balcons du Lac ... 543
Le Domaine de Clairefontaine ... 541
Ferme de Ruthières ... 541
Le Val Fleuri ... 543
Loire
La Bussinière ... 549
Rhône
Chambre d'Hôte M. et Mme Bonnot ... 556
Saint-Romain ... 554
La Terrasse ... 560
Savoie
L'Autantic ... 563
La Croix du Sud ... 562
Flor'Alpes ... 565

WINING & DINING BREAKS

Good food is of course an essential prerequisite for a successful holiday and we should know! We have therefore decided to point out all the hotels and maisons d'hôte whose cuisine is in some way outstanding. The hotels have all been awarded either one or more "Stars" for excellent cooking or a "Bib Gourmand" for good food at moderate prices by the Michelin Red Guide. In the maisons d'hôte, you will tuck into delicious home cooking, often prepared using home-grown produce.

ALSACE
Bas-Rhin
À l'Ami Fritz 20
Au Cheval Blanc 19
Julien 15
Haut-Rhin
Les Alisiers 28
L'Arbre Vert 27
Aux Armes de France 24
Auberge St-Laurent 35

AQUITAINE
Dordogne
La Belle Étoile 46
Hôtel du Château 44
Pyrénées-Atlantiques
Arraya 90
La Belle Auberge 82

AUVERGNE
Cantal
Auberge de l'Aspre 99
Auberge des Montagnes 104
Beauséjour 98
Puy de Dôme
Auberge de Mazayes 114
Castel Hôtel 1904 119

BURGUNDY
Yonne
Auberge le Pot d'Étain 149
Hostellerie des Clos 146

BRITTANY
Finistère
Le Moulin de Rosmadec 169
La Pointe du Cap Coz 165
Ille-et-Vilaine
Relais de la Rance 174
Morbihan
Gavrinis 176
La Marine 179
Relais du Porhoët 178

CENTRE AND UPPER LOIRE VALLEY
Cher
Auberge du Piet à Terre 190
Loir-et-Cher
Hôtel de l'École 207

FRANCHE COMTÉ
Doubs
Le Bon Accueil 241
La Cascade 242
Jura
Le Comtois 248

LANGUEDOC ROUSSILLON
Aude
Auberge de Cucugnan ... 276
Host. du Château de la Pomarède ... 277
La Maison sur la Colline ... 275
Hérault
Auberge de Saugras ... 285
Lozère
Grand Hôtel Prouhèze ... 288

LIMOUSIN
Corrèze
LeManoir de Beaulieu ... 298

LORRAINE
Meuse
Château de Labessière ... 307
Vosges
Le Collet ... 314
Le Val Joli ... 314

MIDI PYRÉNÉES
Aveyron
Hôtel du Vieux Pont ... 320
Midi-papillon ... 323
À la Route d'Argent ... 321
Haute-Garonne
Auberge du Poids Public ... 330
Lot
Moulin de Fresquet ... 338
Les Vieilles Tours ... 342

NORMANDY
Manche
La Croix d'Or ... 395
France et Fuchsias ... 401
Manoir de l'Acherie ... 403
Seine-Maritime
Villa des Houx ... 405

PAYS DE LA LOIRE
Loire-Atlantique
Château de la Sébinière ... 421

PICARDY
Aisne
Auberge le Relais ... 442
La Toque Blanche ... 439

PROVENCE, ALPS AND THE FRENCH RIVIERA
Hautes-Alpes
Auberge la Neyrette ... 482

RHÔNE ALPES
Haute-Savoie
Le Cordonant ... 569
Les Gentianettes ... 569
Isère
Le Châlet Hôtel Prayer ... 542
Le Domaine de Clairefontaine ... 541
Rhône
Saint-Romain ... 554

ACTIVITY BREAKS

Feel like getting away from it all? Ready for a change of scenery? Want to get out into the countryside and work off some stress or extra pounds? The hotels and maisons d'hôte listed below all have a swimming pool at the very least and generally one or several other sports facilities or activities, either on site or very nearby. These include themed or signposted walks, fishing, tennis, golf, a fitness room/mini-gym, or riding, so check out each establishment to discover what is on offer.

ALSACE
Bas-Rhin
Au Cheval Blanc 19

AQUITAINE
Dordogne
Le Branchat 52
Les Charmes de Carlucet 53
La Flambée 41
La Guérinière 44
Le Manoir du Grand Vignoble . 55
Gironde
Dousud 62
Landes
Domaine de Bellegarde 77
Les Lacs d'Halco 75
Lot-et-Garonne
La Cascade aux Fées 79
Château de la Seiglal 79
Moulin de Labique 80

AUVERGNE
Allier
G. H. Montespan-Talleyrand ... 93
La Grande Poterie 94
Cantal
Auberge des Montagnes 104

Hostellerie les Breuils 101
Puy de Dôme
Auberge de Fondain 113
Au Pont de Raffiny 118

BURGUNDY
Côte-d'Or
La Saura 129
Nièvre
Beaumonde 133
Le Colombier de Corvol 134
Yonne
La Grange de Boulay 150

BRITTANY
Finistère
Château de Kerlarec 163

CENTRE AND UPPER LOIRE VALLEY
Loiret
Domaine de la Thiau 210
Le Domaine de Sainte-Barbe .. 213

CHAMPAGNE ARDENNE
Haute-Marne
Le Moulin 224

FRANCHE COMTÉ
Doubs
Taillard 240

ÎLE DE FRANCE AND PARIS
Essonne
Le Clos des Fontaines 268

LANGUEDOC ROUSSILLON
Gard
Vic 280
Pyrénées-Orientales
Auberge les Écureuils 294

LORRAINE
Vosges
Auberge de la Vigotte 312
Jamagne 311
La Résidence 313

MIDI PYRÉNÉES
Ariège
Auberge les Myrtilles 318
Aveyron
Carayon 324
Gers
Au Vieux Pressoir 332
Haute-Garonne
La Halte du Temps 328
La Manufacture 325
Lot
Domaine du Berthiol 337
Les Moynes 343
Tarn-et-Garonne
Les Hortensias 359
Manoir des Chanterelles 357
Le Platane 355

NORMANDY
Manche
Les Isles 396

PAYS DE LA LOIRE
Loire-Atlantique
Château de la Sébinière 421
Le Marini 421
Ty Gwenn 423
Maine-et-Loire
Domaine de la Brégellerie 425
Vendée
Hôtel du Martinet 432

PICARDY
Oise
Domaine du Bois d'Aucourt ... 446

Somme
Chambres d'Hôtes du Bois de Bonance 448

POITOU CHARENTES
Charente-Maritime
Logis Saint-Léonard 455

PROVENCE, ALPS AND THE FRENCH RIVIERA
Alpes-de-Haute-Provence
Auberge Charembeau 472
Alpes-Maritimes
Le Bosquet 488
Les Jardins Fragonard 483
Mas des Cigales 489
Bouches-du-Rhône
Castel Mouisson 493
La Galinière 494
Val Majour 494
Hautes-Alpes
Le Chalet des Alpages 481
Les Chalets de la Meije 479
Le Parlement 479
Var
Domaine le Peyrourier "Une Campagne en Provence" 500
Le Mas des Oliviers 506
Villa Lou Gardian 507
Vaucluse
Le Mas de Guilles 516

RHÔNE ALPES
Ain
Le Nid à Bibi 530
Ardèche
Hostellerie "Mère Biquette" 534
Haute-Savoie
L'Aiguille du Midi 567
Le Bois Joli 570
Fleur des Neiges 572
Isère
Le Châlet Hôtel Prayer 542
Château de Passières 540
Loire
Château de la Motte 550
Rhône
Aucherand 559
Savoie
L'Autantic 563

ALPHABETICAL INDEX OF HOTELS AND MAISONS D'HÔTE

A

À la Thuilerie des Fontaines	39700 Châtenois	247
À l'Ami Fritz	67530 Ottrott-le-Haut	20
A l'hôtel des Trois îles	25220 Chalezeule	239
A Martinella	20245 Galéria	229
A Spelunca	20226 Speloncato	234
A Tramula	20259 Pioggiola	232
Abbaye de Villelongue	11170 Saint-Martin-le-Vieil	279
Abri du Passant	59100 Roubaix	367
L'Agrybella	24560 Saint-Aubin-de-Lanquais	53
Aigle d'Or	67116 Reichstett	21
L'Aiglon	20124 Zonza	235
L'Aiguille du Midi	74400 Chamonix-Mont-Blanc	567
Les Airelles	73710 Pralognan-la-Vanoise	565
Les Albatros	33510 Andernos-les-Bains	61
L'Alcyone	56340 Carnac	176
Les Alisiers	68650 Lapoutroie	28
L'Alliey	05220 Le Monêtier-les-Bains	480
L'Alpage	39130 Bonlieu	246
L'Amandière	13210 Saint-Rémy-de-Provence	498
L'Amphithéatre	13200 Arles	492
An Tiez Bihan	29770 Plogoff	167
L'Ancienne École	14960 Meuvaines	387
Angleterre	65240 Arreau	344
Angleterre	13300 Salon-de-Provence	499
L'Antiquité	85300 Challans	433
Apollon Montparnasse	75014 Paris	256
Les Aquarelles	89450 Vézelay	153
Ar Milin'	35220 Châteaubourg	172
Ar Presbital Koz	29410 Saint-Thégonnec	170
Arbez Franco-Suisse	39220 La Cure	248
Les Arbousiers	40630 Sabres	76
L'Arbre Vert	68240 Kaysersberg	27
Les Arcades	66400 Céret	290
Ar-Men	29990 Île-de-Sein	166
Armenonville	06000 Nice	487
Aux Armes de France	68770 Ammerschwihr	24
Arnold	67140 Itterswiller	17
Arraya	64310 Sare	90
Artistes	69002 Lyon	557
Arvor	22100 Dinan	160
L'Atelier	30400 Villeneuve-lès-Avignon	285
Les Atelleries	41300 Selles-Saint-Denis	209
Au Chasseur	67440 Birkenwald	12
Au Moulin d'Ancy le Franc	89160 Ancy-le-Franc	143
Au Vieux Logis	10220 Brévonnes	218

/Auberge le Pot d'Étain

Au Vieux Pressoir	32100 Caussens	332
L'Auberge	56400 Sainte-Anne-d'Auray	185
L'Auberge Campagnarde	01230 Évosges	528
Auberge Catalane	66760 Latour-de-Carol	292
Auberge Charembeau	04300 Forcalquier	472
Auberge de Campagne du Mollard	01320 Châtillon-la-Palud	527
Auberge de Carcarille	84220 Gordes	512
Auberge de Cucugnan	11350 Cucugnan	276
Auberge de Fondain	63820 Laqueuille	113
Auberge de la Forge	63160 Glaine-Montaigut	112
Auberge de la Motte Jean	35350 Saint-Coulomb	174
Auberge de la Vigotte	88340 Girmont-Val-d'Ajol	312
Auberge de l'Aspre	15140 Fontanges	99
Auberge de l'Orangerie	74700 Sallanches	573
Auberge de Mazayes	63230 Mazaye	114
Auberge de Quelven	56310 Quelven	183
Auberge de Saugras	34380 Argelliers	285
Auberge des Bichonnières	01330 Ambérieux-en-Dombes	526
Auberge des Brizards	89630 Quarré-les-Tombes	150
Auberge des Mésanges	57960 Meisenthal	308
Auberge des Montagnes	15800 Vic-sur-Cère	104
L'Auberge des Moulins	25110 Pont-les-Moulins	243
Auberge des Seigneurs	06140 Vence	490
Auberge du Beau Lieu	76440 Forges-les-Eaux	408
Auberge du Bon Puits	06450 Le Suquet	486
Auberge du Cheval Blanc	77910 Varreddes	265
Auberge du Cheval Blanc	84240 La Bastide-des-Jourdans	513
Auberge du Fel	12140 Entraygues-sur-Truyère	321
Auberge du Mehrbächel	68550 Saint-Amarin	33
Auberge du Piet à Terre	18370 Châteaumeillant	190
Auberge du Poids Public	31540 Saint-Félix-Lauragais	330
Auberge du Pont de Lanau	15260 Lanau	100
L'Auberge du Port des Roches	72800 Luché-Pringé	430
L'Auberge du Soleil	06390 Coaraze	484
Auberge du Spitzemberg	88490 La Petite-Fosse	313
Auberge du Val au Cesne	76190 Yvetot	415
Auberge du Val de l'Oise	02580 Étréaupont	440
Auberge du Vernay	38390 Charrette	540
Auberge du Vieux Chêne	15270 Champs-sur-Tarentaine	98
L'Auberge du Vieux Donjon	27800 Brionne	391
Auberge et Hostellerie Paysanne	68480 Lutter	29
Auberge la Meunière	68590 Thannenkirch	36
Auberge la Neyrette	05250 Saint-Disdier	482
Auberge la Plume d'Oie	24250 La Roque-Gageac	46
Auberge le Fiacre	80120 Quend	449
Auberge le Pot d'Étain	89440 L'Isle-sur-Serein	149

ALPHABETICAL INDEX OF HOTELS AND MAISONS D'HÔTE

Auberge le Râtelier	56340 Carnac	177
Auberge le Relais	02850 Reuilly-Sauvigny	442
Auberge le Tillau	25300 Verrières-de-Joux	244
Auberge le Voutenay	89270 Voutenay-sur-Cure	155
Auberge les Écureuils	66340 Valcebollère	294
Auberge les Grandes Roches	29910 Trégunc	170
Auberge les Murets	07230 Chandolas	532
Auberge les Myrtilles	09000 Foix	318
Auberge les Palmiers	31370 Rieumes	329
Auberge Metzger	67530 Natzwiller	18
Auberge Régordane	48800 La Garde-Guérin	289
Auberge Saint-Fleuret	12190 Estaing	322
Auberge Saint-Simond	73100 Aix-les-Bains	561
Auberge St-Laurent	68510 Sierentz	35
Aucherand	69620 - Saint-Vérand	559
L'Aulnaye	28400 Nogent-le-Rotrou	194
L'Aumônerie	83320 Carqueiranne	501
Aurifat	81170 Cordes-sur-Ciel	352
L'Autantic	73700 Bourg-Saint-Maurice	563
Les Auzières	84110 Roaix	519
L'Avenue	04240 Annot	470
Azteca	04400 Barcelonnette	470

B

La Badelle	84220 Gordes	513
Le Bailliage	15140 Salers	103
La Balance	25200 Montbéliard	242
Les Balcons du Lac	38730 Le Pin	543
Barbary-Lane	40150 Hossegor	75
Le Barry du Grand Chemin	34520 Le Caylar	286
Les Basses Portes	38118 Saint-Baudille-de-la-Tour	545
De Bastard	32700 Lectoure	334
La Bastide de l'Aubetin	77120 Saints	265
La Bastide de Saint-Donat	06480 La Colle-sur-Loup	485
La Bastide des Corbières	11200 Boutenac	274
La Bastide des Senteurs	30500 Saint-Victor-de-Malcap	283
La Bastide Rose	83690 Salernes	507
Les Batarelles	33550 Villenave-de-Rions	73
Les Baudarts	63500 Varennes-sur-Usson	121
Beau Séjour	74290 Menthon-Saint-Bernard	572
Le Beau Site	46500 Rocamadour	341
Beaumonde	58500 Chaulgnes	133
Beauséjour	15340 Calvinet	98
Beausoleil	73530 Saint-Sorlin-d'Arves	566
Beausoleil	74400 Chamonix-Mont-Blanc	568
Le Béguinage	41700 Cour-Cheverny	206
Bel Air	50340 Flamanville	397

Auberge le Râtelier/Le Castel de Burlats

La Bélie	24220 Meyrals	51
La Belle Auberge	64270 Castagnède	82
La Belle Étoile	24250 La Roque-Gageac	46
La Belle Vue	67420 Saulxures	21
Bellevue	77610 Neufmoutiers-en-Brie	262
Bellier	26420 La Chapelle-en-Vercors	536
Belvédère	45200 Amilly	210
Le Belvédère	65400 Salles	349
Le Berger des Abeilles	13670 Saint-Andiol	497
La Bergerie du Moulin	83460 Taradeau	508
La Bergerie St-Michel	40550 St-Michel-d'Escalus	77
Blanche Neige	06470 Valberg	489
Le Blason	37400 Amboise	198
Boileau	75016 Paris	257
Le Bois Joli	74500 La Beunaz	570
Le Bon Accueil	25160 Malbuisson	241
Le Bon Laboureur	58400 La Charité-sur-Loire	135
La Bonbonnière	21240 Talant	132
La Bonne Franquette	67220 Villé	23
Le Bosquet	06580 Pégomas	488
La Boursaultière	51480 Boursault	221
Le Branchat	24170 Sagelat	52
Brikéténia	64210 Guéthary	83
Au Brochet du Lac	51290 Saint-Rémy-en-Bouzemont	224
Brueghel	59000 Lille	366
La Bussinière	42110 Feurs	549
Le Bussy	49730 Montsoreau	427
La Butte de l'Épine	37340 Continvoir	201

C

Cabalus, l'Ancienne Hôtellerie de l'Abbaye	89450 Vézelay	153
Le Cadran Solaire	13690 Graveson	496
Calendal	13200 Arles	492
Le Calounier	89310 Molay	149
Campagne "Le Paradis"	04300 Forcalquier	472
Can Oliba	66200 Elne	291
Les Cancades	83330 Le Beausset	503
Capcazal de Pachiou	40350 Mimbaste	76
Le Caprice des Neiges	73590 Crest-Voland	564
La Caravelle	26110 Nyons	538
Carayon	12380 Saint-Sernin-sur-Rance	324
Casa Del Arte	66300 Thuir	293
La Casa Musicale	20220 Pigna	231
La Cascade	25920 Mouthier-Haute-Pierre	242
La Cascade aux Fées	47230 Barbaste	79
Le Castel de Burlats	81100 Burlats	351

ALPHABETICAL INDEX OF HOTELS AND MAISONS D'HÔTE

Castel Hôtel 1904	63390 Saint-Gervais-d'Auvergne	119
Castel Mouisson	13570 Barbentane	493
Castelet des Alpilles	13210 Saint-Rémy-de-Provence	498
La Cathédrale	57000 Metz	309
La Caussolière	17600 Saint-Sornin	459
Les Cèdres Bleus	43110 Aurec-sur-Loire	105
Au Cep de Vigne	67880 Innenheim	16
Au Cerf	68480 Winkel	36
Le Chalet de la Neverdière	03160 Ygrande	97
Le Chalet de Venise	86280 Saint-Benoît	465
Le Chalet d'En Hô	05100 Névache	480
Le Chalet des Alpages	05500 Poligny	481
Le Chalet du Lac	88400 Gérardmer	311
Le Chalet et Montégut	03000 Coulandon	94
Le Châlet Hôtel Prayer	38650 Gresse-en-Vercors	542
Chalet le Paradou	73210 La Côte-d'Aime	564
Les Chalets de la Meije	05320 La Grave	479
Chambre d'Hôte Arrayoa	64310 Ascain	81
Chambre d'Hôte au Village	24420 Sorges	59
Chambre d'Hôte Bourlenc	07200 Saint-Julien-du-Serre	533
Chambre d'hôte Brie Champagne	77510 Saint-Denis-lès-Rebais	264
Chambre d'Hôte Clos de la Croix Blanche	91490 Moigny-sur-École	268
Chambre d'Hôte de Bosseron	01160 Neuville-sur-Ain	529
Chambre d'Hôte Delong	51390 Saint-Euphraise-et-Clairizet	223
Chambre d'Hôte du Petit Château	80480 Dury	447
Chambre d'hôte Ferme d'Écosse	76110 Manneville-la-Goupil	410
Chambre d'Hôte Gérard Lagneau	69430 Quincié-en-Beaujolais	558
Chambre d'Hôte Hourcazet	32800 Eauze	333
Chambre d'hôte La Calmade	24420 Saint-Vincent-sur-l'Isle	57
Chambre d'hôte La Marmittière	37150 Civray-de-Touraine	201
Chambre d'Hôte La Villa-Florida	76200 Dieppe	406
Chambre d'hôte l'Ambroisie	24310 Bourdeilles	42
Chambre d'hôte le Clos-Vallis	24200 Sarlat-la-Canéda	57
Chambre d'Hôte Le Moulin d'Aries	65230 Castelnau-Magnoac	345
Chambre d'Hôte le Saint-Denis	95510 Chérence	269
Chambre d'Hôte les Brugères	21160 Couchey	127
Chambre d'Hôte Les Égrignes	70150 Cult	250
Chambre d'Hôte M. Bruandet	60650 Hannaches	446
Chambre d'Hôte M. Dormion	77650 Lizines	261
Chambre d'Hôte M. Dumontant	23200 Saint-Pardoux-le-Neuf	301
Chambre d'hôte M. et Mme Asnar	64260 Izeste	86
Chambre d'Hôte M. et Mme Bonnot	69430 Les Ardillats	556
Chambre d'Hôte M. Ladeuix	40220 Tarnos	78
Chambre d'Hôte M. Leclère	02330 Connigis	440
Chambre d'Hôte M. Malherbe	56400 Ploemel	181

Castel Hôtel 1904/Château de Creissels

Chambre d'Hôte M. Mathieu	71600 Poisson	142
Chambre d'Hôte M. Piedallu	89160 Lézinnes	148
Chambre d'Hôte M. Prudent	15140 Salers	103
Chambre d'Hôte M. Stekelorum	27630 Fourges	392
Chambre d'Hôte M. Trouvé	17810 Saint-Georges-des-Coteaux	460
Chambre d'Hôte Madame Bonnet	85420 Maillezais	434
Chambre d'Hôte Madame Bordeau	72190 Coulaines	429
Chambre d'Hôte Madame Faraut	06530 Cabris	482
Chambre d'Hôte Madame Genty	76740 Saint-Aubin-sur-Mer	413
Chambre d'Hôte Madame Gouzer	56570 Saint-Philibert	185
Chambre d'Hôte Madame Pean	72800 Le Lude	430
Chambre d'Hôte Madame Servant	80230 Saint-Valery-sur-Somme	449
Chambre d'hôte Madame Vermeil	65400 Arcizans-Avant	343
Chambre d'Hôte Mme Bacchieri	21500 Rougemont	131
Chambre d'Hôte Mme Bagatelle	21320 Châteauneuf	126
Chambre d'Hôte Mme Beaujeard	63460 Beauregard-Vendon	110
Chambre d'Hôte Mme Boissière	63114 Montpeyroux	114
Chambre d'Hôte Mme Devenat	39130 Charezier	246
Chambre d'Hôte Monsieur Delaleu	95620 Parmain	269
Chambre d'Hôte Monsieur Gener	34530 Montagnac	287
Chambre d'Hôte Paul Gebrillat	63500 Perrier	117
Chambre d'Hôte Peyron-Gaubert	41170 Mondoubleau	207
Une Chambre en Ville	33000 Bordeaux	63
Chambres d'hôtes	28700 Cherville	192
Chambres d'Hôtes du Bois de Bonance	80132 Port-le-Grand	448
Chambres d'Hôtes le Sabathé	32700 Saint-Mézard	336
Chambres d'Hôtes M. Breton	88140 Bulgnéville	310
Chambres d'hôtes M. et Mme Blasselle	17300 Rochefort	457
Les Chandelles	28130 Villiers-le-Morhier	195
Les Charmes de Carlucet	24590 Saint-Crépin-et-Carlucet	53
Au Château	32230 Juillac	333
Château d'Épenoux	70000 Pusy-et-Épenoux	251
Château Blanchard	42140 Chazelles-sur-Lyon	548
Château Cagninacci	20200 San-Martino-di-Lota	233
Château Cantet	47250 Samazan	81
Château Coulon Laurensac	33360 Latresne	66
Château de Bachelard	42120 Commelle-Vernay	549
Château de Bel Air	18340 Arcay	189
Le Château de Boues	64570 Féas	83
Château de Bouesse	36200 Bouesse	196
Château de Chapeau Cornu	38890 Vignieu	548
Château de Charade	63130 Royat	118
Château de Châtel	08250 Châtel-Chéhéry	217
Château de Crazannes	17350 Crazannes	455
Château de Creissels	12100 Millau	322

ALPHABETICAL INDEX OF HOTELS AND MAISONS D'HÔTE

Château de Dampierre	14350 Dampierre	384
Château de Gamot	46130 Loubressac	339
Château de Grand Branet	33550 Capian	64
Château de Jonvilliers	28320 Écrosnes	193
Château de Kerlarec	29300 Arzano	163
Château de la Coste	46700 Grézels	338
Château de la Motte	59740 Liessies	365
Château de la Motte	42640 Noailly	550
Château de la Sébinière	44330 Le Pallet	421
Château de la Seiglal	47380 Monclar-d'Agenais	79
Château de la Vernède	63500 Saint-Rémy-de-Chargnat	120
Château de la Volonière	72340 Poncé-sur-le-Loir	431
Château de Labarom	86380 Cheneché	463
Château de Labessière	55320 Ancemont	307
Château de l'Ormet	03330 Valignat	97
Château de Marigny	58160 Sauvigny-les-Bois	137
Le Château de Mirvault	53200 Château-Gontier	428
Le Château de Pâquier	38650 Saint-Martin-de-la-Cluze	546
Château de Pasredon	63500 Saint-Rémy-de-Chargnat	120
Château de Passières	38930 Chichilianne	540
Château de Prauthoy	52190 Prauthoy	226
Château de Ribourdin	89240 Chevannes	146
Château de Rouillon	77590 Chartrettes	259
Château de Saint-Pierre-Brouck	59630 Saint-Pierre-Brouck	368
Château de Salornay	71870 Hurigny	141
Château de Saulty	62158 Saulty	374
Château de Séguenville	31480 Cabanac-Séguenville	327
Château de Vaumoret	86000 Poitiers	464
Château de Vins	83170 Vins-sur-Caramy	508
Château de Voissieux	63210 Rochefort-Montagne	117
Château de Vouilly	14230 Vouilly	389
Château d'En Haut	59144 Jenlain	365
Château des Jacobins	47000 Agen	78
Château des Marceaux	38650 Avignonet	539
Le Château des Salles	17240 Saint-Fort-sur-Gironde	458
Château des Varennes	31450 Varennes	332
Le Château d'Escolles	71960 Verzé	143
Le Château d'Herbelon	38650 Treffort	547
Château du Max	03240 Le Theil	95
Le Château du Pavillon	85620 Rocheserviere	435
Château du Rey	30570 Le Vigan	281
Château Lantic	33650 Martillac	68
Château Meylet	33330 Saint-Émilion	70
Château Monlot	33330 Saint-Hippolyte	71
Le Chatellier	35260 Cancale	171
La Chaumière	62180 Verton	375

Château de Dampierre/La Cour au Tilleul

La Chaumière de Kervassal	56670 Riantec	184
Les Chaumières de Cahire	56400 Plougoumelen	182
Les Chaumières du Lac	44110 Saint-Lyphard	423
Ché Catrine	73500 Villarodin-Bourget	567
Les Chemins Verts	05500 Buissard	478
Le Cheval Blanc	52200 Langres	225
Au Cheval Blanc	67510 Niedersteinbach	19
Chez les Colin	25650 Hauterive-la-Fresse	240
Christine et Maurice Biron	24300 Nontron	52
Les Cinq Lacs	39130 Le Frasnois	249
Le Clos	21200 Montagny-lès-Beaune	130
Le Clos de la Garenne	17700 Puyravault	457
Le Clos de la Garenne	67700 Saverne	22
Le Clos des Arômes	13260 Cassis	493
Le Clos des Fontaines	91750 Nainville-les-Roches	268
Le Clos des Iris	04360 Moustiers-Sainte-Marie	473
Le Clos des Saumanes	84470 Châteauneuf-de-Gadagne	512
Le Clos du Mûrier	68170 Rixheim	33
Le Clos du Petit Marray	37310 Chambourg-sur-Indre	199
Le Clos du vivier	76540 Valmont	414
Le Clos Fleuri	14450 Saint-Pierre-du-Mont	388
Le Clos Grincourt	62161 Duisans	370
Le Clos Jouvenet	76000 Rouen	411
Clos Sainte-Marie	58000 Nevers	136
Clos Saint-Laurent	28210 Saint-Laurent-la-Gâtine	195
La Closerie de Manou	63240 Le Mont-Dore	113
La Closerie du Guilhat	64270 Salies-de-Béarn	88
Le Collet	88400 Xonrupt-Longemer	314
Les Colombages Champenois	10270 Laubressel	220
Colombier	67210 Obernai	19
Le Colombier de Corvol	58210 Corvol-d'Embernard	134
La Commanderie	62990 Loison-sur-Créquoise	372
Commerce	22800 Quintin	162
Le Comtadin	84200 Carpentras	511
Le Comtois	39130 Doucier	248
Le Conquérant	50760 Barfleur	395
Au Coq En Velours	38490 Aoste	539
La Cordeline	83170 Brignoles	500
Le Cordonant	74700 Cordon	569
La Corne de Cerf	35380 Paimpont	173
La Corniche	20200 San-Martino-di-Lota	233
Cos-Milin	29233 Cléder	164
Côté Rivage	24150 Badefols-sur-Dordogne	40
Le Cottage	14390 Cabourg	381
La Couette de Biéou	65170 Camparan	345
La Cour au Tilleul	46600 Martel	340

ALPHABETICAL INDEX OF HOTELS AND MAISONS D'HÔTE

La Cour des Prés	08290 Rumigny	217
Les Courtils	45430 Chécy	211
Le Couvent	15400 Trizac	104
Le Crêt l'Agneau	25650 La Longeville	241
Crispol	89450 Vézelay	154
La Croix Blanche	49590 Fontevraud-l'Abbaye	426
La Croix de Savoie	74300 Les Carroz-d'Araches	571
La Croix d'Or	50300 Avranches	395
La Croix du Sud	73100 Aix-les-Bains	562
Crystal	51100 Reims	222
Les Cymaises	21140 Semur-en-Auxois	132

D

D'Argouges	14400 Bayeux	381
De Barathe	15130 Giou-de-Mamou	99
De Biencourt	37190 Azay-le-Rideau	198
De Blauvac	84000 Avignon	509
De Lescoff	29770 Plogoff	168
Demeure de Flore	81240 Lacabarède	354
La Demeure de la Presqu'île	64270 Salies-de-Béarn	89
Demeure de la Vignole	49730 Turquant	428
Demeure d'Hauterive	03340 La Ferté-Hauterive	95
La Désirade	07340 Saint-Désirat	533
Aux Deux Clefs	68480 Moernach	30
Diderot	37500 Chinon	200
Domaine Borgnat le Colombier	89290 Escolives-Sainte-Camille	147
Domaine de Beauséjour	37220 Panzoult	203
Domaine de Bellegarde	40140 Soustons	77
Domaine de Carrat	33480 Castelnau-de-Médoc	64
Le Domaine de Clairefontaine	38121 Chonas-L'Amballan	541
Domaine de Coussères	66220 Prugnanes	293
Domaine de Croccano	20100 Sartène	234
Domaine de Gaudon	63520 Ceilloux	111
Domaine de Jean-Pierre	65300 Pinas	347
Domaine de la Brégellerie	49490 Auverse	425
Le Domaine de la Chapelle de Vâtre	69840 Jullié	555
Domaine de la Colombière	38270 Moissieu-sur-Dolon	545
Domaine de la Creuse	10800 Moussey	220
Domaine de La Fouquette	83340 Les Mayons	505
Domaine de la Marmette	24150 Lanquais	47
Domaine de la Pierre Chaude	11490 Portel-des-Corbières	278
Domaine de la Thiau	45250 Briare	210
Domaine de Lafon	82270 Montpezat-de-Quercy	358
Domaine de l'Ermitage	18500 Berry-Bouy	189
Domaine de Loran	32300 Saint-Maur	335
Domaine de Mestré	49590 Fontevraud-l'Abbaye	426
Domaine de Nestuby	83570 Cotignac	501

La Cour des Prés/La Ferme Ancienne de Bellerive

Le Domaine de Paguy	40240 Betbezer-d'Armagnac	74
Domaine de Romarand	69430 Quincié-en-Beaujolais	558
Le Domaine de Sainte-Barbe	45500 Nevoy	213
Domaine de Saint-Jean	11200 Bizanet	274
Domaine de Teinteillac	24320 Bourg-des-Maisons	42
Domaine de Ternant	63870 Orcines	116
Domaine des Patrus	02540 L'Épine-aux-Bois	441
Domaine des Rayes	04200 Saint-Geniez	476
Domaine du Berthiol	46300 Gourdon	337
Domaine du Bois d'Aucourt	60350 Pierrefonds	446
Domaine du Bois Vert	13450 Grans	495
Domaine du Bouxhof	68630 Mittelwihr	30
Le Domaine du Cauze	47600 Nérac	80
Domaine du Château de Marchangy	42190 Saint-Pierre-la-Noaille	552
Domaine du Clos des Garands	69820 Fleurie	554
Domaine du Fontenay	42155 Villemontais	553
Domaine du Mas Boluix	66100 Perpignan	292
Domaine du Mascaret	33290 Parempuyre	69
Domaine du Moulin aux Moines	21190 Meursault	130
Domaine du Voirloup	10190 Estissac	219
Domaine le Peyrourier "Une Campagne en Provence"	83149 Bras	500
Domaine Véga	65250 Saint-Arroman	348
Le Donjon	17470 Aulnay	454
Doumarias	24800 Saint-Pierre-de-Côle	56
Dousud	33430 Bernos-Beaulac	62
Durante	06000 Nice	487

E

L'Échauguette	42155 Saint-Maurice-sur-Loire	551
L'Enclos	24390 Tourtoirac	60
L'Erablais	28300 Saint-Aubin-des-Bois	194
L'Ermitage	61140 Bagnoles-de-l'Orne	404
Ermitage Saint Vincent	43100 Vieille-Brioude	109
Eth Béryè Petit	65400 Beaucens	344
Europe	81100 Castres	352
L'Évêché	84110 Vaison-la-Romaine	520
Eychenne	09200 Saint-Girons	319

F

La Faisanderie	60480 Puits-la-Vallée	447
La Famille Guy Charbaut	51160 Mareuil-sur-Ay	221
La Farigoule	84150 Violès	520
La Fauconnerie du Roy	78124 Montainville	267
Du Faudé	68650 Lapoutroie	28
La Ferme	84000 Avignon	509
La Ferme Ancienne de Bellerive	60170 Cambronne-lès-Ribecourt	444

ALPHABETICAL INDEX OF HOTELS AND MAISONS D'HÔTE

La Ferme aux Sangliers	64570 Issor	84
La Ferme Blanche	59840 Lompret	367
La Ferme Bonne de la Grotte	73360 Saint-Christophe-la-Grotte	566
Ferme de Bonavis	59266 Banteux	363
Ferme de Bray	76440 Sommery	413
La Ferme de Cabourg	50760 Réville	400
Ferme de Guerlan	56400 Plougoumelen	182
La Ferme de la Chapelle	76400 Fécamp	407
Ferme de la Gloire Dieu	10250 Courteron	218
Ferme de la Montagne	02290 Ressons-le-Long	441
La Ferme de la Rançonnière	14480 Crépon	383
Ferme de la Recette	77830 Échouboulains	260
La Ferme de Porz Kloz	29690 Berrien	164
Ferme de Ruthières	38930 Chichilianne	541
La Ferme de Soulan	65170 Saint-Lary-Soulan	348
La Ferme de Toussacq	77480 Grisy-sur-Seine	260
La Ferme de Vaux	60100 Creil	445
La Ferme de Vosves	77190 Vosves	266
Ferme des Glycines	14510 Gonneville-sur-Mer	385
Ferme des Grands Hutains	01300 Brens	526
Ferme des Guezoux	24800 Vaunac	60
La Ferme des Roses	42360 Panissières	550
Ferme du Busset	68370 Orbey	31
La Ferme du Château	28300 Bailleau-l'Évêque	192
La Ferme du Château	39800 Bersaillin	245
Ferme du Chatel	77160 Provins	263
La Ferme du Couvent	77720 Bréau	258
La Ferme du Couvent	04400 Pra-Loup	475
La Ferme du Grand Chesnoy	45260 Chailly-en-Gâtinais	211
La Ferme du Mouchel	14710 Formigny	384
La Ferme du Poulet	69400 Villefranche-sur-Saône	561
La Ferme du Vieux Château	77540 Ormeaux	262
Ferme Etxeberria	64220 Ispoure	84
Ferme le Petit Val	14480 Banville	380
Ferme Musée du Cotentin	50480 Sainte-Mère-Église	401
Les Feuilles d'Acanthe	33490 Saint-Macaire	71
La Flambée	24100 Bergerac	41
Fleur des Neiges	74110 Morzine	572
Le Fleuray	37530 Cangey	199
Floralp	74220 La Clusaz	570
Flor'Alpes	73590 La Giettaz	565
Les Forges	58200 Cosne-Cours-sur-Loire	134
La Fossardière	50440 Omonville-la-Petite	399
France et Fuchsias	50550 Saint-Vaast-la-Hougue	401
Funtana Marina	20220 L'Île-Rousse	230

La Ferme aux Sangliers/Le Griou

G

G. H. Montespan-Talleyrand	03160 Bourbon-L'Archambault	93
Les Gabales	43170 Saugues	108
La Gabetière	38780 Estrablin	542
Gai Soleil	74170 Les Contamines-Montjoie	571
La Galinière	13790 Châteauneuf-le-Rouge	494
La Garance	84410 Bédoin	511
La Garencière	72610 Champfleur	429
La Garlande	32380 Saint-Clar	335
La Gâtine	78125 La Boissière-École	266
Gavrinis	56870 Baden	176
Au Gay Séjour	74210 Seythenex	574
Les Gentianettes	74360 La Chapelle-d'Abondance	569
La Gentilhommière	59269 Artres	363
George V	81000 Albi	350
Les Géraniums	84330 Le Barroux	514
Germinal	35510 Cesson-Sévigné	172
Gimbelhof	67510 Gimbelhof	16
Giniès	38114 Allemont	538
La Girandole	05350 Arvieux	477
Gîte du Val des Nymphes	26700 La Garde-Adhémar	537
La Goélette	62930 Wimereux	376
Golf Hôtel	76470 Le Tréport	409
Gorges de la Diosaz	74310 Servoz	573
Le Grain de Sable	33740 Arès	61
Le Grand Boucaud	33580 Rimons	70
Le Grand Cèdre	65270 Saint-Pé-de-Bigorre	349
Le Grand Cerf	61000 Alençon	403
Le Grand Fumichon	14400 Vaux-sur-Aure	389
Le Grand Hotel	71140 Bourbon-Lancy	138
Grand Hôtel Prouhèze	48130 Aumont-Aubrac	288
Le Grand Talon	49800 Andard	424
La Grande Marque	24440 Marnac	50
La Grande Poterie	03000 Coulandon	94
La Grand'Maison	62179 Escalles	371
Les Grands Crus	21220 Gevrey-Chambertin	128
Les Grands Prés	88240 La Chapelle-aux-Bois	312
La Grange aux Marmottes	65120 Viscos	350
La Grange de Boulay	89570 Neuvy-Sautour	150
La Grange du Moulin	64230 Lescar	87
Les Granges	63210 Nébouzat	115
Les Granges Hautes	24590 Saint-Crépin-et-Carlucet	54
La Grek	56590 Île de Groix	179
La Gribane	80230 Saint-Valery-sur-Somme	450
Grillon	21200 Beaune	125
Le Griou	15800 Saint-Jacques-des-Blats	102

ALPHABETICAL INDEX OF HOTELS AND MAISONS D'HÔTE

La Grosse Haie	51510 Matougues	222
La Guérandière	44350 Guérande	420
La Guérinière	24250 Cénac-et-Saint-Julien	44
Les Gués Rivières	33350 Pujols	69

H

Les Habrans	24310 Brantôme	43
La Halte du Temps	31310 Montesquieu-Volvestre	328
Le Hameau de Charles-Auguste	83340 Le Luc	504
La Haute Chambre	62170 Beussent	369
La Haute Verrerie	83340 Le Cannet-des-Maures	504
Les Hauts de Montguillon	77860 Saint-Germain-sur-Morin	264
Les Hauts de Véroncle	84220 Murs	517
Henri IV	33230 Coutras	65
L'Herminette	43550 Saint-Front	107
L'Hermitage	84210 Pernes-les-Fontaines	518
L'Hermitage Saint-Pierre	12230 Nant	323
Les Hirondelles	68970 Illhaeusern	26
Les Hortensias	17380 Archingeay	453
Les Hortensias	82700 Saint-Porquier	359
Host. du Château de la Pomarède	11400 La Pomarède	277
Host. du Pavillon Saint-Hubert	60270 Gouvieux	445
Hostal dels Trabucayres	66480 Las Illas	291
Hostellerie "Mère Biquette"	07580 Saint-Pons	534
Hostellerie des Clos	89800 Chablis	146
Hostellerie des Remparts	06570 Saint-Paul	488
Hostellerie du Bois	44500 La Baule	420
Hostellerie du Château	21320 Châteauneuf	127
Hostellerie du Château d'As	25110 Baume-les-Dames	239
Hostellerie du Cygne	67160 Wissembourg	23
Hostellerie du Grand Duc	11140 Gincla	277
Hostellerie du Lion d'Or	57680 Gorze	307
Hostellerie du Passeur	24620 Les Eyzies-de-Tayac	48
Hostellerie du Vieux Cordes	81170 Cordes-sur-Ciel	353
Hostellerie François Joseph	84330 Le Barroux	515
Hostellerie la Clé d'Or	77630 Barbizon	258
Hostellerie le Saint-Laurent	69720 Saint-Laurent-de-Mure	559
Hostellerie le Vert	46700 Mauroux	341
Hostellerie les Aiguillons	24320 Saint-Martial-Viveyrols	55
Hostellerie les Breuils	15300 Murat	101
Hostellerie Les Griffons	24310 Bourdeilles	41
Hostellerie les Hirondelles	63870 Orcines	116
Hostellerie Saint-Germain	39210 Saint-Germain-les-Arlay	250
Hostellerie Schwendi	68240 Kientzheim	27
Hôtel - restaurant de la Roue d'Or	86200 Loudun	464
Hôtel - restaurant la Dômerie	12470 Aubrac	320
Hôtel de Garlande	84000 Avignon	510

La Grosse Haie/Leï Souco

Hôtel de Kerlon	56680 Plouhinec	183
Hôtel de la Cathédrale	76000 Rouen	412
Hôtel de la Madeleine	24200 Sarlat-la-Canéda	58
Hôtel de l'École	41400 Pontlevoy	207
Hôtel des Bories	24620 Marquay	51
Hôtel des Canonniers	02100 Saint-Quentin	442
Hôtel des Récollets	24200 Sarlat-la-Canéda	58
Hôtel d'Évreux	27200 Vernon	394
Hôtel du Canal	11400 Castelnaudary	276
Hôtel du Château	24260 Campagne	44
Hôtel du Chêne	64250 Itxassou	85
Hôtel du Comminges	31510 Saint-Bertrand-de-Comminges	330
Hôtel du Golf	77150 Lésigny	261
Hôtel du Mail	49100 Angers	425
Hôtel du Marquais	59216 Sars-Poteries	368
Hôtel du Martinet	85230 Bouin	432
Hôtel du Saumon	27130 Verneuil-sur-Avre	394
Hôtel du Vieux Pont	12390 Belcastel	320
Hotel Laumière	75019 Paris	257
Hôtellerie du Lac	31250 Revel-Saint-Ferréol	329

I

Les Isles	50270 Barneville-Carteret	396

J

La Jabotte	06160 Cap-d'Antibes	484
La Jacquerolle	43160 La Chaise-Dieu	106
Jamagne	88400 Gérardmer	311
Le Jardin de Gustave	25290 Ornans	243
Les Jardins Fragonard	06800 Cagnes-sur-Mer	483
Jas des Nevières	04300 Pierrerue	474
Le Jeu du Mail	07400 Alba-la-Romaine	531
Chez Julie	59134 Beaucamps-Ligny	364
Julien	67130 Fouday	15

K

Le Kandahar	74390 Châtel	568
Kervenel	44350 Saint-Molf	424
Klein	67160 Cleebourg	13
Krumeich	67660 Betschdorf	12

L

La Bastide Vieille	34310 Capestang	286
La Ferme du Vert	62720 Wierre-Effroy	375
Lac des Graves	15590 Lascelle	100
Les Lacs d'Halco	40700 Hagetmau	75
Les Landettes	24260 Journiac	45
Leï Souco	83350 Ramatuelle	506

ALPHABETICAL INDEX OF HOTELS AND MAISONS D'HÔTE

La Lézardière	33540 Saint-Martin-de-Lerm	72
L'hôtel Europe	67700 Saverne	22
Li Fundali	20228 Luri	230
Le Lièvre amoureux	38840 Saint-Lattier	546
L'Inattendu	01400 Châtillon-sur-Chalaronne	527
Le Logis	50520 Juvigny-le-Tertre	398
Le Logis d'Antan	79270 Vallans	462
Logis de la Couperie	85000 La Roche-sur-Yon	433
Le Logis de la Paqueraie	37320 Saint-Branchs	204
Le Logis de l'Aunis	17540 Saint-Sauveur-d'Aunis	459
Les Logis de Lestiac	33550 Lestiac-sur-Garonne	66
Logis Saint-Léonard	17139 Dompierre-sur-Mer	455
Lou Chandel'Aigue	43140 La Séauve-sur-Semène	106
Lou Ferradou	15130 Saint-Étienne-de-Carlat	102
La Lozerette	48400 Cocurès	289

M

Ma Maison de Mer	17420 Saint-Palais-sur-Mer	458
Madame Micheline Denieau	17310 Saint-Pierre-d'Oléron	456
La Magnanerie de Bernas	30630 Montclus	281
La Magnolière	79000 Saint-Liguaire	461
Maïnade	64260 Buzy	82
La Mainaz	01170 Gex	528
La Maison	19120 Beaulieu-sur-Dordogne	297
Maison Bakea	81170 Cordes-sur-Ciel	353
Maison Burret	65200 Montgaillard	346
Maison de la Forêt	24130 Laveyssière	47
Maison de la Grande Ourse	09800 Salsein	319
La Maison de la Treille	63200 Davayat	112
La Maison de Manon	82130 Lamothe-Capdeville	356
La Maison des Chanoines	19500 Turenne	301
Maison des Chevaliers	82700 Escatalens	355
La Maison des Sources	84360 Lauris	514
Maison d'hôte des Méans	04340 Méolans-Revel	473
La Maison du Charron	67370 Pfettisheim	20
La Maison du Prince de Condé	03140 Charroux	93
Maison Elixondoa	64120 Pagolle	87
Maison Errard	37130 Langeais	202
La Maison Fleurie	24310 Brantôme	43
Maison Forte de Clérivaux	26750 Châtillon-saint-Jean	535
Maison Jeanne	31110 Saint-Paul-d'Oueil	331
Maison Léchémia	64270 Salies-de-Béarn	89
Maison Oléa	24260 Le Bugue	48
Maison Rachou	64570 Lanne-en-Barétous	86
La Maison Royale	70140 Pesmes	251
La Maison sur la Colline	11000 Carcassonne	275
Maison Thomas	68770 Ammerschwihr	25

La Lézardière/Les Marmottes

Le Manoir	84550 Mornas	517
Le Manoir de Beaulieu	19120 Beaulieu-sur-Dordogne	298
Manoir de Beaumont	76260 Eu	407
Manoir de Bel Air	41500 Saint-Dyé-sur-Loire	208
Manoir de Bellauney	50700 Tamerville	402
Manoir de Bodrevan	56190 Noyal-Muzillac	180
Manoir de Boisvillers	36200 Argenton-sur-Creuse	196
Manoir de Cantepie	14340 Cambremer	382
Le Manoir de Coat Canton	29140 Rosporden	165
Le Manoir de Crépon	14480 Crépon	383
Le Manoir de la Barbacane	85130 Tiffauges	436
Manoir de la Croix	50530 Montviron	399
Manoir de la Févrerie	50760 Sainte-Geneviève	400
Le Manoir de la Forêt	41160 La Ville-aux-Clercs	206
Manoir de la Salle du Roc	41400 Bourré	205
Manoir de la Semoigne	02130 Villers-Agron-Aiguizy	443
Le Manoir de la Ville Gourio	22400 Morieux	161
Manoir de l'Acherie	50800 Villedieu-les-Poêles	403
Manoir de Lanleya	29610 Plouigneau	169
Le Manoir de l'Engagiste	14290 Orbec	387
Manoir de l'Hermerel	14230 Géfosse-Fontenay	385
Manoir de Mathan	14310 Longvillers	386
Manoir de Rigourdaine	22490 Plouër-sur-Rance	162
Manoir de Tarperon	21510 Aignay-le-Duc	125
Manoir de Tourville	69610 Les Halles	556
Manoir de Troézel Vras	22610 Kerbors	160
Manoir des Chanterelles	82290 Meauzac	357
Le Manoir du Grand Vignoble	24140 Saint-Julien-de-Crempse	55
Le Manoir du Meldick	62730 Marck	372
Manoir du Plessis	35650 Le Rheu	173
Manoir du Plessis	76940 Vatteville-la-Rue	415
Manoir Francis	62170 Marles-sur-Canche	373
Manoir Le Plaix	03320 Pouzy-Mésangy	96
Le Manoir Saint-Clair	31130 Balma	326
Manoir Saint-jean	50110 Tourlaville	402
Manoir Saint-Michel	22240 Sables-d'Or-les-Pins	163
La Manufacture	31190 Auterive	325
Au Marais	79510 Coulon	460
La Mare	26800 Étoile-sur-Rhône	536
Mare e Monti	20225 Feliceto	229
La Marine	14117 Arromanches-les-Bains	380
La Marine	56590 Île de Groix	179
Le Marini	44500 La Baule	421
Marliac	46140 Bélaye	336
La Marmotte	89700 Collan	147
Les Marmottes	05330 Saint-Chaffrey	481

ALPHABETICAL INDEX OF HOTELS AND MAISONS D'HÔTE

Les Marronniers	14340 Cambremer	382
Mas de Bouvau	84150 Violès	521
Le Mas de Castel	24200 Sarlat-la-Caneda	59
Mas de Clairefontaine	06530 Val-du-Tignet	490
Le Mas de Guilles	84160 Lourmarin	516
Mas de la Lause	84330 Le Barroux	515
Le Mas de Magali	84110 Le Crestet	516
Le Mas de Mazan	07200 Mercuer	532
Mas des Aigras	84100 Orange	518
Mas des Cigales	06140 Tourrettes-sur-Loup	489
Le Mas des Oliviers	83390 Puget-Ville	506
Le Mas des Rièges	13460 Les Saintes-Maries-de-la-Mer	496
Le Mas du Caroubier	30700 Saint-Quentin-la-Poterie	283
Mas du Figuier	04200 Bevons	471
Mas Fontclaire	30250 Sommières	284
Maxime	89000 Auxerre	144
La Mazade	30730 Saint-Mamert-du-Gard	282
Le Médiéval	84000 Avignon	510
Les Mésanges	38410 Uriage-les-Bains	547
Messageries	39600 Arbois	245
La Métairie du Bourg	85500 Les Herbiers	434
La Métairie Neuve	81660 Pont-de-Larn	351
La Meulière	37130 Cinq-Mars-la-Pile	200
Meurice	62100 Calais	370
Midi-papillon	12230 Saint-Jean-du-Bruel	323
La Milaudière	37500 Ligré	203
Mimosa	34725 Saint-Saturnin-de-Lucian	288
Aux Mines d'Argent	68160 Sainte-Marie-aux-Mines	34
Le Mirval	06430 La Brigue	485
Monastère de Segriès	04360 Moustiers-Sainte-Marie	474
Chez Monsieur et Madame Perrot	19460 Naves	299
Montarlet	63390 Saint-Gervais-d'Auvergne	119
Montgarni	36230 Sarzay	197
Montségur	11000 Carcassonne	275
Les Mouettes	35430 Saint-Suliac	175
Le Moulin	25380 Vaucluse	244
Le Moulin	52100 Chamouilley	224
Le Moulin	62770 Fillièvres	371
Au Moulin	68127 Sainte-Croix-en-Plaine	34
Moulin Chantepierre	39110 Pont-d'Héry	249
Moulin de Bourgchâteau	71500 Louhans	141
Moulin de Fresquet	46500 Gramat	338
Le Moulin de Hard	14400 Subles	388
Moulin de Huttingue	68480 Oltingue	31
Le Moulin de la Beune	24620 Les Eyzies-de-Tayac	49
Le Moulin de la Butte	50170 Huisnes-sur-Mer	397

Les Marronniers/Parc

Le Moulin de la Coudre	89290 Venoy	152
Le Moulin de la Forge	89350 Tannerre-en-Puisaye	151
Le Moulin de la Renne	41140 Thésée	209
Le Moulin de la Sorinière	79250 Nueil-les-Aubiers	461
Au Moulin de la Walk	67160 Wissembourg	24
Le Moulin de la Wantzenau	67610 La Wantzenau	17
Moulin de Labique	47290 Saint-Eutrope-de-Born	80
Le Moulin de Linthe	72130 Saint-Léonard-des-Bois	432
Le Moulin de Marsaguet	87500 Coussac-Bonneval	302
Le Moulin de Moissac	82200 Moissac	357
Le Moulin de Pommeuse	77515 Pommeuse	263
Le Moulin de Rosmadec	29930 Pont-Aven	169
Le Moulin d'Eguebaude	10190 Estissac	219
Le Moulin des Arbillons	71520 Bourgvilain	139
Le Moulin des Planches	28270 Montigny-sur-Avre	193
Le Moulin des Vernières	63120 Aubusson-d'Auvergne	110
Moulin du Château	04500 Saint-Laurent-du-Verdon	477
Le Moulin du Gastronome	71850 Charnay-lès-Mâcon	140
Le Moulin Neuf	24510 Sainte-Alvère	54
Le Moulinot	89270 Vermenton	152
Les Moynes	46320 Saint-Simon	343

N
Le Nid à Bibi	01960 Servas	530
Chez Norbert	68750 Bergheim	25
Normandie	89000 Auxerre	145
La Nouvelle France	14310 Longvillers	386

O
Les Oliviers	83300 Draguignan	502
L'Ombre de Gozinière	03350 Theneuille	96
L'Orangerie	52190 Prangey	225
L'Orangerie	61290 Longny-au-Perche	404
L'Orée des Vignes	58200 Saint-Père	137
L'Oriel	68340 Riquewihr	32
Les Oussaillès	09140 Aulus-les-Bains	318

P
La Pagnoune	15320 Loubaresse	101
Paix	59000 Lille	366
La Palombière	89450 Vézelay	154
Le Panorama	76480 Duclair	406
Le Panoramique	24620 Les Eyzies-de-Tayac	49
Le Panoramique	38142 Mizoen	544
La Paravent	43700 Chaspinhac	105
Parc	21200 Levernois	129
Parc	34000 Montpellier	287
Parc	13420 Gémenos	495

ALPHABETICAL INDEX OF HOTELS AND MAISONS D'HÔTE

Le Parc de Geoffroy	63300 Thiers	121
Le Parc des Maréchaux	89000 Auxerre	145
Le Parlement	05000 Gap	479
Le Pas-de-l'Île	85230 Saint-Gervais	435
Les Pasquiers	69220 Lancié	555
La Passiflore	07460 Saint-Paul-le-Jeune	534
À la Pastourelle	73480 Bonneval-sur-Arc	563
Le Pavillon de Margaux	33460 Margaux	67
Pavillon Sévigné	31110 Bagnères-de-Luchon	326
Le Pélican	56220 Rochefort-en-Terre	184
La Péniche Soleïado	31250 Ramonville-Saint-Agne	328
Les Perce-Neige	37210 Vernou-sur-Brenne	204
Père Benoit	67960 Entzheim	15
Perreau	58140 Lormes	135
Petit Castel	27210 Beuzeville	390
Le Petit Pont	72230 Moncé-en-Belin	431
La Petite Auberge	67140 Le Hohwald	18
Les Peupliers	05200 Baratier	478
Peyraguey Maison Rouge	33210 Bommes-Sauternes	62
Piaggiola	20166 Porticcio	232
Les Picorettes	69460 Vaux-en-Beaujolais	560
Pierre Nicole	75005 Paris	255
Pierrot-Pierrette	06500 Menton	486
Le Pigeonnier de Picandine	24350 Lisle	50
La Pilleterie	37420 Huismes	202
Les Pins	83510 Lorgues	505
Le Platane	82130 Lafrançaise	355
Platelin	42370 Renaison	551
La Pointe du Cap Coz	29170 Fouesnant	165
La Pointe du Grouin	35260 Cancale	171
La Pomme de Pin	87140 Thouron	303
Au Pont de Raffiny	63660 Saint-Anthème	118
Le Pont d'Or	46100 Figeac	337
Le Pont du Roy	30126 Tavel	284
Le Portail	36170 Saint-Benoît-du-Sault	197
Le Portail Bleu	77610 Châtres	259
Porz-Morvan	29550 Plomodiern	168
Poste	44420 Piriac-sur-Mer	422
La Poste	71120 Charolles	140
Le Poujastou	31110 Juzet-de-Luchon	327
Le Poupat	31420 Alan	324
Le Poutic	40240 Créon-d'Armagnac	74
La Pradasse	31450 Ayguesvives	325
Les Pradets	63114 Montpeyroux	115
Les Prairies	43190 Tence	109
Les Prés d'Ondine	67500 Baldenheim	11

Le Parc de Geoffroy/Residence Vert Galant

Au Président	32300 Mirande	334
Le Pressoir du Mont	27210 Saint-Maclou	393
Le Prieuré	18500 Vignoux-sur-Barangeon	191
Le Prieuré	62180 Tigny-Noyelle	374
Le Prieuré de la Chaise	41400 Saint-Georges-sur-Cher	208
Le Prieuré de Molanes	04400 Pra-Loup	475
Le Prieuré des Fontaines	27500 Les Préaux	392
Le Prieuré Maïalen	78840 Moisson	267
Le Prieuré Sainte-Croix	76470 Le Tréport	410
Prieuré-Saint-Lazare	49590 Fontevraud-L'Abbaye	427
Le Puits d'Athie	89380 Appoigny	144

Q

Quatre Dauphins	13100 Aix-en-Provence	491
Le Quercy	82110 Lauzerte	356
Le Quesnot	50660 Montchaton	398
Quic-en-Groigne	35400 Saint-Malo	175

R

La Raboullière	41700 Contres	205
La Ranquière	81240 Rouairoux	354
La Raze	19500 Collonges-la-Rouge	298
Régence	63140 Chatelguyon	111
Le Régent	02600 Villers-Cotterets	443
Relais Brunehaut	60350 Chelles	444
Relais de la Rance	35290 Quedillac	174
Le Relais de l'Abbaye	76480 Jumièges	408
Le Relais de Lavergne	24150 Bayac	40
Relais de l'Oustau Camarguen	30240 Port-Camargue	282
Le Relais des Abbesses	39210 Château-Chalon	247
Le Relais du Bas Limousin	19270 Donzenac	299
Le Relais du Castera	65150 Nestier	346
Le Relais du Çatey	38080 L'Isle-d'Abeau	544
Au Relais du Château de Mensberg	57480 Manderen	308
Le Relais du Lyon d'Or	86260 Angles-sur-l'Anglin	462
Relais du Porhoët	56490 Guilliers	178
Le Relais du Taurion	87480 Saint-Priest-Taurion	302
Le Relais Guillaume de Normandy	80230 Saint-Valery-sur-Somme	450
Le Relais Rose	88300 Autreville	309
Le Relais Saint Benoît	89130 Villiers-Saint-Benoît	155
Le Relais Saint Vincent	89144 Ligny-le-Chatel	148
Relais Saint-Gilles	44210 Pornic	422
Les Remparts	33890 Gensac	65
La Résidence	11100 Narbonne	278
La Résidence	88340 Le Val-d'Ajol	313
La Résidence	82140 Saint-Antonin-Noble-Val	358
Residence Vert Galant	75013 Paris	256

ALPHABETICAL INDEX OF HOTELS AND MAISONS D'HÔTE

Les Revers	43130 Retournac	107
La Rivoire	42220 Saint-Julien-Molin-Molette	553
Les Rocailles	65100 Omex	347
La Romance	67220 Dieffenbach-au-Val	14
À la Route d'Argent	12340 Bozouls	321
Rue du Château	13150 Tarascon	499

S

Les Sables d'Ocre	84220 Roussillon	519
Saint-Christophe	13100 Aix-en-Provence	491
Saint-Éloi	87110 Solignac	303
Saint-Pierre	61150 Rânes	405
Saint-Romain	69480 Anse	554
Le Saint-Sauveur	48150 Meyrueis	290
Santa Maria	20113 Olmeto	231
La Santoline	07460 Beaulieu	531
Le Sarment d'Or	68340 Riquewihr	32
La Saura	21360 Lusigny-sur-Ouche	129
La Sauvageonne	33820 Saint-Palais	72
La Sérénité	30430 Barjac	279
Sèvres-Azur	75006 Paris	255
SNC les Charmettes	01510 Saint-Martin-de-Bavel	530
Soleil	73500 Aussois	562
La Solognote	18410 Brinon-sur-Sauldre	190
Soubeleta	64250 Itxassou	85
Les Sources Bleues	27500 Aizier	390
Sous le Pic - La Pérolière	42610 Saint-Romain-le-Puy	552
La Souveraine	88140 Contrexéville	310
Sphinx-Hôtel	26200 Montélimar	537
Stiren ar Mor	56470 La Trinité-sur-Mer	180

T

Les 3 Luppars	62000 Arras	369
À la Table de la Bergère	19600 Nespouls	300
Taillard	25470 Goumois	240
La Templerie	16430 Champniers	453
Au Temps d'Autrefois	21340 Nolay	131
La Terrasse	43170 Sauges	108
La Terrasse	46120 Lacapelle-Marival	339
La Terrasse	69240 Thizy	560
La Terrasse	76119 Varengeville-sur-Mer	414
Le Thy	56800 Ploërmel	181
Ti Va Zadou	29253 Île-de-Batz	166
Les Tilleuls	46160 Marcilhac-sur-Célé	340
Les Tilleuls	69480 Lucenay	557
Le Tinailler du Manoir de Champvent	71700 Chardonnay	139
La Tonnelle	30200 La Roque-sur-Cèze	280

Les Revers/Villa Argi-eder

La Toque Blanche	02300 Chauny	439
La Toscane	83310 Grimaud	503
La Touille	24250 Cénac-et-Saint-Julien	45
La Tour	19190 Aubazine	297
La Tour	27340 Pont-de-l'Arche	393
La Tour du Vieux Port	33500 Libourne	67
La Tour Intendance	33000 Bordeaux	63
Les Tourelles	80550 Le Crotoy	448
Les Tourterelles	62290 Noeux-les-Mines	373
La Treille Muscate	26270 Cliousclat	535
Les Trémières	17310 La Cotinière	456
Le Trianon	56410 Étel	178
Le Troubadour	46500 Rocamadour	342
Turenne	68000 Colmar	26
Ty Gwenn	44550 Saint-Malo-de-Guersac	423
Ty Me Mamm	56340 Carnac	177
Ty-boni	40500 Angresse	73
Ty-Dreux	29410 Loc-Eguiner-Saint-Thégonnec	167

U

Univers	51100 Reims	223
Les Usses	45760 Marigny-les-Usages	212

V

Le Val d'Aron	58340 Cercy-la-Tour	133
Le Val Fleuri	38250 Lans-en-Vercors	543
Le Val Joli	88230 Le Valtin	314
Val Majour	13990 Fontvieille	494
Val-Chrétien	02130 Bruyères-sur-Fère	439
Vauban	90000 Belfort	252
La Veaudepierre	86300 Chauvigny	463
Vent d'Ouest	76600 Le Havre	409
Verdun	58000 Nevers	136
Les Vergers	76860 Quiberville	411
Les Vergers de Montourey	83600 Fréjus	502
Vic	30210 Castillon-du-Gard	280
La Vieille Forêt	45240 La Ferté-Saint-Aubin	212
Les Vieilles Fontaines	89270 Sacy	151
Les Vieilles Tours	46500 Rocamadour	342
Le Vieux Carré	76000 Rouen	412
Le Vieux Castel	04500 Roumoules	476
Le Vieux Logis	17500 Clam	454
Le Vieux Logis	74140 Yvoire	574
Le Vieux Pressoir	27210 Conteville	391
À la Vigne	68280 Logelheim	29
Le Vignoble	67650 Dambach-la-Ville	14
Villa Argi-eder	64500 Saint-Jean-de-Luz	88

ALPHABETICAL INDEX OF HOTELS AND MAISONS D'HÔTE

Villa Ashram	33121 Maubuisson	68
Villa des Courtissous	24210 Saint-Rabier	56
Villa des Houx	76390 Aumale	405
La Villa du Lac	68290 Sewen	35
La Villa du Rhône	01700 Miribel	529
Villa du Vieux Puits	71140 Bourbon-Lancy	138
Villa Fleurie	21200 Beaune	126
Villa Gaïa	04000 Digne-les-Bains	471
Villa Hôtel	45500 Poilly-lez-Gien	213
Villa l'Églantier	06400 Cannes	483
Villa les Pins	31340 Vacquiers	331
Villa Lou Gardian	83110 Sanary-sur-Mer	507
Villa Marguerite	22370 Pléneuf-Val-André	161
Villa Marie-Jeanne	13012 Marseille	497
Village Grouchy	50560 Blainville-sur-Mer	396
Villemenard	18500 Vignoux-sur-Barangeon	191
La Violetterie	71740 Saint-Maurice-lès-Châteauneuf	142
Les Voyageurs	19320 Saint-Martin-la-Méanne	300

W
Wilson	21000 Dijon	128
Winzenberg	67650 Blienschwiller	13
Le Withof	59630 Bourbourg	364

Z
Zinckhotel	67140 Andlau	11

PHOTO CREDITS

Photographs of hotels and maisons d'hôte:

Project Manager – Production: Alain LEPRINCE
Agence ACSI – A CHACUN SON IMAGE
2, rue Aristide Maillol, 75015 Paris – Tél. : (33) 01 43 27 90 10
Photo Credits : Philippe GUERSAN, Lawrence BANAHAN, Romain AIX, Annick MEGRET

Except:
L'Hermitage : L'Hermitage/MICHELIN
La ferme de la Rançonnière : La ferme de la Rançonnière/MICHELIN
La Romance : La Romance/MICHELIN
Thuilerie des Fontaines : La Thuilerie des Fontaines/MICHELIN
Une campagne en Provence : Une Campagne en Provence - www.provence4u.com/MICHELIN
Le chalet des Alpages : Le chalet des Alpages/MICHELIN
La Bergerie : La Bergerie/MICHELIN

The Regions – captions and credits

ALSACE : *Andlau, the Route du Vin* R. Mattes/MICHELIN • **AQUITAINE** : *Bassin d'Arcachon* A. Thuillier/MICHELIN • **AUVERGNE** : *Ambert town hall* J. Damase/MICHELIN • **BURGUNDY** : *Briare canal bridge* Ph. Gajic/MICHELIN • **BRITTANY** : *Port du Palais, Belle-Île* G. Guégan/MICHELIN • **CENTRE AND UPPER LOIRE VALLEY** : *Château d'Ussé* Ph. Gajic/MICHELIN • **CHAMPAGNE-ARDENNE** : *Place Ducale, Charleville-Mézières* Ph. Gajic/MICHELIN • **CORSICA** : *Bonifacio* G. Magnin/MICHELIN • **FRANCHE-COMTÉ** : *Château de Joux* G. Benoît à la Guillaumen/MICHELIN • **ÎLE-DE-FRANCE AND PARIS** : *Place de la Concorde* B. Kaufman/MICHELIN • **LANGUEDOC-ROUSSILLON** : *Le Cirque de Navacelles* B. Kaufman/MICHELIN • **LIMOUSIN** : *Sénoueix bridge* S. Sauvignier/MICHELIN • **LORRAINE** : *Bitche* R. Mattes/MICHELIN • **MIDI-PYRÉNÉES** : *Albi Cathedral* B. Kaufman/MICHELIN • **NORD-PAS-DE-CALAIS** : *International Kite Festival at Berck* Y. Tierny/MICHELIN • **NORMANDY** : *The Auge countryside* G. Targat/MICHELIN • **PAYS-DE-LA-LOIRE** : *Harvesting salt at Noirmoutier* M. Thiery/MICHELIN • **PICARDY** : *Marquenterre nature reserve* S. Sauvignier/MICHELIN • **POITOU-CHARENTES** : *Port d'Arçais, Marais poitevin* D. Mar/MICHELIN • **PROVENCE-ALPS – FRENCH RIVIERA** : *Calanque de Sormiou* G. Magnin/MICHELIN • **RHÔNE-ALPS** : *Notre-Dame de la Vie, Saint-Martin de Belleville* S. Sauvignier/MICHELIN

Cover photo: © SIC/Valentin Christophe

MICHELIN
46, avenue de Breteuil – 75324 Paris Cedex 07
☏ 01 45 66 12 34
www.ViaMichelin.fr

Manufacture Française des Pneumatiques Michelin
Société en commandite par actions au capital de 304 000 000 EUR
Place des Carmes-Déchaux, 63 Clermont-Ferrand (France) – R.C.S. Clermont-Fd B 855 200 507
Michelin et Cie, Propriétaires-Editeurs - Dépôt légal Janvier 2006
No part of this publication may be reproduced in any form without the prior permission of the publisher

Printed in Italy 01-2006/4.1

Typesetting: Maury Malesherbes (France)
Printing: STIGE, San Mauro (Italy)

Layout: Studio Maogani
4, rue du Fer à Moulin, 75005 Paris - Tel : 01 47 07 00 06

Layout and Cover: Laurent Muller
Picture research and cover photos: Christelle Le Déan et Maud Burrus

Published in 2006

YOUR OPINION MATTERS!

To help us constantly improve this guide, please fill in this questionnaire and return to:
Michelin Charming Places to Stay France Questionnaire
Hannay House, 39 Clarendon Road
WATFORD WD17 1JA – U.K.

❯ 1- You are a:

Man .... ❒   Woman .... ❒

< 25 years old .... ❒   25 – 35 years old .. ❒

35 – 50 years old .. ❒   > 50 years old ..... ❒

Farmer/Worker in primary industry .... ❒

Employee .... ❒

Service worker, Craftsman, Owner
of small business .... ❒

Manual worker .... ❒

Manager/Executive, Professional .... ❒

Retired .... ❒

Teacher .... ❒

Student .... ❒

Unemployed .... ❒

❯ 2- Did you buy this guide:

For holidays? .... ❒

For a weekend/short break? .... ❒

For business purposes? .... ❒

As a gift? .... ❒

❯ 3- Will you be travelling:

In a couple? .. ❒   With family? ... ❒

Alone? .... ❒   With friends? .. ❒

Other .... ❒

❯ 4- Have you bought a Michelin guide before?

Yes .... ❒   No .... ❒

If so, which one(s)?

The Red Guide
(hotel and restaurant guides) .... ❒

The Green Guide (tourism guides) .... ❒

Another edition of this guide .... ❒

Another Michelin guide (please specify) .. ❒

❯ 5- How often do you use the Internet to find out information on hotels, guesthouses and restaurants?

Never .... ❒

Occasionally .... ❒

Regulary .... ❒

A lot .... ❒

❯ 6- How do you rate the different elements of the guide?

1 = Very good   2 = Good   3 = Acceptable   4 = Poor   5 = Very poor

	1	2	3	4	5
Selection of establishments	❒	❒	❒	❒	❒
Number of establishments	❒	❒	❒	❒	❒
Hotel/Guesthouse mix	❒	❒	❒	❒	❒
Geographical spread of establishments	❒	❒	❒	❒	❒
Room rates	❒	❒	❒	❒	❒
Practical Information (prices, activities…)	❒	❒	❒	❒	❒
Text	❒	❒	❒	❒	❒
Photos	❒	❒	❒	❒	❒
General presentation	❒	❒	❒	❒	❒
Distribution of establishments by region	❒	❒	❒	❒	❒
Themed indexes	❒	❒	❒	❒	❒
Cover	❒	❒	❒	❒	❒
Price of the guide	❒	❒	❒	❒	❒
Other (please specify)	❒	❒	❒	❒	❒

❯ 7- Please rate the guide out of 20:   / 20

❯ 8- Which aspects could we improve?

....
....
....